NOTTS COUNTY

The Magpies:

Flight through The National League

followed by a turbulent EFL season

NOTTS COUNTY

The Magpies:

Flight through The National League

followed by a turbulent EFL season

by

Roger King

Quantum Dot Press

Copyright © 2024 Roger King

All rights reserved

The right of Roger King to be identified as the author of this work has been asserted in accordance with section 77 of the Copyright, Designs and Patents Act 1988.

All rights reserved without limits under copyright reserved above, no parts of this publication may be reproduced, stored in or introduced into a retrieval system, or transmitted in any form, or by any means (electronic, mechanical, photocopying, recording or otherwise) without the prior permission of the copyright owner.

Front cover: Magpies taken by author. Back cover image: supplied by Nick Richardson, Notts County's Head of Media, Communications & Marketing.

Cover design by Lightspeed Dreams

Other photographs were taken from the Notts County website, courtesy of Nick Richardson, or publicly available copyright-free internet sources.

The author and publisher apologize in advance for any unintentional breaches of copyright. They will be pleased to include an appropriate acknowledgement in any future editions.

Table of Contents

About the author i
Introduction ii

Alan Hardy, Nolan, and Kewell - Ardley survives Reedtz brother's arrival

Chapter 1: The Good, The Bad, and The Ugly 1
Chapter 2: Relegation at Swindon 25
Chapter 3: "What's next for Notts?" 28
Chapter 4: A summer of discontent 31
Chapter 5: Alexander and Christoffer Reedtz takeover 42

If at first you don't succeed, try, try again

Chapter 6: National League Here We Come! 47
Chapter 7: The 2019-20 season (and Coronavirus) 53
Chapter 8: So near yet so far 86
Chapter 9: The Coronavirus (COVID-19) pandemic, and lockdown 128
Chapter 10: Restart and lift-off 145
Chapter 11: National League Promotion Final at Wembley 157
Chapter 12: Preparations for a second National League season 169
Chapter 13: The 2020-21 season (to halfway, match 22) 176
Chapter 14: A brutal second half of the season 232
Chapter 15: Neal Ardley departs, Ian Burchnall arrives 241
Chapter 16: Sixteen important league matches for Burchnall 250
Chapter 17: Summer of 2021 293
Chapter 18: The 2021-22 season (to halfway, 22 matches) 302
Chapter 19: The second half of the season 343
Chapter 20: The summer of 2022 - Burchnall 'out', Williams 'in' 383
Chapter 21: The 2022-23 season (first half, matches 1-23) 392
Chapter 22: The second half of the season (matches 24-46) 429

Extra time - a helping hand, and foot!

Chapter 23: Promotion playoffs May 2023 471

Chapter 24: EFL League Two - A turbulent 2023-24 season 490

Luke Williams swan-song
Stuart Maynard's baptism of fire

Acknowledgements 513

At the end of each of the four National League seasons there is a statistical breakdown – results, goal scorers/goal times, player 'starts', substitute appearances, a disciplinary record, Meadow Lane attendances, and a final league table.

About the author

Born in Mansfield, Nottinghamshire, and a Notts County supporter since 1957 when his father took him to see a second division match between bottom of the league Notts and top of the league Leicester City. It was a 0-0 draw, in front of 42,489 spectators.

Nine years later he became a Notts County player, but only for a brief period, as an amateur. His main claim to fame is that, as a 'right-half', he played alongside Dave Watson who went on to win international honours with England.

Roger's playing days ended when he began a shift working career in the Meteorological Office, during which he left Nottinghamshire. However, his support of 'The Magpies' continued, not only visiting Meadow Lane but also many away stadiums.

He was at Wembley Stadium in 1990, 1991, and 2023 to see Notts win three playoff finals.

Roger is married with two sons and five grandchildren, and enjoys retirement in Harrogate, North Yorkshire.

Introduction

It has been said many times in the past that Notts County is one of the most stressful teams to support.

In the seven years this book covers, from the Alan Hardy takeover in January 2017, there were many highs and lows. Relegation into The National League at Swindon in May 2019 was the lowest point. The arrival of new owners Christoffer and Alexander Reedtz, who provided much needed stability and foresight, occurred in July 2019.

The huge disappointment of the relegation was compounded when the team who just avoided relegation in May 2019, Macclesfield Town, were relegated at the end of the following season and then expelled from The National League.

Six managers/head coaches walked through the Meadow Lane gates. Two assistants departed unexpectedly, one to manage another club, and one because of derisory comments he directed at a Notts player.

Notts' four seasons in The National League were never boring. At the end of each season they participated in a playoff campaign, the first three ending in disappointment. There were two visits to Wembley Stadium, the first ended in defeat to Harrogate Town but the second a fantastic victory over Chesterfield.

The 2020-21 season included withdrawal from the FA Cup, due to the coronavirus (COVID-19) pandemic. With this decision Notts drew a comparison with Manchester United, who withdrew from the competition in season 1999-2000 to compete in the Club World Championship.

Ah, the coronavirus pandemic. Obviously, every football club in the UK was affected, but Notts tried harder than many to adhere to the guidelines, restrictions, and rules.

During their final, record breaking (in a positive sense) National League season in 2022-23, there was the very sad loss of respected Chief Executive Officer Jason Turner, who died a young fifty-year-old.

This book evolved as it progressed. Initially I hoped Notts would be members of The National League for only one season. But instead, it was a four-year saga, which ended at Wembley on the afternoon of 13 May 2023. The last chapter of the book is devoted to Notts' turbulent first season back in EFL League Two.

I hope you enjoy the read. It is more than just a chronological record of all the 170 National League, 8 FA Cup, 16 FA Trophy, and 7 playoff matches. I accept responsibility for any (hopefully, few) mistakes or inaccuracies.

Roger King
Harrogate, North Yorkshire
1 May 2024

Chapter 1: The Good, The Bad, and The Ugly

Nottingham businessman Alan Hardy completed his takeover of Notts County, from Ray Trew, in January 2017. Not only were Notts without a manager, they had also lost their last ten consecutive league matches and were twenty second in the League Two table just a point above the relegation zone. A winding-up petition brought by HM Revenue & Customs was also pending, some outstanding debts had to be settled, and a transfer embargo was in place.

Within twenty four hours of the takeover Hardy appointed 34 year old Kevin Nolan as manager. He brought with him an impressive c.v. An attacking midfielder, he had played for, and captained, three clubs: Bolton Wanderers, Newcastle United and West Ham United, with the majority of his appearances in the Premier League. Prior to joining Notts, as player-manager, he had been player-manager at another League Two club, Leyton Orient. Although successful he left Orient in the summer of 2016.

Kevin Nolan welcomed by Alan Hardy

Kevin Nolan did not play in any games during his time at Notts – as far as I can remember he didn't even name himself as a substitute.

On his appointment he said:

> *"This squad is capable of staying in the league. With my input we can start to get away from the current situation. I do not see this as a risk. I see this as something I can build with Alan. Alan knows we have to turn this around slowly. I see this as a challenge. I hope I can make him and Notts County successful and give him back all the faith and confidence he has shown in me."*

Alan Hardy praised his new manager, and acknowledged the despondency of the Notts fans:

> "Kevin Nolan is an outstanding leader and that is what this football club needs. He will provide the leadership on the playing side. Not only is he a very good footballer, but when he went to Orient he had immediate success - and we need to start climbing the table. This is a massive football club but it is not successful on the pitch. These two need to be realigned. The immediate priority is survival and we need to understand what the fans want. We want the product to be right on the pitch but we also want fans to enjoy themselves while they are here. I understand their frustration and anger. The passion and determination in this club needs to go up a few notches. There is a one, three and five-year plan in place."

The transfer embargo was lifted from Notts a few days before the transfer window closed at the end of January, which gave Notts approximately seventy-two hours to complete the signing of new players.

Kevin Nolan's record between his appointment and the end of the 2016-17 season was good: P21 W10 D4 L7 and Notts finished 16th in League Two with 56 points. The only home match lost in this period was against League Two champions Portsmouth. Ironically Notts lost their final match of the season (to a last-minute goal) at Newport County which saved Newport from relegation! Hartlepool and his previous club, Leyton Orient, were the two clubs relegated into The National League.

On 31 August 2017, a few weeks into the new season, Hardy issued the following message to supporters after the closure of the summer transfer window.

> My second transfer window at the helm is now at an end – and what a different experience it was to my first! Back in January we faced a mad dash to exit our transfer embargo before bolstering the squad with a number of late signings to give Kevin Nolan the best possible chance of keeping us in the EFL [English Football League]. He comfortably achieved that, as he promised he would, setting us up nicely for the summer.

> This window, we were keen to get the bulk of our business done early to allow our new signings to settle in properly before the season began, and to help the manager and his coaching staff formulate a strong plan for the season ahead. I'm delighted with the way our business has panned out and I believe our position in the top seven is a good reflection of the positive strides we've made in the transfer market.

> No doubt many of you will have been keeping an eager eye on our website and social media today in the hope of some exciting news, but Kevin and I are happy with our squad and saw no reason to add to it today.

> *We will continue to explore targets with a view to January but, as always, our selection process will be carefully thought-out with the best interests of the club at heart. We have faith in this group and believe they are getting better day after day.*
>
> *Your support, which has been magnificent so far this season, will be vital in helping the players reach their full potential. Stick with us and let's see how far we can go.*
>
> *COYP! (Come On You Pies)*

More good news followed three weeks later, on 20 September, when Notts announced that manager Kevin Nolan had signed a new three-year contract.

He had led the Magpies to second in League Two, after helping them avoid relegation last season. His assistant manager Richard Thomas, and first-team coach Mark Crossley, also signed new deals with the club.

> *"It was an easy decision to make which is why I have been so comfortable talking about it in recent weeks. I'm delighted that Richard and Mark will be staying with me. We have a solid backroom staff here. I was confident of keeping the club up, and getting it into a stable position this season, so we can kick on in the future."*

Nolan and Hardy expressed their delight at getting the deal done.

> *Kevin Nolan continued: "I have to thank Alan because he has been first class since we first met. We hit it off immediately and knew we had something which would be great. Alan backs me with whatever I do. He lets me do my work and that is why we have been so successful. We work together rather than against each other, which is not what I have had in the past," he admitted. "This club is a sleeping giant with the history and facilities we have. We want to be successful here and get the club back to where we feel it belongs but we have to do it in the right way. I'm really excited. I have the same feeling here as I did when I signed my first contract with Bolton Wanderers."*

Alan Hardy was again full of praise for his manager:

> *"When I took over in January we were on a 10-game losing streak and had one foot in The National League. It has been an incredible turnaround. Kevin has brought real pride, optimism, stability and excitement to this club which has not been seen for many years.*
>
> *The key element when I was hiring a manager in January was leadership. We needed someone who was a leader of men and could galvanise the players. Kevin's experience as a captain of Bolton, Newcastle and West Ham stood out. As soon as I met him, he oozed confidence, character and passion.*

It was about understanding how individuals work and ensuring you get the best out of them. Kevin was outstanding in that regard. We are mindful that we still have a big job to do. I have to keep the staff in the office motivated and committed while Kevin has to keep the players grounded.

I am delighted to have agreed a three-year contract to allow Kevin to take the club forward on a fabulous journey.

Who knows where we will be at the end of those three years?"

Nolan, as well as being rewarded with a new three-year contract, became the League Two Manager of the Month for September. The citation read:

Kevin Nolan guided Notts County to six wins from seven games in the month, keeping five clean sheets in the process, as they climbed to the top of the table…. and he has overseen a remarkable turnaround at Meadow Lane since taking on the job in January.

After inheriting a team on a run of 10 successive league defeats, Nolan led the club to safety and has maintained momentum over the summer with some shrewd recruitment, building a squad which has suffered only two defeats in 11 games so far this season.

The Liverpudlian was keen to ensure the praise and recognition for the award was shared among his staff and players.

Crossley, Nolan, Thomas

"This is an extremely proud achievement for me, my staff and my players, who have all made a massive contribution. There's no way I could do this job without Richard Thomas, Mark Crossley and everyone who has supported me behind the scenes. They all thoroughly deserve this recognition. I would also like to thank the chairman once again for the amazing backing he has given me, not only this season but since our arrival in January."

A much-improved performance, on and off the field, during 2017 prompted Alan Hardy to issue the following message to supporters on 1 December:

> Firstly, a huge thank you to all our supporters for making Notts County the fastest-growing football club in the East Midlands. Secondly, a challenge to all of you to help us make Meadow Lane the busiest it has been for 25 years. As many of you will know, I'm an impatient sort of guy. I want success. And I want it yesterday.
>
> But when I allowed myself a moment to take stock of what has been achieved so far this year, I realised how much all of you, the fans, are buying into our Magpies revolution.
>
> My ticket office team told me our average crowd had slumped to just 4,353 when I arrived at the club and the underlying trend was for the average to have dipped below 4,000 within a matter of weeks.
>
> Just how far the club had been allowed to degenerate was characterised by a record of three home victories in the calendar year of 2016.
>
> In the first 10 home league matches at Meadow Lane this season, our average attendance is 7,186. And we've won almost three times as many home games than we did in the whole of 2016! That's a massive crowd increase of 65% - dwarfing any rises made by any of the other clubs in Nottinghamshire.
>
> But we are only just beginning our journey to turn this city 'black and white', as Jimmy Sirrel so famously said in the 60s.
>
> For us to be successful we must continue to sustain major growth in our fan base year-on-year.
>
> That's why I'm challenging all Notts fans to deliver the highest average crowd at Meadow Lane for a quarter of a century. Not since 1992, when Derek Pavis and Neil Warnock had us playing in the top flight, have we had a 10,000-plus average. The best in the following 25 years was the 8,314 in the 1994 campaign - we're not far behind that at the moment. The challenge between now and the end of the season is for us to better that.
>
> Our manager and our players deserve it. Thanks to Kevin Nolan, his coaching staff and playing squad, we boast the third-best home record in the whole of the Premier League and EFL in 2017. We've not been outside the top two in the league for over two months. Our home form is the best it's been for the best part of 20 years.
>
> My commitment to you as supporters is to fund and create an environment in which this club can challenge for promotion, deliver an ongoing programme of improvements to the club's infrastructure and facilities both on and off the pitch and give you a club of

which you can be justifiably proud after two decades of chronic mismanagement and lack of investment.

But I need your help. I need you to support me, support Kevin and support the players. I firmly believe we are the true club of the community in this region. I am a local businessman, born and bred in Eastwood, and a father of five children who all call this community their home.

My businesses are all in the county, we employ local people - I like to think that as a football club chairman I truly understand the heartbeat of this region. Every Saturday morning, every Sunday morning and afternoon I'm in a tracksuit involved in grassroots boys and girls football across the pitches of Nottinghamshire as a coach, referee, ball boy and tea-maker. I even put up the nets and the corner flags, because I love it.

I challenge you to find any other chairman of a professional football club who does that week in, week out? It matters to me that Notts County is successful. It matters to me that we grow this football club.

I know over 3,000 of you have already come back in the past 10 months to watch us regularly. But there are many more of you out there who I know are wanting to come back. Do it, you won't be disappointed.

Let's also nail a myth about our ageing fan base: it isn't. We are attracting more children as a percentage of total support than any other club in the Midlands. We provide a safe, family-friendly environment where local junior teams get the chance to take penalties on the pitch every week. These young people are the future lifeblood of this football club.

We run a host of complimentary ticket schemes for local junior teams which are always oversubscribed. We have created a series of strategic partnerships with local schools to encourage regular attendance. Did you know our Community Day game against Forest Green Rovers attracted the highest individual gate of the League Two campaign of any club so far - 13,267.

In the coming weeks and months, we will be unveiling further ambitious ticket promotions and incentives. I cannot stress the importance of you doing your bit for this football club. Support us in every way possible. Persuade a friend, relative, neighbour or whoever to come on down to Meadow Lane.

I have another challenge to you all as well: I want Meadow Lane to be sold out for at least one game between now and the end of the season. I'll do my bit to make it as affordable as possible for 19,500 fans to come - make sure you do yours.

The atmosphere at our games is unrecognisable compared with 12 months ago.

This season has the potential to be a special one for the club. Make sure you play your part, starting this weekend when we welcome Oxford City for an exciting Emirates FA Cup tie.

Your support will be more important than ever - so see you down at the Lane!

Kevin Nolan's League Two record during the 2017-18 season (up to and including 1 January 2018) was: P26 W14 D8 L4 with Notts 2nd in the table, alternating top spot with Luton Town, and unbeaten at home.

But, in late January Notts lost two home games (both 2-1) in the space of four days, and although they didn't lose again at home until the second leg of the play-off semi-final against Coventry their away form for the remainder of the season was disappointing with only two league wins after Boxing Day.

Notts had a good run in the FA Cup, winning at home to Bristol Rovers (League One) 4-2, and Oxford City (non-league) 3-2, followed by an away win at Brentford (Championship) 1-0. They achieved a 1-1 draw at home to Swansea City (Premiership) in the 4th round but in the replay - televised live on BBC1 on 6 February Notts crashed to an 8-1 defeat!

On loan players Ryan Yates (midfielder, re-called by Nottingham Forest on 11 January after 29 league and cup appearances for Notts with 6 goals) and Mason Bennett (forward, returned to Derby County when injured in his second match on 10 February – he scored in his first on 3 February) were significant departures who could have made 'the difference' if they had remained at Notts until the end of the 2017-18 season

A disappointed Alan Hardy issued the following message to supporters following the conclusion of the season.

I would like to take this opportunity to say a huge thank you to everyone who supported us throughout the campaign. Unfortunately, there was to be no fairy-tale ending and, given some of the refereeing decisions we were subjected to over the course of our play-off semi-final tie, perhaps it simply wasn't meant to be.

(1-1 at Coventry, who equalised with a dubious 87th minute penalty. At home, in the second leg, Notts lost 4-1).

When the dust settles, we will be able to look back on an amazing season of progression on and off the field, culminating in a breath-taking occasion which attracted a record crowd this century (17,615). It's difficult to put into words the level of pride I felt looking around the stadium ahead of kick-off last night. Nearly every seat was filled and there was a terrific atmosphere swirling around Meadow Lane.

We are all united in our desire to have more nights like that and with your continued backing, I'm sure we will. While the players will now have some well-deserved time off with their friends and family, behind the scenes the hard work begins straightaway to ensure we continue on our upward curve. As always, I will keep you informed of the latest developments in our exciting journey.

Thank you once again.

Alan

Following a summer close season during which ten players departed, including the captain Michael O'Connor, six new ones arrived. Alan Hardy was in a buoyant mood when he delivered his pre-season message on 1 August 2018. At the time everything still seemed in place to enjoy a second successful season – possibly even automatic promotion rather than a place in the play-offs.

What a season I hope we have in store for each and every one of you. I genuinely believe these to be truly exciting times for everyone involved with Notts County Football Club.

I always felt we could surprise a lot of people with a successful campaign last season - and a fifth-place finish was a great achievement when you consider that a few months earlier the club had sadly set a club record of 10 consecutive defeats - the worst-ever run in our 156-year history.

Now we are better prepared and have invested substantially to get this club back up the league pyramid. I'll be straight with you. A lot of money has been put on the line this season. We've invested significantly in new players – small change by Premier League standards, but significant by our own.

Throughout my business life and during my time as custodian here at Meadow Lane, I have liked to get on the front foot and make things happen. Patience is not a virtue I have been blessed with. I want to restore the playing fortunes of the world's oldest Football League club - and I want to do it sooner rather than later. I passionately believe we have invested in and created the strongest group of players we have had since my arrival and, for that matter, many a year.

Talent has to be transferred into results but in Kevin Nolan and his coaching team I am sure we have the perfect management group to fulfil our potential.

The response we have received from our supporter base has been brilliant. To attain an average crowd of 8,500 last year was a truly remarkable achievement. A general rule of thumb is that if you get results right on the pitch, most other things will follow. We've certainly seen that with major increases in supporters, hospitality sales, merchandise sales and other revenue streams.

I've lost count of the number of fans who have contacted me to say the atmosphere at the club has changed beyond belief, how lapsed fans are coming back in their droves, how parents and grandparents are bringing their children and grandchildren to Meadow Lane for their first taste of professional football and how we are all enjoying - and not enduring - watching this great club of ours.

Our season ticket holder base has gone up by 35 per cent but that needs to grow still further. Season ticket holders are the lifeblood of our club. If you have not already bought one, please do your very best to do so in the next few days - our current discounted rate is due to expire on Saturday. For those of you unable to buy a season ticket, please make an extra effort to come to as many games as you possibly can. Your support really does make a difference.

I'd like to see a crowd in excess of 6,500 on Saturday for our opening game at home to Colchester. It would mean a huge amount to me, to Kevin and all the players. A league season is a marathon not a sprint but to see you all on Saturday would be a great way to welcome our new signings to Meadow Lane and to show the fighting spirit and passion our support can create.

I hope and believe this can be a very special season and, with your support, it will be.

However, one aspect of the pre-season concerned me. The last three friendlies, before the first league game of the season, ended in defeat for Notts. The matches were against: Derby County (Notts lost 1-4 at Meadow Lane) who went on to reach the Championship play off final – defeated 2-1 by Aston Villa, Leicester City (again Notts lost 1-4 at home) who went on to finish 9th in the Premier League, and Luton Town (Notts lost 2-0 away) who became champions of League One with 94 points. Kevin Nolan was of the opinion that more is learnt from a defeat than a win. This may be true but I think those defeats, to higher league opposition, immediately before the start of the season, weren't exactly confidence boosters!

In the opening game at home to Colchester 7,136 saw a 0-0 draw, and this was the last point gained by Notts during Kevin Nolan's reign as manager!

His record during the calendar year of 2017 was excellent. However, Notts failed to win any of their last four matches at the end of the 2017-18 season, and this poor form continued into the start of the 2018-19 season. Between 11 August and 8 September they lost six consecutive league matches and conceded at least three goals in each of those defeats – the seventh match was a 3-3 draw! After four league matches, on 21 August, Notts dropped to the bottom of League Two, and sadly, five days later, Kevin Nolan and his assistant Richard Thomas were sacked.

A dismayed Kevin Nolan

Alan Hardy issued this statement:

This is a decision we've made with the best interests of Notts County at heart. While the beginning of our 2018-19 campaign has been bitterly disappointing, the board and I believe results and performances throughout 2018 have not been good enough overall. The last eight months have seen us win only eight of our 28 League Two matches, a run which saw us surrender our position in the automatic promotion places before suffering defeat in the play-off semi-finals against Coventry City. Our away form has also been a continuing concern, with only two league victories recorded on the road since the turn of the year.

Ultimately, a continuation of this form would not allow us to meet our targets for the season and, having conceded 16 goals in our last five matches [13 in the league and 3 in the EFL cup at Middlesbrough] *and being without a win in our last ten competitive games, we feel now is the time to move forward with a new manager at the helm.*

Everybody knows of my desire to restore the fortunes of the world's oldest Football League club and I have invested substantial monies to strengthen our playing squad in the summer. Our supporters have responded magnificently by turning out in their droves but, unfortunately, their efforts have not been backed up by performances on the pitch.

This club will nevertheless always owe Kevin a huge debt of gratitude for his work in saving us from relegation from League Two of the EFL in May 2017. It was a truly remarkable turnaround and we wish him and his team every success in the future.

So, after just over nineteen months, Alan Hardy was looking for a new Notts manager. His relationship with Kevin Nolan had been very good. Only a few weeks prior to the dismissals Hardy, in his pre-season message, had said "in Kevin Nolan and his coaching team I am sure we have the perfect management group to fulfil our potential."

Three weeks can be a long time in football!

It didn't take long for Alan Hardy to find a replacement for Kevin Nolan. Within a week, on 1 September 2018, Australian Harry Kewell was appointed the new Notts County manager. At the same time Hardy decided to restructure the football department, with the appointment "of a vastly experienced technical director."

The c.v.'s of Nolan and Kewell were similar. Both were in their thirties when they joined Notts (Harry Kewell was 39). In addition to being an attacking midfielder, Kewell also played as a winger or second striker. In England he had played for two Premier League clubs: Leeds United and Liverpool. When he left Liverpool in 2008 he spent three seasons in Turkey with Super Lig side Galatasaray. He completed his playing career in his native Australia. He also played in more than fifty games for the Australian national team and appeared in the 2006 and 2010 final stages of the World Cup.

Prior to joining Notts, Kewell had been manager of League Two rivals Crawley Town for fifteen months, since May 2017. At the end of the 2017-18 season Crawley finished fourteenth in League Two.

All smiles – Alan Hardy and Harry Kewell

Alan Hardy indicated he had learnt some lessons during his period in charge of Notts, and had decided to make a notable addition to his management team:

> "Having now worked in football for a significant period of time, I have had the opportunity to learn from other clubs what good looks like. I have therefore decided to appoint a technical director, who will set the club's overall footballing philosophy and be on hand to support and mentor the manager as required.
>
> Harry will, however, be solely responsible for our first-team squad, having the final say on transfers, tactics and team selection. He has enjoyed an excellent start to his managerial career and I am hugely impressed with his knowledge and attention to detail.
>
> I thoroughly enjoyed our discussions about the role and have been left with no doubt that he has a fierce ambition to succeed and a real enthusiasm to work for Notts County. I'm excited to see how he implements his exciting methods and look forward to him working with our new technical director."

As part of the restructure, Vice-Chairman Darren Fletcher stood down from his position.

> "Darren and I have come to a very amicable agreement that it would be best to part ways," explained the chairman. "He will remain a close personal friend of mine and I thank him for the tireless effort and support he gave to me."

Soon after Harry Kewell's appointment the new technical director arrived, Paul Hart (age 61) who had been associated with Notts previously. A defender, he had played some games during the 1987-88 season, just before his retirement as a player. For six months at the end of 2014/beginning of 2015 he had been a member of Notts' management team, working with the academy and in a caretaker capacity as team manager for a few games.

> "Paul is a superb addition for us," said Alan Hardy, "Not only is he one of the most respected men in the game, he also knows Harry very well. His remit will be a broad one to match his tremendous knowledge, experience and breadth of contacts.
>
> He will be on hand to mentor and support Harry, while also being responsible for setting the club's overall footballing philosophy with a keen emphasis on our development and academy set-ups. I have every confidence that he and Harry will oversee an upturn in our immediate fortunes and build a footballing infrastructure which will help us achieve our long-term ambitions."

A few weeks into his managerial role Harry Kewell learnt he was to be inducted into the Sport Australia Hall of Fame at a ceremony in Melbourne.

Notts remained at the bottom of League Two until 22 September. The winless sequence, which started on 28 April, of fifteen league and cup matches, finally came to an end on 29 September when they beat Crewe Alexandra 2-1 at Meadow Lane. Notts also won their next two games, so they had won three games in succession in the space of a week. Prior to these three wins Notts had secured two draws – so five games unbeaten! Unfortunately, Notts then suffered a 4-0 league defeat at Bury. Three weeks later another 4-0 defeat at Barnsley, in the first round of the FA Cup, sealed Kewell's fate. The earlier improvement was soon forgotten and after a total of fourteen matches, and just ten weeks into his reign, Harry Kewell (and his assistant Warren Feeney) departed in mid-November.

Harry Kewell was obviously disappointed.

Alan Hardy summed it up:

> *"Harry's passion and commitment as a coach is unquestionable. I enjoyed seeing first-hand his love for the job and it gives me absolutely no pleasure to take that away from him. Unfortunately, however, things quite simply were not working out for him here at Meadow Lane. Results have not been good enough and performance levels are a continuing concern. We see no reason to continue with something we don't think can work. Harry leaves with our best wishes for the future and our search for a new manager begins immediately."*

Two weeks later, at the end of November, the new manager was appointed. Would it be third time lucky for Alan Hardy?

During his (almost) two years as owner and chairman Alan Hardy had appointed two high profile, but young and inexperienced in terms of management, ex-Premier League players. This changed with his third (and final) managerial appointment at the end of November 2018 when Neal Ardley became the new manager of Notts County, with Neil Cox his assistant.

Neal Ardley, 46, was a midfielder, who played in over 400 games during his career, mainly in the Premier League or Division One/Championship, with Wimbledon, Watford, Cardiff and Millwall. He played for Wimbledon for over ten years.

Neil Cox, 47, was a defender, who played in over 500 games during his career, mainly with Aston Villa, Middlesbrough, Bolton, Watford and Cardiff.

They had recently left AFC Wimbledon where they had been together as a management team for just over six years. At the end of their first season (2012-13) at Wimbledon they avoided relegation from League Two into The National League in the final game of the season. Three years later Wimbledon were promoted into League One, after beating Plymouth Argyle in the play-off final.

Ardley was the third longest-serving manager in England's top four divisions before he, and Cox, amicably departed Wimbledon at the beginning of November. This followed a very disappointing start to their 2018-19 season in League One. Chairman Erik Samuelson described Neal Ardley as a 'clear thinker, superb man-manager and fine coach.' These accolades together with over ten years as a player and six years as a manager, with the same club, indicated additional attributes of loyalty and perseverance.

A realistic Alan Hardy acknowledged the qualities of his new manager:

"Having enjoyed very productive discussions with Neal and following close consultation with the board and key staff, I am very confident we have selected the right man to deliver our short and long-term targets. Our biggest priority is preserving our proud status as the world's oldest Football League club and in Neal we have someone who

knows what it takes to survive. Neither he nor I are under any illusions it's going to be easy but we are both confident of achieving this very important aim.

Beyond that, Neal has demonstrated an ability to win promotion from League Two and sustain a club at a higher level. I hope, in time, he will be able to deliver the same for us. Quite rightly, he is a much-loved, respected figure in Wimbledon folklore and his integrity, loyalty, passion and tremendous coaching qualities will all be valuable assets as we look to bounce back from our unexpectedly poor start to the season. As I have come to learn all too well, football is a suffocating environment. Neal gave absolutely everything to Wimbledon in his six years as their manager and is deservedly enjoying a family holiday which he'll be cutting short in order to join us in the middle part of next week."

Neal Ardley thanked the chairman and explained why he had returned to football management sooner than he had planned:

"I would like to say a huge thank you to the chairman for giving me the opportunity to manage such a magnificent club. There are few clubs who could have tempted me into such a quick return to management following what was obviously an emotional departure from Wimbledon, a club I love dearly. But the chance to manage Notts County is one I couldn't let pass and I will come back from my break fully refreshed and determined to drive us up the table."

Before I continue Notts' journey it is appropriate to record that seven weeks after Neal Ardley arrived technical director Paul Hart departed, after just over four months, on 17 January 2019. He had worked with Nathan Jones at Luton Town before joining Notts and had agreed to team up with him again, and become his assistant manager, at Stoke City. Hart said:

"While I am tremendously excited for the challenges ahead with Stoke City, I am sad to be leaving Meadow Lane. Notts County is a club very close to my heart and, especially with the current predicament, this is not a decision I took lightly. I have, however, seen first-hand the hard work and determination of Neal Ardley and Neil Cox, along with everyone else at Meadow Lane, to put things right and I would like to wish the club every success for the rest of the season and beyond."

Alan Hardy concluded:

"This is a magnificent opportunity for Paul and we were not going to stand in his way. It's been a pleasure working with him and his knowledge and experience have been a big help to us. We wish him and Nathan the very best of luck in their new challenge."

[Jones and Hart were sacked by Stoke on 1 November 2019 with the club bottom of the Championship.]

Neal Ardley and Neil Cox inherited a Notts County team whose record in League Two since their win at Macclesfield (bottom of League Two) on 6 October was: P8 W0 D4 L4 F6 A15 - a sequence which started on 20 October with a 4-0 defeat at Bury. Notts were also defeated 4-0 at Barnsley in the first round of the FA Cup on 10 November – Harry Kewell's last game as manager. Their only win in this period was the 4-2 defeat of Doncaster Rovers in the 'Check A Trade' cup, which was Steve Chettle's first game as caretaker manager four days after the Barnsley defeat. The first game for the Ardley/Cox partnership was on 4 December - a 2-0 defeat at Sunderland in the 'Check A Trade' competition. Notts were therefore out of all cup competitions - all they had to concentrate on was the remaining twenty-six league games of the 2018-19 season. They were next to the bottom of League Two with only sixteen points from twenty games:

23rd Notts County P20 W3 D7 L10 (Goal Diff -19) Pts 16

24th Macclesfield P20 W3 D4 L13 (Goal Diff -21) Pts 13

Macclesfield had recently appointed a new manager – ex England and Arsenal central defender Sol Campbell, who played one game for Notts during the Munto Finance debacle of 2009. His arrival had had a positive effect and they had won their last two League games.

There follows a record of the first nine of those twenty-six League Two games:

MATCH	OPPONENT	H/A	RESULT	PLACE	DATE
21	Mansfield Town (6th)	(A)	Lost 2-0	23rd	Dec 8th
22	Tranmere Rovers (7th)	(H)	Won 3-2	23rd	Dec 15th
23	Grimsby Town (18th)	(A)	Lost 4-0	23rd	Dec 22nd
24	Macclesfield Town (24th)	(H)	Lost 1-2	Bottom	Dec 26th
25	Bury (6th)	(H)	Drew 0-0	Bottom	Dec 29th
26	Oldham Athletic (11th)	(A)	Lost 2-0	Bottom	Jan 1st
27	Colchester United (4th)	(A)	Drew 3-3	Bottom	Jan 5th
28	Cambridge United (21st)	(H)	Lost 0-1	Bottom	Jan 12th
29	Yeovil Town (22nd)	(A)	Lost 2-0	Bottom	Jan 19th

The home defeat to Macclesfield on Boxing Day was disappointing, but the home defeat to Cambridge (21st in League Two at the time) before a crowd of 15,026 was even more disappointing. Chairman Alan Hardy reduced admission charges to £2 in an attempt to get a big crowd with everyone 'up for it', but even that didn't work. Notts also fielded three new players: goalkeeper Ryan Schofield (on loan), midfielder Jim O'Brien, and defender Ben Barclay (on loan) who had made his Notts debut the previous week at Colchester. In their next game, at Yeovil (22nd in League Two), they suffered another defeat. Notts then had a two week break due to their next opponent's continuation in the FA Cup. Neal Ardley was of the opinion that this would give him an opportunity to integrate the new players he expected to sign, before the winter transfer window closed on 31 January, and allow injured players to recover and be fully fit for the next league game against top of League Two Lincoln City on 2 February. Ardley also had another concern, which he thought was damaging morale: the presence of clique's among the players. Kevin Nolan had signed players. Harry Kewell had signed players. And now he was about to add more new faces before the closure of the transfer window. It was therefore unlikely to be the most harmonious group to undertake a relegation battle.

However, during the weekend of 26/27 January 2019, with seventeen games remaining, more drama unfolded when Notts County issued the following statement:

> *Notts County Football Club's Owner and Chairman Alan Hardy has 'very reluctantly' put the club up for sale, citing a need to focus on his external business portfolio as the reason for his decision.*

Hardy said:

> *"After considerable soul-searching, I no longer feel I can continue as the owner of Notts County Football Club. I would like to make it clear from the outset that the club's current league position is not a factor in this decision, nor are any of the events which have unfolded in the media this weekend."*

[He had apologised for ("accidentally") posting an embarrassing photo on social media, and it was reported that he had been disqualified from driving for three months after a speeding offence increased his licence penalty points into double figures]

> *"Everyone at Meadow Lane remains staunchly committed to preserving our proud status as the world's oldest Football League club and, until a new buyer is found, I will continue to support that aim. The truth is, my efforts to restore Notts County's fortunes over the last two years mean my other businesses have had to take a back seat. They are now in need of my full attention. Looking back, as a Nottingham-born man, I take huge pride in being able to say I took on the challenge of owning the world's oldest Football League club at a time when its only alternative fate, according to my*

predecessor, was extinction. The football-related creditors had to be paid up immediately, otherwise Notts County would have ceased to exist. The club was virtually down and out with huge debts, a dwindling, disengaged supporter base and staff morale at an all-time low, while suffering the worst run of consecutive defeats in its history.

Over the following 15 months we had a truly wonderful journey. Initially the challenge was to avoid relegation, which we were able to achieve, and last season we qualified for the play-offs, only to lose out against Coventry in highly questionable circumstances. During that time we were able to double attendances, re-engage supporters and attract crowds of up to 17,000 for League Two fixtures.

Clearly, however, this season has been an incredibly difficult challenge and one of monumental under-achievement, which has left us once again fighting for EFL survival. As the owner, the buck stops with me. I take ultimate responsibility for our current situation. But it cannot be said that our poor performance is due to a lack of investment, as is so often the case in business. We are currently engaged in a relegation fight alongside clubs who have one-third of the playing budget we have allocated this season. I have backed every manager with generous wage and transfer budgets and invested heavily in our academy, girls and ladies divisions, facilities and infrastructure. I readily accept there are no guarantees in football but to find ourselves at the foot of the League Two table is an incredibly bitter pill to swallow.

My decision to sell the club does not mean I won't be supporting our manager, Neal Ardley, in his efforts to strengthen our squad in this transfer window. I am not suddenly pulling up the drawbridge, nor will I be absent from matches. I continue to support this club. We have 17 games remaining to fight tooth and nail to save our EFL status.

Moving forward, I am sad to say the time has come for me to pass on the baton to the next owner of Notts County. But I would like to reassure supporters that I will be doing my utmost to ensure this huge honour is bestowed upon someone who has the best interests of the club at heart. I have already held talks with two interested parties and I will keep fans informed of any future developments when appropriate."

To Alan Hardy's credit, this didn't stop movement in the transfer market, with Notts signing five players between 29 and 31 January, the final day of the 'window'. So, in addition to Ben Barclay (on loan from Brighton), Ryan Schofield (on loan from Huddersfield) and Jim O'Brien (Bradford City), who signed earlier in January, came Mitchell 'Mitch' Rose (midfielder, Grimsby), Craig Mackail-Smith (forward, on loan from Wycombe Wanderers), Sam Stubbs (defender, on loan from Middlesbrough), Virgil Gomis (forward, on loan from Nottingham Forest) and Michael Doyle (midfielder, Coventry). Of the eight, O'Brien, Rose, Mackail-Smith and Doyle were the experienced players. Doyle was captain of Portsmouth when they won 3-1 at Meadow Lane in April 2017 to seal promotion to League One, and twelve months later he was Coventry's captain when they won the League Two play-off final at Wembley (after beating Notts in the two-leg semi-final) to earn promotion to League One. The other four were young players with limited experience, but lots of potential. To balance the books eight Notts players departed, six permanently, with two (Dennis and Crawford) going to other clubs on loan. Would this mixture of experience and youth blend with the resident players to extract Notts from their perilous position and escape relegation from the EFL?

The final seventeen games:

Seven of the eight newcomers started the game against Lincoln, and the one who didn't start (Gomis) came on as a substitute (for Mackail-Smith).

MATCH	OPPONENT	H/A	RESULT	PLACE	DATE	SCORER(S)	ATTEND-ANCE
30	Lincoln City (Top)	H	Drew 1-1	Bottom	Feb 2	Stead (pen.)	Att: 10,641
31	Forest Green Rovers (4th)	A	Won 1-2	Bottom	Feb 9	O'Brien, Boldewijn	
32	Mansfield Town (2nd)	H	Won 1-0	Bottom	Feb 16	Mackail-Smith	Att: 12,660
33	Newport County (15th)	H	Lost 1-4	Bottom	Feb 19	Hemmings	Att: 6253
34	Tranmere Rovers (9th)	A	Lost 1-0	Bottom	Feb 23		

With twelve games now remaining yet more complications, and even more drama, unfolded:

25 Feb: Alan Hardy acknowledged the financial difficulties of his company Paragon Interiors Group PLC.

28 Feb: Notts revealed: "a payment to HM Revenue and Customs became due at the beginning of February" and that unfortunately HMRC had taken "an extremely aggressive approach" and rejected Notts' offer of a payment plan "to clear the debt in full" before the end of March. HMRC issued a winding up petition against the club.

1 Mar: Alan Hardy decided not to attend the Port Vale game, citing "the reaction to recent developments has led me to surmise that my attendance would be counter-productive"

MATCH	OPPONENT	H/A	RESULT	PLACE	DATE	SCORER(S)	ATTEND-ANCE
35	Port Vale (22nd)	H	Drew 0-0	Bottom	Mar 2		Att: 7457
36	Cheltenham (17th)	A	Lost 4-1	Bottom	Mar 9	Hemmings (pen.)	
37	Carlisle United (7th)	A	Won 1-3	23rd	Mar 12	Hemmings 2 (1 pen.), Alessandra	

Notts off the bottom, where they had been since 26 December!

MATCH	OPPONENT	H/A	RESULT	PLACE	DATE	SCORER(S)	ATTEND-ANCE
38	Morecambe (19th)	H	Drew 0-0	Bottom	Mar 16		Att: 5813
39	Exeter City (7th)	H	Lost 0-1	Bottom	Mar 23		Att: 9505

Exeter had a player sent off halfway through the first half. Notts had 59% possession, 8 corners, and 21 shots (4 on target). Exeter had 41% possession, 1 corner, 3 shots and scored in the 3rd minute of injury time with their only 'on target' effort, a header!

MATCH	OPPONENT	H/A	RESULT	PLACE	DATE	SCORER(S)	ATTEND-ANCE
40	Stevenage (11th)	A	Won 0-3	23rd	Mar 30	O'Brien, Hemmings, Boldewijn	

On 4 April Alan Hardy issued an update on his attempts to sell the club, and other off-field matters:

I am pleased to confirm I have accepted an offer to purchase Notts County Football Club from a very credible party, who is now undertaking due diligence. As expected, there has been a huge level of interest in the club and I am delighted that we are now at an advanced stage with people who I am confident have Notts County's best interests at heart. They must be given the time and privacy to carry out their checks properly but, as soon as I can reveal more, I will provide a further update.

I would also like to assure staff and supporters that, in light of recent conjecture, the money for April's wages has already been transferred to the bank for payment. As for the debt owed to HMRC, I am expecting this to be paid in full by early May with the approval of the High Court next Wednesday. I hope these updates will be reassuring to everyone connected with the club, whose concerns are understandable during this time of change.

While the takeover gathers pace, I was also thrilled to witness a magnificent performance from the team at Stevenage last weekend. It's been a tough time for Neal Ardley and the players, with recent results failing to reflect the level of dominance we've had in matches, but we certainly banished a few demons with an emphatic, clinical and very encouraging 3-0 win. We are of course very keen to produce a performance of that nature on home soil to further reassure supporters that our battle against the drop is far from over. Hopefully that comes on Saturday [against Northampton Town].

Thanks again for your amazing, loyal support, which was especially evident at Stevenage where our fans cheered loud and proud from the first minute to the last.

| Match 41 | Northampton Town (15th) | H | Drew 2-2 | 23rd | Apr 6 | Rose, Hemmings | Att: 7129 |

Northampton equalised just before half time and took the lead just after half time, from the free kick awarded after goalkeeper Ryan Schofield was sent off!!

On 9 April Macclesfield won their game in hand to move off the bottom to 22nd – bottom two teams relegated into The National League:

Rank	Team	Played	Goal Difference	Points
21	Crawley	41	-20	43
22	Macclesfield	41	-23	39
23	Yeovil	41	-22	37
24	**Notts County**	**41**	**-31**	**37**

The next day, 10 April, Notts issued the following short (and sweet) statement:

> "Notts County have been given until 5 June 2019 to settle their debt to HMRC.
>
> At a High Court hearing today, the judge adjourned the case in order to allow sufficient time for the takeover of the club to be completed".

Two days later, on the 12th, Notts signed Alex Palmer a 22-year-old (6' 3") goalkeeper on emergency loan from West Bromwich Albion. Ryan Schofield was given a one match suspension for his sending off against Northampton. Ross Fitzsimons, the first-choice goalkeeper until January, who came on as a substitute after the dismissal, was unavailable and "withdrawn on doctor's advice due to illness". Never a dull moment at Notts this season!

| Match 42 | Crewe Alexandra (15th) | A | Lost 3-0 | Bottom | Apr 13 |

Described by Neal Ardley

> "I can't defend the performance. Everything was wrong. We weren't a team, like we have been recently. We became 11 individuals who weren't on the same page. We were awful in every shape and form. I could go to town on the players and start blaming them, but that's a load of rubbish. The buck stops with me. The boys have been fighting hard and none of them want this to end badly. They're doing their best but, at times, they're not good enough. We've got four games to go and the players need leadership. They need me to step up and refocus them, like I did after Cheltenham. We were awful there and we bounced back at Carlisle. We've got to do that again. I have to make sure they keep the belief, train hard in the week and step up against one of the best teams in the league [MK Dons] on Friday, like they did against Lincoln and Mansfield [in the first half of February]."

Thankfully Yeovil and Macclesfield also lost so it was 'as you were ' at the bottom end of the table, but the team now in 21st position (Cambridge United) were six points clear of 22nd. As the bottom two clubs are relegated it was becoming increasingly obvious that three teams were fighting for the coveted 22nd position. Notts were two points adrift at the bottom but their inferior goal difference meant that in effect it was like being three points adrift – so… Notts had it all to do!

On 15 April there was yet another twist to this amazing season. The following statement was issued by the club:

Notts County have reported a number of individuals for abusive comments made on social media

The club fully accept this has been a bitterly disappointing and frustrating season for fans and respect their right to voice their displeasure, be that at matches or online. However, Notts officials, players and staff have recently been subjected to an increased number of comments which overstep the line between fair criticism and vile, threatening abuse, many of which have a knock-on effect on the families of those targeted. This cannot and will not be tolerated. The club have been in contact with Nottinghamshire Police to report one particularly malicious tweet, while legal advice is being sought in relation to comments made by other individuals. Formal proceedings against the protagonists are likely to commence shortly and indefinite club bans have been imposed. Recent communications from Leicester Tigers RFC and Crawley Town illustrate that this is a growing – and concerning – problem in professional sport. Notts stand in solidarity with those clubs and implore supporters to consider the potential impact of what they're saying – often in the heat of the moment – before doing so. Notts would like to take this opportunity to once again express their immense gratitude to their supporters, who continue to back the team in huge numbers. Everyone at Meadow Lane is doing their utmost to ensure the season ends on a positive note.

| Match 43 | Milton Keynes Dons (4th) | H | Lost 1-2 | Bottom | Apr 19 | Barclay | Att: 7130 |

As last Saturday, Yeovil and Macclesfield also lost so it's again 'as you were ' at the bottom of the table, but the team still in 21st position (Cambridge United) are now seven points clear of 22nd, so it's almost definitely Notts, Yeovil and Macclesfield fighting for the coveted 22nd position to avoid relegation.

| Match 44 | Crawley Town (18th) | A | Drew 1-1 | Bottom | Apr 22 | Mackail-Smith |

Barclay sent off 54th minute with score 1-1

Yeovil and Macclesfield also drew, so it remained 'as you were' at the bottom.

Next, the final home game of the season for Notts. It was also possible/likely that it would be their final home game as a football league club. They surely had to win, and they did!

| Match 45 | Grimsby Town (17th) | H | Won 2-1 | 23rd | Apr 27 | Mackail-Smith, and an own goal | Att: 8519 |

Macclesfield also won and remained in the coveted 22nd position. Yeovil drew, dropped to the bottom of the league, and were relegated. So, despite the victory over Grimsby, Notts' situation had not really improved, except that they had moved up one position to 23rd. If they had not won they would have remained at the bottom and been relegated with Yeovil. However, they lived to fight another day!

Rank	Team	Played	Goal Difference	Points
21	Cambridge	45	-26	46
22	Macclesfield	45	-26	43
23	**Notts County**	**45**	**-34**	**41**
24	Yeovil	45	-25	39

The scenario for the final games of the 2018-19 season:

If Macclesfield avoided defeat they would not be relegated, unless they only drew and Notts achieved the impossible and won by nine goals to improve their goal difference to minus 25!!!

In reality, Notts needed to win at Swindon and Macclesfield needed to lose, at home to Cambridge United, for Notts to avoid relegation out of the football league for the first time in their 157-year history.

Chapter 2: Relegation at Swindon

The only Swindon Town 'away' tickets available on Notts' website on 30 April were those for the Stratton Bank stand – behind the goal and all seated but uncovered. The 'away' seating in The Arkell's Stand was sold out. I therefore bought our two tickets from Swindon's website, for the same price (£17 each, concession) and in so doing was able to get seats in the upper tier of Arkell's three rows from the front.

My wife and I arrived in Swindon at 13:30 on Saturday 4 May 2019. The afternoon was cool, 12C, with a north-westerly wind, but plenty of sunshine. The showers in the vicinity all missed The County Ground. We had arranged to meet a former Met Office colleague of mine, Clive Thundercliffe (great name for a weatherman), a Swindon season ticket holder, and his son Martin, at 14:15 "outside the chip shop across the road from the fire station", beside 'The Magic Roundabout' - a notorious set of traffic islands where the central large island is surrounded by five satellite islands. We parked in the fire station for £5. Clive and Martin admitted that for once they wanted Swindon to lose (and also Macclesfield). We were seated in different parts of block A4U in The Arkell's Stand. The Thundercliffe's were further back from where we were in seats 94 & 95 of row C near the front, directly behind the team dug-outs and almost opposite the half-way line. The Notts team for this momentous occasion was:

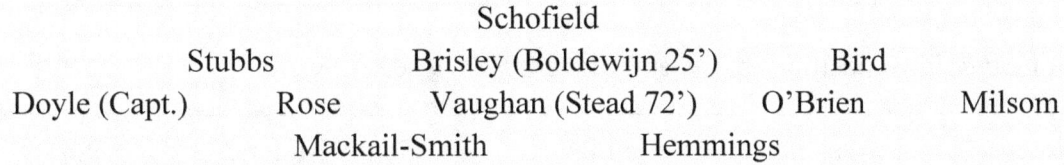

Defender Brisley injured on 25 minutes: Boldewijn (midfielder) substituted. Vaughan replaced by (forward) Stead on 72 minutes. The other (un-used) subs were: Fitzsimons (Gk), Evina, Alessandra, Dunn and Gomis.

When the teams appeared, we were surprised that Notts were playing in blue (admittedly, their away kit) rather than their traditional black and white stripes – especially as Swindon were in all red, and it was possibly going to be Notts' last match as a football league club!

The first half was just about even, although Boldewijn squandered a good chance to give Notts the lead – he failed to connect with a cross from Milsom, when in front of goal on the edge of the six-yard box. Probably the most exciting event occurred just before half time when there was a sudden loud cheering from the Stratton Bank and the adjacent AW block of The Arkell's Stand, where the 2,248 Notts supporters (Att: 8,676) were housed. Macclesfield were losing 1-0 at home to Cambridge.

Not surprisingly Notts started the second half in a purposeful manner, and in the 52nd minute Mackail-Smith was tripped in the penalty area and the referee immediately awarded a penalty. Hemmings calmly scored from the spot to put Notts 0-1 up. For almost twenty minutes Notts were out of the relegation zone, and in the coveted 22nd position of League Two. However, the Swindon fans then started to shout "You're going down" when they discovered that Macclesfield had equalised. This precipitated a disastrous final twenty-five minutes of league football for Notts.

Notts had had chances to increase their lead, but in the 69th minute Woolery received the ball just inside the Notts half and accelerated past Stubbs before he scored with a good left foot finish. Five minutes later Milsom misjudged a Swindon clearance and headed the ball into the path of Robinson who ran on to beat Schofield with a powerful rising shot from the edge of the penalty area. Defeat was confirmed in the second minute of added time when, following a corner, a Swindon header found Robinson almost on the goal line and he cleverly hooked the ball into the net. In the end the 3-1 defeat didn't matter because Macclesfield got the draw (1-1) they needed to confirm their escape, and finish in 22nd position.

| Match 46 | Swindon Town (14th) | A | Lost 3-1 | 23rd | May 4 | Hemmings (pen.) |

So, the final League Two positions at the end of the 2018-19 season were:

Rank	Team	Played	Goal Difference	Points
20	Port Vale	46	-16	49
21	Cambridge	46	-26	47
22	Macclesfield	46	-26	44
23	**Notts County**	**46**	**-36**	**41**
24	Yeovil	46	-25	40

As Notts had been in the bottom two since game 18 on the 17 November 2018 (and therefore throughout Neal Ardley's management) the final outcome was not a big surprise.

Throughout the season Notts had been a poor side. They lost both games against Yeovil (aggregate score 0-6) and both games against Cambridge (agg. 2-4). Their two Port Vale games were drawn. They managed to win 0-1 at Macclesfield thanks to an 82nd minute penalty by Stead but lost the home game 1-2 on Boxing Day. A record of P8 W1 D2 L5 F6 A14 Pts 5 out of 24.

Notts also had the worst defence in League Two with 84 goals conceded. When the Premiership, Championship and League One are included only Rochdale in League One had more goals (87) against. At one stage, in August and September, when for seven consecutive league games Notts had three or more goals scored against them, it looked as if the 'against' total for the season would exceed one hundred!

There were other notable league statistics for Notts at the end of the season:

Bottom of the 'Away form' table with 17 points. Third from bottom of the 'Home form' table with 24 points. Fifth from bottom of the 'Goals scored' table with 48 (Kane Hemmings scored 14 of the goals). Their discipline was also poor with only five teams collecting more yellow cards (bookings) than Notts (79) and only two teams collecting more red cards (sending's-off) than Notts (7).

There is very little to record that is positive, but remarkably their supporters did not desert them. The average home attendance was 7,357 – excellent for a team who produced so many poor performances, and who were in the bottom two (relegation zone) of League Two for most of the season.

During their four seasons in League Two, since their relegation from League One at the end of the 2014-15 season, only last season's fifth from top finish was acceptable. In 2015-16 they finished 17th of 24 and at the end of season 2016-17 they finished 16th of 24.

I don't like admitting this, but Notts probably deserved to be relegated.

Chapter 3: "What's next for Notts?"

Notts County owner and Chairman Alan Hardy issued a statement following the club's relegation to The National League.

Having headed into this season with every intention of challenging for automatic promotion, to find ourselves in this situation is bitterly disappointing for everyone involved with the club.

Once again, I have invested heavily in the playing budget this season, fully supporting each manager with new signings, and having had the best interests of this club at heart since my arrival two and a half years ago, I am as distraught as anybody at today's outcome. But, as owner, I take ultimate responsibility and apologise to our fans, whose support has been unwavering despite the difficulties we've faced.

Staggeringly, we boast the third-highest average attendance in the league – more than 7,000 - while our backing away from home has also been superb. Our supporters don't deserve this, and their frustrations are completely understandable. I also have huge sympathy for the staff at the club, who have worked incredibly hard all season in extremely testing circumstances. I thank them for their efforts.

Naturally, questions will now be raised about the club's immediate future. Conversations with prospective new owners are ongoing and I expect a deal to be completed in the near future. I truly hope the next custodian of Notts County is able to restore our status as the world's oldest Football League club at the earliest opportunity.

Charlie Slater, BBC Radio Nottingham's Notts County correspondent/commentator:

"It is the end of an era and ultimately the darkest day in the football club's 157-year history, undoubtedly. The club will have to restructure and, unfortunately, an inevitable consequence of relegation could be that people will lose their jobs.

From a football standpoint, it's the culmination of a season from hell. Only Notts County could start a campaign as promotion favourites and end it staring into the abyss of non-league. And there is no guarantee that they will bounce straight back up. As far as I am aware, only three teams in the past 15 years have managed immediate promotion following relegation from the EFL.

Obviously, they will hope any stay in non-league will be a short one but the fear is that the end of this era could prompt the start of a new one based largely outside of the league that for so long they have called home."

Mark Stallard, BBC Radio Nottingham's Notts County summariser who works alongside Charlie Slater on match days:

A former Notts striker, he was a player for the club when it was in administration for a record 534 days (almost eighteen months) between 17 June 2002 and 3 December 2003. He said "The Magpies have a compelling case to be top of the tree when it comes to stressing out supporters. They really are put through the mill time and time again. If it's not trouble on the pitch, then it is financial, a takeover or threat of administration. But this is a real low point. It means just about everything to be the oldest professional league club. Even during the hard times, when money was being raised and the club were close to extinction, it's that moniker and history that got people from around the country and world to put their hands in their pocket to help out. To lose it is devastating and it will hit the club hard. To be 'the oldest football league club in the world' again should be the motivator to get back."

There were many comments and quotes on the internet/social media about the downfall of Notts County. Most were sympathetic and expressed sorrow at the situation.

"Notts are arguably the biggest club to have ever suffered relegation into non-league football .... having been one of ten teams to have featured in every season since the formation of the Football League in 1888."

"It is the relegation that has robbed a club of its identity."

"It will feel like a drop into the abyss."

"Death by a thousand cuts."

"It's not just sad for Notts fans - they will be distraught, no doubt - this is one relegation that the general football fan, anyone who loves the history of the game, will also feel."

"They were there at the birth of the professional game."

"To lose their Football League status after so long is tragic, but they have their oldest professional club mantle to cling to."

"Joyous moments, such as winning back-to-back play-off finals at Wembley under Neil Warnock to reach the top flight in 1991, are intertwined with years of financial hardship."

"Even moments of almost fairy-tale fortune have resulted in nightmare endings."
(*A reference to the Munto Finance episode during the summer of 2009.*)

"In July 2009, Sven-Goran Eriksson, just three years after managing England to a World Cup and one year after leaving Manchester City, was lured to Notts by their historical significance and the romance of taking them to the Premier League from the depths of League Two."

"Notts are a club that have experienced more ups and downs than any other, with this their 17th relegation. It would take winning promotion for a 14th time to see them return to the EFL."

Notts County therefore found themselves in a perilous position. It was hoped (rather than expected) their stay outside the English Football League would be short – one season, two season's………but in reality it could be longer.

The pessimistic question was:

Will this be the beginning of the end for Notts County?

The optimistic question was:

How long will it take Notts County to get back where they belong?

Chapter 4: A summer of discontent

On 15 May Notts issued their 'Retained List 2019' - seventeen players **Under Contract**

Pierce Bird, Age 20 Nottingham born. Central defender/left back. Played for local side Dunkirk before joining Notts. Northern Ireland U21 international.

Enzio Boldewijn, Age 26 Winger/striker or midfield. Notts paid a six-figure fee, to Crawley Town of League Two, to bring the Dutchman to Meadow Lane ahead of the 2018-19 season. After a promising start he then missed the latter part of 2018 and the beginning of 2019 with a knee injury.

Remaye Campbell, Age 19 Striker, originally a midfielder. Came through the academy system at Meadow Lane.

Tom Crawford, Age 20 Midfielder. Joined Notts from National League side Chester.

Kristian Dennis, Age 29 Striker, with a good goal scoring record. Signed from League Two Chesterfield. After a disappointing first season with Notts he was expected to make a significant contribution in their National League campaign.

Michael Doyle, (Captain), Age 38 Midfielder. Very experienced, with over 750 appearances for Coventry City, Sheffield Utd, Portsmouth, and Leeds Utd. Republic of Ireland international.

Declan Dunn, Age 18 Midfield or defence. A graduate of the Notts academy.

Ross Fitzsimons, Age 25 Goalkeeper. Played outside the EFL before he joined Notts from Chelmsford City.

Alex Howes, Age 19 Midfielder. Part of Notts' academy since the age of nine.

Sam Osborne, Age 20 Midfielder/winger. Another Notts academy graduate.

Christian Oxlade-Chamberlain, Age 21 Defender/midfielder. Signed from Portsmouth, where he made one appearance.

Mitchell Rose, Age 25 Midfielder. He had made 29 appearances for League Two Grimsby Town, during the first half of the 2018-19 season, before signing for Notts. Has also played in League Two for Mansfield Town and Newport County.

Matt Tootle, Age 28 Defender/full back. Experienced League One and League Two player with Crewe Alexandra and Shrewsbury Town, from where he joined Notts in June 2015.

The following (under contract) players left Notts before the end of August

Kion Etete, Age 17 Forward. After a successful trial, he attracted a bid from Tottenham Hotspur and transferred to the Champions League finalists in June.

Kane Hemmings transferred to Scottish Championship club Dundee on 8 August.

Will Patching and **Andy Kellett** both had their contracts terminated by mutual consent, on 14 August and 27 August respectively.

Offered Development Contracts

Owen Betts, Age 18 Central defender. Came through Notts' academy.

Tyreece Kennedy-Williams, Age 19 Left back. One senior appearance, as a substitute.

Max Culverwell, Age 18 Goalkeeper. Although he had been among the first team substitute's he had not yet made his Notts debut.

Out of Contract, Released

Lewis Alessandra, Shaun Brisley, Richard Duffy, Cedric Evina, Elliott Hewitt, Noor Husin, Dan Jones, Robert Milsom, **Jim O'Brien**, Jon Stead, David Vaughan, Elliott Ward. **O'Brien re-signed 1 August**.

Loans Expired

Ben Barclay (Brighton & Hove Albion), Virgil Gomis (Nottingham Forest), Craig Mackail-Smith (Wycombe Wanderers), Ryan Schofield (Huddersfield Town), Sam Stubbs (Middlesbrough).

Apprentices Under Contract

Rasharn Altaf, **Tiernan Brooks**, Corey Bucalossi, Kieran Cummings, Leo Marshall, Mazhi Simmons, Charlie Wilde. **Brooks (Goalkeeper) still with Notts on their return to EFL League Two in May 2023**.

New Apprentice Intake/Released

Taylor Conway, Bill Harrison, Stern Irvine, Kayne McKenna Crofts, Morgan Mellors, Syme Mulvany, Tyreace Palmer, Cameron Smith, James Snedden, Emillio Stavrou.

Released Harry Bugg, Coden Duncan, Jack Henchcliffe, Owen Newell, Oscar Ramirez Inscoe.

The following two months, June and July, were (not for the first time in Notts' history) momentous: court appearances, disputes, salaries not paid, acts of kindness, and the continuation of a protracted takeover which eventually led to a change of ownership.

The next significant news came on 5 June when Notts issued the following statement:

HMRC hearing

Notts County have this morning been given more time to settle their debt to HMRC.

The High Court have adjourned the case until 10 July in recognition of the ongoing takeover process.

Notts fully understand supporters' frustrations and concerns surrounding the club's ownership situation but stress that strict confidentiality measures must be adhered to in order to ensure a deal is completed professionally and in line with all regulations.

As soon as the club are in a position to comment further, a statement will be released.

The HMRC debt was reported to be at least £250,000.

There had been no information forthcoming, regarding the position of manager Neal Ardley, in the thirty two days since the Swindon defeat on 4 May. His position was obviously insecure. New owners often appoint a new manager on, or shortly after, takeover. However, it was reported at the end of the season that he wanted to stay at Notts. In some ways this was not a surprise - loyalty and perseverance seemed to be two of his attributes.

Anyway, on 14 June Alan Hardy issued the following update regarding the takeover of the club:

Due to increasing and understandable levels of frustration within the fan base I would like to provide assurances that talks with prospective buyers are continuing in a constructive manner.

An issue out of the club's control is currently delaying matters but I am extremely confident it will be resolved so we can reach a positive outcome.

Everyone involved is acutely aware that time is of the essence and we are working around the clock to get a deal done at the earliest opportunity.

I'm sorry that I can't reveal more but, as is normal practice, non-disclosure agreements have been signed, limiting what I can tell you at this stage.

Thank you for your continued support and patience.

The "issue out of the club's control" was, allegedly, the serious illness and hospitalisation of the person (Terry Pritchard) leading negotiations on behalf of those considering the takeover of the club – believed to be a South African consortium. More bad luck! They subsequently withdrew their interest before the (adjourned) 10 July court hearing.

Three days before the players returned for pre-season training on Monday 24 June, Notts announced:

> Mark Crossley will leave Notts County when his contract expires this month.
>
> The former goalkeeper arrived at Meadow Lane in 2016, taking on the role of assistant manager to John Sheridan, and went on to become a key part of the first-team coaching set-up at Meadow Lane.
>
> Notts thank Mark for his service and wish him well for the future.

Presumably a total of nineteen players returned - the sixteen under contract (the retained list had been reduced from seventeen by the transfer of Kion Etete to Spurs), plus the three offered development contracts.

It must be remembered that Notts were unable to sign any new players as they were under a transfer embargo until all debts had been paid etc. It was not the only embargo in place: manager Neal Ardley and the players were not allowed to give interviews to anyone.

Finally, to give everyone associated with the club a confidence boost, and to improve morale, at the end of the week staff were informed that they wouldn't be receiving their June salaries!

However, a light appeared at the end of the tunnel on 1 July when Alan Hardy issued another update on his attempts to find a buyer for the club.

> I am very pleased to say that, following hugely constructive talks today and over the weekend, I am extremely confident that a sale will be completed ahead of our upcoming court hearing on 10 July.
>
> Conversations with a group who I am certain have Notts' footballing fortunes at heart are now at an advanced stage and I am sure supporters will be delighted to hear their plans for the club.
>
> Apologies, once again, that I am unable to reveal any identities. At the request of all parties, this remains private business until formalities are completed. I can, however, confirm that we have ceased talks with the group associated with Alex May.
>
> Should our talks progress further as planned, I will be liaising with the prospective new owners to rectify the current situation regarding player and staff salaries at the earliest

opportunity. I deeply regret being unable to fulfil this obligation to my employees and hope - and expect - there will be a speedy resolution.

I am also aware that a great deal of cynicism is likely to come my way in response to this update, which I can understand following an immensely frustrating and disappointing chapter in the club's history.

However, I felt it was only right to bring supporters up to speed following the significant developments of the last few days.

Despite all this turmoil Notts played their first pre-season friendly of the summer on 6 July with a trip to Nuneaton Borough, where Notts won 2-0. Four days later the following statement was issued:

HMRC hearing

Notts County have this morning been granted a further extension by the High Court in order to settle their debt to HMRC. The Magpies' case has been adjourned until 31 July after lawyers were able to demonstrate that a takeover of the club will soon be finalised. Alan Hardy said: "While I hoped and expected a takeover to have been completed before today's hearing, I am pleased to say I will be exchanging contracts with the new owners of the club in the coming days. I would like to thank all our supporters for their continued patience. I will provide a further update in due course."

The people now reported to be the takeover favourites were a Danish group headed by brothers Christoffer and Alexander Reedtz, directors of Football Radar Limited (HQ 31 Vernon Street, London W14 0RN, with offices in Liverpool and Plovdiv, Bulgaria). On their website Football Radar described themselves…

'Football Radar is a leading provider of football betting advice. We specialise in predicting the outcome of matches and competitions, and have helped our clients achieve outstanding returns in the betting markets for the past 10 years.'

Unfortunately, the next day (11 July) the 'Nottingham Post' revealed:

Alan Hardy storms out of Meadow Lane meeting with staff as tensions at Notts County over the club's financial crisis reached boiling point.

Nottinghamshire Live has been told the Magpies chairman this afternoon met with anxious employees, who are yet to receive their June salaries. But no assurances were given about when they can expect their wages which has angered the players, who were informed by Hardy earlier in the week that he hoped to pay them on Wednesday or today.

After realising no money had been deposited into their accounts, several senior players are understood to have vented their frustrations in a heated discussion with Hardy who then stormed out of the room. The squad is understood to have become increasingly tired of being told when they will be paid, only for no money to be forthcoming.

There are now fears a dressing room revolt could take place, while rank and file staff at Meadow Lane are also said to be close to breaking point. It has also since emerged that, during a meeting with the players last week, one player is understood to have interrupted Hardy when he began talking about how much money he has lost since buying the Magpies in January 2017.

The news comes just 24 hours after the club avoided being wound-up in the High Court for the third time, after Judge Clive Jones gave them until July 31 to complete a sale of the club to a Danish consortium. Barrister Hilary Stonefrost told the court the prospective new owners had passed the Football Association's fit and proper person test, with a sale purchase agreement drafted up. It is believed a meeting with The National League and brothers Christoffer and Alexander Reedtz, who own the betting statistics firm Football Radar, was also scheduled for today.

Two days later Notts won (5-0) their second pre-season friendly at Ilkeston Town. A collection was made and a total of £2,483 was raised for Notts County's unpaid staff. Those who entered via designated 'Notts County' turnstiles saw their admission fee added to the fund, with a total of £1,485 being raised in this way. The club's **O**fficial **S**upporters' **A**ssociation also conducted a bucket collection inside the ground, when an additional £998 was collected. Staff who needed it most benefited from the fundraising, and the club thanked everyone who had contributed for their support.

On 18 July, two days before Notts won their third pre-season friendly (2-1 at Meadow Lane at home to Walsall), another contribution was received, this time from **LIFELINE**:

Lifeline has made a donation of £25,000 to Notts County in order to contribute to the unpaid salaries of club staff. The donation, which has been ratified by the membership committee, is being shared among employees who do not benefit from any external financial assistance. The monies have been gratefully received by all beneficiaries, who would like to thank Lifeline's members and committee for their generosity and support. Lifeline coordinator Lynn Lawson said:

"On behalf of my fellow Lifeline committee members Daphne Mounteney, Les Bradd and Colin Slater, who we hope you all agree have the club's best interests at heart, we would like to say thank you to our members, who continue to make Lifeline a success ever since it was launched 33 years ago. This is a record of which you and we should all be very proud. As a committee we meet on a quarterly basis, and more often if urgent business requires us to do so. Our agendas include many aspects of issues

associated with Lifeline, with membership of the scheme and distribution of the money raised being among the regular items. It needs to be emphasised that all monies raised are always donated to the club - not ever to any individual. In the instance of our most recent donation, the club's Human Resources and Finance departments have worked together to distribute the funds in a fair and honest way. Under the current ownership, £211,000 (including today's donation) has been released for the benefit of the club, funding the following important projects:

- *Installation of a state-of-the-art indoor training surface in the Haydn Green Family Stand (a facility used by all age groups)*

- *Maintenance and upkeep of the Meadow Lane playing surface*

- *Essential boiler repairs*

- *The purchase of a new first-team kit van*

- *Renovation of the club's IT infrastructure, enabling contactless payments at the ticket office and concourse kiosks*

- *Player/match sponsorship and other initiatives, all of which help to promote, grow and maintain Lifeline*

- *Lifeline server replacement/upgrade*

"Finally, as an assurance, at its regular meetings the Lifeline committee always considers any issues raised by members of the scheme and will continue to do so. Your part in helping us grow Lifeline is absolutely vital to our continued success so please continue your loyal, excellent and much-appreciated support."

LIFELINE HISTORY

Monday 15 September 1986 was one of the most significant occasions in the long history of Notts County Football Club.

This was the night that 1500 supporters packed into the Astoria Ballroom with hundreds locked outside as they gathered to hear of the financial crisis that threatened the future of the club.

Notts had been struggling financially for a long time and it was only the financial support of then chairman Jack Dunnett that enabled the club to continue.

At the time of the meeting the club's debt had reached £1.8million, which would not have been dissimilar to the figure involved when the club went into administration in 2003.

Just as there was tremendous enthusiasm shown by Notts fans during the 2003 crisis, so it was then.

The players were all on the platform, led by captain Steve Sims, pledging their support and listened to the speeches from amongst others Tommy Lawton, Don Masson and Jimmy Sirrel.

To rousing cheers, Sirrel said: "With the passion you are showing tonight there is no chance the club will die."

John Mounteney, Notts' former vice-chairman said on the night: "We are staggered to find so many people turning out for Notts County. The club belongs to you. We as directors are just stewards of an institution that has been running 120 years and it is our duty to preserve it for the generations of supporters to come."

And so Lifeline was launched with John Mounteney as chairman, backed by the tremendous enthusiasm from Neil Hook and Les Bradd, and membership numbers were soon approaching the maximum 2,500. 33 years later, following a surge in support amid the 2020 coronavirus pandemic, Lifeline membership hit full capacity for the very first time, leading to the introduction of a waiting list for new members - which soon filled up!

The wave of new joiners means the scheme, which has contributed over £3million to the club since its formation, is thriving more than ever.

Colin Slater's tribute to Mr Dunnett, who died in October 2019 aged 97:

It was with the west London club, Brentford, that Jack Dunnett first became a director of a Football League club, later switching to Notts after a local businessman, Bill Hopcroft, had rescued the club from financial oblivion.

At Brentford Mr Dunnett had become an admirer of Jimmy Sirrel, who was part of the managerial set-up, and after his own election as chairman to succeed Mr Hopcroft he soon embarked on the task of bringing Sirrel to Meadow Lane which he achieved early in November, 1969.

The club was then in the Fourth Division, since re-branded as League Two, and earned three great promotions to take them, ultimately, to the top flight of the English game. The first lifted Notts into the Third Division in 1971, the second into the old Second Division (now the Championship) in 1973 and the third into the old First Division (now the Premier League) in 1981.

Mr Dunnett was one of four men who, throughout this transformation, held key positions the others being Jimmy Sirrel, Captain Don Masson and trainer-coach Jack Wheeler. In addition, Mr Dunnett became a significant figure on the national scene as President of the Football League, the only director in Notts' long history to be elected to such a lofty position.

When he retired from the Meadow Lane board in 1987 he was succeeded by Derek Pavis, who was responsible for the complete redesign and rebuilding of the Meadow Lane stadium in only two years, 1991 and 1992. His vice-chairman was the late John Mounteney who held the same position under Jack Dunnett. He was also a key figure in Nottingham's political fortunes as a Labour Member of Parliament for Nottingham Central, then after constituency boundary changes, Nottingham East.

Our thoughts are with Mr Dunnett's family at this very sad time.

In the middle of July 2019, the 'Nottingham Post' reported:

Juventus offered to supply Notts County with a new kit - but they had to turn them down.
We can exclusively reveal the Italian giants were ready to help in the Magpies' hour of need.

Juventus made the incredible gesture of supplying Notts County with new shirts for next season but the club had to turn down the offer because of their contract with Puma. Nottinghamshire Live revealed in midweek how Lilian Greenwood MP had written to the Serie A giants in the hope they would repay a 116 year debt after the Magpies had supplied Juventus with their black and white shirts.

Juventus chairman Andrea Agnelli was willing to supply Notts with new kit through Adidas and wrote to the club informing them of their willingness to lend a hand. But Notts had to respectfully turn down the offer because of their contract with Puma who are awaiting payment for new shirts that are currently in a warehouse waiting to be delivered.

In a letter seen by Nottinghamshire Live, Juventus' head of communications Claudio Albanese explained to Ms Greenwood how Juventus had been willing to help Notts during their hour of need. "Considering the long-lasting relation between the two clubs, Juventus would have gladly assisted in providing new kits for next season," he wrote. "We have already held talks with our technical sponsor, Adidas, to inform them of the situation and they immediately contacted Notts County to arrange equipment supply. Unfortunately, as it turns out, the club has a two-year binding agreement with Puma that doesn't allow them to wear any other brand.

Thank you for the letter. We wish Notts County all the best for the future."

Juventus' gesture shows the incredible bond between the two clubs which was formed in 1903 when Notts had supplied them with their iconic black and white shirts. In 2011, Juventus invited Notts to open their new stadium with the Magpies the first English team to play at the Allianz Stadium where the teams fought out a 1-1 draw.

Notts played their fourth pre-season friendly, a 1-1 draw at Meadow Lane on Tuesday 23 July at home to Ipswich Town. The next day staff were informed they wouldn't be receiving their July wages. Following this announcement Nottingham Forest's website confirmed........

"....a collection will be held prior to Friday night's pre-season friendly against Real Sociedad to help the staff of Notts County. The club would like to reassure all supporters wishing to donate that 100% of the money raised will go towards the staff at Meadow Lane. Collectors will be easily identifiable around The City Ground prior to kick-off and Nottingham Forest do not endorse any unauthorised collections taking place and urge supporters to check before donating."

Rumours of a sale began to circulate, and Notts' fifth, and penultimate, pre-season friendly at Alfreton Town (Notts lost 1-0) kicked off just after the sale announcement at 19:00 hours on Friday 26 July 2019.

(An acknowledgement of the Nottingham Forest bucket collection was posted on Notts' official website on 30 July.......

> *"...with Notts' takeover now complete and all outstanding wages paid by new owners Christoffer and Alexander Reedtz, Magpies staff have decided the money should go to worthwhile causes of the two clubs' choosing………..Everyone at Meadow Lane would like to thank all connected with Forest for their kindness and generosity."*)

Notts County's staff and players deserved great credit for the way they continued to perform their duty in the most trying of circumstances, especially when the club suffered relegation out of the football league. Throughout all the turmoil their fortitude and dedication was outstanding. The leadership and inspiration of Jason Turner (Football Operations Director, later CEO), manager Neal Ardley and his assistant Neil Cox, captain Michael Doyle, strength and conditioning coach Erik Svendsen, and the medical services team, gave everyone some unity and belief.

Before discussing the arrival of the new owners I would like to conclude this chapter with a few words about the main protagonist in this saga: Alan Hardy. At times he was his own worst enemy. Luck was against him on occasions. He admitted to impatience. He made mistakes, and some would question his judgement. However, although not all will agree, he departed with some credit. In the end, whether by luck or judgement, he achieved two of his goals – if you'll pardon the pun. First, when he put the club up for sale in January 2019, he wanted to reassure supporters that he would do his utmost to ensure the new owner(s) had the best interests of the club at heart. Second, he hoped the next custodian of Notts County would be able to restore Notts' status as the world's oldest Football League club at the earliest opportunity.

So, Alan Hardy's remarkable two and a half years, since he became owner and chairman of Notts County in January 2017, had finally come to what appeared to be a satisfactory conclusion.

Chapter 5: Alexander and Christoffer Reedtz takeover

Danish brothers acquire Notts County

Alexander and Christoffer Reedtz have released the following statement after acquiring Notts County from Alan Hardy

It is with great pleasure that we are able to announce today that we are the new owners of Notts County Football Club. We are delighted that the deal has been completed, and that the uncertainty about the club's future has come to an end. We can now all shift our focus towards the exciting new football season which is just around the corner.

As you may be aware, we run a football analysis company called Football Radar, which has its headquarters in London and further offices in Liverpool and Plovdiv, Bulgaria. Ever since we founded the company 10 years ago it has been our goal to own a professional football club, and we are thrilled that the day has come where we have fulfilled this ambition. While football is business for us it is also our lifelong passion and to now have the opportunity to own a club with such heritage as Notts County is a dream come true for both of us.

Why Notts County? It goes without saying that Notts County are a big club with a proud history, and its status as the world's oldest professional football club is something that we, and anyone else who loves football, find absolutely compelling. What also appealed to us about Notts County is the city of Nottingham itself, and the support the club enjoys here. The club's results in recent years have not lived up to the high expectations, but the fans have continued to support their team wholeheartedly. In our view, the fans are the foundation of any successful football club. The passion and loyalty that the Notts County fans demonstrate is truly admirable, and of essential importance to the club's future. We look forward to getting to know the fans better and to working with them to take Notts County forward.

We are very much going to need the support of the fans in the upcoming season, which will not be easy. The National League is a strong league and the gap between it and League Two isn't massive. With only two promotion spots at stake for 24 teams, and twice the number of relegation places, the competition is going to be tough. The preparations for the new season, of course, haven't been ideal, with many players leaving and the club unable to sign replacements until now due to the financial circumstances. Having said all that, our ambition is to bring Notts County back to the Football League as soon as possible. We will work intensively with Neal Ardley and the rest of the team to bring in the right players in order to have a squad that has the necessary quality and depth to hopefully challenge for promotion this season.

A key element in our future strategy for Notts County will be the work we do at Football Radar. We believe that the unique data and knowledge we have access to through Football Radar, when used alongside the extensive expertise that already exists within the club, can help Notts County become very successful.

Finally, we would like to say that we feel very proud and humbled to be in charge of this fantastic football club. We know how important Notts County are to the fans and to the city of Nottingham, and we can guarantee that we will do our utmost to bring success to the club. It is now our responsibility to carry forward the great traditions of Notts County, to ensure that the world's oldest professional football club endures, and last, but not least, to win an awful lot of football matches!

With the arrival of the Reedtz brothers the ban on manager Neal Ardley, and the players, doing interviews to the media was lifted. The manager's first interview, summarised on Notts' website, before the York game:

He had enjoyed a short meeting with the new owners before the Alfreton friendly.

"Obviously, it's a huge relief," he said. "Hopefully this is going to be the start of something good. The new owners want to put a model in place that grows success over a longer period of time and they're really enthusiastic. In the coming days, we'll be in a position to start strengthening the squad which will be fantastic so, all in all, it's really positive."

Ardley also took the opportunity to praise club staff, who he says have been an inspiration to him and others on the football side of the business.

"My job hasn't been easy, but it's not been the hardest job at the club," he said. "The work Jason Turner (Football Operations Director) and Beverley Markland (HR Director)

have done has been fantastic and the office staff have kept their spirits high and turned up every day – they've been an inspiration."

Notts' sixth, and final, pre-season friendly was at York City (Bootham Crescent) on Saturday 27 July – a match Notts lost 3-1.

Captain Michael Doyle gave a frank interview <u>after</u> the York game:

He believed the completion of the club's takeover should draw a line under what he admitted had been a 'tough' summer, and it was now time to look forward.

"The massive thing about the takeover is that there are no excuses anymore," he said. "We can get our heads down, concentrate on football and get this club back in the Football League, where it belongs. Last year was tough but in a strange way I think it's brought everyone together – fans, players and staff – and we've got to use that as motivation so we can reward everyone for their efforts and support."

Despite the club's difficulties over the summer, Doyle and his team-mates had remained committed to the cause. The 37-year-old, with a long and established career in the EFL, said it never crossed his mind to move on.

"For me personally, when we went down it was so tough – but I never thought about leaving the club so I could stay in the League," he said. "I came back in and felt like I wanted to be part of taking this club back up, because you certainly feel responsible for it going down. I know how big Notts County is and I didn't want to step in when I did, only to run away if the worst happened. I wasn't making any phone calls to get out, I was just hoping the takeover could get done as quickly as possible. Now we're hopefully in a position where the owners and the manager can add a few players as they see fit, and we can kick on."

The next day, after Neal Ardley had had time to reflect on a hectic forty-eight hours he summed up his thoughts in an interview with Leigh Curtis of the 'Nottingham Post':

Ardley, who deliberately selected physical opponents for the latter stages of pre-season, said the performances proved what he and his staff have known to be true all summer.

"We need to become a more physical team to be able to cope with The National League," he said. "At York we got beaten up and out-run and the same happened at Alfreton. It was the reason we got relegated last season. We certainly need to man-up as a team."

Ardley had not ruled out making a move for some of the club's trialists.

"They're all there for discussion," he said. "It's not fair to single anyone out at the minute, but I think it's clear we need to add some physical qualities to the squad. Can we find them in the next week? We'll certainly work hard. We'd like to get two or three in before Saturday to at least get us started on the right foot. We have to give up every hour to do it."

On Tuesday 30 July The National League confirmed that Notts had settled all outstanding payments to HMRC, staff, players and creditors and as a result the transfer embargo had been lifted. A few hours after this excellent news the new Notts County board structure was revealed. Christoffer Reedtz became chairman. He was to be supported by three directors: his brother, Alexander, Richard Montague (Head of Analysis at Football Radar) and Jason Turner (Notts' Football Operations Director).

Christoffer said: "I am confident that between us we have the knowledge, experience and enthusiasm to drive Notts County forward. While Alexander, Richard and I are new to working within a club, we feel the skills and expertise we can bring from other areas of football and business will be very useful. Jason, meanwhile, has been at Meadow Lane for a number of years now and has an excellent knowledge of the club's culture, along with vast experience of football administration. We look forward to working with him closely."

You will probably have come to the conclusion from the events and revelations of the last five days that the court appearance planned for Wednesday 31 July did not happen. The new owners had settled the clubs debts after completing their takeover, on Friday 26 July, from Alan Hardy. Court officials therefore confirmed that the winding-up petition had been dismissed.

As there was no summer transfer window for clubs in The National League, ("Transfer window" is the unofficial term commonly used by the media for the concept of "registration period" as described in regulations) Notts could continue to sign players after the EFL window closed at the end of August.

THE FOOTBALL CONFERENCE LIMITED
KNOWN AS THE NATIONAL LEAGUE

FA STANDARDISED MEMBERSHIP RULES 2019/20 SEASON

6.2 REGISTRATION PERIOD
6.2.1

In any Playing Season the Registration Period for that season for The National League, National League North and National League South Clubs shall be the period commencing at midnight on the last day of the immediately preceding Playing Season and ending at 5.00pm on the fourth Thursday in March next following.

> *After 5.00pm on the fourth Thursday in March each Playing Season new registrations, new loans, and transfer of registrations will be declined or will be approved subject to such limitations and restrictions as the Board may determine and, if so determined, the Player shall only be eligible to play in the matches for which permission is granted by the Board.*

Notts could therefore manage the arrival/departure of players until the end of the current registration period on Thursday 26 March 2020. Little did we know that by then sport, including football, would be suspended due to the coronavirus (COVID-19) pandemic. However, for now, with the lifting of the transfer embargo, the question was: How many players would Notts sign before their first ever National League game, on Saturday 3 August 2019, and beyond?

A few weeks after their takeover of Notts County, Colin Slater interviewed the Reedtz brothers. We all knew of Colin's passion for Notts County and the ability he had to obtain answers to his insightful questions. This interview was not only revealing but it also proved how lucky Notts County were to have such level-headed and articulate owners who spoke with clarity and intelligence. Chairman Christoffer was asked what had pleased him most since his (and Alexander's) arrival. He gave an answer which praised the people and staff associated with Notts, in particular Jason Turner and manager Neal Ardley who were "great to work with and doing a fantastic job". He had been impressed with the "many competent and dedicated people at the club". The supporters had not only been "very welcoming" but also "outstanding, despite the relegation". He described their attendance at away games as "brilliant" and said they obviously have "a passion for Notts County". Alexander talked about his (and Christoffer's) interest in most sports, particularly football, and his love for tennis which he had played professionally. The brothers play six-a-side football to keep themselves fit and be "ready if Neal Ardley wants us for the team!" He also gave a detailed description of the work undertaken by their company 'Football Radar', founded by Christoffer in 2009. It now has 235 employees based in London, Liverpool and Bulgaria. Analysts rate teams in fifty leagues across the world and use mathematical models to predict the outcome of matches, and provide advice and guidance to the betting industry. Players are also analysed and rated. To conclude the interview Colin asked Christoffer what his "priorities for the near future" were, to which he answered:

- Build and improve the scouting structure
- Identify other sources of revenue, and to spend money efficiently
- Improve the spectator experience at Meadow Lane
- Promote the club throughout Nottingham ("a great city") and the whole community

Colin thanked Christoffer and Alexander and finished by saying "I can assure you of this, there isn't a single person in this room who doesn't wish you all the best and every success."

Chapter 6: National League Here We Come!

Within a couple of days of the transfer embargo being lifted Notts signed seven players before their first National League fixture at Eastleigh on 3 August 2019. These additions to the remaining sixteen 'Under Contract' from last seasons retained list gave the first team squad a strength of twenty-three for the Eastleigh game.

Ben Turner, Age 31
A powerful and dominant 6'4" centre back, who had played in each of England's top four tiers, including 31 appearances in the Premier League for Cardiff City in season 2013-14. With Mansfield in the second half of last season. Ardley: "He brings aerial dominance, leadership, experience and know-how."

Zoumana Bakayogo, Age 33
Experienced, League One/League Two, left sided attacking full back or wing back. Signed from Tranmere Rovers. Born in Paris, he has represented Ivory Coast at U23 level. Ardley: "….he has mentality, drive and physicality…"

Sam Slocombe, Age 31
Goalkeeper, who had played most of his games in Leagues One and Two. After spending seven seasons with his hometown club, Scunthorpe United, he moved to Oxford United and then Blackpool. Joined Notts after being released by Bristol Rovers at the end of last season.

Damien McCrory, Age 29
Left back or centre of defence. Had spent the majority of his career at Burton Albion, during which time they were promoted from League Two to League One, and then the Championship. Released by Burton at the end of last season. A successful pre-season trialist.

Dion Kelly-Evans, Age 22
Right full back or wing back. League One experience with Coventry City. Played for non-league Kettering Town last season. A successful pre-season trialist.

Nathan Tyson, Age 37
A much travelled and vastly experienced (centre) forward/striker. At Nottingham Forest from November 2005 to May 2011, followed by two seasons with Derby County. Joined Notts from League One Wycombe Wanderers following a successful pre-season trial.

Jim O'Brien, Age 31
An experienced midfield player, whose playing career had alternated between the Scottish Premier League and the Championship (Barnsley) and League One (mainly Coventry City). Initially signed

for Notts in January 2019, from Bradford City. "In truth, I never really left. I was back in pre-season on the first day and involved in the uncertainty, which was a frustrating time for everyone, but I think its built togetherness."

Between 8-27 August three 'Under Contract' players departed:

Kane Hemmings, last season's leading goalscorer transferred to Dundee.
Will Patching and **Andy Kellett** had their contracts terminated by mutual consent.

Following the Eastleigh game, another eight players were signed between 5 August and 5 September:

Connell Rawlinson, Age 27
Central defender. He had spent most of his career with the very successful **The New Saints** in the Welsh Premier League. Signed from Port Vale after being with them since May 2018. Ardley: "He's got a voice, experience, is very good in the air and is an intelligent player."

Sam Graham, Age 18
Central defender on a season long loan from Premier League Sheffield United. Ardley: "An unbelievable athlete, very powerful." Unfortunately, his loan ended in mid-September when he suffered a ruptured Achilles in training. In his short stay he started seven games and came on as a substitute in three.

Regan Booty, Age 21
Central midfielder. Booty had been with Huddersfield from the age of eight and had been on the fringes of the first team prior to their promotion to the Premier League. He spent last season on loan at fellow National League club Aldershot Town. Joined Notts after his Huddersfield contract expired.

Wes Thomas, Age 32
A much travelled and experienced (centre) forward/striker. During a fifteen year playing career, with twelve league clubs, most of his appearances had been in League One and the Championship. Released by League Two Grimsby Town at the end of last season.

Kyle Wootton, Age 22
A big 6'3" central striker on a season long loan from Scunthorpe United, his only permanent club, where he had made a number of League One appearances. Ardley: "Our intention is to use him as a target man, but he can do more. He's mobile, and I believe he'll score and create goals."

Richard Brindley, Age 26
Right full back/wing back. Most of his appearances had been in Leagues One and Two, principally with Colchester United. Last season he played over 30 games for Bromley in The National League.

Sean Shields, Age 27
Winger/wide midfielder on a season long loan from fellow National League club Ebbsfleet United. Although he had played a few games at League Two level, the rest of his appearances had been in non-league football, and mostly with St. Albans and Ebbsfleet.

Jake Kean, Age 28
Goalkeeping coach. Subsequently registered as a player. Had played one game in the Premiership (for Blackburn Rovers at Chelsea on 13 May 2012) and 36 games in the Championship (also for Blackburn). His other appearances had been in Leagues One and Two when on loan.

On 5 September the strength of the first team squad was therefore 28, plus three 'Development Contract' players.

Notts County 2019-20

Back Row: ? ?   Brindley, Booty, Campbell, Oxlade-Chamberlain, Howes, Dennis, Bakayogo, Osborne, Dunn   ?
Mid Row: ? Kean, Thomas, Turner, Graham, Culverwell, Slocombe, Fitzsimons, Wootton, Crawford, Rawlinson, Boldewijn ? ?
Front Row: Tyson, Rose, Kelly-Evans, O'Brien, Doyle (Capt.) Neal Ardley (Manager), Christoffer Reedtz (Chairman), Alexander Reedtz (Director) Neil Cox (Ass. Man.), Betts, Kennedy-Williams, Shields, McCrory, Tootle (Pierce) Bird was on international duty when this photo was taken. A total of 31 players.

My apologies to the six (standing) unnamed staff (?); very important people whose contribution should not be underestimated – thank you.

Despite the relief and euphoria at the arrival of new owners Christoffer and Alexander Reedtz in late July, August was a challenging month for manager Neal Ardley and his assistant Neil Cox. The fifteen new players, and the 'Under Contract' sixteen, had to gel and get to know each other. Not only that but some of the new players hadn't had a complete pre-season of training, so there was an imbalance in the levels of fitness. This problem wasn't helped by the punishing schedule of the first four league games, Saturday/Tuesday, Saturday/Tuesday, which meant there was not much time for tactics and training. Anyway, the departure for their National League journey was scheduled for Saturday 3 August 2019 at 15:00 hours from Eastleigh, a suburb of Southampton. So, ready or not, Notts had to get on with it and do the best they could in these chaotic circumstances.

A thought about Notts' start in the Southampton suburb of Eastleigh:

Over the years many had sailed from Southampton on (cruise) ships, embarking to commence journeys to locations worldwide. The ex-Cunard liner Queen Elizabeth 2 (QE2) was probably the most famous ship to be associated with the port. However, there was one vessel whose journey started in Southampton with which Notts had to avoid comparison. The Titanic sailed in 1912, was struck by an iceberg, and sank on its maiden voyage!

No further players were signed until early November when the permanent replacement for the injured Sam Graham arrived:

Alex Lacey, Age 26
Central defender, given a contract until the end of the 2019-20 season. After spending his early career with Luton Town, he transferred to League Two Yeovil Town in July 2015 where he was named Player of the Season 2016-17. For the next two seasons he played at League One Gillingham before he departed, upon the expiration of his contract, last May.

Manager Neal Ardley thought a squad of thirty-one was too big. He had hoped that a few more of the 'fringe' players would have departed (on loan) but this had not, so far, materialised. Only three youngsters, Campbell, Dunn, and Culverwell, had taken season long loans. Two others, Howes and Betts, had taken short term loans. Following Lacey's arrival Pierce Bird departed to National League North club Boston Utd 'for the remainder of 2019'.

As Notts didn't have a reserve side it meant that a number of players were not involved on match days. A maximum of five substitutes were permitted in The National League (seven were allowed in the EFL) so seventeen or eighteen players would be named in the squad for each fixture. After suspensions, injuries and illness were taken into consideration those on the periphery had to rely on the occasional 'behind closed doors' arranged friendly, and training matches, in an attempt to maintain match fitness and be ready if/when called upon.

(Tootle and Oxlade-Chamberlain were subsequently loaned. Tootle to local rivals Chesterfield for the remainder of the season, and Oxlade-Chamberlain to Ilkeston Town until the end of December.)

The following appeared on 'Club News', just after the 2019-20 season had started:

16 August 2019

The National League Chairman Brian Barwick notes a significant date in the division's history this weekend.

This weekend, The National League celebrates its 40th anniversary, since the first fixtures took place in the then-called Alliance Premier League. An allocation of 20 Clubs made up the fifth tier, with Altrincham claiming the title in the inaugural season. The Noel Kelly trophy - named after the former Nuneaton Borough Chairman - remained at Moss Lane (Altrincham) at the end of the first two campaigns. The pyramid shaped trophy represented a transition to the structure of Non-League football, which has been integral in shaping the game in this country.

With automatic promotion introduced from 1987, even the smallest Clubs could dream of a meteoric rise into the Football League and beyond. Football power-brokers Jim Thompson and Noel White, were just two of a number of key people who influenced this ground-breaking change - and many others, like the influential Bill King, Peter Hunter and current President Brian Lee, have tirelessly steered the League through its many adventures over the past four decades.

The addition of the play-offs in 2003, then the North and South divisions a year later, has added a new dimension to the competition and created more wonderful memories.

Not only has the league had three titles, with the Football Conference in use for nearly 30 years, there has also been a total of six title sponsors. All of which have helped create an identity for the competition, as we know it today.

From a football perspective, there has been a huge number of significant moments throughout The National League's history. Wealdstone became the first Club to win the "Non-League double" of league title and FA Trophy success back in 1985. Colchester United matched this achievement in 1992, then Martin O'Neill's Wycombe Wanderers the following season.

Many managers and players have gone on to have hugely successful careers in the game. Similar to O'Neill, the likes of Neil Warnock, Jamie Vardy and Joe Hart have made their mark at the top level.

And who can forget the more recent FA Cup runs of Lincoln City and Sutton United just over two years ago? Managers Danny Crowley and Paul Doswell performed heroics with their respective sides, showcasing their efforts in front of global audiences.

Our current commercial partnerships with Vanarama, LV Bet and BT Sport are flourishing, and the estimated money generated by the season-long competition is now at over £80 million.

From small acorns, The National League has become a well-established part of English football - and its profile is growing season-by-season. Extensive live match day TV coverage on BT Sport and a greater awareness of our three divisions across the breadth of both traditional and modern media continues to grow. Last season, over two million spectators attended our matches. It's incredibly encouraging to see so many people coming through the turnstiles at our Football Clubs, the heartbeats of their communities. The figure is substantially larger than a decade ago.

Most importantly our competition remains friendly, welcoming and open to all. It is a National League but with wonderful Local Values.

Happy Birthday! And here's to the next forty years.

Chapter 7: The 2019-20 season (and Coronavirus)

To achieve promotion back into the **E**nglish **F**ootball **L**eague (League Two) Notts had to do one of two things:

1. Finish as champions of The National League, and be automatically promoted.
2. At the end of the season finish in one of the six places below the champions, and achieve promotion via the play-off system.

Until 2017 the four teams below the champions played against each other in semi-finals over two legs, with second playing fifth and third playing fourth. The winner of each semi-final then played a single final game, known as the Promotion Final, with the winner getting the second promotion place.

However, at the end of season 2017-18 the play-off system changed with the six clubs below the champions (instead of four) taking part in play-offs for the other promotion place. Two eliminator games take place before the semi-finals: Match A - 5th place vs 6th place, Match B - 4th place vs 7th place.

The clubs who finished the season in 2nd and 3rd automatically proceed to a semi-final at their home ground, with 2nd place vs winner of Match A and 3rd place vs winner of Match B.

The Promotion Final is played at Wembley Stadium.

2018-19 season play-off results:

Match A: AFC Fylde 3 Harrogate Town 1; Match B: Wrexham 0 Eastleigh 1 a.e.t.

Semi-Final: Solihull Moors 0 AFC Fylde 1

Semi-Final: Salford City 1 Eastleigh 1
(Salford won 4-3 on penalties)

Final: AFC Fylde 0 Salford City 3

Salford promoted to League Two with champions Leyton Orient.

Would Notts County defy the odds and return to League Two of the EFL at the first attempt?

Match 1	Eastleigh 1 Notts County 0	Att: 2,668
Sat 3 Aug 2019 15:00	goal 13' mins	(796 Notts supporters)

Only four players survived from the side relegated three months ago – Doyle, Rose, O'Brien and Bird, although Boldewijn came on as a substitute at Swindon. Six of the seven players signed after the transfer embargo was lifted on 30 July started – Slocombe, Kelly-Evans, McCrory, Bakayogo, Tyson and O'Brien (re-signed after his contract expired at the end of last season). The one who didn't play was Turner as he was not considered match fit due to very little game time during pre-season.

Slocombe

Oxlade-Chamberlain (Tootle 75')   Bird (Turner 75')   McCrory

Kelly-Evans (Hemmings 60')   Bakayogo

Doyle (Capt.)   Rose   O'Brien

Tyson   Boldewijn

Subs: Fitzsimons (Gk), Tootle, Turner, Dunn, Hemmings

Eastleigh finished in 7th position at the end of last season and were beaten in the promotion play-offs. So, a difficult start for Notts – to be expected following the events during the close season and the influx of new players in the last few days of pre-season.

The disappointment experienced by nearly eight hundred Notts supporters was accentuated by the fact that two players, Michael Doyle in the 75th minute (slap/punch) and Damien McCrory in the 90th minute (dangerous tackle), were sent off after receiving straight red cards. Both were suspended for the next three games.

Eastleigh's goal (in the unlucky 13th minute) was a header from a corner.

Meadow Lane, the home of Notts County FC

Match 2	**Notts Co** (19th) **1 Stockport Co** (20th) **1**	Att: 5,820
Tue 6 Aug 2019 19:45	O'Brien 36' goal 71'	

```
                          Slocombe
        Graham            Rawlinson           Bird (Turner 62')
             Kelly-Evans           Bakayogo
             Rose (Capt.)          O'Brien
        Hemmings       Tyson (Dunn 28')      Boldewijn
```

Subs: Fitzsimons (Gk), Tootle, Turner, Dunn, Campbell

Central defenders Sam Graham and Connell Rawlinson made their debuts after joining Notts yesterday.

Stockport, who suffered a home defeat on the opening day, were promoted from The National League (North) at the end of last season after finishing as champions.

Notts' first ever goal in non-league football was an excellent shot by Jim O'Brien, who did well to keep his balance as he turned and angled his shot into the corner from the edge of the penalty area.

Stockport's equaliser was well worked, with close passing followed by a good placement from near the penalty spot.

Match 3	**Notts Co** (20th) **1 Barnet** (8th) **2**	Att: 4,096
Sat 10 Aug 2019 17:20	Boldewijn 9' goals 28', 75'	
Shown live on BT Sport		

                            Slocombe

Rawlinson   Turner (Tootle 61')   Graham

      Kelly-Evans (Campbell 84')   Bakayogo

Rose (Capt.)   Dunn   O'Brien (Dennis 50')

        Tyson   Boldewijn

Subs: Fitzsimons (Gk), Tootle, Bird, Dennis, Campbell

Ben Turner was now fit enough to make his first Notts start and young midfielder Declan Dunn made his debut.

Barnet finished in mid-table (13th) last season and were unbeaten, with a win and a draw, in their first two games of this season.

Notts' goal was unstoppable: Enzio Boldewijn cut in from the left wing and struck a right foot shot into the top corner from twenty yards.

Barnet's equaliser followed a corner when three of their players were allowed to head the ball on its way into the net. Their winner came after a good through ball was lifted over the advancing Slocombe, from fifteen yards.

The end of a difficult and disappointing first week of the season for Notts was not helped by the suspensions of Doyle and McCrory. Their inability to win either of their first two home games had given more cause for concern. They were next to the bottom of the league with just one point!

Place	Team	Played	Goal Diff	Points
20th	Boreham Wood	3	- 1	2
21st	Chesterfield	3	- 1	2
22nd	Stockport County	3	- 1	2
23rd	**Notts County**	**3**	**- 2**	**1**
24th	Ebbsfleet United	3	- 6	0

Match 4	Harrogate (9th) 0 Notts Co (23rd) 2	Att: 1,863
Tue 13 Aug 2019 19:45	Dennis 45' (pen), Boldewijn 88'	(682 Notts supporters)

<pre>
                         Slocombe
   Kelly-Evans   Rawlinson   Turner   Bakayogo
                    Rose (Capt.)   Booty
   Osborne (Graham 90')   Boldewijn
              Tyson (Thomas 66')   Dennis (Dunn 79')
</pre>

Subs: Fitzsimons (Gk), Graham, Dunn, Thomas, Campbell

Notts gave an immediate debut to midfielder Regan Booty (signed yesterday, along with Wes Thomas). Sam Osborne also made his first start of the season. Both played very well, especially Booty.

Harrogate Town, who play on a 3G (artificial grass) pitch, were excellent last season (their first in The National League, and the highest level they had ever played) finishing sixth before losing in the promotion play-offs.

On a warm, cloudless, evening in Harrogate an incredible following from Nottingham (nearly seven hundred supporters) were rewarded when Notts achieved a first ever victory in non-league football after 157 years of history.

In an entertaining game, Harrogate missed a penalty (given away by Kelly-Evans) in the fortieth minute. Then, just before half time, Notts were awarded a penalty following a goal line 'save' by a Harrogate defender, for which he was given a straight red card and sent off. Dennis scored from the spot kick.

Notts' win was sealed by Boldewijn two minutes from the end when he stooped to steer a low header into the corner of the net from seven yards, following a Booty free kick from near the right touchline.

Match 5	**Notts Co** (15ᵗʰ) **1 Wrexham** (9ᵗʰ) **1**	Att: 6,263
Sun 18 Aug 2019 15:00	Dennis 69' goal 74'	

Slocombe
Graham   Rawlinson   Turner   McCrory
Doyle (Capt.)   Rose   Booty (O'Brien 76')
Boldewijn   Dennis (Tyson 76')   Thomas (Osborne 88')

Subs: Fitzsimons (Gk), Bakayogo, O'Brien, Tyson, Osborne

Wes Thomas made his first start for Notts. Doyle and McCrory returned after serving three game suspensions following their dismissals in the first game at Eastleigh.

Wrexham finished fourth last season but lost in the promotion play-offs. In their last game they narrowly defeated top of the league Halifax Town.

As at Harrogate five days ago, Booty supplied the cross for the goal. This time he swung the ball in from the left touchline to the far post and Dennis ran in to cleverly steer the ball into the net, with his head, from a tight angle.

Wrexham's equaliser was a good shot from eighteen yards.

Of the five games Notts had played so far, three had been against teams who reached The National League promotion play-off's last season, with another against a promoted club from the sixth tier.

So, Notts were still without a home win this season.

Match 6	Ebbsfleet Utd (24th) 2 Notts Co (17th) 2	Att: 1,293
Sat 24 Aug 2019 15:00	goals 45'+1 Turner 11'	(? Notts
	61' (O'Brien og) Booty 48'	supporters)

                         Slocombe
      Graham   Rawlinson (O'Brien 46')   Turner   McCrory
              Doyle (Capt.)   Rose   Booty
      Boldewijn   Dennis (Tyson 70')   Thomas

Subs: Fitzsimons (Gk), Bakayogo, O'Brien, Tyson, Osborne

For the first time this season Notts fielded an unchanged side from last Sunday's draw against Wrexham, with the same five substitutes.

Although Ebbsfleet finished eighth last season, their form this season had been very poor: five games, five defeats, bottom of the league; so this was their first point.

Both of Notts' goals were created by Boldewijn. For the first he crossed from the right and Turner planted a powerful header into the corner of the net from ten yards – his first Notts goal. The second also came from a right wing cross: Thomas attempted a diving header but he couldn't reach the ball and Booty, backing-up, scored with a cross shot from ten yards.

A scrappy goal, on the stroke of half time, provided Ebbsfleet with their first equaliser: following a long throw the ball was eventually tapped in from three yards. Their second equaliser came courtesy of Jim O'Brien's own goal: his attempt to slowly steer the ball back to Slocombe failed and instead it evaded the goalkeeper and trickled into the net!

A third consecutive game undefeated for Notts, and an indication that they were beginning to 'find their feet' in The National League.

Match 7 Mon 26 Aug 2019 15:00	**Notts Co** (17th) **5 Chorley** (23rd) **1** Tyson 30' goal 9' Boldewijn 49' Dennis 53' Thomas 65', 71'	Att: 5,082

Slocombe

Kelly-Evans (Graham 75')   Turner   McCrory   Bakayogo (Booty 75')

Doyle (Capt.)   Rose   O'Brien

Boldewijn   Dennis   Tyson (Thomas 60')

Subs: Fitzsimons (Gk), Graham, Booty, Thomas, Osborne

Chorley, promoted from The National League (North) at the end of last season, hadn't won any of their first six games (drawn 4 lost 2). However, they made a good start and took an early lead with a header from six yards following an in-swinging corner. They were eventually overwhelmed by Notts and finished the game with ten men when they had a player sent off for a second bookable offence. This defeat sent them to the bottom of the league.

In the end it was a comfortable second win of the season for Notts, with five left footed goals:

Tyson brought the scores level with a clean strike from twelve yards after Jim O'Brien had nodded the ball down to him.

Boldewijn put Notts ahead when he moved purposefully forward and scored with a powerful shot from the edge of the penalty box.

Dennis extended the lead when he finished off a good passing move, turned and swept the ball into the corner of the net from twenty yards.

Thomas, soon after his arrival from the substitute's bench, then scored twice in six minutes. His first was a tap in from five yards after some slick Notts passing. For his second he unleashed an unstoppable drive from twenty five yards.

Notts secured their first home win at the fourth attempt.

Match 8 Sat 31 Aug 2019 15:00	**Yeovil Town** (18th) **3 Notts Co** (12th) **1** goals 40', 81', 84' Dennis 90'+4 (pen.)	Att: 2,424 (? Notts supporters)

                          Slocombe
  Kelly-Evans   Graham (Rawlinson 82')   Turner   McCrory
  Doyle (Capt.) Booty (Wootton 71')   O'Brien
  Boldewijn   Dennis   Thomas

Subs: Fitzsimons (Gk), Rawlinson, Bakayogo, Wootton, Osborne

Kyle Wootton, signed on a season long loan yesterday, made his debut from the substitute's bench.

Yeovil, who were relegated from League Two (with Notts) at the end of last season, had lost their previous three league games.

To someone not at the game the result would indicate a poor Notts performance and a comprehensive defeat. However, this was not the case. Notts played well for most of the game, especially in the second half when they had a number of chances to equalise and take the lead, but in the last ten minutes – with Notts continually pressing for the equaliser - Yeovil scored twice!

Unfortunately, goalkeeper Slocombe was not at his best on two occasions. Yeovil took the lead when he and Graham, in a misunderstanding, allowed their player to capitalise and score a simple goal. For the third goal he allowed a shot from twenty yards to squirm under his diving body. In between Yeovil had extended their lead with a (second) header following a free kick.

Dennis scored from the penalty spot in added time at the end of the second half, after Boldewijn had been tripped, to give Notts a consolation goal, and add a little respectability to the score line.

So, Notts' four game unbeaten run came to an end despite a good performance.

This win for Yeovil was the start of a sequence of seven successive victories – they won all their six league games in September, which saw them become promotion candidates rather than relegation contenders.

Match 9	Notts Co (15th) 0 Solihull Moors (7th) 0	Att: 4,152
Tue 3 Sep 2019 19:45		

```
                          Slocombe
      Kelly-Evans     Graham      Turner      McCrory
           Doyle (Capt.)      Rose           O'Brien
      Boldewijn (Dennis 66')   Wootton       Thomas
```

Subs: Fitzsimons (Gk), Rawlinson, Bakayogo, Booty, Dennis

Wootton made his first start, after his substitute appearance last week at Yeovil.

Solihull finished last season as runners-up to champions Leyton Orient, before losing in the play-offs. After five games (a draw on the opening day followed by four wins) they were top of the league. However, since then their three games prior to this match had ended in defeat.

In a drab goalless draw scoring opportunities were scarce. Solihull hit the bar with a free kick at the start of the second half, and McCrory headed over the bar, with a great chance, just before the final whistle.

Two days later, on 5 September, Notts manager Neal Ardley gave an update on the progress Notts had made and declared that, with the signings of Richard Brindley, on a permanent deal, and Sean Shields (on a season long loan from Ebbsfleet) he had at last assembled a balanced squad and didn't plan any further additions to the playing staff. Fourteen (excluding goalkeeping coach Jake Kean) new players had been signed since the transfer embargo was lifted on 30th July. At the time he didn't know that before the end of the month injuries (and a suspension) would lead him to reconsider the position. During his "Incomings completed" interview he said:

> "We're done with signings now. We looked at the balance that we thought we'd need for the season and have worked hard to get there. It's been about putting the team together and creating a culture and an environment that will take us forwards, and the owners have been fantastic throughout the overhaul that we knew was needed. The work we've put in has been 10 out of 10 but it will be judged by winning games of football and that's when I'll be able to enjoy it".

> "We knew the first month or two would be tough but there have been promising signs. We want to be towards the top end of the table and pushing towards promotion to give everybody some excitement and something to look forward to. If we can perform like we did in the games against Wrexham and Yeovil and cut out the mistakes in the same manner as the Solihull fixture, we'll be a match for anyone."

Match 10	**Sutton Utd** (17th) **1 Notts Co** (15th) **1**	Att: 2,059
Sat 7 Sep 2019 15:00	goal 11' Wootton 52'	(? Notts supporters)

Slocombe

Kelly-Evans   Rawlinson (Graham 89')   Turner   McCrory

Doyle (Capt.)   Rose   Booty (Shields 76')

Boldewijn   Wootton   Dennis (Thomas 76')

Subs: Graham, Bakayogo, O'Brien, Thomas, Shields (no substitute goalkeeper)

Sean Shields made his debut from the substitute's bench.

This was Notts' second game of the season on a 3G pitch. On their first experience of an artificial grass surface they won 2-0 at Harrogate.

Sutton made a good start to the season, and after their fifth game (two wins, three draws) they were in sixth position. However, since then their four games prior to this match had ended in one draw and three defeats.

Sutton took the lead with a tap in from inside the six yard box when a cross from the right wing was not cleared. Wootton's equaliser, and first goal for Notts, was a powerful right footed shot from twenty five yards. Sutton's goalkeeper subsequently made two excellent saves to ensure a draw.

Most football 'experts' agree that after ten games the league table begins to indicate realistic positions. So, where were Notts at this stage? Answer: Just below halfway in fourteenth position.

	P	W	D	L	F	A	GD	Pts
14th Notts County	10	2	5	3	14	12	+2	11

Fifty percent of their games had ended in a draw. Of those, if you class three as two points dropped (i.e. opponents equalised) and one as a point gained (i.e. Notts equalised) with the other 0-0 it's not unreasonable to suggest that Notts had dropped five points. I know it's not a very scientific conclusion, but if this far-fetched hypothesis was accepted Notts would have sixteen points and be in a play-off position – possibly as high as 5th!

At this stage my report would read "A difficult, but promising, start."

Match 11	**Notts Co** (14th) **1 FC Halifax Town** (2nd) **0**	Att: 5,188
Sat 14 Sep 2019 15:00	Wootton 57'	

                              Slocombe

Brindley   Graham   Turner (Rawlinson 70')   McCrory

    Doyle (Capt.)   Rose   O'Brien

Boldewijn   Wootton   Thomas (Booty 84')

Subs: Fitzsimons (Gk), Rawlinson, Bakayogo, Booty, Dennis

Richard Brindley made his debut for Notts.

Halifax had made an excellent start to the season. They had won seven of their first nine games. The (home) defeat in their last game knocked them off the top of the league.

Notts were down to ten men when Wootton scored the winner - the ball fell to him near the penalty spot and he scored with a right foot volley. Doyle had been sent off ten minutes before, for the second time this season, after receiving a straight red card for a dangerous tackle. He was again suspended, this time for the next four games.

To make matters worse, five days later on 19 September, Notts reported that central defender Sam Graham had suffered a ruptured Achilles in training and was likely to miss the rest of the season. He had therefore returned to his parent club, Sheffield United.

Ben Turner also had a calf injury. So, just as Notts seemed to be settling down and showing some good form they lose two players to injury, both central defenders, and one to suspension.

Match 12	Bromley (2nd) 2 Notts Co (13th) 1	Att: 3,122
Sat 21 Sep 2019 15:00	goals 2', 73' Wootton 35'	(? Notts supporters)

Slocombe

Brindley   Rawlinson   McCrory   Bakayogo (Bird 82')

Rose (Capt.)   Booty   O'Brien (Osborne 90')

Dennis (Thomas 69')   Wootton   Boldewijn

Subs: Kean (Gk), Bird, Dunn, Thomas, Osborne

Jake Kean, who became Notts' goalkeeping coach a few weeks ago, was also registered as a player and he replaced the injured Ross Fitzsimons on the substitute's bench.

Notts arrived in southeast London with a good recent record of only one defeat in their last eight games.

Bromley took an early lead when a cross from the left found a player unmarked inside the six yard box and he duly smashed the ball into the net. Their winning goal was well taken with a shot into the corner of the net from the edge of the penalty area.

Wootton equalised when he scored for the third successive game. Another with his right foot, this time curled in from the edge of the penalty box.

There was another setback for Notts in the last minute of the game – an (arm) injury to midfielder Jim O'Brien. The Scot walked off the pitch breathing gas and air, following a collision with a Bromley defender, and was taken to hospital to learn the severity of his injury.

It was discovered he had suffered a double fracture and dislocation to his (left) arm which would require surgery, and he was expected to miss up to three months of action.

So, O'Brien joined Doyle and Turner (and Graham) on the unavailable list.

Bromley, who like Harrogate and Sutton play on a 3G (artificial grass) surface, moved to the top of the league with this win. They remained the only unbeaten side with seven wins and five draws.

Match 13	Boreham Wood (12th) 1	Notts Co (16th) 2	Att: 756
Tue 24 Sep 2019 19:45	goal 84' (pen.)	Boldewijn 41'	(289 Notts
		Osborne 66'	supporters)

Slocombe

Brindley Rawlinson McCrory Bakayogo

Rose (Capt.) Booty

Osborne (Shields 78') Boldewijn (Bird 90' +2)

Thomas Wootton

Subs: Kean (Gk), Bird, Dunn, Dennis, Shields

Boreham Wood just escaped relegation at the end of last season – they finished 20th, but eight points clear of the relegation zone. Following a poor start to this season, when they won only one of their first seven games, their recent form had improved with only one defeat in the last five.

Boldewijn gave Notts the lead just before half-time when a twenty yard shot from Thomas was pushed to the right by the diving goalkeeper - Enzio's left footed shot then hit the far post and then the near post before it crossed the goal line. Sam Osborne's first senior goal was one to remember - a twenty yard right foot shot into the top corner.

The penalty awarded to Boreham Wood near the end was given away by Brindley.

Two years ago, in July 2017, the then Arsenal manager, Arsene Wenger opened Boreham Wood's brand-new (FIFA approved) 5th Generation Astro Turf pitch. They claim it is one of the newest and most advanced artificial surfaces available which will play just like natural grass.

Wenger said: "It's a pleasure to help Boreham Wood open their new pitch. Our women's and academy teams play their home matches here at Meadow Park, so of course it's important for us that the facilities are the best they can be".

This was Notts' third away game in succession played on an artificial pitch, and they have now played at all four clubs with such a surface – the others being Harrogate, Sutton and Bromley.

Match 14	Notts Co (11th) 2 AFC Fylde (15th) 0	Att: 9,090
Sat 28 Sep 2019 15:00	Thomas 19'	
	McCrory 80'	

Slocombe

Brindley　　　Rawlinson　　　McCrory　　　Bakayogo

Rose (Capt.)　　　　　　Booty

Osborne (Shields 60')　　　　Boldewijn (Bird 74')

Thomas (Dennis 66')　　　　Wootton

Subs: Kean (Gk), Bird, Dunn, Dennis, Shields

For the second time this season Notts were unchanged from the previous game, including the substitutes. It was their first back-to-back win of the season and the third successive home game they had kept a 'clean sheet'.

Fylde reached The National League play-off final at the end of last season but were defeated, at Wembley, by Salford City who replaced Notts in League Two of the **E**nglish **F**ootball **L**eague. However, the following week they beat The National League champions Leyton Orient in the FA Trophy final, also at Wembley. This season their twelve games had been evenly split (W4 D4 L4). Although they had won their last two (home) games they had not won away since the opening day of the season.

Thomas put Notts ahead when, twenty-five yards from goal, he controlled a difficult Rawlinson pass, ran on and out maneuvered three defenders, before he smashed the ball into the roof of the net from the corner of the six-yard box. An excellent individual goal. McCrory's first goal for Notts was a header after a Booty corner had been flicked on, at the near post, by Bird.

~ ~ ~

Notts' average home attendance prior to this game was 5,100, the best in The National League. The reason for the four thousand increase for this game can be explained….

Adult tickets purchased in advance for this home match were priced at only £3 (usual price £22). Tickets for supporters aged 65 and over and 18-21 cost £2 (instead of £16), under 18s only £1 (£9), under 16 £1 (£5), under 12* £1 (£1) and under sevens* free (free). *Tickets for supporters aged 12 and under purchased in the same transaction as an adult purchase.*

This initiative followed on from the success of Notts' unique £2 ticket promotions, which attracted big crowds to Meadow Lane, in recent seasons.

A bumper attendance was expected for the visit of the Lancastrians. Prices reverted to the usual match day rates at midnight before the match.

Hospitality prices were also reduced.

Notts also celebrated their annual Lifeline Day. Lifeline, which has been in existence for more than thirty-three years, is a membership scheme which gives supporters the opportunity to win weekly prizes while helping the club financially. Special activities for this match included a £10,000 annual jackpot draw, made by owner and Chairman Christoffer Reedtz.

Match 15	**Dover** (7th) **2** **Notts Co** (10th) **2**	Att: 1,463
Sat 5 Oct 2019 15:00	goals 35', 57' Rose 41' (pen)	(355 Notts supporters)
	Dennis 90'	

Slocombe

Brindley Rawlinson Turner Bakayogo

Rose (Capt.) Booty

Osborne (Shields 75') Thomas (Dennis 80') Wootton Boldewijn

Subs: Bird, Dunn, Dennis, Tyson, Shields (no substitute goalkeeper)

Although Dover occupied a play-off position, this was thanks to their excellent away record. Their home record was poor with only one victory achieved in seven games.

Dover's first goal came when a twenty yard direct free kick was superbly placed into the top corner – good goal. Their second followed a long free kick into Notts' penalty area which was allowed to bounce to an unmarked Dover forward who had plenty of time to place his shot into the net – defensive error(s).

Rose was responsible for both Notts equalisers. First he scored with a penalty, just before half-time, after Brindley had been tripped as he sprinted into the penalty area. On the second occasion, in the last minute of the game, he lobbed the ball from just outside the penalty area towards substitute Dennis, who saw the goalkeeper coming of his line and cleverly headed the ball over him into the corner of the net.

~ ~ ~

Notts were now one third of their way through the season and the fixture list had not given them the easiest start to life in non-league football.

In their first fifteen games they had played five teams who had been involved in The National League promotion play-off's at the end of last season: Eastleigh (A), Harrogate (A), Wrexham (H), Solihull Moors (H) and Fylde (H) winning two, drawing two, losing one.

They had also played at home to the two clubs promoted from The National League North: Stockport (draw) and Chorley (won 5-1, Notts' highest score to date).

Halifax (H) and Bromley (A) were faced in successive weeks when both clubs were next to the top of the league at the time. They beat Halifax but lost to Bromley.

Six of their eight away games had involved long trips, to Eastleigh (Hampshire), Ebbsfleet (near Gravesend, Kent), Yeovil (Somerset), Sutton and Bromley (both Greater London, south of the Thames) and Dover (a coastal town in southeast Kent). At least they had all been Saturday afternoon fixtures. Only one game, a Tuesday evening at Harrogate, had been north of Nottingham. The other (evening) game was at Boreham Wood (Herts).

They had also played at all four grounds with artificial grass pitches: Harrogate, Sutton, Bromley and Boreham Wood.

The following National League table shows the positions one third of the way through the season, after fifteen of the forty-six games. Notts were exactly halfway, in twelfth place, only three points off a play-off position.

Considering the upheaval of the summer, the new players signed in a short space of time at the beginning of the season (who all had to 'gel'), the subsequent imbalance of fitness, the difficult fixture list and some long journeys for away games, Notts' position was good.

With a bit of luck, they could have been higher than twelfth.

National League Table
5 October 2019

	Team	P	Home					Away					Overall					GD	PTS
			W	D	L	F	A	W	D	L	F	A	W	D	L	F	A		
1	Halifax Town	15	5	0	2	13	7	5	1	2	13	7	10	1	4	26	14	12	**31**
2	Bromley	15	5	2	1	15	10	3	3	1	9	8	8	5	2	24	18	6	**29**
3	Yeovil Town	15	5	1	1	13	7	4	0	4	12	9	9	1	5	25	16	9	**28**
4	Woking	15	3	3	2	11	9	4	2	1	12	6	7	5	3	23	15	8	**26**
5	Barrow	15	4	0	3	9	6	4	1	3	17	13	8	1	6	26	19	7	**25**
6	Barnet	15	3	3	1	8	5	3	3	2	13	12	6	6	3	21	17	4	**24**
7	Dagenham & Redbridge	15	3	3	2	12	12	3	3	1	7	4	6	6	3	19	16	3	**24**
8	Dover Athletic	15	1	3	4	9	13	6	0	1	12	6	7	3	5	21	19	2	**24**
9	Torquay United	15	4	1	3	13	11	2	3	2	12	11	6	4	5	25	22	3	**22**
10	Harrogate Town	15	4	2	2	10	7	2	2	3	9	10	6	4	5	19	17	2	**22**
11	Boreham Wood	15	3	2	3	14	10	3	1	3	9	7	6	3	6	23	17	6	**21**
12	**Notts County**	**15**	**3**	**3**	**1**	**11**	**5**	**2**	**3**	**3**	**11**	**12**	**5**	**6**	**4**	**22**	**17**	**5**	**21**
13	Solihull Moors	15	5	0	2	13	6	1	3	4	9	11	6	3	6	22	17	5	**21**
14	Eastleigh	15	2	4	1	8	6	3	1	4	9	13	5	5	5	17	19	-2	**20**
15	Hartlepool United	15	2	3	3	13	15	3	2	2	6	7	5	5	5	19	22	-3	**20**
16	Maidenhead United	15	1	2	5	8	10	4	1	2	10	6	5	3	7	18	16	2	**18**
17	Stockport County	15	4	0	3	10	10	1	3	4	5	14	5	3	7	15	24	-9	**18**
18	Sutton United	15	1	4	3	9	11	2	3	2	7	7	3	7	5	16	18	-2	**16**
19	Fylde	15	3	2	2	8	11	1	2	5	11	18	4	4	7	19	29	-10	**16**
20	Wrexham	15	3	3	1	9	7	0	3	5	10	17	3	6	6	19	24	-5	**15**
21	Aldershot Town	15	1	2	4	6	10	3	1	4	7	10	4	3	8	13	20	-7	**15**
22	Chesterfield	15	2	2	4	11	13	0	4	3	7	14	2	6	7	18	27	-9	**12**
23	Chorley	15	1	4	3	7	13	0	4	3	5	14	1	8	6	12	27	-15	**11**
24	Ebbsfleet	15	1	2	4	9	15	1	2	5	7	13	2	4	9	16	28	-12	**10**

Top = Promoted to EFL League Two. Positions 2-7 = play-off's to decide the other promoted team. Positions 21-24 relegated.

Match 16 Tue 8 Oct 2019 19:45	**Notts Co** (12th) **2 Dagenham & Redbridge** (7th) **0** Booty 24' Dennis 87'	Att: 3,670

<pre>
                         Slocombe
    Brindley   Rawlinson   Turner   Bakayogo (Bird 79')
              Rose (Capt.)   Booty
    Shields (Dennis 61')   Thomas (Doyle 61')   Wootton   Boldewijn
</pre>

Subs: Bird, Doyle, Dennis, Tyson, Osborne
(No substitute goalkeeper, for the third time this season)

Sean Shields made his first start for Notts. Captain Michael Doyle was available again after completion of his four-match suspension.

Prior to this game Dagenham had gone eleven games unbeaten. They also had a very good away record, with only one defeat in seven games. However, these seven games had only produced eleven goals: seven scored and only four conceded!

Notts' opening goal was direct from a nineteen-yard free kick. Booty struck the ball cleanly with his left foot, through a gap in the defensive wall, and found the bottom corner of the net. For the second goal Boldewijn ran through the middle and squared a pass to substitute Dennis, who swung his left foot at the ball and his twenty-two-yard shot curled in off the far post with the goalkeeper motionless - beaten by flight and speed.

Match 17 Sat 12 Oct 2019 15:00	**Notts Co** (7th) **2** Torquay Utd (6th) **0** Brindley 8' Dennis 48'	Att: 5,265

Slocombe

Brindley   Rawlinson   Turner   Bakayogo (Kelly-Evans 61')

Doyle (Capt.)   Rose

Boldewijn   Dennis (Thomas 79')   Wootton   Shields (Booty 76')

Subs: Kelly-Evans, Bird, Booty, Thomas, Osborne
(No substitute goalkeeper, for the fourth time)

Captain Michael Doyle regained his place in the Notts team.

Torquay had won their last three games, two of which had been away from home with four goals scored in both victories. It was Notts' third successive fixture against opponents in a play-off position at the start of the game.

Brindley scored his first Notts goal with a brilliant right footed drive from thirty yards which skimmed into the bottom corner past nine defenders (one of whom had made the clearance) and the goalkeeper who was rooted to the spot, plus four Notts players. For Notts' second, a Shields free kick from near the left touchline reached Dennis who guided his header into the far corner of the net from ten yards - his third goal in as many games.

Notts last conceded a goal at Meadow Lane on 26 August, and it was their fifth home game in succession with a 'clean sheet'. With this win Notts moved to their highest league position so far, 5th.

FA Cup – Final Qualifying Round	**Notts Co 2**	**Belper Town 1**	Att: 5,729
Sat 19 Oct 2019 15:00	Boldewijn 29'	goal 11'	
	Wootton 76'		

                                       Slocombe

Kelly-Evans   Rawlinson   Turner   McCrory

            Doyle (Capt.)   Booty

Boldewijn   Dennis (Thomas 83')   Wootton   Shields (Tyson 83')

Subs: Fitzsimons (Gk), Brindley, Bakayogo, Rose, Tyson, Thomas, Osborne

For Notts, and the other twenty-three National League teams (level five), this was the first game of the season in the FA Cup, with a place in the first round proper, on Saturday 9 November, at stake.

Local Derbyshire side Belper Town, members of the Northern Premier League – Division 1 South East, played three levels below Notts in level eight of English football, and in the same league as Ilkeston Town, against whom Notts won their second pre-season friendly 5-0 on 13 July when Nathan Tyson scored a hat-trick.

Belper's record this season had been outstanding. Due to their successful FA Cup run (unbeaten in six including replays) they had only played six (unbeaten) league games. In total, a sequence of twelve games without defeat since the beginning of the season. However, they had lost for the first time in their final game before the Meadow Lane visit – a 3-0 defeat in the FA Trophy.

After Belper had taken an early lead, with a great shot from twenty-five yards, Enzio Boldewijn equalised when he received the ball on the right side of the penalty area, found some space with a stepover, and then bent a left-footed shot across goal into the bottom corner. The winner arrived when Booty threaded a delightful through ball in behind the defence and Wootton scored with a left footed shot from ten yards into the corner of the net.

A resilient Belper Town were finally beaten in an exciting game.

Match 18	**Chesterfield** (18th) **1 Notts Co** (5th) **0**	Att: 5,432
Sat 26 Oct 2019 17:20	goal 27'	(1,422 Notts
Shown live on BT Sport.		supporters)

Slocombe

Brindley   Turner   McCrory   Bakayogo (Booty 64')

Doyle (Capt.)   Rose

Boldewijn   Dennis (Thomas 64')   Wootton   Shields (Tyson 86')

Subs: Kelly-Evans, Booty, Thomas, Tyson, Osborne
(again, no substitute goalkeeper (Ross Fitzsimons the No.2)
for the fifth time in a league game this season)

Chesterfield were bottom of the league after ten games and without a win. However, since that bad start they had only been beaten twice in seven league games, although they had suffered a narrow defeat in the FA Cup following a replay.

Notts dominated this game with good possession/passing, but they struggled to create any good scoring chances. Neal Ardley said in his after-match interview "we lacked a cutting edge" even though Notts had scored two goals in each of their last six league and FA Cup games. He also thought this performance and the one at Yeovil were Notts' two best away performances of the season, but both had ended in defeat!

This was, therefore, a disappointing result for Notts. In their last fourteen league games they had only been defeated twice and had risen to 5th from the top – only five points behind leaders Halifax.

Chesterfield had taken their only real chance in the game with a good goal following a right wing cross and, for the second time this season, Notts had lost in a live televised (BT Sport) fixture.

Match 19 Tues 29 Oct 2019 19:45	**Woking (6th) 0 Notts Co (8th) 4** Boldewijn 7', 73' Thomas 18', 60'	Att: 2,175 (? Notts supporters)

                    Slocombe

Brindley   Rawlinson   Turner   McCrory

      Doyle (Capt.)   Rose   Booty

    Boldewijn   Thomas (Shields 80')   Wootton

Subs: Kelly-Evans, Bakayogo, Dennis, Osborne, Shields
(again, no substitute goalkeeper for the sixth time in a league game this season)

Notts returned to winning, and scoring, form after their defeat at Chesterfield three days prior to this fixture.

Woking won seven of their first eight league games, but since their last win on 31st August, when they were top of the league, they had gone twelve league/F A Cup games without a win (eight of the twelve were drawn).

Notts' opening goal was a(nother) 'goal of the season' contender from Boldewijn. He received the ball in the centre circle, ran on and unleashed an unstoppable right footed shot into the top corner from twenty five yards. The second goal was scored after Wootton's low cross shot, from the left hand side of the penalty area, clipped the diving goalkeeper's fingers on the way to the far post where Thomas bundled the ball into the net from close range. Notts' third came after a shot from Brindley was side-footed into the corner of the net, from 10 yards, by Thomas. The last goal was another superb effort from Boldewijn, who cut inside from the left touchline and scored with his left foot as the goalkeeper and two defenders converged.

Match 20	**Notts Co** (7ᵗʰ) **2**	**Hartlepool Utd** (12ᵗʰ) **2**	Att: 5,258
Sat 2 Nov 2019 15:00	Thomas 44', 61'	goals 8', 42'	

```
                        Slocombe
    Brindley      Rawlinson        Turner       McCrory
    Doyle (Capt.)      Rose        Shields (Booty 46')
      Boldewijn      Wootton       Thomas (Dennis 88')
```

Subs: Bakayogo, Booty, Dennis, Tyson, Osborne
again no substitute goalkeeper

Hartlepool had had a caretaker manager for the last three weeks. Since then, however, they had been unbeaten winning all three games (two in the league, one in the FA Cup) without conceding a goal.

They took an early lead when a shot from the edge of the penalty area was deflected past Slocombe. This eighth minute goal was the first Notts had conceded at Meadow Lane since the ninth minute of their game against Chorley on Bank Holiday Monday, 26 August. That's one minute short of nine hours. If time added at the end of each half of those six games is included the approximate total becomes nine and a half hours since the last home league goal was conceded! Hartlepool's second goal was a good finish from ten yards after they had penetrated the Notts defence with some slick passing.

Wes Thomas got Notts back in the game just before half time with the first of his two goals. He chased McCrory's long ball out of defence and, as a defender stumbled and the goalkeeper approached with a half-hearted dive, he prodded the ball into the corner of the net. His equaliser came when he met a Booty cross, from the left edge of the penalty area, to head home from inside the six-yard box. Thomas had scored a second double in three days!

~ ~ ~

After this (their 20ᵗʰ) league game Notts were in 7ᵗʰ position (the last play-off place) with thirty-one points - five behind top of the league Bromley. They had the best 'Goal Difference', +12, and the joint best defence with twenty goals conceded. Steady progress was being made.

On 7 November 'Club News' announced that Notts had completed the signing of former Gillingham defender Alex Lacey on a contract for the remainder of the season, following a successful trial period. Prior to his two seasons at League One Gillingham he had spent two seasons at League Two Yeovil, whom he had joined from his first club Luton Town.

Twenty-six-year-old Lacey had trained with League One Bury during the summer, but their off-field problems, which led to expulsion from the EFL at the end of August, meant they were unable to offer him a contract.

Neal Ardley said he wanted to add another defender to the squad to replace Sam Graham, the loanee central defender who had returned to Sheffield United in September after he acquired a serious leg injury.

> *"We looked at him in the summer and held some discussions but, with Bury in for him, League One was obviously appealing," said Ardley.*
>
> *"He's a very good option. He's bright, clever, mobile and athletic. He reads the game really well and isn't bad on the ball either.*
>
> *"He's a good centre half who adds competition in a position I felt we needed because of the hole Sam's injury left us with.*
>
> *"He's been promoted out of this league with Luton and, because we'd done our homework on him already, bringing him in seemed the right thing to do."*

Lacey made his debut for Notts in their 1-0 victory at Chesterfield in the first round of the FA Trophy on 14 December.

FA Cup – 1st Round	Ebbsfleet Utd 2	Notts Co 3	Att: 1,206
Sat 9 Nov 2019 15:00	goals 7', 89' (pen)	Wootton 33', 58' Turner 90'+3	(? Notts supporters)

```
                        Slocombe
      Brindley     Rawlinson      Turner        McCrory
   Doyle (Capt.)        Rose         Booty (Bakayogo 90'+5)
        Boldewijn    Thomas (Tyson 85')    Wootton
```

Subs: Kean (Gk), Kelly-Evans, Bakayogo, Dennis, Tyson, Osborne.
Only six substitutes named, even though seven are allowed in the FA Cup. Shields (on loan from Ebbsfleet) was ineligible to play against his parent club, as part of the loan deal.

There were two changes to the Notts side that drew 2-2 at Ebbsfleet on 24 August in the sixth league game of the season. Graham and Dennis were the two missing, with Brindley and Wootton the replacements.

Ebbsfleet (like Hartlepool last week) had had a caretaker manager since early October. However, in the four weeks they had only been beaten once in four league games and had progressed in the FA Cup following a replay. The caretaker manager's position had recently been made permanent. They were 22nd in The National League (17 points) with the worst defensive record (thirty eight goals conceded in their twenty games. Their goal scoring record was reasonable, twenty eight gave them a goal difference of minus 10.

Ebbsfleet took an early lead with a great shot from thirty five yards! Notts equalised with a disputed goal. Following a Booty low pass corner kick, the assistant referee (linesman) indicated Wootton's first time right footed shot had crossed the goal line. There was no doubt about his second goal. Thomas received the ball on the half way line, turned a defender and ran to the edge of the penalty area before he slid a perfect pass to Wootton who scored with another right footed shot, into the far corner of the net, from fifteen yards.

In a dramatic finale, with one minute of normal time left, Ebbsfleet equalised from the penalty spot after Brindley was harshly adjudged to have handled the ball. But, with a replay at Meadow Lane looking certain, a Booty corner skimmed off a defenders head at the near post and Turner nodded the ball into the net at the far post to take Notts into the second round of the FA Cup.

Match 21	Notts Co (8th) 0 Barrow (4th) 3	Att: 5,287
Sat 16 Nov 2019 15:00	goals 10', 13', 87'	

Slocombe

Brindley   Rawlinson   Turner   McCrory

Doyle (Capt.)   Rose   Booty

Boldewijn (Shields 70')   Thomas (Dennis 70')   Wootton

Subs: Kelly-Evans, Bakayogo, Dennis, Tyson, Shields
again no substitute goalkeeper

Notts were unchanged from their FA Cup victory at Ebbsfleet last week.

Barrow lost six of their first nine league games but had been defeated only once in ten league games since 3 September, scoring 23 goals with 8 against. The only defeat was at Torquay, 4-2.

Barrow were the better side and deserved their victory. They got off to a flying start and scored twice in the first thirteen minutes. For the first a defence splitting pass was turned back in the penalty area for a ruthless ten-yard finish. Unfortunately, the second was due to a dreadful attempted back pass by Boldewijn, from fifteen yards inside the Barrow half. Goalkeeper Slocombe raced out to try and beat a Barrow forward to the ball but it was flicked beyond him and the player ran on and squared the ball, which the recipient tapped into the net. Barrow sealed their victory just before the end when a low centre from the right was confidently dispatched from the edge of the six-yard box.

So, Notts' excellent recent home record (five wins, three draws, with only four goals conceded) came to an end. They had experienced only three defeats in their previous nineteen league and FA Cup games. This was their heaviest defeat of the season. The only consolation for Notts was that they had been beaten by a team whose form had been impressive during the last two months.

With this victory Barrow went to the top of The National League.

Match 22	**Aldershot Tn** (19th) **2**	**Notts Co** (9th) **1**	Att: 2,211
Sat 23 Nov 2019 15:00	goals 27', 43'	Wootton 36'	(346 Notts supporters)

Slocombe

Brindley   Rawlinson   Turner   McCrory

Doyle (Capt.)   Rose (Dennis 76')   Booty

Boldewijn (Shields 76')   Thomas (Tyson 84')   Wootton

Subs: Kelly-Evans, Bakayogo, Dennis, Tyson, Shields
again no substitute goalkeeper

For the third successive game Notts were unchanged.

Aldershot had spent the season in, or just above, the relegation zone. Last week they lost 6-1 at Dagenham & Redbridge but they, rather than Notts after their home defeat against Barrow, were the team who 'bounced back'.

Aldershot took the lead with a good, powerful, header from ten yards following a right wing cross. Notts equalised after Booty's deep cross was headed away from goal but only as far as Doyle, whose shot was diverted past the goalkeeper by Wootton. Just before half time Aldershot got, what proved to be, the winner. Turner's pass put Doyle under pressure and he lost the ball, which allowed their player to shoot as Slocombe advanced.

Notts suffered back-to-back defeats for the first time this season. It was the fourth consecutive game they had conceded two or more goals. Three weeks ago they had the joint best defence in the league.

An angry Neal Ardley did not try to defend Notts' performance. He complained about "a lack of intensity and individual errors" and wanted "more aggression and zip" in the next game.

Match 23 Tue 26 Nov 2019 19:45	**Notts Co** (11th) **2** Wootton 30' & 41'	**Boreham Wood** (12th) **2** goals 15' & 90'+1 (pen)	Att: 3,256

                        Slocombe

Brindley   Rawlinson   Turner   McCrory

            Doyle (Capt.)   Rose

            Boldewijn   Shields (Booty 85')

            Thomas (Tyson 78')   Wootton

Subs: Kelly-Evans, Bakayogo, Booty, Dennis, Tyson
again no substitute goalkeeper

Fitzsimons was the substitute goalkeeper for ten of the first eleven league games of the season; Kean then had three games as the named substitute towards the end of September. This was the ninth successive league game with no substitute goalkeeper.

Neal Ardley made his first change to the starting eleven in four games with Shields coming into the side in place of Booty.

This game was the first return fixture of the season so far. Since 24 September when they lost 1-2 at home to Notts, Boreham Wood's record was P9 W4 D3 L2 F11 A10 so they were in a reasonable run of form.

Notts made a poor start to the game, and it wasn't a surprise when Boreham Wood scored. A cross from the right was calmly headed into the net by an unmarked forward. However, Notts improved and managed to reach half time in the lead. Both goals were Wootton headers; the first (the equaliser) followed a right-wing cross by Brindley and the second came after a left wing cross by Thomas. Notts controlled most of the second half but in the 90' a Rawlinson foul gave Boreham Wood a penalty, and the equaliser. Rawlinson was sent off.

This last-minute drama meant that Notts hadn't won a league game in November – two draws and two defeats – despite three of the four being at Meadow Lane.

Notts' recent loss of form, which had revealed itself in the first half of the home game against Hartlepool on 2 November, had halted the momentum they had steadily generated since the middle of August.

Notts successfully appealed against the straight red card shown to Connell Rawlinson. The central defender would have been banned from playing in the next three games. He had been dismissed on the grounds of serious foul play for a challenge which also resulted in a dubious penalty being awarded. The tackle appeared to occur just outside the penalty area. The Football Association decided not to impose a suspension.

~ ~ ~

Neal Ardley and his assistant, Neil Cox, were appointed twelve months ago, on 27 November 2018. Their record at the end of their first twelve months was:

	P	W	D	L	F	A	Win %
League Two	26	6	7	13	26	43	23.1
National League	23	8	8	7	35	27	34.8
	49	**14**	**15**	**20**	**61**	**70**	**28.6**
If the 3 Cup games are inc.	**52**	**16**	**15**	**21**	**66**	**75**	**30.8**

At this halfway stage in the season Notts had thirty-two points. A simple doubling of the points would give a total of sixty-four at the end of the season. The final National League table at the end of 2018-19 indicated that sixty-four points would result in a mid-table position of eleventh, ten points off a play-off place, and twenty-five points below the champions. Although Notts had had a reasonably good first half of this season a significant improvement was required if they were to stand any chance of promotion.

National League Table 26 November 2019		Home					Away					Overall						
#	Team	P	W	D	L	F	A	W	D	L	F	A	W	D	L	F	A	GD	PT
1	Barrow	22	7	1	3	17	10	6	1	4	24	17	13	2	7	41	27	14	**41**
2	Solihull Moors	23	9	0	2	22	9	3	4	5	15	14	12	4	7	37	23	14	**40**
3	Bromley	23	6	4	1	25	15	5	3	4	15	14	11	7	5	40	29	11	**40**
4	Woking	23	4	5	3	14	15	6	3	2	21	14	10	8	5	35	29	6	**38**
5	Halifax Town	23	5	2	4	16	14	6	3	3	16	14	11	5	7	32	28	4	**38**
6	Yeovil Town	22	6	3	3	20	14	5	1	4	17	13	11	4	7	37	27	10	**37**
7	Harrogate Town	23	7	3	2	18	11	3	4	4	17	19	10	7	6	35	30	5	**37**
8	Torquay United	23	6	1	4	19	15	4	3	5	22	21	10	4	9	41	36	5	**34**
9	Notts County	23	5	5	2	19	12	3	3	5	16	15	8	8	7	35	27	8	**32**
10	Hartlepool United	23	3	4	4	17	18	5	4	3	19	14	8	8	7	36	32	4	**32**
11	Eastleigh	22	5	5	1	17	11	3	3	5	12	18	8	8	6	29	29	0	**32**
12	Dover Athletic	22	2	4	6	16	20	7	1	2	13	10	9	5	8	29	30	-1	**32**
13	Stockport County	23	6	1	5	16	19	3	4	4	10	17	9	5	9	26	36	-10	**32**
14	Boreham Wood	23	4	3	4	16	13	4	4	4	17	15	8	7	8	33	28	5	**31**
15	Barnet	23	5	4	3	19	14	3	3	5	15	18	8	7	8	34	32	2	**31**
16	Dagenham & Redbridge	23	5	3	4	21	18	3	3	5	8	12	8	6	9	29	30	-1	**30**
17	Maidenhead United	23	2	3	6	12	14	6	1	5	18	16	8	4	11	30	30	0	**28**
18	Fylde	22	4	3	3	12	14	3	3	6	16	22	7	6	9	28	36	-8	**27**
19	Aldershot Town	23	4	2	5	14	14	3	3	6	10	19	7	5	11	24	33	-9	**26**
20	Sutton United	22	1	4	6	11	17	4	3	4	11	12	5	7	10	22	29	-7	**22**
21	Chesterfield	22	3	2	6	15	21	2	5	4	14	20	5	7	10	29	41	-12	**22**
22	Wrexham	22	4	5	3	14	13	0	3	7	11	20	4	8	10	25	33	-8	**20**
23	Chorley	23	2	4	5	9	19	1	7	4	11	20	3	11	9	20	39	-19	**20**
24	Ebbsfleet	23	1	4	6	16	25	3	3	6	17	21	4	7	12	33	46	-13	**19**

Top = Promoted to EFL League Two. Positions 2-7 = play-off's to decide the other promoted team. Positions 21-24 relegated.

FA Cup – 2nd Round	Northampton Town 3	Notts Co 1	Att: 4,489
Sun 1 Dec 2019 14:00	goals 3', 25', 76'	Dennis 84'	(1,041 Notts supporters)

                                      Slocombe

Brindley   Rawlinson   Turner   McCrory

Doyle (Capt.)   Rose   Booty (Shields 46')

                                      Boldewijn

Thomas (Dennis 77')   Wootton (Tyson 85')

Subs: Kean (Gk), Kelly-Evans, Bakayogo, Dennis, Tyson, Osborne, Shields

Neal Ardley reinstated the starting eleven he had picked for the three games before last Tuesday night's game. The only change involved the same two players – Booty in, Shields out.

Northampton's recent form had been good, whereas Notts' had been poor with only one win (FA Cup 1st Round at Ebbsfleet) in their last five fixtures, so the result wasn't really a surprise. Northampton were sixth in League Two and had won five of their last six league games (the other was drawn), scoring fourteen goals with only three conceded. In the first round of the FA Cup, away at non-league Chippenham Town, Northampton had a comfortable 3-0 victory.

Notts, once again, conceded an early goal, just as they had done in their previous two FA Cup ties, against Belper and Ebbsfleet. It was the eleventh time they had conceded a goal in the first fifteen minutes, in league and cup, this season.

All three of Northampton's goals were scored from headers; the first from a corner and the other two from crosses, one from the left and one from the right.

A much improved second half performance was in vain – chances were created, but not taken. Notts did, however, get the consolation goal they deserved when substitute Dennis tapped the ball into the net after Boldewijn's low cross had been parried away by the goalkeeper.

At the end of October, after the 4-0 win at Woking, Notts had the best defensive record in The National League, but since that game they have conceded at least two goals in each of their last six league and FA Cup games.

So, Notts were knocked out of the FA Cup but two weeks later they undertook the short journey to Chesterfield in the first round of the FA Trophy and won 1-0.

A trip to Wembley was still a possibility.

Chapter 8: So near yet so far

Match 24	**Notts Co** (11th) **1 Sutton Utd** (20th) **1**	Att: 5,652
Sat 7 Dec 2019 15:00	Thomas 14' goal 76'	

                                Slocombe
    Brindley   Rawlinson   Turner   McCrory
                   Doyle (Capt.)   Rose
                   Boldewijn   Shields (Booty 72')
                   Thomas (Dennis 79')   Wootton

Subs: Kelly-Evans, Bakayogo, Booty, Dennis, Osborne
(no substitute goalkeeper)

It was the same team as the one which was knocked out of the FA Cup six days ago except this time it was Shields in, Booty out!

Notts drew 1-1 at Sutton on 7 September.

Sutton did not win a league game in October, and were knocked out of the FA Cup, by National League South club Billericay Town, losing 5-2. However, their recent form had improved, and they had won three of their last four league games.

After a reasonable first quarter of an hour, Notts disappointed once again despite taking the lead. Boldewijn drippled into the penalty area and had what looked like a mis-directed shot forced home by Thomas from the edge of the six-yard box.

Thereafter, instead of an increase in momentum from Notts the opposite happened, and it wasn't a surprise when Sutton equalised. Poor defensive work, after a cross from the left, allowed their forward to squeeze the ball into the net from close range.

This was Notts' fifth league game without a win, and four of those games had been at Meadow Lane! Their only victory in November was at Ebbsfleet in the first round of the FA Cup courtesy of Ben Turner's 90' +3 header. Following this draw Notts slipped one place to a mid table position.

A frustrated Neal Ardley gave an honest assessment of the game:

"I saw an anxious team." he said. *"We turned into 11 individuals because of it and it looked like people were passing the buck. It's difficult when you see the players clamming up and too many went missing as the game wore on. They didn't want the ball and weren't brave enough, so we got progressively worse as the match continued."*

He put the anxiety down to a desperation to bring an end to the winless run of five league matches.

"When you've not won in a few, you try and see the game out. We've got to cure the nerves and anxiety. We need to find a result, lift our spirits and build momentum from there. Mentality is a big thing. We've gone from free-flowing and trusting each other to having that bit of doubt. We've become an average team and we have to turn that around quickly because we have another nine games between now and mid-January. Our season could fade away if we don't improve, and a win will do us the world of good."

Ardley admitted it wasn't a fine spectacle against Sutton.

"It was a horrible game to watch," he conceded. *"It's rare I've said that because we've been quite entertaining at times this season. If we had kept a clean sheet, I'd have been here saying 'it's a poor performance but at least we're back on the winning trail', but that wasn't to be. If the players perform like they did today, without taking responsibility and showing bravery to do what they're good at, it becomes tough here. After where we were a few weeks ago, I'm frustrated that we're at this point now. It's my job to find the answers."*

FA Trophy - 1st Round	Chesterfield 0 Notts Co 1	Att: 931
Sat 14 Dec 2019 13:00	Dennis 72'	(336 Notts supporters)

Slocombe (Kean 37')

Kelly-Evans   Rawlinson   Lacey   Bakayogo

O'Brien (Capt.) (Doyle 27')   Booty

Osborne   Shields

Dennis   Tyson (Crawford 81')

Subs: Kean (Gk), McCrory, Doyle, Crawford, Thomas

Some players were rested. Nevertheless, Neal Ardley made eight changes to the side who disappointed against Sutton last weekend. Alex Lacey, signed in early November, made his debut and Tom Crawford made his first appearance of the season. Jim O'Brien returned for his first game since breaking his arm nearly three months ago.

Chesterfield had a home win (1-0) over Notts in a league game on 26th October. Since that victory they had played seven league games (drawn two and lost five). They had scored in each of those seven games but had conceded nineteen goals. As a consequence, they were now joint bottom of the league (23rd). Notts were a mid table 12th.

During a poor first half, not surprising with two out of form teams, O'Brien (a deep eight-inch gash/cut down the middle of his thigh, with a possible tear in the muscle where the stud entered) and Slocombe (groin injury) had to be replaced by Doyle and Kean respectively. Notts' winner was scored by ex-Chesterfield player Dennis when he slid the ball into the net from close range after a good run, and low cross, by winger Osborne who had intercepted the ball inside the Notts half of the field.

At last, Notts ended their poor run of form with a hard-earned victory, and they had kept a 'clean sheet'. Since they won 4-0 in the league at Woking, at the end of October, Notts had conceded fifteen goals in five league and two FA Cup games.

Although this game was not the greatest of spectacles it turned out to be the win that set Notts on a resurgent run through Christmas and the start of 2020.

Match 25	**Halifax Tn** (7th) **2 Notts Co** (12th) **4**	Att: 2,491
Sat 21 Dec 2019 15:00	goals 45', 57' Wootton 48', 90' + 8	(? Notts
	Rose 60', 81' (pen)	supporters)

<pre>
                            Fitzsimons
   Brindley (Kelly-Evans 78')   Rawlinson   Lacey   McCrory
                    Doyle (Capt.)   Rose (Crawford 90' + 4)
                       Boldewijn   Shields (Dennis 83')
                          Thomas   Wootton
</pre>

Subs: Kean (Gk), Kelly-Evans, Bird, Crawford, Dennis

Pierce Bird was recalled from his loan (at Boston) due to Ben Turner's (hamstring) injury. Goalkeeper Ross Fitzsimons made his first appearance since 6th April. Alex Lacey made his league debut for the injured Turner.

Notts defeated Halifax 1-0 at Meadow Lane on 14 September.

Halifax were one of the better teams in the league. To date they had not been outside the play-off positions and had topped the league. However, their recent form had been poor, winning only two of their last eleven games, in league and cup. The second win was last week in the FA Trophy.

At the end of an uneventful first half Notts fell behind when a shot was deflected, and left Fitzsimons stranded.

Notts responded at the beginning of the second half when Wootton equalised with a shot from twelve yards following a poor headed clearance by a Halifax defender. Three minutes after Halifax had taken the lead for the second time Rose equalised with a wonderful right footed volley, from the edge of the penalty area, following another poor defensive header. Two minutes later he hit the crossbar! Notts took the lead with a penalty kick (taken by Rose) after Boldewijn, who had an excellent second half, had been fouled. Victory was sealed when a Fitzsimons clearance was well controlled by Dennis on the left wing. He passed inside to Wootton who side footed the ball into the corner of the net from fifteen yards.

Neal Ardley classed this game as the first of the five to be played over the holiday period. As Notts were now unbeaten in their last three league games it was confirmed that their poor November form had come to an end.

| **Match 26**
Thurs. 26 Dec 2019 15:00 | **Notts Co** (11ᵗʰ) **3 Maidenhead Utd** (16ᵗʰ) **0**
Wootton 21'
Osborne 29'
Dennis 43' | Att: 5,129 |

```
                         Slocombe
    Kelly-Evans     Rawlinson      Lacey          McCrory
           Doyle (Capt.)        Rose (Crawford 73')
              Osborne          Boldewijn (Bird 87')
              Dennis           Wootton (Thomas 73')
```

Subs: Fitzsimons (Gk), Brindley, Bird, Crawford, Thomas

Notts had a double header against Maidenhead over Christmas and the New Year - the return fixture was on New Year's Day.

Maidenhead made a good start to the season, but generally their form had been inconsistent. However, they had one of the best away records in the league.

An excellent first half display produced three quality goals for Notts.

Wootton gave them the lead with a powerful header direct from Boldewijn's corner kick. Osborne's goal was an unstoppable left footed shot from sixteen yards into the top corner of the net, following a series of passes out of defence – a great team goal. Dennis completed Notts' best first half performance of the season so far, just before half-time, after Boldewijn skipped down the right wing and crossed low for Dennis to side foot the ball into the net from twelve yards.

The second half was more even, but Notts' game management was good and they earned their second win of the (five game) Christmas/New Year period.

Match 27	Solihull Moors (5th) 0 Notts Co (9th) 1	Att: 3,212
Sat 28 Dec 2019 15:00	Thomas 72'	(1000? Notts supporters)

Slocombe

Kelly-Evans Rawlinson Lacey Bakayogo

Doyle (Capt.) Rose Crawford (Osborne 70')

Thomas (Bird 86') Wootton Tyson (Boldewijn 70')

Subs: McCrory, Bird, Boldewijn, Osborne, Dennis
(no substitute goalkeeper)

Midfielder Tom Crawford made his first start of the season.

McCrory, Boldewijn, Osborne and Dennis were rested.

Notts and Solihull drew 0-0 at Meadow Lane on 3 September.

Solihull had been in, or just below, the play-off positions throughout. They were undefeated during November, and at the halfway stage of the season they were next to the top with the best home record in the league. However, earlier this month, they experienced a calamitous home defeat to League One Rotherham in the second round of the FA Cup; a 3-0 lead, with fourteen minutes to go, was wiped out and they lost 4-3! Since that defeat they had drawn two and lost one.

Notts took the lead when Wootton's persistence down the left wing enabled him to rob a defender of the ball, run on, and centre to Thomas who tapped home at the far post.

Following this set back Solihull, as expected, pressed hard for the equaliser. They were denied by an excellent goal line clearance by Rose in the 90' and a great save by Slocombe three minutes later.

With three of the five festive games now played Notts had gained maximum points, nine, and were now up to sixth in The National League.

Match 28	**Maidenhead Utd** (17th) **0 Notts Co** (6th) **0**	Att: 1,657
Wed 1 Jan 2020 15:00		(? Notts supporters)

Slocombe

Kelly-Evans   Rawlinson   Lacey   McCrory

Doyle (Capt.)   Rose

Boldewijn   Osborne (Tyson 68')

Dennis (Thomas 75')   Wootton

Subs: Bird, Bakayogo, Crawford, Thomas, Tyson
(no substitute goalkeeper)

Neal Ardley made four changes to the team victorious at Solihull Moors. He reverted to the same eleven who started the game when the sides met six days ago. The four rested against Solihull returned in place of Bakayogo, Crawford, Thomas and Tyson.

On this occasion Notts didn't perform as they had done in the first game when they led 3-0 at half time, and the play followed a similar pattern to the second half of the Meadow Lane fixture. Both sides gave plenty of endeavour and had/missed chances. Played on a pitch with a slope and an uneven surface a draw was probably a fair result, secured in the 87' when Dion Kelly-Evans made a superb clearance to deny Maidenhead a goal. Four Notts players were booked by the referee (given yellow cards) in the second half – Kelly-Evans, McCrory, Doyle and Wootton.

So, at the end of the fourth game of five in the festive period, Notts had earned ten points from a possible twelve keeping three clean sheets in the process. If the FA Trophy game at Chesterfield is included Notts had kept four clean sheets out of five since central defender Alex Lacey made his debut in that game.

Match 29	Notts Co (7th) 2 Bromley (3rd) 1	Att: 5,192
Sat 4 Jan 2020 15:00	Thomas 4' goal 50'	
	Rawlinson 70'	

                          Slocombe
        Brindley   Rawlinson   Lacey   McCrory
                    Doyle (Capt.)   Rose
                  Boldewijn   Osborne (Bird 83')
                    Thomas (Dennis 83')   Wootton

        Subs: Bird, Bakayogo, Crawford, Dennis, Tyson
                  (no substitute goalkeeper)

Notts lost 2-1 at Bromley on 21 September.

Bromley had had a tremendous season to date. They had been in the top three since mid-August, were unbeaten in the league until their fourteenth game at the end of September, and until mid-November they were mostly in top position.

It was a very entertaining game: Notts scored an early goal and fifteen minutes later missed a penalty, Bromley had a goal disallowed but equalised with an excellent twenty five yard shot, Rawlinson's scored his first goal for Notts, and a Bromley player (long throw-in specialist Bush) was sent off just before the final whistle.

A three man move gave Notts a dream start to the game. Slocombe found Osborne on the left wing with a great throw. His initial run forward was halted but the ball fell to Thomas. He returned the ball to Osborne who ran on, beat a defender, and rolled the ball back for the advancing Thomas to score with a powerful left footed shot from sixteen yards. Rose missed a twentieth minute penalty when his shot struck a post and Boldewijn shot over the bar from the rebound. Connell Rawlinson's winner came when he headed home Doyle's cross following a short corner.

Neal Ardley praised Bromley for their "relentless" play and Notts for dealing with the challenge they presented.

The fifth festive game therefore ended with another victory, which meant Notts had earned more league points (thirteen out of fifteen) than any other club over Christmas and the New Year. Notts extended their undefeated league run to seven games and moved up to fifth from the top. Bromley dropped down to fourth.

Neal Ardley had become increasingly concerned about Kyle Wootton's situation, particularly with the opening of 'The Transfer Window' on 1 January. His form for Notts had been good since his arrival on a season long loan from Scunthorpe United at the end of August 2019. In twenty four league and cup appearances he had scored twelve goals, and Ardley's concern was that he might leave Notts if he was enticed by a club from a higher league.

Since his arrival at Notts Wootton and Ardley had developed a good working relationship to improve his game, and the fifty percent strike rate was evidence that this training had had a positive effect. Ardley, Jason Turner (Chief Executive Officer ex Football Operations Director) and the new owners (Christoffer and Alexander Reedtz), had indicated to Kyle Wootton's agent, and Scunthorpe, that they did want to lose Wootton. Ardley said they had done all they could to prevent his departure.

On 8 January Notts made the following announcement:

Wootton signs permanent deal

We have completed the permanent signing of Kyle Wootton from Scunthorpe United.

The striker has been a big hit at Meadow Lane since joining us on loan in late August and leads our scoring charts with 12 goals in all competitions. Neal Ardley revealed last week we have been working for two months on turning the transfer into a permanent one, and the efforts of the manager and other senior officials at the club have now paid off as the 23-year-old becomes a Notts County player. Wootton has signed a deal that runs until the end of the 2021-22 season and everyone concerned will hope he continues his fine form in black and white with his long-term future now secured.

"I'm absolutely delighted to get it done," smiled Wootton. "I couldn't be happier and I'm ready to keep improving and helping the club go in the right direction. I've been here on loan and it's felt like home – that's a really important thing for me. I was at Scunthorpe for 13 years and it was a massive part of my life but it's the right time to move on. This club has a big place in my heart and I'm ready to keep moving forwards with Notts now."

Wootton's been a firm favourite among supporters and he cited his relationships with everyone involved with the club as one of the factors behind his decision.

"Everything has made me want to stay," revealed the striker. "That's the staff, players and fans. I can't thank the supporters enough for their backing since the day I arrived and I'm really happy to give them something back – hopefully they're pleased to see me staying on. All of the staff are great and that's huge for me. I have a really good relationship with Neal Ardley and Neil Cox, which shows on the pitch, and that has been a massive part of things. The lads have been brilliant, too. The situation has been

dragging on a bit but I've just tried to cancel it all out and the lads have helped me keep my head down and focus on each game."

Neal Ardley was both relieved and pleased:

"Kyle has already been through a pressurised time, which people don't realise. While it's only recently come out in the press, this has been going on for a long time behind the scenes.

"As a player, whenever I was in the middle of contract talks or if there was speculation about my future, I struggled to hold my form. It plays on your mind and you feel extra pressure to play well so you can justify what the club are offering you. Kyle's held his form throughout all of that. I think he's now been through the hardest part and he knows all he's got to do is relax, give everything for the team and be unselfish – the rest will take care of itself.

"My aim for Kyle, if he can continue to earn his place in the team, is to try and get to 20 goals this season. If you look at his record in previous seasons, that would represent a dramatic turnaround for him to get there. As a coach, I take pride in that side of things – the development of players."

Ardley admitted losing Wootton would have been a big blow at a bad time, so he was delighted the matter was now resolved.

"I think we were all worried that, if we lost him, anyone who came in probably wouldn't have been the same type of player. We'd have lost the fact Kyle knows how we play and what we expect. Obviously, he's a very, very good player. Keeping Kyle gives us a great chance of maintaining some momentum for the remaining games and it'll give the fans a huge lift, too."

Ardley also believed the acquisition of Wootton was a positive reflection of the improved culture and transfer strategy at the club.

"Our owners have been very generous and supportive in making this happen – but they haven't been stupid. In the past, as we know, this club's thrown everything into signing players and it hasn't always worked. But they have stuck to their principles and managed to get it done. I can't praise them enough. Players now know they're not coming here for the money because anything over and above market value isn't viable for us anymore. You're coming here because we've got good staff and a really nice feel about the place. Hopefully that will help us grow."

A few days later, Neal Ardley was named Vanarama National League Manager of the Month for December.

"It's Team of the Month really," he suggested. "I'm looking at the effort of the players and the sacrifices the staff made, so I receive it on behalf of them".

FA Trophy - 2nd Round	Notts Co 2 Dagenham & Redbridge 1	Att: 2,385
Sat 11 Jan 2020 15:00	Dennis 53' goal 76'	
	Doyle 90'+3	

Fitzsimons

Kelly-Evans   Lacey   McCrory   Bakayogo

Doyle (Capt.)   Crawford

Osborne   Shields (Boldewijn 77')

Dennis (Wootton 77')   Thomas

Subs: Slocombe (Gk), Brindley, Rawlinson, Rose, Boldewijn, Wootton, Howes

Of last Saturday's starting eleven five retained their place and the other six were rested, following the hectic Christmas/New Year schedule. It was the first time this season that Alex Howes had reached a team sheet.

Notts beat Dagenham and Redbridge 2-0 at Meadow Lane in the league on 8th October. Since then the Daggers form had been poor, winning only two of fourteen league games and they had not won in the league since mid-November. This fixture was also the first game in charge for their new manager.

In the FA Trophy this season if the scores were level after 90' extra time would be played. If at the end of extra time the scores were still level penalty kicks would decide the winner. However, both teams had to agree this scenario for it to occur. Dag & Red had decided against this and had insisted on a reply if the scores were level at the end of 90'.

In an entertaining first half a cross from Shields struck the bar, Dennis had a goal disallowed and Thomas hit a post. Dag & Red missed a great chance on the half hour.

The second half was eight minutes old when a wonderful long pass by Crawford found Bakayogo on the left wing. His low cross was neatly turned into the net by Dennis from close range. Following a Dag & Red free kick, Fitzsimons made two tremendous saves but in the ensuing scramble the ball just crossed the line for the equaliser. Captain Michael Doyle, after going close with two shots earlier in the game, finally got his first goal for Notts with the last kick of the match – and what a kick it was. Thomas was almost put through on goal by a good Osborne pass from inside the Notts half. However, the Dag & Red goalkeeper charged out of his goal area and kicked the ball straight to Doyle who was standing on the left-hand side of the half way line, where it intersects the centre circle. With his left foot he controlled the ball and from fifty plus yards released a shot which travelled like an Exocet missile to enter the net just underneath the crossbar, with the goalkeeper and a defender stranded and floundering in the six-yard box! Wow, what a goal!

Captain Michael Doyle

Notts' next fixture was scheduled for three days later at relegation threatened AFC Fylde, but the evening game was postponed at 18:00 – less than two hours before kick-off – due to a waterlogged pitch.

On 15 January Notts' 'Club News' issued an update from Chief Executive Officer Jason Turner

Our chief executive, Jason Turner, has given his thoughts on yesterday's postponement and provided an update on a number of club issues.

I'd like to begin by empathising with our supporters who booked time off work and made the journey to last night's match at AFC Fylde only for the fixture to be postponed at late notice.

I, like many of you, had arrived in Fylde before the decision was made and, having seen the pitch myself, I don't understand why this decision could not have been made earlier in the day.

What's more, the first we heard of the 5.30pm pitch inspection – and the subsequent confirmation that the match had been postponed – was via Fylde's Twitter account, which gave us little opportunity to notify you of the latest developments.

I have expressed my frustrations to The National League today over what I believe was an entirely avoidable sequence of events, and we await their response.

Since returning to the role of Chief Executive in the summer, having become Football Operations Director under the previous ownership, I have to say it's been a hugely positive – and busy – time at Meadow Lane.

I've thoroughly enjoyed working closely alongside our new owners, Christoffer and Alexander Reedtz, who I'm sure you'll agree have made an excellent start to their time at the helm, and I'm very excited about what the future holds for the club.

I should say a huge thank you to you, our supporters, for the tremendous backing you've given the team this season. Despite everything we've been through and some tough runs on the pitch in the early part of the season, we boast by far the highest average attendance in the league. Your loyalty does not go unnoticed and I'm delighted you've been rewarded with such a terrific run of results.

I was also ecstatic for Neal Ardley after his brilliant work was recognised with December's Manager of the Month award. While our form on the field made him an obvious choice for the accolade, I see first-hand the effort he, Neil Cox and the entire backroom staff put in behind the scenes and I can assure you it's richly deserved!

Well done, also, to our skipper Michael Doyle for firing us into the third round of the Buildbase FA Trophy in such sensational style. I've worked in football for 25 years but I don't think I've ever seen a better goal live! It was brilliant to see his effort receive more than half-a-million views across our social media channels over the weekend, with supporters of Michael's former clubs all congratulating him on a magnificent strike.

We face a very difficult trip to Yeovil Town in the next round but, the way Neal and our entire squad are going, I see no reason why we can't take another step towards Wembley!

Here's an update on some of the other big things happening at the club…

SCOREBOARDS

As I'm sure you'll be well aware by now, two new scoreboards are to be installed on the Air-IT Kop and Haydn Green Family stands later this month.

Plans are progressing smoothly, with the old scoreboard now removed allowing for contractors to begin work on the frames which will hold the new screens. A big thank you to the Notts County Supporters' Club, who've covered the costs of the plant hire to allow for these essential works to take place.

All being well, both scoreboards should be in place and fully operational in time for the Chesterfield match on 1 February.

Not only will they greatly improve the match day experience at Meadow Lane, they'll also help us generate extra revenue through advertising and help us communicate key messages to you.

As you know, the screens were paid for by the amazing fundraising efforts of our Official Supporters Association and Lifeline, whose continued backing is hugely appreciated.

Keep an eye on our digital channels for further updates!

PUMA

I hope you'll agree that it's great news <u>we've reached an agreement with PUMA</u> which will see them continue to provide us with our match, training and replica kit for the foreseeable future.

They've been brilliant to work with since our partnership began in 2017-18 and, crucially, they offer us the chance to create our own bespoke kits, rather than us having to choose from 'off-the-shelf' options which may also be used by other clubs.

From a commercial perspective they're an excellent fit for us and the quality of their products is superb, too.

Our owners and I thoroughly enjoyed the process of selecting next season's kits and we look forward to sharing the designs with you in the summer.

KYLE WOOTTON

It was certainly a huge weight off my shoulders when Kyle signed on the dotted line last week, bringing to an end a lengthy period of negotiations.

You always feel a little pressure when you're trying to get a deal like this done – especially once the news reaches the public domain – but deep down we were always confident that Kyle felt this was the best place for him to further his career.

It was great to see such a huge wave of positivity after we announced the good news and we're looking forward to seeing Kyle kick on now his long-term future is decided.

I'd like to express my gratitude to Scunthorpe United for their assistance throughout the process.

HERITAGE

Last week we remembered the late, great Jack Wheeler on the anniversary of his passing by reverting the 'Carlsberg Club' to the 'Wheeler Suite' with immediate effect.

This followed the news from earlier in the season when Club 155 was returned to the 1862 Suite.

At our monthly board meetings, I discuss with our owners a range of topics concerning the club's heritage and we're committed to doing all we can to honour our great history.

JOIN US FOR THE RUN-IN!

There's still time for those of you without a (half) season ticket to purchase an eight-game ticket bundle.

Not only will your preferred seat be guaranteed for each of our final home matches, you'll also benefit from priority purchase periods for in-demand matches – which could come in very handy should we reach the play-offs and the latter stages of the Trophy.

You'll save up to £4.50 a game (based on an adult match day price), so if you're not planning on missing a kick between now and the end of the season it's a no-brainer!

The next day, Thursday 16 January, goalkeeper Ross Fitzsimons moved to Chesterfield on loan for the remainder of the season. However, it was agreed he would not be selected for Chesterfield against Notts on 1 February. Notts also had the right to recall him at any time before the end of the season, if required.

Fitzsimons had instigated the move after becoming dis-satisfied at playing in only two games this season, plus the fact that Neal Ardley does not usually select a goalkeeper among the five allowed substitutes for National League fixtures.

Although Notts had an injury to goalkeeper Sam Slocombe, during the FA Trophy game at Chesterfield just before Christmas, statistically injury is much more common with outfield players. For this reason the manager usually preferred to take the risk and name five outfield players to give additional cover, and more formation options. In the FA Trophy seven substitutes are allowed and with goalkeeping coach Jake Kean a named substitute he replaced Slocombe! Apparently, Kristian Dennis would become the goalkeeper in an emergency.

Match 30	Notts Co (5th) 0 Dover Athletic (13th) 0	Att: 5,157
Sat 18 Jan 2020 15:00		

Slocombe

Brindley   Rawlinson   Lacey   McCrory

Doyle (Capt.)   Rose

Boldewijn   Osborne (Tyson 79')

Thomas (Dennis 69')   Wootton

Subs: Bird, Bakayogo, Crawford, Dennis, Tyson
(no substitute goalkeeper)

It wasn't a major surprise to discover that Neal Ardley decided to field the same starting eleven (the five substitutes were also the same) that defeated high flying Bromley in the last league game a fortnight ago. There were therefore six changes to the side victorious in last Saturday's FA Trophy game.

Notts drew 2-2 at Dover on 5 October.

Going into this game Notts were undefeated in their last seven league games.

Mid-table Dover's recent league record was P6 W2 D2 L2 F6 A7. However, their away form was very good – three defeats in thirteen away games (fifteen scored and fourteen conceded) and only top of the league Barrow were above them in the 'Away Table'.

In a tight game, Notts probably (just about) deserved all three points.

In the first half Dover's goalkeeper saved Boldewijn's powerful seventeen yard shot, from just inside the corner of the penalty box, with his legs and the ball rebounded off a defenders foot into his grateful arms. He also made an excellent save midway through the second half to deny Thomas, who had received a great through ball from Doyle, one of many excellent passes given by Doyle during the match.

Notts almost won in the 90' +10. Just after six minutes added time had been indicated there was a four minute delay caused by an injury to a Dover player which extended the time added from 6' to 10'. A direct free kick, in a good central position twenty one yards from goal, was taken by Boldewijn and his shot hit a post! Dover's defence cleared the rebound and the final whistle was immediately blown by the referee.

The Dover game meant the season was now at least two thirds of the way through for the majority of National League clubs. Notts had transformed their season during the last six weeks with some excellent performances and were undefeated in their last eight league games (nine in league and cup).

They were now in a play-off position (6th) eleven points below first place, whereas at the half way stage they were ninth, five points off the play-off's but nine points adrift of the summit.

Apart from Barrow, who were top of the league and unbeaten in their last thirteen league games (fifteen in league and cup) going back to 26 October, Harrogate and Boreham Wood, Notts were one of the in-form teams. Like Barrow they had lost the fewest league games – seven. Only five teams had scored more goals than Notts, only two teams had a better defensive record and only two a better goal difference. However, Notts had drawn eleven games (only one side had drawn more). In five of those draws Notts had dropped two points (i.e. their opponents equalised) and in three they had gained a point (i.e. Notts equalised). The other three were goalless draws. Goalkeeper Slocombe had so far kept eleven 'clean sheets', with four in the last five league games.

Also, Notts had new owners (the Reedtz brothers) who were well liked and progressive, supported by a knowledgeable board, an experienced and dedicated management team (Neal Ardley and Neil Cox, and their backroom staff), players who were now adaptable and fully aware of their responsibilities, an excellent fan base of appreciative supporters who had given Notts the highest average home attendance in the league (5,222), a great stadium, and enthusiastic and hardworking office administrative/support staff.

Of the teams currently in the play-off positions Notts had played Halifax, Boreham Wood and Bromley, twice, but still had return fixtures against Yeovil (last game of the season) and Harrogate at Meadow Lane, and top club Barrow away.

With sixteen league games to play everything was in place to achieve a successful end to the season. Surely Notts would finish in the top seven to make the play-offs, hopefully in third or second to get the guarantee of a direct place into a semi-final with the advantage of a home tie. If Barrow's form dipped maybe the top spot, and automatic promotion into League Two, could be achieved!

National League Table 18 January 2020

	Team	P	Home					Away					Overall					GD	PT
			W	D	L	F	A	W	D	L	F	A	W	D	L	F	A		
1	Barrow	29	10	2	3	28	11	8	2	4	31	19	18	4	7	59	30	29	**58**
2	Harrogate Town	31	10	3	2	25	13	6	4	6	24	24	16	7	8	49	37	12	**55**
3	Yeovil Town	31	8	5	3	30	18	7	3	5	26	20	15	8	8	56	38	18	**53**
4	Bromley	31	8	5	2	34	19	6	3	7	18	22	14	8	9	52	41	11	**50**
5	Boreham Wood	30	6	5	4	21	16	7	4	4	24	16	13	9	8	45	32	13	**48**
6	Notts County	30	7	7	2	25	14	5	4	5	21	17	12	11	7	46	31	15	**47**
7	Halifax Town	30	7	3	5	24	20	6	4	5	18	22	13	7	10	42	42	0	**46**
8	Stockport County	31	8	2	6	26	25	5	5	5	18	21	13	7	11	44	46	-2	**46**
9	Solihull Moors	29	10	0	4	25	12	3	6	6	17	18	13	6	10	42	30	12	**45**
10	Woking	30	6	5	4	17	18	6	3	6	24	28	12	8	10	41	46	-5	**44**
11	Hartlepool United	31	5	5	5	22	22	5	6	5	24	23	10	11	10	46	45	1	**41**
12	Dover Athletic	29	3	5	7	20	23	8	3	3	15	14	11	8	10	35	37	-2	**41**
13	Torquay United	31	7	1	7	24	26	5	4	7	28	31	12	5	14	52	57	-5	**41**
14	Barnet	28	6	5	3	22	16	4	5	5	19	19	10	10	8	41	35	6	**40**
15	Sutton United	31	5	4	6	26	23	5	6	5	14	14	10	10	11	40	37	3	**40**
16	Aldershot Town	30	6	5	5	24	21	4	3	7	12	21	10	8	12	36	42	-6	**38**
17	Eastleigh	29	5	6	3	18	16	4	4	7	19	27	9	10	10	37	43	-6	**37**
18	Wrexham	31	7	5	4	23	16	2	3	10	17	27	9	8	14	40	43	-3	**35**
19	Maidenhead United	31	3	4	8	15	22	7	1	8	22	26	10	5	16	37	48	-11	**35**
20	Dagenham & Redbridge	30	5	5	5	23	21	3	4	8	9	18	8	9	13	32	39	-7	**33**
21	Chesterfield	31	4	3	8	20	27	4	6	6	21	26	8	9	14	41	53	-12	**33**
22	Fylde	29	4	5	6	17	22	3	4	7	18	25	7	9	13	35	47	-12	**30**
23	Ebbsfleet	30	2	5	8	19	30	3	5	7	19	30	5	10	15	38	60	-22	**25**
24	Chorley	31	3	5	7	11	24	1	8	7	17	31	4	13	14	28	55	-27	**25**

Top = Promoted to EFL League Two.

Positions 2-7 = play-off's to decide the other promoted team.

Positions 21-24 relegated.

On 20 January 2020 Notts signed 22-year-old Callum Roberts from Blyth Spartans, of The National League (North) - tier six of English football. First thoughts were that this was an underwhelming signing. However, investigation revealed that this may not be the case.

An attacking winger he had had a good first season with Blyth, scoring seventeen goals in twenty-five games. Before Blyth he was a Newcastle United player, from the age of eight, and had grown through their academy to become a professional and make a few first team appearances. It was a big surprise to Callum, and many Newcastle supporters, when he was released at the end of last season.

Although he had no bitterness towards Newcastle, he became disillusioned with football and experienced a frustrating summer trying to find another club. The Blyth manager, Lee Clark, a former Newcastle player (and coach) who was aware of his talents, persuaded him to resume his football career and he had regained his enthusiasm for the game and his desire, one day, to become a Premier League player.

Lee Clark negotiated a sell-on clause as part of the deal which meant Blyth would receive a percentage of any future transfer fee. He was of the opinion that Callum, whose contract with Notts runs until the end of season 2021-22, should be playing in the EFL.

Neal Ardley was delighted to have signed such a young, talented, attacking player, who had the ability, and desire, to play at a higher level.

> *"I've said in recent weeks that we'd only make additions if we felt they were going to improve us and offer us something different, and we're confident Callum Roberts does that," he said.*

> *"He's an exciting winger who loves to run at people, get crosses into the box and score goals – all of which he's been doing in abundance for Blyth this season.*

> *"Cal arrives with great pedigree having come through the academy at Newcastle. He was in and around the first-team squad in the Premier League under Rafael Benitez, so it was a big shock and disappointment for him when he was released in the summer.*

> *"To come that close to making it for your boyhood club only to be let go is a huge test of your character and determination to succeed, but he's responded in the right way by committing himself to Blyth, getting his head down and delivering strong performances in a tough, physical league.*

> *"He's an ambitious lad who we know will come here determined to better himself, which can only benefit us. We're really looking forward to working with him.*

"Once again, I have to say a huge thank you to our owners for sanctioning this signing. We feel Cal has the potential to be an excellent investment for the club and we'll continue to work together to identify players who can add value to our squad."

There was more good news the next day, Tuesday 21 January.

Jim O'Brien, who had had so much bad luck with injury this season, was near to full fitness. He played the first half of the game against AFC Mansfield in the Nottinghamshire FA Saturday Senior Cup, and came through unscathed.

Although not ready for first team consideration, he was expected to be by the beginning of February.

He suffered a broken arm on 21 September at Bromley and then, in his first match after that injury, a deep gash down the middle of his thigh on 14 December at Chesterfield.

There were two other pieces of news before the end of the week, both concerning Chesterfield:

First, it was announced that forward Nathan Tyson had departed on (a remainder of the season) loan. There was no recall clause in the agreement, but he would not be eligible for Chesterfield at Meadow Lane on 1 February.

Second, goalkeeper Ross Fitzsimons, loaned to Chesterfield until the end of the season only last week, was recalled after Sam Slocombe injured his thigh in training.

Match 31	**Dagenham & Redbridge** (20th) **2 Notts Co** (6th) **0**	Att: 1,697
Sat 25 Jan 2020 15:00	goals 61', 80'	(472 Notts supporters)

                          Fitzsimons

Brindley   Rawlinson   Lacey   Bakayogo

           Doyle (Capt.)   Rose

     Roberts (O'Brien 68')   Boldewijn

      Dennis (Thomas 68')   Wootton

Subs: Bird, O'Brien, Crawford, Thomas, Osborne
(no substitute goalkeeper)

Callum Roberts made his debut for Notts, and Jim O'Brien returned after injury.

This was the third meeting of the season between the two clubs. Notts were victorious on both occasions at Meadow Lane: 2-0 in a league fixture on 8 October and 2-1 in the second round of the FA Trophy two weeks ago. As their scheduled fixture last weekend was postponed, Dag & Red hadn't played since.

Following a good start to the season, Dag & Red were 5th from the top at the end of September. However, their only victory since the middle of November had been in the first round of the FA Trophy. Only bottom of the league Chorley had scored fewer goals than the Daggers but their defensive record was reasonable with only thirty-nine conceded, good for a team only one place above the relegation zone.

Although Notts had some good attempts on goal, obviously they were disappointed with the result. The two Dag & Red second half goals should have been avoided. The first followed a corner, which bounced twice before it was tapped home from inside the six yard box. The second came after Fitzsimons failed to gather a twenty yard shot which rebounded off his chest and the loose ball was prodded into the net. Between those goals Michael Doyle was sent off (66') for the THIRD time this season when he received a second yellow card. As he was running into a defensive position he was adjudged to have tripped a player who ran across him - it looked a harsh decision. It meant he would serve another suspension!

This was Alex Lacey's ninth game for Notts and his first experience of a defeat!

Match 32	**Notts Co** (7ᵗʰ) **3 Chesterfield** (21ˢᵗ) **0**	Att: 6,347
Sat 1 Feb 2020 17:20	Boldewijn 51'	(inc. 1,462 from
Shown live on BT Sport.	Wootton 59', 76'	Chesterfield)

Fitzsimons

Brindley   Rawlinson   Lacey   Kelly-Evans

Rose (Capt.)   O'Brien (Crawford 79')

Roberts (Bird 82')   Boldewijn

Thomas (Dennis 77')   Wootton

Subs: Bird, Crawford, Dennis, Osborne, Shields
(no substitute goalkeeper)

Jim O'Brien's re-appearance at Meadow Lane (his first since 14 September) was only his ninth start of the season, following his two serious injuries. He replaced Captain Michael Doyle who was suspended for three games because of his dismissal last weekend. Normally a second yellow card (= red card) resulted in a one game ban but as it was Doyle's third red card of the season he received a one game ban plus two more for the other two red cards!

This was the third meeting of the season between the two clubs. The first two games were at Chesterfield. Notts were defeated 1-0 in the league fixture on 26 October but won 1-0 in the first round of the FA Trophy on 14 December. Since that FA Trophy defeat Chesterfield's form had improved and they had only lost two of their last seven league games.

Chesterfield had been without a manager since John Sheridan (former Notts manager) was sacked on 2 January. They were unbeaten in the three games they had played under the caretaker manager, although they remained in the relegation zone. Their squad had been strengthened by three Notts players on loan until the end of the season: Matt Tootle (ineligible), Nathan Tyson (ineligible) and goalkeeper Ross Fitzsimons (would have been ineligible) but who was recalled by Notts last week when Sam Slocombe was injured in training.

Notts eventually won comfortably, but Chesterfield had their moments in an entertaining game. One of the most dramatic featured Fitzsimons!

Notts nearly took the lead twice in the first twenty minutes. First Rawlinson headed a Boldewijn cross against a post and then Boldewijn struck the cross bar with a free kick. However, Chesterfield should have taken the lead just before half time but a penalty, awarded for a foul by Brindley, was saved by the recalled Fitzsimons!

Notts took the lead when 'Man of the Match' Boldewijn moved purposely forward from near the half way line before unleashing a terrific right footed shot into the top corner of the net from twenty five yards – his first goal since the end of October, but what a goal! Chesterfield nearly equalised a few minutes later when Notts' crossbar was struck by a vicious twenty yard shot. A Wootton double secured the win for Notts. His first was a header, following a good cross from Roberts, and the second a tap in after Boldewijn's shot from the edge of the penalty area was fumbled by the goalkeeper. In between Wootton's goals Fitzsimons made an excellent, flying, one handed save from a twenty yard shot.

At last Notts put on a good performance in a televised match, after the disappointments of two defeats against Barnet (2-1) and Chesterfield (1-0) earlier in the season. No Notts supporter will forget two BBC televised FA Cup defeats: November 2015 at Salford City (2-0) who were then a non-league club in what is now known as The National League (North) and Notts were three leagues higher, in League One. February 2018 at Premier League Swansea City (8-1, yes eight - one), admittedly in a replay following a 1-1 draw at Meadow Lane. Although less than two years ago, not one of the eighteen players who were in that squad (the eleven who started plus seven substitutes) are still with Notts County.

Two days after the Chesterfield game (3 February) Notts announced that Ross Fitzsimons had decided to return to Chesterfield on loan (this time without a recall clause) for the remainder of the season. As a replacement Notts signed goalkeeper Joe McDonnell, age twenty five, on a deal until the end of the season. His contract at League One AFC Wimbledon expired on 31 January. He had worked with Neal Ardley and Neil Cox when they were the management duo at Wimbledon. Fitzsimons' departure meant goalkeeping coach Jake Kean would provide McDonnell with competition/cover for the number one position.

It was revealed that the injured Sam Slocombe would be side-lined for the foreseeable future - six to eight weeks.

FA Trophy – 3rd Round	**Yeovil Town 1 Notts Co 2**	Att: 1,946
Sat 8 Feb 2020 15:00.	goal 77' Rawlinson 8' Wootton 69'	(214 Notts supporters)

McDonnell

Kelly-Evans   Rawlinson   Lacey   McCrory

O'Brien (Capt.)   Crawford

Osborne (Rose 65')   Shields (Brindley 46')

Dennis (Wootton 65')   Thomas

Subs: Kean (Gk), Brindley, Rose, Boldewijn, Wootton, Betts

Among the Notts changes from the side that beat Chesterfield seven days ago, Joe McDonnell made his debut in goal. Roberts and Bird were cup-tied having played in the competition for Blyth and Boston respectively. Brindley, Rose, Boldewijn and Wootton were rested.

Although Notts fielded a strong side they weren't at full strength. In addition to the players mentioned above there were four others unavailable through injury: Sam Slocombe (goalkeeper, last played 18 January), Ben Turner (central defender, last played 7 December), Zoumana Bakayogo (left sided wing back, last played 25 January) and Regan Booty (midfielder, last played 14 December).

Notts were unluckily defeated 3-1 at Yeovil, in a league game, on 31 August.

Following that victory Yeovil won their next six league games – all in September – and moved into third place, one point off top spot. They had since remained in a play-off position. However, their last league victory was on New Year's Day, and in their last game, at home to bottom club Chorley, they scored two minutes from the end of the match to secure a draw.

Yeovil fourth, Notts sixth, in The National League. Weather 'Storm Ciara' was approaching the UK from the west, but this stormy game was completed before its wind and rain arrived.

This eventful game was Notts' most dramatic of the season so far. A total of ninety nine incident packed minutes (45' + 3' at the end of the first half and 45' + 6' at the end of the second half) were played; for sixty two of those minutes Notts played with ten men, and from the 79' Notts played with nine men!

8' – Rawlinson gave Notts the lead. Dennis chipped the ball into the six yard box which the goalkeeper (under pressure from his own defender) punched into the air and Rawlinson headed the ball over the line.

17' – O'Brien yellow card for a foul.

37' – Thomas given a straight red card and sent off, following an altercation with a Yeovil player. A few minutes before this two Yeovil players (one was the player involved in the fracas with Thomas) were shown yellow cards.

43' – Dennis yellow card for a push.

Just before half time a third Yeovil player was shown a yellow card.

During the interval Neal Ardley replaced Shields with substitute Brindley which meant Notts had five in their back line! The break took some of the heat out of what had been a feisty first half, and little of note occurred in the first twenty minutes of the second half.

65' – Dennis and Osborne replaced by substitutes Wootton and Rose.

69' – Wootton scored Notts' second goal. Rawlinson (yes, central defender Rawlinson) jinked past a defender, crossed low from the left hand side of the penalty area and Wootton's shot hit the crossbar and bounced down over the goal line.

77' – Yeovil scored and reduced the deficit (1-2).

79' – McCrory injured and unable to continue, and Notts had used their three permitted substitutes.

82' – A Yeovil shot hits the crossbar.

Not surprisingly Notts were under pressure for the remainder of the game, but a great team performance of grit, determination and desire (together with a little luck) was rewarded with a place in the quarter finals of the FA Trophy, and a Wembley final just two rounds away!

Match 33	**Notts Co** (8ᵗʰ) **1 Woking** (12ᵗʰ) **1**	Att: 5,074
Sat 15 Feb 2020 15:00	Dennis 70' goal 50'	

<pre>
                        McDonnell
      Brindley   Rawlinson   Bird   Kelly-Evans
              Rose (Capt.)   O'Brien
                 Roberts   Boldewijn
                    Dennis   Wootton
</pre>

Subs: Kean (Gk), Crawford, Osborne, Shields, Bagan

Pierce Bird started for the third time this season in place of the injured Lacey. In all there were six changes to the team which started, and won, at Yeovil in the FA Trophy last Saturday. Thomas was absent for the first of his three-game suspension.

You may have noticed the name (Joel) Bagan as one of the substitutes. The eighteen year old left back was signed yesterday, on a one month loan from Championship side Cardiff City, to provide cover for the injured McCrory and Bakayogo. His one and only start for Cardiff came in their recent FA Cup fourth round replay at home to Reading, when he had an impressive debut.

Notts won 4-0 at Woking on 29 October, when Boldewijn and Thomas each scored twice.

At the beginning of December Woking were in fourth place (eight points ahead of Notts who were twelfth). Since mid-December, when they lost in the FA Trophy, their form had been poor with nineteen league goals conceded in six defeats, and two (1-0) home victories. They had lost their last six away league games; seven if the FA Trophy defeat was included.

Notts had the better of the first half, but Woking took the lead early in the second half when a header, following a driven right wing cross, entered the net via a post. The goal unsettled Notts and for a short while they struggled. However, they regained their composure and twenty minutes later equalised when Roberts and Wootton combined to provide Dennis with the opportunity.

Weather 'Storm Dennis' was affecting the UK, so conditions were overcast and very windy with (outbreaks of) rain. All but three of the fixtures in The National League were postponed. It was therefore apt that Dennis was Notts' goal scorer.

Match 34	**Hartlepool Utd** (12th) **2 Notts Co** (6th) **0**	Att: 3,839
Sat 22 Feb 2020 15:00	goals 47', 58'	(422 Notts supporters)

McDonnell

Brindley   Rawlinson   Long   Kelly-Evans

Doyle (Capt.)   Rose (Crawford 81')

Roberts (Osborne 81')   Boldewijn

Dennis (O'Brien 46')   Wootton

Subs: Bird, O'Brien, Crawford, Osborne, Bagan
(no substitute goalkeeper)

Captain Michael Doyle returned following the completion of his three game suspension, with Jim O'Brien dropped to substitute.

For the second game in succession a new player was in the squad, but whereas Joel Bagan was only a named substitute last week, on this occasion Adam Long made his debut in place of Pierce Bird. The nineteen year old central defender was signed two days ago, on a one month loan from Championship side Wigan Athletic, to provide cover for the injured Turner and Lacey. Long had made two first team appearances for Wigan. This season he'd been a regular member of their very successful Under 23s.

Since they drew 2-2 at Meadow Lane on 2 November Hartlepool had experienced indifferent form and mixed results. However, their recent league form had been better with only one defeat in the last six games and they had won their last three home games.

In cold, windy, showery conditions Notts struggled for most of the game. They were fortunate to get to half time level, with Hartlepool in the ascendency for most of the first forty five minutes. Hartlepool took the lead when a cross from the left and the swirling wind deceived goalkeeper McDonnell. Although he got his hand to the ball, he was unable to keep it out of the net. The second goal came when a direct free kick, also from the left and by the same player who scored the first goal, evaded everyone and finished in the far corner of the net. It had been a very disappointing afternoon for Notts and their supporters.

(Nathan Tyson, the Notts striker on loan at Chesterfield until the end of the season, scored a twenty three minute hat-trick while Notts toiled away in vain at Hartlepool. Goalkeeper Ross Fitzsimons, also on loan from Notts until the end of the season, was again an unused substitute.)

Notts' next fixture was scheduled for three days later at relegation threatened AFC Fylde, but the evening game was AGAIN postponed, and AGAIN at very short notice – just one hour before the 19:45 kick off. Earlier in the day the pitch had passed two inspections, but after a late afternoon shower an area of the pitch was subsequently deemed unsafe for the players.

Despite the disappointment of a second wasted journey to Fylde, and the frustration that a fixture backlog was now unavoidable, Neal Ardley and Neil Cox agreed with the decision.

However, the next day there was controversy when The National League granted Fylde's proposal to rearrange the twice postponed fixture for the evening of Tuesday 3 March, despite strong objections from Notts.

CEO Jason Turner issued a statement:

> *On behalf of the club I would like to place on record my disappointment that The National League have approved this date and that Fylde would not agree to another available option later in the season.*
>
> *This decision, we feel, is at a huge disadvantage to our supporters who, having already lost time and money on two wasted journeys, must now make the necessary working and travel arrangements to return to the same venue in only five days' time.*
>
> *As a club we have also unnecessarily spent thousands of pounds on coach travel and accommodation in preparation for two matches only for them to be postponed within two hours of kick-off. With the weather forecast remaining bleak, we are concerned that next week's match could still be in doubt and therefore feel the decision to play on this day commits us and our supporters to further expenditure amid continued uncertainty.*
>
> *I must also warn our supporters that, should either ours or Fylde's FA Trophy fixtures fall foul of the forecasted poor weather this weekend, any rearranged Trophy match would be scheduled for Tuesday – meaning our trip to Fylde will have to be rearranged yet again. I would urge our supporters to be mindful of this before making firm arrangements to travel.*

(Notts won. Fylde lost at home to Harrogate)

> *We did our very best to set a date which we feel would have been fair for both clubs and their supporters. However, Fylde informed us that they wished to leave this date free in case they progress to the semi-final of the FA Trophy. I am baffled as to why a currently free date for both clubs can be ruled out and how a hypothetical situation can take precedence over our fixture? This simply cannot be right.*

> *Despite us submitting a very strong argument in our favour, the league cited fixture congestion and FA Trophy scheduling as their reason to agree to Fylde's request. I can only apologise to our own supporters for any inconvenience today's developments will cause them.*

To their credit Fylde responded with a goodwill gesture:

> *AFC Fylde is offering Notts County supporters, who attended either of the two postponed fixtures, a full refund and a complimentary ticket to Tuesday night's game.*
>
> *As well as the free ticket, AFC Fylde will also fully fund two coaches for the Notts County supporters who wish to travel up on the night.*
>
> *As a community-based club Fylde recognise that it's the supporters who are most affected by late postponements, and as such we felt we needed to do something.*
>
> *The Chairman, David Haythornthwaite, has been upset by what he considers unfair criticism of the club and wanted to do something personally to try and rectify the situation.*

On 28 February Notts signed forward Scott Wilson from League Two Oldham Athletic on a loan deal until the end of the 2019-20 season.

The 27-year-old spent the early part of his career in non-league football and was Macclesfield Town's top scorer with fourteen goals when they won promotion from The National League as champions in 2017-18.

He remained at Macclesfield last season and, ironically, helped them avoid relegation from League Two at Notts' expense. On Boxing Day 2018 he scored both goals for Macclesfield in their 2-1 win at Meadow Lane! The clubs swapped places at the bottom of League Two, where Notts remained for the next twelve games before being relegated (in 23rd position) at the end of the season. Macclesfield finished in 22nd position and escaped.

Last summer he transferred to Oldham and had been a regular member of their first team squad until he joined Notts.

FA Trophy – Quarter Final	**Notts County 5 Aveley 0**	Att: 4,893
Sat 29 Feb 2020 12:30	O'Brien 32', Crawford 38'	
	Osborne 44', Wootton 60',	
	Wilson 64'	

                          McDonnell

Kelly-Evans   Rawlinson (Betts 71')   Long   Bagan

Doyle (Capt.) (Shields 61')   Crawford   O'Brien

                          Osborne

           Dennis   Wootton (Wilson 61')

Subs: Kean (Gk), Brindley, Rose, Boldewijn, Shields, Wilson, Betts

This game was Michael Doyle's 800th career appearance – what an achievement. Adam Long made his home debut and Joel Bagan his debut. Scott Wilson and Owen Betts (on a Notts development contract) both made their debuts from the substitute's bench, and Wilson scored within three minutes!

Aveley Football Club, from Essex, were the lowest ranked side left in the competition and members of the Isthmian League Division One North – level 8 of the football pyramid (National League = level 5).

A professional Notts performance resulted in a stylish, comprehensive, victory. This meant that Notts would now play a two leg semi-final (home and away) against Harrogate Town (National League), Concord Rangers (17th of 22 in National League South, level 6) or Halesowen Town (next to the top of Southern League Division One Central, level 8).

Notts (3rd in The National League) were drawn against Harrogate (2nd)!!

Semi-Final: Winners receive **£15,000**, losers receive **£5,000**
Final: Winner **£60,000**, loser **£30,000**

Match 35	AFC Fylde (23rd) **1** Notts Co (10th) **2**	Att: 1,353
Tue 3 Mar 2020 19:45	goal 18' Boldewijn 13'
Long 76'	(150? Notts supporters)

McDonnell

Brindley   Rawlinson   Long   Kelly-Evans

Doyle (Capt.)   Rose

Roberts (Dennis 74')   Boldewijn (Wilson 74')

Thomas (O'Brien 60')   Wootton

Subs: Bird, O'Brien, Crawford, Dennis, Wilson
(no substitute goalkeeper)

This game was the fourth attempt to play the fixture. The first (scheduled for 30th November) was postponed because of Notts' second round FA Cup tie at Northampton. The second (scheduled for Tuesday evening 14 January) and third (scheduled for Tuesday evening 25 February) were postponed due to the weather. Notts beat Fylde 2-0 at home on 28 September.

Fylde's last league win was on 26 November. Since then they had played eleven league games without a victory. Despite their poor league form Fylde reached the third round of the FA Cup (narrowly beaten at Premier League Sheffield United). Like Notts they also reached the quarter final of the FA Trophy, but whereas Notts won their game Fylde lost at home to Harrogate after extra time.

Before this fixture Notts' form could be looked at in two different ways: they had lost only three of their last seventeen games in league and cup, **or**, so far in 2020 they had won only two of their seven league games. In four of those they had failed to score, and hadn't scored in the league away from Meadow Lane!

Boldewijn consigned that final statistic to the waste bin after just thirteen minutes when he gave Notts the lead with a direct free kick from twenty yards – his low shot beat the defensive 'wall' and squirmed underneath the goalkeepers dive. Five minutes later Fylde equalised, against the run of play, with an excellent low shot from the edge of the penalty box into the far corner. Notts' winner was scored by young, on loan, central defender Adam Long in only his third game for Notts – a header direct from an O'Brien corner.

Neal Ardley described this victory as "the best and most satisfying win of the season". Next, away at top of the league Barrow!

Match 36	**Barrow** (1st) **0 Notts Co** (6th) **2**	Att: 3,307
Sat 7 Mar 2020 15:00	Crawford 67'	(433 Notts supporters)
	Roberts 72'	

McDonnell

Brindley   Rawlinson   Lacey   McCrory   Bagan (Long 83')

Doyle (Capt.)   Crawford   O'Brien

Wilson (Wootton 58')   Thomas (Roberts 58')

Subs: Long, Boldewijn, Roberts, Wootton, Dennis
(no substitute goalkeeper)

Prior to this game Neal Ardley had said he would be rotating players during the remainder of the season as he was of the opinion that the Saturday / Tuesday fixture schedule was too demanding to expect the same eleven for every game. Joel Bagan and Scott Wilson made their first league starts. Lacey and McCrory returned after being injured in the FA Trophy victory at Yeovil on 8th February. Rose and Kelly-Evans weren't even in the squad. With a change in formation, and only five who started in the victory at Fylde four days ago retained, the side Ardley chose was a surprise.

When Barrow beat Notts 3-0 at Meadow Lane in mid-November (Notts' heaviest defeat of the season, so far) they moved to the top of The National League, and had not been dislodged since. In the intervening sixteen weeks they had played twenty league and FA Trophy games and only lost two, both away from home. The first defeat was in the league on 4 February and the other was in the FA Trophy four days later on 8 February.

Barrow had scored the most goals in The National League, sixty eight. They had the league's leading goal scorer, Quigley, with twenty and Rooney was only three behind with seventeen goals. Their defensive record was the joint best in the league with only thirty seven conceded (the same as Notts and Solihull) and their goal difference of thirty one was by far the best in the league.

The game was played with a strong and gusty south-westerly wind blowing in the direction goal to goal. Notts faced the wind in the first half and had to defend for most of the time. On the quarter hour mark, McCrory wrestled Quigley to the ground and the referee immediately awarded a penalty. Barrow captain John Rooney (younger brother of former England captain Wayne Rooney) missed the penalty – the ball hit a post and rebounded away for a throw-in. Fifteen minutes later he struck the outside of the opposite post with a direct free kick from thirty yards. Notts got to half-time with the score level.

In the sixty second minute Quigley was shown a straight red card by the referee, and sent off, for a late challenge on goalkeeper McDonnell. This dismissal, just a few minutes after Notts had introduced substitutes Wootton and Roberts, unsettled Barrow and they fell behind when Crawford scored his first league goal, with a header, following a Roberts corner. Five minutes later a fine individual goal by Roberts, his first for Notts, sealed victory. He received the ball from Crawford on the edge of the penalty area, and with close control he dribbled past three defenders and placed the ball into the far corner of the net from just inside the six yard box. Notts played out the final twenty minutes with relative ease.

Manager Neal Ardley's strategy had proved to be correct.

The top half of The National League table on **7 March 2020**			Home				Away				Overall						
	Team	P	W	D	L	F	A	W	D	L	F	A	W	D	L	F	A	GD	Pts
1	Barrow	37	13	2	4	33	15	8	5	5	35	24	21	7	9	68	39	29	**70**
2	Harrogate Town	37	12	4	3	32	16	7	5	6	29	28	19	9	9	61	44	17	**66**
3	Yeovil Town	37	9	6	3	34	19	8	3	8	27	25	17	9	11	61	44	17	**60**
4	Boreham Wood	37	7	7	4	24	18	9	5	5	31	22	16	12	9	55	40	15	**60**
5	Halifax Town	36	10	3	6	31	25	7	4	6	19	23	17	7	12	50	48	2	**58**
6	**Notts County**	**36**	**8**	**8**	**2**	**29**	**15**	**7**	**4**	**7**	**25**	**22**	**15**	**12**	**9**	**54**	**37**	**17**	**57**
7	Solihull Moors	38	12	1	6	29	15	3	9	7	19	22	15	10	13	48	37	11	**55**
8	Woking	37	8	6	4	21	19	7	4	8	28	33	15	10	12	49	52	-3	**55**
9	Stockport County	38	9	3	7	28	28	6	7	6	21	25	15	10	13	49	53	-4	**55**
10	Hartlepool United	38	8	5	6	28	23	6	7	6	27	26	14	12	12	55	49	6	**54**
11	Dover Athletic	37	6	5	8	29	26	9	3	6	19	22	15	8	14	48	48	0	**53**
12	Bromley	38	8	6	5	37	26	6	4	9	20	26	14	10	14	57	52	5	**52**
13	Barnet	34	7	6	3	26	19	6	6	6	23	22	13	12	9	49	41	8	**51**

Top = Promoted to EFL League Two.
Positions 2-7 = play-off's to decide the other promoted team.

Notts now had ten league games to play (five at home and five away) before the end of the season on Saturday 25 April, when Yeovil were the visitors to Meadow Lane.

They also had a two leg FA Trophy semi-final against Harrogate, to be played on Saturday's 21 and 28 March, with the added complication that the league fixtures scheduled for those two dates had been rearranged by The National League. Notts had agreed mutually convenient alternative dates with both opponents which they considered more reasonable for both players and supporters. However, Notts were instructed to play on the dates decided by the league.

A total of twelve games in the next seven weeks. Three of those games (the two leg FA Trophy semi-final followed by a home league fixture) were against second in the table Harrogate!

Although Notts had a game in hand over both Barrow and Harrogate, it was unlikely they could overtake either. However, the reward for a second or third place finish was a guaranteed semi-final play-off with the fixture at Meadow Lane. A finish between fourth and seventh would mean an additional play-off game, with a victory an away semi-final fixture.

In the corresponding games earlier in the season against the ten opponents Notts still had to play, their record was mediocre:

P10 W3 D3 L4 F16 A13 Pts 12

With a repeat of those results Notts would finish with 57 Pts +12 Pts = 69 Pts. Last season The National League champions earned 89 Pts, second 86 Pts, third 85 Pts and seventh 74 Pts.

Although Notts' current form was good, and the momentum gained from the excellent results over the Christmas and New Year period had been maintained (apart from the disappointments at Dagenham and Redbridge and Hartlepool) there was obviously no room for complacency. Despite their victory at league leaders Barrow the management duo of Ardley and Cox (and the players) were aware that any dip in form would be difficult to rectify with the end of the season so near. A final position outside the play-offs would now be a huge disappointment.

But more importantly, two months ago in early January, the world began to realise that a new highly contagious mystery virus was likely to become a worldwide pandemic. Coronavirus (COVID-19) had arrived!

Match 37	Notts Co (6th) 3 Aldershot Tn (17th) 1	Att: 4,287
Tue 10 Mar 2020 19:45	Roberts 35' goal 17'	
	Dennis 59', 67'	

McDonnell

Kelly-Evans   Long (Rawlinson 60')   Lacey   McCrory

Rose (Capt.) (Crawford 83')   O'Brien

Roberts (Doyle 76')   Boldewijn

Dennis   Wootton

Subs: Rawlinson, Doyle, Crawford, Thomas, Wilson
(no substitute goalkeeper)

Manager Neal Ardley continued his squad rotation policy and made seven changes to the team who beat top of the table Barrow three days ago.

Notts lost 2-1 at Aldershot on 23 November.

Aldershot's results since that victory, and indeed since the start of the season, had been mixed. They had remained in the bottom half of the league throughout.

This game was a wonderful opportunity for Notts to move into third place in the league with a victory, but they made a poor start and went a goal behind when Aldershot scored with a simple header from six yards following a cross from the right side of the penalty area.

Following this setback Notts gradually improved and ten minutes before half time they equalised when Roberts scored his second goal in as many games. With close control he moved forward and arrowed a low left footed shot into the net from the edge of the penalty area. Just before Notts took the lead on the hour, McDonnell made a great save when he tipped a ferocious thirty yard shot on to the crossbar. Within a minute Wootton hit the Aldershot crossbar with a thunderous shot from the edge of the penalty area. Moments later a long clearance by McDonnell was well controlled by Dennis who then beat the goalkeeper with a brilliant lob from twenty yards. Notts continued to put their opponents under pressure and Dennis scored his second, with a powerful header from near the penalty spot, following an excellent cross by Kelly-Evans.

So, three league victories in a week. They had risen to third from the top, their highest ever position in non-league football, with nine fixtures to be played. COYP ('Come On You Pies').

Match 38	Notts Co (3rd) 4 Eastleigh (16th) 0	Att: 4,942
Sat 14 Mar 2020 15:00	Wootton 15', 62'	
	Dennis 54', Roberts 70'	

McDonnell

Brindley　　Rawlinson　　Lacey　　Bagan

Doyle (Capt.)　　Rose (Crawford 72')

Roberts (Wilson 78')　　Boldewijn

Dennis (Thomas 72')　　Wootton

Subs: O'Brien, Long, Crawford, Thomas, Wilson
(no substitute goalkeeper)

Neal Ardley made four changes to the team victorious over Aldershot four days ago. One was the inclusion of Joel Bagan, who yesterday had his initial month long loan from Cardiff City extended until the end of the season.

Notts lost 1-0 at Eastleigh on 3 August, the opening day of the 2019-20 season.

[The day before this game The Football Association, Premier League, EFL, Barclays FA Women's Super League and FA Women's Championship collectively agreed to postpone the professional game in England until Friday 3 April at the earliest. The suspension also applied to all FA competitions e.g. FA Trophy.

This action was taken due to the increasing numbers of clubs taking steps to isolate their players and staff because of the coronavirus (COVID-19) pandemic.

The FA also stated that they were liaising with The National League pyramids (men's and women's) and would continue to offer guidance and support, but any decision to continue playing or to postpone their respective competitions was a matter for each league. It was expected that The National League would soon issue a similar directive. This game was one of only six which survived a postponement.]

Eastleigh's results throughout had been mixed and for the majority of the period since they had been in the bottom half of the table. After losing their first four league games of 2020, they had lost only one of their last six league games and had kept three 'clean sheets' in the process. Despite Eastleigh's recent improved form Notts were dominant for most of the game and they consolidated their league position (3rd) with a comprehensive victory.

Notts made a good start and took the lead when a pin-point cross by Dennis was headed home by Wootton. Their second goal, just after half-time, came from Dennis who nodded the ball home following a chipped cross, to the far post, by Roberts. A few minutes later Wootton scored his second when Rose cut the ball back for him to side foot the ball into the net from the edge of the penalty area. Roberts completed the scoring when he fired a left footed shot low into the corner of the net from a central position twenty yards from goal.

If The National League was suspended Notts were well placed to respond if further restrictions were introduced, and subsequently lifted:

They were top of the 'current form' table. In their four successive league victories (all in March) Notts had scored eleven and conceded two. Their goal difference of twenty-three was now only bettered by league leaders Barrow. Harrogate, in second, and Yeovil, in fourth, both had a goal difference of seventeen, and they had yet to visit Meadow Lane!

Notts had lost only three of their last twenty-one games in league and cup since the end of November, were in third position in the league and in the semi-final of the FA Trophy.

The players were united and confident and, because of Notts' fixture congestion until the last week of the season, had accepted Neal Ardley's squad rotation policy. The long-term injured players, goalkeeper Slocombe, central defender Turner, midfielder Booty and wing back Bakayogo, were all close to regaining full fitness and they were expected to be in contention for a return to the team during April.

Examination of the leading scorers (ten or more goals) in The National League, revealed three players from Notts County: Wootton (13), Dennis (12 inc. 2 penalties), and Thomas (10). Boldewijn was just outside the list with 8.

If 'minutes per goal' was scrutinised Dennis, with only 16 'starts' plus 14 as a substitute, would be top of the table with a goal every 122 minutes. Murphy (Yeovil, 17 inc. 2 penalties) with a goal every 133 minutes would be second. The league's leading scorer (20 goals, no penalties), Barrow's Quigley, with a goal every 141 minutes would be third.

As the Eastleigh game was likely to be the last before The National League suspended fixtures, the top half of the league table (as on Monday **16 March 2020**) is reproduced here:

Team	P	GD	PTS
1 Barrow	37	29	70
2 Harrogate Town	37	17	66
3 **Notts County**	**38**	**23**	**63**
4 Yeovil Town	37	17	60
5 Boreham Wood	37	15	60
6 Halifax Town	37	1	58
7 Stockport County	39	-3	58
8 Solihull Moors	38	11	55
9 Hartlepool United	39	6	55
10 Woking	38	-5	55
11 Barnet	35	10	54
12 Dover Athletic	38	0	54

Position 1 = Automatic promotion to EFL League Two.
Positions 2-7 Play-offs to decide other promoted club.
(A finish in positions 2 & 3 = clubs guaranteed a home semi-final against winner(s) of positions 4 to 7)

With the UK, and most of the rest of the world, now becoming increasingly consumed and alarmed by the seriousness of the coronavirus (COVID-19) pandemic it wasn't a surprise when, on Monday 16 March, The National League issued the following statement:

National League Competition Suspended

At its Board Meeting on Friday, The National League decided to use its best endeavours to keep its season going in the face of unprecedented adversity

However, with the current coronavirus (COVID-19) reaching global pandemic levels it has to accept that the situation is now out of its own control.

In the knowledge of the government measures now announced including not to support sporting events with emergency services workers it is clearly not practical for its fixtures to be fulfilled in the immediate future.

In those circumstances and in line with The Football Association and the Professional Game, at a Board Meeting today, The National League has decided that its competition is now suspended until at least 3rd April 2020.

The National League will continue to monitor the situation, but trusts that its loyal clubs, fans, players, officials, staff, volunteers and sponsors will accept that it has had no other choice but to reach this decision.

It wishes everybody connected with the competition and indeed the whole country a safe passage through these turbulent times.

As a result of the above statement, Notts immediately issued the following:

Season suspended - Meadow Lane closure

Following today's announcement that the Vanarama National League has been suspended until at least 3 April, along with the FA's decision to suspend the Buildbase FA Trophy, our board of directors have decided to close Meadow Lane Stadium for the rest of this week.

The FA statement read: "In light of the most recent update from the Government on the coronavirus, we have decided to postpone all matches across all FA Competitions, including those outside of the Professional Game, until 3 April. We are committed to trying to complete all competition fixtures and will be liaising with the relevant parties to establish appropriate options to do so."

The decisions of both the league and FA leave us without a scheduled first-team fixture for the foreseeable future and, in the best interests of our supporters, staff and players, the stadium will be closed until next Monday, 23 March. The situation will be reviewed towards the end of this week, with a more prolonged closure possible.

Our chief executive, Jason Turner, said: "While we are of course all disappointed that such an exciting end to our season has been put on hold, we welcome the clarity today's decisions have brought and feel it's only right that Meadow Lane should close for the time being.

"I'd like to make it clear that this is a precautionary measure. No-one connected with the club has tested positive for Covid-19, nor shown any symptoms, and our staff will be working from home throughout the closure.

"Our first-team manager Neal Ardley has prepared for this eventuality and, with the help of his staff, will ensure our playing squad are able to do all they can in order to return to action in the best possible condition when the time is right. I'd like to thank our fans for their loyal support at this challenging time."

All ticket sales have been suspended and an update for season ticket holders, along with those who have purchased a match ticket for any of our forthcoming home or away fixtures, will be provided in due course. Please note that, in line with expert advice, non-essential business such as player appearances, commercial activities, stadium tours, etc. will also be postponed indefinitely. We will continue to review our position on an ongoing basis and provide updates when appropriate. We will be remotely operating our usual opening hours throughout the closure and phone lines have been diverted where possible.

On 17 March Christoffer and Alexander Reedtz, issued a message of reassurance to supporters following the suspension of the season and the closure of Meadow Lane:

Firstly, we would like to thank you for your incredible support so far this season, and for the warm welcome you all continue to extend to us.

This is obviously an extremely challenging period worldwide, not only for football, and we wholeheartedly support the suspension of all football activities at this time. Health will always trump sporting considerations, however much we have been enjoying the season and our recent run of results!

We would like to reassure you all that our commitment to the club is unwavering, even if there is to be a long break from football being played. We are in constant communication with Jason Turner, our CEO, and Neal Ardley, our manager, to make sure that on and off the pitch we are as prepared as possible for whatever the next few months will bring. Your continued support is very much appreciated by us all and rest assured the club will keep you informed of any developments.

Chris and Alex

So, no football until…….?

What will happen in the next few months?

An uncertain future lay ahead for everyone!

Chapter 9: The Coronavirus (COVID-19) pandemic, and lockdown

The following is a brief resume of the coronavirus (COVID-19) pandemic. My aim is to highlight the main aspects and the impact it had on the outcome of the 2019-20 football season. But, with worldwide death's increasing, football was not the most important thing for many people.

This new virus was unknown before the outbreak began in the city of Wuhan, China, in December 2019. In early January 2020, the World Health Organization was notified by China that 41 people in Wuhan, had been hospitalized with what appeared to be a mystery strain of pneumonia. Many were reported to be workers in, or visitors to, a live animal market. It soon became evident that the disease was spreading worldwide.

The key symptoms were: fever and tiredness, continuous cough, and breathing difficulties. Later, loss of smell (anosmia) was added to the official list of symptoms. Also, some people experienced a loss of taste.

STAY AT HOME

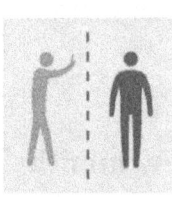
AVOID CONTACT WITH OTHERS

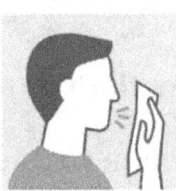
COVER YOUR NOSE AND MOUTH WITH TISSUE OR ELBOW WHEN SNEEZING

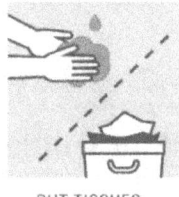
PUT TISSUES IN THE TRASH BIN AND WASH HANDS

KEEP OBJECTS AND SURFACES CLEAN

When venturing outside people were expected to keep a distance of at least two metres from anyone – known as 'social distancing'. In the majority of cases the virus lasted about five days and was mild, but for people over seventy, particularly those with an underlying serious medical condition, the virus could be life threatening. Fortunately, children were relatively free from infection. Men were more likely to get the disease than women.

On 30 January, the WHO declared the coronavirus (COVID-19) outbreak a Public Health Emergency of International Concern (PHEIC). By 14 February the virus had been confirmed in 24 other countries on several continents. On 11 March, WHO characterized COVID-19 as a pandemic.

The WHO Director-General's opening remarks at the media briefing:

In the past two weeks, the number of cases of COVID-19 outside China has increased 13-fold, and the number of affected countries has tripled. There are now more than 118,000 cases in 114 countries, and 4,291 people have lost their lives. Thousands more are fighting for their lives in hospitals.

In the days and weeks ahead, we expect to see the number of cases, the number of deaths, and the number of affected countries climb even higher. WHO has been assessing this outbreak around the clock and we are deeply concerned both by the alarming levels of spread and severity, and by the alarming levels of inaction. We have therefore made the assessment that COVID-19 can be characterized as a pandemic.

Pandemic is not a word to use lightly or carelessly. It is a word that, if misused, can cause unreasonable fear, or unjustified acceptance that the fight is over, leading to unnecessary suffering and death.

Describing the situation as a pandemic does not change the WHO's assessment of the threat posed by this virus. It doesn't change what WHO is doing, and it doesn't change what countries should do.

We have never before seen a pandemic sparked by a coronavirus. This is the first pandemic caused by a coronavirus. And we have never before seen a pandemic that can be controlled, at the same time. WHO has been in full response mode since we were notified of the first cases. And we have called every day for countries to take urgent and aggressive action. We have rung the alarm bell loud and clear.

Apprehension, fear, panic (call it what you like) had slowly gathered momentum, not only in the UK but also in most of the rest of the world, particularly in Europe and the USA.

It wasn't a surprise, therefore, when sporting fixtures worldwide started to be cancelled. Although largely an outdoor entertainment, crowds huddled closely together could only accelerate the spread of the disease. The last major sporting event to go ahead in the UK was the Cheltenham (Horse Racing) Festival 10-13 March. There were 251,684 racegoers in attendance across the four days.

The last Premier League game was on 9 March, the last Championship game on 8 March, and the last in Leagues One and Two were played on Tuesday 10 March. On Wednesday 11 March, when Spain were even more seriously affected with COVID-19 than the UK, Liverpool lost 2-3 (aet) at home to Atletico Madrid, and were eliminated from the Champions League competition – the attendance that night at Anfield was 52,267. In hindsight this game and the Cheltenham Festival should not have taken place.

The National League was suspended on Saturday 14 March, when Notts played, what turned out to be, their final game of the 2019-20 season – a 4-0 victory at home to Eastleigh. Five days later it was announced that "English football will be suspended until at least 30 April because of the continued spread of coronavirus". The next day the Meadow Lane closure was extended for another week, with staff continuing to work from home.

The National Health Service was in danger of becoming overwhelmed.

The new Chancellor of the Exchequer Rishi Sunak (only appointed just over a month ago, on 13 February) announced generous economic assistance to individuals and businesses. The measures introduced were astronomical in terms of cost, but considered necessary to mitigate the likely financial hardship to millions of UK citizens. [The Governor of the Bank of England, Andrew Bailey, had been in that position for only a few days - since 16 March.]

The Prime Minister, Boris Johnson, introduced stringent 'lockdown' measures in an attempt to curb the spread of the virus.

On Monday 23 March (the day from which schools were closed, except for the children of key workers and vulnerable children) the Prime Minister addressed the nation in an evening television broadcast. I reproduce his statement in full as it illustrates the seriousness of the situation.

The Rt Hon Boris Johnson MP

Good Evening,

The coronavirus is the biggest threat this country has faced for decades – and this country is not alone. All over the world we are seeing the devastating impact of this invisible killer.

And so tonight I want to update you on the latest steps we are taking to fight the disease and what you can do to help. I want to begin by reminding you why the UK has been taking the approach that we have.

Without a huge national effort to halt the growth of this virus, there will come a moment when no health service in the world could possibly cope; because there won't be enough ventilators, enough intensive care beds, enough doctors and nurses.

As we have seen elsewhere, in other countries that also have fantastic health care systems that is the moment of real danger. To put it simply, if too many people become seriously unwell at one time, the NHS will be unable to handle it - meaning more people are likely to die, not just from Coronavirus but from other illnesses as well.

So it's vital to slow the spread of the disease. Because that is the way we reduce the number of people needing hospital treatment at any one time, so we can protect the NHS's ability to cope - and save more lives.

That's why we have been asking people to stay at home during this pandemic. Although huge numbers are complying - and I thank you all - the time has now come for us all to do more. From this evening I must give the British people a very simple instruction - you must stay at home. The critical thing we must do is stop the disease spreading between households.

That is why people will only be allowed to leave their home for the following very limited purposes:

- *shopping for basic necessities, as infrequently as possible*
- *one form of exercise a day - for example a run, walk, or cycle - alone or with members of your household;*
- *any medical need, to provide care or to help a vulnerable person; and*
- *travelling to and from work, but only where this is absolutely necessary and cannot be done from home.*

That's all - these are the only reasons you should leave your home.

You should not be meeting friends. If your friends ask you to meet, you should say no. You should not be meeting family members who do not live in your home. You should not be going shopping except for essentials like food and medicine - and you should do this as little as you can. Use food delivery services where you can.

If you don't follow the rules the police will have the powers to enforce them, including through fines and dispersing gatherings.

To ensure compliance with the Government's instruction to stay at home, we will immediately:

- *close all shops selling non-essential goods, including clothing and electronic stores and other premises including libraries, playgrounds and outdoor gyms, and places of worship;*
- *we will stop all gatherings of more than two people in public – excluding people you live with;*
- *we will stop all social events, including weddings, baptisms and other ceremonies, but excluding funerals.*

Parks will remain open for exercise but gatherings will be dispersed.

No Prime Minister wants to enact measures like this.

I know the damage that this disruption is doing and will do to people's lives, to their businesses and to their jobs. That's why we have produced a huge and unprecedented programme of support both for workers and for business.

I can assure you that we will keep these restrictions under constant review. We will look again in three weeks and relax them if the evidence shows we are able to. But at present there are just no easy options. The way ahead is hard, and it is still true that many lives will sadly be lost.

And yet it is also true that there is a clear way through.

Day by day we are strengthening our amazing NHS with 7500 former clinicians now coming back to the service.

With the time you buy - by simply staying at home - we are increasing our stocks of equipment. We are accelerating our search for treatments. We are pioneering work on a vaccine. And we are buying millions of testing kits that will enable us to turn the tide on this invisible killer.

I want to thank everyone who is working flat out to beat the virus. Everyone from the supermarket staff to the transport workers to the carers to the nurses and doctors on the frontline.

But in this fight we can be in no doubt that each and every one of us is directly enlisted. Each and every one of us is now obliged to join together to halt the spread of this disease. To protect our NHS and to save many many thousands of lives.

And I know that as they have in the past so many times, the people of this country will rise to that challenge and we will come through it stronger than ever.

We will beat the coronavirus and we will beat it together. And therefore I urge you at this moment of national emergency to stay at home, protect our NHS and save lives.

Thank you.

After suffering from the symptoms of coronavirus for ten days, Boris Johnson was admitted to St Thomas' Hospital in central London on Sunday 5 April. The next day he was transferred into the Intensive Care Unit, where he remained for three days. He then made good progress and was allowed to leave hospital on Easter Sunday 12 April to continue his recovery at home, Chequers.

Following the PM's address Notts announced that the Meadow Lane closure would be extended "until 13 April at the earliest". The Notts County board of directors then issued the following message to supporters following the media's publication of a National League statement to clubs, the content of which suggested the league intended to close the 2019-20 season as soon as possible.

> *We appreciate that today's media coverage has caused a great deal of confusion and concern to our fans who are very keen to see us complete our season. Naturally, we share their desire to continue our push for at least a play-off position and a place in the Buildbase FA Trophy final.*
>
> *While we have yet to be officially consulted by The National League, we'd like to assure our supporters that we have already strongly stated our case for all remaining fixtures to be played so that promotion and relegation matters can come to a natural conclusion. It's our firm belief that a dynamic approach needs to be taken in order to preserve the integrity of both The National League and the FA Trophy and we have shared several ideas with the league, the EFL and the FA on how we feel this can be achieved.*
>
> *As the EFL's decision on the best way forward will directly impact The National League in terms of promotion and relegation to/from League Two, we don't anticipate The National League will rush into any decisions without exhausting all possible options, and hope they will take the time to carefully consider the several viable suggestions we believe we have presented to them.*
>
> *We look forward to receiving further correspondence from the league and hopefully returning to the 2019-20 campaign when it is safe to do so.*

At the end of another difficult week for all in the UK, and also for many millions of people worldwide, the outcome for the 2019-20 football season paled into insignificance when the COVID-19 **global** numbers were examined.

Total confirmed cases 509,164 (46,484 in the last 24 hours) with 23,335 deaths (2501 in the last 24 hours). On Saturday 28 March the number of deaths in the UK passed 1000!

The following week commenced with an operational update from Notts' CEO Jason Turner:

First and foremost, I hope our supporters and their loved ones are keeping safe and well as we continue our collective battle against a virus which has immeasurably changed the way we are all currently living.

As is the case for all clubs, and particularly those further down the pyramid, Covid-19 has and will continue to have a significant financial impact. The board have held numerous conversations over the past week, with decisions being taken as we look for the best possible way to safely navigate Notts County through these unprecedented times.

As our supporters will know from our previous updates, Meadow Lane has now been closed for the past two weeks with all employees, other than those with an essential need to carry out their roles on-site, working remotely.

However, having kept a close eye on government updates and advice it is unlikely that we will return to Meadow Lane in the very near future, so we have now taken the decision to furlough a number of our administrative and football staff under the Coronavirus Job Retention Scheme.

Our considerate owners, Chris and Alex Reedtz, will ensure that all furloughed staff receive their full salary, so nobody will be out of pocket during this time. I'm sure this gesture will be hugely appreciated, particularly as many of our staff are now experiencing their second successive spring/summer of uncertainty following the well-documented events which preceded the Reedtz brothers' takeover last year.

Having spoken to all staff affected by these temporary arrangements, they are fully supportive and understand why this decision has been taken and all look forward to returning to their jobs at the earliest opportunity.

Our playing staff are as yet unaffected and will continue to keep themselves fit in line with social distancing guidelines with a view to returning to training in the best possible condition when it's safe to do so.

While we eagerly await the time for us to resume our normal working routine, a small number of employees across all departments will continue to perform their roles remotely, and in some cases on-site, to ensure the club is able to operate and communicate as best it can.

We have received several messages from supporters asking how they can help us at this challenging time and, while we are sure the financial security of the club will not be compromised, we appreciate the sentiment and are working on initiatives which will enable them to do so.

For now, I'd encourage all supporters who have not yet signed up to Lifeline to please do so. The popular scheme, which gives you an opportunity to win cash and other prizes while supporting the club with £2 a week, will continue to operate as normal and it would be brilliant to see us close in on the maximum membership of 2,500.

Our online shop also remains open for business. While orders may take a little longer to process, we are dispatching on a weekly basis.

On a final note, we have already received more than 200 nominations for supporters deserving of a phone call following our appeal on Saturday. The response has been staggering and we're working through them as quickly as we can.

I hope this update has provided you all with some assurances that the club has a clear vision for how we move forward on an operational basis. We remain in close contact with the football authorities with regards to the completion of the 2019-20 season and will provide further updates on this subject as and when appropriate.

We would like to thank our fans for the support they continue to show us at this challenging and unprecedented time. Stay at home, stay safe and I hope to see you soon.

The next day (31 March) The National League Board, which had reviewed its prior decision to suspend the competition until at least 3 April, issued the following statement:

Competition Suspended Indefinitely

In consideration of the very serious and unprecedented national public health emergency caused by the coronavirus, the Board has taken the decision to suspend The National League, National League North and National League South competitions indefinitely.

The National League is currently obtaining specialist legal advice, is consulting regularly with The Football Association and other stakeholders, and is committed to involving its member clubs in a pending decision on how best to conclude the 2019/20 season.

On 9 April following much debate, deliberation and discussion (not forgetting media analysis and speculation) The Football Association/National League System confirmed that the 2019-20 season was at an end, with all results expunged, for clubs in Steps 3-7 of the NLS, Tiers 3 and below of the women's football pyramid, and the wider grassroots game.

So, for the time being at least, no decision had been made regarding The National League (Step 1), The National Leagues North and South (Step 2), the Premier League, the English Football League (Championship, League One, League Two) and the Women's Super League and Championship.

Also, as the 2019-20 FA Cup, Women's FA Cup, FA Trophy (remember, Notts had progressed to the semi-final stage and were scheduled to play Harrogate Town over two legs) and FA Vase were all at an advanced stage, The FA were keeping their options under review for those competitions. They had expressed a desire that, if possible, they be completed whenever it was safe and appropriate to do so. It was appreciated that the clubs involved were close to reaching a major final, and for those clubs and supporters The FA wanted to keep the Wembley dream alive.

The weather in the UK during the autumn and winter of 2019-20 had been very wet. Since early March, the weather had been much better, with a lot of dry and often sunny weather, for most. This, together with longer days (GMT became BST on 29 March), had helped to ease the burden of the 'lockdown'. The weather remained good over the long Easter weekend, and beyond.

However, there had been little else to cheer people up. The number infected had continued to increase at an alarming rate. Officially the UK total, on Easter Sunday 12 April, was 84,279 but unofficially the number was thought to be much higher. Hospital deaths in the UK had also risen dramatically - from the first death on 5 March, to over 1,000 on 28 March, to 10,612 on 12 April, when the UK became the fifth country to surpass 10,000 deaths related to coronavirus. The other four were the USA, Spain, Italy and France.

It was, therefore, no surprise when it was announced on 16 April that the lockdown restrictions imposed by PM Boris Johnson three weeks ago would remain in force for at least the next three weeks.

The prospect of a restart and continuation of the 2019-20 football season was still very uncertain, and it was impossible to contemplate if, or when, it would happen!

Six days elapsed before the next piece of significant football news. When it came it wasn't a shock to Notts, but it was a disappointment. The National League announced, on 22 April, that a majority of member clubs had voted to cancel all scheduled remaining league fixtures for the 2019-20 season.

The full National League statement read as follows:

> *National League Clubs were asked to support an ordinary resolution on 9 April to end the Playing Season for all fixtures scheduled up to and including 25 April 2020.*

With almost 90% of responses returned it is evident a clear majority of Clubs are in favour, including a majority of Clubs in each of The National League, National League North and National League South divisions.

In the knowledge that the ordinary resolution has passed, the League's Board has chosen to communicate the decision now and before the last few responses are received, which will not change the outcome, to enable Clubs to make business decisions with greater clarity as soon as possible. Clubs yet to respond still have an opportunity to do so, and the League wishes to include as many preferences as possible before the final voting result is declared.

National League Chief Executive Officer, Michael Tattersall, commented, "At a time when the entire country is wrestling with the devastating impact of Covid-19, the cancellation of the remaining normal season matches brings a degree of certainty to our Clubs coping with the business implications of the virus."

The options concerning the sporting outcomes of the 2019/20 season remain under careful and timely consideration, and further updates will be given in due course.

With a further vote to follow on how the outcomes of the campaign should be decided, the Notts board of directors responded:

We would like to place on record our disappointment that the 2019-20 Vanarama National League season has been brought to a premature end. While we appreciate the views of other clubs and respect the overall outcome of this vote as a representation of opinion across the three divisions, our stance has always been that The National League should operate in tandem with the EFL due to the intrinsic link between the two leagues.

We were therefore opposed to this vote being imposed – particularly as there was no clear indication of what the next steps would be in terms of deciding the conclusion of the season, including end-of-season play-offs and matters concerning promotion and relegation.

We have written to The National League on a number of occasions over the past month with detailed, constructive and well-considered options for how we believe the league can be concluded, thus giving clubs involved at both ends of the table a fair opportunity to compete for what they deserve.

One of such proposals would lead to clubs in less promising or precarious positions being able to conclude their season once and for all, leaving the others to resolve matters in the spirit of the competition over a short time period.

We thank The National League for allowing us to submit our thoughts and hope they are duly considered by the board and its executive to enable them to provide a fair way of deciding these huge outcomes in the next stage of voting.

To be clear, while all remaining scheduled league matches have been cancelled, we are not ruling out a return to action in some form between now and the formal conclusion of the 2019-20 campaign. We will therefore continue to ask our players to train remotely and, as a club, we'll make sure we're ready to resume our push for promotion if we're given the opportunity we feel we and others deserve.

We'd also like to advise our supporters that no decision has yet been taken by the FA on how this season's Trophy campaign will be concluded. We're mindful that hundreds of our fans purchased tickets for the first leg of our semi-final away to Harrogate Town and appreciate their patience. As soon as we have an update on what's planned for the competition, we'll circulate it.

In the meantime we look forward to hearing from The National League with regards to what the next round of voting will entail, with the continued hope that our fight for an immediate return to the EFL isn't over. Stay home, stay safe and thank you for your amazing continued support.

So, Notts County's eight remaining fixtures of the 2019-20 season were cancelled. Those fixtures were: Torquay United, Stockport County, Barnet, Chorley and Wrexham 'away' and Harrogate, Ebbsfleet United and Yeovil at Meadow Lane. The season had started at Eastleigh on 3 August with a 1-0 defeat and had ended at home to Eastleigh on 14 March with a 4-0 victory. This was an indication of the improvement and progress Notts had made in the intervening seven months.

The excellent April weather continued until the last few days of the month (April 2020 was the sunniest April on record, and also dry in most of the UK) but the COVID-19 statistics continued to make grim reading. On Saturday 25 April (the day Notts should have been playing their final league game of the season at home to Yeovil) it was announced that coronavirus deaths in UK hospitals had passed 20,000 (20,319) and that 16,411 were in hospital suffering with the disease.

The USA, Italy, Spain and France were the other countries who had experienced over 20,000 deaths. The USA had had by far the most deaths to date = 52,058 with the state of New York easily top of the US league table with 21,411.

The UK figure of 20,319 did not include deaths in care homes, or in the community. The number of people hospitalised had fallen slightly. It was thought that, maybe, the peak of the outbreak had been reached.

On 29 April the government started to include deaths in care homes and the wider community (revised total 26,097). The Italian (27,359) and French (23,660) statistics included care home deaths, but it was unclear if deaths in care homes were included in the total from Spain (23,822).

The revised UK figure indicated that approximately 4,000 care home patients had died since the first UK death from coronavirus at the beginning of March. The 26,097 total only included people who had died after testing positive for coronavirus, so the actual figure was likely to be even higher.

Despite the fact that the Prime Minister confirmed that we had "passed the peak" it was still debateable if the second review of the lockdown measures, expected on 7 May, would introduce a significant relaxation of the social distancing instructions.

There was much speculation about what, and how, restrictions would be eased. The government were, understandably, very concerned that too much easing could lead to a second coronavirus peak amongst the population, so it was expected they would take a cautious approach with a slow and gradual return to something like normality.

It was interesting to note that on the Sunday before the second review, television news referred to the review day as "next Sunday, the 10 May". I think the government delayed the review because Thursday 7 May was the day before the VE Day Public Holiday – they had moved the early May public holiday back by four days for the whole of the UK to coincide with the 75th anniversary of VE Day. If you gave (the general public) a small concession, especially before a holiday weekend, then 'given an inch they'll take a mile' may have been the reason behind the change of date!

Having said all that, to date, the vast majority of people had been very supportive of all the government lockdown instructions. However, with everyone now enduring the seventh week of lockdown most were looking for a 'light at the end of the tunnel' to offer hope that the beginning of the end, of the difficult and unpleasant situation, was in sight.

Would football matches (the relative few that remained of the 2019-20 season) return? Unlikely, unless behind closed doors and possibly at a neutral venue.

Would children return to nurseries/schools? Again, an immediate return to the classroom was unlikely. To be frivolous, would we be able to visit a hairdresser?

The ramifications of society are such that the impact of COVID-19 would remain with everyone for many months, if not years, to come. It was hoped a vaccine would become available during 2021!

Although different countries had different ways of counting deaths, by 5 May only the USA had recorded more deaths than the UK. Our total (all COVID-19 deaths in all settings) was now almost

32,000. When Prime Minister, Boris Johnson, addressed the nation in the televised broadcast on the evening of Sunday 10 May it wasn't a surprise that he gave a cautious message….

> *"to beat the virus and provide the first sketch of a road map for reopening society…we are taking the first careful steps to modify our measures…although we have a plan, it is a conditional plan. And since our priority is to protect the public and save lives, we cannot move forward unless we satisfy the five tests.*
>
> *We must protect our NHS.*
>
> *We must see sustained falls in the death rate.*
>
> *We must see sustained and considerable falls in the rate of infection.*
>
> *We must sort out our challenges in getting enough PPE (Personal Protective Equipment) to the people who need it, and yes, it is a global problem but we must fix it.*
>
> *And last, we must make sure that any measures we take do not force the reproduction rate of the disease - the **R** - back up over one, so that we have the kind of exponential growth we were facing a few weeks ago.*
>
> *To chart our progress and to avoid going back to square one, we are establishing a new Covid Alert System run by a new Joint Biosecurity Centre.*
>
> *And that Covid Alert Level will be determined primarily by **R** and the number of coronavirus cases.*
>
> *And in turn that Covid Alert Level will tell us how tough we have to be in our social distancing measures – the lower the level the fewer the measures.*
>
> *The higher the level, the tougher and stricter we will have to be. There will be five alert levels.*
>
> *Level One means the disease is no longer present in the UK and Level Five is the most critical – the kind of situation we could have had if the NHS had been overwhelmed.*
>
> *Over the period of the lockdown we have been in Level Four, and it is thanks to your sacrifice we are now in a position to begin to move in steps to Level Three.*
>
> *We are taking the first careful steps to modify our (lockdown) measures.*
>
> ***The first step** is a change of emphasis that we hope that people will act on this week. We said that you should work from home if you can, and only go to work if you must.*

We now need to stress that anyone who can't work from home, for instance those in construction or manufacturing, should be actively encouraged to go to work.

And we want it to be safe for you to get to work. So you should avoid public transport if at all possible – because we must and will maintain social distancing, and capacity will therefore be limited.

So work from home if you can, but you should go to work if you can't work from home.

And to ensure you are safe at work we have been working to establish new guidance for employers to make workplaces COVID-secure.

And when you do go to work, if possible do so by car or even better by walking or bicycle. But just as with workplaces, public transport operators will also be following COVID-secure standards.

And from this Wednesday, we want to encourage people to take more and even unlimited amounts of outdoor exercise.

You can sit in the sun in your local park, you can drive to other destinations, and you can even play sports but only with members of your own household.

You must obey the rules on social distancing and to enforce those rules we will increase the fines for the small minority who break them.

*And so every day, with ever increasing data, we will be monitoring the **R** and the number of new infections, and the progress we are making, and if we as a nation begin to fulfil the conditions I have set out, then in the next few weeks and months we may be able to go further.*

In step two *– at the earliest by June 1 – after half term – we believe we may be in a position to begin the phased reopening of shops and to get primary pupils back into schools, in stages, beginning with reception, Year 1 and Year 6.*

Our ambition is that secondary pupils facing exams next year will get at least some time with their teachers before the holidays. And we will shortly be setting out detailed guidance on how to make it work in schools and shops and on transport.

And step three *- at the earliest by July - and subject to all these conditions and further scientific advice; if and only if the numbers support it, we will hope to re-open at least some of the hospitality industry and other public places, provided they are safe and enforce social distancing.*

Throughout this period of the next two months we will be driven not by mere hope or economic necessity. We are going to be driven by the science, the data and public health….

…of course we will be monitoring our progress locally, regionally, and nationally and if there are outbreaks, if there are problems, we will not hesitate to put on the brakes.

We have been through the initial peak – but it is coming down the mountain that is often more dangerous.

We have a route, and we have a plan, and everyone in government has the all-consuming pressure and challenge to save lives, restore livelihoods and gradually restore the freedoms that we need.

But in the end this is a plan that everyone must make work.

And though the UK will be changed by this experience, I believe we can be stronger and better than ever before. More resilient, more innovative, more economically dynamic, but also more generous and more sharing.

But for now we must stay alert, control the virus and save lives."

R - The reproduction number is a way of rating a disease's ability to spread.

It's the number of people that one infected person will pass the virus on to, on average. If the reproduction number is higher than one, then the number of cases increases exponentially. If the number is lower than one, the disease will eventually peter out as not enough new people are being infected to sustain the outbreak. At the moment our **R**-value was between 0.5 and 0.9, with some regional variability.

COVID-19 was slowly being beaten into submission, but its capacity to fight back wasn't being underestimated. So, how did the above affect professional football? The government published a 50-page guidance document detailing how England planned to ease lockdown measures.

Step two of that plan - not to start before 1 June - stated "permitting cultural and sporting events to take place behind closed doors for broadcast, while avoiding the risk of large-scale social contact".

Speaking in the House of Commons the day after his second televised address, Prime Minister Boris Johnson said being able to hold sporting events behind closed doors could "provide a much-needed boost to national morale".

The document also stated that reopening venues that attract large crowds, such as sports grounds, "may only be fully possible significantly later depending on the reduction in numbers of infections".

The guidance document also provided an answer to my frivolous question about a visit to the hairdresser. That possibility was part of the step three criteria and wouldn't be allowed until July at the earliest!

To summarise: Football, even behind closed doors, would not be staged in England before 1 June. The cautious optimism expressed by Prime Minister Boris Johnson in his televised address to the nation on 10 May, that the public could look forward to a slow and gradual easing of some of the lockdown measures, materialised.

The number of new confirmed cases, daily hospital admissions, the number of people in hospital, the percentage of patients requiring mechanical ventilation, and the daily death rate of those who had tested positive, all steadily (rather than spectacularly) decreased during May.

Towards the end of May with little change to the Alert State (still four, slowly moving down towards three) and the **R** number (still as high as 0.9 in some areas) a significant number of medical professionals and advisors, together with some MP's, expressed concern that the easing of the lockdown rules were not supported by enough scientific evidence and were therefore "too much, too soon". Maybe the excellent weather was partly responsible for the disregard shown, by some people, to social distancing, as they lengthened their car journeys, particularly to the coast and countryside, as a return to more social freedom gathered momentum.

The government confirmed that their five tests were being met and lockdown restrictions could therefore be eased, as planned, on 1 June.

The Office for National Statistics (ONS) 'Deaths involving COVID-19' up to 29 May were 45,748 registered in England and Wales – 25,359 men and 20,389 women. The majority of deaths had been among people aged 65 years and over – 40,796 out of 45,748, with 47% (19,183) in the aged 85 years and over group.

The (provisional) ONS figures include all deaths registered where "COVID-19" was mentioned on the death certificate, whether in or out of hospital, for England and Wales.

Finally, on 31 May, the Department of Health and Social Care (DHSC) published a figure of 38,489 UK cumulative deaths in all settings (30,861 in hospitals, the measure until 29 April). The DHSC figure = the total number of deaths reported to them among patients who had tested positive for COVID-19, regardless of place of death and wherever the deaths occurred in the UK.

Approximate World Health Organisation Worldwide COVID-19 deaths by 31 May 2020 for Selected Countries

World	**371,166**
USA	102,640
UK	38,489
Italy	33,415
Spain	29,045
Brazil	28,834
France	28,746
Mexico	9,779
Belgium	9,467
Germany	8,511
Iran	7,797
Canada	7,092
Netherlands	5,956
India	5,394
Russia	4,855
China	4,645

Chapter 10: Restart and lift-off

During the coronavirus lockdown Notts had remained active in a number of ways:

- To acknowledge the wonderful effort by all in the National Health Service Notts announced that the first home league match following the coronavirus pandemic would be dedicated to the NHS, whose staff would be offered free tickets for the occasion. (At the time 'behind closed doors' hadn't been considered).
- Neal Ardley, Neil Cox, ex player Les Bradd (now a Notts 'ambassador'), and the first team squad made themselves available to make telephone calls to deserving elderly/vulnerable supporters, or key workers, who required a 'pick-me-up'. The recipients were nominated by completion of an online form by a friend, relative or colleague. Neal and Les played a huge part and nearly 400 fans benefited.
- Following CEO Jason Turner's operational update at the end of March, nearly 250 supporters became new Lifeline members. By the beginning of May membership had reached the maximum allowed by the scheme – 2500, and for the first time there was a waiting list!
- At the beginning of April a 'Support Notts County and Age UK' appeal was launched. This was to raise money for Notts and the local Age UK branch, while offering supporters the opportunity to pre-order various ticket bundles, hospitality packages, experiences and commercial opportunities for the 2020-21 season.
- Notts were confident the financial security of the club wouldn't be compromised by the suspension of football. However, they had been inundated with messages from supporters who wanted to know how they could help the club through this tough, uncertain time. The money raised assisted with their cash flow when most of their income streams had ceased. The target, by the end of April, was £20,000 with 10% of the money raised donated to Age UK Nottingham and Nottinghamshire to help them continue to provide their services to the community.
- The response was magnificent, and by mid-April the £20,000 target had been reached, with eleven days to spare. Notts then increased the fundraising target to £25,000. At the close on 29 April, £25,495 had been raised and Notts rounded up the 10% donation to Age UK to £3000.
- In mid-April the Meadow Lane annual pitch renovation commenced, with essential works on the playing surface. A more extensive summer renovation had been planned (the replacement of the top 25mm with the addition of more fibre sand). Basic work now (the replacement of the top 8mm to remove all the unwanted organic matter and any weed grasses) ensured a suitable surface for the year ahead.
- Notts made sixteen of their seventeen (the exception was the game at AFC Fylde) league victories available for viewing on social media. The games, complete with BBC Radio Nottingham commentary, were shown on Facebook or You Tube.

Monday 1 June 2020 was an important day for many people in England. Since the lockdown began in late March the vast majority of the UK's 67 million population had been at home, unable to meet anyone other than members of the same household. They were only allowed to leave home, infrequently, for basic shopping necessities, one form of exercise a day, any medical need, and to travel to/from work if unable to work from home. Some had lost their jobs or had been furloughed. This restriction was modified on 1 June to allow family and friends to meet in groups of up to six people in outdoor spaces, like private gardens and parks, provided they maintained social distancing and remained at least two metres apart. Lockdown restrictions were eased in three core areas – schools, retail outlets, social contact.

However, Notts County's immediate future remained uncertain. Last year they experienced 'A summer of discontent'. The outcome of the summer of 2020 was impossible to predict. Although the balance of The National League fixtures were cancelled on 22 April, many questions remained unanswered.

Would the season be declared null and void with all results expunged? If not, how would promotion and relegation issues be determined? Would the FA Trophy semi-final (against Harrogate Town) be played? Would players out of contract (which usually expire on 30 June) be allowed to play in a resurrected play-off campaign and the FA Trophy? When would the 2020-21 season start?

Anyway, on 3 June Notts issued a 'SQUAD UPDATE'.

Manager Neal Ardley selected a 24-man training squad to prepare for a possible National League play-off campaign. Eleven players who had been on the periphery of the first team during the season were informed they would not be required to return and would be released from their contracts when they expired on 30 June. It was anticipated that if the play-offs occurred, players with contracts due to expire on 30 June would be allowed to participate.

Play-off training squad

Goalkeepers: Sam Slocombe, Joe McDonnell, Jake Kean, Tiernan Brooks (recently graduated from the academy to a professional contract)

Defenders: Damien McCrory, Ben Turner, Connell Rawlinson, Dion Kelly-Evans, Zoumana Bakayogo, Richard Brindley, Alex Lacey, Adam Long

Midfielders: Michael Doyle (Captain), Mitch Rose, Jim O'Brien, Regan Booty, Tom Crawford

Forwards: Sam Osborne, Wes Thomas, Kristian Dennis, Enzio Boldewijn, Kyle Wootton, Scott Wilson, Cal Roberts

Released players

Goalkeepers: Ross Fitzsimons, Max Culverwell

Matt Tootle, Christian Oxlade-Chamberlain, Pierce Bird, Declan Dunn, Owen Betts, Tyreece Kennedy-Williams, Alex Howes, Nathan Tyson, Remaye Campbell

Loan players returned to parent clubs

Sam Graham, Joel Bagan, Sean Shields

Five days later CEO Jason Turner provided a lengthy and detailed operational update on several club matters amid the ongoing COVID-19 pandemic. Some of the topics have already been mentioned but below is a precis, and a few quotations:

In the hope that a league play-off competition would soon be announced, and the Football Association would give the go ahead for the two-legged semi-final of the FA Trophy to be played at some stage, he had been in regular dialogue with manager Neal Ardley regarding the safe return to action of the 24-man training squad. When the 2019-20 season was officially concluded a full and final retained list would be confirmed. Following the annual Meadow Lane pitch renovation he stated that it was "more than ready" to stage football matches and congratulated head groundsman Matt Hallam, and his staff, for their excellent remedial work.

To avoid misinterpretation the following were taken direct from the update:

> *While the club remains closed and the majority of our staff continue to be furloughed, recent government updates and growing confidence that the play-offs will take place means we've been escalating our plans to return club operations to a more normal level in the coming weeks.*

> *As well as leading on that, I've been holding several conversations with the board to reflect on how certain objectives and expectancies have materialised during their first year at the helm. When Chris and Alex arrived as our new owners, the club was losing over £2.5million a year. While they were – and continue to be - happy to invest a significant amount of money each year to help the club prosper on and off the pitch, losses of that magnitude clearly aren't sustainable for any business. They therefore asked me to undertake a comprehensive evaluation of the club and the structure of all departments in the first 12 months of their tenure, with a view to reducing the operating losses without compromising key areas of the club moving into their second year.*

> *As a result of this review, the board have taken the decision to streamline our academy operation to bring it more in line with other Category 3 clubs, the majority of whom play in League One or Two. Chris, Alex, Rich (Montague) and myself recognise the importance of having an academy and how much it means to our supporters in*

particular, and we have therefore had to make some difficult decisions in order to preserve its financial viability heading into next season, when it will be operating with a new structure intended to reduce running costs while enabling us to continue to provide the best coaching and care we can to our academy players. I'd like to thank our Academy Manager, Craig Wallace, for his input and assistance towards these updated arrangements.

We have also received several very kind messages from 2019-20 season ticket holders assuring us that they will not be seeking a refund for the three home matches they have missed due to the cancellation of our regular season. To put things into perspective, should all season ticket holders claim a refund the club stands to lose more than £70,000 at a time when the vast majority of our income has dried up. I fully appreciate this is a period of hardship for many and that in some cases a refund may be required, but for those who can afford to support the club by not requesting a refund I would ask them to please do so. If however you do wish to apply for a refund, please email your full name and membership number to season.tickets@nottscountyfc.co.uk or call....

The Premiership and Championship were about to resume their revised fixtures to complete the 2019-20 season. Leagues One and Two had voted by an overwhelming majority to formally end the season, with all remaining fixtures cancelled, except for the promotion play-offs and relegations. Final league positions were decided on an unweighted point's per game basis. There was a growing frustration that no decision had been made about how The National League would be finalised. It wasn't until the middle of June that some significant information was revealed concerning its completion. The enlightenment came from the Notts board of directors who issued the following statement in response to The National League's proposal of an Ordinary Resolution to decide the sporting outcomes of the 2019-20 season. The National League asked clubs to submit their vote by 5pm on Wednesday 17 June. Notts confirmed:

We will be voting in support of The National League's Ordinary Resolution which, if passed, would see us compete in a play-off competition to determine who joins champions-elect Barrow in winning promotion to League Two.

The proposal mirrors the resolution of the League Two season, which in our view is fair and correct, and we are already very well prepared to challenge for play-off success should the resolution pass.

We would like to thank our fans for their continued support and positivity, which has not gone unnoticed in recent weeks, and we look forward to providing further updates as soon as we have them.

Shortly after the 5pm deadline, The National League issued the following statement:

Following a vote by all member Clubs, and subject to FA Council approval, The National League, National League North and National League South seasons 2019/20 will be concluded with final league tables compiled on an "Unweighted Points Per Game" basis.

The outcome is Barrow AFC are champions of The National League, King's Lynn Town are champions of National League North and Wealdstone are champions of National League South.

The end of season Play-Offs will now proceed with the Clubs that qualify, subject to the competition rules and the applicable government guidance on the phased return of elite sport.

The number of Clubs to be relegated from The National League will be determined so as to maintain a National Division of 24 Clubs after any relegation from EFL League Two, promotion to EFL League Two and promotion from The National League North and National League South divisions. There shall be no relegation from National League North and National League South.

Chief Executive Officer Michael Tattersall commented: "I congratulate each of our champions Clubs on their successful campaigns. The enforced curtailment of our season does nothing to discredit the quality of the football played and I am pleased that our Clubs have overwhelmingly supported the award of their titles. We can now also look towards the completion of end of season Play-Offs."

National League Clubs were asked to support an Ordinary Resolution to conclude the season with final leagues tables compiled on an "Unweighted Points Per Game" basis. The resolution received the support of a significant majority of member Clubs in each division.

"Unweighted Points Per Game" is defined as: The method for calculating the final points total of each Club in the Division concerned, calculated in accordance with the following formula, rounding the final points total up to three decimal places:

$$PT / CM \times LMS = \text{Final Points Total}$$

Where "PT" means a Club's points total in the 2019/20 Season at the point when the Competition was suspended on 16 March 2020.

Where "CM" means the number of Competition Matches a Club has played in the 2019/20 Season at the point the Competition was suspended on 16 March 2020.

Where "LMS" means the number of Competition Matches originally scheduled to be played by each Club in the 2019/20 Season, being (a) 46 for National League Clubs; and (b) 42 for National League North and National League South Clubs.

Worked Example:

Club A is in National League North and has played 32 Competition Matches and has a point's total of 43 points. Applying the formula, Club A's final points tally will be:

$$43 / 32 \times 42 = 56.438$$

Predictably Notts, delighted with the news, made an immediate response to The National League vote:

Subject to FA Council approval, The National League's Ordinary Resolution has passed and we will participate in a play-off competition to challenge for promotion to League Two.

A significant majority of member clubs in each division voted in favour of the league's proposals, which means the final 2019-20 National League tables have been determined on an unweighted points-per-game basis.

By this measure, we finish third in our division and will now face the winners of Yeovil Town (fourth) v Barnet (seventh) in a behind-closed doors play-off semi-final at Meadow Lane, on a date to be announced in due course.

Second-placed Harrogate Town will play the winners of Boreham Wood (fifth) v FC Halifax Town (sixth) in the other semi-final, while Barrow are promoted as champions.

All play-off matches will be broadcast live on BT Sport.

A statement from our board of directors reads: We are very pleased that an overwhelming majority of clubs have voted in favour of The National League's Ordinary Resolution, which we feel provided the fairest method of deciding the sporting outcomes of the season.

Our congratulations go to Barrow on their successful campaign, and to King's Lynn Town and Wealdstone who are promoted as champions from North and South respectively.

We have long been preparing for this eventuality and we're now looking forward to providing our players and staff with a safe return ahead of what we hope will be an exciting and successful play-off campaign.

We're very sorry that our supporters can't be with us on the latest step of our journey but the club will be doing all it can to bring them the best possible information and insight over the coming weeks.

While we await further instruction and advice from The National League and FA, we will this week be comprehensively testing our 24-man training squad along with several members of staff. The results of these tests will allow for a safe and informed return to Stage One training from next Monday in accordance with government guidance. Further details on training methods and the safety protocols we're deploying will follow in the coming days.

When will the matches be played?

Although we are yet to receive confirmed match dates, The National League have previously communicated to clubs that the play-offs, beginning with the quarter-final matches involving Yeovil, Boreham Wood, Halifax and Barnet, should commence no later than 18 July, while the final should be played by 31 July.

Revised National League final table (top half only)

		P	GD	Points	
1	Barrow	37/46	29	87.027	Promoted to League Two
2	Harrogate Town	37/46	17	82.054	Home semi-final play-off
3	**Notts County**	**38/46**	**23**	**76.263**	**Home semi-final play-off**
4	Yeovil Town	37/46	17	74.595	*Winner to play*…
5	Boreham Wood	37/46	15	74.595	Winner away
6	FC Halifax Town	37/46	1	72.108	at Harrogate
7	Barnet	35/46	10	70.971	…*at Meadow Lane*
8	Stockport County	39/46	-3	68.410	
9	Solihull Moors	38/46	11	66.579	
10	Woking	38/46	-5	66.579	
11	Dover Athletic	38/46	0	65.368	
12	Hartlepool United	39/46	6	64.872	

Changes to 16 March 2020 positions:

The top six were unchanged. Barnet up from 11th to 7th and qualified for the play-offs at the expense of Stockport. Solihull down one position. Hartlepool down from 9th and Dover up from 12th.

On Thursday 18 June, in preparation for the play-offs, Notts' 24-man training squad, along with manager Neal Ardley and others, attended Meadow Lane to be tested for coronavirus (COVID-19). It was subsequently confirmed that all had tested negative. The players and key personnel were then tested on a weekly basis. The following Monday, Stage One training commenced on the 'new' Meadow Lane pitch. During Stage One only two groups of five players were permitted on the pitch at one time, with social distancing guidelines adhered to throughout. Despite being a very warm week, with temperatures approaching 30°C, there were no injuries and all again tested negative for COVID-19. Stage Two contact training with larger groups started the following week. Neal Ardley and his staff, Neil Cox (Assistant Manager), Erik Svendsen (Strength and Conditioning Coach), Marco Ferreira (Head of Medical Services), Craig Heiden (First Team Sports Scientist) and Jimmy Redfern (Performance Analyst) were aware of the difficult training schedule that lay ahead.

Usually, players had a six to eight week break at the end of a season, followed by about six weeks of pre-season training with friendly matches played. The three-month layoff caused by the coronavirus pandemic had therefore created a longer than normal close season followed by a shorter 'pre-season'. Although friendly matches were difficult to arrange due to the retention of social distancing and the associated complications involved to create and maintain a safe playing environment for all concerned, management revealed that discussions were advanced with a couple of suitable opponents, and it was hoped that at least one behind closed doors friendly would be arranged before the play-off semi-final.

Although all the players had been given a fitness and activity programme to follow when the suspension commenced in mid-March, and they were in lockdown, the return to training was obviously a significant challenge. With the play-offs scheduled for the second half of July, there was an increased risk that players would be injured if training was too intense too soon. A careful balancing act was required but Neal Ardley acknowledged that it was almost inevitable there would be some (hopefully minor) injuries.

In early July the dates for the play-offs were announced:

> Fri 17 July: Boreham Wood v FC Halifax Town, and Sat 18 July: Yeovil Town v Barnet
>
> Sat 25 July: Harrogate Town v Boreham Wood or Halifax, and **Notts County** v Yeovil or Barnet

It was confirmed that the promotion final would be played at Wembley Stadium on Sunday 2 August 2020 at 3pm. All five games to be played behind closed doors:

Notts' play-off preparations continued, and the weekly coronavirus tests remained negative for all. However, Neal Ardley revealed that two players would not be available for play-off selection due to injury, defender Damien McCrory (knee surgery) and midfielder Regan Booty (recurrence of his back problem). Cardiff City (and the Football Association) agreed to Notts' request to allow Joel Bagan to return on loan, as cover for McCrory.

There was also another 'newcomer', forward Scott Wilson, one of the 24-man squad selected for the play-offs, who had originally arrived at Meadow Lane in late February on loan until the end of the season. After being released by Oldham Athletic he had been allowed to re-join Notts on a short-term deal.

Neal Ardley also revealed that a friendly fixture had been arranged with Dorking Wanderers. Despite losing their last five league games, before the coronavirus suspension, they still finished in seventh position in National League South after the final league table was determined on an unweighted points per game basis. They had, therefore, also qualified for the play-offs and a possible promotion into The National League. The game was played behind closed doors at Meadow Lane on Saturday 11 July. Although Notts suffered a defeat assistant manager Neil Cox was pleased at the end of the game:

> *"We got 45 minutes into everybody's legs and it was a great workout. Dorking were about a week ahead of us in terms of fitness and we didn't pick-up any injuries, so that's another good thing. We know we've got to work harder in training next week".*

As well as the obvious benefits of a friendly/practice match, one of the other reasons was to familiarise the players (and management) with the strict operational guidelines to be adhered to regarding safety at all behind closed doors games during the coronavirus pandemic. These included: an opportunity to practice match day protocols, the use of red, amber and green zones in the stadium, one way systems, split team dressing rooms, the location for team talks, only three allowed in team dug-outs etc. On semi-final day players, management and coaching staff would therefore be more relaxed and able to concentrate fully on the game rather than on where they should be and what they should be doing.

Notts played their second, and final, friendly/practice match behind closed doors on the evening of Thursday 16 July at Meadow Lane. Their opponents were Boston United who had finished in third position in National League North after the final league table was determined on an unweighted point's per game basis. They had, therefore, also qualified for the play-offs, with, like Notts, an automatic home semi-final game on Saturday 25 July, and a possible promotion into The National League. After a competitive 3-3 draw manager Neal Ardley was generally happy with the performance, despite Notts conceding three goals as they did in the defeat to Dorking:

"Again, it was a case of getting sixty minutes into some players and forty five minutes into others. There were no injuries, only a few impact knocks which you might not get in training. We were much sharper than against Dorking, with more tempo and intensity, and there were loads of positives. The game did highlight some things we need to do better and it indicated which players were a little behind where they could or should be in terms of fitness. It helped me as I start to consider team selection for next week's semi-final."

On the evening of Friday 17 July Boreham Wood beat Halifax Town 2-1. The next day Notts discovered that their semi-final opponents would be Barnet, who defeated Yeovil 2-0 in the other quarter-final. The Barnet head coach, Darren Currie, admitted that they hadn't played particularly well, and their victory was down to a solid defensive display and some luck. Unfortunate Yeovil hit the crossbar, a goal post, had attempts cleared off the goal line and missed some good scoring opportunities. Barnet's first goal was scored by Paul McCallum during a counterattack after 53 minutes. It was his fifth goal in six games since he joined on loan from Solihull Moors at the end of January. Barnet's leading scorer with fifteen goals, Simeon Akinola, didn't feature at Yeovil because of injury. Their goalkeeper, Nottingham born Scott Loach, was a Notts player for two seasons (2015-16, signed by manager Ricardo Moniz, and 2016-17, released by manager Kevin Nolan). In all he made twenty-three appearances for Notts whose other goalkeepers at the time were Roy Carroll and Adam Collin.

Notts lost 2-1 to Barnet at Meadow Lane, in the third game of the season at the beginning of August. Enzio Boldewijn gave Notts an early lead, but Akinola scored the winner fifteen minutes from the end. The defeat, shown live on BT Sport, meant that Notts dropped to next to the bottom of the league. The return was not played due to the coronavirus pandemic and the subsequent cancellation of all remaining scheduled league fixtures for the season.

The run-up to the Barnet game went smoothly and Neal Ardley said the players were ready and (with the exception of the injured McCrory and Booty) all were fit, coronavirus free, and available for selection. He also repeated his earlier comment "The fittest, sharpest and most mentally-ready players will be the ones who start on 25 July. My team selection will not be influenced by the fact we won our last four prior to lockdown."

He made three changes to the team which defeated Eastleigh 4-0 on 14 March, in Notts' last competitive game 133 days ago. Slocombe (last game 18 January, due to injury) replaced McDonnell in goal, Turner (last game 7 December, due to injury) replaced Rawlinson, and O'Brien came in for Boldewijn.

National League play-off semi-final	**Notts Co 2**	**Barnet 0**	Played behind closed
Sat 25 July 2020 17:00	Dennis 37'		doors at Meadow Lane
	Roberts 59'		

Slocombe

Brindley　　　Lacey　　　Turner　　　Bagan

Doyle (Capt.)　　　Rose　　　O'Brien

Roberts (Thomas 86')　　　Wootton　　　Dennis (Boldewijn 74')

Subs: McDonnell (Gk), Kelly-Evans, Rawlinson, Crawford, Boldewijn, Thomas

Adam Long, Zoumana Bakayogo, Sam Osborne and Scott Wilson were the fit outfield players who didn't make the seventeen-man squad.

Due to the three-month lockdown, the shortage of match fitness and the warmth of mid-summer, there were some changes to the usual game format:

Drinks and Cooling Breaks: There was a one-minute drinks break midway through each half.

Substitutes: The number of substitutions permitted for use by each team was increased from three to five, and up to six substitutes could be named instead of five. A maximum of three substitution opportunities were permitted during the match, not including an additional opportunity at the end of half-time before the second-half started.

Removal of Extra Time: If the scores had been level after ninety minutes a penalty shootout, rather than extra time, would have determined the winner.

During a first half played in torrential thundery rain, Cal Roberts was denied an opening goal after fifteen minutes when he had a curling free-kick well saved by Loach. With half-time approaching Notts took the lead. Jim O'Brien made an excellent run down the left wing, crossed superbly, and Kristian Dennis threw himself at the ball to head home from six yards. Soon after Roberts had a good opportunity to give Notts a second goal but he dragged his shot wide of the far post, following a headed flick on by Kyle Wootton.

The weather improved for the second half and Slocombe had to make a good early save following a fierce fifteen-yard shot. On the hour, just after Loach had made a double save to deny Dennis, Roberts scored Notts' second goal with a brilliant solo effort. Excellent close control enabled him to beat two defenders in the penalty area before sliding the ball into the far corner of the net, with his left foot, from the right-hand side of the six yard box. The goal was almost identical to the one he scored at Barrow, and it was his fourth in successive games. In a bid to reduce the deficit Barnet introduced substitute Akinola, their top scorer who missed the game at Yeovil through injury, but he only played seventeen minutes before he had to be replaced. A last chance for Barnet came near the end of the game, but the resultant header was directed well clear of Slocombe's cross bar.

A dominant and professional display by Notts gave them a deserved victory. In the other semi-final Harrogate Town defeated Boreham Wood 1-0 and so they became Notts' opponents in the Wembley final played on Sunday 2 August at 3pm.

Chapter 11: National League Promotion Final at Wembley

On Friday 31 July 2020, two days before the final, Notts received the results of their last round of pre-Wembley COVID-19 tests. The weekly tests had commenced on the 18 June and throughout all had returned negative. Excellent news. The 31 July was a very hot day over most of the UK, but particularly so in southern England. London (Heathrow) recorded a maximum temperature of 37.8C (100 deg. F) the warmest day of the year so far, and the third hottest UK day on record. But there was even more good news. During Friday night cooler Atlantic air re-established itself, and although the weather in London remained fine over the weekend temperatures dropped markedly – Heathrow recorded 28C on Saturday 1st and 25C on the big day.

Notts travelled south down the M1 on Sunday morning full of confidence with an almost fully fit squad (only Damien McCrory and Regan Booty were injured). McCrory didn't play in the one meeting during the season between Harrogate and Notts, at Wetherby Road in mid-August. He (and Michael Doyle) were absent due to a three match suspension each received when both were sent off in the first game of the season at Eastleigh. Booty made his Notts debut at Harrogate and had an excellent game. Notts won 2-0 and it was their first ever victory in non-league football.

Neal Ardley gave two reasons for travelling on Sunday morning. First, he thought the players would benefit from a pre-match night at home in familiar surroundings rather than in a strange hotel where there would be plenty of time to think about the Wembley occasion. Second, where distance had necessitated an overnight stay in a hotel before an away fixture, results were not as good as in the games when they travelled on the day of the game. He also said that if this had been a 'normal' fixture the two-and-a-half-hour journey (about 120 miles from Nottingham to north London) would have been undertaken on the day.

Notts' play-off squad consisted of twenty-five players; the twenty four named on 3 June plus Joel Bagan on loan from Cardiff as cover for the injured McCrory. Harrogate's play-off squad was five smaller than Notts' with twenty players.

National League play-off final	**Notts County 1**	**Harrogate Town 3**	Played behind closed
Sun 2 Aug 2020 15:00	Roberts 47'	Thomson 5'	doors at Wembley
		Hall 28'	Stadium, London
		Diamond 70'	

```
                          Slocombe
   Brindley (Kelly-Evans 87')      Lacey           Turner            Bagan
        Doyle (Capt.)              Rose         O'Brien (Boldewijn 46')
           Roberts                Wootton        Dennis (Thomas 46')
```

Subs: McDonnell (Gk), Kelly-Evans, Rawlinson, Crawford, Boldewijn, Thomas

The Notts team and substitutes were unchanged from their victory over Barnet in the semi-final eight days before.

For one reason or another, only four players (Slocombe, Turner, Rose and Dennis) from the victorious team which started at Harrogate less than a year ago were included in the starting eleven. The seven not in this starting eleven were: Kelly-Evans, Rawlinson, Bakayogo, Booty, Osborne, Boldewijn, and Tyson. For Harrogate, twelve who were in their squad on that sunny evening were in their seventeen-man squad.

Notts looked nervous and sluggish from the start and they conceded a goal after only five minutes when Thomson beat Turner to a low cross and stabbed the ball into the net at the near post. Notts' play failed to improve and Harrogate nearly increased their lead twice with shots that flew narrowly wide. In a rare Notts attack Dennis had a shot blocked by a defender, but it wasn't a surprise when Harrogate scored a second goal. Bagan was harshly booked for a foul and from the free kick Turner and Slocombe were unable to prevent Hall tapping the ball into the net from close range. On forty minutes Harrogate hit a post and Notts were fortunate to reach half time only two goals behind. Their first half performance was very poor. How such a fit, in-form, and experienced team could play so poorly after such a good performance against Barnet was incomprehensible!

Neal Ardley replaced O'Brien and Dennis at the beginning of the second half with Boldewijn and Thomas, and within two minutes of the restart a deficit that could/should have been three at half time was reduced to one when Roberts scored with a direct free kick from twenty yards. It was his fifth goal in his last five games. Notts then had an improved twenty-minute period and Harrogate's defence was put under pressure. Roberts, who was booked shortly after his goal, nearly equalised when his twenty-yard shot bent away from the angle of post and crossbar at the last moment. Wootton then forced the goalkeeper into a good save at his near post. Just before the second half drinks break Harrogate nearly scored a third when a shot went close following a goalmouth scramble. However, two minutes after the drinks break they broke away and scored their third goal. Lacey and Brindley were unable to prevent Sunderland loanee Diamond turning a good low cross beyond Slocombe into the corner of the net from six yards. As time ticked away Thomas had a shot well saved and Doyle twice came close. Near the end ex Notts striker Jon Stead, who had earlier come on as a Harrogate substitute, had a good chance to score against his former club when his well-placed shot beat Slocombe but struck a post and rebounded to safety.

Harrogate were worthy winners and deserved their promotion into League Two of the English Football League, to experience league football for the first time in their one hundred- and six-year history. The hope and expectation that Notts would regain their league status after just one year in The National League did not materialise. Their progress, both on and off the pitch, since new owner's Christoffer and Alexander Reedtz took over from Alan Hardy in July 2019, had been remarkable. The players and everyone at the club were to be congratulated for their endeavours since relegation, especially when the coronavirus pandemic is taken into consideration.

To conclude the 2019-20 season, below is the update issued by CEO Jason Turner on 5 August:

> *Despite a difficult weekend for all connected with the club, I'm pleased to report that there remains a very positive atmosphere behind the scenes as we embark on the latest chapter of the exciting story we began one year ago.*
>
> *Neal spoke a lot in the build-up to our play-off final about the way the whole club has come together since Chris and Alex's takeover, and that team spirit shone through last weekend as all who were fortunate enough to attend the game – staff, guests, players and the board – came together for some post-match refreshments at a hotel close to Wembley.*
>
> *It was lovely to hear Chris address the whole room and thank everyone for their efforts over the course of the season, while Neal also spoke brilliantly. Yes, we were all disappointed with how the match went, but the determination from everyone to go one better next year was clear to see.*

When we returned to Meadow Lane on Monday to begin planning for next season we were greeted by a number of supporter flags tied to the stadium gates. It was heart-warming to come home to such supportive messages and I'm sure you'll all agree that the flags displayed at Wembley looked fantastic, too.

The first item on this week's agenda was our retained list. While we were pleased to give several players the opportunity to stay with us, we were also sad to say goodbye to a number of others who have served us with huge commitment and pride. We wish all outgoing players the very best for the future and look forward to hopefully bringing you news of new contracts – and signings – in the coming weeks.

We're very nearly in a position to share the designs of our 2020-21 home kit and pre-orders will be available straight away, so keep your eyes peeled for updates on our digital channels. As we're still negotiating with a potential sponsor for our away kit we're unable to bring you any updates as yet but we hope we're not too far away.

As I'm sure you'll have seen, a new home kit brings a new sponsor in Sharpes of Nottingham. We have a wonderful long-running relationship with Sharpes, who have been our official travel partners for many years, so we're delighted that Cadbury chose them as one of the beneficiaries of our exciting new partnership.

In the near future I'll be attending a National League Zoom meeting to learn more about what next season will look like. A start date of 3 October has been confirmed and it's hoped that over the next few weeks we'll understand more about if, how and when crowds will be able to return to matches. Until this picture is clearer we're unable to confirm details of our 2020-21 season ticket offering but please rest assured we will act as quickly as possible when we're in a position to do so.

As the EFL season begins three weeks before ours, our pre-season opponents will all need to come from our level or below and, while our friendlies will most likely all be played behind closed doors, there is potential for us to stream them live on social media. We'll let you know the details as soon as we have them.

We're also still awaiting news on the plans to conclude the 2019-20 FA Trophy and, until a decision has been reached, we'll be unable to refund any tickets purchased for either leg of our semi-final. We really appreciate your patience on this matter and hope to have a resolution soon.

As the new season draws closer we'll be able to begin delivering more of the rewards purchased during our successful Crowdfunder campaign over lockdown.

So, in summary, there's plenty going on at the Lane and we're already focussing on next season. Everyone at every level of the club remains determined to deliver success and we'll be working harder than ever in 2020-21 to give ourselves the best possible chance of returning to the EFL.

Thank you for your loyal support – and COYP!

RETAINED LIST *following conclusion of the 2019-20 National League season.*

Ten players remain under contract for next season, while seven others have been offered the opportunity to extend their stay at Meadow Lane. Sadly, however, five players have been released following the expiration of their contracts and our manager Neal Ardley has praised the contributions they have made towards the club's resurgence.

"This is always the toughest day in a manager's calendar, but it's especially difficult this year as we are saying goodbye to great lads who have given their absolute all to the cause. The relationship I have with these boys goes beyond that of a typical manager and player. They have all bought into mine and the club's philosophy and helped take us to a play-off final and an FA Trophy semi, achievements we could only have dreamed of at this stage last year. Unfortunately football is a cruel sport and disappointing news is par for the course in any player's career. All I can do is publicly thank each of them for their efforts and wish them all the very best for the future."

Under contract

Tiernan Brooks (Gk), Enzio Boldewijn, Damien McCrory, Jim O'Brien, Connell Rawlinson, Callum Roberts, Sam Slocombe (Gk), Wes Thomas, Ben Turner and Kyle Wootton

Out of contract, offered new deal

Richard Brindley, Kristian Dennis, Michael Doyle, Dion Kelly-Evans, Alex Lacey, Joe McDonnell (Gk) and Sam Osborne

Out of contract, released

Zoumana Bakayogo, Regan Booty, Tom Crawford, Mitch Rose, Scott Wilson

Loan players returning to clubs

Joel Bagan and Adam Long

Perhaps the biggest surprise was the release of Regan Booty. When he played (seventeen starts in league and cup, plus seven substitute appearances) he looked good, and he made an excellent debut at Harrogate on 13 August 2019. However, his long-running back injury problem may have been the reason behind the decision. Mitch Rose started more games in the season (forty) than any other player but scored only three goals - a disappointing return, especially as two were penalties.

Finally, the end of season awards were won by:

- Connell Rawlinson (Supporters' Player)
- Kyle Wootton and Connell Rawlinson (Players' Players)
- Michael Doyle (Goal of the Season v Dagenham in the FA Trophy)
- Kyle Wootton (Golden Boot with 18 goals)
- Sam Osborne (Young Player of the Season)
- Rounding off this year's winners was club Hall of Famer Les Bradd, whose continued outstanding work alongside FITC (Football in the Community), as well as his tremendous efforts in calling the vulnerable and elderly during the coronavirus lockdown, earned him the Community Champion award.

Connell Rawlinson was (somewhat surprisingly) overlooked, in favour of Ben Turner, for the two games against Barnet and Harrogate. He was an unused substitute. Also, Sam Osborne was not in the play-off squads, and a few weeks later he (reluctantly) decided it was the right time to leave Notts in order to seek more regular first team football. In the season just ended he appeared 16 times for Notts in league and cup (12 'starts') and scored three goals.

At the end of the pandemic affected 2019-20 season, Barrow and Harrogate were promoted into EFL League Two, with only bottom club Macclesfield Town relegated into The National League instead of the bottom two. The EFL wanted to keep a total of 24 clubs in League Two. (Bury were expelled from the EFL in August 2019 because of financial irregularities and the collapse of a takeover bid). As a result, after the ponts-per-game revision of The National League table, only three clubs - **Chorley, Fylde, and Ebbsfleet** - rather than the usual four, were relegated. The other clubs in the bottom half of the table, Bromley, Sutton, Torquay, Aldershot, Eastleigh, Dagenham & Redbridge, Chesterfield, Wrexham, and Maidenhead remained in The National League.

Actually, Jason Turner's update and the awards did not conclude the 2019-20 season. There was one outstanding fixture – the FA Trophy semi-final against (now League Two) Harrogate Town. In early September it was announced that the game would not now be to a two-legged affair but a single game to take place at Meadow Lane on Tuesday 22 September, behind closed doors, with a 7.45pm kick-off. A description of this game is given in the next chapter.

Notts now looked forward to the start of the 2020-21 season on 3 October. Would they be promoted back into the football league at the second attempt?

Notts County National League Results 2019-20

Date	Home	Away	F-A	Scorers	Att	Pos
2019						
3/8/		Eastleigh	0-1		2668 (796)*	19
6/8	**Stockport Co**		**1-1**	O'Brien	5820	20
10/8	**Barnet**		**1-2**	Boldewijn	4096	23
13/8		Harrogate Town	2-0	Dennis (p) Boldewijn	1863 (682)*	15
18/8	**Wrexham**		**1-1**	Dennis	6263	17
24/8		Ebbsfleet Utd	2-2	Turner, Booty	1293 (?)*	17
26/8	**Chorley**		**5-1**	Tyson, Boldewijn Dennis, Thomas (2)	5082	12
31/8		Yeovil Town	1-3	Dennis (p)	2424 (?)*	15
3/9	**Solihull Moors**		**0-0**		4152	15
7/9		Sutton Utd	1-1	Wootton	2059 (?)*	14
14/9	**Halifax Town**		**1-0**	Wootton	5188	13
21/9		Bromley	1-2	Wootton	3122 (?)*	16
24/9		Boreham Wood	2-1	Boldewijn, Osborne	756 (289)*	11
28/9	**AFC Fylde**		**2-0**	Thomas, McCrory	9090**	8
5/10		Dover Athletic	2-2	Rose (p) Dennis	1463 (355)*	12
8/10	**Dagenham & Redbridge**		**2-0**	Booty, Dennis	3670	7
12/10	**Torquay Utd**		**2-0**	Brindley, Dennis	5265	5
26/10		Chesterfield	0-1		5432 (1422)*	8
29/10		Woking	4-0	Boldewijn (2), Thomas (2)	2175 (?)*	7
2/11	**Hartlepool Utd**		**2-2**	Thomas (2)	5258	7
16/11	**Barrow**		**0-3**		5287	9
23/11		Aldershot Town	1-2	Wootton	2211 (346)*	11
26/11	**Boreham Wood**		**2-2**	Wootton (2)	3256	9
7/12	**Sutton Utd**		**1-1**	Thomas	5652**	12
21/12		Halifax Town	4-2	Wootton (2), Rose (2 inc pen)	2491 (?)*	11
26/12	**Maidenhead Utd**		**3-0**	Wootton, Osborne, Dennis	5129	9
28/12		Solihull Moors	1-0	Thomas	3212 (1000?)*	6
2020						
1/1/		Maidenhead Utd	0-0		1657 (?)*	7
4/1	**Bromley**		**2-1**	Thomas, Rawlinson	5192	5
18/1	**Dover Athletic**		**0-0**		5157	6
25/1		Dagenham & Redbridge	0-2		1697 (472)*	7
1/2	**Chesterfield**		**3-0**	Boldewijn, Wootton (2)	6347	6
15/2	**Woking**		**1-1**	Dennis	5074	6
22/2		Hartlepool Utd	0-2		3839 (422)*	7
3/3		AFC Fylde	2-1	Boldewijn, Long	1353 (150?)*	6
7/3		Barrow	2-0	Crawford, Roberts	3307 (433)*	6
10/3	**Aldershot Town**		**3-1**	Roberts, Dennis (2)	4287	3
14/3	**Eastleigh**		**4-0**	Wootton (2), Dennis, Roberts	4942	3

*Notts supporters
** Discounted admission

Notts County National League Results 2019-20 (cont.)

Date	Home	Away	F-A	Scorers	Att	Pos
16/3		Coronavirus (COVID-19) suspension				
17/3		Torquay Utd	C			
24/3		Stockport County	A			
4/4		Barnet	N			
7/4	**Harrogate Town**		C			
10/4		Chorley	E			
13/4	**Ebbsfleet Utd**		L			
18/4		Wrexham	L			
25/4	**Yeovil Town**		E			
			D			
25/7	**Barnet (play-off semi-final)**		2-0	Dennis, Roberts	0 played behind	
2/8	**Harrogate Town (play-off final, Wembley)**		1-3	Roberts	0 closed doors	

Notts County FA Cup and FA Trophy Results 2019-20

Date	Home	Away	F-A	Scorers	Att	Round
19/10/19	**Belper Town**		2-1	Boldewijn, Wootton	5729	4th Q FA Cup
9/11/19		Ebbsfleet United	3-2	Wootton (2) Turner	1206 (?)	1st FA Cup
1/12/19		Northampton Town	1-3	Dennis	4489 (1041)	2nd FA Cup
14/12/19		Chesterfield	1-0	Dennis	931 (336)	1st FA Trophy
11/1/20	**Dagenham & Redbridge**		2-1	**Dennis, Doyle**	2385	2nd FA Trophy
8/2/20		Yeovil Town	2-1	Rawlinson, Wootton	1946 (214)	3rd FA Trophy
29/2/20	**Aveley**		5-0	**O'Brien, Crawford, Osborne, Wootton, Wilson**	4893	**Quarter Final FA Trophy**
16/3/20		Coronavirus (Covid-19) suspension				
~~21/3/20~~		~~Harrogate Town~~				~~1st Semi Final~~
~~28/3/20~~	~~Harrogate Town~~					~~2nd Semi Final~~
22/9/20	**Harrogate Town**		0-1		Behind closed doors (one leg only)	

Notts County 2019-20
League +Cup 'Starts', (+Sub appearances) & Goals

	Name	Starts	(Sub)	Goals	Yellow/Red (Cards)
Gk	Slocombe	31+5	(0+0)		2
"	McDonnell	06+2	(0+0)		
"	Fitzsimons	03+1	(0+0)		
"	Kean	00+0	(0+1)		
D	Rawlinson	31+7	(3+0)	1+1	1/1 straight red
E	McCrory	25+5	(0+0)	1+0	4/1 straight red
F	Brindley	26+3	(0+1)	1+0	5
E	Turner	21+3	(2+0)	1+1	2
N	Kelly-Evans	16+5	(3+1)		4
D	Bakayogo	14+2	(0+1)		
E	Lacey	13+3	(0+0)		1 yellow FA Trophy
R	Graham	07+1	(3+0)		
S	Long	03+1	(1+0)	1+0	
"	Bird	03+0	(8+0)		
"	Bagan	04+1	(0+0)		2
"	Oxlade-Chamberlain	01+0	(0+0)		
"	Tootle	00+0	(2+0)		
"	Betts	00+0	(0+1)		
M	Rose (Vice Capt.)	38+2	(0+1)	3+0	9 + 1 yellow FA Cup
I	Doyle (Capt.)	29+6	(2+1)	0+1	5/3 (2 straight reds)
D	Booty	13+4	(7+0)	2+0	
F	O'Brien (Vice Capt.)	14+3	(5+0)	1+1	3
I	Crawford	02+3	(6+1)	1+1	
E	Dunn	01+0	(2+0)		1
L	Howes	00+0	(0+0 unused sub in FA Trophy)		
D					
A	Boldewijn	36+3	(3+2)	8+1	4
T	Wootton	31+5	(2+2)	13+5	4
T	Thomas	22+5	(12+1)	10+0	2/1 str red FATrophy
A	Dennis	18+5	(14+1)	13+3	1
C	Osborne	08+4	(4+0)	2+1	
K	Shields	07+4	(7+2)		
E	Roberts	09+1	(1+0)	5+0	2
R	Tyson	06+1	(7+3)	1+0	
S	Wilson	01+0	(2+1)	0+1	1
"	Hemmings	01+0	(1+0)		
"	Campbell	00+0	(1+0)		

Culverwell (Gk) and **Kennedy-Williams** no appearances. **Chicksen, Reeves, Rodrigues** and **Sam** (sub) FA Trophy semi-final 22/9/2020

Notts County League & (Cup) goal scorers 2019-20

Wootton	13	(5)	=18	
Dennis	13 inc. 2 pens	(3)	=16	
Thomas	10		=10	
Boldewijn	8	(1)	=9	
Roberts	5		=5	
Rose	3 inc. 2 pens		=3	
Osborne	2	(1)	=3	
Booty	2		=2	
Rawlinson	1	(1)	=2	
Turner	1	(1)	=2	
O'Brien	1	(1)	=2	
Crawford	1	(1)	=2	
Brindley	1		=1	
McCrory	1		=1	
Tyson	1		=1	
Long	1		=1	
Doyle		(1)	=1	
Wilson		(1)	=1	
Total	64	(16)	=80	inc. the two play-off games

Notts County Goal Times League (& Cup) 2019-20

First 23 league (& FA Cup) games

\	\	\	For	\	\	\
0-15 min	16-30 min	31 min - HT	46-60 min	61-75 min	76-90 min	90+
4	5 (1)	8 (1)	7 (1)	6	4 (2)	1 (1)
\	\	\	Against	\	\	\
0-15 min	16-30 min	31 min - HT	46-60 min	61-75 min	76-90 min	90+
8 (3)	3 (1)	5	2	4	4 (2)	1

Second 15 league (& FA Trophy) games

\	\	\	For	\	\	\
0-15 min	16-30 min	31 min - HT	46-60 min	61-75 min	76-90 min	90+
4 (1)	2 (0)	3 (3)	8 (2)	8 (3)	3 (0)	1 (1)
\	\	\	Against	\	\	\
0-15 min	16-30 min	31 min - HT	46-60 min	61-75 min	76-90 min	90+
1 (0)	3 (0)	1 (1)	5 (0)	2 (0)	2 (2)	0 (0)

Including the semi-final and final play-off games and the FA Trophy semi-final on 22/9/2020

Notts County home attendances 2019-20

Att.	Opponents	Date (k.o. 15:00 unless stated)	
9,090	AFC Fylde	28 Sep	Admission prices reduced
6,347	Chesterfield	1 Feb, 17:20	Live on BT Sport – 1,462 from Chesterfield
6,263	Wrexham	18 Aug, Sun	
5,820	Stockport Co	6 Aug, 19:45	First home league game of season
5,729	Belper Town	19 Oct	FA Cup – 1,718 from Belper!
5,652	Sutton Utd	7 Dec	Admission prices discounted
5,287	Barrow	16 Nov	
5,265	Torquay Utd	12 Oct	
5,258	Hartlepool Utd	2 Nov	
5,192	Bromley	4 Jan	
5,188	Halifax Town	14 Sep	
5,157	Dover Athletic	18 Jan	
5,129	Maidenhead Utd	26 Dec	
5,082	Chorley	26 Aug, Mon	
5,074	Woking	15 Feb	
4,942	Eastleigh	14 Mar	Coronavirus apprehension?
4,893	Aveley	29 Feb, 12:30	FA Trophy – 530 from Aveley, Essex
4,287	Aldershot Town	10 Mar, 19:45	
4,152	Solihull Moors	3 Sep, 19:45	
4,096	Barnet	10 Aug, 17:20	Live on BT Sport
3,670	Dagenham & Red	8 Oct, 19:45	
3,256	Boreham Wood	26 Nov, 19:45	
2,385	Dag & Redbridge	11 Jan	FA Trophy

Harrogate Town   }
Ebbsfleet Utd   } All 3 cancelled 22 April (Coronavirus   COVID-19)
Yeovil Town   }

Not including the play-off semi-final against Barnet and the FA Trophy semi-final against Harrogate Town – both played behind closed doors

National League Average: 104,207 = 5,210
FA Cup/FA Trophy Average: 13,007 = 4,336
Combined Average: 117,214 = 5,096

Chapter 12: Preparations for a second National League season

No sooner had the 2019-20 season ended before preparations for the beginning of the 2020-21 season started. Only five days after the disappointment of the Wembley play-off defeat there was a departure and an arrival.

Notts' assistant manager Neil Cox, who had worked alongside Neal Ardley for almost eight years since they came together at AFC Wimbledon in October 2012, left Notts to become manager of League Two Scunthorpe United.

Cox was born in Scunthorpe, joined his local club when a youngster and made his first team debut for them in the 1990-1991 season.

He said, "When I left this club 29 years ago, I didn't really want to leave but I had no option. When I had the conversation with the chairman I couldn't wait to get here. I'm raring to go."

A philosophical Neal Ardley was full of praise for his long-time friend, "Neil has been a very loyal assistant manager and an excellent coach who has always given me everything. He deserves this opportunity and I couldn't stand in his way. While I will miss working with him immensely I wish him the very best."

Notts' first summer signing, on 7 August, was Portuguese attacking midfielder Ruben da Rocha Rodrigues, from Dutch club FC Den Bosch. The first Portuguese player to play for Notts, his family moved to the Netherlands when he was very young. Neal Ardley was pleased to have secured the signature of the twenty four year old.

> *"Rúben is the player I watched more than any other during (the coronavirus) lockdown. The recruitment team and I believe we have found an exciting talent who will improve the squad and get better with age. He can play as an attacking midfielder, a number ten or even as a striker and we hope he fulfils his talent with us."*

Ruben Rodrigues scored 12 goals and was credited with seven assists before coronavirus ended his 2019-20 season

In a revealing and articulate twenty five minute press conference with journalists he answered questions in perfect English. Due to a lack of match fitness he commenced training immediately.

The responses from the seven players 'out of contract, offered new deal' were:

Michael Doyle: Re-signed 8 August

Alex Lacey: Re-signed 11 August

Richard Brindley: Re-signed 13 August

Dion Kelly-Evans: Re-signed 19 August

Kristian Dennis: Signed for Scottish Premier League club St Mirren 19 August.

Joe McDonnell (Gk): Signed for fellow National League club Eastleigh in mid-August (as did Pierce Bird whose Notts contract expired on 30 June).

Sam Osborne: Declined a new deal and decided to leave Notts. Signed for Leamington FC of The National League North.

A few days before the players returned for a second pre-season on Monday 24 August there were two more player signings and the arrival of a new assistant manager.

Jake Reeves, a 27-year-old midfielder from League Two Bradford City, signed on the 18 August. Following a long term (almost two years) groin injury he had proved his fitness by playing in Bradford's final 18 league fixtures before the coronavirus lockdown in March. He had previously played over 100 games for Neal Ardley at AFC Wimbledon and was a regular in their side which gained promotion to League One in May 2016.

The other newcomer was another midfielder, 28 year old Casper Sloth, who signed following a disappointing six months with Scottish Premier League club Motherwell. Prior to that he had played mostly in Denmark, but he had a two year spell (2014-2016) with Leeds United in the Championship. Earlier in his career he represented Denmark and won eight international caps for his native country, including a Wembley appearance against England in a World Cup warm-up match in 2014 – just before he joined Leeds. Six weeks later, on 5 October, his contract was terminated "by mutual consent" following a disagreement with Neal Ardley.

The replacement for Neil Cox, as assistant manager, was Greg Abbott. He had been in the same role at Meadow Lane, when he worked alongside former manager Shaun Derry, between November 2013 and March 2015.

Manager Neal Ardley said:

"Greg's got incredible experience and standing in the game and achieved fantastic things alongside Derry when he was here before. He's got a wealth of knowledge in terms of players, recruitment, coaching, management and assistant managing. It's going to be a change – but change can bring positives, and I think Greg's certainly going to do that. He has a huge personality and, with the strong characters we've got in the dressing room, I think he will help recreate the incredible atmosphere we had last season."

So, to re-cap, the following personnel were the principals when pre-season training commenced on Monday 24 August:

Manager	Neal Ardley
Assistant Manager	Greg Abbott
Goalkeeper Coach	Jake Kean
Strength and Conditioning Coach	Erik Svendsen
Head of Medical Services	Marco Ferreira
Performance Analyst	Jimmy Redfern

17 Players: Sam Slocombe & Tiernan Brooks (Gk's)

Richard Brindley
Dion Kelly-Evans
Connell Rawlinson
Ben Turner
Alex Lacey
Damien McCrory

Michael Doyle (Captain)
Jake Reeves
~~Casper Sloth~~ contract terminated 5/10/20
Jim O'Brien

Callum Roberts
Wes Thomas
Kyle Wootton
Ruben Rodrigues
Enzio Boldewijn

One week later, on Monday 31 August, the squad was strengthened further when a fourth summer signing was announced. Notts continued their recent trend of signing foreign players, with three of the four new arrivals so far for the new season being Portuguese (Ruben Rodrigues), Danish (Casper Sloth), and now Belgian (Elisha Sam) - a 23-year-old 6ft 5" centre forward. Sam was born in Antwerp and a graduate of Standard Liege's academy. After playing in Israel for a year, he rose to prominence at Dutch second-tier side FC Eindhoven where he appeared 33 times and scored eight goals. Before he arrived at Meadow Lane he had been playing in the top tier of the Bulgarian football league. In his first interview he spoke with clarity in perfect English.

A delighted Neal Ardley said:

"It's rare to find someone with a target man's build who's also mobile and quick. We thought it was going to be a long shot to get Elisha and there's been a lot of hard work to get it to this point. He's come out extremely strongly in all our research and his movement is the thing that really took me by surprise. He enjoys dropping into pockets and technically he's very, very good. He's a really pleasant young man who's worked hard for every team he's played for – we've done our research on that as well. We feel he'll fit into everything we're trying to grow here and that he'll be an exciting addition.

It's never easy coming to a new country so we've got to be a little bit patient with him but he's well above his years in his maturity and I think he'll take it in his stride."

During the first ten days of September there were four further additions to the squad. Luke Pilling, a 23-year-old goalkeeper, had been with Tranmere Rovers since an early age but had had only limited first team opportunities.

Neal Ardley commented "Tiernan Brooks, is a real prospect, but is still young and this signing will allow him to gain further experience out on loan".

The second arrival was an old face – 20-year-old Sam Graham, on loan from Premier League Sheffield United until the end of the year. The central defender made ten National League appearances for Notts at the beginning of last season before suffering a serious Achilles injury in training, after which he returned to his parent club for treatment and rehabilitation.

The final two players were at each end of the experience scale. Jimmy Knowles, a promising 18 year old striker who had made a handful of appearances for near neighbours Mansfield Town of League Two, was a loan signing until the end of the season. A local young man, born in Sutton-in-Ashfield, his first interview indicated maturity and a willingness to learn.

Adam Chicksen, a 28-year-old left back had previously played for eight clubs and amassed over 200 appearances during his career, with the vast majority at League One level. A free agent since leaving Bolton Wanderers in January, he had recently been training with Notts and played the second half of the friendly game against Ilkeston Town on 5 September which Notts won 2-0.

Neal Ardley confirmed that these four signings had brought Notts' pre-season recruitment to an end. With four of the 23-man squad goalkeepers (Jake Kean the goalkeeping coach was registered as a player), 19 were outfield players – eight defenders, four midfielders and seven forwards.

During September, before the opening fixture of The National League season on 3 October, Notts played five games - four friendlies and the outstanding (now one-leg instead of two) FA Trophy semi-final against Harrogate Town:

> Saturday 5 September (3pm): Ilkeston Town 0-2 Notts (Wootton scored both goals)
> Saturday 12 September (3pm): Alfreton Town 1-2 Notts (Thomas, Wootton pen.)
> Saturday 19 September (3pm): Telford United 1-3 Notts (Lacey, own goal, Thomas)

FA Trophy - Semi-Final	Notts County 0-1 Harrogate Town
Tuesday 22 September 2020 7.45pm	

Slocombe

Brindley　　Rawlinson　　Graham　　Chicksen

Doyle (Capt.)　　Reeves

Roberts (Kelly-Evans 78')　　Rodrigues (Boldewijn 69')

Thomas (Sam 69')　　Wootton

Subs: Pilling (Gk), Kelly-Evans, Lacey, McCrory, Boldewijn, Sam

Of Notts' 19 outfield players, Turner, O'Brien and Sloth were injured. Knowles, although he had made a good impression against Alfreton and Telford, did not make the squad.

Although Notts 'huffed and puffed' Harrogate were the better team for most of the game and, as in the play-off final, deserved to win. They scored the winning goal with a header a minute before half-time. This was Harrogate's sixth competitive fixture since their season started on 5 September, and it showed – they looked fitter/sharper than Notts. Notts' disappointment at failing to reach the Wembley final was enhanced by what looked like a serious ankle injury to Cal Roberts, following a bad tackle. After a lengthy delay he was carried off on a stretcher. However, he subsequently made a good recovery and was declared fit for the first game of the season at Dover 11 days later.

Saturday 26 September (3pm): Notts 0-3 York City

Notts gave a pedestrian and disjointed display. Losing 2-0 at half-time, an improvement was expected in the second half but it didn't materialise and, as on Tuesday against Harrogate, they were beaten by the better side.

Alfreton, Telford and York were members of National League North, one tier below Notts. All five pre-season games were played behind closed doors except for the game at Ilkeston where a few hundred spectators were allowed access. However all the games were 'streamed' live (and free) on Notts' website and their YouTube channel, complete with commentary.

With increasing concerns about the financial position of all football clubs because of the coronavirus pandemic, and fixtures being played behind closed doors, it was announced on Friday 2 October that The National League would receive financial support from the government in the form of a £10 million emergency grant over three months to compensate clubs for the revenue lost from supporters not able to attend games. In addition to the government grant clubs decided to get more much needed revenue by 'streaming' their games live, provided they were not televised (by BT Sport).

In mid-September Macclesfield Town were wound up in the High Court over debts totalling in the region of half a million pounds. The decision to wind-up the club came after they were relegated from the English Football League (League Two) at the end of last season. On 29 September, they were expelled from The National League, four days before the commencement of the 2020-21 season on 3 October. The expulsion took effect from 12 October with the club suspended until then and their three scheduled fixtures cancelled.

So, on Saturday 3 October 2020, Notts played the opening fixture of their second season in The National League – away to Dover Athletic, who streamed the game live via a video link to their website at a cost of £8 per 'ticket'.

Bookmakers were divided on favouritism for the team to be promoted as champions. Two clubs dominated the betting, Notts and Stockport County, with Wrexham, Yeovil, Dagenham & Redbridge, Hartlepool and Solihull Moors the strong play-off candidates.

Chapter 13: The 2020-21 season (to halfway, match 22)

Match 1 Sat 3 Oct 2020 15:00	Dover Athletic 1 - 0 Notts County goal 89'	Played behind closed doors

Slocombe

Brindley   Rawlinson   Lacey   Chicksen

Doyle (Capt.)   Reeves

Roberts   O'Brien (Boldewijn 85')

Wootton   Thomas (Knowles 80')

Subs: Kelly-Evans, Graham, Boldewijn, Rodrigues, Knowles
(As in many games last season, no substitute goalkeeper. I wonder if Luke Pilling
was aware of this Neal Ardley tactic when he signed in early September.)

Only five players who were named in the 16-man squad for Game 1 at the start of last season were present – Slocombe, Doyle, O'Brien, Kelly-Evans and Boldewijn.

The two games with Dover last season were drawn (2-2, 0-0 at Meadow Lane).

Dover were in twelfth position at lockdown in mid-March and rose one place after the points per game calculation decided the final positions of the season.

On a poor pitch (Dover's manager apologised to Neal Ardley for its condition) Notts didn't deserve to lose, but, especially in the first half, they created few clear cut goal scoring opportunities. Just as the fourth official displayed '4' minutes of added time at the end of the second half Dover won a corner and scored from the resultant cross – a powerful header crashed against the underside of the crossbar on its way into the net.

Notts were defeated 1-0 (at Eastleigh) on the opening day last season when the goal was… a header from a corner! For the record, Stockport County, joint favourites with Notts to become National League champions this season, also lost 1-0 to a last-minute goal at Torquay.

Two days after this game the contract of midfield player Casper Sloth was terminated by mutual consent. Despite a recent injury and lack of match fitness he thought he should be in the squad at Dover. Neal Ardley disagreed.

Match 2	**Notts County 3 - 1 Altrincham**	Played behind closed
Wed 7 Oct 2020 19:45	Wootton 15' 27' goal 77'	doors, but televised by
	Reeves 65'	BT Sport

Slocombe
Brindley   Rawlinson   Lacey   Kelly-Evans
Doyle (Capt.)   Reeves
Roberts (Boldewijn 73')   O'Brien
Wootton (Sam 73')   Thomas (Rodrigues 86')

Subs: Graham, Boldewijn, Rodrigues, Sam, Knowles
(no substitute goalkeeper)

Notts made one change from the side defeated at Dover – Kelly-Evans replaced Chicksen.

Altrincham, promoted from National League North via the play-offs at the end of last season, drew their opening game 0-0 at home to National League South play-off winners Weymouth.

Both Notts' first half goals followed excellent play between Wootton and Thomas down the left hand channel. For the first they swapped passes cleverly before Wootton scored from the corner of the six yard box. The second came after Thomas tenaciously chased a defender, robbed him of the ball and then chipped a cross into the centre of the goal for Wootton to glance a simple header into the corner of the net. Five minutes before half-time Wootton was fouled in the penalty area, but the goalkeeper denied him his hat-trick when he dived to his left to push Wootton's spot kick away for a corner.

Wootton nearly scored at the beginning of the second half when he skilfully created space for himself, but his shot was then blocked. Soon afterwards a Roberts shot, from the edge of the penalty area, hit the outside of the post. It was Reeves who got the third goal, his first for Notts, with a powerful shot from 25 yards. Altrincham's consolation goal was well deserved – a determined forward run ended with an excellent shot from twenty yards which gave Slocombe no chance.

This was an entertaining game with both sides playing good football and passing the ball accurately. Although Notts deserved to win Altrincham were not outclassed, they came up against a team who were determined to overcome the disappointment of a first day defeat.

The next day Notts announced details of their internet 'streaming' package. With fixtures being played behind closed doors for the foreseeable future due to coronavirus (COVID-19), they had been working hard to establish a professional and reliable service to enable fans and supporters all over the world the opportunity to view games live.

The package, introduced to provide live comprehensive coverage of non-televised home games, included a four-camera multi-angle feed, commentary (in-sync with BBC Radio Nottingham), slow-motion replays, half-time highlights and the ability to rewind to any point during the match.

Supporters could stream each game for £12, although those who wished to provide extra financial support to the club could choose £16 or £20 options. It was stressed that the 'stream' would remain the same no matter which price was chosen.

> Notts' CEO, Jason Turner, said: "We are very pleased to share our streaming plans with supporters following a thorough review process. We've known all along the importance of providing a reliable service to our fans and we're very confident we will deliver that, starting on Saturday with the visit of Barnet. We had a number of options available to us, including the potential to continue with our one-camera pre-season offering, but the results of our streaming questionnaire showed that the vast majority of supporters were happy to pay a little more for a better service. It's been very humbling to see so many fans offering to pay the price of a season ticket to access a stream of all our home matches. Unfortunately, rules dictate we're unable to offer seasonal streaming passes or bundles, but hopefully the option to pay up to £20 will be a good alternative. A huge 'thank you' in advance to anyone who generously decides to pay more. Don't forget, home clubs keep all the revenue from league matches so please tune in and cheer on the boys from home!"

The replacement for Casper Sloth was announced in mid-October – Matty Wolfe, a twenty year old midfielder from Championship club Barnsley on loan until 3 January. His only appearance for Barnsley, in their penultimate fixture last season, had been as a substitute during a victory over our near neighbours Nottingham Forest last July. He was in the Barnsley squad for their last five fixtures during which they unexpectedly avoided relegation, an indication that Barnsley were confident in his ability at such a critical stage in the season.

Match 3 Sat 10 Oct 2020 15:00	**Notts County** (8th) **4 - 2 Barnet** (14th) Roberts 14' goals 45' 75' Wootton 17' Boldewijn 23' Doyle 90'+4	Played behind closed doors

Slocombe

Kelly-Evans   Rawlinson   Graham   McCrory

Doyle (Capt.)   Reeves   Rodrigues (O'Brien 67')

Roberts (Brindley 90')   Wootton   Boldewijn (Thomas 67')

Subs: Brindley, Lacey, O'Brien, Thomas, Sam
(no substitute goalkeeper)

Notts made one positional change (Kelly-Evans) and four changes from the side victorious over Altrincham with Graham, McCrory, Rodrigues and Boldewijn making their first starts of the season. Manager Neal Ardley had indicated that due to the frequency of games he was likely to rotate players, which he did last season when fixtures were congested.

Barnet finished in 7th position (after the points per game calculation) at the end of last season and played Notts in the play-off semi-final on 25 July when they were defeated 2-0 at Meadow Lane. Notts only played them once in the league – a 1-2 defeat in Nottingham. The away fixture was cancelled due to the coronavirus lockdown. Barnet's opening game last Saturday ended in a disastrous 5-1 home defeat to Eastleigh, but they redeemed themselves in mid-week when two late goals gave them a 2-1 victory at Dagenham & Redbridge.

Notts started were they left off against Altrincham and Wootton hit the post after just four minutes. Notts continued to pass the ball with confidence, speed and accuracy and ten minutes later Wootton, following good close control, flicked the ball to Roberts who stroked it into the net from just outside the penalty area. Roberts then became the provider with two assists, the first for Wootton to poke the ball home from close range and the second for Boldewijn to score with a powerful drive from twenty yards. After a superb thirty minutes Notts lost their impetus and Barnet scored on the stroke of half-time. During a more even second half Barnet reduced the deficit further when Slocombe's good save ran loose and was tapped home from close range. However, a nervy Notts regained enough composure for Doyle to steer the ball into the net in stoppage time after Wootton allowed a low cross from Reeves to reach the Notts captain who was unmarked near the penalty spot.

Although Notts deservedly won the game they were taught a lesson. They must not become complacent and allow opponents back into a game. Notts should have reached half-time with a lead of at least 4-0, but in the end Barnet gave them a scare and nearly achieved a draw!

Match 4	Sutton United (2nd) 0 - 1 Notts County (5th)	Played behind closed
Tue 13 Oct 2020 19:45	Wootton 90'+4	doors

Slocombe

Brindley   Rawlinson   Lacey   Kelly-Evans

Doyle (Capt.)   Reeves   O'Brien

Boldewijn (Knowles 76')   Wootton   Rodrigues (Roberts 70')

Subs: Pilling (Gk), McCrory, Graham, Roberts, Knowles

Notts made one positional change (Kelly-Evans returned to the left sided position) and three changes from the side which defeated Barnet with Brindley, Lacey and O'Brien restored to the starting eleven. Roberts was not 100% fit so was one of the substitutes.

The two fixtures last season both ended in 1-1 draws. Sutton, who play on a 3G (artificial grass) pitch, finished in the bottom half of the table but had made a 100% winning start to this season with victories in all three games – scoring six goals with just one conceded. Only Hartlepool Utd were above them in the league table.

This was a game involving two well organised teams, with (on the night) two strong defences. Reeves had a good chance in the second minute but shot over the crossbar. After 20 minutes a Boldewijn goal attempt bounced before it struck the top of the crossbar on its way out for a goal kick. On a soft grass pitch (there had been a wet start to October) it may not have bounced as high! On the hour a good Lacey header from near the penalty spot was just too high following a short corner and cross. In the latter stages of the second half Wootton twice came close to scoring, before, in added time he did score his fourth goal in three games. The Sutton goalkeeper made a poor clearance (not for the first time in the game) straight to Doyle whose first time pass found Knowles. He advanced into the penalty area and the goalkeeper saved his shot but the ball ran loose to Wootton who gleefully swept it into the corner of the net from twelve yards.

We saw a different side to Notts from the one which outplayed Barnet, in the first thirty minutes, three days ago. Most neutrals would probably have said a draw would have been a fair result, but a third successive win and a 'clean sheet' for Notts meant they rose to third in the table.

As a footnote:

Stockport County, the bookmaker's joint favourites with Notts for the title, had also won three on the trot since their opening day defeat and were second with a slightly better goal difference than Notts. Hartlepool were top with ten points from their four games. Dover, who were fortunate to beat Notts ten days ago, had lost their three subsequent games with twelve goals conceded!

Match 5	**Notts Co** (3rd) **2-3 Maidenhead United** (19th)	Played behind closed
Sat 17 Oct 2020 15:00	Knowles 3' goals 14' 64' 75'	doors
	Rodrigues 29'	

Slocombe
McCrory   Rawlinson   Lacey (Turner 84')   Chicksen
Doyle (Capt.)   Reeves
Boldewijn (Sam 78')   Rodrigues (Wolfe 69')
Knowles   Wootton

Subs: Pilling (Gk), Turner, Graham, Wolfe, Sam

A few hours before kick-off Notts announced that four players had tested positive for coronavirus but, following consultation with National League medical officers and Maidenhead, the game went ahead as planned. The five outfield players not in today's squad were Brindley, Kelly-Evans, O'Brien, Roberts and Thomas. Those infected would now self-isolate for ten days from either the point they first experienced symptoms or returned a positive test.

The two fixtures last season were played over Christmas/New Year. Notts secured a comprehensive 3-0 victory at Meadow Lane on Boxing Day but were then held to a goalless draw in the return on New Year's Day.

Maidenhead had lost their first three fixtures, conceding ten goals, but they bucked the trend in midweek with a 1-0 victory at Wrexham.

Notts started brightly and went ahead in the third minute when Knowles scored his first Notts goal on his full league debut. A good Reeves pass released McCrory on the right and his low cross was turned into the net by Knowles from the edge of the six yard box. Soon after Boldewijn missed a good chance to put Notts further ahead. Maidenhead equalised when a scramble in the Notts penalty area, following a free kick, resulted in a loose ball which was duly smashed into the net from ten yards. Rodrigues restored Notts' lead when he scored his first goal for Notts. After controlling a loose ball he moved forward with skill and composure, outmanoeuvred two defenders and placed the ball into the corner of the net from the edge of the penalty area.

Despite the score line Maidenhead had given a good account of themselves in the game and they equalised when a corner kick was headed home by an unmarked forward. With fifteen minutes to play they went ahead for the first time. A poor kick by their goalkeeper was flicked on, the Notts defence were outpaced and Slocombe was beaten by a well-placed shot from sixteen yards.

A frustrating and disappointing day for Notts ended with a dramatic defeat. Maidenhead's perseverance and 'never say die' attitude meant few would begrudge them their hard earned victory. The match was well refereed by a woman, Rebecca Welch, the highest ranked female referee in England. So, four firsts for Notts in one day – players with coronavirus, goals for Knowles and Rodrigues and a female in charge!

During the week following the Maidenhead defeat there were two significant events in the history of Notts County Football Club.

More detail was released concerning the announcement, at the beginning of October, of financial support from the government to compensate National League clubs for revenue lost due to games being played behind closed doors, after the return of supporters was paused due to rising coronavirus infection rates. There was confirmation as to how the £10 million funding, over three months, would be distributed amongst the 66 clubs in The National League (23, Macclesfield Town were expelled on 12 October) and National Leagues North (22) and South (21), the fifth and six tiers of English football. The money for the initiative came from a National Lottery promotional fund following a unique deal brokered by the government.

Quote from the government press release:

> *"The £10 million emergency support package, which will reach clubs quickly via the Football Association (FA), is in recognition of the important role National League clubs play in their local areas – being a source of pride to their towns, giving children opportunities to get active, and being at the heart of their communities. Many clubs and their supporters have also been very active in their areas throughout the pandemic, rallying round to help the elderly and isolated, and raising money for front-line charities."*

Distribution was on an average attendance basis with seven former Football League clubs (Notts County, Stockport County, Yeovil Town, Hartlepool United, Chesterfield, Torquay and Wrexham) receiving the largest proportion - £95,000 a month. The remaining National League Clubs received £84,000 a month.

In National Leagues North and South, the majority of clubs received £30,000 a month, although five got £36,000 a month on a similar distribution model used for The National League.

The second significant event is best explained by the reproduction of the announcement made on Notts County's website:

> **Two more of our players have tested positive for Covid-19 and as a result we have withdrawn from the Emirates FA Cup and postponed our upcoming Vanarama National League matches away to FC Halifax Town and Aldershot Town.**
>
> *After four members of our squad tested positive for the virus last week, we scheduled another round of testing this Wednesday to identify any further infections. Unfortunately this has resulted in two more positive results and, following consultation with the FA and National League's medical officers, we have taken the difficult but responsible decision not to travel to King's Lynn Town on Saturday and to temporarily halt our league campaign. King's Lynn will be awarded a bye to the first round and our trips to Halifax and Aldershot will be rearranged for later in the season. We would like to thank each club for their cooperation and understanding.*
>
> ***Our chief executive Jason Turner said:*** *"Our thoughts are with the players affected by the virus, who are all receiving the best possible care and support to ensure they return to us safe and well. Naturally, we are incredibly disappointed to withdraw from the FA Cup – a competition, as past winners, we have a wonderful association with – but with only 14 available players and several positions we're now unable to cover, on top of the clear risk of more infections coming to light in the coming days, it is only right that we take decisive action to cease training and playing for the time being. I am hugely proud of the way the club has conducted itself throughout the pandemic and would once again like to pay tribute to our owners, Chris and Alex Reedtz, for continuing to fund regular testing despite this not being mandatory, thus ensuring we are doing all we can to protect our players, staff and the wider public."*
>
> *"Chris and Alex's diligence has drawn huge praise from the authorities and allowed us to take informed decisions since the outbreak in March. With some of our infected players not displaying symptoms, our efforts have probably prevented us from unknowingly and irresponsibly spreading the virus to any of our aforementioned opponents. With no matches now scheduled until our home fixture against Stockport County on Wednesday 11 November, our focus is on minimising a further outbreak within the club, devising a return-to-play protocol for our affected players and helping our fit players maintain their conditioning remotely to ensure we're ready to continue our strong start to the season next month."*

Our manager, Neal Ardley, added: *"While I'm devastated that I won't have the opportunity to put together a cup run for the club this season, the safety of my players, staff, the opposition and their families have to be the priority at this terrible time. As we're all aware, it's taken some people many months to recover from this illness and we therefore need to tread very carefully when it comes to rehabilitating our affected players. This is a new situation for everyone and I'm in close dialogue with our medical department to ensure we have careful and considered procedures in place. I'm hugely proud to represent a club that cares so strongly about its employees and community and I would like to join Jason in thanking our owners for their unwavering commitment to our safety."*

There was a link to both the above events. Surely it should have been stipulated that a percentage of the money provided to each club be used to pay for some coronavirus pandemic testing. It was not mandatory for National League clubs to test players and Notts were of the opinion that "a wider testing regime was required". Notts had tested at least five times since their return in the summer. As well as the tests they had also been very proactive in their protocols to prevent the infiltration of the disease into the club. Masks were worn indoors, including in the gym. Equipment was frequently wiped and sanitised, as were footballs, bibs and cones. Social distancing was practised and two changing rooms were used. They felt they had done at least as much as, and possibly a lot more than, most other football clubs to prevent the spread of coronavirus. Ironically, Notts County, admittedly in a 'High' COVID Alert Level area, had still fallen victim to the disease. It was almost certain that many players, throughout football, had played with a coronavirus infection since the second wave of the pandemic commenced in September. The following extract from the government Press Release describes the three local COVID Alert Levels (sometimes referred to as 'Tiers' or known as a 'local lockdown'), brought into operation for England in mid-October, for local authorities, residents and workers, about what to do and how to manage the outbreak in their area.

Local COVID Alert Level – Medium (Tier 1)

This is for areas where national restrictions continue to be in place. This means:

All businesses and venues can continue to operate, in a COVID-19 Secure manner, other than those that remain closed in law, such as nightclubs.

Certain businesses selling food or drink on their premises are required to close between 10pm and 5am.

Businesses and venues selling food for consumption off the premises can continue to do so after 10pm as long as this is through delivery service, click-and-collect or drive-thru.

Schools, universities and places of worship remain open.

Weddings and funerals can go ahead with restrictions on the number of attendees.

Organised indoor sport and exercise classes can continue to take place, provided the Rule of Six is followed.

People must not meet in groups larger than 6, indoors or outdoors.

Local COVID Alert Level – High (Tier 2)

This is for areas with a higher level of infections. This means the following additional measures are in place:

People must not meet with anybody outside their household or support bubble in any indoor setting, whether at home or in a public place

People must not meet in a group of more than 6 outside, including in a garden or other space.

People should aim to reduce the number of journeys they make where possible. If they need to travel, they should walk or cycle where possible, or to plan ahead and avoid busy times and routes on public transport.

Local COVID Alert Level – Very High (Tier 3)

This is for areas with a very high level of infections. The Government will set a baseline of measures for any area in this local alert level. Consultation with local authorities will determine additional measures.

The baseline means the below additional measures are in place:

Pubs and bars must close, and can only remain open where they operate as if they were a restaurant – which means serving substantial meals, like a main lunchtime or evening meal. They may only serve alcohol as part of such a meal.

Wedding receptions are not allowed

People must not meet with anybody outside their household or support bubble in any indoor or outdoor setting, whether at home or in a public space. The Rule of Six applies in open public spaces like parks and beaches.

People should try to avoid travelling outside the 'Very High' area they are in, or entering a 'Very High' area, other than for things like work, education, accessing youth services, to meet caring responsibilities or if they are in transit.

People should avoid staying overnight in another part of the UK if they are resident in a 'Very High' area, or avoid staying overnight in a 'Very High' area if they are resident elsewhere.

In addition to the three Local COVID Alert Levels it was stressed

In the fourth, and last, FA Cup qualifying round on 24 October, much smaller clubs than Notts completed their fixtures. Skelmersdale Utd, the lowest ranked club (level 9) still in the competition, (West Lancashire, currently an area with a 'Very High' Alert Level), Marine (Crosby, Liverpool, also a 'Very High', risk area), Marske Utd (Redcar and Cleveland, in a 'High' risk area), Guiseley (Leeds = 'High' area), Cray Valley Paper Mills (Royal Borough of Greenwich, London = 'High' area), Leiston (East Suffolk = 'Medium' area) and Sholing (Eastleigh, Southampton = 'Medium'), to highlight just some of the less well known clubs involved. Interestingly three of the above made it into the first round proper, Skelmersdale, Marine, and Cray Valley Paper Mills who did what Notts couldn't do last Saturday – they beat Maidenhead!

King's Lynn Town v Notts County was the only FA Cup fixture cancelled in the fourth qualifying round, although a few clubs had withdrawn in earlier qualifying rounds because of coronavirus.

I think Notts therefore became the highest ranked club to withdraw from the FA Cup since Manchester United withdrew from the 1999-2000 competition. In May 1999 United, managed by (Sir) Alex Ferguson, completed a Premier League, FA Cup and UEFA Champions League treble which meant they were eligible to compete in the inaugural FIFA World Club Championship in Brazil in early January 2000. United's decision to withdraw was widely criticised. With the holder's not participating it was said the competition would be de-valued and possibly set a precedence to allow others to withdraw in the future. Fixture congestion and travel fatigue were two reasons given for the withdrawal. Another reason was the government and the Football Association thought that if United failed to participate in Brazil the FA's bid to stage the 2006 World Cup would be jeopardised. Now, it is not unusual for higher level clubs to field understrength teams especially in cup competitions in the early part of a season. For the record Manchester United disappointed in Brazil and were eliminated. England were unsuccessful in their 2006 World Cup bid!

To summarise a hectic period in the club's history Notts' CEO Jason Turner issued an update on 23 October:

> *As you can no doubt imagine, it's been a challenging couple of weeks at Meadow Lane following a number of our players testing positive for COVID-19. This led us to make the incredibly hard but correct decision yesterday to cease training and playing for a short time to create a 'firebreak' process at the club.*
>
> *Withdrawing from this season's Emirates FA Cup was a particularly difficult call but, with so many players unavailable and the possibility of further cases evolving despite good infection prevention and control measures within the club, it would have been negligent and irresponsible of us to travel to King's Lynn, and subsequently to Halifax and Aldershot next week for our National League fixtures. We're in dialogue with the latter clubs to rearrange both matches and will provide an update in due course, but we're hopeful of catching up quite quickly.*
>
> *While a few players who tested positive are still experiencing symptoms, I'm pleased to report that they are all looking forward to returning to training when the time is right. Thankfully, some are already symptom free and raring to go, while others will need a little more time before getting back to work. They will then, no doubt, need to regain some of the fitness they have lost as a result of the virus and lack of training, so we'll have to be patient while they get back up to full speed.*
>
> *This disruption to our season, particularly following such a strong start, is hugely disappointing. We are, nevertheless, proud of the proactive approach we have taken which has led us to identify the cases within our camp. Testing is by no means a cheap exercise, nor is it mandatory, but our owners Chris and Alex Reedtz have generously funded a regular programme and will continue to do so in the interests of protecting the health of our employees and public health. We absolutely believe this is the right thing to do and that the league should reconsider their position on this for other member clubs.*
>
> *The FA's Chief Medical Officer, who I was in close dialogue with earlier this week, was very complimentary about our approach throughout the pandemic and we will continue to act diligently and responsibly to limit the risk of the virus spreading within our club and into the wider community. We're planning to test all players and staff again next Friday before welcoming them back to training the following week to commence preparations for our currently scheduled return to action on Wednesday 11 November, when we host Stockport County in front of the BT Sport cameras.*
>
> *Our live streaming service returns for our following home game, against Wealdstone on Friday 27 November, and we've been absolutely delighted with the response so far with more than 2,100 match passes being sold for both of our streamed matches to*

date. Barring a couple of minor teething problems, both streams have been a tremendous success and with so many of you generously choosing to pay above the base price of £12 I'm very confident streaming will provide us with an important income stream over the course of the campaign. Unfortunately, however, it won't make up for the revenue we've lost due to not being able to welcome our supporters back to Meadow Lane.

We had hoped that our share of the well-publicised £10million funding package kindly made available by the National Lottery would have gone a long way to making up the shortfall. But, while we appreciate the Government, FA and National League's efforts in securing this funding, the allocation of the monies does not accord with the criteria set out earlier this month, when Government made it clear it should be used to subsidise clubs for their lost gate revenue.

How can it be right, therefore, that we receive only £11,000 per month more than the likes of Boreham Wood, Wealdstone and Weymouth despite our average attendances being more than five times theirs? They and a host of other clubs are now actually in a stronger financial position than they would have been if crowds were permitted at matches and, as a result, have gained an unfair competitive advantage over clubs like ours who have been left significantly worse off. The allocation is profoundly flawed to the extent that it seriously and adversely impacts the very integrity of the competition.

All clubs were asked to provide the league with financial information at the end of September and to specifically detail their estimated lost gate revenue. While we understand these figures are merely indicative, alongside average attendances over say a two-year period they should have provided enough information to enable the league to work out a sensible banding of teams rather than adopting this purely arbitrary system. If the funds were distributed in an optimal way, it is conceivable that all clubs could have received close to their lost gate receipts for the first three months of the season, with further potential to replace other lost revenue streams with live streaming and creative sponsorship and marketing initiatives. In a letter to the league I have offered to provide a number of options for a more considered and structured distribution based on various scenarios using the above information. I am yet to receive a response!

On Monday I will be speaking with Lilian Greenwood MP to ask for her support, alongside other MPs, in demanding The National League revisit their decision and distribute these very welcome funds in a manner which meets their mandated use. While we are of course grateful to receive this help and accepting of the fact we may not recover all our losses, we cannot accept other clubs profiting from the grant while many others are left short. I would like to thank Lilian in advance for her support and assistance in this matter.

Moving on to operational matters, I'd like to bring you up to speed on a number of staff changes at the club in recent months. Mike Townsend's arrival as ticketing supervisor coincides with our former ticket office manager Jordan Worthington's promotion to the role of commercial operations manager.

There has also been a change in our academy, with Craig Wallace stepping back from his role as academy manager to take on a new full-time role away from the club. Craig will, however, continue to look after our academy recruitment, with Dave Plant promoted to academy manager. Congratulations to both Jordan and Dave on their well-deserved promotions.

While the club remains closed to visitors in line with our COVID protocols, our club shop will continue to open on Thursdays (9am-5pm), Fridays (9am-5pm) and Saturdays (9am-1pm) and our hardworking backroom team will continue to answer your telephone queries throughout the week.

My colleague, Alice Kelk, will be particularly delighted to hear from all of you who wish to sign the young Notts fan in your life up to our 2020-21 Young Pies membership, which carries a host of exciting benefits!

Jason

Before moving on I wish to expand upon Jason's displeasure regarding the distribution of the monthly funding that Notts and the other National League clubs are receiving. I am a friend of Notts' honorary club historian, Michael Chappell, and in a recent exchange of emails he provided a stark example of the money distribution inequality. I quote Michael:

"......I can't fault the manner in which he (Jason) has responded to the ineptitude of The National League Big-Whigs. I just hope he can resolve the current injustice of the National Lottery Fund allocations which mean that the likes of Boreham Wood (800 gates x £20 = £16,000 per home match) who are having a laugh at our expense (5200 gates x £20 = £104,000 per home match, not to mention hospitality revenue). Pro rata (an average of 2.5 home games per month) this approximates to £40,000 per month compared to £260,000 per month, so why do Notts only get £11,000 per month more than the minnows who are far better off playing in empty stadiums?"

I assume Michael has allocated £20 per attendee, based on admission charge, possible purchase of a programme and consumption of some basic refreshments, to arrive at the £20 figure. Obviously Notts' average National League home attendance (5210 in season 2019-20) receipts include not only the full adult admission charge (£22) but a reduced charge for concessions (£16) and under 18's., so the £20 should be treated as an approximation/estimate. Nevertheless, his example does indicate the significant difference in lost gate revenue between Notts (who receive £95,000 a month) and

Boreham Wood (£84,000 per month). Boreham Wood are better off playing behind closed doors as they are making a profit of £44,000 per month while Notts are making a loss of 165,000.

Alternative: £95,000/5210 = £18.23 per supporter and £84,000/800 = £105.

After a ten day 'firebreak' Notts announced that following further COVID-19 testing for players and staff, when one further player tested positive and was required to self-isolate for ten days, the available squad members would return to training on Monday 2 November in preparation for the rearranged match at Aldershot five days later. It was also stated that there would be another round of testing before that game, including an additional antibody test to help identify anyone who contracted the virus between Notts' play-off campaign and the resumption of the testing regime ahead of the 2020-21 season.

On the same day as the above announcement the Nottingham(shire) infection rate had increased to such an extent that the city and the county were moved up from the 'High' to the 'Very High' COVID Alert Level - a local lockdown.

Notts should have played two league games in the week ending Saturday 31 October but they had postponed both due to the outbreak of coronavirus in the club. The vast majority of clubs were playing as normal. The Premier League and Championship had (so far) played all fixtures as scheduled. A few clubs in EFL League One and in EFL League Two had postponed games in October. On Tuesday evening 27 October (when Notts should have played at Halifax) The National League had no other postponements in a full programme of fixtures, but on the 31 (when Notts should have played at Aldershot) three other clubs postponed their games due to coronavirus – Dagenham & Redbridge, Halifax Town and Wrexham. Earlier in October two other clubs, Altrincham and Barnet, had postponed fixtures due to the coronavirus pandemic. It is worth noting that Notts played these clubs on 7 and 10 October respectively.

However, in a fast developing and changing coronavirus situation there was a dramatic turn of events on the evening of Saturday 31 October. The Prime Minister, Boris Johnson, in a live televised broadcast, announced that despite local lockdowns in existence in some regions of England a more effective way to combat the spread of coronavirus would be to introduce a national lockdown affecting everyone in England. (It was estimated that approximately 11 million people, nearly 20% of the population, were now living under the tightest local COVID Alert Level restrictions – 'Very High' Tier 3). This national lockdown was programmed to last four weeks, starting on Thursday 5 November and ending on Wednesday 2 December, but with the possibility that, if the situation was still critical at the end of November, an extension may have to be considered.

An important indicator as to the success, or otherwise, of the lockdown was the value of the 'Reproduction Number' (R). This is the average number of secondary infections produced by one infected person. In other words the R number represents the rate of spread of COVID-19 across the country. If the R number is higher than one (currently estimated between 1.1 and 1.3 for England with a growth rate – new infections – of between 3% and 5% per day) the infection rate is rising - the higher the R number the higher the growth rate of new infections. An R number between 1.1 and 1.3 means that on average every ten people infected will infect between 11 and 13 other people. To reverse this trend the government will hope the R number is below one by the end of November. It was below one during the summer, after the first lockdown, but during September the R number climbed above one as the second coronavirus wave became established.

The lockdown was required to help prevent hospitals and the National Health Service from being overwhelmed, as infections and deaths were increasing rapidly during this second wave of the coronavirus pandemic. The main difference from the spring national lockdown was that schools, colleges and universities would remain open. Football was allowed to continue, behind closed doors, for clubs in level six (National Leagues North and South) and above. The 'non-elite' clubs were only allowed to play in the FA Cup.

On the subject of the FA Cup:

The weekend of November 7/8 was the First Round proper.

Clubs participating included Tonbridge Angels (lost 7-0), Canvey Island (won), South Shields (lost), Marine (won), Hampton & Richmond (lost), Maldon & Tiptree (lost), Hayes & Yeading (lost), Cray Valley Paper Mills (lost), Skelmersdale (lost, at Harrogate), but not Notts County following their honourable withdrawal. King's Lynn, the beneficiary of Notts' withdrawal, won through to the second round, when they would be one of 14 non-league teams involved.

| **Match 6** | **Aldershot Town** (21st) **1-0 Notts Co** (10th) | Played behind closed |
| Sat 7 Nov 2020 15:00 | goal 64' | doors |

Slocombe

Brindley   Graham (Turner 78')   Lacey   Chicksen

Doyle (Capt.)   Reeves   O'Brien

Thomas (Sam 78')   Wootton   Rodrigues (Boldewijn 68')

Subs: Turner, Kelly-Evans, Boldewijn, Knowles, Sam
(no substitute goalkeeper)

Of the 19 outfield players in the squad, Rawlinson (ill), McCrory (injured), Roberts (injured) and Wolfe were missing.

In the two fixtures last season Notts lost 2-1 at Aldershot, towards the end of November, but then went unbeaten in their following eight league games. Notts gained revenge at Meadow Lane, in their penultimate game before the first National lockdown in March, with a 3-1 victory.

Notts' 'firebreak' had seen them fall from 3rd to 10th in the league table. Aldershot finished last season just above the relegation zone. Like Notts they had only played five league games to date, and were joint bottom of the league in 21st position. Their only win was at Dover 0-5! In their last game (27 October) they lost 1-4 at home to Torquay.

An un-distinguished first half for Notts, not surprising following their coronavirus three week break, except for an O'Brien shot (just before half time) from the corner of the penalty area which clipped the crossbar. There was some improvement in the second half and, on the hour mark, Wootton missed a good chance. Ten minutes later the goalkeeper made a wonderful save from his header, following an O'Brien corner kick. However, in-between those attempts by Wootton, Aldershot took the lead when indecision, and a misdirected pass, by Lacey allowed an Aldershot forward to score with a good shot from 20 yards. Sam had a chance near the end, but, in a scrappy and error strewn game, Notts' performance was below par. They played like a side suffering from the disruption of an illness lay-off. A very unhappy Neal Ardley refused to offer any excuses: "I'm as disappointed as I've ever been as Notts County manager".

The season had a long way to go although three defeats in the first six games (to supposedly weak teams) was not what the doctor ordered! Two days later Notts announced that Wednesday's fixture at home to Stockport County, scheduled to be televised live by BT Sport, had been postponed "due to several COVID-19 events being reported by Stockport, including a positive test result".

At the end of the week (Friday 13th!) there were two pieces of news, one bad and one good. First the bad news:

Erik Svendsen, the first-team strength and conditioning coach, resigned. For family reasons he, and his fiancée, had to return home to Norway. He acknowledged the timing of his decision was bad (for Notts) "but unfortunately life sometimes takes away your ability to decide".

Neal Ardley, added:

> "Everyone here is sad to see him go. He's a big part of what we do. I trust his opinions and the sports science side of things here is right up there with the best I've seen and been involved with. It will be very difficult to replace Erik's qualities. Whoever comes in will need to be strong enough to give me their opinion on players and physical data. I don't want a 'yes' man."

Now the good news:

Cal Roberts signed a new contract which will keep him at Meadow Lane until the end of the 2022-23 season. The winger had become a hugely popular figure since arriving from Blyth Spartans at the beginning of the year. With Notts he had scored eight goals, created a number of assists, and confused defenders with his pace and trickery. It was a huge surprise when Newcastle United released him at the end of last season. He has always maintained that he can (and will) play in the Premier League.

Neil Ardley was obviously pleased:

> "I talk to Cal all the time about how we can give him the tools to be able to do what he does at a high level. The one thing I remind him of is that Premier League and Championship players are super-fit, super-fast and super-athletic – you can't rest on your laurels because you're doing well at the lower levels. You have to make sure you get everything right if you want to play at the top."

Roberts, who missed the defeat at Aldershot with a calf strain, today returned to training with the hope that he would be fit for Notts' next match against Halifax Town next Tuesday. He said:

> "Firstly, I'd like to thank the club for repaying me for what I've done on the pitch. Like I said when I first came, if I work hard I'll get the rewards – and I've been rewarded with a new contract, so I'm really happy about that. Coming here was a no-brainer and signing a new contract is a no-brainer again. The club's going in the right direction and it's a great place to be at the minute. The manager and the lads are brilliant and I enjoy

training every day. Now we just want to get back to our best after the coronavirus break."

Notts should have returned to action before the Halifax game but Saturday's fixture at home to Macclesfield Town was cancelled after the club were expelled from The National League last month because of financial problems and regulation breaches last season, for which they were deducted points and subsequently relegated from League Two. Remember, Macclesfield were the club who escaped relegation, when Notts didn't, in the last match of the 2018-19 season.

Match 7	**Halifax Town** (20th) **1-1 Notts County** (12th)	Played behind closed
Tue 17 Nov 2020 19:45	goal 90'+4 Sam 6'	doors

Slocombe
Brindley   Rawlinson   Lacey (Turner 46')   Kelly-Evans
Doyle (Capt.)   Reeves   O'Brien
Boldewijn
Sam (Roberts 67')   Wootton

Subs: Turner, Wolfe, Rodrigues, Roberts, Knowles
(no substitute goalkeeper)

Neal Ardley made four changes to the team beaten at Aldershot. Rawlinson returned after illness and replaced Graham. With McCrory still injured and Chicksen away on international duty with Zimbabwe, Kelly-Evans was selected at left full-back. Boldewijn and Sam replaced Rodrigues and Thomas (ill) respectively. It was Sam's first league start for Notts.

Notts completed the double over Halifax last season, winning 1-0 at Meadow Lane and 4-2 in the away fixture. Wootton scored three of Notts' five goals. Halifax lost in the promotion play-offs. Like Notts they had only played six league games to date (only four goals scored and only four conceded), but whereas Notts were 12th Halifax were 20th. They had not won a game since the opening day of the season.

Sam took only six minutes to score his first Notts goal. Reeves split the Halifax defence with a wonderful through ball which Sam controlled and swept cleanly into the net from near the penalty spot. The remainder of the first half was fairly even but just before half-time Notts almost conceded twice. First Brindley made an excellent intervention in the six yard box when he averted danger by putting the ball out for a corner. Slocombe then made an unbelievable reflex save with his legs – the goal bound shot from close range rebounded off a post and Halifax were unable to press home the advantage.

In an even second half Notts almost scored a second in the 76th minute when a powerful 25 yard shot by Reeves was tipped over the crossbar by the goalkeeper. A few minutes later Roberts missed a great chance when he shot well wide with only the goalkeeper to beat. Halifax then missed an equally good scoring opportunity, but with the last kick of the match they equalised. Notts, in an attempt to keep possession near the Halifax corner flag, gave the ball away and it was launched towards the centre circle. Turner hesitated and didn't clear the ball. Under pressure he stumbled over. The forward ran on and shot from the edge of the penalty area and, as Slocombe advanced, the ball hit his legs but it had enough momentum to carry on into the net. Notts probably didn't deserve to win but to concede in such a calamitous manner so late in the game was very disappointing. Neal Ardley described it as "a car crash of a goal". Notts' match commentator Charlie Slater (BBC Radio Nottingham) didn't mince his words: "It's a shocker. A stinking piece of defensive work and a stinking way to spend the final minute of your Tuesday night in Halifax".

Match 8	**Chesterfield** (21st) **2-3 Notts County** (12th)	Played behind closed
Sat 21 Nov 2020 15:00	goals 33', 77' Boldewijn 22'	doors
	Rodrigues 90'+1	
	Wootton 90'+3'	

Slocombe
Brindley   Rawlinson   Turner   Kelly-Evans
Doyle (Capt.)   Reeves   O'Brien (Rodrigues 59')
Roberts   Wootton   Boldewijn (Sam 59')

Subs: Graham, Chicksen, Rodrigues, Sam, Knowles
(no substitute goalkeeper)

Neal Ardley made two changes after the draw at Halifax. The two who came on in that game Turner (for Lacey) and Roberts (for Sam) retained their places.

Notts played Chesterfield three times last season. In the league Notts won 3-0 at Meadow Lane but lost 1-0 in the away fixture. Notts won 1-0 at Chesterfield in the FA Trophy. Since they were relegated from League Two at the end of the 2017-18 season, Chesterfield had struggled in The National League. In the following two seasons they finished 15th and then 19th. This season the struggle had continued and six defeats in their first eight League games meant they were in 21st position. A few days before this fixture they sacked their manager.

Notts started the game brightly and after three minutes Boldewijn moved in from the left to shot narrowly wide from 20 yards. Ten minutes later Roberts drifted in from the right and tried his luck from the edge of the penalty area but the ball hit a post. Notts took the lead when, following an O'Brien corner, a Turner header resulted in a goal mouth scramble and Boldewijn managed to hook the ball in from inside the six yard box. Chesterfield equalised with a good goal after a series of quick, neat, passes. Although Slocombe dived and managed to get his fingertips on the ball the powerful shot from the edge of the penalty area nestled into the bottom corner of the net. With rain falling Notts' disappointed for most of the second half and Chesterfield went ahead with 15 minutes remaining when a cross from the left was met with a diving header which skidded off the wet surface into the corner of the net. Soon afterwards a Doyle cross gave Wootton a chance to equalise but, under pressure, he was unable to make sufficient contact with the ball. However, in added time, Notts, incredibly, won the game with two headed goals – one from Rodrigues and one from Wootton. The equaliser came after a poor defensive header, following a Doyle free kick, which dropped for Rodrigues to direct into the net from twelve yards. Two minutes later another free kick, taken by Rodrigues near the right touchline, was met by Wootton who guided the ball into the net from ten yards.

An interesting statistic: Notts have scored fourteen league goals this season. Of the five scored in the second half four have been in time added on after the 90th minute!

Match 9 Fri 27 Nov 2020 19:45	**Notts County** (12th) **3-0 Wealdstone** (4th) Boldewijn 15', Sam 19' Knowles 89'	Played behind closed doors

Slocombe

Brindley   Rawlinson   Turner   Kelly-Evans

Doyle (Capt.)   Reeves

Boldewijn   Rodrigues (O'Brien 74')   Sam (Knowles 88')

Wootton

Subs: Pilling (Gk), Chicksen, O'Brien, Wolfe, Knowles

Neal Ardley (a few days after his second anniversary as Notts' manager) made two changes to the team who achieved the dramatic victory at Chesterfield. Rodrigues replaced O'Brien who dropped to the substitute's bench and Sam came in for the injured Roberts.

Wealdstone were promoted as champions of The National League South at the end of last season. This season, between mid-October and early November they won five consecutive league matches, but were defeated at home by a seventh tier side in the FA Cup. In ten league games they had scored 19 goals (only league leaders Torquay had more) but only two clubs had conceded in excess of Wealdstone's 20.

Notts were very good at home to Altrincham and Barnet in early October. In this game though, especially in the first half, they were even better and could have been four or five goals ahead by half time but for an inspired display by the Wealdstone goalkeeper – Isted. The most remarkable of his many first half saves came in the fifth minute when he made a remarkable double save. An excellent 50yd cross field pass by Rodrigues, from right to left, found Sam who moved forward and unleashed a powerful shot from the edge of the penalty area which Isted tipped on to the crossbar. From the rebound Wootton directed a header towards the corner of the net which Isted palmed over for a corner kick. Notts took the lead on 15 minutes when Isted dived to save another powerful shot, this time from Rodrigues, but the ball ran loose and Boldewijn was on hand to score easily from ten yards. Four minutes later Sam scored an excellent individual goal when he moved in from the left wing, dribbled past a defender, and from a tight angle smashed the ball into the far corner of the net. Just before the half hour Isted produced another fine double save, first from Sam and then the follow-up from Rodrigues. With the last kick of the first half Wealdstone almost scored when a curling shot from the edge of the penalty area flew inches wide of Slocombe's left hand post. A very impressive first half display by Notts who dominated throughout.

In the second half Notts were still good, particularly in the first fifteen minutes, but thereafter the game was more even. For their third goal, Boldewijn blocked a defensive clearance and the ball fell to Wootton. He passed to an unmarked Knowles who, with his first touch after coming on as a substitute, had an easy tap in from inside the six-yard box.

Before the current lockdown in England was introduced on 5 November, because of the second wave of the coronavirus (COVID-19) pandemic, Nottingham and Nottinghamshire were in Tier 3 restrictions, the most restrictive level.

At the end of November, the Government confirmed that the city and county would re-enter (the enhanced) Tier 3 restrictions when England's second lockdown ended on 2 December. This meant that Notts would not be permitted to welcome supporters back to Meadow Lane for the time being.

Elite football clubs based in Tier 1 and Tier 2 areas of the country would be permitted to play competitive matches in front of a limited number of supporters for the first time since the 2019-20 season was curtailed in March, but those in Tier 3 must continue to play behind closed doors.

Notts' CEO Jason Turner stated:

"Our supporters should rest assured that we will continue to plan for their return to Meadow Lane so we can act quickly when Nottingham's Tier 3 restrictions are lifted."

From Wednesday 2 December 2020 the Government definitions, as they applied to Large (Sporting) Events, were:

Public attendance at spectator sport and business events can resume inside and outside, subject to social contact rules, and limited to whichever is lower: 50% capacity, or either 4,000 people outdoors **(Tier 1 Medium Alert)** *or either 2000 people outdoors* **(Tier 2 High Alert)** *or 1000 people indoors.*

Tier 3: Very High alert

There should be no public attendance at spectator sport or indoor performances and large business events should not be taking place. Elite sport events may continue to take place without spectators.

Nottingham and Nottinghamshire	**Very high (Tier 3)**	There has been an improvement, but case rates remain very high in the over 60s at 211 per 100,000. The overall case rate is 244 per 100,000 and positivity is 10%. The proportion of hospital beds taken up by COVID-19 patients is high but appears to be falling.

In reality the Government placed almost everyone in Tiers 2 or 3 with only Cornwall, the Isles of Scilly and the Isle of Wight in Tier 1. Notts' next match, at Dagenham & Redbridge on the evening of Wednesday 2 December, was played in a Tier 2 area – the London Borough of Barking and Dagenham – so a restricted number of spectators were allowed to attend. However, The National League and D & R were unable to guarantee the stringent COVID-19 protocols wouldn't be compromised so the game was played behind closed doors.

| Match 10 | **Dagenham &** (18th) 0-0 Notts County (7th) | Played behind closed |
| Wed 2 Dec 2020 19:00 | **Redbridge** | doors |

Slocombe

Kelly-Evans   Rawlinson   Turner   Chicksen

Doyle (Capt.)   Reeves

Boldewijn (Walker 67')   Sam (O'Brien 82')   Rodrigues (Knowles 70')

Wootton

Subs: Pilling (Gk), O'Brien, Wolfe, Knowles, Walker

Just one change after the impressive victory over Wealdstone. Brindley was injured so Kelly-Evans moved to right back with Chicksen coming in at left back.

Notice the name Walker among the substitutes. Tom Walker, aged 24, was signed from League Two Harrogate Town two days ago on a five-week loan deal until 3January 2021. He joined Harrogate in the summer but, surprisingly, had been unable to command a regular first team place. Walker said his preferred position was right/left wing, or attacking from mid-field. Neal Ardley had been an admirer of the player for some time and saw him as a replacement for the injured Cal Roberts, whose groin injury was likely to keep him out of contention until the New Year.

Both last season's league games ended with a score line of 2-0, Notts winning at home but losing away. However, Notts won 2-1 at Meadow Lane in the second round of the FA Trophy. D & R had lost four of their eight league games this season and had scored only five times but had conceded only nine!

Notts made another very good start to the game with Sam and Rodrigues testing the home goalkeeper. With 12 minutes gone Doyle took a short corner to Boldewijn who passed to Reeves whose 20-yard shot hit a post. The quick tempo bombardment of the D & R goal continued as the first half progressed, but after half an hour D & R changed their shape and their play improved. Despite all Notts' domination, pressure (and chances) they nearly fell behind in the 40th minute when D & R had (what looked like) a good goal disallowed for hand ball. Notts should have taken the lead, or been given a penalty, with the second half two minutes old. Sam found Boldewijn with an excellent through ball. He squared it to Rodrigues who was pushed over as he was about to roll the ball into the net. So, no goal and the referee decided it wasn't a penalty. Notts continued to press but D & R gradually eased themselves into the game and on 75 minutes hit the post with a tremendous free kick from twenty-five yards. A few minutes later Notts had another nervy moment when D & R came close to taking the lead. However, Notts retaliated and with two minutes to go an O'Brien shot from the edge of the penalty area was deflected narrowly wide. Notts deserved to win, but at least they got a point and kept a 'clean sheet' for the second successive match.

NATIONAL LEAGUE TABLE Friday 4 December 2020			Home				Away					Overall						
	Team	P	W	D	L	F	A	W	D	L	F	A	W	D	L	F	A	GD	PT
1	Torquay United	10	3	1	0	6	2	5	0	1	16	6	8	1	1	22	8	14	25
2	Sutton United	11	3	1	1	10	3	4	1	1	9	9	7	2	2	19	12	7	23
3	Bromley	11	2	2	2	11	9	3	2	0	10	4	5	4	2	21	13	8	19
4	Altrincham	13	2	1	3	6	7	3	2	2	6	6	5	3	5	12	13	-1	18
5	Eastleigh	8	2	2	0	7	4	3	0	1	12	6	5	2	1	19	10	9	17
6	**Notts County**	**10**	**3**	**0**	**1**	**12**	**6**	**2**	**2**	**2**	**5**	**5**	**5**	**2**	**3**	**17**	**11**	**6**	**17**
7	Woking	11	3	2	1	9	4	2	0	3	8	9	5	2	4	17	13	4	17
8	Wrexham	11	3	1	2	7	3	2	1	2	6	6	5	2	4	13	9	4	17
9	Maidenhead United	11	2	1	2	9	11	3	1	2	6	8	5	2	4	15	19	-4	17
10	Wealdstone	12	3	1	2	14	15	2	1	3	6	10	5	2	5	20	25	-5	17
11	Solihull Moors	8	4	0	0	9	0	1	1	2	4	5	5	1	2	13	5	8	16
12	Hartlepool United	10	1	2	2	3	8	3	1	1	9	4	4	3	3	12	12	0	15
13	Stockport County	7	2	1	1	6	3	2	0	1	7	4	4	1	2	13	7	6	13
14	King's Lynn Town	11	2	1	3	10	14	2	0	3	7	14	4	1	6	17	28	-11	13
15	Aldershot Town	10	1	1	2	3	6	2	2	2	10	6	3	3	4	13	12	1	12
16	Halifax Town	10	2	2	2	10	7	0	2	2	1	3	2	4	4	11	10	1	10
17	Chesterfield	11	1	1	4	9	9	2	0	3	8	9	3	1	7	17	18	-1	10
18	Boreham Wood	9	1	1	2	1	2	1	2	2	6	5	2	3	4	7	7	0	9
19	Dagenham & Redbridge	9	1	2	1	2	2	1	1	3	3	7	2	3	4	5	9	-4	9
20	Barnet	10	1	1	3	3	10	1	1	3	7	14	2	2	6	10	24	-14	8
21	Weymouth	8	1	0	3	3	5	1	1	2	4	5	2	1	5	7	10	-3	7
22	Dover Athletic	9	2	0	3	5	13	0	0	4	1	11	2	0	7	6	24	-18	6
23	Yeovil Town	10	0	1	5	5	12	0	4	0	4	4	0	5	5	9	16	-7	5
24	Macclesfield Town (Expelled 12th October)	0	0	0	0	0	0	0	0	0	0	0	0	0	0	0	0	0	0

The uneven number of games played was due to postponements caused by the coronavirus pandemic.

Match 11 Sat 5 Dec 2020 15:00	Notts County (6th) 1-0 Woking (7th) Wootton 80'	Played behind closed doors

Slocombe

Brindley   Rawlinson   Turner   Kelly-Evans

Doyle (Capt.)   Reeves

Walker (Knowles 81')   Sam (Boldewijn 60')   Rodrigues (O'Brien 68')

Wootton

Subs: Pilling (Gk), Chicksen, O'Brien, Boldewijn, Knowles

There were two changes to the side held to a goalless draw by Dagenham & Redbridge. Brindley returned with Kelly-Evans reverting to left back at the expense of Chicksen. Tom Walker made his first start for Notts which meant Boldewijn was omitted.

Woking finished just below the play-off places last season, when Notts had a comprehensive 4-0 victory away from home but were held to a 1-1 at Meadow Lane. This season Woking had made a solid start in the league.

Woking were the first to threaten a goal when a powerful shot from 22 yards just cleared Notts' crossbar. Notts responded with a Walker shot which flew narrowly wide and a Wootton shot was deflected for a corner. Just before half time Walker dummied a defender, streaked away down the right wing, and produced a superb low cross but Sam arrived in the six yard box just too late and the chance was gone. Woking went close with the last action of the half when a long throw was headed backwards by Rawlinson and an attacker's header went inches over the crossbar. The second half was only eight minutes old when Notts had an opportunity to take the lead. Wootton was fouled in the penalty area and as the two penalty takers of last season had left Notts (Rose and Dennis) it was Wootton who stepped up to take the penalty. Unfortunately his shot wasn't the best and the Woking goalkeeper dived to his right to push the ball away for a corner. After this miss, and with the introduction of Boldewijn and O'Brien from the substitute's bench, Notts became more focused. Their increase in tempo paid off in the 80th minute, when Boldewijn let a Doyle pass bounce of his chest before he moved forward into the penalty area. With close control and strength he held off two defenders before side footing the ball to Wootton who scored easily from eight yards. Notts continued to apply pressure to the Woking defence, although Kelly-Evans made an excellent block after 85 minutes when Woking looked to have an opportunity to equalise. O'Brien then had a powerful shot deflected narrowly wide for a corner, and Notts had earned a significant victory.

In comparison to the four previous home games so far this season, this game was a more subdued affair, with defences often getting the upper hand. Goal scoring opportunities were in short supply. Woking gave a good account of themselves and provided a stern test of Notts' capabilities. Unbeaten in their last five games, with three successive clean sheets, Notts moved up to their highest position in the league this season, third.

Our charitable arm, Notts County Football in the Community, today (7 December 2020) become **Notts County Foundation**.

The rebrand was announced by the Foundation's CEO, Ian Boyd, who said: "As Notts County FC's charity, we are extremely proud of the community work we've been carrying out in the local area since 1989. Connected to the world's oldest professional football club, the work that we have undertaken has grown rapidly and will continue to increase as we fulfil the needs of our local community.

"Over the past 12 months we have initiated an extensive consultation exercise with beneficiaries and stakeholders. This consultation was wide-ranging and the feedback has directly impacted the strategic plans for the future. Pride in our relationship with the football club was a theme which resonated throughout the feedback; a relationship which we want to further strengthen going forward.

"The consultation also allowed us to hear that people were not fully aware of the breadth of work that we undertake within our community, nor its full impact. This encouraged us to reflect on our 'brand' and the message it sends; to consider raising our independent charitable profile and to draw further attention to the excellent work taking place across the city and the county of which the wider public is often unaware.

"We firmly believe that the time is now right for a rebrand in order to successfully communicate the outstanding work which we deliver through our many positive S.H.I.N.E. outcomes. Activities delivered throughout the following themes of: Sport, Health, Inclusion, NCS, Education and the operation of Portland Leisure Centre in the Meadows.

"I therefore take great pride in announcing that, as of today, our charity will now be known as Notts County Foundation. Today marks the start of our evolution as we celebrate our past history and successes as Football in the Community, and begin that transition across to the rebranded Foundation. There will be a coordinated set of promotional and delivery activities that will support this journey over the next twelve months.

"This refresh began in a pre-covid environment but is being delivered as the world around us is adapting to a new normal. The challenges we have and will continue to face as a result of the virus are significant. Being flexible and creative, whilst remaining true to our past will be important; as will practicing resilience for the future.

"If anything, the pandemic has brought some issues into sharper focus and strengthened our resolve to address them. Themes such as Equality, Diversity and Inclusion, challenging Health Inequalities, deepening our placed based approach, as we empower and co-create with communities, will all be key to our delivery going forward.

"We are an independent, regional sports development charity supporting the people of Nottinghamshire. We use the power of sport, physical activity and Notts County Football Club to engage and empower local communities and the individuals they serve. We are Notts County Foundation."

Notts County chief executive Jason Turner added: "On behalf of the football club I would like to congratulate the Foundation on their rebrand and wish them every success moving forward. We look forward to continuing close collaboration with our charitable arm to use the incredible Notts County brand as a force for good in the local community."

Match 12	Notts County (3rd) **0-1** Boreham Wood (17th)	Played behind closed
Tue 8 Dec 2020 19:45	goal 71'	doors

Slocombe

Brindley   Rawlinson   Turner   Kelly-Evans

Reeves   Doyle (Capt.)   O'Brien (Sam 77')

Walker (Rodrigues 72')   Wootton   Boldewijn

Subs: Pilling (Gk), Lacey, Rodrigues, Sam, Knowles

There were two changes to the side who defeated Woking three days ago. O'Brien returned in place of Rodrigues, and Boldewijn was preferred to Sam.

Last season Boreham Wood were beaten in the play-off semi-final by Harrogate, (Notts know what that feels like!). In the league Notts won 2-1 in the away fixture but were held to a 2-2 draw at Meadow Lane in late November. Although currently in the lower half of the league Boreham Wood's ten games had been close affairs with only nine scored and eight conceded, giving them the next to the best defensive record in the league. They had also reached the third round of the FA Cup.

On a cold, rainy, evening at Meadow Lane, Notts could (should) have scored twice in the first four minutes. Wootton headed a Reeves cross inches wide when well placed and moments later Boldewijn, after being released by O'Brien, muscled his way past two defenders into the penalty area to give himself a clear chance from 12 yards but the goalkeeper saved his shot with his legs.

For the rest of the first half Boreham Wood were in control and they put Notts under pressure. In the 24th minute a good shot from 15 yards hit a post with Slocombe beaten. However, just before half time, an excellent cross by Kelly-Evans just eluded the on rushing O'Brien as he arrived in the six-yard box.

Notts began the second half with purpose. A 25-yard shot by Brindley flew just wide of the far post and a few minutes later a similar shot from O'Brien rebounded of the goalkeeper and was scrambled clear. Boreham Wood then raised their game and, on the hour, a header direct from a corner kick was only just off target. Ten minutes later they took the lead when they directed a header from a free kick into the six-yard box for their centre half to steer home, yes, with a header! Following this set back Notts pushed forward and twenty-yard shots by Reeves and then Rodrigues were well saved by the goalkeeper, and an O'Brien shot was deflected into the side netting. Unfortunately, Notts' late pressure was in vain and Boreham Wood held on for victory in what had been an entertaining game.

Match 13 Tue 15 Dec 2020 19:45	**Notts County** (7th) **1-0 Stockport Co** (9th) Reeves 35'	Played behind closed doors (but televised by BT Sport)

Slocombe

Brindley   Rawlinson   Turner   Kelly-Evans

Reeves   Doyle (Capt.)   O'Brien

Boldewijn   Wootton   Rodrigues (Walker 75')

Subs: Lacey, Chicksen, Sam, Knowles, Walker
(no substitute goalkeeper)

The only change to the side who were defeated by Boreham Wood a week ago was Rodrigues in for Walker.

On Saturday 14 March (when the final National League fixtures of last season were played, before the rest of the season was cancelled due to the coronavirus pandemic) Stockport were in the last promotion play-off position (7th). The subsequent revision of the league table on a 'points per game' calculation meant they dropped to 8th. Because of the cancelled fixtures Notts only played Stockport once, a 1-1 draw at Meadow Lane on 6 August. To recap, that was Notts' first ever home game (attendance 5,820), and point, in non-league football. Jim O'Brien scored the goal. At the start of this season Notts and Stockport were the bookmaker's joint favourites to finish as champions.

Stockport were unbeaten since 31 October with victories in their last five league and FA Cup games, in which they scored thirteen goals. They also had the best defensive record in the league with only eight goals conceded, although because of coronavirus postponements they had only played nine league games to date. In the third round of the FA Cup they had been drawn at home to Premier League West Ham United.

The first effort on goal was from Stockport, when a good shot from the corner of the penalty area flew a yard past Slocombe's left hand post. Notts retaliated with two twenty yard shots, the first from Reeves which went narrowly wide, and the second from Wootton which the goalkeeper saved comfortably. Perhaps Stockport should have taken the lead in the 23rd minute when Rooney tried to place the ball from sixteen yards but his shot lacked power and Slocombe dived to his right and made a good save. Rodriques then made an excellent run from the half way line but his shot from the edge of the penalty area was saved.

Notts' took the lead after they had executed **fifteen** consecutive passes. Brindley ran into the penalty area to collect an excellent through ball (pass number thirteen) by Rodrigues. The Stockport full back should have dealt with the situation but he didn't and this allowed Brindley to pass to Wootton, who in turn passed to Reeves who then calmly side footed the ball into the corner of the net from twelve yards despite the presence of three defenders!

Notts were in control for most of a closely contested second half and Stockport were restricted to two off target attempts on goal. Two Wootton headers both came to nothing. A well-deserved win for Notts, who moved up to third again.

FA Trophy on Saturday, with the next league game a week later on Boxing Day.

FA Trophy 3rd Round Sat 19 Dec 2020 15:00	**Morpeth Town 0-3 Notts County** Sam 5' Graham 58' Knowles 63'	Played behind closed doors

<pre>
                          Pilling
   Brindley (Kelly-Evans 46')   Graham   Lacey   Chicksen
       O'Brien (Capt.)   Wolfe   Rodrigues (Boldewijn 65')
                     Walker   Knowles   Sam
</pre>

Subs: Kean (Gk), Rawlinson, Kelly-Evans, Doyle, Wootton, Boldewijn

There had been five rounds in the FA Trophy (three qualifying plus first and second rounds) before National League teams joined the competition. It is the equivalent of the FA Cup, but for non-league teams.

This FA Trophy (first/third round) fixture gave Neal Ardley the chance to get match fitness into two of the five injured players who had missed games - Lacey (heel) and Graham (back). Unfortunately, McCrory (knee), Thomas (kidney stone) and Roberts (groin) remained side-lined. He also took the opportunity to include players who had not had much game time in recent weeks. So, a much changed Notts team, and only three who played against Stockport County retained their place in the starting eleven. Goalkeeper Luke Pilling made his Notts debut and Matty Wolfe his first start.

Morpeth, in 16th position in the Northern Premier League the seventh tier of English football, two tiers below Notts, last played a league game nearly seven weeks ago, on 3 November. This was because of the coronavirus (COVID-19) restrictions and the suspension of the season. They had only been allowed to compete in the earlier (two qualifying) rounds of the FA Trophy. In the second of these they were scheduled to play at Blyth Spartans, but they had to forfeit the tie due to coronavirus in the squad.

Sam scored early when he received the ball from Walker on the edge of the penalty area and beat the goalkeeper at his near post with a well struck low shot. Notts increased their lead in the second half with two quick goals either side of the hour mark. First Graham stooped low at the back post to head home a Walker corner and five minutes later Notts scored again, this time from a counter attack after Sam collected a loose ball following a Morpeth corner kick and passed to Knowles who ran on and rounded the goalkeeper before placing the ball into the empty net. Just before the end Lacey denied Morpeth a consolation goal when he cleared a header off the goal line.

The pitch was playable but after all the recent rain it was soft and uneven, so another good performance by Notts on a difficult playing surface.

Later in the week there was disappointing news for Damien McCrory and Cal Roberts when it was announced that both players required operations. McCrory's opposite knee to the one which was operated on after the first lockdown had now 'broken down'. Roberts' was to rectify his groin problem.

Match 14	**Notts County** (4th) 0-1 **Hartlepool United** (3rd)	Played behind
Mon 28 Dec 2020 15:00	goal 19'	closed doors

Slocombe

Brindley　　Rawlinson　　Turner　　Kelly-Evans

Reeves

Doyle (Capt.)　　Rodrigues (Knowles 75')

Walker (Sam 65')　　Wootton　　Boldewijn

Subs: Lacey, Chicksen, O'Brien, Sam, Knowles
(no substitute goalkeeper)

Despite the good performance, with a win, at Morpeth in the FA Trophy, Neal Ardley reverted to ten of the eleven victorious over Stockport in the last league game a fortnight ago. The one change was Walker instead of O'Brien.

Notts failed to beat Hartlepool last season. They were held to a 2-2 draw at Meadow Lane and lost 2-0 in the away fixture. Hartlepool made a good start to the season, but since a defeat (0-5) at home to leaders Torquay Utd on 31 October their form had been mixed. However, they had won their last two league games – at home, to Stockport (4-0) and Halifax (3-1) on Boxing Day.

Notts started well and Boldewijn had two (off target) shots in the first five minutes. However, as the first half progressed Hartlepool became the more purposeful team, and after nineteen minutes they took the lead. In a sprint along the side of the penalty area Brindley was unable to prevent a forward from making an excellent low, fast, cross which evaded Slocombe and an onrushing attacker slotted the ball into the net from close range. Notts responded positively and an excellent free kick by Walker just evaded Rawlinson and Turner in the six-yard box. In a breakaway Walker ran from the halfway line but dragged his early 25 yard shot well wide.

Within three minutes of the start of the second half Hartlepool had a chance to increase their lead when Turner passed straight to a forward, unmarked on the edge of the penalty area. Fortunately, for Notts, he rushed his shot and the attempt went well wide. Shortly afterwards a Rodrigues shot hit a post and from the rebound Boldewijn teed up Doyle who fired the ball over the crossbar. From then on Notts dominated the remainder of the second half and created many opportunities to score, but in the 82nd minute Rawlinson, under pressure, headed the ball towards Turner who, in his attempt at a clearance, raised his foot to head height and kicked an opponent in the face. He was given a straight red card by the referee and sent off for dangerous play. In the final minute a centre by Reeves was headed on by Sam to Knowles who confidently found the corner of the net, but he was deemed to be (incorrectly) offside and the goal was disallowed. A combination of poor finishing, bad luck and incompetent officials meant Notts were unable to find an equaliser despite their dominance, especially in the second half.

Notts' last four league matches, at home because of coronavirus postponements at Yeovil and King's Lynn, had produced two 1-0 victories and two 0-1 defeats! (This was the fifth consecutive Hartlepool match when an opponent had been sent off).

With the turn of the year (2020 to 2021) it is an appropriate time to give a brief resume of the weeks since Notts returned to action, on 7 Novembers with a 1-0 defeat at Aldershot, following their coronavirus (COVID-19) outbreak. Two days before (5 November) Prime Minister Boris Johnson announced a four week national lockdown to combat a second wave of the pandemic. The first lockdown started on 23 March and was gradually eased as the summer progressed.

During this second coronavirus lockdown four fixtures were subsequently postponed by Notts' opponents: Stockport County (in the rearranged [home] game Notts won 1-0), Yeovil (away), and King's Lynn [home and away] over Christmas and the New Year. Notts had therefore had a spasmodic stop/start existence in recent weeks, as had most other teams in The National League. At least the season wasn't suspended as it was in March. This time the Premier League, the EFL, The National League and National Leagues North and South continued. Premier League and

Championship fixtures had few postponements, but Leagues One and Two and The National League(s) were not so fortunate with games called off, sometimes at very short notice.

The November lockdown ended in early December but on the first working day of 2021, Monday 4 January, Boris Johnson introduced a third national lockdown for England and instructed people to stay at home to control the virus, protect the National Health Service and save lives. The following was taken from the www.gov.uk website:

> *The decision follows a rapid rise in infections, hospital admissions and case rates across the country, and our hospitals are now under more pressure than they have been at any other point throughout the pandemic.*
>
> *This drastic jump in cases has been attributed to the new variant of COVID-19, which our scientists have now confirmed is between 50 and 70 per cent more transmissible.*
>
> *On 4 January, there were 26,626 Covid patients in hospital in England, an increase of over 30% in one week, and the April 2020 hospital admissions peak has now been surpassed by 40%.*
>
> *The case rate in England up to 29 December was 478.5 per 100k, three times higher than on 1 December when the case rate was 151.3.*
>
> *On 3 January, 454 deaths were reported, with 4,228 over the last 7 days – a 24% increase on the previous 7 days.*
>
> *This afternoon, the four UK Chief Medical Officers have advised that the COVID threat level should move from level four to level five, indicating that if action is not taken NHS capacity may be overwhelmed within 21 days.*

Obviously the full list and description as to what people can and cannot do was long and exhaustive. The above illustrates the very serious situation in England (and Scotland, Wales and Northern Ireland). Although not very important in the context of everyday life, once gain the leagues mentioned above were allowed to fulfil their fixtures 'behind closed doors'. Prior to this lockdown a few clubs, in areas least infected, had been allowed a very limited number of spectators inside their stadiums provided stringent restrictions and protocols were followed.

Notts tried to continue as normal, but on 5 January they announced that Saturday's fixture at Eastleigh had been postponed:

> *"….following a Covid-19 case in the Eastleigh camp. The south-coast side were due to travel to Stockport County this evening but the game was called off following a positive test result. The league have now informed both clubs that Saturday's fixture cannot go ahead."*

A decision regarding the immediate future of two on loan player's, Matty Wolfe and Tom Walker, whose deals ended on 3 January, was announced. The pair had been on loan at Meadow Lane from Barnsley and Harrogate respectively.

Despite making only two appearances so far this season, Wolfe had impressed manager Neal Ardley with his development since his mid-October arrival and Barnsley had agreed he could stay with Notts for the remainder of the season.

Walker, who had made six appearances as cover for Cal Roberts, had decided to return to Harrogate.

> *Ardley said: "Tom indicated to us that he would prefer to return to Harrogate to fight for his place and we fully respect his decision. He leaves with our best wishes. Cal has been working hard in the gym and is making good progress, so we're hopeful Tom's departure shouldn't hit us too hard. With Matty, we're really looking forward to continuing our work with him and I would like to thank Barnsley for trusting us with his continued development. It's been a challenging season so far for him. He caught coronavirus at an unfortunate time. We value him as an important part of our squad and can see him learning every day from the likes of Michael Doyle, Jim O'Brien and Jake Reeves. Opportunities will come for Matty between now and the end of the season and we're excited to see more of him. I'm in regular dialogue with our owners to explore ways we could further improve the squad – we're assessing our options and if we feel we can do something to benefit the club, we'll act."*

One week later two "on loan until the end of the season" players arrived.

Inih Effiong, 29 years of age and 6'4", joined from League Two Stevenage. With two thirds of the season still to be played, and a congested fixture list, Neal Ardley wanted to ease the pressure on Kyle Wootton. Effiong was an experienced player. The vast majority of his 400 plus career games had been in non-league football, including 120 appearances in The National League (35 goals scored).

Calvin Miller, 23 years of age who joined from League Two Harrogate, for whom he signed in the summer. A skilful forward who can play on either wing, and provide cover at full back. He made his debut for boyhood club Celtic in the Scottish Premier League four years ago and gained further experience with loan spells at Dundee and Ayr United. Miller was a Scotland U21 international.

FA Trophy 4th Round	**Stockport County 1-2 Notts County**	Played behind closed
Sat 16 Jan 2021 15:00	goal 37' Knowles 32'	doors
	Wootton 89'	

Pilling

Brindley   Graham   Lacey (Rawlinson 57')   Miller

Reeves (Capt.) (Doyle 68')   Wolfe   Rodrigues

Boldewijn (Wootton 51')   Knowles   Sam

Subs: Slocombe (Gk), Rawlinson, Kelly-Evans, Chicksen, Doyle, O'Brien, Wootton

Effiong was cup-tied. He played in the third round when on loan at Barnet. For Ben Turner this game was the first of his three-match suspension after being sent off against Hartlepool.

Neal Ardley made three changes to the team victorious at Morpeth, in round three, a month ago. Calvin Miller, on his debut, replaced Chicksen as a wing back. Reeves and Boldewijn came in for O'Brien and Walker.

Due to two coronavirus postponements this was Notts' first match of 2021.

Since Stockport were defeated (1-0) at Meadow Lane in the league a month ago, they had played four league games (lost one, won one and drawn two). In The National League table Stockport and Notts have almost identical records. Stockport are 4th with 24 points and Notts are 7th with 23 points. Both have played 14 games with a goal difference of plus six.

Last Monday evening, on a heavy pitch in pouring rain, Stockport lost (0-1) at home to Premiership side West Ham United in the third round of the FA Cup.

The first half hour of this game was largely uneventful and contested in midfield. However, Notts then took the lead when Boldewijn collected the ball near the half-way line and ran to the edge of the penalty area. His attempted pass to Knowles bounced off a defender but Rodrigues continued the attack and successfully passed to Knowles who stabbed the ball into the net from ten yards. Five minutes later Stockport equalised when a corner kick was headed on from the near post to the back post where the ball was ushered over the line. Just before half-time Pilling made an excellent save (with his feet) when he advanced as a forward shot for goal.

The second half was fairly even although Stockport hit a post with twenty minutes remaining and soon afterwards Pilling made another good save when he pushed a shot away for a corner. Five minutes from full time Stockport missed a close range opportunity to win the game. With penalties looking certain (no extra time or replay this season) Wootton scored Notts' winner when, with strength, he dispossessed a defender and his 25 yard shot was deflected into the net with the home goalkeeper stranded.

This game turned out to be central defender Sam Graham's last for Notts. Two days later it was announced that, with his loan period now at end, he would be returning to his parent club, Premier League Sheffield United.

Match 15 Sat 23 Jan 2021 15:00	**Notts County** (7th) **0-0 Torquay United** (1st)	Played behind closed doors

Slocombe

Brindley (Miller 87')   Rawlinson   Lacey   Kelly-Evans

Reeves   Doyle (Capt.)

Boldewijn (O'Brien 76')   Rodrigues

Effiong (Sam 62')   Wootton

Subs: O'Brien, Wolfe, Sam, Knowles, Miller
(no substitute goalkeeper)

For Notts' first league game of 2021 Neal Ardley reverted to his 'league eleven' following last weekend's FA Trophy victory. However, there were two changes from their last league game at home to Hartlepool. Lacey was in for the suspended Turner and Effiong (his Notts debut) replaced Walker, now back at Harrogate after his loan spell.

Torquay finished in the bottom half at the end of last seasons curtailed campaign, when Notts only played them once and secured a 2-0 victory at Meadow Lane. However, this season they currently had an eight-point lead at the top of the league, with 38 points from 17 games, and were the only team with a positive goal difference in double figures, +21. (+6 for Notts). They had scored an impressive 38 goals. Notts' recent defensive record of only two goals conceded in their last six league games (three conceded in their last eight league and cup fixtures) therefore indicated an intriguing confrontation. A concern for Notts was the fact that they had scored only two goals in their last five league games, the last four of which had been at Meadow Lane. Like Notts, Torquay had reached the fifth round of the FA Trophy.

This game, between two good teams who obviously respected each other, was a competitive encounter but most of the action was in a fiercely contested midfield. When it came to the final third of the pitch there was a lack of creativity, with both sides unable to generate more than a few clear-cut openings. There were chances, of course, but these were squandered.

Neither side hit a post/crossbar, had an attempt cleared off the goal line, had a goal disallowed, and the work required of both goalkeepers could be described as "routine". On the BBC Sport website the report (supplied by the Press Association) of the game was summarised with the comment "both sides struggled to create chances in a game lacking in inspiration". In the end, although a disappointment for Notts, a draw was a fair result.

Notts' last five league games had now been at Meadow Lane, with a record of:

W2 D1 L2 Scored 2 Conceded 2. The game prior to the five at home was a 0-0 away draw! Therefore in their last six league games they had W2 D2 L2 F2 A2.

The stop/start circumstances since mid-December, due to postponements caused by the coronavirus (COVID-19) pandemic, had hindered Notts. Near the end of January and only one third of their way through The National League season!

The Premier League, Championship and Leagues One & Two were half way through their fixtures. However, in The National League the number of fixtures completed by clubs ranged from 13 to 19. National Leagues North and South, with a suspension of fixtures currently in force from 23 January to 2 February, were even further behind with a range of games played 11 to 17 and there was speculation that their season may be brought to a conclusion and declared null and void. The number of postponements, initially because of the lockdown/coronavirus pandemic, had increased in recent weeks due to wintry weather – waterlogged, frozen or snow covered pitches.

A snow covered Meadow Lane on Monday 25 January

Wes Thomas' last game for Notts was at Aldershot on 7 November, when Notts returned to action following their coronavirus outbreak. However, more illness together with continued concerns about coronavirus (COVID-19) and its impact on him and his family prompted Thomas to ask for permission to train away from the rest of the players. Notts agreed to his request and created a bespoke fitness programme in a bid to keep him fit in the hope he would return to action when he felt it was safe to do so. However, on Monday 25th Notts issued the following statement:

> *We have reluctantly accepted Wes Thomas' request to terminate his contract. The forward, who joined us in 2019, cited family reasons behind his decision and departs with our best wishes for the future. This season he had made four league appearances without scoring. Last season he made 37 league and cup appearances and scored ten goals, all in the league.*

On the subject of COVID-19, the next day (26 January) the Government announced that the UK had passed the grim milestone of 100,000 coronavirus deaths since the pandemic reached our shores approximately one year ago!

Although life had to carry on, when you digest the above statistic it puts Wes Thomas' decision into context.

Following snowfall over the Midlands, Solihull informed Notts that their pitch was unlikely to be fit for the fixture on the evening of Tuesday 26 January. With the weather forecast good in the short term Notts were confident they could clear Meadow Lane to allow the game to go ahead if the kick-off was delayed 24 hours. With league approval this was confirmed and the fixtures were reversed with Notts instead travelling to Solihull on the evening of Tuesday 13 April.

Match 16	**Notts County** (8th) **2-0 Solihull Moors** (7th)	Played behind closed
Wed 27 Jan 2021 19:45	Wootton 79' & 87'	doors

Slocombe

Kelly-Evans   Rawlinson   Lacey   Miller

Reeves   Doyle (Capt.)   O'Brien (Rodrigues 67')

Boldewijn

Effiong (Knowles 67')   Wootton

Subs: Chicksen, Rodrigues, Wolfe, Sam, Knowles
(no substitute goalkeeper)

Near Ardley made two changes to the team which drew 0-0 with Torquay. Brindley (badly bruised, cut and swollen nose) was replaced by Miller, with Kelly-Evans moved to the right hand side of the back four, and O'Brien was preferred to Rodrigues.

Solihull finished just below the play-off places at the end of last season. Their results against Notts were 0-0 at Meadow Lane with Notts winning the away fixture 1-0. They currently lay one place above Notts with 25 points from 14 games and a goal difference of +7. (Notts 24 points from 15 games, goal difference +6). Both have an excellent defensive record this season with only 13 league goals conceded. Solihull had won three of their last four league games.

Solihull started the game impressively and in the first minute a 25 yard shot flew inches wide of Slocombe's right hand post. Two minutes later, from a corner kick, a header just cleared the Notts crossbar. They continued to dominate the first half and on 32 minutes they should have taken the lead. A sequence of incisive passes arrived at the feet of an unmarked forward ten yards from goal, but a tame shot gave Slocombe the chance to save at the second attempt. Although Notts had plenty of midfield possession their attacking threat was disappointing. The Solihull goalkeeper had a very quiet first half.

Solihull started the second half as they had started the first and Slocombe was in action on a couple of occasions. However, Notts then began to be more imaginative going forward and with 63 minutes played almost took the lead when an excellent low cross from Boldewijn, into the six yard box, was ushered into the goalkeeper's hands by a defender with Effiong in attendance. After 76 minutes a 20 yard shot by Kelly-Evans hit the top of the crossbar. Three minutes later Notts took the lead. Boldewijn received a pass (Notts' ninth in succession) turned and ran with determination into the penalty area before he slid the ball to Wootton who stroked it into the net from near the penalty spot. Notts sealed victory with three minutes of normal time to play. A Kelly-Evans pass found Knowles in the penalty area and he pulled the ball back to Rodrigues. He out manoeuvred three defenders before he squared the ball to Wootton who made no mistake from six yards.

A much improved display by Notts in the second half when good team work created two excellent goals, the second of which involved both substitutes. They have now conceded only three goals in their last ten league and cup games.

| Match 17 | Weymouth (21ˢᵗ) 0-1 Notts County (7ᵗʰ) | Played behind closed |
| Sat 30 Jan 2021 15:00 | Sam 51' | doors |

Slocombe

Kelly-Evans   Rawlinson   Lacey   Miller

Reeves   Doyle (Capt.)   Rodrigues (O'Brien 74')

Boldewijn   Sam (Effiong 74')

Wootton

Subs: Turner, O'Brien, Wolfe, Effiong, Knowles
(no substitute goalkeeper)

Neal Ardley made two changes to the team which beat Solihull. Rodrigues replaced O'Brien and Sam was preferred to Effiong.

Notts' last away league game was nearly two months ago, on 2 December. Their away record so far this season is: P6 W2 D2 L2 F5 A5.

This was the first ever meeting between the two clubs. At the end of last season Weymouth were promoted from The National League South when they were victorious in the play-off final. They had found life more difficult this season and had won only four of 18 games, although they had earned victories in their last two league games without conceding a goal. However, in eleven home games they had suffered eight defeats and conceded 24 goals in the process!

In conditions not ideal for good football – an overcast, wet and cold afternoon with a blustery easterly wind – Notts started brightly, and with eight minutes played Boldewijn cut in from the right to send a low shot wide of the far post. Ten minutes later he had a better shot from the edge of the penalty area which the goalkeeper tipped over the crossbar. On the half hour a good Kelly-Evans cross found Wootton but his header lacked power and was easily saved. Although Notts dominated the first half it was by no means one sided and Weymouth looked dangerous on the counterattack.

The second half was only six minutes old when Notts took the lead. Sam collected a pass from Rodrigues on the halfway line and ran down the left into the penalty area from where he had a shot-cum-cross which was deflected as a defender tackled him and the ball flew over the goalkeeper into the net. Five minutes later he nearly made it two when a powerful low 20-yard shot went just wide. In the last half hour Weymouth were denied an equaliser when Slocombe made two good saves. A loose throw out by the home goalkeeper gave Notts possession but Rodrigues was unable to capitalise and the 'keeper redeemed himself with a good save. Thereafter Weymouth continued to press for the equaliser but Notts stood firm and collected three valuable points.

A hard earned victory for Notts who denied a spirited Weymouth team.

On Monday 1 February The National League issued the following:

The National League has distributed resolutions this evening for Member Clubs to consider the outcome of the 2020/21 season.

The resolutions are formed of four parts: one Special Resolution and three Ordinary Resolutions based on the outcome of the first. A Special Resolution requires a 75% majority to be passed, whereas an Ordinary Resolution requires a more than 50% majority. Resolution 1 and 4 votes will be counted under prescribed voting conditions. Resolution 2 and 3 will be counted with one vote per Member Club.

Should Resolution 1 pass, Resolution 2 and 3 will be counted, with Resolution 4 disregarded. Should Resolution 1 be voted against, Resolution 4 will be counted, with Resolution 2 and 3 votes disregarded.

Under The National League's Articles of Association, Member Clubs have 28 days to return voting submissions.

The resolutions are as follows:

Resolution 1 (All Clubs)

That Resolution 2 about whether to end the 2020/21 Playing Season of The National League (Step 1) be taken only by Clubs in The National League and that Resolution 3 about whether to end the 2020/21 Playing Season of The National League North and The National League South (Step 2) be taken only by Clubs that play in The National League North or The National League South with votes cast for Resolution 3 being counted on a one member, one vote basis for National League North and National League South Clubs.

Resolution 2 (National League Only)

That, conditional upon Resolution 1 being passed, the 2020/21 Playing Season of The National League (Step 1) shall immediately end on the date this Resolution 2 is passed and be declared null and void and subject to the approval of The Football Association, those Regulations that provide for promotion and relegation to and from Step 1 be suspended for the 2020/21 Playing Season.

Resolution 3 (National League North and South Only)

That, conditional upon Resolution 1 being passed, the 2020/21 Playing Season of The National League North and The National League South (Step 2) shall immediately end on the date this Resolution 3 is passed and be declared null and void and subject to the approval of The Football Association those Regulations that provide for promotion and relegation to and from Step 2 be suspended for the 2020/21 Playing Season.

Resolution 4 (All Clubs)

That conditional upon Resolution 1 not being passed, the 2020/21 Playing Seasons of The National League (Step 1) and The National League North and The National League South (Step 2) shall immediately end on the date this Resolution 4 is passed and be declared null and void and subject to the approval of The Football Association, those Regulations that provide for promotion to and relegation from Step 1 and Step 2 be suspended for the 2020/21 Playing Season.

On Friday 5 February the Notts board of directors issued their response:

*"We have voted **for** Special Resolution One and **against** Ordinary Resolutions Two and Four, meaning we believe the season should continue and that clubs should decide the outcome of their own divisions.*

We look forward to learning the full results of the vote and hopefully continuing our push for promotion."

FA Trophy 5th Round Sat 6 Feb 2021 13:00	**Havant and Waterlooville 2-2 Notts County** goals 33', 48' Wolfe 14' Knowles (pen) 71' **Notts won the penalty shoot-out 4-2**	Played behind closed doors

Pilling
Brindley   Turner   Lacey   Barnett
O'Brien (Capt.)   Wolfe
Miller (Boldewijn 64')   Chicksen (Rodrigues 64')
Knowles   Sam (Palmer 64')

Subs: Brooks (Gk), Kelly-Evans, Reeves, Rodrigues, Boldewijn, Palmer

Effiong cup-tied. The game was played on a 3G (artificial grass) pitch.

Neal Ardley included a mixture of his 'league' and 'cup' squads, but he obviously also had player rotation in mind because of the scheduled fixture congestion in the weeks and months ahead – dependant on the outcome of The National League resolutions! A debut was given to 21 year old Jordan Barnett, signed from League Two Oldham Athletic earlier in the week on a contract until the end of the season. A versatile left sided player, his usual position was left back but he could play in midfield or on the wing. This season he had made 25 appearances for Oldham in all competitions. Among Notts' substitutes were forward Tyreace Palmer (what a debut he had!), captain of Notts' under 18s team, and young goalkeeper Tiernan Brooks.

Due to the recent two week suspension of fixtures for National Leagues North and South, because of issues (funding, with some clubs threatening not to fulfil fixtures) caused by the coronavirus (COVID-19) pandemic, this was Havant and Waterlooville's first game since Tuesday 19 January. They had been defeated (both 2-1) in their last two National League South league games, before the suspension, and were currently in ninth position. In the previous round Altrincham forfeited the cup-tie due to their coronavirus outbreak.

Notts took the lead when Wolfe scored his first Notts goal after Knowles squared the ball to him near the six yard box. H & W equalised when a quick free kick to a forward caught Notts unprepared and he took advantage with a shot from 18 yards. Three minutes into the second half a header direct from a corner put H & W ahead. Five minutes after he came off the substitute's bench for his Notts debut Palmer was fouled in the penalty area (the H & W defender was sent off) and Knowles equalised with the spot kick. Palmer had only been on the pitch for 22 minutes before he was sent off when he received a second yellow card for a foul on the goalkeeper – his first yellow card had been for simulation to obtain a penalty. So, both teams down to ten men! Rodrigues should have won the game for Notts with the last kick of the match in the 95th minute. With no extra time this meant the game was settled by penalty kicks. Both teams missed their first penalty (O'Brien hit a post, Pilling hade a good save). Knowles, Boldewijn and Rodrigues then scored before Pilling saved H & W's fourth penalty. Brindley's kick put Notts into the quarter-final of the FA Trophy. Phew!

Match 18	**Notts County** (6th) **3-1 Dagenham & Redbridge** (17th)		
Tue 9 Feb 2021 18:00	Wootton 10', 45'+3 Rodrigues 34'	goal 90'+1	Played behind closed doors

```
                       Slocombe
     Kelly-Evans    Rawlinson      Lacey       Barnett
                 Reeves    Doyle (Capt.)
                Boldewijn      Rodrigues
           Knowles (Effiong 75')   Wootton
```

Subs: Brindley, Turner, O'Brien, Sam, Effiong
(no substitute goalkeeper)

Miller and Wolfe were not considered for "personal reasons".

Barnett made his league/home debut. Knowles was given his second start of the season following good form in the FA Trophy matches and when coming on as a substitute in recent league games.

Notts drew 0-0 at D & R on the evening of 2 December. In an inconsistent season to date, one of D & R's four away victories was a surprise 1-0 win at runaway league leaders Torquay United in mid December – achieved in a game they had a player sent off in the 41st minute, so they know how to win with ten men! Although they had scored four goals in their last two games (both 2-2 draws) they had only scored 18 in 19 league games.

Notts' last game at Havant and Waterlooville three days ago, particularly the second half, was an exciting spectacle, but this game was even better. Read on.

On a freezing evening with snow showers, the first half was one of the most dramatic 45 minutes in Notts County's history! Notts took the lead in the tenth minute. A brilliant cross by Rodrigues was headed by Knowles and the goalkeeper made a superb save but Wootton was on hand to stab the loose ball into the net from six yards. Eight minutes later Notts' goalkeeper Sam Slocombe was sent off. After losing control of the ball at his feet, following a back pass, he fouled a D & R player in the penalty area. The referee awarded a penalty and adjudged Slocombe's lunge to be dangerous play and he was shown a red card. Neal Ardley had again not named a substitute goalkeeper – a calculated risk to allow more flexibility for outfield changes. Following a delay while Notts re-organised, Captain Michael Doyle (39 years of age and 5'9" tall, so not the youngest or tallest goalkeeper) took over in goal. The penalty kick was taken by their top scorer but his shot smacked against the right hand post and rebounded to him without any other player touching the ball so Notts were awarded a free kick.

Throughout the remainder of the first half Notts were brilliant. They continued to attack and after 34 minutes they increased their lead. Rodrigues collected the ball 40 yards from goal, powered forward past defenders, and unleashed a 20 yard thunderbolt which flew into the roof of the net. During the five minutes of time added at the end of the first half Boldewijn ran from the centre circle to the edge of the penalty area before he slid a pass to Wootton who curled his shot into the top corner of the net from 15 yards.

As snow fell, and the pitch became whiter and whiter, Notts remained in control throughout the second half. Wootton should have completed his hat-trick three minutes after the restart, when Boldewijn teed up the ball for him inside the penalty area, but with time and space to shoot he skied the ball high and wide. Knowles and Boldewijn also had chances to increase Notts' lead. Despite playing with ten men for most of the game Neal Ardley made only one change – substitute Effiong replaced Knowles with 15 minutes remaining.

Dagenham & Redbridge scored a consolation goal in added time when a speculative low shot from 20 yards, although not very powerful, crept passed the Notts defence on its way into the corner of the net. Unfortunately it meant Michael Doyle didn't keep the 'clean sheet' his faultless display deserved. For Notts it would have been a fourth consecutive league game without conceding a goal – although it was their fourth straight win in league and cup.

Michael Doyle about to face
the penalty at the kop end

The commitment, aptitude and professionalism of every Notts player was excellent. What a shame no supporters were there to witness such a magnificent display.

One final word about Michael Doyle. Just over a year ago, at Meadow Lane on 11 January 2020, he launched his exocet missile shot to score from the half way line in the 90th minute of the second round of the FA Trophy – to give Notts a 2-1 win…over Dagenham & Redbridge!

Match 19	King's Lynn Town (21st) 0-1 Notts County (5th)	Played behind
Tue 16 Feb 2021 19:45	Reeves 54'	closed doors

                                      Pilling

Kelly-Evans   Rawlinson   Lacey   Barnett

                Reeves   Doyle (Capt.)

Boldewijn (Effiong 83')   Rodrigues (Turner 83')

      Knowles (Miller 69')   Wootton

Subs: Turner, O'Brien, Sam, Effiong, Miller
(no substitute goalkeeper)

Brindley was not considered due to a groin injury. The only change to the side victorious over Dagenham & Redbridge was Luke Pilling, who was making his Notts league debut, in goal for the suspended Sam Slocombe.

Last season The National League North was abandoned due to the coronavirus (COVID-19) pandemic. At that time King's Lynn were in second position, two points behind the leaders with two games in hand. The final league table was based on a points-per-game basis, which resulted in King's Lynn being declared champions with promotion to the National League. This season their home record had been poor with only two wins in nine games. In a sequence since the end of November they had won only two of eleven league and cup games including defeat in their last three league games.

The first chance of the game came after eight minutes when a good cross by Kelly-Evans found Rodrigues but his downward header bounced into the arms of the goalkeeper. Fifteen minutes later an excellent free kick by Barnett brushed against a post with the goalkeeper beaten. King's Lynn then forced Pilling into his first real save and as half-time approached one effort, from 15 yards, went wide and another forced Pilling into a good save. From the resultant corner and goalmouth scramble Lacey headed off the goal line.

Notts took the lead nine minutes into the second half when Reeves struck a thunderous 25 yard shot which swerved into the far top corner of the net - a goal of the season contender. Knowles nearly put Notts further ahead but his low cross cum shot, from inside the penalty area, whistled wide of the far post. From then on King's Lynn pressed hard for the equaliser. Pilling made a brilliant save and a few minutes later a low cross flashed through Notts' six yard box. Notts responded with a dangerous Barnett free kick from the left which just evaded Wootton and Rawlinson and went out for a goal kick. In the last minute King's Lynn wasted another good scoring opportunity when a shot from 15 yards was ballooned over the crossbar.

Although the victory moved Notts up to third in the table, with games in hand, their overall performance was very disappointing. This was reflected by Neal Ardley in his post-match interview:

> "We didn't deserve to win, the best team lost. At times, other than at the start of the second half, we were loose and at sixes and sevens. We got worse as the game went on."

On Thursday 18 February The National League issued the following statement:

Earlier this month, The National League distributed four resolutions for Member Clubs to consider the outcome of the 2020/21 season.

With relevant voting thresholds now met for each resolution, The National League can confirm the outcome of this process as follows.

Resolution One

In summary: Steps 1 and 2 to be split in deciding the outcome of 2020/21 Playing Season. As a Special Resolution, a voting percentage of 75% or higher under standardised National League voting criteria was required to pass.

*[Step 1] National League: (**for**) 21- (**against**) 0*
[Step 2] National League North: 16-6
[Step 2] National League South: 9-12

Result: Passed

As a result, **Resolution Four is disregarded***.*

Resolution Two (National League only)

In summary: The National League 2020/21 Playing Season (Step One) to be declared null and void. A minimum 51% majority was required for Resolution Two to pass.

National League: 7-13

Result: Not Passed

As a result, The National League National Division will continue to operate for the remainder of the season.

Resolution Three (National League North and South only)

In summary: The National League North and South 2020/21 Playing Season (Step Two) to be declared null and void. A minimum 51% majority was required for Resolution Three to pass.

National League North: 15-7
National League South: 9-12

Result: Passed

Resolution is passed and consequently the season at Step Two is null and void.

Note – There are 2 votes from the National Division that have not yet been cast, however, the outcome of the resolutions cannot be affected by these votes, however they are cast.

With the voting procedure now closed, National League North and South fixtures will cease with immediate effect.

The Board will take the resolution outcome to The Football Association for ratification. This will include dialogue regarding promotion and relegation.

There were therefore at least <u>seven</u> clubs in Step 1 who voted for the season to be declared null and void. Presumably one of those clubs was bottom of the league Dover Athletic who had already ceased playing their fixtures.

Notts were happy:

Our board of directors have released a statement following The National League's announcement that our season will continue.

We are very pleased that the league's consultation of member clubs in relation to the outcomes of the 2020-21 campaign will result in step one of The National League continuing. This, we feel, is a conclusion which protects the competition's integrity and rewards the efforts of all clubs who have imparted great effort into the season so far. We're also delighted for our loyal supporters who have backed us so staunchly from afar.

It is noted that The National League have now asked the Football Association to ratify the outcome of this vote and that dialogue is set to take place between the league and FA regarding promotion. We look forward to hearing more in due course.

For now, however, we would like to congratulate Neal Ardley and the team on their excellent recent form and wish them well for Saturday's exciting derby against Chesterfield.

Match 20 Sat 20 Feb 2021 15:00	**Notts County** (3rd) **0-1 Chesterfield** (17th) goal 31'	Played behind closed doors

Pilling

Kelly-Evans   Rawlinson   Lacey   Miller (Effiong 86')

Reeves   Doyle (Capt.)

Boldewijn   Rodrigues

Wootton   Sam (Knowles 73')

Subs: Turner, O'Brien, Effiong, Knowles, Wolfe
(no substitute goalkeeper)

There were two changes from the team victorious at King's Lynn. Miller (at left back) for Barnett, whose accumulation of yellow cards (all but one at his previous club Oldham Athletic) had resulted in a one match suspension, and Sam replaced Knowles.

Since Notts visited Chesterfield at the end of November (Notts won 3-2 with two goals in time added at the end of the second half) Chesterfield had been defeated only once in eleven league and FA Trophy matches. However, due to a coronavirus (COVID-19) outbreak in the club (the reason they had to forfeit their fifth round FA Trophy fixture) and bad weather, their last game was on 30 January.

Notts made a positive start. In the first five minutes they had three attempts on the Chesterfield goal. A powerful long range shot by Reeves flew well wide. Sam tried to lob the goalkeeper but the ball landed on the roof of the net. The effort by Rodrigues was the best – an 18 yard shot which just cleared the crossbar, after Boldewijn had created the opportunity. However, from then on it was Chesterfield who dominated the remainder of the first half, with Pilling and the Notts defence under almost constant pressure. On the half hour Miller was shown a yellow card for a bad foul. The subsequent free kick was lifted into the six yard box, where the ball evaded everyone and skidded on into the corner of the net. During the half Chesterfield had a total of nine corner kicks and their long throw specialist hurled the same number of throw-in's into the penalty area. Notts offered little in return.

Notts gave an improved performance in the second half, and dominated possession, but for all their pressure (including six corner kicks) they failed to create any clear cut chances – the final pass often lacked quality. The best chance almost fell to Knowles, but the goalkeeper was quick to leave his area and fly kick the ball away, following an excellent through ball by Rodrigues. Chesterfield nearly added to their lead towards the end but poor finishing and a good Pilling save, in the 96th minute, meant the second half was goalless.

Notts have the best defensive record in The National League, and in possession they look good, but 26 goals in 20 league games is an indication that some improvement is required in front of goal. In their last eleven league games (eight of them at Meadow Lane) they have scored only nine goals, with just four conceded.

| **Match 21** | **Stockport County** (6th) 0-0 **Notts County** (5th) | Played behind |
| Tue 23 Feb 2021 19:45 | | closed doors |

Pilling

Kelly-Evans   Rawlinson   Lacey   Barnett

Doyle (Capt.)   Wolfe (Knowles 78')   O'Brien

Boldewijn   Rodrigues (Roberts 78')

Wootton

Subs: Turner, Sam, Roberts, Knowles, Miller
(no substitute goalkeeper)

There were three changes to the team defeated by Chesterfield. Barnett returned after suspension in place of Miller. O'Brien replaced the ever present Reeves. Wolfe made his league debut, with Sam relegated to substitute. Also on the substitutes bench was Roberts, who had been out injured since the end of November. In the Stockport side was forward Tom Walker who made six appearances for Notts in December when on loan from Harrogate.

This was the third meeting between the two clubs since mid-December. Notts won the two previous games: 1-0 at Meadow Lane in the league and 2-1 at Stockport in the fourth round of the FA Trophy in mid-January. Five days after that defeat Stockport sacked their manager. They had played two games more than Notts to obtain the same number of points (36). Their February form had been poor: P5 W1 D2 L2 F1 A3 - the one goal was scored over five and a half hours ago (337 minutes)!

On a wet and windy evening, Pilling had some luck in the eighth minute when he attempted to punch clear a cross but the ball spun away for a corner. The first significant action of the game occurred in the 28th minute when Stockport had a goal disallowed. Pilling made a good save although the ball ran loose and was stabbed into the net, but the goal was ruled offside. Just before half time Notts had their first attempt on goal when a twenty five yard shot from Doyle cleared the crossbar.

Stockport made a good start to the second half and should have taken the lead after 55 minutes. Kelly-Evans failed to control the ball, near the half way line but in the Stockport half, and a forward was put through on goal for a one-on-one with Pilling but the Notts goalkeeper timed his dive and saved the shot. Soon after Notts had another escape. Following a corner and a goalmouth scramble the ball was cleared off the line by Doyle. Notts retaliated with two good attempts. First a Barnett cross-cum-shot landed on the roof of the net and, a few minutes later, a downward header by Rawlinson, following a corner, struck the goalkeepers legs before he claimed the ball. In the last minute Pilling made another good save, direct from a 25 yard free kick after a foul by Lacey, when he pushed the shot away for a corner.

So, another solid defensive display, together with some luck and good goalkeeping, earned Notts a goalless draw. In their last thirteen league games Notts had conceded just four goals, but once again they were disappointing in front of goal. It was a case of 'job done', in poor weather on a difficult pitch.

FA Trophy Quarter-Final	**Notts County 3-1 Oxford City**		Played behind closed doors
Sat 27 Feb 2021 15:00	Sam 48', 72' Knowles 90'+3	goal 26'	

Slocombe
Golden (Kelly-Evans 40')   ~~Turner~~ Rawlinson   Lacey   Chicksen
Wolfe (Doyle 88')   O'Brien (Capt.)
Miller   Sam
Knowles   Palmer (Wootton 60')

Subs: Pilling (Gk), Kelly-Evans, ~~Rawlinson~~, Barnett, Doyle, Boldewijn, Wootton

Initially there were eight changes to the team which earned a goalless draw at Stockport in the league four days ago. This became seven when Turner injured his calf in the warm-up and was replaced by Rawlinson. Tylor Golden, a 21-year-old right back signed last week from League Two Salford City on loan until 23 March, made his Notts debut. He had made eleven appearances for Salford this season in league and cup. Tyreace Palmer made his first start following his dramatic substitute appearance in the previous round, when he was sent off after 22 minutes. Goalkeeper Sam Slocombe returned after completing his three-match suspension.

Oxford City were in fourth position in The National League South when the remainder of the season in Step 2 (National Leagues North and South) of non-league football was declared null and void on 18 February, due to issues caused by the coronavirus (COVID-19) pandemic. However, clubs still in the FA Trophy were allowed to continue in that competition.

When their league season ended Oxford were unbeaten in their last twelve league and FA Trophy games, going back to the end of November. They had won their last six league and cup games with a goal difference of plus 14. This game was the second time the two clubs had been drawn together in a cup competition in the last three years. In December 2017, in the second round of the FA Cup, 5,092 attended Meadow Lane to see Notts secure a 3-2 victory with a goal in the 95th minute! Not one player from Notts' eighteen-man squad for that televised (BT Sport) game was still at Meadow Lane.

On a cloudless afternoon the 'Jimmy Sirrel Stand', and the quarter of the pitch in front of it, was bathed in glorious sunshine. Notts started brightly and Palmer missed a great chance to put Notts ahead in the tenth minute. A shot by Sam was deflected and the ball dropped kindly to Palmer, unmarked, ten yards from goal, but he got neither pace nor direction on his free header and the chance was gone. Thereafter Oxford came more into the game and they began to exert pressure on the Notts defence. After 20 minutes Golden sustained an ankle injury, but after treatment was able to play on. However, his misfortune continued when, five minutes later, his mis-placed pass presented a forward with a chance but Slocombe pushed the shot away. The resultant Oxford corner kick was cleared but they regained possession on the left and a cross-cum-shot struck Golden and was deflected beyond the stranded Slocombe. Just before half time Golden's ankle injury caused his substitution. During a disappointing first half performance Notts repeatedly gave the ball away or got caught in possession. Slocombe was by far the busier of the two goalkeepers.

Oxford started the second half with a good 18 yard shot which flew just wide, but within three minutes of the restart Sam equalised. He won the ball on the left and moved into the penalty area to place a shot into the corner of the net from the edge of the six yard box. Although Oxford still posed a threat and Slocombe had to be alert on a number of occasions, Notts began to assert themselves. One minute after coming off the substitute's bench a Wootton shot rattled the crossbar after a Knowles pass. On 69 minutes Chicksen showed his experience when he was confronted with a forward in a one-on-one situation, but he calmly dispossessed the attacker to avert the danger. Three minutes later Notts took the lead. Chicksen was again involved but this time it was with a cross from the left which found Sam near the penalty spot who scored with a 'Scorpion' kick! With his back to goal he swung his right foot, momentum turned him, and he watched the ball crash into the roof of the net off his heel! In time added at the end of the second half Oxford won a corner and all their player's, including the goalkeeper, were in the Notts penalty area when the ball was headed clear. It fell to Knowles who, chased by opponents, ran from the Notts half to place the ball into the empty net.

In the semi-final Notts were drawn at home to Hornchurch FC who play in the Isthmian Premier League, two steps below Notts. They are the lowest ranked side of the four who remain in the FA Trophy. The game, to be played on Saturday 27 March meant a league postponement and therefore another rearranged fixture for Notts.

Match 22	**Notts County** (7th) **2-2 King's Lynn Town** (20th)	Played behind
Tue 2 Mar 2021 19:45	Wootton 38' & 43' goals 1' & 90'+3	closed doors

Slocombe
Kelly-Evans   Rawlinson   Lacey   Barnett
Reeves   Doyle (Capt.)
Boldewijn (O'Brien 80')   Rodrigues (Wolfe 90')
Knowles (Effiong 80')   Wootton

Subs: O'Brien, Wolfe, Sam, Effiong, Miller
(no substitute goalkeeper)

Cal Roberts, who made a brief substitute appearance against Stockport seven days ago, had suffered a setback and was unlikely to be fully fit before the end of March.

The only change to the team victorious (1-0) at King's Lynn a fortnight ago was Slocombe in place of Pilling as goalkeeper.

Three days after that defeat King's Lynn issued a statement to their supporters:

> "…..in light of the ongoing consequences caused by the Coronavirus Pandemic…….We are unable to confirm that we will play any further fixtures after February 27th……"

They issued an update yesterday to confirm

> "…the next two National League fixtures will go ahead as scheduled."

The 'ongoing consequences' were financial, after the government discontinued the grants they had provided during October, November and December. Since their defeat to Notts they had played two home games – a 5-1 victory over Barnet (22nd position) and a 2-2 draw with Weymouth (21st position).

There was a shock for Notts if the first minute when King's Lynn took the lead. Slocombe had no chance when a brilliant 25 yard shot flew into the top corner of his net. For the next half hour Notts were second best as King's Lynn dominated the game. But for an excellent save by Slocombe, a bad miss and a timely clearance by Kelly-Evans they would have increased their lead, although Wootton nearly scored after 15 minutes when, following a corner kick, the ball struck his thigh and rebounded on to a post and out for a goal kick. Against the run of play Notts scored twice just before half-time. The equaliser came when a Reeves cross hit a defender and bounced to Wootton and his well-placed header, from close range, found the corner of the net. He then gave Notts the lead when he met a Barnett cross and powered his header into the net from twelve yards despite the presence of a defender.

In the second half both teams created scoring chances as the game ebbed and flowed. Notts' best chance fell to an unmarked Rodrigues after 52 minutes when he headed a Knowles cross over the crossbar from a central position seven yards from goal. This miss proved to be costly for Notts when King's Lynn equalised in stoppage time. Effiong committed an unnecessary foul just outside the penalty area. The free kick was headed on into the six yard box from where it was bundled in the net.

Almost a victory for Notts, but in truth they didn't deserve to win. In an open and entertaining game King's Lynn created some good goal scoring opportunities and, at times, Notts' defence looked nothing like the secure unit it had been in the previous thirteen league games (nine clean sheets). Other than against Dagenham & Redbridge three weeks ago, when for most of the game they played with ten men but still won 3-1, Notts' recent form had been disappointing.

However, it is acknowledged that even promotion chasing teams only perform to a high standard in about one quarter of their games. In the remainder they have good luck, bad luck, grind out results and play indifferently, so Notts should really be congratulated as they have been in one of the play-off positions for most of the season.

Although Kyle Wootton was second in The National League 'top scorers' chart with his twelve league goals, Notts' scoring record (28) was the lowest in the top half of The National League. Their next highest scorers were Boldewijn, Rodrigues, Reeves and Sam with three each. If Wootton picked up an injury or lost form where would the goals come from?

NATIONAL LEAGUE TABLE Tuesday 2 March 2021			Home					Away					Overall						
	Team	P	W	D	L	F	A	W	D	L	F	A	W	D	L	F	A	GD	PTS
1	Torquay United	24	6	3	3	21	12	8	2	2	25	12	14	5	5	46	24	22	**47**
2	Sutton United	22	8	2	2	28	10	6	2	2	13	11	14	4	4	41	21	20	**46**
3	Hartlepool United	25	9	2	3	22	13	4	3	4	12	11	13	5	7	34	24	10	**44**
4	Stockport County	24	5	5	2	14	8	6	2	4	18	13	11	7	6	32	21	11	**40**
5	Wrexham	25	6	4	2	18	7	5	2	6	16	20	11	6	8	34	27	7	**39**
6	Notts County	22	7	2	4	21	12	4	3	2	7	5	11	5	6	28	17	11	**38**
7	Eastleigh	24	6	5	2	16	9	4	3	4	16	15	10	8	6	32	24	8	**38**
8	Altrincham	27	4	2	5	13	13	6	4	6	18	21	10	6	11	31	34	-3	**36**
9	Boreham Wood	25	3	4	4	11	12	6	4	4	18	13	9	8	8	29	25	4	**35**
10	Yeovil Town	25	6	1	5	19	15	4	4	5	20	22	10	5	10	39	37	2	**35**
11	Bromley	24	5	4	5	24	20	4	3	3	15	11	9	7	8	39	31	8	**34**
12	Aldershot Town	24	5	1	5	15	16	5	3	5	21	19	10	4	10	36	35	1	**34**
13	Chesterfield	22	6	1	4	20	10	4	2	5	13	15	10	3	9	33	25	8	**33**
14	Maidenhead United	21	4	2	4	19	18	5	3	3	13	14	9	5	7	32	32	0	**32**
15	Halifax Town	23	4	3	3	19	14	4	4	5	18	16	8	7	8	37	30	7	**31**
16	Solihull Moors	22	6	0	3	14	6	3	4	6	13	18	9	4	9	27	24	3	**31**
17	Dagenham & Redbridge	24	3	3	4	9	11	5	2	7	13	20	8	5	11	22	31	-9	**29**
18	Woking	22	4	4	3	13	9	3	1	7	12	18	7	5	10	25	27	-2	**26**
19	Wealdstone	23	5	2	3	20	20	2	3	8	10	28	7	5	11	30	48	-18	**26**
20	King's Lynn Town	22	3	4	5	18	21	3	1	6	12	23	6	5	11	30	44	-14	**23**
21	Weymouth	24	3	2	9	15	26	2	3	5	10	13	5	5	14	25	39	-14	**20**
22	Barnet	23	2	2	9	8	26	1	1	8	10	31	3	3	17	18	57	-39	**12**
23	Dover Athletic	15	3	1	5	9	18	0	0	6	3	17	3	1	11	12	35	-23	**10**
24	Macclesfield Town (Expelled 12 October 2020)	0	0	0	0	0	0	0	0	0	0	0	0	0	0	0	0	0	

The uneven number of games played was mainly due to postponements caused by the coronavirus pandemic.

Dover Athletic had failed to fulfil their last nine fixtures and been charged with a breach of Rule 8.39. They had confirmed they would be unable to fulfil further fixtures until appropriate funding was made available to prevent the club from insolvency.

Chapter 14: A brutal second half of the season

So, at last, Notts had reached the half-way stage of their league campaign – it had taken five months! Of Notts' remaining 22 league games only nine were at Meadow Lane. Thirteen were away from home, with some long trips involved e.g. Torquay, Eastleigh (Southampton), Yeovil, Hartlepool. Notts' nine game away record so far had produced only twelve goals (P9 W4 D3 L2 F7 A5)! The next three months, before the final game of the season on Saturday 29 May, would be difficult, both physically and mentally.

Neal Ardley was well aware of the fixture congestion and he had described the second half of the season as "brutal" with two fixtures a week scheduled for the remainder of the season until the penultimate Saturday on 22 May.

However, it was likely Notts would be without a game on Saturday 15 May when they were scheduled to play Dover Athletic at Meadow Lane. Bottom of the league Dover (P15 with only 10Pts) last played on 30 January, and they had failed to fulfil their last nine fixtures. All management, players and staff had been furloughed to safeguard the club's long-term future and prevent it from becoming insolvent. They had confirmed they would be unable to fulfil further National League fixtures until appropriate funding was made available.

Due to the coronavirus (COVID-19) pandemic all games this season had been played behind closed doors, with little spectator revenue except for match streaming on the internet. Government grants were provided to clubs during October, November and December to compensate National League clubs, but the funding had ceased.

The National League charged Dover with a breach of Rule 8.39.

> *8.39 Where a match has been postponed for any reason…...*
> *Any Club without just cause failing to fulfil an engagement to play a Competition match on the appointed date shall for each offence be liable to expulsion from the Competition and/or such other disciplinary action the Board may determine….*

If Dover were expelled presumably their fifteen-game record would be expunged. This would benefit Notts as they were beaten (1-0) at Dover on the opening day of the season, so they would not be deducted any points!

Last season (2019-20) Notts reached the mid-point (23 games played) on 26 November 2019. They were two places below the play-off's in ninth position with a record of: **P23 W8 D8 L7 F35 A27 GD+8 Pts 32** - five points behind Harrogate Town (7th) who had 37 points from 23 games. Barrow were top of the league with 41 points from 22 games. At the end of the season Barrow were promoted as champions and Harrogate beat Notts in the play-off final at Wembley.

The second half of this season got off to a bad start when, on Thursday 4 March, the scheduled visitor's to Meadow Lane on Saturday (Aldershot) announced a positive coronavirus infection at the club. League rules dictated that they must isolate for ten days and, as a result, the Notts match was postponed.

On Monday 8 March Notts revealed that it was now mandatory for National League clubs to carry out COVID-19 tests the day before each match. This obligation had been placed on clubs following the commencement of the government's free COVID-19 testing programme, which provided registered workplaces with access to rapid testing. A statement from Notts' board of directors read:

> *Having funded our own regular testing programme, which has helped identify a number of positive cases, we are pleased that the league have now imposed this directive on all clubs. While the long-term picture is beginning to look a little brighter, Covid still poses a huge risk to society and, as a club, we feel we have a duty to protect our players, staff, opponents and the wider public as best we can.*

The recent injuries to centre half Ben Turner and right full back Tylor Golden, together with the absence of two other injured defenders (McCrory and Brindley) meant Notts were short of fit defensive players. The fixture congestion added to the urgency to sign cover. With the deadline for signing players near

> *National League Rule 6.2 REGISTRATION PERIOD*
>
> *......After 5.00pm on the fourth Thursday in March (this season the 25th) each Playing Season new registrations, new loans, and transfer of registrations will be declined or will be approved subject to such limitations and restrictions as the Board may determine and, if so determined, the Player shall only be eligible to play in the matches for which permission is granted by the Board.*

Neal Ardley signed Kenton Richardson (right full back) and Mark Ellis (centre half) to strengthen the defence – Richardson on loan until 5 April and Ellis on loan for the rest of the season.

Richardson (21) joined Sunderland last summer from Hartlepool United, where he made over 50 appearances in League Two and The National League. Injury had limited his Sunderland experience to four recent Under-23 appearances.

Ellis (32) had made over 400 appearances, mainly in League Two, for seven clubs. He had been out of favour with his current club, Tranmere Rovers of League Two, since November. Neal Ardley likened him to Connell Rawlinson.

In addition there was also a permanent signing, Lewis Knight (age 22) from National League North Bradford Park Avenue, on a two and a half year contract until the summer of 2023. Originally a member of the Leeds United Academy, he had been with Bradford since 2018. Although initially a winger, this season he had been successful in a more central striker position and was Bradford's top scorer with 11 goals from 15 appearances.

Match 23	**Notts County** (6th) **1-2 Halifax Town** (13th)	Played behind closed
Tue 9 Mar 2021 19:45	Boldewijn 74' goals 27' & 83'	doors

Slocombe
Richardson   Rawlinson   Lacey   Barnett
Reeves   Doyle (Capt.)
Boldewijn   Rodrigues
Knowles (Sam 59')   Wootton

Subs: Kelly-Evans, Ellis, O'Brien, Sam, Miller
(no substitute goalkeeper)

The only change to the team which drew at home to King's Lynn a week ago was Richardson (Notts debut) for Kelly-Evans.

Notts drew 1-1 at Halifax in mid-November. Three weeks ago Halifax lost at Barnet (then bottom of the league) but four days later they won at top of the league Torquay! Since that victory they had earned a draw and a win, so their recent form was good.

The first half of this game was identical to the one a week ago – then King's Lynn dominated the first half hour, this time Halifax had the territorial advantage and put the Notts defence under almost constant pressure. Once again Notts' control was poor, as was their passing, with the ball given away too easily. Slocombe had to make two good saves in the first six minutes. The only real effort from Notts came when Barnett drove a 25 yard shot just beyond the angle of crossbar and post in the 12th minute. Halifax deservedly took the lead in the 27th minute when a forward moved purposefully into the penalty area and squared the ball for his teammate to tap into the net from six yards. Notts showed some improvement thereafter. A Wootton header sailed over the crossbar, a Rodrigues shot was easily saved and Boldewijn weaved his way into the penalty area but the goalkeeper saved his shot. Despite the improvement it was a forgettable 45 minutes for Notts.

Halifax were not as dominant in the second half and the referee gave Notts the chance of an equaliser in the 72nd minute when he gave them a penalty after Rodrigues was fouled. Sam's kick was low but too straight and the goalkeeper dived to his right to make the save before the ball was scrambled away for a corner. However, two minutes later Notts did equalise. Boldewijn cut inside from the right touchline and, with defenders in his wake, shot powerfully into the corner of the net from the edge of the penalty area. But, ten minutes after that excellent equaliser, Halifax got the victory their overall performance deserved. Slocombe dived to his right and got his hand on the ball but couldn't prevent the powerful, rising, 18 yard shot from entering the roof of the net.

Yet another disappointing night for Notts. It was their fourth game without a victory and three of those four games had been at home. Although they remained in sixth position Notts were now twelve points behind the new league leaders, Sutton United, and only two points ahead of Chesterfield in twelfth. Fortunately they still had a few games in hand over all but Chesterfield.

| **Match 24** | **Wealdstone** (19th) **0-1 Notts County** (6th) | Played behind closed |
| Sat 13 Mar 2021 15:00 | Ellis 63' | doors |

Slocombe

Rawlinson   Ellis   Lacey

Kelly-Evans   Miller

Doyle (Capt.)   O'Brien

Boldewijn

Effiong (Sam 85')   Wootton

Subs: Turner, Barnett, Rodrigues, Sam, Knowles
(no substitute goalkeeper)

In a change of formation there were five changes to the side defeated by Halifax. Mark Ellis made his debut in central defence. Kelly-Evans and Miller replaced Richardson and Barnett. O'Brien returned to midfield in place of Reeves and Effiong came in for Knowles. Rodrigues became a substitute.

Notts convincingly defeated Wealdstone 3-0 at Meadow Lane at the end of November. Since then Wealdstone's form had been inconsistent, although this was their fourth consecutive home game and they had won two of the previous three.

Notts started better than in recent games and were in control for most of the first half. The only concern for Slocombe was a Wealdstone free kick from 20 yards which just cleared the crossbar. Just before half time the Wealdstone goalkeeper dived to his right to make a superb save when a low, well struck, Doyle shot from the edge of the penalty area looked destined for the corner of the net. Notts' enterprise was rewarded with just over one hour played, and the goal scorer was debutant Ellis. A Slocombe clearance was headed on by Ellis to Boldewijn who kept control of the ball before passing to Kelly-Evans. He squared a pass to Doyle who lifted the ball into the penalty area where Ellis headed the ball over the goalkeeper into the top corner of the net from six yards. In the last ten minutes only two excellent saves by the home goalkeeper, from O'Brien and Miller, prevented Notts from increasing their lead.

A solid all round performance by Notts who deserved the three points. So, a win after four league games without a victory. However, although their recent home form had been disappointing, their away record this season had been exceptional. Including today, in league and FA Trophy they were last defeated away from home on 7 November, when they returned to action following their three week enforced break due to a coronavirus infection at Meadow Lane. In the intervening four months they had gone ten away games undefeated (W7 D3), and this was the fifth consecutive away league game without conceding a goal.

Match 25	**Boreham Wood** (10th) **2-2 Notts County** (6th)		Played behind closed
Tue 16 Mar 2021 19:45	goals 1' & 54'	Lacey 76'	doors
		Effiong 87' pen.	

Slocombe

Rawlinson (Knowles 67')   Ellis   Lacey

Boldewijn   Miller

Reeves   Doyle (Capt.)   Rodrigues (O'Brien 90')

Wootton   Sam (Effiong 67')

Subs: Kelly-Evans, Turner, O'Brien, Effiong, Knowles
(no substitute goalkeeper)

There were three changes to the side victorious at Wealdstone. Kelly-Evans, O'Brien and Effiong were replaced by Rodrigues, Sam and Reeves who returned following a one game suspension for yellow card accumulation.

Boreham Wood won 1-0 at Meadow Lane at the beginning of December. They had won only one of their last nine league games, but five of their last six matches had been drawn - the last two 0-0. Although only three points behind Notts they had played four games more.

There was a repeat of the start of the King's Lynn game played two weeks ago – a first minute goal for the opposition. Slocombe dived but was beaten by a good 25 yard shot which hit a post and nestled in the opposite corner of his net. However, on this occasion there was a better response from Notts as they searched for the equaliser. Just a few minutes later a long throw-in by Ellis (which reached the penalty spot!) was headed on by Rawlinson and Wootton stooped to head the ball towards goal but the goalkeeper made a comfortable save. A Boldewijn cross then reached Ellis (yes, he is a central defender) in the penalty area and he stabbed the ball wide of the far post from a good position. Although Boreham Wood remained a threat, Notts nearly equalised just before half time when a Rodrigues free kick was flicked on by Rawlinson's head but the goalkeeper's save was hacked away by a defender.

At the start of the second half Notts were put under pressure. A fierce 22 yard free kick was tipped onto the crossbar by Slocombe and Lacey headed the rebound out for a corner kick. From the corner a header went narrowly wide. Notts fell further behind when Sam was caught in possession near the centre circle and a few passes later a well struck 15 yard cross shot flew past Slocombe into the corner of the net. With time running out Notts managed to reduce the deficit when a corner kick was missed by the goalkeeper. The ball rebounded off a defender and then the goalkeeper for Lacey to tap into the net from close range. Boreham Wood had an excellent chance to seal victory but then gave Notts a penalty, with five minutes to go, when Wootton's goal bound header was handled. Effiong calmly stroked the penalty home for his first Notts goal. In the final minute Rodrigues headed over when well placed and, in time added, Boldewijn made a good clearance with Slocombe stranded at the edge of the penalty area after he had attempted to prevent a shot.

A good fight back by Notts who 'snatched a draw out of the jaws of defeat' to preserve their exceptional away record, just! More a point gained than two lost.

Match 26 Sat 20 Mar 2021 15:00	**Notts County** (7th) **2-0 Yeovil Town** (12th) Reeves 40' Barnett 78'	Played behind closed doors

                Slocombe
Rawlinson   Ellis   Lacey (Turner 50')
     Boldewijn   Barnett
  Reeves   Doyle (Capt.)   O'Brien
   Effiong (Knowles 90')   Wootton

Subs: Kelly-Evans, Turner, Rodrigues, Sam, Knowles
(no substitute goalkeeper)

There were three changes to the side which fought back to draw at Boreham Wood. Miller, Rodrigues and Sam were replaced by Barnett, O'Brien and Effiong.

This was the first game of a double-header – Notts' next game was away to Yeovil on Tuesday.

Last season Yeovil were beaten in the promotion play-off's. Notts played them twice, both away fixtures. In the league they lost 3-1 but in the third round of the FA Trophy Notts won 2-1. The Meadow Lane league fixture was cancelled due to the coronavirus pandemic. Yeovil made a dreadful start to this season and were bottom of the league on 1 December after being without a victory in their first ten games (five draws and five defeats). Their form then improved and they were in tenth position at the beginning of March. However, they had lost three of the last four games, and hadn't made a draw since mid-November!

Notts played with more confidence and a better tempo and, unlike recent home games, the first half was an even contest. After 23 minutes a fierce Reeves shot from the edge of the penalty area was pushed over the bar by the goalkeeper. Five minutes before half time he went one better when he gave Notts a deserved lead with a brilliant free kick. His 30-yard strike just cleared the defensive wall and flew into the top corner of the net.

In the second half Barnett was twice denied by the Yeovil goalkeeper before he increased Notts' lead with just over ten minutes to go. Boldewijn's good control and movement allowed him to release the ball to Reeves who flicked it beyond a defender with his heel and Barnett ran on to the ball and smashed an unstoppable left footed shot into the net from 25 yards. What a way to score your first goal in professional football.

In the end a much improved performance by Notts who achieved a comfortable win, and they made the long midweek journey to Huish Park three days later boosted by their victory.

Match 27	**Yeovil Town** (14th) **2-2 Notts County** (6th)	Played behind closed
Tue 23 Mar 2021 19:45	goals 29' & 38' pen. Boldewijn 78'	doors
	Rodrigues 86'	

Slocombe

Rawlinson   Ellis   Turner (Kelly-Evans 46')

Boldewijn   Barnett

Reeves   Doyle (Capt.)   O'Brien (Rodrigues 63')

Effiong (Knowles 46')   Wootton

Subs: Kelly-Evans, Chicksen, Rodrigues, Sam, Knowles

(no substitute goalkeeper)

Just one change from the first meeting at Meadow Lane – Turner replaced the injured Lacey.

This was the third attempt to fulfil the fixture – Yeovil postponed the first two (12 December and 19 January) due to the coronavirus pandemic.

Yeovil were the better side during the first ten minutes and they had a chance to take the lead but Slocombe made a good save with his legs. Notts then came more into the game and had five corners in quick succession. From one of them Turner headed over the crossbar. Soon after, against the run of play, Yeovil took the lead. A corner was headed on at the near post and the ball was tapped into the net at the far post. Notts' defence then came under pressure and ten minutes later they conceded a second goal from the penalty spot. Turner was unable to cope with the pace and tenacity of a forward and he pulled him back to give away a penalty. In the final minute of the first half a through pass almost found Wootton but the Yeovil goalkeeper was alert to the danger and claimed the ball.

Notts brought on Kelly-Evans (for Turner) and Knowles (for Effiong) at the start of the second half. Although dominant, Notts had a lucky escape in the 58th minute when Slocombe charged out to the edge of the penalty area and a forward slipped the ball past him but fortunately it travelled just wide of the empty net. Yeovil's defence continued to play well and it took a brilliant goal by Boldewijn, with twelve minutes left to play, to get Notts back into the game. At the corner of the penalty area, with his back to goal, he controlled a bouncing ball, swivelled, and hooked it into the far corner of the net. Minutes later Doyle just cleared the crossbar with an 18 yard shot. Notts completed their comeback when an unmarked Rodrigues tapped a low Knowles cross from the right into the net from close range. Incredibly Notts should have won the game in time added at the end of the second half. Another Knowles cross found Wootton six yards from goal but he sliced his shot wide!

So, just as they had done a week ago at Boreham Wood, Notts 'snatched a draw out of the jaws of defeat' with two late goals to preserve their exceptional away record. But, less than 24 hours later, Notts' 'Club News' dropped a bombshell!

Chapter 15: Neal Ardley departs, Ian Burchnall arrives

On Wednesday 24 March, Notts announced:

We have parted company with our first-team manager Neal Ardley and assistant manager Greg Abbott.

[Neal] Ardley, who took charge in November 2018, left his post this afternoon following an amicable meeting with our owners, Chris and Alex Reedtz, who have issued the following statement:

"We wish to place on record the huge respect we have for Neal both as a manager and a man.

"He stuck by this club through some of its darkest hours and has played a leading role in stabilising us following a devastating relegation, helping to maintain a close connection between the players, staff and supporters in the most trying of circumstances.

"We will never forget the job he did in guiding us to last season's play-off final at Wembley and some of the excellent performances he has extracted from the team during our time at the helm.

"It has also been pleasing to see an upturn in recent results, including another spirited fightback last night, and we understand, therefore, that this announcement may come as a surprise to our supporters, who we know share our view that Neal is an excellent ambassador for the club.

"We do not, however, apply short-term thinking to decisions of this magnitude. We consider many factors which far outweigh our results in the last few matches and these deliberations have ultimately led us to conclude that we can be better, and that a change is needed to take us to the next level.

"Neal has always said that when the time comes for him to depart Meadow Lane, he will leave having helped to create a far better footballing environment than he inherited. He has undoubtedly achieved that and we will forever be grateful to him for his efforts in rebuilding a platform for the club to go on and achieve success.

"We would also like to express our gratitude to Greg, who has been a terrific support to Neal and a valuable member of our backroom team since his arrival last year. He and Neal depart with our very best wishes."

We are not inviting applications for the manager's position. A further update will be provided to supporters in the near future.

During his two years and four months as manager of Notts County, Neal Ardley's league and cup record was:

	P	W	D	L	F	A	
Season 2018-19	26	6	7	13	26	43	
Season 2019-20	40	18	12	10	64	41	(inc. play-off's)
Season 2020-21	27	13	7	7	36	23	
	93	37	26	30	126	107	
Cup games 2018-2021	13	10	0	3	26	15	(1 Check-a-Trade, 3 FA Cup, 9 FA Trophy)
	106	47	26	33	152	122	

Neal Ardley did not look back in anger after his departure as Notts County manager.

Neal Ardley released the following statement through the League Managers Association:

NEAL ARDLEY
STATEMENT

"I would like to share my gratitude to the owners Chris and Alex Reedtz for trusting me to lead Notts County through one of the club's most challenging times. After the huge disappointment of that day at Swindon and the following summer of uncertainty, Chris and Alex breathed new life into one of the most traditional football clubs in England, providing hope to some of the most loyal fans around.

"Building a squad from scratch was not easy, so to achieve this the following season and finish one game away from a quick return to the Football League was a remarkable effort from everybody at the club. As history suggests, the National League is one of the toughest leagues to gain promotion from, with only one automatic spot, and many huge clubs have taken a while to achieve this.

"I am naturally disappointed not to have the opportunity to finish off what I, and the players, vowed to do at the start of the season, which was to gain promotion. Being in the play-off positions, with games in hand, and being one game away from another Wembley visit in The FA Trophy, I had hoped to deliver the success the fans richly deserve. I firmly believe it would've happened and still hope it will.

"To all the staff I worked with, both from the football and office departments, I thank you for your hard work, loyalty and friendship. Along with the local press and reporters, I have met so many great people.

"To the players, I thank you for your hard work and professionalism during my time and I wish you the barnstorming end to the season we were striving for.

"To the new management team, I sincerely wish you good luck in your venture with this great club.

"Finally, I would like to thank the fans for making me welcome and helping me through one of the clubs most challenging times. I am immensely proud to have managed your great football club and will continue to support from a distance, hoping you will be celebrating good times soon. With Chris and Alex at the helm, I am sure it won't be long."

Neal

Neal Ardley didn't mention the upheaval caused by the coronavirus (COVID-19) pandemic since January 2020, that Notts had been in a promotion play-off position for most of this season, that Notts had lost just two of their last sixteen league and FA Trophy games in 2021, that Notts were unbeaten in their last twelve league and FA Trophy games away from Meadow Lane (going back to early November), that Notts had the best defensive record in The National League, that he had 'lost' (transfer) Kristian Dennis (16 goals in 38 appearances last season) and been without Cal Roberts (5 goals in 11 appearances last season) who had been absent through injury since November (except for 12 minutes as a substitute on 23 February), and that he had devoted nearly two and a half years to Notts County.

OK, Neal made some mistakes, as we all do, and I'm sure there were things he did that, with hindsight, he would have done differently or better, but it is worth repeating here the words expressed by the Chief Executive Officer of his previous club Erik Samuelson, AFC Wimbledon, "he is a clear thinker, superb man-manager and fine coach". Although I only knew Neal Ardley through the many interviews he gave to BBC Radio Nottingham, his weekly press conferences and the occasional Q & A session on social media, I'd like to add that I thought he displayed characteristics of allegiance (loyalty) and application (diligence). Another club will benefit from his many fine attributes in the future.

Obviously the last two sentences of the statement issued on the departure of Neal Ardley and Greg Abbott told us that their successors had been chosen, and on the morning of Thursday 25 March the names of the new head coach and his assistant were revealed.

We are delighted to announce the appointment of Ian Burchnall as our new head coach.

Burchnall, 38, arrives with eight years' experience working in the Scandinavian top tiers and is regarded as one of football's most exciting young coaches.

Possessing a background in youth coaching, Burchnall's first senior role came as Brian Deane's assistant at Norwegian side Sarpsborg in 2012. He then took the same job at Viking FK, paving the way for him to become their manager in 2017. Off-field issues led to his departure, much to the disappointment of Viking's supporters, but he was quickly invited to move across the Swedish border to replace now-Brighton manager Graham Potter at Ostersund FK.

Potter had led the club on a meteoric rise through the Swedish football system, culminating in the club's remarkable qualification for the Europa League, and Burchnall, who had previously worked with Potter while coaching university football in Leeds, was chosen as the man to fill his boots. Despite the club's decision to sell numerous key players, Burchnall led Ostersund to a sixth-place finish, one point and a place below the record set by Potter the previous year. His second season began strongly before off-field problems emerged once again, eventually leading Burchnall to leave his post last summer to pursue his next opportunity in the UK.

And our owners, Chris and Alex Reedtz, are thrilled that Burchnall has chosen Meadow Lane as his next destination.

"We are tremendously excited to welcome Ian to the role of head coach.

"As part of our ongoing extensive research, we compile detailed profiles of many different coaches and Ian stands out as an outstanding prospect. Despite his young age, he has tremendous experience of working in top-flight football and has been linked with several international and club roles since his departure from Ostersund. We feel very lucky to have him and have every confidence that he is the right man to complement our model.

"It's our hope that Ian will be able to continue our push for promotion this season but we understand it will take him time to fully implement our philosophy. He is a long-term appointment for this club and his performance in the role will be judged on that basis.

"We think supporters will share our appreciation of Ian's passion for coaching and his willingness to take risks and meet difficult challenges head-on, as he did during his time in Scandinavia, and we're very excited to see him lead the team for the first time in Saturday's Buildbase FA Trophy semi-final against AFC Hornchurch."

Burchnall will be assisted by former Scotland and Rangers full-back Maurice Ross, who has also coached in Scandinavia before most recently being Motherwell's first-team coach.

Maurice Ross   Ian Burchnall

A matter of hours after Ian Burchnall and Maurice (Mo) Ross joined Notts there were two issues in their favour.

The first was the non-closure of the transfer window for National League clubs at 5pm on the fourth Thursday of March, which usually meant clubs could not sign any new players for the remainder of the season. However, due to the impact of the coronavirus (COVID-19) pandemic Rule 6.2.1 had been 'temporarily amended or disapplied' and clubs could sign players until 22 April.

The second, 24 hours later on Friday 26 March, was the announcement by The National League of the punishment issued to bottom club Dover Athletic for failing to fulfil fixtures. Their fifteen results were expunged and as a result Notts moved up one place in the league table from 6th to 5th because they were defeated by a last minute goal at Dover on the opening day of the season. The records of the top two teams in the league, Sutton United and Hartlepool United, were unaffected as they had not played Dover.

With the arrival of Burchnall and Ross it is also appropriate to introduce the 'new' Strength & Conditioning Coach, Ian Hutton, who replaced Erik Svendsen a few months ago following his resignation for family reasons. (Coincidentally Svendsen returned to Sweden, from where our new duo departed last summer). Ian Hutton had previously held a similar position at Solihull Moors and Cheltenham Town.

NATIONAL LEAGUE (Top 12 of 22 clubs)
Fri 26 March 2021

		P	W	D	L	GD	PTS
1	Sutton United	28	18	6	4	25	60
2	Hartlepool United	31	16	8	7	13	56
3	Torquay United	28	15	6	7	19	51
4	Stockport County	28	13	8	7	16	47
5	**Notts County**	**26**	**13**	**7**	**6**	**14**	**46**
6	Wrexham	28	12	8	8	9	44
7	Halifax Town	28	12	7	9	10	43
8	Eastleigh	28	11	10	7	6	43
9	Chesterfield	27	13	3	11	11	42
10	Bromley	28	11	8	9	6	41
11	Maidenhead United	25	11	6	8	4	39
12	Boreham Wood	29	9	12	8	4	39

The season would now be completed when all clubs had played 42 games.

Position 1 = Automatic promotion to League Two
Positions 2&3 = Automatic Play-off semi-final with home fixture
Positions 4-7 = 4 at home to 7 and 5 at home to 6
(4 or 7 away at 2 and 5 or 6 away at 3)

The revised (full) league table incorporated:

1. Dover Athletics' punishment, ordered by an Independent Panel commissioned by The National League, for breaches of Rule 8.39 - failing to meet fixture obligations (between 16-27 February). As a result it was confirmed that Dover would play no further part in the 2020-21 season, with their existing (15) league results expunged. They had played their last fixture at the end of January. (Dover were also given a 12-point deduction for the 2021-22 league season and fined £40,000).
2. The demise of Macclesfield Town, who never started the season before their expulsion in October 2020.

Notts County's remaining 16 National League fixtures of the 2020-21 season for Ian Burchnall and Maurice Ross to manage:

	Home	Away	Round Trip (miles)
Tue 30 March	**Aldershot**		
Fri 2 April	**Wrexham**		
Mon 5 April		Woking	282
Sat 10 April		Hartlepool	278
Tue 13 April		Solihull Moors	99
Sat 17 April	**Eastleigh**		
Sat 24 April		Torquay	462
Tue 27 April		Eastleigh	330
Sat 1 May		Altrincham	173
Mon 3 May	**Sutton**		
Sat 8 May		Barnet	232
Tue 11 May		Maidenhead	260
Sat 15 May	**Bromley**		
Tue 18 May		Wrexham	186
Sat 22 May	**Weymouth**		
Sat 29 May		Bromley	325
			2627

10 of the 16 were against clubs in the top 12 with Wrexham, Eastleigh and Bromley to be played home and away. But first there was the outstanding FA Trophy semi-final against Hornchurch FC to negotiate.

FA Trophy Semi-Final	**Notts County 3-3 Hornchurch FC**	Played behind closed
Sat 27 Mar 2021 15:00	Wootton 10' Rawlinson (og) 37'	doors. Hornchurch won
	Rodrigues 42' goal 45'+2	5-4 after penalties.
	Sam 77' goal 90'+1	

Slocombe

Kelly-Evans   Ellis   Rawlinson   Barnett

Reeves   Doyle (Capt.)   Rodrigues (O'Brien 54')

Miller (Sam 74')   Boldewijn (Knowles 67')

Wootton

Subs: Pilling (Gk), Golden, Turner, Chicksen, O'Brien, Sam, Knowles

For his first Notts game in charge Ian Burchnall made eight changes to the side victorious in the quarter-final of the FA Trophy (three changes to the side which forced a draw at Yeovil in Neal Ardley's last match).

Lewis Knight was unavailable - cup-tied as he had played for Bradford Park Avenue in an earlier round before his transfer to Notts. Effiong was also cup-tied. Tylor Golden, injured in the first half of his Notts debut in the quarter-final of the FA Trophy, was initially on loan from Salford until 23 March. However, as he had been injured throughout, his loan period had been extended until 27 April.

Hornchurch FC were a part-time club who played in the Isthmian Premier League (two levels below The National League). Due to the coronavirus (COVID-19) pandemic their season was officially curtailed at the end of February, with no further league matches this season, but clubs in the FA Trophy were allowed to continue in that competition until defeated. In reality the last league game they played was on 3rd November 2020, at which point they were in ninth position. During December they played two friendlies and three FA Trophy games, and won them all. In 2021 their only fixtures had been three more FA Trophy games, the last of which was the quarter-final victory on 27th February.

Notts dominated the first half hour, territorially and in possession, with good quick passing and movement and they looked much the better side. They deservedly took the lead after ten minutes when Wootton headed home a Barnett cross from the left. A couple of minutes later only an excellent save by the goalkeeper from another Wootton header prevented Notts increasing their lead. However, Hornchurch equalised when a speculative 25-yard shot, which would have gone yards wide, hit Rawlinson's shin 17 yards from goal and the ball was deflected beyond the wrong footed Slocombe. Notts regained the lead just before half-time when Rodrigues side-footed a Boldewijn pass into the net from ten yards. Hornchurch had adopted a way of upsetting Notts' rhythm by slowing the game down and giving away a few free kicks. As a result there were four minutes of added time at the end of the first half during which they equalised for a second time. A forward was given time and space to cross the ball low from the left side of the penalty area into the six yard box from where it was bundled into the net by an onrushing player.

The second half was more evenly contested, and Notts began to look ragged with passes going astray. The closest they came was when Wootton, following a good build-up, had his shot blocked when in a good position. However, they took the lead again with thirteen minutes to play when an O'Brien shot found Sam who had the simple task of tapping the ball into the net from three yards. The goal steadied Notts and it was expected they would manage the remainder of the game and progress to the Wembley final. But, once again, in time added at the end of the half, Hornchurch equalised for the third time when the ball was cleverly lifted, inside the penalty area, towards an onrushing player who stooped to nod the ball forward and it was tapped into the net from close range.

With no extra-time in the FA Trophy this season the game was decided by a penalty shoot-out, with sudden death if the score was still level after each side had taken five penalties. Hornchurch scored their first five but although Wootton, O'Brien, Knowles and Sam were successful Reeves, who took Notts' third penalty, was not, and so Hornchurch won the shoot-out 5-4.

Of course, it was all desperately disappointing from a Notts point of view and for Ian Burchnall and Mo Ross. Supporters gave a scathing assessment on social media with "Notts beaten by a team who played like a Sunday pub side" a common theme in the criticism. Burchnall said that Notts didn't cope with the tactics adopted by Hornchurch, but acknowledged that they should have done and offered no excuse. He went on to say "the Hornchurch technical area was lively today, make no mistake about that" but he admitted that Jake Kean had been out of order when he shouted and made a noise as Hornchurch took their second penalty. So, for the second consecutive season Notts were beaten at the semi-final stage in the FA Trophy. This defeat was a massive shock, but the message was to move on and concentrate on the final 16 league games and get the results that would ensure Notts return to the football league!

Chapter 16: Sixteen important league matches for Burchnall

(the first nine with assistant Maurice Ross, the last seven with assistance from Michael Doyle)

Match 1 (27 exc. Dover) Tue 30 Mar 2021 19:00	**Notts County** (6th) **0-1 Aldershot Town** (16th)	goal 4' (pen.)	Played behind closed doors

Slocombe
Kelly-Evans   Ellis   Turner   Barnett
Reeves (Capt.)   O'Brien
Miller (Rodrigues 75')   Boldewijn (Effiong 85')
Wootton   Sam (Knowles 55')

Subs: Rawlinson, Chicksen, Rodrigues, Effiong, Knowles
(no substitute goalkeeper)

For his first National League game Ian Burchnall made three changes to the side beaten by Hornchurch in the FA Trophy. Turner replaced Rawlinson, O'Brien came in for the injured Doyle and Sam was preferred to Rodrigues.

Notts lost 1-0 at Aldershot in early November. It was Notts' first game after their three week break due to a coronavirus (COVID-19) outbreak at the club. Since that defeat Notts had been unbeaten in twelve games away from Meadow Lane in the league and FA Trophy. Aldershot's recent form had been poor with four games without a win – a draw and three 1-0 defeats.

On a warm, cloudless, evening Aldershot took the lead in the fourth minute when the referee awarded them a very dubious penalty. Ellis and a forward were running side by side in the penalty area and the forward fell (some would say dived). To add insult to injury Ellis was given a yellow card! Aldershot nearly scored a second in the 34th minute when the player who won and scored the penalty hit the crossbar with a fierce shot. Notts responded immediately when a good pass by Kelly-Evans down the right released Sam who squared the ball, but it ran just behind Wootton near the penalty spot and just too far ahead of Boldewijn. From then on, until half-time, Notts showed some improvement, but the Aldershot defence was never in danger.

The second half was ten minutes old when Aldershot almost scored a second goal. Reeves, running towards the Notts goal inside the penalty area, was dispossessed, but Slocombe advanced and the subsequent shot rebounded off him and over the crossbar for a corner. In the final five minutes Knowles was twice responsible for giving the Aldershot goalkeeper his only anxious moments in the whole game. First, he received a header from Reeves and shot from twelve yards but the goalkeeper saved with his legs. A minute later he collected an Effiong header but hooked his shot into the side netting. With the last kick of the match, following an Aldershot breakaway, Slocombe pawed a 20-yard shot beyond his right-hand post after which the referee blew the final whistle.

For Notts it was a forgettable evening. An ordinary Aldershot team, given an early goal by a poor refereeing decision, was then too good for an un-imaginative Notts.

Match 2 (28 exc. Dover) (Good) Fri 2 Apr 2021 12:15	**Notts County** (6th) **1-0 Wrexham** (5th) Ellis 80'	Played behind closed doors but televisted by BT Sport

Slocombe
Rawlinson   Ellis   Chicksen
Boldewijn   Reeves (Capt.)   Griffiths   O'Brien (Roberts 78')   Barnett
Knowles (Knight 68')   Wootton

Subs: Kelly-Evans, Rodrigues, Miller, Roberts, Knight
(no substitute goalkeeper)

Ian Burchnall made four changes to the side beaten by Aldershot. Rawlinson replaced Turner and Chicksen (last league game early December) returned at the expense of Kelly-Evans. Knowles was preferred to Sam and Miller made way for debutant Regan Griffiths, a 20 year old midfield player signed from League One Crewe Alexandra on loan for the remainder of the season. He had made four appearances for Crewe this season, two in the EFL Cup and two as a substitute in the league. He was cover for the injured Doyle and Wolfe.

Notts had not played Wrexham since August 2019 when the game, at Meadow Lane, ended in a 1-1 draw. Due to the curtailment of the 2019-20 season the away fixture was cancelled. So far during 2021 promotion rivals Wrexham had played 16 league games and only been beaten twice – the last time eight games ago – so their current form was good.

Wrexham started the game well and Slocombe came to Notts' rescue three times in the first ten minutes. Thereafter Notts gradually settled and play became more even. Halfway through the first half Notts appealed strongly for a penalty when a Wootton header seemed to hit a defenders arm near the goal line before going over the crossbar.

Although there were opportunities for both teams in the second half, Notts' improvement continued and they began to look solid and inventive. In a bid to add more variety to their attacking play Burchnall introduced another debutant, Lewis Knight, followed by the charismatic Cal Roberts after a long absence through injury. However, it was the two central defenders who combined to put Notts in the lead with ten minutes to go. A Barnett corner was met by Rawlinson whose downward header was volleyed into the net by Ellis. More drama followed as five minutes of added time was announced at the end of the game. Wootton was adjudged to have used his arm in an attempt to out jump a defender, who was subsequently carried off with a head injury, and the referee gave the Notts player a second yellow card and he was sent off. In the remaining minutes Wrexham attacked but were unable to find an equaliser.

Notts weren't back to their fluent best but there were indications that confidence had returned and in the end they just about deserved their victory.

Match 3 (29 exc. Dover)   **Woking** (18th) **2 - 4 Notts County** (5th)   Played behind
(Easter) Mon 5 Apr 2021 15:00   goals 28'(pen.), 33' Ellis 20'   closed doors
                                                      Knowles 60', 65', 79'

Slocombe
Rawlinson   Ellis   Chicksen
Boldewijn (Kelly-Evans 88')   Barnett
Reeves (Capt.)   Griffiths (Rodrigues 46')   O'Brien
Knowles   Sam (Knight 55')

Subs: Kelly-Evans, Golden, Rodrigues, Miller, Knight
(no substitute goalkeeper)

The only change to the side victorious over Wrexham, was the one enforced by Wootton's one match suspension. His replacement was Elisha Sam. Two on loan players, Inih Effiong and Kenton Richardson, had recently returned to their parent clubs, Stevenage and Sunderland respectively.

Wootton scored the only goal when Notts won the home fixture at the beginning of December. Like Notts, Woking were beaten in the FA Trophy semi-final by a club from a lower tier. Their league form since the beginning of March had been mixed – P8 W2 D2 L4 F6 A6. Only one club had scored fewer league goals than their 26, but defensively they were sound – only 31 conceded.

Notts made a good start and deservedly took the lead on 20 minutes when central defender Ellis scored his third goal in only his eighth appearance. Boldewijn returned a poor defensive clearance into the penalty area from where Ellis let the ball bounce before he smashed it into the net. However, Notts' joy was short-lived as Woking then scored two quick goals. The first from the penalty spot after Barnett had fouled an attacker. The second when, following a free kick, the ball glanced off Reeves' head to the far post from where it was headed back and then forced into the net from close range.

The first sign of what was to come in a very entertaining second half occurred in the 50th minute. Woking had a claim for another penalty ignored by the referee and in the counterattack a Barnett cross found Reeves but his downward header bounced harmlessly into the goalkeeper's arms. Knight then had an opportunity, but he dragged his shot wide of the far post. On the hour Notts equalised when a defender failed to intercept a Boldewijn pass, and Knowles ran the ball into the penalty area and slid it confidently into the corner of the goal. Five minutes later Notts took the lead after the goalkeeper rushed to the edge of his penalty area, failed to clear a Barnett cross, and Knowles gained possession and shot into the unguarded net. Knight was presented with another opportunity, by a good O'Brien through ball, but his mishit 20 yard shot bounced wide of the goal. Knowles then completed his (twenty minute) hat-trick when a Reeves lob put him in the clear and he ran through on goal and gave the goalkeeper no chance with a smart finish. The last action of the game saw Slocombe make a brilliant save and in the ensuing scramble Boldewijn blocked a goal bound shot.

Notts' tenth successive league game, away from Meadow Lane, without defeat!

Match 4 (30 exc. Dover)	Hartlepool United (2ⁿᵈ) 2-0 Notts Co. (5ᵗʰ)	Played behind closed
Sat 10 Apr 2021 17:20	goals 45', 86'	doors but televised by BT Sport

Slocombe

Rawlinson   Ellis   Chicksen

Boldewijn (Roberts 70')   Barnett (Kelly-Evans 70')

Reeves (Capt.)   Griffiths (Knight 37')   O'Brien

Knowles   Wootton

Subs: Kelly-Evans, Lacey, Rodrigues, Roberts, Knight
(no substitute goalkeeper)

The only change to the side that demolished Woking was Wootton's return, after his one game suspension, in place of Sam.

In the last league game of 2020 Hartlepool defeated Notts 1-0 at Meadow Lane. Since that win they had lost just twice in 18 games, with the last defeat in mid-February. During their unbeaten 13 game run, they had achieved seven draws and six victories – so Notts were up against a team in good form.

Hartlepool dominated the first half hour which meant Slocombe was the busier of the two goalkeepers. However, it was Notts who created the best chance, after 35 minutes, when Griffiths ran through the penalty area and crossed superbly to Wootton whose powerful header from ten yards went inches over the crossbar. Just two minutes later Burchnall made a tactical change when forward Knight replaced midfielder Griffiths. On the stroke of half time Hartlepool took the lead when Notts failed to clear a cross from the left and in the subsequent scramble the ball was swept into the corner of the net from ten yards.

In the second half Notts were the better side. Reeves and Knowles (twice) both went close, and Roberts was introduced to push for the equaliser. His first effort on goal was deflected for a corner but a couple of minutes later, when passing the ball to the right, he pulled up with what looked like the return of his 'hip flexor' injury. As Notts had already introduced three substitutes they were reduced to ten men and Hartlepool took advantage with a second goal just before the final whistle which involved three of their players. A corner kick was back headed to the far post area from where the third player controlled the ball with his right foot and flashed it into the net with his left foot.

Notts' last eight league games, before today, had seen them score 13 (only 2 in the first half) with 9 conceded (7 in the first half). In other words they had become a much better second half team! This was the case today, but still their fine away record came to an end and they also lost the title 'best defence in the league'.

So, Hartlepool completed the double over Notts, just as Aldershot had done after Ian Burchnall's first league game in charge, and moved to the top of the league – twelve points ahead of Notts (remained fifth), but they had played five games more!

Match 5 (31 exc. Dover)	**Solihull Moors** (15th) **2-1 Notts County** (5th)	Played behind
Tue 13 Apr 2021 19:00	goals 65' & 79' Knowles 11'	closed doors

Slocombe

Rawlinson   Ellis (Rodrigues 84')   Lacey

Kelly-Evans   Chicksen

Reeves (Capt.)   Griffiths

Knight (Sam 72')   Wootton   Knowles (Boldewijn 84')

Subs: Barnett, O'Brien, Rodrigues, Boldewijn, Sam
(no substitute goalkeeper)

Ian Burchnall made three changes to the side defeated at Hartlepool. Kelly-Evans, Lacey and Knight were preferred to Barnett, O'Brien and Boldewijn. For Lewis Knight it was his first Notts start after three appearances as a substitute.

Notts defeated Solihull 2-0 at Meadow Lane in late January, after which a poor run of form saw them drop down the league table. Although only three clubs had scored fewer goals, they were undefeated in their last four games – three of them victories without conceding a goal. The fourth was a goalless draw at home to, then, top of the league Sutton United.

Notts, for a change, started the game positively and they took an early lead. Wootton swept the ball out to Kelly-Evans on the right who passed to Knight, as he ran into the penalty area, and his excellent cross found Knowles who volleyed confidently into the corner of the net. Although Solihull had created a couple of good opportunities, it was Notts who nearly increased their lead on the half hour. A Kelly-Evans cross gave Wootton a chance but, as the goalkeeper advanced, he headed high over the crossbar. At the start of the second half Notts continued in the ascendency. Lacey found the goalkeeper when well placed. A few minutes later Wootton was twice denied by the goalkeeper who pushed a shot beyond the post for a corner, from which he saved Wootton's header. After 56 minutes Slocombe made a brilliant save when he tipped a fierce 30 yard shot on to the angle of crossbar and post and the ball rebounded into his hands! Ten minutes later Solihull equalised when a cross was nodded down for a forward to stab the ball into the net from close range. Soon after this setback the referee ignored Notts claims for a penalty when Wootton was hauled to the ground. With ten minutes remaining Solihull took the lead with another scrappy goal. A long throw into the penalty area, <u>where all ten Notts outfield players were assembled</u>, still managed to find its way to the giant Solihull centre forward (Hudlin 6'9"). Miraculously the ball fell to his feet and he was given time to perform a back heel which eluded Slocombe and trickled into the corner of the net! A Chicksen pass gave Rodrigues the chance to equalise in the last minute but he shot over the bar from near the penalty spot.

Notts' performance overall was good but missed chances and two defensive lapses meant they suffered back to back league defeats for the second time this season, and for the fifth consecutive away game conceded two goals.

Match 6 (32 exc. Dover)   **Notts County** (6th) **0-1 Eastleigh** (10th)   Played behind closed
Sat 17 Apr 2021 12:30   goal 45'+2   doors

                              Slocombe
           Rawlinson   Turner (O'Brien 72')   Lacey
   Kelly-Evans   Chicksen
           Reeves (Capt.)   Griffiths (Miller 72')
   Knight (Boldewijn 57')   Wootton   Knowles

Subs: Ellis, Doyle, O'Brien, Boldewijn, Miller
(no substitute goalkeeper)

Ian Burchnall made just one change to the side unfortunate to lose at Solihull - Turner was preferred to Ellis.

Due to an earlier postponement by Eastleigh (coronavirus) this was the first meeting of the season. Following a good start Eastleigh had a poor run of form and had fallen to 18th towards the end of January. However, by the beginning of March they had risen to 4th. More recently their form had dipped again with only two victories in their last eleven games.

On a gloriously sunny afternoon, it was also cloudless at Windsor Castle for the funeral of Prince Philip at 3pm – the reason the kick-off time had been brought forward. Notts had a good first half hour during which a Rawlinson cross found Chicksen but his first time shot from seven yards just cleared the crossbar. Following Notts' first corner kick the ball fell to Turner who had a shot blocked in the six-yard box. Unfortunately, Notts then began to lose control of the game and, in time added at the end of the half, Eastleigh took the lead after their first corner. The ball wasn't cleared and, with some neat passes, it reached a forward who beat Slocombe at his near post from fifteen yards. It was their one and only attempt of the half.

Notts started the second half on the front foot and, in their first attack the Eastleigh goalkeeper (McDonnell, who made eight appearances for Notts last season) turned a 25 yard shot from Griffiths out for a corner. A few minutes later a Knowles strike from the corner of the penalty area flew just wide. However, Notts then began to struggle and, with 60 minutes played, Eastleigh missed a chance to increase their lead after Slocombe could only palm the ball towards the penalty spot but the shot cleared the crossbar. Ten minutes later Slocombe kept them in the game when he made an excellent save with his legs. Notts' passing lost its crispness with little penetration into the attacking third of the pitch. Apart from a good Knowles shot (McDonnell saved), Notts resorted to aimless crosses into the penalty area which didn't trouble the goalkeeper. Eastleigh just about deserved their narrow victory.

So, for the first time in non-league football Notts suffered three consecutive defeats and dropped to eighth – one below the playoff positions, where they had been for the majority of the season. An out of form Notts County now had just ten league games left to turn things around and regain some momentum! They deserve (and need) a change of fortune.

National League
Table After results Saturday 17 April 2021

Top Half Only

		GP	W	D	L	GF	GA	GD	Pts	PPG	last 8
1	Hartlepool	36	19	10	7	54	33	+21	67	1.86	2.25
2	Sutton Utd	33	19	9	5	55	27	+28	66	2.00	1.63
3	Torquay Utd	33	19	6	8	53	31	+22	63	1.91	2.25
4	Stockport	34	16	11	7	52	28	+24	59	1.74	2.00
5	Wrexham	34	15	8	11	48	33	+15	53	1.56	1.63
6	Halifax Town	33	15	8	10	53	43	+10	53	1.61	2.00
7	Chesterfield	32	16	4	12	44	31	+13	52	1.63	2.00
8	**Notts County**	**32**	**15**	**7**	**10**	**42**	**30**	**+12**	**52**	**1.63**	**1.25**
9	Bromley	34	14	10	10	52	46	+6	52	1.53	1.75
10	Eastleigh	34	13	11	10	37	33	+4	50	1.47	1.25
11	Boreham Wood	34	10	15	9	40	35	+5	45	1.32	1.13

PPG = Points Per Game: percentage of points picked up by the team relative to maximum possible points
Games to complete the season = 42

League table			Form table (last 8)			Home			Away		
	GP	Pts		GP	Pts		GP	Pts		GP	Pts
Hartlepool	36	67	Hartlepool	8	18	Hartlepool	18	39	Sutton Utd	17	35
Sutton Utd	33	66	Torquay Utd	8	18	Sutton Utd	16	31	Torquay Utd	17	33
Torquay Utd	33	63	Stockport	8	16	Torquay Utd	16	30	Stockport	17	30
Stockport	34	59	Chesterfield	8	16	Stockport	17	29	Hartlepool	18	28
Wrexham	34	53	Halifax Town	8	16	**Notts County**	18	29	Bromley	16	28
Halifax Town	33	53	Bromley	8	14	Solihull Moors	15	29	Wrexham	18	27
Chesterfield	32	52	Wrexham	8	13	Halifax Town	16	28	Chesterfield	16	26
Notts County	32	52	Sutton Utd	8	13	Eastleigh	17	27	Halifax Town	17	25
Bromley	34	52	Solihull Moors	8	13	Chesterfield	16	26	Boreham Wood	18	25
Eastleigh	34	50	Dagenham & R.	8	12	Wrexham	16	26	Aldershot Town	18	24
Boreham Wood	34	45	Aldershot Town	8	10	Yeovil Town	16	26	**Notts County**	14	23
Aldershot Town	33	44	**Notts County**	8	10	Dagenham & R.	18	26	Eastleigh	17	23
Dagenham & R.	34	43	Yeovil Town	8	10	Bromley	18	24	Altrincham	19	23
Solihull Moors	32	42	Eastleigh	8	10	Wealdstone	16	23	Maidenhead Utd	15	20
Yeovil Town	32	42	Boreham Wood	8	9	Maidenhead Utd	15	21	Dagenham & R.	16	17
Maidenhead Utd	30	41	Maidenhead Utd	8	8	Woking	17	21	Yeovil Town	16	16
Altrincham	35	41	Weymouth	8	7	Boreham Wood	16	20	Solihull Moors	17	13
Wealdstone	33	33	Altrincham	8	7	Aldershot Town	15	20	Woking	15	11
Woking	32	32	Kings Lynn	8	7	Weymouth	18	20	Weymouth	15	10
Weymouth	33	30	Woking	8	5	Altrincham	16	18	Kings Lynn	16	10
Kings Lynn	32	27	Barnet	8	5	Kings Lynn	16	17	Wealdstone	17	10
Barnet	31	17	Wealdstone	8	4	Barnet	17	11	Barnet	14	6
Dover Athletic	0	0	Dover Athletic	0	0	Dover Athletic	0	0	Dover Athletic	0	0

Match 7 (33 exc. Dover)	**Torquay United** (3rd)	**2-2 Notts County** (8th)	Played behind
Sat 24 Apr 2021 15:00	goals 75' & 90'+8	Kelly-Evans 38'	closed doors
		Ellis 49'	

```
                        Steele
          Rawlinson    Ellis        Lacey (Miller 46')
Kelly-Evans                                      Chicksen
          Reeves     Doyle (Capt.)  O'Brien (Griffiths 67')
                     Wootton       Knowles (Knight 58')
```

Subs: Pilling (Gk), Boldewijn, Griffiths, Knight, Miller

Goalkeeper Sam Slocombe received a groin injury in the defeat to Eastleigh. To provide experienced cover Notts signed Luke Steele, 36, on a short term contract until the end of the season. A free agent without a club, he had not played a game this season, but had amassed nearly 400 career appearances in the Championship and with Panathinaikos (Super League Greece).

There were three other changes to the side. Ellis was preferred to Turner, Doyle returned after injury to replace Griffiths and O'Brien came in for Knight.

The game at Meadow Lane towards the end of January ended goalless. From early February to mid-March Torquay experienced an indifferent run of form which saw them lose their position as league leaders. However, they had won seven of their last eight league games with only two goals conceded, including five consecutive victories in their April fixtures to date.

On a sunny afternoon in Devon, Notts were much the better side in the first half and they were unlucky not to take the lead after 26 minutes. A cross by Kelly-Evans found Knowles and his header hit the crossbar, and Wootton's header from the rebound was saved. With half-time approaching Notts scored a deserved goal. O'Brien chased what appeared to be a lost cause and won the ball off a defender. He passed to Knowles who lost control but the ball ran loose to Kelly-Evans, and his left foot shot from inside the penalty area curled into the corner of the net - his first goal for Notts. With the last action of the half O'Brien passed to Reeves but his first time shot from inside the penalty area was pushed over the crossbar by the goalkeeper.

An injury to Lacey meant he was replaced by Miller from the start of the second half, which was barely five minutes old when Notts increased their lead. Central defender Ellis scored his fourth goal in only his tenth league appearance. Following a short corner kick, Rawlinson headed the cross towards goal and the ball found Ellis who shot calmly into the net from close range. Notts continued in the ascendency and O'Brien gathered a superb Reeves through ball but a defender made a crucial intervention, which looked suspiciously like a foul, on the edge of the penalty area. Unfortunately O'Brien was injured in the process and was substituted by Griffiths. With 75 minutes played Torquay, who had created a couple of chances during the game, reduced their deficit. A cross from the left to the far post was driven first time into the far corner of the net from a tight angle by one of three unmarked attackers. With just over five minutes of normal time left Reeves created a chance for Griffiths but a defender managed to block his goal bound shot. Torquay were then reduced to ten men when a player was sent off after he received yellow cards, in quick succession, for two aggressive aerial challenges on Ellis. But the treatment Ellis required meant eight minutes were added at the end of normal time and in the 98th minute Torquay equalised when, following a long throw-in and a goalmouth scramble, a shot struck a post and was adjudged to have crossed the line before it was cleared.......by the head bandaged Ellis!

Torquay moved to the top of the league. Notts dropped to their lowest league position (ninth) since November.

National League Table

Top Half Only		GP	W	D	L	GF	GA	GD	Pts	PPG	Last 8
1	Torquay Utd	35	20	7	8	57	33	+24	**67**	1.91	2.38
2	Hartlepool	36	19	10	7	54	33	+21	**67**	1.86	2.25
3	Sutton Utd	34	19	9	6	55	28	+27	**66**	1.94	1.25
4	Stockport	35	17	11	7	55	28	+27	**62**	1.77	2.25
5	Halifax Town	35	16	8	11	56	46	+10	**56**	1.60	1.63
6	Bromley	35	15	10	10	54	47	+7	**55**	1.57	1.75
7	Wrexham	35	15	9	11	48	33	+15	**54**	1.54	1.38
8	Chesterfield	34	16	5	13	45	33	+12	**53**	1.56	1.75
9	**Notts County**	**33**	**15**	**8**	**10**	**44**	**32**	**+12**	**53**	**1.61**	**1.00**
10	Eastleigh	35	14	11	10	38	33	+5	**53**	1.51	1.25
11	Aldershot Town	35	14	6	15	47	48	-1	**48**	1.37	1.63

Match 8 (34 exc. Dover)	**Eastleigh** (10th) **2-0 Notts County** (9th)	Played behind closed doors
Tue 27 Apr 2021 19:45	goals 57' & 75'	

```
                        Steele
           Rawlinson    Turner         Ellis (Knowles 78')
Kelly-Evans                                      Chicksen
           Reeves   Doyle (Capt.)   Griffiths (Boldewijn 60')
                    Wootton        Knight (Rodrigues 70')
```

Subs: Brindley, Barnett, Boldewijn, Rodrigues, Knowles
(no substitute goalkeeper)

For the second long trip south in four days there were three changes to the side held to a draw at Torquay. Two were due to injury – Turner instead of Lacey and Griffiths instead of O'Brien. For the other change Knight was preferred to Knowles.

Since the reverse fixture at Meadow Lane ten days ago Eastleigh, like Notts, had played one game. At home they had defeated, then second placed, Sutton United 1-0.

Notts dominated the first half and were the better side. After 13 minutes Knight received a pass from Wootton, ran into the penalty area and shot but (ex Notts) goalkeeper McDonnell made a good save. On the half hour McDonnell was in action again – this time with a remarkable double save. An excellent Reeves cross was met by Wootton but his header was pushed away to Knight, who, from a tight angle chose to cross rather than shoot, and a header by Griffiths was again pushed away by the goalkeeper. Just before half time a Rawlinson cross was met by Chicksen but, unmarked, he headed wide from a good position.

Against the run of play Eastleigh took the lead after 57 minutes when a cross from the left was headed into the corner of the net from the edge of the six-yard box. It was their first attempt on target! The goal transferred momentum to Eastleigh and just over fifteen minutes later they scored a second goal. A forward gained possession of a loose ball, played a quick one-two, and when he reached the corner of the penalty area (with Rawlinson in pursuit) he arrowed his shot, low and hard, into the far corner of the net.

With ten minutes left Turner had a great chance to reduce the deficit but in a central position about five yards from goal his header lacked power and the ball was hooked away.

Notts had opportunities to win the game but they failed to make the most of their chances. Eastleigh, who had scored the fewest number of goals in the top half of the league, had two attempts on target and scored on both occasions.

So, for the seventh consecutive away league game (W1 D3 L3) Notts conceded two goals. Also they had been defeated in four of their last five games (one point earned out of a possible fifteen) – their worst run of form in non-league football. With this defeat they dropped to tenth, three points below a play-off position, but still with at least one game in hand over the nine teams above.

Club News 28 April 2021
Club recognised for Covid response

We're immensely proud to have been named finalists in the 'Best Covid-19 Community Response' category at the 2021 Football Business Awards.

The award recognises the outstanding work undertaken by a club to support its community during the pandemic and has been split into Premier League and Non-Premier League categories.

This amazing recognition comes as a result of various initiatives throughout the pandemic, which began with our first-team management, players and club legend Les Bradd making more than 350 phone calls to elderly, vulnerable and key-worker supporters to bring them some cheer and companionship in the first lockdown.

We also launched a Crowdfunder campaign for Age UK Notts which later blossomed into an official partnership, paving the way for us to raise more vital funds at such a crucial and pressurised time for the charity.

Our community-led approach has been carried into our commercial operations this season, too, with us forging a unique partnership with Cadbury which saw the world-famous chocolate company become our home shirt sponsors before donating the inventory to our travel partners, Sharpes of Nottingham, whose business had been decimated by the pandemic.

We have been nominated alongside the following clubs/organisations and will be attending the ceremony at the Brewery, London, on Tuesday 6 July.

Ashton Gate Stadium – Bristol City FC

Brentford FC

Bristol Rovers FC

Derby County FC Community Trust

Dons Local Action Group with AFC Wimbledon Foundation

Port Vale Foundation Trust

Rangers Charity Foundation

A statement from our board of directors reads: "We are absolutely delighted that the club's efforts to engage and support the local community during such a challenging time have been recognised.

"We understand and respect the important role we have to play in our local area and have been humbled by the response to our initiatives from supporters and members of the community alike.

"This recognition also reflects the incredible work of our staff who have worked so hard this year to deliver our many amazing projects. We say a huge thank you to them and will have our fingers crossed that they bring the award home to Meadow Lane."

Is this the start of the deserved (and needed) change of fortune for Notts?

Match 9 (35 exc. Dover)	**Altrincham** (17th) **1-1 Notts County** (10th)	Played behind closed doors
Sat 1 May 2021 15:00	goal 23' Rodrigues 45'+1	

```
                        Steele
            Rawlinson    Turner (Knight 46')    Ellis
     Brindley                                      Barnett (Chicksen 46')
                 Reeves       Doyle (Capt.)
            Boldewijn               Rodrigues (Knowles 74')
                        Wootton
```

Subs: Kelly-Evans, Chicksen, Griffiths, Knight, Knowles
(no substitute goalkeeper)

For the sixth game away from Meadow Lane out of the last seven fixtures, Ian Burchnall made four changes to the side defeated at Eastleigh. Brindley and Barnett replaced Kelly-Evans and Chicksen as wing backs. Boldewijn and Rodrigues were preferred to Griffiths and Knight.

Notts played Altrincham at the beginning of October, in their first home game of the season, and secured a 3-1 victory. At the halfway stage in their season (early February) Altrincham won at the (then) runaway leaders Torquay and moved up to fourth position. However, in their last 16 matches they had been beaten 11 times, including four consecutive defeats in their last four fixtures, all in April - the last three at home!

On an uneven, spongy, pitch the first half was an uninspiring affair. Notts looked ponderous and Altrincham looked ordinary – not surprising from two out of form teams. However, both goals were good. Altrincham took the lead at the midpoint of the half when a forward advanced down the right and passed inside where a teammate unleashed a powerful shot from 25 yards, and the ball skimmed the grass on its way into the corner of the net. In time added at the end of the half a Rodrigues free kick, from a central position just outside the penalty area, beat the five man defensive wall and the goalkeeper's dive.

For the start of the second half Burchnall changed to a 4-4-2 formation and Knight and Chicksen replaced Turner and Barnett. The first action was an identical Rodrigues free kick to the one he converted at the end of the first half, but this time his shot was easily saved. Wootton had a 20 yard shot pushed behind by the goalkeeper, and a penetrating through ball by Rodrigues allowed Boldewijn to run into the penalty area but the goalkeeper advanced and saved the shot with his legs for another corner kick. However, as the game wore on Notts began to lack urgency and it was Altrincham who had the better goal scoring opportunities. Two 15 yard shots just cleared the bar and a post, and Steele also made two outstanding saves.

It was a disappointing afternoon for Notts who remained in tenth position. Unfortunately this draw extended their winless run to six games, with just two points gained from a possible eighteen. Fortunately they still had one, or two, games in hand over their rivals for a playoff position.

However, as if Notts didn't have enough problems to overcome on the field, two days later, on a cold wet and windy May Day Public Holiday, Notts dropped a (nother) bombshell. A terse statement read:

Assistant head coach Maurice Ross has this afternoon left the club with immediate effect. We will be making no further comment.

Maurice Ross was sacked (resigned?) following an incident at Altrincham last Saturday. Ross immediately apologised after his contract was terminated for gross misconduct (derogatory comments). He had only been with Notts for just over five weeks. In a statement he said:

"During Saturday's match at Altrincham, I made an ill-judged comment to a member of our playing staff which has led to my departure from the club.

"I deeply regret the comment, which is not a reflection of the type of person I am, and would like to place on record my apologies to the player in question for the upset I have caused.

"While it was said in the heat of the moment with no malice intended, it was nevertheless unacceptable and I'm devastated by the impact it's caused.

"I would also like to apologise to the club's board of directors, supporters and Ian Burchnall, all of whom I have enjoyed working with immensely.

"The club have handled today's events impeccably and everyone at Meadow Lane has my full support for the rest of the season and beyond.

> *"I will be taking some time to reflect on my actions and learn from this experience before continuing my coaching journey."*

The next day, just before the game at home to Sutton United, Notts announced that their vastly experienced club captain Michael Doyle would assist Ian Burchnall with coaching duties until the end of the season.

Recently I had suggested that Notts deserved (and needed) a change of fortune. On a bright, but cold and blustery, May evening…

Match 10 (36 exc. Dover) Tue 4 May 2021 17:00	**Notts Co** (10th) **3 - 2 Sutton United** (2nd) Rodrigues 8' Rodrigues 90'+4 (pen.) Wootton 48'	goals 20', 62'	Played behind closed doors but televised by BT Sport

```
                    Slocombe
         Rawlinson    Ellis    Chicksen
Kelly-Evans                              Miller (Brindley 72')
         Reeves   Doyle (Capt.)   Rodrigues (Turner 90'+5)
                Wootton    Knowles (Sam 46')
```

Subs: Brindley, Turner, Griffiths, Boldewijn, Sam
(no substitute goalkeeper)

Ian Burchnall made five changes after the disappointment at Altrincham. Goalkeeper Slocombe returned after injury. Chicksen, Kelly-Evans and Miller replaced Barnett, Brindley and Turner. Knowles was preferred to Boldewijn.

Notts visited Sutton at the beginning of the season (mid-October) when a Wootton goal in the 94th minute gave them a 0-1 victory. Sutton's form throughout had been very good and they were top of the league in mid-April following an unbeaten sequence of 14 league games (W9 D5 L0). In their five games since they had won three and lost two but were still in contention to return to the top and achieve automatic promotion. Only one team had conceded fewer goals than their 29 and they had the next best goal difference (+30).

Sutton created the first scoring opportunity, but Kelly-Evans raced back to block the shot and divert the ball for a corner. The first half was only eight minutes old when Notts took the lead. Tenacity by Reeves and Rodrigues on the edge of the penalty area gave Rodrigues the chance to shoot, and he angled the ball through defenders into the corner of the net. Twelve minutes later Sutton equalised, after Doyle lost possession near the halfway line and the ball was passed to the left wing. From there a forward ran into the penalty area and, as he was challenged by Rawlinson, lifted the ball over Slocombe into the far corner of the net from 15 yards. On the half hour Slocombe produced an excellent save when he dived low to his right to parry a 20-yard shot away from his goal. Just before halftime an excellent Kelly-Evans cross was met by Knowles, in a good position, but he was unable to generate power and direction in his header. The first 45 minutes were entertaining with Notts sharper and much more focussed than at Altrincham.

Notts started the second half on the front foot and, after three minutes, went into the lead for the second time. The goalkeeper failed to hold a Rodrigues shot from near the penalty spot and Wootton ended his (13 game) goal drought when he tapped home the rebound. It was his first league goal since 2 March. On 60 minutes Rodrigues presented Miller with an excellent opportunity to increase Notts' lead but he dragged his shot across goal and wide. Sutton responded with the equaliser when, against the run of play, a cross from the left found its way into the six-yard box and the ball was tapped home. Five minutes later a foul by Kelly-Evans earned him a second yellow card and he was sent off the field. The subsequent free kick nearly produced a goal for Sutton but Slocombe made a good save from an on target header. Although down to ten men it was Notts who held the ascendency in the final 25 minutes. They thought they had taken the lead again but an 'own goal' was ruled out when Sam was flagged offside. A few minutes later Wootton had the ball in the net again with a neat shot but he was adjudged to have handled the ball. In time added after the scheduled 90 minutes Notts scored the winner. An Ellis header, following a cross from the right by Rodrigues, ran loose and, when he tried to retrieve the ball, he was fouled (in the penalty area). The excellent Rodrigues stepped up and, with coolness and authority, sent the goalkeeper the wrong way with a well-placed shot from the spot!

It was an excellent team performance against a very good Sutton side, but one player stood out. Ruben Rodrigues orchestrated play with a series of excellent penetrative passes and crosses – he seemed to be everywhere!

[Mark Ellis suffered a head injury just before the end of the game at Torquay ten days ago, which required twenty stitches at hospital! During the time added for his treatment Notts conceded the equaliser to Torquay in the 98th minute. This game was his third since the injury and in all three he had worn a head bandage for protection. Against Sutton he must have headed the ball at least a dozen times, and at the final whistle, after an outstanding contribution to the victory, the bandage was heavily blood stained!]

So, after a dramatic game, Notts deservedly completed the double over Sutton (the only team to achieve the feat so far) and moved up to eighth, one point below the last playoff position but still with at least one game in hand.

National League Table

Top Half Only			GP	W	D	L	GF	GA	GD	Pts	Form	PPG	last 8
1	Torquay Utd		38	23	7	8	64	35	+29	76		2.00	2.75
2	Sutton Utd		37	21	9	7	61	32	+29	72		1.95	1.38
3	Stockport		38	20	11	7	64	28	+36	71		1.87	2.50
4	Hartlepool		38	20	10	8	57	35	+22	70		1.84	2.13
5	Halifax Town		38	18	8	12	60	47	+13	62		1.63	1.88
6	Wrexham		37	16	10	11	52	36	+16	58		1.57	1.38
7	Bromley		37	16	10	11	56	49	+7	58		1.57	2.13
8	**Notts County**		**36**	**16**	**9**	**11**	**48**	**37**	**+11**	**57**		**1.58**	**1.00**
9	Chesterfield		37	17	5	15	48	39	+9	56		1.51	1.00
10	Eastleigh		37	15	11	11	41	36	+5	56		1.51	1.63
11	Dagenham & R.		37	15	7	15	42	44	-2	52		1.41	1.88

Match 11 (37 exc. Dover)	**Barnet** (22nd) **1-4 Notts County** (8th)	Played behind closed doors
Sat 8 May 2021 15:00	goal 89' Ellis 45'+2	
	Rodrigues 46'	
	own goal 55'	
	Boldewijn 85'	

Slocombe

Rawlinson   Ellis   Chicksen

Brindley   Miller

Reeves   Doyle (Capt.) (Griffiths 68')   Rodrigues (O'Brien 81')

Wootton (Boldewijn 74')   Sam

Subs: Turner, O'Brien, Griffiths, Boldewijn, Knowles
(no substitute goalkeeper)

There were two changes to the side so impressive in the victory over Sutton. Brindley replaced the suspended Kelly-Evans and Sam was preferred to Knowles.

After four games this season Barnet had won two and lost two. The second of those defeats was to Notts (4-2) at Meadow Lane on 10 October. Between late October and Easter Monday on 5 April they played 25 league games and won just one. However, despite the fact they remained bottom of the league (the 'retired' Dover – results expunged – below) their form had improved in the last seven games (P7 W3 D2 L2 F8 A6) which included three 'clean sheets'.

Morning rain gave way to a dry, but overcast and windy, afternoon. Notts played against the wind and dominated the first half but it wasn't until the last action of the half that they took the lead, following a Reeves corner. The scorer was central defender Mark Ellis with his fifth goal in only his 14th league game – a header from close range after the ball had bounced around in the penalty area. Slocombe's only concern in the first 45 minutes was an excellent 25 yard shot with flew inches wide of his right-hand post.

In the first action of the second half Notts increased their lead. This time the scorer was Tuesday's man-of-the match Ruben Rodrigues, with his fourth goal in three games. A long Chicksen pass found Miller who ran to the byline and then pulled the ball back for Rodrigues to side foot the ball into the net from seven yards. Miller provided another 'assist' ten minutes later when a defender turned his low cross over the goal line (just) for an 'own goal' – Notts' first 'present' of the season gave them their third goal. After 72 minutes only a brilliant save by the goalkeeper prevented a

Wootton goal. With five minutes left the maligned Enzio Boldewijn ended his difficult week with Notts' fourth when he moved in from the left and struck the ball with his right foot into the far corner of the net from the edge of the penalty area. Barnet scored a consolation goal just before the commencement of added time.

Notts moved up to seventh, the final promotion playoff position – but still with game(s) in hand. League leaders Torquay were held to a goalless draw by Bromley who dropped out of the playoffs despite the point earned. Two of Notts' five remaining fixtures were against Bromley, first at home, and then away in the final game of the season!

Match 12 (38 exc. Dover) Tue 11 May 2021 19:45	**Maidenhead United** (12th) **0-4 Notts Co** (7th) O'Brien 10', 65' O'Brien 75' (pen) Rodrigues 83'	Played behind closed doors

Slocombe

Rawlinson   Ellis   Chicksen

Kelly-Evans   Miller (Brindley 85')

Reeves   Doyle (Capt.) (Griffiths 83')   O'Brien

Rodrigues (Sam 83')

Wootton

Subs: Brindley, Turner, Griffiths, Boldewijn, Sam
(no substitute goalkeeper)

There were two changes to the side victorious over Barnet. Kelly-Evans returned, after his one match suspension, to replace Brindley, and O'Brien was preferred to Sam.

Maidenhead defeated Notts (2-3) at Meadow Lane in mid-October. Notts then didn't play again for three weeks due to coronavirus (COVID-19) infections at the club. Maidenhead's form this season had been inconsistent and unpredictable. This was illustrated by their results since they defeated Torquay in mid-March. In six home games they had won just once, but had suffered defeat in only one of their last eight games. Their goal scoring record was one of the best in the league, and the two players responsible for the majority of the goals scored all four in their victory at Hartlepool three days ago, which almost certainly ended Hartlepool's automatic promotion chances (top spot). Orsi-Dadomo's goal took him to 17 for the season and Barratt's hat-trick took his tally to 15. The same duo scored the goals in the victory at Meadow Lane. However, there was a surprise when

Maidenhead's team was announced – there was no Barratt and no explanation was given for his absence. Also Maidenhead only named four substitutes (five allowed) and the four didn't include a goalkeeper. With the second half only a few minutes old their goalkeeper (Lovett) had to retire injured and an outfield player took over. As the players walked off at half time the Maidenhead manager had an altercation with the referee and was shown a red card – in other words he was banned from the dug-out for the second half.

During an unusual evening Jim O'Brien scored his first goal(s) of the season and completed a hat trick – the first he had achieved in professional football!

In the first ten minutes of the game Notts were excellent. Wootton and Rodrigues created three chances between them but a goal saving tackle, a save by the goalkeeper and a shot which flashed narrowly wide meant the score remained goalless. However, in the tenth minute Doyle spotted an attacking run by O'Brien and lifted a superb through ball which O'Brien brought under control and then shot. His first attempt bounced off the goalkeeper but he headed home the rebound. Maidenhead then gradually came more into the game but they failed to trouble Slocombe. Notts regained the ascendency as half time approached with Miller and Rodrigues the protagonists. Just before the break only a brilliant save from a Rodrigues header prevented a second Notts goal. The goalkeeper, who was injured in the process when he collided with a goalpost, continued following lengthy treatment and completed the seven minutes of added time.

However, the second half was only five minutes old when the Maidenhead goalkeeper (Lovett) signalled his inability to continue and he was replaced by an outfield player. Five minutes later Slocombe had his only anxious moment of the evening when a Maidenhead shot flew narrowly wide. It wasn't a surprise when Notts increased their lead after 65 minutes. Miller ran to the byline and pulled the ball back for Wootton to tap to O'Brien who shot home from near the penalty spot. Miller then had a shot, from point blank range, luckily saved by the stand-in goalkeeper and Rodrigues' follow up was blocked. A minute later Wootton was brought down in the penalty area and O'Brien converted the spot kick to complete his hat trick. With seven minutes remaining a pass out of defence by Kelly-Evans found Rodrigues near the half way line and in the breakaway, chased by two defenders, he ran into the penalty area and slipped the ball beyond the diving goalkeeper to score his fifth goal in four games.

Notts moved up to fifth and they still had one game in hand over teams in positions 6-8. Wrexham (9th) had played the same number of games and were Notts' next opponents away from home. Realistically, with four games to play, Notts were now poised to finish fifth which would guarantee a home fixture in the first round of the playoffs.

National League Table

Top Half Only		GP	W	D	L	GF	GA	GD	Pts	Form	PPG	last 8
1	Sutton Utd	39	23	9	7	66	34	+32	78		2.00	1.88
2	Torquay Utd	39	23	8	8	64	35	+29	77		1.97	2.50
3	Stockport	39	20	12	7	65	29	+36	72		1.85	2.50
4	Hartlepool	39	20	10	9	59	39	+20	70		1.79	1.75
5	**Notts County**	**38**	**18**	**9**	**11**	**56**	**38**	**+18**	**63**		**1.66**	**1.38**
6	Chesterfield	39	19	5	15	56	41	+15	62		1.59	1.25
7	Halifax Town	39	18	8	13	60	48	+12	62		1.59	1.50
8	Bromley	39	17	11	11	57	49	+8	62		1.59	2.38
9	Wrexham	38	17	10	11	55	36	+19	61		1.61	1.75
10	Eastleigh	37	15	11	11	41	36	+5	56		1.51	1.63
11	Dagenham & R.	39	16	8	15	48	45	+3	56		1.44	2.38

Match 13 (39 exc. Dover) **Notts County** (5th) **2-2 Bromley** (8th) Played behind closed
Sat 15 May 2021 15:00 Wootton 53' goals 27' & 75' doors for the last time
Rodrigues 62' at Meadow Lane

                        Slocombe
            Brindley   Ellis   Chicksen
    Kelly-Evans (Boldewijn 46')   Miller
            Reeves   Doyle (Capt.)   O'Brien (Sam 80')
                        Rodrigues
                        Wootton

Subs: Turner, McCrory, Griffiths, Boldewijn, Sam
(no substitute goalkeeper)

Damien McCrory had made just two starts this season due to injury – the last was on 17 October 2020. As a reminder his position is (left) full back, but he has played as a central defender!

Ian Burchnall made one change to the team which comprehensively defeated Maidenhead. Brindley took the place of the injured Rawlinson.

This was the first meeting between the sides this season. The fixture was originally scheduled for early February but was postponed due to a waterlogged Meadow Lane pitch. Notts were due to play

Dover (season terminated with results expunged) and Bromley were due to play Macclesfield (expelled before they had played a game), so this was a free date to accommodate the re-arranged fixture.

Bromley finished in mid-table last season. They beat Notts 2-1 at home and lost 2-1 at Meadow Lane. They had been in the top half of the league for the majority of this season. Following a defeat at Wrexham at the end of March Bromley appointed a new manager and to date, after ten games, he had only experienced one loss. In six away games under his tenure they had won four and drawn two before today, and had kept a clean sheet in their last three games. In 39 league games played they had failed to score only six times – the best in the league. Forward Michael Cheek was The National League's leading scorer with 20 goals, but he hadn't scored in his last four games.

Notts dominated the first 25 minutes with confident movement and passing, although Bromley had a chance to take the lead in the 14th minute when a shot from near the penalty spot was sliced wide. Against the run of play they did take the lead after 27 minutes when Cheek, near the far post, headed a cross from the right into the six yard box and Ellis, under pressure, headed into his own net. Slocombe had to make a good save five minutes later. Notts regained the initiative as half time approached and O'Brien nearly equalised when, from ten yards, he headed Wootton's cross inches wide. For all their possession this was the best chance Notts created in an entertaining first half.

At the start of the second half Boldewijn replaced Kelly-Evans, and Notts continued to dominate the game. Just after Miller shot wide from 20 yards the goalkeeper saved a Reeves shot with his legs which lead to the first of three Notts corner kicks in quick succession. The pressure finally told on the Bromley defence and Wootton equalised from close range when he received a Rodrigues pass from the left side of the penalty area. Notts continued to press and ten minutes later a Boldewijn cross from the right found Miller near the far post and the goalkeeper could only palm his excellent header to Rodrigues who tapped the ball home from six yards to give Notts the lead. It was his sixth goal in the last five games! Notts were now relentless, and a 25 yard O'Brien shot smashed against a post and a 25 yard free kick by Rodrigues rattled the crossbar. Notts could have been 4-1 ahead, but with a quarter of an hour left Bromley, again against the run of play, equalised when a forward stooped low to head a cross from the right into the net from six yards. In the final minutes Sam had a goal bound shot blocked and moments later, when he tried to hook the ball into the goalmouth, a penalty appeal for hand ball was rejected by the referee.

Notts deserved all three points but Bromley defended well and contributed to an excellent game of football. This game, Notts' penultimate Meadow Lane fixture of the season, was their last 'behind closed doors'. The coronavirus (COVID-19) lockdown restrictions in England were eased by the government on Monday 17 May. The next day Notts had a fixture at Wrexham to negotiate. Examination of the table (see below) indicated the importance of that game, for both clubs. It was the only midweek fixture of direct relevance to playoff positions, although Eastleigh's victory at Aldershot moved them up to ninth (on goal difference) and therefore still in contention for a playoff place as they had a game in hand over everyone else.

Table after Sat 15 May results

Top Half Only		GP	W	D	L	GF	GA	GD	Pts	Form	PPG	last 8
1	Sutton Utd	40	24	9	7	69	34	+35	81		2.03	2.25
2	Torquay Utd	40	23	9	8	66	37	+29	78		1.95	2.25
3	Stockport	40	20	13	7	67	31	+36	73		1.83	2.25
4	Hartlepool	40	21	10	9	62	40	+22	73		1.83	2.00
5	Wrexham	39	18	10	11	58	38	+20	64		1.64	2.13
6	**Notts County**	**39**	**18**	**10**	**11**	**58**	**40**	**+18**	**64**		**1.64**	**1.50**
7	Chesterfield	40	19	6	15	56	41	+15	63		1.58	1.38
8	Bromley	40	17	12	11	59	51	+8	63		1.58	2.13
9	Halifax Town	40	18	8	14	60	51	+9	62		1.55	1.50
10	Eastleigh	38	16	11	11	44	36	+8	59		1.55	2.00
11	Dagenham & R.	40	17	8	15	51	45	+6	59		1.48	2.75

Match 14 (40 exc. Dover) Tue 18 May 2021 19:00	**Wrexham** (5th) **0-1 Notts County** (6th) Reeves 26'	Played behind closed doors

Slocombe
Brindley   Ellis   Chicksen
Kelly-Evans   Miller (McCrory 77')
Reeves   Doyle (Capt.)   O'Brien
Rodrigues (Sam 67')
Wootton

Subs: Turner, McCrory, Griffiths, Boldewijn, Sam
(no substitute goalkeeper)

There were no changes, to the starting eleven and the substitutes, to the squad that made a draw against Bromley.

This game was originally scheduled for mid-February but was postponed because of a frozen pitch. After losing 1-0 at Meadow Lane on Good Friday (2 April) Wrexham lost their next two games.

They then began their current sequence of seven unbeaten – W5 D2. (Notts' last seven W3 D3 L1). The Welsh Government had taken a different approach to that in England regarding the safe return of supporters to football matches. As a consequence, there were no spectator's at the game.

During the first 35 minutes Notts were excellent. Their passing was crisp, their movement was impressive, and they amassed eight corner kicks. The Wrexham goalkeeper made two very good saves, first from a 20-yard Reeves shot and then a 25 yard shot from O'Brien. It was no surprise when Notts took a deserved lead in the 26th minute. Rodrigues slid the ball to the unmarked Reeves 35 yards from goal. He had time to control the ball, move forward a couple of yards, and unleash a powerful low drive which arrowed its way into the corner of the net with the goalkeeper well beaten. Wrexham's only foray into the Notts half resulted in a 25-yard shot of their own which flew just wide. However, in the ten minutes before half time Wrexham came more into the game and started to put the Notts defence under pressure.

Wrexham continued the assault on the Notts defence throughout most of the second half. On the hour mark a series of penetrative passes out of defence resulted in a Kelly-Evans shot being blocked. Notts continued to defend bravely and, in particular, Slocombe and Ellis were magnificent. Notts showed tremendous character throughout and gave a wonderful, solid, team performance. They showed fluency and class in the opening 35 minutes and then gave a dogged, but assured, defensive display in the second half. Notts up to fifth, Wrexham down to sixth!

The game was refereed by Rebecca Welch who had made history on Easter Monday when she became the first woman to referee a men's English Football League match from the start - Harrogate Town v Port Vale in League Two. She also refereed the Meadow Lane game against Maidenhead on 17 October 2020.

Match 15 (41 exc. Dover)	**Notts County (5th) 3-0 Weymouth (18th)**	Attendance 4,197
Sat 22 May 2021 15:00	Rodrigues 24' (pen.)	
	Wootton 28'	
	Boldewijn 64'	

Slocombe

Brindley   Ellis   Chicksen

Kelly-Evans (Boldewijn 61')   Miller

Reeves (Sam 80')   Doyle (Capt.)   O'Brien

Rodrigues (Griffiths 83')

Wootton

Subs: Turner, Rawlinson, Griffiths, Boldewijn, Sam

(no substitute goalkeeper)

Ian Burchnall named an unchanged team for the third successive game.

Due to the coronavirus (COVID-19) pandemic, this was Notts' first fixture at Meadow Lane with spectators in attendance since 14 March 2020 – fourteen months ago – when they defeated Eastleigh 4-0 before a crowd of 4,942. Their National League average attendance last season, before the lockdown, was 5,210. Although the government had eased restrictions considerably, following extensive dialogue with the relevant authorities a maximum attendance of 4,400 was sanctioned. In addition to the 4,197 present there were 1,165 streamers = total 'attendance' 5,362.

Notts won 0-1 at Weymouth, who had been in the bottom third of the league table throughout the season, at the end of January. Since their last draw, in mid-March, Weymouth had played thirteen games – won 5 lost 8. They had lost four of their last five games and only three teams had conceded more goals than their 64. Notts were unbeaten in their last six outings.

Once again Notts were excellent in the first half hour and went into a two goal lead. The first goal came from a penalty, following an incisive passing move which ended with a Rodrigues shot but the goalkeeper palmed the ball away. Wootton retrieved the ball and slid it to Reeves who was fouled as he was about to shoot into the net from a central position seven yards out. Rodrigues calmly placed the penalty into the corner of the net as the goalkeeper dived in the opposite direction. The second goal was unusual in that a Rodrigues free kick from 30 yards struck the defensive wall and the ball looped some distance into the air, the goalkeeper slipped and Wootton was on hand to tap the rebound home from very close range. Notts then relaxed a little and Weymouth had two opportunities to reduce the arrears. Ellis attempted to back head the ball to Slocombe but only succeeded in giving it to Weymouth's Dallas (their on loan top scorer with 12 goals in 24 games) but his 15 yard shot went just over the crossbar. A few minutes later Rodrigues was caught in possession and the ball ran to Dallas but Slocombe saved his 25 yard shot. In the last minute of the first half Ellis headed a corner kick to Brindley but his header hit the crossbar.

For most of the second half Weymouth were outplayed and Notts should have increased their lead by more than the one scored by Boldewijn. His goal came courtesy of the unselfish Wootton who presented him with the chance and he side-footed the ball into the corner of the spion kop net from 15 yards. Only a superb save by the goalkeeper prevented the industrious Miller from getting his deserved first Notts goal. Rodrigues hit a post, his shot from the rebound was cleared off the line and Boldewijn's follow up shot was blocked. There were other opportunities but Notts had to settle for just the three goals. As the referee blew the final whistle the sun shone (after a cool, wet, May to date) over Meadow Lane and the crowd rose to acknowledge Notts' performance. The whole playing squad and coaching staff responded by applauding as they paraded around the perimeter of the pitch.

Once again 39 year old Michael Doyle (captain and assistant head coach) gave an outstanding and inspiring performance in midfield. You don't make almost 850 career appearances (including nearly 100 for Notts) without being the ultimate professional.

The victory kept Notts in fifth position and guaranteed their participation in the playoffs, with one game (away at Bromley) to complete the season. It also extended their unbeaten run to seven (P7 W5 D2 L0 F18 A6 Pts 17) since the start of the sequence on 1 May.

The next day Sutton defeated Hartlepool 3-0 and became champions to earn automatic promotion to EFL League Two. Incidentally Notts were the only team to complete the double over Sutton - they won 1-0 away from home in mid-October and then won 3-2 at Meadow Lane six games ago.

Over is the top half of The National League table, with just the final fixtures to complete the season on Saturday 29 May.

(Following their victory over Hartlepool, Sutton lost their final game of the season 2-0 at bottom of the league Barnet!)

National League Table

Top Half Only

#	Team	GP	W	D	L	GF	GA	GD	Pts	Form	PPG	last 8
1	Sutton Utd	41	25	9	7	72	34	+38	84	Promoted	2.05	2.25
2	Torquay Utd	41	23	10	8	68	39	+29	79		1.93	2.00
3	Stockport	41	20	14	7	68	32	+36	74		1.80	2.00
4	Hartlepool	41	21	10	10	62	43	+19	73		1.78	1.63
5	**Notts County**	**41**	**20**	**10**	**11**	**62**	**40**	**+22**	**70**		**1.71**	**2.13**
6	Wrexham	41	19	10	12	63	42	+21	67		1.63	2.13
7	Chesterfield	41	20	6	15	58	42	+16	66		1.61	1.75
8	Eastleigh	41	18	12	11	49	38	+11	66		1.61	2.38
9	Bromley	41	18	12	11	62	53	+9	66		1.61	2.13
10	Halifax Town	41	19	8	14	62	52	+10	65		1.59	1.50
11	Solihull Moors	41	18	7	16	56	48	+8	61		1.49	2.00

A few days before the final game of the season at Bromley, Jason Turner provided an update on the future of the academy.

Should the first team not win promotion to the EFL this season the club would no longer receive academy grant aid funding, leaving an annual shortfall of more than £200k against this season's external support.

Our board of directors are, however, committed to providing significant financial support to enable the academy to continue in a similar format to now, albeit outside the parameters of the Elite Player Performance Plan, should the club remain in The National League.

"As a board, we recognise the importance of providing a pathway for young, local players to become our potential stars of the future," said Turner.

"We are also very aware that our supporters take great pride in the academy and the many excellent players it has produced over the years.

"It therefore gives us great pleasure to reassure fans, staff, players and parents that we will continue to have an academy next season, across all age groups, no matter which division the club finds itself in.

"Along with financial support from our owners, the academy will continue to benefit from the dedicated work of our Official Supporters' Association whose fundraising efforts have been hugely helpful over the years.

"Following last season's title success for our Under 18s, and the rise to prominence of Tyreace Palmer, we can all look forward to what will hopefully be a prosperous future for our youth development programme.

"Operating outside of EPPP would raise many new challenges but we are determined to tackle these head-on in the interests of providing the best possible platform for our young players."

Tyreace Palmer signed a professional contract in the summer of 2021. After his recovery from an injury, and then regaining his fitness, in the autumn of 2021, he had loan spells at Melton Town and Basford United. Unfortunately, however, in the summer of 2022 he was released by Notts.

Match 16 (42 exc. Dover)	**Bromley** (9th) **1-0 Notts County** (5th)	Attendance 1,344
Sat 29 May 2021 12:30	goal 64'	

Slocombe

Rawlinson　　Ellis　　Chicksen

Brindley　　　　　　　　　　　　Miller (Sam 76')

Reeves (Boldewijn 46')　　Doyle (Capt.)　　　O'Brien

Rodrigues (Griffiths 85')

Wootton

Subs: Turner, Kelly-Evans, Griffiths, Boldewijn, Sam
(no substitute goalkeeper)

For the final league game of the season Ian Burchnall, determined to maintain momentum, made one change to the team which outplayed Weymouth. Rawlinson returned after injury with Kelly-Evans relegated to the substitutes bench.

Since the drawn game at Meadow Lane a fortnight ago Bromley had played one game – a victory at Aldershot – while Notts had won at Wrexham and defeated Weymouth. Bromley needed to win to participate in the playoffs.

On a 3G (artificial grass) pitch, Notts controlled the majority of the first half. However, both sides could have taken the lead in the first five minutes. First Bromley's Michael Cheek, The National League's leading scorer with 21 goals, sent a header just wide when well placed. Notts retaliated, with what turned out to be their best chance of the half, when Wootton lifted the ball over the goalkeeper but his shot hit the underside of the crossbar. Rodrigues did well to get the rebound back to Wootton who side footed the ball to O'Brien but he then shot wide from ten yards. Notts created other opportunities but were unable to make the breakthrough their play deserved.

Due to an injury Reeves was replaced by Boldewijn at the start of the second half. Rodrigues had a good chance to open the scoring but his shot, from near the penalty spot, went wide. Bromley then began to take control of the game and their pressure brought a goal in the 64th minute. Following a corner, after Slocombe had pushed a 20-yard shot behind, a shot struck a post and from the rebound another shot was helped into the net from close range. Notts responded when the goalkeeper saved a Rodrigues shot with his feet and Miller's follow-up volley was blocked on the line. However, Bromley regained the initiative and a header hit the crossbar and Slocombe made some good saves.

After the game Ian Burchnall described the hard 3G pitch as a "nightmare". He thought it was responsible for Reeves' heel injury, and the cramp suffered by Miller and Rodrigues. Following a good first half performance, Notts disappointed in the second half and they were defeated for the first time in eight games. However, other results were in their favour and they finished the season in fifth position which gave them a home fixture in the eliminator playoff against the team who finished in sixth place – near neighbours Chesterfield.

The final National League table for season 2020-21

	Team	GP	W	D	L	GF	GA	GD	Pts	Form	PPG	last 8
1	Sutton Utd	42	25	9	8	72	36	+36	84	Promoted to EFL League Two	2.00	2.25
2	Torquay Utd	42	23	11	8	68	39	+29	80		1.90	1.75
3	Stockport	42	21	14	7	69	32	+37	77		1.83	2.25
4	Hartlepool	42	22	10	10	66	43	+23	76	Promoted	1.81	1.88
5	**Notts County**	**42**	**20**	**10**	**12**	**62**	**41**	**+21**	**70**		**1.67**	**2.13**
6	Chesterfield	42	21	6	15	60	43	+17	69		1.64	2.00
7	Bromley	42	19	12	11	63	53	+10	69		1.64	2.13
8	Wrexham	42	19	11	12	64	43	+21	68		1.62	1.88
9	Eastleigh	42	18	12	12	49	40	+9	66		1.57	2.00
10	Halifax Town	42	19	8	15	63	54	+9	65		1.55	1.13
11	Solihull Moors	42	19	7	16	58	48	+10	64		1.52	2.38
12	Dagenham & R.	42	17	9	16	53	48	+5	60		1.43	2.13
13	Maidenhead Utd	42	15	11	16	62	60	+2	56		1.33	1.00
14	Boreham Wood	42	13	16	13	52	48	+4	55		1.31	1.25
15	Aldershot Town	42	15	7	20	59	66	-7	52		1.24	0.88
16	Yeovil Town	42	15	7	20	58	68	-10	52		1.24	0.88
17	Altrincham	42	12	11	19	46	60	-14	47		1.12	0.75
18	Weymouth	42	11	6	25	45	71	-26	39		0.93	0.75
19	Wealdstone	42	10	7	25	49	99	-50	37		0.88	0.50
20	Woking	42	8	9	25	42	69	-27	33		0.79	0.13
21	Kings Lynn	42	7	10	25	50	98	-48	31		0.74	0.38
22	Barnet	42	8	7	27	37	88	-51	31		0.74	1.25
23	Dover Athletic	0	0	0	0	0	0	0	0		0	0

No relegations this season.

So, as the season ended and before the playoff(s) commenced, Ian Burchnall's record was:
P16 W7 D3 L6 F26 A19 Pts 24.

Neal Ardley's league record for the part of the season he was manager was:
P26 W13 D7 L6 F36 A22 Pts 46.

After Neal's final game in charge at Yeovil, Notts were in 6th position. At the end of the season, under Ian, Notts finished 5th.

This comparison was not included to indicate the merits of Ian or Neal, as many factors needed to be taken into consideration before a rational judgement was made.

Playoff Quarter-Final/ Eliminator Sat 5 June 2021 16:00	**Notts County** (5th) **3-2 Chesterfield** (6th) Wootton 30', 71' goals 27', 42' Ellis 90'	Restricted Attendance 4,569

```
                      Slocombe
    Rawlinson (Knowles 46')    Ellis              Chicksen
Brindley                                             Miller
         Reeves (Kelly-Evans 90')    Doyle (Capt.)
               Boldewijn         Rodrigues
                       Wootton

    Subs: Turner, Kelly-Evans, Barnett, Griffiths, Knowles
                  (no substitute goalkeeper)
```

There was just one change to the team defeated at Bromley in the final game of the season. Boldewijn replaced the injured O'Brien.

Chesterfield were unbeaten in their last five league games of the season. They won 4 and drew 1. Three of those games were against strugglers Woking (20th), King's Lynn (21st) and Wealdstone (19th) who held them to a 0-0 draw, despite having the worst defensive record in the league. In their ten league fixtures against the other playoff contenders they lost 8 and won 2. Admittedly both victories were away from home, at Meadow Lane 0-1 and at Bromley 1-2.

The first 30 minutes of this enthralling game were fairly even. Chesterfield took the lead after Reeves committed a foul thirty yards from goal. Slocombe dived to his right and got his hand on the thunderous free kick but the power of the shot was such that it still flew into the roof of the net. Three minutes later Notts equalised when Rodrigues charged down an attempted defensive clearance and ran on into the Chesterfield penalty area where he was brought down by the goalkeeper, but the referee allowed play to continue as Wootton collected the loose ball and calmly side footed it into the net as four defenders tried to retrieve the situation. As half time approached Notts began to dominate the game, but after an attack was halted a Chesterfield breakaway ended with a cross from the left which was swept into the corner of Slocombe's net from the edge of the six yard box.

In a tactical change, at the start of the second half, forward Knowles was introduced in place of defender Rawlinson and Notts continued to dominate the game. The Chesterfield goalkeeper received a leg injury, but after lengthy treatment he continued as, like Notts, they hadn't named a goalkeeper among their five substitutes. Notts equalised for a second time when, following a Rodrigues corner kick, Ellis headed the ball down to Wootton who volleyed into the net from six yards for his 19th (league and cup) goal of the season. Although Notts were bombarding the Chesterfield defence, with 15 minutes remaining Slocombe came to Notts' rescue. Ex Notts forward Nathan Tyson (17 league and cup appearances for Notts last season but just one goal), on the pitch as a Chesterfield substitute, received the ball near the half way line and sped towards the Notts goal. Slocombe advanced and saved the shot with his legs. The tension mounted and **in the final minute of normal time Notts took the lead** for the first time in the game. Rodrigues, on the left wing, withstood some fierce challenges and finally the referee awarded a free kick. He floated the ball into the goalmouth where Ellis (the goal scoring central defender) weaved his way from the edge of the penalty area towards the dropping ball and thundered it into the net with a powerful header, and Meadow Lane erupted with delight. It was his sixth goal in twenty league games since his arrival, on loan from Tranmere Rovers, at the beginning of March. But the game wasn't over and Slocombe again rescued Notts with a brilliant save when he dived to his left to tip a bullet of a shot from 20 yards over the crossbar. With the last action of the game, following a Chesterfield corner, there was a goalmouth scramble when the ball ran loose. Thankfully, after it had pin-balled around, Slocombe smothered it on the goal line and kissed the ball as the referee then blew the final whistle. Everyone breathed a big sigh of relieve!

So, a dramatic late afternoon ended in Notts' favour but not without a battle and some scary moments. A great all round team performance, complemented with Wootton's opportunism, Ellis's heading ability, Slocombe's outstanding saves and Doyle's control in midfield, earned Notts a playoff semi-final at Torquay Utd on 12 June.

In the other playoff quarter-final/eliminator, Hartlepool Utd defeated Bromley (3-2) to earn a semi-final trip to Stockport County.

Playoff Semi-Final	**Torquay United** (2nd) **4-2 Notts County** (5th)	Restricted attendance
Sat 12 June 2021 12:00	*After Extra Time*	1,709 – no visiting
	goals 1', 48'　　　　　Rodrigues 39'	supporters permitted
	102', 105'+4(pen.)　　Chicksen 51'	

```
                        Slocombe
         Brindley        Ellis        Chicksen (Rawlinson 105')
Kelly-Evans                                       Miller (Barnett 85')
   Reeves (Griffiths 105')           Doyle (Capt.)
       Boldewijn (Knowles 73')          Rodrigues
                        Wootton
```

Subs: Turner, Rawlinson, Barnett, Griffiths, Knowles
(no substitute goalkeeper)

There was just one change to the starting eleven which dramatically defeated Chesterfield in the quarter-final/eliminator; Kelly-Evans replaced Rawlinson.

Torquay drew 0-0 at Meadow Lane and were fortunate to earn a draw (2-2) in the return fixture, with Notts losing a two-goal lead. Their equaliser came in the 98th minute!

Torquay were top of the league from late October until early March. At the turn of the year they had an 11 point lead over second place! In 12 games against the other teams in the top seven they suffered only one defeat – at home to Hartlepool. They were unbeaten in their last 13 league games of the season (W8 D5 F20 A9) – their last defeat was on 27 March. However, their last four games had ended in a draw.

The game was **less than one minute old** when Torquay took the lead. A harmless looking cross from the left was headed by their centre forward and struck the challenging Chicksen on its way past Slocombe. Notts equalised six minutes before half time with a brilliant goal, following a sequence of 16 passes, when Rodrigues dived to connect with a Kelly-Evans cross and steered his powerful header into the net from ten yards. As half time approached a Brindley shot from 25 yards just cleared the crossbar, Rodrigues had a shot blocked and Wootton headed a Boldewijn cross over when well placed.

The second half was barely three minutes old when Torquay regained the lead. A low cross from the right was clinically swept into the net from 12 yards by the scorer of their first goal. Back came

Notts almost immediately, this time courtesy of Chicksen's first goal for the club. Following a Rodrigues corner kick the ball was headed down by Brindley and Chicksen reacted quickly to flash it into the roof of the net with a shot on the turn. Soon afterwards Slocombe made an excellent save when he dived to palm away a shot following a quick Torquay counter attack. Notts retaliated with a Rodrigues shot from the edge of the penalty area which crept just wide. Torquay then created two opportunities - a shot from near the penalty spot went over the crossbar and another shot was blocked. Just before the end of normal time a 20-yard shot by Wootton was well saved by the goalkeeper. In the first (15 minute) period of extra time Wootton worked himself into a good position but then shot over the crossbar. Towards the end of the first period of extra time Notts conceded twice in quick succession. Torquay took the lead for a third time when a corner kick was bravely headed into the net from eight yards. The scorer received a head injury in the process, as Wootton challenged him, and he required lengthy treatment. In time added Torquay increased their lead when Ellis was harshly adjudged to have committed a foul, as he stretched his foot out to dispossess an attacker, and the referee awarded a penalty. Notts nearly reduced the arrears when a Wootton header was saved by the goalkeeper and Rodrigues hit the crossbar from the rebound. In the second period of extra time Griffiths shot <u>just</u> wide and after another good cross by Kelly-Evans a Wootton 'bicycle kick' from near the penalty spot <u>just</u> cleared the crossbar. After an excellent game of football Notts deserved better during extra time and were unfortunate not to get a penalty shoot-out.

Notts made the worst possible start to what became a pulsating encounter. Throughout they tried (and succeeded) to play constructive football whereas Torquay had a more basic and direct (but nonetheless effective) approach to the game. The penalty was described by the BT Sport commentary team as "very harsh" (Ellis played the ball). Although Notts tried to produce another comeback in the second period of extra time, it wasn't to be and they had to accept a cruel disappointing defeat, and a third season in non-league football.

In the other semi-final Hartlepool Utd visited Stockport County and won (0-1). So, the two teams who were the bookies favourites for promotion at the start of the season, Notts County and Stockport County, failed in their attempt to return to the English Football League. Two clubs at the extremities of England, approximately 370 miles apart, therefore contested the final at Ashton Gate – the home of Bristol City. Wembley was unavailable due to their (joint) hosting of the delayed 2020 UEFA European Championship. In their two National League meetings, Torquay won 5-0 at Hartlepool at the end of October but then succumbed to a 1-0 defeat in the return fixture in Devon at the beginning of March.

In the playoff final the Torquay goalkeeper (Covolan Cauagnari) equalised with a header in the 95th minute to take the game into extra time, after which the score remained 1-1. In the penalty shootout Hartlepool's first two penalties were saved by Cauagnari, but Hartlepool still won the shootout 5-4 and achieved promotion to EFL League Two.

A thought… about Connell Rawlinson. Would Notts have conceded two headed goals (one in the first minute) if he had played in his central defensive position? Should he, at least, have started the Torquay game to provide the additional security of a back four, rather than a back three?

This season he made 37 starts in The National League out of 42, plus three appearances in the FA Trophy (Notts withdrew from the FA Cup). Although he played the first half of the Chesterfield playoff he was omitted from the starting eleven against Torquay. Last season he made 31 starts in the league out of 38, plus six in cup competitions. However, he was an unused substitute for the promotion playoff semi-final and the final at Wembley when Notts lost 3-1 to Harrogate Town.

A dependable and experienced defender, who last season was the Supporters' 'Player of the Season' and joint winner (with Kyle Wootton) of the Players' 'Player of the Season', the unfortunate Rawlinson must have been disappointed when omitted by Ian Burchnall and Neal Ardley.

Notts County National League Results 2020-21
(5 months to reach the midpoint – ~~22~~ 21 games)

Date	Home	Away	F-A	Scorers	Attendance	Pos
2020						
3/10/		~~Dover Athletic~~	~~0-1~~	Result expunged March 2021	0 (RK=Stream)	20
7/10	Altrincham		3-1	Wootton (2), Reeves	0 (Televised-BT Sport)	8
10/10	Barnet		4-2	Wootton, Roberts, Boldewijn, Doyle	2160 Streamers	5
13/10		Sutton Utd	1-0	Wootton	0 (RK=S)	3
17/10	Maidenhead Utd		2-3	Knowles, Rodrigues	2000+ Streamers	5
27/10		Halifax Town		Postponed by Notts – COVID-19		
31/10		Aldershot Town		Postponed by Notts – COVID-19		
R 7/11		Aldershot Town	0-1		0	10
11/11	Stockport County			Postponed by Stockport – COVID-19		
14/11	Macclesfield Town			Cancelled – Macclesfield expelled from league in Oct.		
R 17/11		Halifax Town	1-1	Sam	0	12
21/11		Chesterfield	3-2	Boldewijn, Rodrigues, Wootton	0	10
27/11	Wealdstone		3-0	Boldewijn, Sam, Knowles	2296 Streamers	7
2/12		Dagenham & Redbridge	0-0		0	6
5/12	Woking		1-0	Wootton	2000+ Streamers	3
8/12	Boreham Wood		0-1		2000+ Streamers	3
12/12		Yeovil Town		Postponed by Yeovil – COVID-19		
R 15/12	Stockport County		1-0	Reeves	0 (Televised-BT Sport)	3
26/12		King's Lynn Town		Postponed by King's Lynn – COVID-19		
28/12	Hartlepool Utd		0-1		3000+ Streamers	5
2021						
2/1	King's Lynn Town			Postponed by King's Lynn – COVID-19		
9/1		Eastleigh		Postponed by Eastleigh – COVID-19		
R 19/1		Yeovil Town		Postponed by Yeovil – COVID-19		
23/1	Torquay Utd		0-0		2000+ Streamers	8
27/1	Solihull Moors		2-0	Wootton (2)	2000+ Streamers	7
30/1		Weymouth	1-0	Sam	0	5
2/2	Bromley			Postponed – waterlogged pitch		
9/2	Dagenham & Redbridge		3-1	Wootton (2), Rodrigues	2000+Streamers	5
13/2		Wrexham		Postponed – frozen pitch		
R 16/2		King's Lynn Town	1-0	Reeves	0	3
20/2	Chesterfield		0-1		3800 Streamers	5
23/2		Stockport County	0-0		0	5
R 2/3	King's Lynn Town		2-2	Wootton (2)	2000+ Streamers	6

R = Rearranged fixture

Notts County National League Results 2020-21
(only 3 months to reach the 42nd and final game)

Date	Home	Away	F-A	Scorers	Attendance	Pos
6/3/2021	Aldershot Town			Postponed by **Aldershot** - coronavirus (COVID-19)		
9/3	**Halifax Town**		**1-2**	**Boldewijn**	**2000+ Streamers**	**6**
13/3		Wealdstone	1-0	Ellis	0	6
16/3		Boreham Wood	2-2	Lacey, Effiong (pen)	0	7
20/3	**Yeovil Town**		**2-0**	**Reeves, Barnett**	**2000+Streamers**	**6**
R 23/3		Yeovil Town	2-2	Boldewijn, Rodrigues	0 (RK=S)	6
		(Neal Ardley's last game)				
		Ian Burchnall's 16 games >				
R 30/3	**Aldershot Town**		**0-1**		**2000+Streamers**	**6**
2/4	**Wrexham**		**1-0**	**Ellis**	**0 (Televised-BT Sport)**	**5**
5/4		Woking	4-2	Ellis, Knowles (3)	0	5
10/4		Hartlepool United	0-2		0 (Televised-BT Sport)	5
13/4		Solihull Moors	1-2	Knowles	0	6
17/4	**Eastleigh**		**0-1**		**2000+Streamers**	**8**
24/4		Torquay United	2-2	Kelly-Evans, Ellis	0	9
R 27/4		Eastleigh	0-2		0	10
1/5		Altrincham	1-1	Rodrigues	0 (RK=S)	10
4/5	**Sutton United**		**3-2**	**Rodrigues (2, 1 pen.), Wootton**	**0 (Televised-BT Sport)**	**8**
8/5		Barnet	4-1	Ellis, Rodrigues, o.g., Boldewijn	0	7
11/5		Maidenhead United	4-0	O'Brien (3 inc. pen), Rodrigues	0	5
~~15/5~~	~~Dover Athletic~~	Cancelled – Dover's results expunged in March				
R 15/5	**Bromley**		**2-2**	**Wootton, Rodrigues**	**2000+Streamers**	**6**
R 18/5		Wrexham	1-0	Reeves	0 (RK=S)	5
22/5	**Weymouth**		**3-0**	**Rodrigues (pen.), Wootton Boldewijn**	**4,197 inc. RK, plus 1,165 Streamers = 5,362***	**5**
29/5		Bromley	0-1		1,344	5
		Playoffs (Televised by BT Sport)				
5/6	Chesterfield		3-2	Wootton (2), Ellis	4,569 **COVID-19 restrictions (home fans only)**	
12/6		Torquay United	2-4 aet	Rodrigues, Chicksen	1,709	

* = Last season Notts' average league attendance was **5,210**
R = Rearranged fixture

The only home game I failed to 'stream' via the internet was Yeovil on 20 March.

The cost of a pass was £12, but you could pay £16 or £20 if you wanted to give the extra – the service was the same whatever you paid. The BT Sport (monthly) pass was £25.

Live streaming review

Multimedia Editor Steven Carter gave us the low-down on what it's been like to manage our popular live streaming service this season.

What were your initial thoughts about leading on such a unique project?

It was an exciting challenge to take on. I had a decent understanding of streaming at the time, so it felt good to be putting that to use. With fans facing a season of not being able to visit Meadow Lane, it was vital to get it right.

Talk us through the process of building our streaming platform...

After having to wait for confirmation that the season was going ahead and that streaming would be permitted, we didn't have long to get things in place. We'd successfully streamed a number of our pre-season friendlies on YouTube but finding a way of monetising our streams required hours of research and virtual meetings with potential paywall and platform providers. We ultimately decided to partner with InPlayer and JW Player, which proved to be a good call.

During pre-season we'd used a basic one-camera set-up but I wanted to expand our offering to multiple cameras with replays, with the aim of providing the best service in The National League. As soon as this was suggested to the board there was no hesitation from them, which was brilliant.

We then made financial projections based on estimates of how many passes we would sell on a match-by-match basis. The feedback from fans who participated in our live streaming questionnaire told us that most were happy to pay more for an advanced product, so we were confident we could invest in the production side of things and still generate vital income for the club.

Do you think going for a high-end production was the right call?

While we'll never know how sales figures would have differed if we'd only offered a basic, one-camera stream, I'm certain we wouldn't have sold anywhere near as many passes across the season.

The additional angles and replays add so much during the live event and also when it comes to producing highlights – imagine if we could only have watched Eli Sam's Puskas Award contender from just the one angle!

It's also worth mentioning how grateful we are to BBC Radio Nottingham for allowing us to use their amazing impartial commentary which adds a real element of class to the output.

What's your role been like on a match day?

Pretty stressful most of the time! With internet-based streaming there can quite often be unexpected connection drop-outs. Thankfully we didn't experience too many of them, but I was constantly in a state of dread waiting for one!

Once each match was underway and supporters were logged on it was a case of monitoring the broadcast and keeping in contact with our production crew to make sure there were no issues and everything was to a high standard. Once we got through to full-time without any issues I could finally begin to relax and focus on recording our post-match interviews.

There were some nervy moments, then?

Whenever we had drops-outs we had an influx of calls, emails and messages from supporters and the pressure was really on to get things back up and running.

In January, a number of £16 purchasers were locked out of the Torquay stream due to an issue which only reared its head about 15 minutes before kick-off. I have to admit, I was panicking! It's an awful feeling knowing people are trying to watch their team but can't. Thankfully we managed to grant most people access and that one ended goalless, so they didn't miss much!

So, how many people match passes did we sell?

Our average figure per match was around 2,300, which means in total we sold well over 40,000 passes. You have to remember that an entire family could watch with only one streaming pass, so the total viewing figures will be much higher than those numbers.

The Chesterfield game was our highest figure at 3,800 and if BT hadn't chosen to broadcast our home games against Stockport and Wrexham I'd have expected similar figures for those games.

We'd conservatively estimated that we'd sell around 1,500 passes per game, so we're delighted with these numbers and would like to thank everyone who supported the service.

Overall do you think the project was a success?

Definitely! We've received lots of kind emails from supporters and many comments online saying that ours is the best service in the division. We should take great pride in that as a club.

Will the club continue to stream games next season?

We'd love to, however we expect UEFA to reintroduce the 3pm blackout which would stop us from streaming live in the UK. Whether we'd be able to provide a service to overseas supporters remains to be seen as the EFL and National League have different rules.

Watch this space – but we'll almost certainly be back in some form for pre-season!

Notts County 2020-21
League +Cup 'Starts', (Sub appearances) & Goals

	Name	Starts	(Sub)	Goals	Yellow/Red (Cards)
Gk	Slocombe	38+2	(0+0)		1/1 Straight red
"	Pilling	3+3	(0+0)		
"	Steele	3+0	(0+0)		
"	Brooks & Kean	0+0	(0+0)		
D	Rawlinson	38+2	(1+1)	0+0	7
E	Kelly-Evans	31+1	(4+2)	1+0	6/1 (second yellow)
F	Ellis (loan)	21+1	(0+0)	6+0	3
E	Lacey	20+4	(0+0)	1+0	1
N	Brindley	19+3	(3+0)	0+0	
D	Chicksen	19+3	(1+0)	1+0	
E	Barnett	12+2	(1+0)	1+0	3
R	Turner	12+1	(6+0)	0+0	4/1 Straight red
S	McCrory	2+0	(1+0)	0+0	
"	Graham (loan)	2+2	(0+0)	0+1	
"	Richardson (loan)	1+0	(0+0)	0+0	
"	Golden (loan)	0+1	(0+0)	0+0	
M	Doyle (Capt.)	38+1	(0+2)	1+0	4
I	Reeves (Vice Capt.)	42+2	(0+0)	5+0	6
D	O'Brien (Vice Capt.)	22+3	(10+1)	3+0	1
F	Griffiths (loan)	6+0	(6+0)	0+0	1
I	Wolfe (loan)	1+4	(2+0)	0+1	
E	~~Sloth~~ Nil				
L			own goals	1+0	
D					
A	Wootton	43+1	(0+2)	17+2	9/1 (second yellow)
T	Boldewijn	30+2	(10+2)	7+0	3
T	Rodrigues	28+3	(9+1)	12+1	5
A	Miller (loan)	15+4	(4+0)	0+0	4
C	Knowles (loan)	12+4	(16+1)	6+4	2
K	Sam	10+4	(16+1)	3+4	3
E	Roberts	3+0	(5+0)	1+0	
R	Knight	3+0	(5+0)	0+0	2
S	Effiong (loan)	5+0	(7+0)	1+0	
"	Walker (loan)	3+1	(2+0)	0+0	
"	Thomas (retired)	2+0	(1+0)	0+0	
"	Palmer	0+1	(0+1)	0+0	0/1 (second yellow)
		484+55		67+13	yellow totals may not be
		exc. Dover (1-0) but inc. playoffs			100% accurate

Notts County League (& Cup) goal scorers 2020-21

Wootton	17	(2)	=19	
Rodrigues	12*	(1)	=13	*inc. 2 pens
Knowles (loan)	6	(4)*	=10	*inc. 1 pen.
Boldewijn	7	(0)	=7	
Sam	3	(4)	=7	
Ellis (loan)	6	(0)	=6	
Reeves	5	(0)	=5	
O'Brien	3*	(0)	=3	*inc. 1 pen.
Roberts	1	(0)	=1	
Doyle	1	(0)	=1	
Lacey	1	(0)	=1	
Barnett	1	(0)	=1	
Kelly-Evans	1	(0)	=1	
Chicksen	1	(0)	=1	
Effiong (loan)	1*	(0)	=1	*pen.
Own goals	1	(0)	=1	
Graham (loan)	0	(1)	=1	
Wolfe (loan)	0	(1)	=1	
Rawlinson	0	(0)	=0	
Turner	0	(0)	=0	
Brindley	0	(0)	=0	
McCrory	0	(0)	=0	
Knight	0	(0)	=0	
Miller	0	(0)	=0	
Griffiths	0	(0)	=0	
Palmer	0	(0)	=0	
Thomas	0	(0)	=0	
Walker	0	(0)	=0	
Golden	0	(0)	=0	
Richardson	0	(0)	=0	
~~Sloth~~ Nil				
Total	**67**	(13)	=80	
	Inc. Playoffs		**Inc. Playoffs**	

Notts County FA Cup and FA Trophy Results 2020-21

Date	Home	Away	F-A	Scorers	Attendance	Round
24/10/20		King's Lynn Town	Notts withdrew from the FA Cup due to a coronavirus (COVID-19) outbreak at the club. King's Lynn given a bye into the 1st round proper			4th Qualifying
19/12/20		Morpeth Town	3-0	Sam, Graham, Knowles	0	3rd FA Trophy
16/1/21		Stockport County	2-1	Knowles, Wootton	0 (RK=S)	4th FA Trophy
6/2/21		Havant and Waterlooville	2-2	Wolfe, Knowles (pen) Notts won 4-2 in penalty shoot-out	0	5th FA Trophy
27/2/21	Oxford City		3-1	Sam (2), Knowles	2000+Streamers (RK)	Quarter-Final
27/3/21	Hornchurch FC		3-3	Wootton, Rodrigues, Sam Hornchurch won 5-4 in penalty shoot-out	2000+Streamers (RK)	Semi-Final

22 May 2021 Hornchurch won the FA Trophy at Wembley when they defeated Hereford 3-1 (Hornchurch were losing 1-0 with 15 minutes remaining)

Notts County Goal Times - League (& Cup) 2020-21
First 21 league (& 4 FA Trophy) games

			For			
0-15 min	16-30 min	31 min - HT	46-60 min	61-75 min	76-90 min	90+
6 (2)	6 (0)	5 (1)	2 (2)	1 (3)	4 (1)	4 (1)
			Against (exc. Dover)			
0-15 min	16-30 min	31 min - HT	46-60 min	61-75 min	76-90 min	90+
2 (0)	1 (1)	3 (2)	0 (1)	5 (0)	~~3~~ 2 (0)	3 (0)

Second 21 league (& FA Trophy semi-final) games

			For			
0-15 min	16-30 min	31 min - HT	46-60 min	61-75 min	76-90 min	90+
3 (1)	4 (0)	4 (1)	6 (0)	7 (0)	9 (1)	1 (0)
			Against			
0-15 min	16-30 min	31 min - HT	46-60 min	61-75 min	76-90 min	90+
2 (0)	6 (0)	4 (2)	2 (0)	6 (0)	4 (0)	1 (1)

Chapter 17: Summer of 2021

Three days after the playoff defeat to Torquay the 'Retained List' was published. A statement from the board of directors read:

We would like to place on record our sincere gratitude to all departing players for their efforts throughout their time at the club. Saying goodbye is never easy but those moving on to new challenges can all leave in the knowledge they gave their all for Notts County.

Enzio (Boldewijn) in particular has provided many special memories, including several wonderful goals, and we're sure he will always be held in the highest regard by our supporters.

As fans will see, we are making every effort to retain a strong core of the squad which we feel performed exceptionally well towards the end of last season.

We believe an element of stability will be key to building on our excellent recent form, while we will of course be looking to make several strong new additions to the squad. We are hopeful that this will include the retention of one of this season's loan players.

(On 18 June Mark Ellis signed for EFL League Two Barrow, and Regan Griffiths signed a new contract with League One Crewe. Calvin Miller signed for Chesterfield on 25 June.)

Our recruitment team have been working closely with head coach Ian Burchnall since his arrival to identify players we believe can help us realise our goal of returning to the EFL as soon as possible and we look forward to welcoming fresh talent to the squad in the coming weeks.

Under contract

Kyle Wootton - Players' 'Player of the Season' 2020-21. Also included in The National League 'Team of the Season' 2020-21

Ruben Rodrigues - Supporters' 'Player of the Season' 2020-21

Elisha Sam - won 'Goal of the Season' with his Puskas kick v Oxford City in the FAT

Alex Lacey, Richard Brindley, Callum Roberts, Lewis Knight

~~*Jake Reeves*~~ [Transferred to Stevenage, League Two, on 21 June]

Offered new contract

Goalkeepers Sam Slocombe [re-signed 22 June] *and Tiernan Brooks* [re-signed 1 July]

Connell Rawlinson [re-signed 24 June], *Adam Chicksen* [re-signed 29 June]

Jim O'Brien [re-signed 6 July], *Dion Kelly-Evans* [re-signed 9 July]

Offered role of assistant head coach on a permanent basis Captain, Michael Doyle [he accepted, and remained a registered player].

Released

Luke Pilling, Luke Steele, Ben Turner, Damien McCrory [allowed to return for pre-season training to maintain his fitness], *Jordan Barnett, Enzio Boldewijn* [signed for promoted Sutton Utd]

Loan players returning to clubs

Mark Ellis [Tranmere], *Calvin Miller* [Harrogate], *Regan Griffiths* [Crewe Alexandra], *Jimmy Knowles* [Mansfield], *Matty Wolfe* [Barnsley].

Tyreace **Palmer**, **O**fficial **S**upporters **A**ssociation 'Young Player of the Season', graduated from the academy, and signed a professional contract on 1 July.

On 21 June season tickets went on sale for the 2021-22 season. Initially the tickets were available at renewal and early bird prices, which were frozen at the 2019-20 rate. Due to the coronavirus (COVID-19) pandemic no season tickets were available for the 2020-21 campaign.

Key dates

Monday 21 June (9am) – Renewals begin for 2019-20 season ticket holders and the early bird window opens for new purchasers

Saturday 24 July (1pm) – Renewal and early bird periods end. 2019-20 season ticket holders must renew prior to this time if they wish to retain their seat. Renewal prices will not be available after this date and all seat reservations that have not been paid for will be released for general sale

Monday 26 July (9am) – Season tickets go on general sale

Prices (per game in brackets)

Renewals

	PAVIS	KOP	FAMILY
Adult	£345 (£15.68)	£276 (£12.54)	£276 (£12.54)
65 and over	£207 (£9.40)	£184 (£8.36)	£184 (£8.36)
22-25	£184 (£8.36)	£184 (£8.36)	£184 (£8.36)
18-21	£100 (£4.54)	£100 (£4.54)	£100 (£4.54)
12-17	£45 (£2.04)	£45 (£2.04)	£45 (£2.04)
Under 12	£25 (£1.13)	£25 (£1.13)	£25 (£1.13)

New early bird purchasers

	PAVIS	KOP	FAMILY
Adult	£368 (£16.72)	£299 (£13.59)	£299 (£13.59)
65 and over	£230 (£10.45)	£207 (£9.40)	£207 (£9.40)
22-25	£184 (£8.36)	£184 (£8.36)	£184 (£8.36)
18-21	£100 (£4.54)	£100 (£4.54)	£100 (£4.54)
12-17	£45 (£2.04)	£45 (£2.04)	£45 (£2.04)
Under 12	£25 (£1.13)	£25 (£1.13)	£25 (£1.13)

When the tickets went on general sale the prices were higher (e.g. £400 for an adult in the Pavis stand and £350 for an adult in the Kop and Family stands). The 'Under 12' price remained at £25. The Jimmy Sirrel Stand was the designated accommodation for away supporters.

More than 1,000 tickets were sold within the first 24 hours! In early July the number sold had risen to "more than 2,200".

[When the renewal and early bird price deadline expired on 24 July the 3,000 milestone had been achieved, and then the number sold soon surpassed the total figure for the 2019-20 campaign – no season tickets last season due to the pandemic.]

On Monday 12 July the players commenced pre-season training in readiness for the first game of the new season on Saturday 21 August (Notts away at Barnet). Cal Roberts had been training throughout in order to slowly return to full fitness after his long lay-off. Prior to the commencement of the 2021-22 season Notts signed seven players:

Kyle Cameron = Age 24, central or left-sided defender, from Torquay United on 25 June – two-year deal.

Following loan spells with York City and Newport County (both League Two), and Queen of the South (Scottish Championship), where he gained first team experience, he was released by Premier League Newcastle United in the summer of 2018. He then signed for Torquay United and made just over 100 appearances for them in his three seasons with the club. Played against Notts in the playoff semi-final! An ex-teammate of Callum Roberts at Newcastle. Succeeded Michael Doyle as Notts' club captain. (Kyle Wootton new vice-captain).

Frank Vincent = Age 22, central midfielder, from AFC Bournemouth on 2 July – two-year deal. After spending four years at Bournemouth he was released in the summer of 2021 after they had finished sixth in the Championship. Prior to last season Bournemouth had been in the Premier League for five seasons. His first team experience had been gained on loan at Torquay, and Scunthorpe and Walsall (both League Two).

Joel Taylor = Age 25, left wing back, from Chesterfield on 13 July - two-year deal. Although he had appeared for the Stoke City U23 team (Stoke were relegated from the Premier League at the end of the 2017-18 season) most of his experience, since being released in July 2017, had been gained with two National League North clubs, Kidderminster Harriers and Chester City. He transferred from Chester to National League Chesterfield in December 2020 and was a regular member of their squad during the remainder of their 2020-21 season.

Ed Francis = Age 21, holding midfielder, from Harrogate Town on 20 July - two-year deal. A Manchester City academy graduate (originally a left-sided centre back at levels up to U23) he transferred to another Premier League club, Wolverhampton Wanderers, in January 2019 where he also made U23 appearances. He captained at both clubs. In order to play regular first team football he signed for Harrogate town in mid-December 2020 and then made 20 appearances in League Two before he was released. Seen as the replacement for Michael Doyle in midfield.

Aaron Nemane = Age 23, forward (wide or central), from Torquay United on 20 July - two-year deal. Another Manchester City academy graduate (appeared up to U23 level) but released in July 2019, after loans to clubs in the Netherlands and Belgium, and also Glasgow Rangers. In mid-December 2019 he joined Torquay United but rejected their offer of another contract to join Notts.

Matt Palmer = Age 26, midfielder, from Swindon Town on 21 July – two-year deal. A first taste of non-league football for an experienced player who had made over 250 appearances in the English Football League and in cup competitions – the majority with Burton Albion in their rise from League Two to the Championship. He was released by League One Swindon Town in May 2021. Likely to play a similar role to that of the departed Jake Reeves.

Kairo Mitchell = Age 23, centre forward, from Chesterfield on 3 August – two-year deal. A product of Leicester City's academy he played for them at levels up to U23. After he was released in June 2017 (one year after Leicester had won the Premier league title) he joined Nuneaton Borough, and then Coalville Town. Latterly he had been with National League clubs, Kings Lynn Town and Chesterfield. He had represented Grenada at international level.

2021-22 pre-season schedule of seven friendlies

Sat 17 July, 15:00 - Coalville Town, Southern League Premier Central (A) **Won 0-2** (McCrory 64', trialist Kyle Bennett 77'). Hot and sunny, 30°C!

Sat 24 July, 15:00 - AFC Telford United, National League North (A) **Won 0-1** (Roberts 68').

Tue 27 July, 19:45 - Boston United, National League North (A) **Won 1-3** (Trialist Andre Wright 17', Wootton 26', Sam 64'. Boston scored just before the end. Unfortunately, prior to the game Ruben Rodrigues tested positive for COVID-19 and was required to isolate for ten days, which also meant he was unavailable for the Derby County fixture. Lewis Knight injured (hamstring) on 25 minutes. Cal Roberts was rested with a view to starting against Derby.

Sun 1 August, 13:00 - Derby County, EFL Championship (H) **Lost 0-2** = goals 42' and 85' (pen.). Managed by Wayne Rooney ex. Manchester United, Everton and England (120 caps). Record goalscorer for both Manchester United (253) and England (53).

Slocombe
Brindley   Rawlinson (McGregor 86')   Cameron (Capt.)
Kelly-Evans (Nemane 76')   Taylor (Chicksen 46')
M. Palmer   Francis   O'Brien (Hondermarck 76')
Roberts (Sam 62')   Wootton

Subs: Brooks (gk), Chicksen, Hondermarck (Trialist), Nemane, Sam, Brad McGregor (Notts Academy)
Injured: Lacey, Vincent, Knight, Ty Palmer. Unavailable: Rodrigues.

Notts' Match Report on their website summed up the game as follows:

> *Kyle Wootton had been unable to convert two well-worked opportunities with the score at 1-0 and there were plenty of promising performances as Ian Burchnall's men continued their 2021-22 preparations with a competitive performance against the Sky Bet Championship side.*

The first opportunity: Wootton's shot hit the crossbar. The second: his shot hit a defender and was eventually cleared. Both attempts were from a central position on the edge of the six-yard box. Derby's first goal was a good header following a corner kick. Cameron gave away the penalty. Attendance 4,849

Sat 7 August, 15:00 Notts County 2 - 3 York City National League North Att: 2,095	
Roberts 28' goals 18', 50', 83'	
Taylor 37'	

<pre>
                         Slocombe
           Brindley   Cameron (Capt.)   Chicksen (Rawlinson 46')
      Kelly-Evans (Nemane 62')   Taylor
        Roberts (O'Brien 76')   Francis   M. Palmer
                  Wootton   Mitchell (Sam 62')
</pre>

Subs: Brooks (gk), Rawlinson, O'Brien, Nemane, Sam, McGregor
Injured: Lacey, Vincent, Knight, Ty Palmer. Now available but not match fit: Rodrigues.

York goal 18'. Roberts equalised 28' with a spectacular 18 yard shot which hit the underside of the crossbar and the rebound fell just over the goal line. After 37' a cross from the left by Taylor was deflected and the ball looped over the goalkeeper to put Notts ahead. Roberts then hit a post with a terrific 20-yard free kick. York equalised 50' and scored the winner (against the run of play) after 83'.

Tue 10 August Tamworth, Southern League Premier Central (A)
Cancelled by Tamworth on the evening of 7 August. A friendly match against Nottingham Forest Under 23s 'behind closed doors' was arranged in lieu. The two sides played out a 0-0 draw over three 20-minute periods. Vincent played 40 minutes and Rodrigues 30 minutes.

Sat 14 August, 15:00	**Solihull Moors** 2 - 2 **Notts County**	Solihull managed by
	goals 10', 17' Roberts 68'	Neal Ardley, Notts'
	Rodrigues 78'	previous manager.

                                     Slocombe

              Brindley   Rawlinson   Cameron (Capt.)

Kelly-Evans   Chicksen (Taylor 46')

Roberts (Nemane 78')   Francis (O'Brien 60')   M. Palmer

       Wootton (Rodrigues 46')   Mitchell (Sam 78')

Subs: Taylor, O'Brien, Vincent, Rodrigues, Nemane, Sam, McGregor

Injured: Lacey, Knight, Ty Palmer.

Brooks (gk) now on loan at Worksop Town.

Jake Keen (goalkeeper coach) registered as a player.

In this National League friendly, Notts made a good start with plenty of possession. However, after ten minutes Solihull took the lead with a well worked goal following a swift counterattack.

Five minutes later there was a bizarre incident. A long clearance from the Solihull penalty area arrived in the Notts half and Rawlinson, under pressure from a Solihull forward, was adjudged to have brought down the opponent. The referee decided that the forward was deprived of a one-on-one with Slocombe and the foul therefore deserved a red card. Neal Ardley then walked 40 yards along the touchline from his technical area to protest to the referee (and then the assistant referee as he walked back to his technical area) for sending off Rawlinson! From the subsequent free kick Solihull increased their lead when the cross was headed firmly into the net from the edge of the six-yard box. So, Notts were two goals down and reduced to ten men after seventeen minutes. They didn't panic and were rewarded with two late goals. The deficit was reduced in the 68th minute when Roberts and O'Brien exchanged passes and Roberts moved into the penalty area and placed a left footed shot into the corner of the net from 12 yards. Ten minutes later Rodrigues equalised from the penalty spot after Kelly-Evans had been fouled in the area.

Four days before the start of the 2021-22 season Notts announced the appointment of a 'first team coach' - Alex Clapham.

> *Boasting an impressive CV which includes senior coaching roles in academies in the UK and overseas, as well as a recent spell as head coach at Swedish side Ytterhogdals IK, Clapham will lead our approach to set pieces and contribute to opposition analysis. He will support Ian Burchnall and Michael Doyle with individual player development*

plans and coaching, while also providing tactical and technical advice on match days. Clapham cut his coaching teeth in Spain where he attained UEFA's highest coaching qualification, the Pro Licence, and Burchnall is delighted to add him to his backroom team.

"In Alex we have found someone who's dedicated themselves to analysing and coaching set pieces, which isn't easy as specialised coaching remains a relatively new thing in football – especially at our level," said the head coach.

"The fantastic infrastructure we've got at the club means we have access to a mass of data surrounding opponents and set pieces and, working closely alongside our head of performance analysis Joao Alves, Alex will be using his analytical skills to drill into the numbers before devising and delivering coaching strategies to the players".

(Performance Analyst Jimmy Redfern recently left Notts to join Walsall, League Two)

We were fortunate to interview several strong candidates for this role but Alex really impressed us with the depth of detail he went into and his ideas about how we can get better.

It's important to stress that we won't see overnight improvements and that Alex is very much part of the wider coaching team – we share responsibility for all aspects of the team's performance.

But we do feel he will be a huge help to us in an area where, while being a long way off the worst in the league, we were behind many of our direct competitors last season.

[Postscript: In June 2022, after just one season at Meadow Lane, Clapham departed to take up a post at an unnamed club, soon after Burchnall and Doyle had departed to join Forest Green Rovers.]

For the 2021-22 season there were 23 clubs in The National League instead of the usual 24. The reason was the demise of Macclesfield Town (expelled from The National League in October 2020) together with no relegations last season, and no promotions from National Leagues North and South, all because of the problems caused by the COVID-19 pandemic.

Wrexham and Stockport County were the joint favourites with most bookmaker's to be 2021-22 champions of The National League. Notts were third favourite. The odds at the start of the season for all 23 clubs, given by two organisations, were:

	SkyBet	BETVICTOR
Wrexham	10/3	11/4
Stockport County	4/1	7/2
Notts County	**8/1**	**8/1**
Chesterfield	9/1	9/1
Grimsby	9/1	9/1
Southend	10/1	8/1
Torquay	12/1	12/1
BAR 7		
Dagenham & Redbridge	20/1	20/1
Solihull Moors	22/1	20/1
FC Halifax	22/1	50/1
Bromley	33/1	33/1
Yeovil	33/1	33/1
Boreham Wood	33/1	66/1
Barnet	40/1	50/1
Eastleigh	50/1	40/1
Aldershot	50/1	80/1
Maidenhead	66/1	80/1
Woking	80/1	66/1
Altrincham	100/1	200/1
Weymouth	150/1	250/1
Kings Lynn	150/1	500/1
Wealdstone	250/1	500/1
Dover	500/1	1000/1

(Started the season with a point's deduction of minus 12)

Notts had played at home on the opening day of the season only once since season 2010-11 – a 0-0 draw at Meadow Lane on 4 August 2018 against Colchester United. At the end of that 2018-19 season Notts were relegated from League Two into The National League. Seasons 2019-20 and 2020-21 had started on the south coast, at Eastleigh and Dover respectively, and both games had ended in a 1-0 defeat. Notts had failed to score on the opening day in the last five seasons.

Chapter 18: The 2021-22 season (to halfway, 22 matches)

Back row, left to right: Alex Clapham (First-Team Coach), Adam **Chicksen**, Ed **Francis**, Tyreace **Palmer**, Joel **Taylor**, Lewis **Knight**, Joao Alves (Analyst)

Middle row, left to right: Craig Heiden (Sports Therapist), Jake Kean (Goalkeeper Coach), Richard **Brindley**, Ruben **Rodrigues**, Connell **Rawlinson**, Tiernan **Brooks**, Sam **Slocombe**, Elisha **Sam**, Kairo **Mitchell**, Alex **Lacey**, Lewis Saleem (Kit & Equipment Manager), Ian Hutton (Strength & Conditioning Coach)

Front row, left to right: Matt **Palmer**, Dion **Kelly-Evans**, Jim **O'Brien**, Kyle **Wootton**, Michael Doyle (Assistant Head Coach), Ian Burchnall (Head Coach), Kyle **Cameron**, Cal **Roberts**, Frank **Vincent**, Aaron **Nemane**

Absent: Marco Ferreira (Head of Medical Services)

So, twenty-one players (plus two registered but unlikely to play, midfielder Michael Doyle and goalkeeper coach Jake Keen) started Notts' journey to find a route back into the English Football League (League Two) at the third attempt.

Notts' opening fixture of the new season was, once again, away from Meadow Lane, at Barnet who ended last season in 22ⁿᵈ position – bottom of the league if Dover's expunged results and 23ʳᵈ position finish was ignored.

Match 1 Sat 21 Aug 2021 15:00	**Barnet 0 – 5 Notts County** Rodrigues 47', 54' Roberts 68' (pen.) Wootton 79', O'Brien 90'+5	Attendance 2,067

Slocombe

Brindley   Rawlinson (Chicksen 79')   Cameron (Capt.)

Kelly-Evans (Nemane 87')   Taylor

Roberts   Francis   M. Palmer   Rodrigues (O'Brien 65')

Wootton

Subs: Chicksen, O'Brien, Nemane, Mitchell, Sam
(no substitute goalkeeper)

Ian Burchnall gave full league debuts to four players: Kyle Cameron, Joel Taylor, Ed Francis, Matt Palmer and Aaron Nemane as a substitute.

It was estimated that at least 1,000 Notts supporters were in attendance – >50% of the crowd – and they were rewarded with an excellent performance, especially in the second half. Barnet were managed by Harry Kewell, who was in charge at Meadow Lane for three months in the autumn of 2018.

Notts made a good start, and Roberts struck a post with a shot from the corner of the penalty area after ten minutes, but as the first half progressed Barnet came more into the game and Slocombe had to make two good saves.

However, within the first ten minutes of the second half Notts scored twice through Rodrigues. Kelly-Evans provided the assist for the first goal when his cross from the right was confidently headed home from twelve yards. The second was a well-placed first time shot from near the penalty spot following a Palmer cross.

On 67 minutes a series of nineteen passes came to an end when Roberts was brought down in the penalty area and the assailant was shown a straight red card and sent off. Roberts scored from the spot. Notts' recognised penalty taker, Rodrigues, had been substituted a few minutes earlier (not yet fully fit after his recent COVID-19 positivity and a slight hamstring strain) and so he missed the opportunity to register a hat-trick.

Wootton put Notts further ahead when a 40-yard pass by Cameron split the Barnet defence and O'Brien ran clear, squared the ball and last season's top scorer opened his account when, unchallenged, he walked the ball towards the net before tapping home from five yards. With almost the last kick of the game the industrious O'Brien scored the fifth goal with an excellent left footed drive, which struck a post on its way into the net, following a good pass by Francis.

So, an excellent second 45 minutes gave Notts a convincing victory and with such an impressive first game score line they were top of the league!

Match 2	**Notts County (1st) 1-1 Torquay Utd (19th)**	Attendance 6,934
Sat 28 Aug 2021 15:00	Wootton 69' goal 37'	

```
                         Slocombe
           Brindley      Rawlinson         Cameron (Capt.)
      Kelly-Evans (Nemane 46')                Chicksen
 Roberts    Francis (O'Brien 46')  M. Palmer   Rodrigues (Mitchell 84')
                         Wootton
```

Subs: Lacey, O'Brien, Nemane, Mitchell, Sam
(no substitute goalkeeper)

Kairo Mitchell made his first league appearance for Notts from the substitute's bench.

In their first game of the season Torquay, last season's beaten promotion play-off finalist, suffered a home defeat against Altrincham (1-3).

After the performance and result at Barnet on the opening day of the season, the first half was a disappointment for nearly 7,000 Notts supporters. The closest Notts came to a goal was when Rodrigues headed a Chicksen cross against a post after ten minutes. Roberts shot narrowly wide, Rodrigues had a shot well saved and Rawlinson headed a Roberts free kick over the crossbar. Either side of these three opportunities Torquay were reduced to ten men, after 25 minutes, when their centre half was sent off (straight red card) for a rash tackle (just outside the penalty area) on Wootton as he chased a Rodrigues pass. Despite this set back they took the lead eight minutes before half time when a long free kick by the goalkeeper into the Notts' penalty area caused confusion between

Slocombe and Rawlinson and Torquay's centre forward took advantage of their misunderstanding and nodded the ball into the net.

With the onus on Notts to put pressure on Torquay's ten men, Ian Burchnall made two changes for the second half and was rewarded with an improved attacking display. The equaliser was scored by Wootton when he moved toward a Chicksen cross and steered a diving header into the corner of the net. From then on Torquay's gamesmanship (time-wasting, slow recovery when injured etc.) frustrated the crowd, and the Notts players, and the encounter gradually petered out with Notts unable to create a second goal.

Match 3	**Wrexham (6th) 1-1 Notts County (5th)**	Attendance 5,454
Mon 30 Aug 2021 19:30	goal 53' Wootton 44'	

Slocombe

Brindley   Rawlinson (Chicksen 69')   Cameron (Capt.)

Kelly-Evans   Taylor

Francis (Roberts 55')   M. Palmer   O'Brien

Wootton   Mitchell (Rodrigues 55')

Subs: Chicksen, Rodrigues, Roberts, Nemane, Sam
(no substitute goalkeeper)

Mitchell made his first league start for Notts. It was a surprise that Roberts and Rodrigues failed to make the starting eleven. Burchnall explained that he wanted to give Roberts some recuperation time after his traumatic injury and illness problems of the last year, and Rodrigues needed to fully recover from his interrupted pre-season (positive COVID-19 test and tight hamstring). The match, only just over 48 hours after Saturday's fixtures for both teams, was televised live by BT Sport.

Wrexham just failed to reach a promotion play-off place at the end of last season. They finished in eighth position just two points behind Notts. This was their first home fixture of the new season, following an away draw and an away win.

Wrexham started well and Slocombe had to make a good early save. Notts retaliated and an unmarked Kelly-Evans shot over the crossbar after an excellent lay-off by Wootton. However, they were forced to defend for most of the first half and were fortunate when Wrexham had what appeared to be a good goal disallowed for offside following an excellent attacking move which ended with a fierce 20-yard shot. However, Notts withstood the pressure and against the run of play took the lead a minute before half-time. Cameron's delightful cross was met by Wootton who superbly headed the ball home into the far corner of the net from the edge of the six-yard box.

The second half was less than ten minutes old when Wrexham equalised. A hesitant Slocombe was beaten to a cross from the right and the ball was bravely headed into the net from within the six-yard box. Thereafter, in what had been an entertaining confrontation between two good teams, the game became less intense and Notts earned the point their defensive display deserved.

Match 4 Sat 4 Sep 2021 15:00	**Notts County (7th) 3– 2 Aldershot Town (21st)** Wootton 38' Cameron 52' Roberts 64'	goals 44', 50'	Attendance 5,921

Slocombe
Brindley (Mitchell 46')   Lacey (Rawlinson 75')   Cameron (Capt.)
Kelly-Evans   Taylor
Roberts   M. Palmer   O'Brien (Francis 82')   Rodrigues
Wootton

Subs: Rawlinson, Chicksen, Francis, Mitchell, Sam
(no substitute goalkeeper)

Alex Lacey made his first appearance of the season following injury.

Aldershot were pointless with three defeats from their opening three fixtures. However, they completed the double over Notts last season, winning both matches 1-0.

Notts had a goal disallowed after 25 mins. Following a good cross by Taylor, Kelly-Evans' first-time shot was saved by the goalkeeper and then the referee decided that he had control of the ball when KE followed on and stabbed it into the net. However, Notts took the lead as half-time approached when Rodrigues controlled a long Lacey pass and slid the ball to Wootton whose 16-yard shot, although not struck cleanly, nestled into the corner of the net. Although Notts had the majority of possession in the first half, Aldershot were their equal in terms of chances created and attempts on goal and with their last attack of the half they equalised when a cross from the left was turned into the corner of the net from the edge of the six-yard box.

Aldershot took the lead five minutes into the second half when a long defensive clearance was misjudged by Cameron (he claimed he was impeded) and the scorer of their first goal ran on and side footed the ball past Slocombe from the edge of the penalty area. But two minutes later Cameron equalised when he scored with a header from a Roberts corner kick. With just over one hour played Notts regained the lead when O'Brien floated the ball to Roberts. He chested it down to Rodrigues who then back healed the ball back to him, and Roberts curled his shot into the corner of the net from 18 yards. However, in the 72nd minute, only some desperate defending and a brilliant save by Slocombe prevented an Aldershot equaliser. A few minutes later Notts had another goal disallowed when O'Brien's composed finish was adjudged offside.

So, an entertaining game saw Notts maintain their unbeaten start to the season, but not without some anxious moments against a spirited Aldershot team.

Match 5	**Weymouth (12th) 1-1 Notts County (4th)**	Attendance 1,783
Sat 11 Sep 2021 15:00	goal 69' Roberts 59'	

Slocombe
Brindley   Lacey   Cameron (Capt.)
Kelly-Evans (Nemane 72')   Taylor
M. Palmer   O'Brien (Mitchell 72')
Roberts (Francis 81')   Wootton   Rodrigues

Subs: Chicksen, Francis, Mitchell, Nemane, Sam
(no substitute goalkeeper)

Notts unchanged from their victory over Aldershot. Rawlinson injured (ankle).

Mid-table Weymouth, who had been victorious in their last two matches after losing their first two, started brightly and they won three corners in the first six minutes. After one corner found its way to the opposite side of the pitch Slocombe had to be alert, when the cross was headed goalwards, and back pedal to turn the dropping ball over the crossbar. Notts gradually began to dominate and midway through the first half Wootton had two opportunities in a minute to give Notts the lead. With the first chance, following a Roberts free kick, he was denied by ex Notts goalkeeper Ross Fitzsimons and the second chance, from a Cameron cross, struck him and went out for a goal kick.

In the second half Notts maintained their superiority and they deservedly took the lead on the hour when, after a foul on Rodrigues, Roberts curled the 20-yard free kick into the top corner of the Weymouth net with Fitzsimons well beaten. However the lead lasted only ten minutes. Weymouth took advantage of a misplaced Kelly-Evans pass and a subsequent series of passes lead to a shot from the edge of the penalty area, and although Slocombe dived and got his fingers to the ball he was unable to prevent the goal. Thereafter Notts tried to get the victory they deserved but the closest they came was in the 85th minute when an excellent Francis free kick just evaded Wootton and Brindley lifted the ball over the crossbar from three yards. Mitchell then ran into the penalty area to receive a Nemane pass but he scuffed his shot and Fitzsimons made an easy save.

In each half Rodrigues also had a good opportunity from inside the penalty area but on both occasions, the second with virtually the last kick of the match, he blazed the ball over the bar. So, a well organised Weymouth team frustrated a still unbeaten Notts who, for the third time in their last four matches, had to settle for a 1-1 draw.

Match 6	**Notts County (5th) 3-2 Wealdstone (15th)**	Attendance 5,213
Tue 14 Sep 2021 19:45	Roberts 41' goals 31' & 65'	
	Wootton 45'	
	Cameron 58'	

Slocombe
Brindley   Lacey   Cameron (Capt.)   Taylor
Roberts (Sam 87')   Francis   M. Palmer   Rodrigues (O'Brien 70')
Wootton   Mitchell (Kelly-Evans 80')

Subs: Chicksen, Kelly-Evans, O'Brien, Nemane, Sam
(no substitute goalkeeper)

After losing their first two matches Wealdstone then drew two followed by a first victory of the season in their last match (penalty in injury time).

On a wet evening, Notts had a goal disallowed for offside (scored by Roberts) after ten minutes. Thereafter Wealdstone gave Notts some anxious moments and it wasn't a surprise when they took the lead. Francis, five minutes after the goalkeeper had saved his 20-yard shot, was shown a yellow card for a foul. From the free kick three Wealdstone touches (a header then a shot which rebounded off a forwards chest) planted the ball in the Notts net. This set-back energised Notts and they scored twice as half-time approached. Roberts got the equaliser, against the run of play, when he turned an excellent cross from the left by Mitchell into the net with a first-time side-footed placement. Wootton then put Notts ahead when he pounced on a loose ball in the penalty area and drove his shot into the corner of the net from 12 yards.

Notts were much the better team at the beginning of the second half and they deservedly increased their lead just before the hour mark when Cameron headed powerfully into the net from Palmer's corner kick. However, seven minutes later Wealdstone drove their way through the Notts defence and the scorer of their first goal was given time and space to beat Slocombe from close range. Soon after Roberts gave Palmer the chance to score his first Notts goal, and extend the lead, but he shot tamely wide from the edge of the six-yard box. As in the first half Wealdstone then started to give Notts problems and with six minutes remaining Slocombe made an excellent save to deny them the equaliser.

In his after the match interview Ian Burchnall gave credit to Wealdstone, and singled out Wootton ("outstanding leading the line"), Palmer ("unbelievable the amount of ground he covered, and his composure with the ball") and Roberts as Notts' stand out performers.

An entertaining match but a somewhat erratic performance by Notts who in the end managed to hold on, earn three points and remain unbeaten. Their last two home matches had been won 3-2 with the same trio of goal scorers!

Match 7   **Notts County (5th) 1-0 Maidenhead Utd (14th)**   Attendance 5,748
Sat 18 Sep 2021 15:00   Lacey 48'

Slocombe

Brindley   Lacey   Cameron (Capt.) (Chicksen 58')   Taylor

Roberts (Kelly-Evans 90')   Francis   M. Palmer   Rodrigues

Wootton   Mitchell (O'Brien 58')

Subs: Chicksen, Kelly-Evans, O'Brien, Nemane, Sam
(no substitute goalkeeper)

No changes to the team (or substitutes) – the same squad that defeated Wealdstone four days ago.

After winning their first two matches, Maidenhead had lost the last three.

In contrast to the wet evening four days ago, the afternoon was dry, warm and sunny. Maidenhead were the better team in the first half and they created the best opportunities. In comparison Notts looked laboured and, despite having more possession, their performance was disappointing. The consolation was that Notts reached half time on level terms. So far this season Notts' six matches had produced 21 goals but (also including today) none of those goals had been scored or conceded in the first 30 minutes!

The second half was only three minutes old when Notts took the lead. Following a Roberts corner kick Cameron headed the ball back towards goal and Lacey got the final touch from inside the six-yard box. Ten minutes later Cameron pulled up (hamstring injury?) and was replaced by Chicksen. Notts had the chance to double their lead after 68 minutes when they were awarded a penalty after Rodrigues was pushed over in the penalty area but Roberts' shot was saved by the goalkeeper. A minute later Taylor jinked his way into the penalty area and shot powerfully at goal but the goalkeeper made an excellent save. On 77 minutes Rodrigues and Roberts combined but the latter then shot over the crossbar from near the penalty spot.

An improved, but not too convincing, display by Notts in the second half gave them another victory and their first clean sheet since the opening day. A frustrating afternoon for Cal Roberts who had another good match but he missed a penalty, a chance, and received his fourth yellow card of the season!

When a team finish as champions of a league they only play like champions for the full 90 minutes on a handful of occasions during the season. Top performances were usually for a half, or a period, in a match. Notts were unbeaten in seven matches and had so far been in a play-off position throughout. They averaged 2.14 goals per match – the next best record in the league, and they were able to win, or avoid defeat, when not at their best. But all that changed for Notts seven days later when they failed to score and suffered their first defeat of the 2021-22 season.

Match 8	**Altrincham (15th) 1-0 Notts County (4th)**	Attendance 2,569
Sat 25 Sep 2021 15:00	goal 29'	

Patterson
Brindley   Brennan   Chicksen
Kelly-Evans (Nemane 60')   Taylor (Mitchell 76')
Roberts   Francis (O'Brien 54')   M. Palmer   Rodrigues
Wootton (Capt.)

Subs: O'Brien, Vincent, Mitchell, Nemane, Sam
(no substitute goalkeeper)

There were five changes, including two newcomers, to the team that defeated Maidenhead. Ciaran Brennan had signed as cover for the injured defenders Rawlinson (ankle), Cameron (hamstring) and Lacey (knock in training) and Anthony Patterson as cover for goalkeeper Slocombe (knock in training). The four absentees were unlikely to be fit again before early/mid-October.

21-year-old central defender Brennan signed on loan until 27 November, from League One Sheffield Wednesday, at the beginning of the week. In all he had made five starts for Wednesday – four last season in the FA Cup and EFL Cup and one this season in the EFL Trophy.

21-year-old goalkeeper Patterson signed on loan until 26 Oct (subsequently extended until 9 Jan 2022), from League One Sunderland, at the end of the week. In all he had made six starts for Sunderland – two last season in the EFL Trophy and four this season – two in League One and two in the EFL Cup.

Due to a positive COVID-19 test in their squad, Altrincham hadn't played for a fortnight and had only completed four matches (won two, lost two = WLWL).

The match (watched by an estimated 800 Notts supporters) was an unremarkable affair, as was Altrincham's winner – a cross cum shot prodded home from close range. Notts were unable to produce any real quality in front of goal. Palmer, in the first half, and Rodrigues, in the second half, missed the best chances to equalise. To complete a miserable day Roberts received another yellow card – his fifth of the season.

Match 9	**Notts County (6th) 1-4 Woking (12th)**	Attendance 5,807
Sat 2 Oct 2021 15:00	Rodrigues 29'	goals 70', 75', 78', 90'+4

Patterson
Brindley   Brennan   Lacey   Chicksen
O'Brien (Vincent 84')   M. Palmer   Rodrigues
Nemane (Knight 76', Kelly-Evans 90')   Wootton (Capt.)   Mitchell

Subs: Kelly-Evans, Taylor, Francis, Vincent, Knight
(no substitute goalkeeper)

Four changes following the first defeat of the season at Altrincham, including a first start for Aaron Nemane for Roberts who was serving a one match suspension for his collection of five yellow cards.

Due to a positive COVID-19 test in their squad a few weeks ago, Woking were behind in their fixtures – six matches played (won three, lost three = WLWLLW). In their last match, at home to second placed Chesterfield, they won 3-1.

On a cold, wet and windy afternoon Woking fielded two players who had played, on loan, for Notts - forwards Tahvon Campbell (six goals already this season) and Inih Effiong (one goal).

In difficult conditions Notts carried the greater attacking threat during the first half and they took the lead in the 29th minute. A good build up ended with O'Brien sliding the ball to Rodrigues who confidently placed the ball into the corner of the net from just inside the penalty area. It was Notts' first goal of the season scored within the first half hour of a match.

Just before half time, following a header from a corner, Patterson made an excellent save and after an incredible goalmouth scramble (with the ball very close to the goal line) Notts were awarded a free kick after the referee consulted his assistant!

Notts continued their domination in the first 25 minutes of the second half, but a disastrous final 20+ minutes saw Woking score four goals, three of which came in the space of eight minutes. They equalised after 70 minutes when Effiong scored with a good cross shot from the corner of the six yard box which entered the net via a post. Five minutes later Woking took the lead when a header following a corner kick glanced off the head of Brindley and flew into the corner of the net. The third came after a free kick wasn't cleared and Campbell pounced to shoot the loose ball into the net from ten yards. Notts lost their discipline and became frustrated. Rodrigues and Brennan were shown yellow cards. To complete a calamitous end, Lewis Knight, who had just completed his first fifteen minutes of the season after coming on as a substitute, was injured (hamstring). In added time Campbell scored his second goal (his fourth double of the season) and Notts suffered a second successive defeat.

Match 10	Halifax Town (5th) 3-2 Notts County (7th)	Attendance 2,023
Tue 5 Oct 2021 19:45	goals 79', 86', 90'+10 Rodrigues 30'	
	Lacey 56'	

                          Patterson
  Brindley (Kelly-Evans 77')   Brennan   Lacey   Chicksen
           Rodrigues (Mitchell 80')   M. Palmer   O'Brien
           Roberts   Wootton (Capt.)   Nemane (Sam 87')

Subs: Kelly-Evans, Francis, Vincent, Mitchell, Sam
(no substitute goalkeeper)

The only change following the knockout blow delivered by Woking was the return of Roberts after the completion of his one match suspension, with Mitchell relegated to the substitutes bench.

Halifax were undefeated in their last five matches and had kept a 'clean sheet' in their last three.

On a cold, wet and windy evening Notts had the better opportunities in the first half but Halifax had more possession. Notts took the lead when the Halifax goalkeeper ran out for the ball but realised he wasn't going to reach it and he became stranded. Rodrigues lobbed the ball into the net from fully 40 yards.

Notts' 447 travelling supporters were rewarded with a second goal ten minutes into the second half when Lacey scored with a good header following a Roberts free kick. Five minutes later the Halifax centre half clashed with Rodrigues and, following a scuffle involving players from both sides, the referee showed the defender a red card and sent him off. Ten-man Halifax then 'did a Woking' on Notts and scored twice in the space of seven minutes. They reduced their arrears with a good 20 yard shot which flew between Patterson and his near post. The equaliser was a controlled side-footed first time shot into the corner of the net from ten yards following a cross from the right. In a grandstand finish Notts should have had a penalty when Mitchell's shirt was pulled and he fell to the ground. Then, just as ten minutes of added time was signalled Brennan headed the ball into the net from a Palmer corner but the goal was disallowed for a foul on the goalkeeper (by Chicksen). On 98 minutes, from another Palmer corner, Lacey rose above everyone but from his header the goalkeeper made a brilliant diving save. Two minutes later, with the last kick of the match in the 100th minute, Halifax won when a ferocious 20-yard shot gave Patterson no chance.

In a fiercely contested, exciting, match, with five excellent goals, the weather improved in the second half but the mood of both players and management did not. At the end there were more scuffles, arguing and threatening behaviour. Unbelievably a naïve Notts, with poor game management, surrendered a two-goal lead against ten men, were defeated for the third consecutive match, and dropped to their lowest position of the season - tenth.

Match 11	Yeovil Town (14th) 0-2 Notts County (10th)	Attendance 2,438
Sat 9 Oct 2021 15:00	Rodrigues 17', 81'	

Patterson

Brindley   Brennan   Cameron (Capt.)   Chicksen (Kelly-Evans 70')

O'Brien   M. Palmer   Rodrigues

Roberts   Wootton (Francis 88')   Nemane (Mitchell 80')

Subs: Kelly-Evans, Francis, Vincent, Mitchell, Sam
(no substitute goalkeeper)

Ian Burchnall made just one change following the disaster at Halifax – Cameron returned after injury. He replaced Lacey who had been playing recent games when not fully fit with a knee injury.

Due to a positive COVID-19 test in their squad at the beginning of the season, Yeovil were behind in their fixtures. Their last three matches had ended with two defeats and, in their last fixture, a 0-0 draw.

Notts and Yeovil were relegated together at the end of the 2018-19 season.

On a calm, warm and sunny, autumn afternoon Notts took an early lead following a patient build up, and good work towards the end by Nemane and Palmer. The 22 preceding passes presented Rodrigues with an opportunity from the edge of the penalty area and he shot confidently into the net for his third goal in successive matches. Notts had chances to increase their lead as they dominated the first half against a disappointing Yeovil but had to settle for a slender lead.

Notts continued to be the superior team in the second half and with nine minutes remaining Rodrigues scored his second of the afternoon with a glancing header into the corner of the net from inside the six yard box, following a Palmer corner. As the match edged towards its conclusion Yeovil pressed Notts and Patterson had to make two good saves.

A strong away performance by Notts and a vital win, but not perfect (they had five players booked). With Notts' next fixture an FA Cup match at Tamworth it was imperative they didn't extend their losing league run to four matches. In his post-match interview a relieved Ian Burchnall revealed that Rawlinson and Slocombe would hopefully be ready to start the cup match.

Rodrigues (4) and central defender Lacey (2) were the only Notts goal scorers in the last five matches.

For Notts this much needed victory meant they had completed one quarter of their league fixtures for the season, so The National League table (as of Tuesday 12 October) is shown below.

National League Table 12 October 2021

		GP	W	D	L	GF	GA	GD	Pts
1	Grimsby Town	11	8	2	1	25	11	+14	26
2	Boreham Wood	11	7	3	1	17	9	+8	24
3	Halifax Town	11	7	2	2	20	10	+10	23
4	Chesterfield	11	6	4	1	22	10	+12	22
5	Bromley	9	6	1	2	20	10	+10	19
6	Dagenham & Red.	11	6	1	4	24	16	+8	19
7	Altrincham	10	6	1	3	19	13	+6	19
1 Auto promotion 2-7 playoffs									
8	Solihull Moors	11	5	4	2	17	15	+2	19
9	**Notts County**	**11**	**5**	**3**	**3**	**20**	**15**	**+5**	**18**
10	Stockport County	10	5	2	3	9	11	-2	17
11	Woking	9	5	0	4	18	11	+7	15
12	Wrexham	9	3	4	2	12	11	+1	13
13	Eastleigh	10	3	3	4	14	17	-3	12
14	Yeovil Town	9	3	2	4	9	10	-1	11
15	Torquay Utd	11	3	2	6	16	22	-6	11
16	Wealdstone	11	2	4	5	10	18	-8	10
17	Barnet	11	2	4	5	13	22	-9	10
18	Maidenhead Utd	10	2	2	6	11	17	-6	8
19	Kings Lynn	10	2	2	6	11	18	-7	8
20	Southend Utd	10	2	2	6	7	16	-9	8
21	Weymouth	11	2	2	7	13	23	-10	8
22	Aldershot Town	10	2	1	7	11	17	-6	7
23	Dover Athletic	11	0	3	8	6	22	-16	-9

Dover deducted 12 points for failing to fulfil fixtures last season

Notts County	Average per game	League ranking
Possession	61%	1
Passes	487	1
Passing accuracy	86%	1
Final third entries	43	1
Touches in opposition penalty area	23	1
Shots on goal	14	3

Notts should be higher in the league than ninth!

FA Cup 4th Qualifying round **Tamworth 0-0 Notts County** Attendance 1,813
Sat 16 Oct 2021 15:00

Patterson

Kelly-Evans   Brennan   Cameron (Capt.)   Taylor

Francis   M. Palmer

Roberts (Sam 81')   Mitchell (Wootton 65')   Rodrigues   Nemane

Subs: Kean (gk), Brindley, Rawlinson, Chicksen, Vincent, Wootton, Sam

With the luxury of seven substitutes allowed in FA Cup matches Notts, for the first time this season, named a substitute goalkeeper. A coronavirus (COVID-19) outbreak at the club prevented Notts from participating in the competition last season.

Ian Burchnall made four changes to the side victorious at Yeovil. It was a surprise that Vincent failed to make the starting eleven for the first time.

Tamworth were a part time club and members of the Southern League Premier Central, two levels below Notts. In their last league match on Tuesday 12th October, at home to lowly Stourbridge, they won 4-0 and moved up to fifth position in the league table. Six of their nine league games had ended in a victory, with one draw and two defeats.

The match, played on a 3G (artificial grass) pitch on a pleasant autumn afternoon, was dominated by Notts who had the lion's share of possession and created the best scoring opportunities. If it had been a boxing match Notts would have clearly won on points, but their problem was an inability to deliver a knockout goal!

They almost took the lead in the 27th minute when a superb Rodrigues free kick hit the underside of the crossbar and the rebound was cleared. In the second half the Tamworth goalkeeper (Singh) who had already made a number of good saves in the first half made another, on this occasion to deny Roberts by diving to his right and pushing the ball away for a corner.

The 800 Notts supporters who made the short journey witnessed a good Notts performance which deserved a victory. But, in order to determine who would progress into the first-round proper of the FA Cup, a replay at Meadow Lane took place three days later.

FA Cup 4th Qualifying round (Replay) Tue 19 Oct 2021 19:45	**Notts County 4-0 Tamworth** Mitchell 21', 49' Wootton 52' Vincent 58'	Attendance 2,594

Patterson

Brindley   Rawlinson   Chicksen

Kelly-Evans (Nemane 74')   Taylor

Francis   Vincent (Sam 81')

Rodrigues (O'Brien 63')

Wootton (Capt.)   Mitchell

Subs: Kean (gk), Lacey, Cameron, Brennan, O'Brien, Nemane, Sam

Ian Burchnall made five changes to the side held to a goalless draw three days ago. The most significant was the inclusion of Frank Vincent for his first Notts start. Rawlinson returned after injury for his first appearance since early September. Roberts was absent with a slight hamstring strain.

On a wet, but very mild, evening, Notts were totally dominant throughout the first half and the Tamworth goalkeeper (Singh) made two excellent saves in the first 15 minutes to deny Vincent. However, Singh had no chance with the shot that gave Notts the lead. Mitchell, on the turn from 25 yards, scored his first Notts goal with a terrific strike into the far corner of the net. Despite all their first half possession, with nine shots (five on target) and eight corners, Notts were unable to capitalise and score further goals.

Notts soon took the match away from Tamworth at the beginning of the second half with three goals in quick succession. First, Mitchell scored his second goal with a firm glancing header into the corner of the net from six yards following a Kelly-Evans cross from the right. Wootton joined the party when he calmly slotted the ball home from a Kelly-Evans pass. Vincent then got the goal he thoroughly deserved when he collected the ball from a short corner kick, moved forward and his hard, low, shot from the corner of the penalty area flew past Singh at his near post.

It was a clinical, professional, performance by Notts who, at the second attempt, were easy winners over a part time team from a league two levels below Notts. In the first round proper of the FA Cup Notts were drawn away at League Two Rochdale.

Match 12	**Notts County (9th) 2-1 Stockport County (10th)**	Attendance 7,418
Sat 23 Oct 2021 15:00	Wootton 54' goal 90'+3 (pen.)	
	Vincent 68'	

Patterson
Brindley   Rawlinson   Cameron (Capt.)
Kelly-Evans   Taylor
O'Brien (Roberts 77')   M. Palmer   Vincent
Wootton   Rodrigues (Mitchell 90')

Subs: Chicksen, Francis, Nemane, Roberts, Mitchell
(no substitute goalkeeper)

There were three changes to the team so convincing against Tamworth in the FA Cup replay. Vincent's impressive debut meant he retained his midfield place but two-goal Mitchell was relegated to the substitute's bench.

Stockport's recent form had been good with three successive league victories before progress to the first round of the FA Cup in their last match. However, they had scored only nine goals (11 conceded) in their ten league matches to date.

On a pleasant afternoon the two teams produced an entertaining first half. Notts (once again) had the greater share of possession but on the half hour only a goal line clearance by Cameron prevented Stockport from taking the lead. In the final ten minutes of the half Wootton had two golden opportunities to put Notts ahead. The first chance was provided by Rodrigues but Wootton's low right footed shot from 12 yards, after he had moved forward into the penalty area, lacked power and placement and the goalkeeper made the save. The second chance was provided by Taylor whose pass found him in the six-yard box but his attempt went over the crossbar. In between those Notts chances a Stockport goal bound shot was diverted off target by one of their players!

Wootton made amends for his earlier misses nine minutes into the second half when he put Notts ahead. He linked well with Vincent who cut the ball back to him near the penalty spot and his powerful first-time shot was deflected into the top corner of the net. Notts increased their lead when the impressive Vincent scored the second goal. He won the ball in Notts' half just outside the penalty box and, after he had passed the ball to Wootton, he sprinted forward. Wootton found Rodrigues and he fed the onrushing Vincent who moved into the right-hand side of the penalty area and calmly slotted the ball home with his left foot as the goalkeeper advanced. Although Stockport gave Notts a few anxious moments in the second half, and scored a consolation goal from the penalty spot after a foul by Rawlinson, Notts thoroughly deserved to win with their best complete performance of the season.

Match 13	**Notts County (8th) 1-1 Bromley (6th)**	Attendance 5,331
Tue 26 Oct 2021 19:45	Cameron 46' goal 80'	

```
                        Patterson
            Brindley    Rawlinson    Cameron (Capt.)
   Kelly-Evans                                    Taylor
            O'Brien     M. Palmer    Vincent (Roberts 66')
                Wootton       Rodrigues (Mitchell 81')

         Subs: Chicksen, Francis, Nemane, Roberts, Mitchell
                    (no substitute goalkeeper)
```

It wasn't a surprise that Notts were unchanged (starting eleven and substitutes) following their impressive victory over Stockport.

Bromley (like Notts) were also through to the first round of the FA Cup. In addition they had won their last six league matches in which they had scored 14 goals and achieved four clean sheets.

During the first half both defences were on top with few chances created. Notts' best opportunity, after five minutes, fell to Wootton. Rodrigues received a pass from Vincent and cleverly back healed the ball to Wootton but his tame shot was saved by the goalkeeper. The ball ran loose and only a superb covering challenge then denied Vincent. Bromley's best chance came just before half time.

However, Notts took the lead in the first minute of the second half. A series of neat passes found Cameron and his sublime shot from just outside the penalty curled into the corner of the net. Bromley's equaliser, with ten minutes plus stoppage time to play, was a lucky, scrappy, affair. Following a free kick a forward headed the ball into the penalty area and Patterson made a good save from the subsequent shot. A scramble in the six yard box ensued and after the ball had pin-balled around it trickled into the corner of the net. The goal was credited to Cheek, second in the National League 'Top Scorers' chart, which gave him his tenth goal of the season. Notts, who had much the better of the second half, responded with a shot by Roberts but his ferocious 22 yard drive thudded against the crossbar with the goalkeeper beaten. In added time an O'Brien pass gave a final chance to Mitchell, unmarked in a central position just inside the penalty area, but his shot lacked power and the goalkeeper made an easy save.

Notts deserved to win but once again they conceded in the latter stages of the second half and had to settle for a point. Most of the goals in Notts matches occur in the second half (16 of the 23 scored in the league; 13 of the 17 conceded). They had scored first in ten of their 13 league matches.

Match 14   **Grimsby Town (1ˢᵗ) 0-1 Notts County (8ᵗʰ)**   Attendance 7,213
Sat 30 Oct 2021 15:00   Rodrigues 90'

Patterson

Brindley   Rawlinson   Cameron (Capt.)

Kelly-Evans (Roberts 46')   Taylor

O'Brien (Nemane 46')   M. Palmer   Vincent (Francis 78')

Wootton   Rodrigues

Subs: Chicksen, Francis, Nemane, Roberts, Mitchell
(no substitute goalkeeper)

For the third match in succession Notts were unchanged (starting eleven and substitutes) following excellent performances against Stockport and Bromley.

Grimsby were relegated from the English Football League at the end of last season when they finished bottom of League Two. Although the current league leaders they were defeated 1-0 (at Wealdstone) in their previous match. Prior to that they had won five on the trot, including a victory to progress into the first round of the FA Cup. Before this match they had a 100% home record with six league victories – 18 scored, 4 conceded, and four clean sheets in the process.

Following morning rain, the first half commenced in bright sunshine with a fresh southwesterly breeze. There was little between the teams in the first 30 minutes until a Grimsby shot from the corner of the penalty area hit the top of the Notts' crossbar on its way out for a goal kick. From then on Grimsby were in the ascendency and just before half time Kelly-Evans blocked a goal bound shot, from the same player who hit the crossbar.

Notts changed their formation (to 4-2-4) for the second half, with Roberts and Nemane wide playing forwards. However, it wasn't until the hour mark that Notts had their first real attempt on goal when the Grimsby goalkeeper dived to his right to push away a Roberts shot from the edge of the penalty area and prevent Notts taking the lead. Grimsby had been the dominant team for most of the half but as the fourth official indicated three minutes of added time Notts scored. Wootton headed a long clearance by Brindley into the path of Palmer on the right, who ran on before he powerfully crossed the ball. The goalkeeper could only palm the ball into the air and it fell to Rodrigues near the penalty spot who shot into the corner of the net.

The 'smash-and-grab' goal was scored in front of the stand which housed most of the 1,087 Notts supporters who had made the trip to Cleethorpes. A resilient Notts weren't at their best but they defended well and earned their sixth clean sheet of the season – four in the league and two in the FA Cup.

FA Cup First round	**Rochdale 1-1 Notts County**	Attendance 2,587
Sun 7 Nov 2021 15:00	goal 45' Wootton 61'	

Patterson
Brindley   Cameron (Capt.)   Chicksen
Kelly-Evans (Nemane 58')   Taylor
M. Palmer   O'Brien
Roberts (Vincent 78')   Wootton   Rodrigues

Subs: Slocombe (gk), Rawlinson, Lacey, Brennan, Francis, Vincent, Mitchell, Nemane, Sam

In the first-round proper of the FA Cup clubs were allowed to nominate nine substitutes which meant the only Notts player not involved in the squad was the injured Lewis Knight. Forward Tyreace Palmer was loaned to Melton Town (four levels below Notts), until 9 January, earlier in the week. (Goalkeeper Tiernan Brooks was loaned to Worksop Town at the beginning of the season). A few days after the match central defender Ciaran Brennan was recalled by his parent club, Sheffield Wednesday – the loan was scheduled to end on 27 November.

Rochdale were just below halfway in League Two with a record to date of P15 W5 D5 L5 F19 A19. At home their record was P7 W2 D2 L3 F6 A7. They were undefeated in their last four league games but in their most recent match suffered a 0-3 home defeat (to Bolton) in the EFL Trophy.

In an even, and entertaining, first half Notts more than matched their higher league opponents. Both sides had opportunities, but it was Notts who fell behind with almost the final action of the half. Following a short corner and then a cross the ball was not cleared and Patterson had no chance with a shot into the top corner from inside the penalty area.

The entertainment continued in a similar vein in the second half. Patterson kept Notts in the match when he made an excellent save (with his legs) on 58 minutes. Nemane then had a fierce goal bound shot deflected for a corner kick from which Palmer found Wootton in the six yard box, at the near post, and, under pressure from the goalkeeper, he headed confidently into the net. With minutes to play Rochdale had a penalty appeal ignored by the referee after a player fell to the ground following a strong challenge by Brindley.

Both teams had ten attempts on goal during the match and chances to win but in the end a draw, between two competitive sides, was a fair result. The replay took place at Meadow Lane on the evening of Tuesday 16 November.

Match 15	Notts County (7th) 2-0 Solihull Moors (6th)	Attendance: 12,843 *
Sat 13 Nov 2021 15:00	Wootton 55', Mitchell 83'	

* The highest ever in The National League. Admittedly admission prices were reduced – adults = £5 and under 16 = £1.

                        Patterson

Brindley   Lacey (Rawlinson 57')   Chicksen

Kelly-Evans   Taylor

M. Palmer   Vincent (Francis 90')   Roberts (Mitchell 81')

Wootton (Capt.)   Rodrigues

Subs: Rawlinson, Francis, Nemane, Mitchell, Sam
(no substitute goalkeeper)
Cameron and O'Brien were absent due to illness.

Since their last defeat at the end of September, Solihull, with ex Notts manager Neal Ardley in charge, had played six league matches (P6 W4 D2 L0 F6 A1). In their last match (first round of the FA Cup) at Wigan Athletic they held the League One leaders to a goalless draw. They had conceded only one goal in their last eight matches!

Notts were the better side in the first half, during which they hit a post twice. After 11 minutes Taylor back heeled the ball to Rodrigues and his cross-shot hit the base of a post. On 36 minutes a good move ended with a Vincent shot from the edge of the penalty area which rattled the woodwork.

Notts deservedly took the lead ten minutes into the second half. A wonderful defence splitting pass by Roberts found the galloping Taylor and he crossed to Wootton who, as the ball dropped, stroked it into the net with a first time volley from six yards. In the 71st minute a Rodrigues header, from another good cross by Taylor, brought an excellent save from the goalkeeper and Vincent shot over the bar on follow up. A ten minute period of Solihull pressure came to an end when Mitchell, a couple of minutes after his arrival off the substitute's bench, scored his first league goal for Notts. The determination of Vincent and then Rodrigues presented him with the opportunity and he placed the ball into the corner of the net with a neat finish.

Although Solihull played well, an excellent controlled performance by Notts gave them a convincing victory. It was also Notts' dedicated Remembrance Day match and a record crowd saw them at their best.

FA Cup First round (replay)	**Notts County 1-2 Rochdale**	Attendance 4,416
Tue 16 Nov 2021 19:45	own goal 62' goals 15' & 90'	

Patterson
Brindley   Rawlinson   Chicksen
Nemane (Kelly-Evans 75')   Taylor
M. Palmer   Vincent (Francis 89')   Rodrigues
Wootton (Capt.)   Mitchell (Roberts 57')

Subs: Slocombe (gk), Kelly-Evans, Francis, Doyle, Roberts, Sam

With Cameron and O'Brien again absent due to illness, Lacey injured (back), Knight not yet fully fit, Ty Palmer out on loan and Brennan's return to Sheffield Wednesday, Notts only named six substitutes (nine permitted).

Rochdale had played once since the drawn first match – they equalised in the 90th minute at home to Leyton Orient.

Both teams started the match brightly, but it was Rochdale who took the lead after 15 minutes when a cross from the right fell to an unmarked player and the ball was volleyed into the corner of the net from six yards. Notts almost equalised seven minutes later. Mitchell and Wootton exchanged passes before the ball was released to Rodrigues who, from just outside the corner of the penalty area, unleashed a ferocious drive which hit the underside of the crossbar. On the half hour a Rochdale lob went inches wide and they then dominated the remainder of the first half.

Notts drew level 17 minutes into the second half when Roberts passed to Chicksen who crossed to the far post where a defender, under pressure from Nemane, turned the ball into his own net. With 13 minutes remaining only a good save by the goalkeeper, after Rodrigues had shot from near the penalty spot, prevented a Notts goal. In the final minutes Patterson made an excellent double save. However, Rochdale pressure finally paid off and they scored the winner after the Notts defence, in four attempts, failed to clear the ball, and when a cross arrived from the left Patterson was beaten by a glancing header from ten yards.

So, after a good entertaining cup tie Notts' unbeaten run of eight matches in league and cup, since early October, came to an end.

Match 16	**Eastleigh (15th) 2-0 Notts County (5th)**	Attendance: 2,817
Sat 20 Nov 2021 15:00	goals 40' & 68'	

Slocombe
Brindley   Rawlinson   Chicksen (Cameron 86')
Kelly-Evans (Nemane 69')   Taylor
M. Palmer   Vincent (Francis 46')   Roberts
Wootton (Capt.)   Rodrigues

Subs: Cameron, Francis, Nemane, Mitchell, Sam
(no substitute goalkeeper)

Sam Slocombe returned in goal in place of Patterson, who had been recalled off his loan by parent club Sunderland. Ian Burchnall said, "We're keen to see Anthony return and have had positive dialogue with Sunderland to that effect."

[It was also revealed that goalkeeping coach Jake Keen had joined League One Burton Albion and goalkeeper Tiernan Brooks had returned from his loan spell at Worksop Town.]

Defeated in their last two matches, both away from home (one league, one FA Cup), Eastleigh had had a mixed season to date. However, their home record was good with only one defeat – on the opening day of the season in August.

After a bright start by Notts their tempo dropped after a delay, due to a head injury sustained by Rodrigues, on ten minutes. Eastleigh scored just before half time when a cross from the left fell between Brindley and Rawlinson and the ball was nodded home from close range. They increased their lead mid way through the second half following a corner kick. Slocombe back-pedalled but was unable to palm the dropping ball away and it bounced off an Eastleigh player and found its way into the net. In the latter stages of the match Slocombe made three good saves.

Notts were restricted to some (decent) long range shots. Ian Burchnall acknowledged that Notts' overall performance had been poor and "lacked purpose, intensity and creativity, and we didn't deserve anything from the game".

Following the FA Cup exit in their last fixture, this match ended a run of five unbeaten league games. It was only the second time (this season) that Notts had failed to score in the league. Their non-league journey began at Eastleigh on 3 August 2019 and this was their third visit to the ground. They had suffered defeat in all three fixtures (1-0, 2-0, and 2-0). At Meadow Lane a win (4-0) and another defeat (0-1) was the record.

Match 17	**Boreham Wood (2nd) 1-1 Notts County (6th)**	Attendance: 821
Tue 23 Nov 2021 19:45	goal 64' Rodrigues 31'	

Slocombe

Brindley   Lacey   Cameron (Capt.)

Kelly-Evans   Taylor

M. Palmer   Vincent   Roberts (Mitchell 68')

Wootton   Rodrigues

Subs: Brooks (gk), Chicksen, Francis, Mitchell, Sam

Cameron and Lacey returned in place of Chicksen and Rawlinson (ill) respectively.

Boreham Wood had been beaten only twice this season. In their last 11 matches in league and FA Cup they had suffered only one defeat – 2-1 at current league leaders Chesterfield. Their defensive record was the best in the league with only 12 conceded and they had kept a clean sheet in their last four home matches.

Notts looked comfortable in the first half and they took a deserved lead on 31 minutes with a good goal. From a free kick Roberts produced and excellent cross to Rodrigues who, from near the penalty spot, gave the goalkeeper no chance with a powerful, well directed, header.

During an open, and more even, second half Boreham Wood equalised with a scrappy goal just after the hour mark. The ball pin-balled around and then fell kindly to an unmarked player who prodded it into the corner of the net from ten yards. Slocombe made a good safe in the 85th minute to thwart a possible BW victory.

A disappointing attendance of only 821 meant the match was played with a lack of atmosphere. Charlie Slater, the BBC Radio Nottingham commentator, thought there were as many Notts supporters as there were home supporters! A draw was probably a fair result in the circumstances.

On Friday 26 November Notts signed Connor Parsons (age 21) on a two month loan – until 29 January 2022 – from League One Wycombe Wanderers. A creative (left) winger/wing back he had played three EFL Trophy matches for Wycombe this season. Although all three ended in defeat he scored one goal. His arrival was due to an Aaron Nemane wrist injury.

Match 18 Sat 27 Nov 2021 17:20	**Notts County (6th) 2-1 Dagenham & Redbridge (10th)** Vincent 35' goal 42' Wootton 74'	Attendance: 4,889 Televised live by BT Sport

Slocombe

Brindley   Lacey   Cameron (Capt.)

Parsons (O'Brien 60')   Taylor

M. Palmer   Vincent (Francis 85')   Roberts

Wootton   Rodrigues (Mitchell 90'+2)

Subs: Rawlinson, Francis, O'Brien, Mitchell, Sam
(no substitute goalkeeper)

O'Brien returned to the squad after illness. Connor Parsons made his debut in place of the ill Kelly-Evans.

Dagenham & Redbridge made an excellent start to the season (defeated only once in their first eight matches). They were top of the league at the end of September. However, their recent form had been inconsistent with defeat in three of their last four matches, including an exit from the FA Cup.

During the previous 24 hours, meteorological storm 'Arwen' had battered most of the UK and the match was played in a strong, cold, northerly wind.

Notts dominated the first 25 minutes, but Slocombe then had to make three good saves in quick succession. Notts regained the initiative and took the lead in the 35th minute. From a Palmer corner kick Cameron headed the ball into the six-yard box and Vincent glanced a header into the corner of the net. Against the run of play D&R equalised just before half-time, also from a header following a corner.

In a more even second half, Roberts moved to the right with the introduction of O'Brien. In the 64th minute Rodrigues, who ten minutes earlier had missed an excellent chance, met a Roberts cross but, unmarked, he planted his diving header wide. However, ten minutes later, when Roberts produced another pin-point cross, Wootton headed confidently into the net from six yards to restore Notts' lead. It was his tenth goal of the season. During the four minutes of added time Slocombe made another good save from a 30-yard shot and Taylor fired just wide of the far post in reply.

Both teams provided good entertainment in difficult conditions. D&R illustrated why they had been at the top of the league earlier in the season and scored 33 goals in their previous 17 matches.

Ian Burchnall with Tom Weal

On 30 November Notts appointed Tom Weal as the new goalkeeper coach following Jake Kean's departure to Burton Albion.

It was Tom's first senior role. He joined from Norwich City, where he was head of academy goalkeeping. He had also coached goalkeepers in Huddersfield Town's academy and Nottingham Forest's academy.

Tom remarked:

"This is a massive club that you can see is going places and Ian Burchnall is a very exciting person to work for. He has a great team underneath him and I want to be part of the collective effort to get the club back to where it should be. I know Ian sees his

goalkeepers as having a crucial role in the way he wants the team to operate and that really appeals to me – it means I'll be responsible for coaching a lot of in-possession stuff on top of simply defending the goal, which is great."

Burchnall added:

"Tom comes highly recommended by a good friend of mine at Liverpool, who certainly knows his goalkeeping. He may be young, but he's an experienced coach who will be able to take a fresh look at Sam Slocombe and Tiernan Brooks and hopefully take them on to the next level."

Brooks had only recently returned from a three-month loan at Worksop Town when he was selected to attend an England goalkeeping development camp at (The Football Association's) St George's Park (near Burton-on-Trent) in early December. The camp was designed to give talented keepers the chance to showcase their skills, develop areas of their game and experience how England players prepare and train for national-team duty.

Notts' fixture at top of the table Chesterfield on 4 December was postponed because the Spireites were involved in a second round FA Cup tie.

On 7 December Notts signed Nottingham born Jayden Richardson (age 21) on a one-month loan from Championship neighbours Nottingham Forest. A defender (right (wing) back) he had made four appearances for Forest this season – two full matches in the EFL Cup then two from the substitute's bench in the league. However, in two recent season-long loans with Exeter City and Forest Green Rovers (both League two) he had made 64 appearances in all competitions, including a Wembley play-off final.

Match 19 Sat 11 Dec 2021 15:00	**Notts County (7th) 4-1 Southend Utd (19th)** Roberts 31' goal 10' Wootton 63' & 71' Cameron 89'	Attendance 6,206

Slocombe
Brindley   Lacey   Cameron (Capt.)
Richardson   Taylor (Parsons 57')
Vincent (O'Brien 78')   M. Palmer   Roberts (Francis 86')
Wootton   Rodrigues

Subs: Chicksen, Francis, O'Brien, Parsons, Mitchell
(no substitute goalkeeper)

Following their two-week break Notts introduced debutant Richardson at the expense of the other loanee, Parsons.

Southend were relegated from the EFL at the end of last season when they finished next to bottom of League Two. Their poor form had continued into this season. They had scored only 14 goals (joint worst in the league with Dover) and conceded 26 (only Eastleigh had a better defensive record in the lower half of the league). In October they appointed a new head coach.

Notts were the first to create a chance when, after four minutes, a Wootton header from a Vincent cross was palmed over the crossbar by the goalkeeper. However, it was Southend who took the lead on ten minutes when some indecisive defensive play gave a forward the opportunity to shot home from 10 yards. But, on the half hour, as rain began to fall, Notts equalised when Vincent won a tackle outside the penalty area. Wootton then gathered the ball and slid it to Roberts who scored from eight yards for his first goal since mid-September.

The second half was 15 minutes old when, following a goalmouth scramble, Southend should have scored but an unmarked player shot straight at Slocombe. A few minutes later Notts took the lead. Cameron, Vincent and Richardson combined and the Forest man's low cross to the far post was tapped home by Wootton. It was all Notts, and a marauding run by Parsons, followed by a low cross, found Rodrigues eight yards from goal in a central position but he shot way over the crossbar! Notts' third goal arrived after Lacey passed to Vincent and he fed Wootton who, from ten yards, rifled a shot past the goalkeeper at the near post. With ten minutes remaining the injured Southend goalkeeper was replaced by an outfield player (like Notts, no substitute goalkeeper) and he was beaten in the last minute of normal time after a sequence of passes on the right released Francis and Cameron headed his cross home from the edge of the six-yard box. In time added Southend had the ball in the net but it was disallowed for offside. After a slow start Notts produced an excellent second half display and in the end achieved a convincing victory.

FA Trophy Third Round	**Notts County 2 – 1 Altrincham**	Attendance 1,248
Sat 18 Dec 2021 19:30	Rodrigues 14' (pen.) goal 24' Wootton 42' (his 50th career goal for Notts)	+971 streamers (FA permitted stream outside 14:45-17:15 blocked hours)

                            Slocombe

            Brindley   Rawlinson (Lacey 65')   Cameron (Capt.)

Richardson   Parsons

              M. Palmer   Vincent (Roberts 80')   Rodrigues

                   Wootton (Francis 46')   Mitchell

Subs: Brooks (gk), Lacey, Chicksen, Francis, Roberts, Sam

Parsons returned to the starting 11 at the expense of the injured Taylor. Mitchell made his first start since the FA Cup replay against Rochdale.

Altrincham were 12th (mid-table) in the National League where they had won only one of their last ten league matches. They beat Notts 1-0 on 25 September.

Notts took an early lead from the penalty spot. Vincent passed to Palmer who was brought down, but Vincent seized the loose ball and side-footed it into the net from 17 yards. However, the referee had blown his whistle for the foul on Palmer and awarded a penalty to Notts. Rodrigues sent the goalkeeper the wrong way with his 12-yard shot into the corner of the net. Altrincham equalised ten minutes later when Slocombe fumbled and dropped a tame header and a forward tapped the ball into the net from three yards. Soon after a cross from the left almost found an Altrincham player unmarked on the edge of the six-yard box but he was unable to convert the chance. Just before half-time Notts regained the lead after Rodrigues split the defence with a pass to Richardson and he cut the ball back for Wootton who confidently swept the ball home from ten yards.

Although there were no goals in the second half, the match continued to provide interest and the goalkeepers of both teams were kept busy. The Altrincham 'keeper made good saves from Palmer, Mitchell and a Rodrigues free kick. Slocombe experienced 'The Good' (saves on 64 and 73 minutes), 'The Bad' (a poor throw out on 79 minutes; the subsequent shot went just wide) and 'The Ugly' (punched the ball up in the air from a corner rather than away). He also had luck on 70 minutes when he was beaten by a 25-yard shot but the ball hit a post on its way out for a goal kick. Finally, in the last minute of normal time, the referee decided a foul was just outside the penalty area!

Altrincham made a significant contribution to an entertaining evening, as did the referee who allowed the game to flow rather than stopping play to give soft free-kicks. Notts were not perfect, but they were good enough to get the job done.

Notts played only two matches in the whole of December, both at Meadow Lane – one in the league (a 4-1 win over Southend) and one in the FA Trophy (a 2-1 win over Altrincham). The re-arranged Chesterfield away fixture, scheduled for the evening of Tuesday 21 December, was postponed for a second time due to a COVID-19 outbreak at the Spireites. The Boxing Day (26 December) match at King's Lynn was postponed one hour before kick-off, without any prior warning, because of a waterlogged pitch! Notts were without a fixture on 28 December as the National League consisted of 23 teams this season and it was their turn for a day off.

To add to the frustration of the quiet end to 2021 from a playing point of view (Notts' inactivity meant they had dropped to ninth position in the league table) Ian Burchnall then revealed that Notts had:

> *"several COVID-19 cases in the camp among the squad and staff… but we've got a strong squad and I believe our strength in depth can shine through this weekend and throughout the rest of the season. I really want to play the game"* (at home to Wrexham on Sunday 2 January).

On New Year's Eve it was announced that Sunderland goalkeeper Anthony Patterson had returned to Notts on loan until the end of the season. The 21-year-old had made 12 league and cup appearances for Notts earlier in the season before he was recalled in mid-November from his initial loan because of injury to the other Sunderland goalkeepers.

Prior to the Wrexham match Notts' owners Alexander and Christoffer Reedtz issued the following New Year message to supporters:

> *As we head into what we all hope will be an exciting and successful 2022, we would like to say thank you to our fans for their incredible support throughout the past year.*

> *We also thank Ian Burchnall, his staff and players for their efforts so far this campaign, which have put us in a healthy position to compete for our ultimate aim of promotion. Despite it being a very tight league with many strong teams who have strengthened compared with last year, we're confident we will be firmly in contention come the end of the season.*

January brings the opening of the transfer window and, while this of course doesn't directly affect National League teams, we are aware of speculation that EFL clubs are monitoring a number of our players. This, in our opinion, should be viewed as a positive reflection of the team's performances and style of play.

We do, however, understand the prospect of losing players at this important stage of the season is concerning to supporters and would therefore like to reaffirm our stance that, for any sale to be approved, the terms of the deal would need to be seen as significantly beneficial for the club and helpful towards our ambition of returning to the EFL as soon as possible.

In the interests of transparency, we have received no formal offers for any of our players and Ian is very much planning for the second half of the season with his current squad intact.

Moving on to incoming transfers, you will no doubt have seen the good news that Anthony Patterson has returned to us on loan until the end of the season, which leaves us with two excellent options in the goalkeeping department. We're very pleased with the quality we've added via the loan market this season and will continue to use it as a tool to supplement the core of what we believe is a strong squad.

We are, as ever, closely monitoring several interesting potential signings. Particularly at this pivotal point of the season, when we are looking to climb further up the table, we will act if we believe the right opportunity presents itself to improve the quality at Ian's disposal.

As well as closely monitoring the team's performance, as a board we regularly analyse, discuss and improve our own methods to identify ways we can help the club achieve its targets. We do this in close consultation with Ian and take into consideration the huge amount we have learned since our arrival two and a half years ago. We look forward to assessing the success these improvements bring and making further enhancements in the future.

We have also been continuing our very close dialogue with our CEO Jason Turner to support our administrative team's excellent efforts to drive the club forward off the field. We would now like to make fans aware of another exciting project we have planned for 2022.

As some of you may have seen, we have recently been granted planning permission for a new four-court padel centre on the land behind the Kop.

Padel, which you could describe as a mix between tennis and squash, is really fun, easy to learn and sociable. It's also the fastest-growing sport in the UK and the world and, with no courts within a 40-mile radius of Meadow Lane, we see this as a very exciting investment opportunity which can drive new revenue for the club and enhance Nottingham's reputation as an incredible city of sport.

Football's relationship with padel is already strong, with Liverpool building a court at their training centre, several clubs incorporating padel sessions in their pre-season camps and the likes of Messi, Ronaldo, Neymar and Pogba all playing regularly. Ian also developed a love for the sport during his time in Scandinavia and we're sure he and the players will see this as a fantastic improvement to our facilities at Meadow Lane.

The development will also enhance the look and feel of that area of the stadium, with new tarmac to be laid down complete with allocated parking bays. We're confident the facility will attract people from across the East Midlands and we're looking forward to seeing the courts in action.

We're currently in discussions with various stakeholders to move things to the next phase and the club will keep supporters updated of future developments.

Supporters will be aware that we have had a number of Covid-19 cases in the club recently. We wish those affected a speedy recovery and commend the way Ian, Jason and their teams continue to work tirelessly to provide the safest possible environment at the club.

We also echo Ian's sentiments regarding doing all we can to play Sunday's game against Wrexham despite the recent disruption. As a club we have worked hard to build a strong squad for this season and we have utmost faith in all our available players to earn us the victory we all want.

Moving forward, we will await further government updates in the hope that it's not necessary for any further restrictions to be imposed and we can continue our collective journey back towards normality.

Thank you once again for your tremendous backing and we wish you a very happy new year.

Alex and Chris

Match 20	**Notts County (9th) 3-1 Wrexham (3rd)**	Attendance 8,890
Sun 2 Jan 2022 15:00	Wootton 10'(pen), 39' goal 4'	
	Richardson 67'	

                            Patterson

             Brindley   Lacey   Cameron (Capt.)

Richardson   Chicksen

           M. Palmer   Francis   Vincent

               Wootton   Mitchell (Sam 46')

Subs: Slocombe (gk), Roberts, Nemane, Sam (no fifth sub. available)

The players not considered due to COVID-19 or injury were: [Brooks (gk)], Rawlinson, Kelly-Evans, Taylor, O'Brien, Parsons, Knight, Ty Palmer. Rodrigues was absent because of a one match suspension for his five yellow card bookings.

Wrexham had won their last four matches, in league and FA Trophy, without conceding a goal. They had won their last five away league matches with sixteen scored and only three conceded. This was a match between the team with the best away record against the team with the best home record, Notts.

The 1,992 Wrexham supporters were in ecstasy after four minutes when their player survived a Palmer challenge, ran on and unleashed a terrific shot from 25 yards which flew past Patterson at his near post. Five minutes later Cameron and Chicksen combined to set up Mitchell but his goal bound shot was handled near the goal line by a defender. The referee deemed the offence to be deliberate, sent the player off, and awarded Notts a penalty which Wootton calmly slotted home. Thereafter the high standard of play, by both teams, continued but it was Notts who took the lead as half-time approached. In pouring rain, a Cameron cross was deflected and the ball fell to Wootton who headed into the net from close range for his 12th league goal of the season.

The second half was ten minutes old when Wrexham were given the chance to equalise from the penalty spot, after Vincent tried to hook the ball clear but then made contact with a forward and the referee awarded a penalty. However, Patterson dived to his right to push away the low shot from Wrexham's leading scorer Paul Mullin. At the mid-point of the half, as the rain ceased and the cloud broke, Notts scored a dramatic third goal. Chicksen dribbled his way to the byline at the edge of the penalty area and delivered a delightful cross which Richardson headed goalwards. The ball was headed clear from underneath the crossbar but the referee and his assistant signalled it had crossed the line.

An enthralling encounter, which was a fantastic advert for non-league football. It had just about everything. Promotion rivals and form team Wrexham were beaten by a superb Notts performance, and Ian Burchnall's faith in his squad was vindicated. What a way to start 2022.

Two days after the Wrexham victory Notts signed Zak Brunt from Championship club Sheffield United, on loan for the rest of the season. The twenty-year-old midfielder had made his debut for Sheffield United at the beginning of the season when he played in two (both for the full 90 minutes) victorious EFL Cup matches. Since then he had started nine matches, on loan, for fellow National League club Southend United – he was in their team defeated at Meadow Lane last month.

Three days later it was announced that Patterson had been temporarily recalled by Sunderland because of COVID-19 issues affecting their goalkeepers, and Richardson's loan spell from Nottingham Forest had been extended until the end of the season.

The next day (8th January) Notts' fixture at bottom club Dover Athletic was postponed. It is appropriate to include the statement published on the Notts website to explain the circumstances of that postponement:

First and foremost, we would like to express our sympathy to supporters who, following the Boxing Day postponement at King's Lynn, have now made two wasted journeys in atrocious conditions. We sincerely hope they return home safely.

Mindful of the lack of warning provided to us and our supporters on Boxing Day, and having closely monitored the very poor weather forecasted in Dover this weekend, we made contact with our opponents at 11am today only to be categorically told that there were no concerns over the match going ahead – a message we then communicated to our supporters.

Having received no further information from Dover, club officials were incredibly frustrated to arrive at the stadium two hours later only to be told by stewards that the match had been postponed. Head coach Ian Burchnall, still on the team bus with his staff and players 10 minutes from the ground, received a call from the match referee around the same time explaining that the pitch was completely unplayable.

Our chief executive Jason Turner then met with the referee who explained that, shortly after Dover had told us the game wasn't in doubt, they had made contact with him to enquire about his arrival time as they wanted him to assess the playing surface. We were not made aware of this dialogue, nor of any increasing concern Dover had of the match not going ahead.

At the time of publishing (4.30pm, Saturday), we are yet to receive any communication from Dover officials, let alone an apology for failing to provide any warning of a potential postponement despite them expressing concern to the referee, the persistent rain falling over the stadium and the poor forecast for the rest of the afternoon.

We have made initial contact with the National League to discuss this matter and will be providing a full report to them early next week.

Burchnall said: "Today has been a disgrace. Fans have sacrificed their Saturday, and a lot of money, to travel four hours in support of their football club and they have been massively let down by a complete lack of communication from Dover – just as they were at King's Lynn [two weeks ago].

"We understand that weather conditions can worsen even in a short time period, but to not inform us of the game coming under question shows a complete lack of respect to our supporters and us as a club. Last season, when games were being played behind closed doors, proved just how important fans are to football, particularly at this level of the game. It's disgraceful that Dover have allowed this completely avoidable situation to play out as it has. Our supporters have been badly let down once again and the National League need to address this for the good of all clubs."

Supporters are advised that King's Lynn's home fixture against Woking was postponed this afternoon due to a waterlogged pitch. We will maintain regular dialogue with King's Lynn and the league in the build-up to Tuesday's scheduled rearranged match to provide supporters with the latest information.

Match 21	**King's Lynn Town (22nd) 2-4 Notts County (7th)**	Attendance
Tue 11 Jan 2022 19:45	goals 9', 82' Roberts 52', 57', 67' Vincent 78'	1,505

Slocombe

Brindley   Lacey   Chicksen

Richardson   Roberts (Sam 83')

M. Palmer   Francis (Brunt 46')   Vincent

Wootton (Capt.)   Rodrigues (Mitchell 79')

Subs: Rawlinson, Nemane, Brunt, Mitchell, Sam
(no substitute goalkeeper)

Slocombe returned in goal in place of Patterson. Cameron's absence through illness meant Wootton became captain. Newcomer Brunt was one of the substitutes. Rodrigues returned after serving his one match suspension.

King's Lynn had resided near, or inside, the relegation zone for most of the season. They had lost 10 of their last 11 league matches. The exception was their defeat of bottom club Dover Athletic on 11 December, the day after a new manager was appointed.

Notts were disappointing in the first half and fell behind early on when, following a cross from the right, a forward headed home at the far post.

For the start of the second half Notts changed to a 4-3-3 formation. Debutant Zak Brunt replaced Francis and Roberts switched to the right-hand side of the front three. The change brought instant results – Roberts scored a hat trick in the space of 15 minutes. For his first he cut inside from the right and arrowed the ball into the corner of the net with his left foot from 15 yards. His second came when, following a 50-yard run down the right, he exchanged passes with Vincent and shot home from inside the penalty area. His hat trick came after an excellent team move and a Brunt low cross which he slid joyfully into the net from six yards. The impressive Vincent scored Notts' fourth when he lashed home a superb Wootton pass. King's Lynn reduced their deficit when a 25-yard shot from a free kick hit the underside of the crossbar as it flew past Slocombe.

The 524 Notts supporters witnessed a much improved second half display by the Magpies, who in the end were comfortable winners.

FA Trophy Fourth Round	**Notts County 2-1 Eastleigh**	Attendance 2,609
Sat 15 Jan 2022 15:00	Sam 9', 87' goal 7'	

Slocombe

Rawlinson   Cameron (Capt.)   Chicksen

Nemane (Taylor 62')   Parsons (Richardson 71')

Roberts   Francis   Vincent

Mitchell (Rodrigues 62')   Sam

Subs: Brooks (gk), Richardson, Lacey, Taylor, Palmer, Wootton, Rodrigues

Ian Burchnall took the opportunity (of a cup fixture) to rotate the squad following player illness/injury and match postponements in recent weeks. Elisha Sam made his first start of the season. Zak Brunt was ineligible as he had played for Southend in the third round of the FA Trophy when on loan at the Essex club. In all Notts made six changes to the team victorious at King's Lynn.

Notts, in 4th position in the league table, were defeated (2-0) at Eastleigh on 20th November. Since then Eastleigh had played six league matches (P6 W3 D1 L2 F6 A10), and were in 13th position in the league. They lost (4-1) their last match, at Halifax who ascended to the top of the league with the victory.

Before the match there was a minute's silence in memory of Colin Slater. Colin, for so many years the BBC Radio Nottingham commentator for Notts matches, helped the club in many ways during his 50+ years of involvement with the Magpies. He died, at the age of 87, earlier in the week – Monday, 10th January.

For the fourth time in the last five matches Notts conceded a goal in the first ten minutes to go one behind. On this occasion, from a corner kick, an Eastleigh forward volleyed the ball home with a back heel flick at the corner of the six-yard box! Notts equalised within two minutes when an excellent team move of incisive passes ended with a Vincent pass to Sam and he tapped the ball into the net from six yards, for his first goal of the season. Notts had the better of the remainder of the first half, but despite their superiority they failed to score again.

In a quiet start to the second half an Eastleigh glancing header brushed Slocombe's post on its way out for a goal kick. When Taylor replaced Nemane he went to left wing back with Parsons moving to right wing back. There was little between the two teams, but it was Notts who took the lead as full time approached. Rodrigues, under pressure, managed to squeeze the ball to Sam near the penalty spot and he shot accurately into the corner of the net.

On a cold, misty, afternoon a much-changed Notts team persevered to get the victory their first half performance deserved.

Notts were scheduled to play Barnet at Meadow Lane on the evening of Friday 21 January – brought forward a day due to a fixture clash with Nottingham Forest (v Derby). However, on the morning of the match, The National League postponed the fixture on medical advice following a number of positive COVID-19 cases, and injuries, at Barnet.

The match was to have been dedicated to Colin Slater MBE. Colin, who sadly passed away on 10 January, will be remembered for his immense contribution to the club and local community in a variety of ways. Notts were considering further permanent options to recognise him, beyond his induction into the Hall of Fame in 2014, his appointment as an honorary vice-president following his retirement, and the naming of the Meadow Lane media lounge in his honour. A special edition of 'The MAG' programme had been produced.

The tribute and commemorations were moved to the next fixture at Meadow Lane: the visit of Grimsby Town on 5 February.

I highly recommend a read of Colin's book 'Tied Up With Notts', his personal and revealing record of Notts County from 1959 to 2011.

Notts had been very unfortunate since early December with five postponements:

4	December	– away at Chesterfield who had an FA Cup second round fixture
21	December	– the rearranged match with Chesterfield who had COVID issues
26	December	– away at King's Lynn (waterlogged pitch)
8	January	– away at Dover (waterlogged pitch)
21	January	– home to Barnet…

As a result, Notts had not reached the half way point of the season (22 league matches) in the **five months** since the start of the season on 21 August. No club in the EFL or National League had played fewer than Notts' 21. The season was scheduled to end on Sunday 15 May. **So, 23 matches in less than four months!**

Match 22	**Wealdstone (20th) 0-0 Notts County (7th)**	Attendance 1,547
Tue 25 Jan 2022 19:45		

Slocombe
Brindley   Lacey   Cameron (Capt.)
Richardson   Chicksen (Parsons 69')
Roberts   M. Palmer   Vincent (Brunt 46')
Wootton   Rodrigues (Sam 72')

Subs: Parsons, Francis, Brunt, Mitchell, Sam
(no substitute goalkeeper)

Ian Burchnall made six changes to the team which started in the victory over Eastleigh in the FA Trophy. There was only one change to the team which started the last league match at King's Lynn - the inclusion of Cameron with the exclusion of Francis.

Wealdstone, one place above the relegation zone, had lost six or their last eight league and FA Trophy matches. The exceptions were the defeat of bottom club Dover Athletic, twice, in late November and mid-January. Despite their lowly position Wealdstone's defensive record was reasonable with 33 conceded in 22 matches – only eight more than Notts.

Statistics indicate that Notts are often not at their best in the first half of league matches (only four scored in the first 30 minutes, which included one penalty, out of a total of just 12 in the first 45 minutes). It was certainly true in this match. They had the most possession but failed to create any clear chances.

Although Wealdstone gave Notts a few anxious moments in the second half, the Magpies were much better. With 67 minutes played an excellent 35-yard drive from Brindley was tipped over the crossbar by the Wealdstone 'keeper. However, it wasn't until near the end that Notts created their two best chances. Richardson had a shot cleared off the line and in time added Roberts ran 40 yards down the right, jinked his way to the edge of the penalty area, and passed to Wootton but his shot was blocked and diverted for a corner kick.

So, a frustrating evening for the Notts players – and their supporters. Charlie Slater (BBC Radio Nottingham match commentator) estimated there were at least 500 Notts supporters in attendance. Wealdstone's average this season was just under 1,500. Their last two home matches had attracted <1,000 spectators. The main positive was Notts kept a 'clean sheet' for the first time since mid-November, during which time they had played six league and three cup matches.

This goalless draw (Ian Burchnall's first in his 40th league match in charge – there was a 0-0 draw at Tamworth in the FA Cup) meant Notts dropped to eighth position, one below a play-off place. However, they were only six points behind top of the league Stockport with two matches in hand.

National League Table 26 January 2022

		GP	W	D	L	GF	GA	GD	Pts
1	Stockport	24	15	3	6	47	24	+23	**48**
2	Chesterfield	23	13	8	2	44	20	+24	**47**
3	Halifax Town	25	14	5	6	38	20	+18	**47**
4	Bromley	24	14	5	5	41	26	+15	**47**
5	Boreham Wood	22	13	7	2	31	14	+17	**46**
6	Wrexham	24	13	6	5	41	24	+17	**45**
7	Dagenham & R.	25	13	3	9	47	32	+15	**42**

1 Auto promotion 2-7 playoffs

		GP	W	D	L	GF	GA	GD	Pts
8	**Notts County**	**22**	**12**	**6**	**4**	**40**	**25**	**+15**	**42**
9	Solihull Moors	24	12	6	6	36	23	+13	**42**
10	Grimsby	24	11	3	10	35	26	+9	**36**
11	Torquay Utd	25	10	4	11	38	40	-2	**34**
12	Woking	24	10	1	13	38	37	+1	**31**
13	Yeovil Town	22	9	4	9	23	24	-1	**31**
14	Eastleigh	23	9	4	10	26	35	-9	**31**
15	Aldershot Town	25	7	6	12	29	38	-9	**27**
16	Barnet	22	7	6	9	26	36	-10	**27**
17	Altrincham	25	7	5	13	37	45	-8	**26**
18	Southend Utd	23	7	5	11	22	34	-12	**26**
19	Wealdstone	23	6	7	10	21	33	-12	**25**
20	Maidenhead Utd	23	7	4	12	25	44	-19	**25**
21	Weymouth	23	4	4	15	25	45	-20	**16**
22	Kings Lynn	22	3	2	17	20	47	-27	**11**
23	Dover Athletic	25	1	4	20	20	58	-38	**-5**

Dover deducted 12 points for failing to fulfil fixtures last season
Positions 21-23 relegation zone

Dagenham & Redbridge (7th) were above Notts because they had scored more goals.

Brindley, Matty Palmer and Wootton (12 league goals) had started all 22 matches. Mitchell had appeared 12 times as a substitute and Francis 8 times.

Capt. Cameron had made 16 league starts (plus four in FA Cup/FA Trophy) and had yet to experience a defeat (he came on as a late sub. in the 2-0 defeat at Eastleigh).

In the second half of matches, Notts had scored 28 of their 40 goals and conceded 16 of the 25 against.

Notts were unbeaten in their last eight matches (six league, two FA Trophy).

In ten matches against teams currently in the top half of the table (they had yet to play Chesterfield) Notts had only been beaten once. The defeat was at Halifax where they allowed their opponents to come back in the second half from a two-goal deficit. Notts conceded three goals – Halifax equalised in the 86th minute and won the match in the tenth minute of added time!

The fixture list appeared to present Notts with a straightforward challenge towards the end of the season. They had Dover to play twice and they, together with King's Lynn and Weymouth, were scheduled to visit Meadow Lane in April and May. Their run-in was not the most difficult – at least on paper!

Earlier in the week Notts were informed by Sunderland that goalkeeper Anthony Patterson would not be allowed to return to Meadow Lane, as one of their senior goalkeepers was medically unfit due to heart problem.

Notts therefore signed 20-year-old Czech youth international Vitezslav Jaros, on loan until the end of the season, from Premier League giants Liverpool. He signed for Liverpool in July 2017 and two years later played in the final of the FA Youth Cup when the U18's beat Manchester City U18's. Although he had made only one senior appearance (in a friendly, July 2019) he had been in Liverpool's UEFA Champions League squad on two occasions in the autumn of 2020. He was loaned to Irish Premier League club St. Patrick's Athletic for their 2021 season (contested between March and November) where he played 39 matches, which included a winner's medal in the FAI Cup Final. He was St Patrick's Player of the Season and the League of Ireland's Goalkeeper of the Year.

At this point it should be recorded that although Sam Slocombe's form had been a little erratic at times, after Patterson originally returned to Sunderland in mid-November, he had not been playing badly. Ian Burchnall wanted competition in the goalkeeping department.

After the arrival of Jaros, the highly rated Tiernan Brooks was loaned to Coalville Town for him to get more match experience in men's football.

Chapter 19: The second half of the season

Match 23	**Bromley (4th) 1-0 Notts County (8th)**	Attendance: 3,606
Sat 29 Jan 2022 15:00	goal 45'+2	

                          Slocombe
        Brindley (Mitchell 65')   Lacey   Cameron (Capt.)
   Richardson   Taylor
        Roberts (Sam 82')   M. Palmer   Brunt (Vincent 65')
                 Wootton   Rodrigues

Subs: Chicksen, Francis, Vincent, Mitchell, Sam
(no substitute goalkeeper)

Ian Burchnall made two changes to the team held to a goalless draw at Wealdstone. Taylor, last start seven weeks ago, returned in place of Chicksen. Newcomer Brunt, favoured ahead of Vincent, was given his first start.

Bromley had won their last three league matches and, like Notts, had reached the fifth round of the FA Trophy. They (currently) had the best home record in the league. The match was played on Bromley's 3G (artificial grass) pitch.

Notts almost opened the scoring when Rodrigues hit a post in the tenth minute with a shot from the edge of the penalty area. After 22 minutes the Bromley 'keeper made two good saves from Roberts in the space of 60 seconds. On 30 minutes Richardson cut the ball back (to no one) inside the penalty area when he probably should have shot, and just before half time he sprinted with the ball almost the length of the pitch to earn Notts a corner kick. In stoppage time at the end of the first half a Bromley corner wasn't cleared and in the subsequent scramble a forward stabbed the ball into Slocombe's net from close range. Notts had much the better of the first half but Bromley, limited to a few dangerous counter attacks, took an undeserved lead into the break.

Bromley had an excellent opportunity to score a second goal at the start of the second half, but rather than a pass to an unmarked forward their player shot high and wide. Bromley's superiority continued and a shot went just wide of a post on the hour mark. Notts tried to inject some momentum by changing to a 4-2-4 formation in the 65th minute. With time running out Slocombe made a brilliant save, with his feet, and Mitchell went close at the other end. In stoppage time a Sam header was saved.

A lack lustre display by Notts in the second 45 minutes meant that for the third time in three seasons they lost at Bromley. Notts had failed to score in four league matches this season - all had been away from home. So, another good following of away supporters saw Notts defeated for the first time in ten weeks.

Match 24	**Notts County (8th) 1-2 Grimsby Town (10th)**	Attendance 9,305
Sat 5 Feb 2022 15:00	Roberts 15' goals 76', 90'	

Jaros

Brindley   Lacey   Cameron (Capt.)

Richardson   Taylor (Mitchell 84')

Roberts   M. Palmer   Brunt (Vincent 64')

Wootton   Rodrigues (Sam 68')

Subs: Chicksen, Francis, Vincent, Mitchell, Sam
(no substitute goalkeeper)

The only change in the starting eleven and substitutes to the side defeated at Bromley was the debut of Vitezslav Jaros as goalkeeper in place of Slocombe.

Grimsby were defeated (0-1) by Notts at their Cleethorpes ground on 30 October. To date their season had consisted of two contrasting fortunes. They lost only one of their first 12 league matches and were four points clear at the top of the table on 23 October. In their next 12 league matches they were defeated nine times, although they had won the latest (match 25) 2-1 at home to Wealdstone.

There were commemorations to honour the life of Colin Slater. His funeral service was held at St. Mary's, High Pavement, Nottingham on 31 January, when the hearse travelled to Meadow Lane before it commenced its poignant journey to the church.

In front of the second highest attendance at Meadow Lane this season, Notts dominated from the start, and they went into an early lead with a superb solo goal by Roberts. He received the ball near the centre circle, moved forward leaving defenders in his wake, and shot clinically into the corner of the net from inside the penalty area. However, Notts' rhythm was broken when Grimsby were awarded a <u>very debateable</u> penalty kick on the half hour for an alleged foul by Cameron. Jaros dived to his left and would probably have saved the kick, but the ball hit a post and rebounded to safety. From then, despite Rodrigues and Roberts going close, the visitors were in control. Only a final block by Brindley prevented a likely goal towards the end of an entertaining first half.

Grimsby's incessant pressure continued during the second half, and it was no surprise when they equalised as the match entered its latter stages. Jaros dived to cut out a low cross but could only palm the ball to a forward who shot into the net from seven yards. Notts then began to play better, and they had a couple of goal scoring opportunities, but in stoppage time the 2,454 Grimsby supporters saw their team score the winner when a free kick was nodded back into the six-yard box from where the ball was tapped home. Prior to this match Grimsby had suffered eight consecutive away defeats, six in the league, one in the FA Cup and one in the FA Trophy. Oh, dear Notts!

Match 25	**Notts County (8th) 6-1 Barnet (17th)**	Attendance 5,657
Tue 8 Feb 2022 19:45	Sam 7', 29' goal 66'	
	Roberts 11'	
	Rodrigues 48'	
	Wootton 72'	
	M Palmer 90'+1	

Jaros

Richardson　　Brindley　　Cameron (Capt.)　　Chicksen

M. Palmer　　Francis

Roberts　　Rodrigues (Brunt 61')　　Sam (Nemane 70')

Wootton (Mitchell 76')

Subs: Rawlinson, Vincent, Brunt, Nemane, Mitchell
(no substitute goalkeeper)

Following the Grimsby defeat Ian Burchnall changed the formation to 4-2-3-1 and made three changes. Lacey and Taylor were rested with Chicksen and Francis restored. Sam, given his first league start of the season, replaced Brunt.

Barnet made a dreadful start to the season. On the opening day they lost 0-5 at home to Notts. On 20 September they sacked head coach Harry Kewell (Notts manager for just 14 matches in the autumn of 2018) after five defeats and two draws in their first seven matches. After a temporary improvement, their form again dipped, although they had ended a run of six matches without a win by recording a 1-3 victory at Aldershot three days ago.

For the first half hour Notts ran Barnet ragged. Sam opened the scoring when the Barnet goalkeeper fumbled a Rodrigues shot and Sam followed up to tap the ball into the net. Roberts soon added a second when he cut inside from the right and let fly with his left foot from 20 yards. For his second goal Sam received a delightful 50-yard pass from Cameron on the edge of the penalty area, controlled the ball and fired home from 12 yards. Just before half time the referee stopped play for five minutes after one of the Barnet players was racially abused by a Notts supporter in the spion cop stand. The supporter was ejected from the stadium and arrested by police. The referee indicated that the match would be abandoned if there was a repeat of such behaviour.

With the exception of a lapse in concentration in the 66th minute, Notts also controlled the second half with goals from Rodrigues (he dispossessed a defender near the touchline, ran into the penalty area and beat the 'keeper with a cross shot), Wootton (who finished off a good Notts move when he converted a Roberts pass from the edge of the six yard box) and Palmer (his first Notts goal was a crisp shot from near the penalty spot).

Notts last scored six at Meadow Lane in December 1983 when they defeated Sunderland 6-1. The following week Notts lost 5-0 at Liverpool, and over Christmas drew 3-3 at Manchester United. Unfortunately, Notts were relegated from Division 1 (the top tier of English football) at the end of that season!

FA Trophy Fifth Round	**Halifax Town 1-2 Notts County**	Attendance 1,406
Sat 12 Feb 2022 15:00	goal 60' Rodrigues 3' Mitchell 86'	

Slocombe

Kelly-Evans (Richardson 77')   Rawlinson   Lacey   Taylor

Vincent   Francis   Rodrigues

Mitchell   Wootton (Capt.) (Nemane 77')   Sam (Roberts 66')

Subs: Jaros (gk), Richardson, Brindley, Cameron, Chicksen, Nemane, Roberts

Apart from the three players out on loan (Ty Palmer, Knight, and Brooks) only three of the squad were absent: Matty Palmer (rested), O'Brien (unfit), Brunt (ineligible). In all Ian Burchnall made seven changes to the team which pulverised Barnet. Rawlinson became captain when Wootton was substituted.

A week ago, Halifax's home game was postponed due to a waterlogged pitch. Today's forecast was for a wet and windy afternoon. As a result, the referee made two pitch inspections, at 8.30 am and 1 pm, before he declared the pitch playable. Despite this 283 Notts supporters attended. Halifax were in 3rd position in The National League. Notts, in 8th position, were defeated (3-2) at Halifax in a dramatic end to that league match in early October. Only one team had conceded fewer league goals than Halifax's 21 from 26 matches.

Notts made a good start and went ahead following a good team move. The ball eventually arrived at the feet of Rodrigues, and he passed to Kelly-Evans in the right-hand side of the penalty area. K-E's shot but the goalkeeper saved with his feet. The loose ball ran back to the unmarked Rodrigues near the penalty spot, and he shot emphatically into the net.

The cup-tie was one hour old when Halifax equalised. Their forwards combined effectively, and the resultant ten-yard shot gave Slocombe no chance. The match seemed to be heading to a penalty shoot-out (no extra time at this stage in the competition) but Notts won with a goal created by two of their substitutes. Richardson ran 50 yards with the ball before he passed to Roberts who gave the tireless Mitchell an easy chance from close range. In stoppage time Rawlinson headed the ball off the Notts goal-line.

So, Notts progressed to the quarter-final stage of the FA Trophy for the third time in their three National League seasons. The draw paired Notts with Wrexham, one of five fellow National League promotion rivals still in the competition, at Meadow Lane. The others were Stockport, Bromley, Solihull, and Dagenham & Redbridge. The remaining two clubs were York City (National League North – Step 2 of the Non-League Football Pyramid) and Needham Market (Southern League Premier Division, Central – Step 3) from Suffolk.

On Tuesday evening 15 February Notts were scheduled to play their rearranged fixture at, bottom of the league, Dover Athletic. Instead of a report of the match, below is the statement Notts released after it was postponed for a second time due to a waterlogged pitch:

> *It is hugely disappointing and frustrating to once again be addressing issues regarding a postponed trip to Dover, not least due to the inconvenience and cost to supporters – many of whom had set off on the understanding that the Crabble Athletic Ground pitch was 'perfectly playable'.*
>
> *On Monday, Dover's club secretary contacted our chief executive Jason Turner to advise that their view was that the pitch was in satisfactory condition but, due to the events leading to the late postponement of the initial fixture on 8 January, they had arranged for a referee from the Kent FA to conduct a provisional pitch inspection at 11am today (Tuesday). We were told that the match referee was unavailable at this time, but that his FA colleague would liaise with him immediately thereafter. We*

therefore communicated to our supporters that, while Dover had expressed no immediate concerns, plans were in place to reassess the situation if necessary and that updates would follow in due course.

It therefore came as a surprise to Turner when, at 11.10am today – 10 minutes after the provisional inspection had been scheduled to start – he received a call from the match referee to say the aforementioned official was no longer available and that Dover believed their surface to be playable having carried out groundworks on Friday. They had advised him the earliest they could schedule another provisional inspection would be for 12.20pm and, based on this information, the match referee informed us that he was instead going to endeavour to inspect the pitch himself at 4pm.

Turner informed him that he wasn't comfortable with our supporters departing Nottingham without a qualified external individual providing their assessment of the pitch, insisting that due to past experience, the weather forecast, the distance and significant cost to fans, it was imperative that the pitch was assessed in the early afternoon. The National League were in agreement and made arrangements for an official of the required level to conduct a pitch inspection shortly after 12.30pm.

Having received no communication from Dover regarding the outcome of said inspection, Turner called their club secretary at 1pm and was categorically assured that the pitch had been deemed perfectly playable and that the appointed official had no concerns about the match going ahead. Turner informed Dover that this information would be communicated immediately via our digital channels to help supporters make what we believed would have been an informed decision as to whether to travel, with the assurance that we would maintain dialogue with all parties in the event of a change in circumstances.

The next communication received by Turner came from the match referee at 2.10pm, informing him that based on the pitch inspection report and weather forecast, he had decided to postpone the match. It is clear, therefore, that Dover's communication to us following the inspection was either misjudged or misleading.

Following the announcement of the postponement, Dover published an interview with their chairman Jim Parmenter in which he inferred that the postponement can only have come as a result of 'undue pressure from Notts County'. While we firmly stand by our decision to ask questions of Dover regarding the condition of their pitch and of The National League to arrange an earlier inspection, this was simply to ensure that our supporters were provided with the best possible information before deciding whether or not to travel. We vehemently reject Parmenter's inference that we were seeking for the match to be postponed. Not only have we once again incurred considerable team travel and hotel costs, but this week's training schedule has now been severely affected. We have already experienced severe disruption to our season for various reasons and were desperate to play this evening's match and continue the momentum we have built in our back-to-back wins over Barnet and Halifax.

We will continue our dialogue with The National League as part of our efforts to promote the importance of clear, open and accurate communication between clubs for the benefit of supporters.

The third journey to Dover was rearranged for the evening of Tuesday 26 April. With the two grounds approximately 210 miles apart, for the three return journeys the distance travelled by Notts to play the match was 420 x 3 = 1260 miles! I wonder how many Notts supporters also made those journeys?

* * * * *

With a very busy schedule of fixtures ahead - 19 league matches to play in the next 12 weeks (plus at least one FA Trophy cup-tie) - Ian Burchnall expected player rotation to become an important consideration in his team selections, during the congested period to the end of the season on 15 May.

He confirmed that currently he had 20 of his 21-player squad available for selection. Jim O'Brien was the only Notts player unfit and therefore unavailable.

Because of illness and injury Jim's last full match was at Rochdale in the FA Cup on 7 November. Since then, he had appeared twice as a substitute - the last time on 11 December - and played a total of just 42 minutes.

Match 26	**Notts County (9ᵗʰ) 2-0 Eastleigh (14ᵗʰ)**	Attendance 5,682
Sat 19 Feb 2022 15:00	Roberts 35'	
	Wootton 41'	

Jaros

Richardson   Brindley   Cameron (Capt.)   Chicksen

M. Palmer   Francis

Roberts (Nemane 85')   Rodrigues   Sam (Mitchell 71')

Wootton

Subs: Rawlinson, Vincent, Brunt, Nemane, Mitchell
(no substitute goalkeeper)

The starting eleven and substitutes were the same as in the last league game – the 6-1 demolition of Barnet.

Since Notts defeated Eastleigh in the fourth round of the FA Trophy five weeks ago the Hampshire club had lost four and drawn two league matches. They had failed to score in five of the six, and even allowed bottom of the league Dover to achieve their first victory since January 2021.

Other than for a brief period around the half hour mark when Eastleigh missed a good chance, Notts dominated throughout the first 45 minutes. However, both their goals had an element of good fortune. Roberts, who, with Richardson, had given defenders a torrid time down the right-hand side, produced another excellent cross but the in-swinging ball bounced and skidded on beyond the diving(ex-Notts) goalkeeper Joe McDonnell into the far corner of the net. A few minutes later McDonnell received a straightforward back pass from a defender and trotted, with the ball at his feet, away from the goalmouth. He panicked as Wootton advanced towards him and was easily dispossessed. Notts' leading goalscorer then slid and scooped the ball, from the edge of the penalty area, into the unguarded net.

Notts' domination continued in the second half, and they squandered further opportunities to increase their lead, and improve their goal difference from its present plus 20 – only bettered by Stockport and Chesterfield.

A controlled and comfortable victory, in a very one-sided encounter, placed Notts just one point below a play-off position. They still had at least one match in hand over most of their promotion rivals.

Match 27	Notts County (8th) 1-1 Halifax Town (4th)	Attendance 5,603
Tue 22 Feb 2022 19:45	Sam 43' goal 18'	

                             Jaros
         Richardson   Brindley   Cameron (Capt.)   Chicksen
                   M. Palmer   Francis (Brunt 70'= Vincent 86')
              Roberts   Rodrigues   Sam (Mitchell 86')
                             Wootton

Subs: Rawlinson, Vincent, Brunt, Nemane, Mitchell
(no substitute goalkeeper)

Notts were unchanged for the third league match in succession - starting eleven and substitutes.

Due to postponements, Halifax had only played one match so far in February – when they were defeated by Notts in the fifth round of the FA Trophy ten days ago. Although four places higher than Notts only two points separated the teams, with the same number of matches played – 26.

Halifax were the better side for the first ten minutes, but Notts then took over. However, it was Halifax who scored first. A forward chased a long pass which Jaros should have collected at the edge of his penalty area. Unfortunately, his approach lacked conviction, the forward tapped the ball beyond him and side-footed it into the empty net. A few minutes later Sam received the ball on the left wing, cut inside, and from just inside the penalty area unleashed a powerful right-foot shot which hit the far post and rebounded to safety. With ten minutes left of the first half a Halifax defender was sent off after the referee issued him with two yellow cards in quick succession. Notts got the equaliser they thoroughly deserved just before half-time when Sam again moved inside from the left and this time his powerful right-foot shot from 22 yards beat the goalkeeper at his near post. It was Notts' 50th league goal of the season.

Notts put ten-man Halifax under constant pressure throughout the second 45 minutes but, despite their superiority and many opportunities, they were unable to create a second goal and get the three points they deserved. The closest they came was in the first of the seven minutes of added time when a Cameron shot hit the crossbar.

Notts gave a very impressive performance throughout and also had two strong appeals for a penalty turned down by the referee in an exciting and dramatic first half. Cameron was clearly held as he ran to make contact with a corner kick at the back post, and a 20-yard shot by Francis struck the arm of a defender. Brunt's appearance as a substitute lasted only 15 minutes before he was injured. So, 392 Halifax supporters saw their team give a dogged defensive display which deprived Notts of two points. Notts remained in eighth position – still one below the play-off places.

Match 28 Woking (15th) 0-2 Notts County (8th)   Attendance 3,141
Sat 26 Feb 2022 15:00   Rodrigues 43'
                        Sam 76'

Jaros

Richardson   Brindley   Cameron (Capt.)   Chicksen

M. Palmer   Francis (Mitchell 85')

Nemane (Vincent 83')   Rodrigues   Sam

Wootton

Subs: Rawlinson, Lacey, Vincent, Brunt, Mitchell
(no substitute goalkeeper)

Ian Burchnall was forced into his first change(s) in four league matches. Aaron Nemane was promoted from the substitutes bench to replace the injured Roberts and Lacey returned to the squad as a substitute.

Woking defeated Notts 4-1 at the beginning of October - the heaviest defeat of the season (so far) for Notts. However, they had won only one of their eight league matches in 2022. In their 14 home matches they had suffered nine defeats (won five) and had yet to draw. Their leading goalscorer was Inih Effiong (11 goals). In January 2021 Neal Ardley (then Notts manager) signed Effiong on loan until the end of the season from League Two Stevenage, but he scored just one goal in 12 appearances – and that was a penalty.

Rodrigues brought a scrappy and largely uneventful first half to life just before half time. First he volleyed just wide as he received a wonderful long pass from Cameron, and a minute later he gave Notts the lead. The ball arrived at his feet curtesy of Nemane and his low 18-yard shot went through a crowded penalty area into the corner of the net.

Woking offered little as an attacking force in the second half, and Notts, although not at their best, gave an improved performance. Wootton and Nemane forced the goalkeeper into good saves in the 50th and 66th minutes respectively, but it was Sam who scored Notts' second goal. Nemane carried the ball forward and found Sam who shot emphatically into the net from just inside the penalty area.

Mainly due to a change of referee midway through the second half there was ten minutes of added time. Notts were untroubled and in the end were comfortable winners and moved into a play-off position. Nemane, who assisted both goals, started in the FA Trophy win over Eastleigh on 15 January but his last league start was at the beginning of October.

On a pleasant, sunny, afternoon, over 500 Notts supporters were in attendance – 517 to be exact. Notts had already sold all their ticket allocation for their next match – away at high flying, and near neighbours, Chesterfield.

Match 29	**Chesterfield (2nd) 3-1 Notts County (7th)**	Attendance 7,912
Tue 1 March 2022 19:45	goals 60', 86', 90' pen Sam 40'	

Jaros

Richardson   Brindley   Cameron (Capt.)   Chicksen

M. Palmer   Vincent (Brunt 58')

Roberts   Rodrigues   Sam (Nemane 85')

Wootton (Mitchell 81')

Subs: Rawlinson, Kelly-Evans, Brunt, Nemane, Mitchell
(no substitute goalkeeper)

There were two changes to the team victorious at Woking: Roberts returned in place of Nemane, and Vincent came in for the injured Francis.

Chesterfield suffered only their second league defeat of the season on 18 January. Six days later their manager, James Rowe, was suspended pending an investigation into allegations of misconduct. On 4 February Rowe departed "with immediate effect by mutual consent". Six days later they appointed a new manager, Paul Cook, but in his first match in charge Chesterfield's (and The National League) leading scorer with 24 goals, Tshimanga, was seriously injured and was unlikely to play again this season. In their last match they ended a sequence of two draws and two defeats with a home victory over Yeovil.

In a competitive first half it was not until the 17th minute that Notts created an opportunity when, following a Richardson cross, Sam's header was saved by ex-Notts goalkeeper Scott Loach. Although it was Chesterfield who looked the more threatening it was Notts who took the lead five minutes before the break. Palmer and Sam exchanged passes and Sam ran to the left corner of the penalty area from where his powerful right foot shot curled into the far top corner of the net. It was his fifth league goal in five matches since he made his first league start of the season only three weeks ago, and his seventh goal since 15 January when he scored both goals in the FA Trophy victory over Eastleigh.

Chesterfield put Notts under pressure at the beginning of the second half and it was not a surprise when they equalised with one hour played. A cross from the left was headed home from close range at the back post. Notts attacked only sporadically, and Jaros was much the busier of the two goalkeepers. Chesterfield won the match in the final five minutes. They took the lead after a corner kick was scrambled into the net, again from close range. To complete a painful evening for Notts, and their 1,793 supporters, Brindley then committed a foul in the penalty area and the spot kick was dispatched with ease. In stoppage time Loach made a great save from a Cameron header.

On a difficult pitch, Notts were exposed defensively. A disappointed Ian Burchnall admitted that Chesterfield were the better team in the second half and deserved their victory. The fixture had previously been postponed twice.

Match 30	**Notts County (7th) 1-1 Yeovil Town (13th)**	Attendance 6,943
Sat 5 March 2022 15:00	Lacey 90'+4 goal 47'	

Jaros

Richardson (Kelly-Evans 58')   Rawlinson   Cameron (Capt.) (Lacey 25')   Chicksen

M. Palmer   Francis (Mitchell 80')

Roberts   Rodrigues   Sam

Wootton

Subs: Lacey, Kelly-Evans, Brunt, Nemane, Mitchell
(no substitute goalkeeper)

Notts made two changes to the team defeated at Chesterfield: Francis returned in place of Vincent. Brindley missed his first league match of the season through injury. His place was taken by Rawlinson for his first league appearance since 20 November, although he had played three cup matches.

Notts won 2-0 at Yeovil at the beginning of October – Rodrigues scored both goals. Since Boxing Day (26 December) Yeovil had won just one of 11 league matches and had been knocked out of the FA Cup and FA Trophy. Defensively they had conceded 29 goals (only five of the top six had a better record) whereas Notts had conceded 33, but only the bottom two teams had scored fewer than Yeovil's 27 goals. In their last match they lost 1-0 at Chesterfield.

Both teams had their moments in the first half, but it was Notts who created two good chances. The first fell to Sam on ten minutes but his header, from a Roberts cross, was cleared near the goal line and the goalkeeper then saved Wootton's attempt after he had diverted a Chicksen shot. On 23 minutes an even better chance fell to the unmarked Rodrigues, following another good cross by Roberts, but his diving header lacked power and direction and went harmlessly wide. Two minutes later Cameron, the Notts captain, pulled up with a hamstring injury and Lacey substituted.

Notts made a disastrous start to the second half when a Francis header back towards Jaros lacked power and was intercepted. The goalkeeper saved the first shot but from the rebound Yeovil took the lead when the ball was driven into the net from 25 yards. Five minutes later Roberts supplied Rodrigues who shot, but the Yeovil 'keeper denied him a goal with an excellent save. The remainder of the match was forgetful from a Notts point of view - until the fourth minute of the nine minutes of stoppage time, when Lacey ran on to a Palmer free kick and headed home from near the penalty spot to give Notts the equaliser. Before the end Rawlinson made an important defensive block and shortly after his attacking header nearly found Wootton but the goalkeeper made a brave save.

So, in an ill-disciplined second half when Notts had three players booked, they salvaged a point and remained in a play-off position – seventh.

Match 31	**Solihull Moors (6th) 3-3 Notts County (7th)**	Attendance 2,120
Tue 8 March 2022 19:45	goals 7' pen, 70', 85' Rodrigues 18', 72'	
	Lacey 56'	

Jaros

Kelly-Evans (Taylor 78')   Rawlinson   Lacey   Chicksen

Brunt   Francis   Vincent (Nemane 64')

Roberts   Wootton (Capt.)   Rodrigues

Subs: Slocombe (gk), Richardson, Taylor, Nemane, Mitchell

Notts had to make fours changes to the team held to a draw by Yeovil. Matty Palmer, who had played every minute of every league match this season, and Sam, were ill. Cameron was injured, and Kelly-Evans replaced, a not 100 per cent fit, Richardson. Notts only had the above 16 to choose from!

Before the match Notts announced that Cal Roberts and Richard Brindley had been selected in the 16-man England 'C' squad to play Wales 'C' on 30 March.

Solihull had the distinction of playing Notts (won 2-0) in mid-November in front of the highest Meadow Lane crowd (12,843) of the season so far. They had drawn their last two league matches but were unbeaten in their last eight. Like Notts they had reached the quarter final stage of the FA Trophy.

The first goal threat came from Solihull when a shot struck the outside of a post in the third minute. Soon after they took the lead with a penalty after central defender Mark Ellis (in all, he played 22 matches for Notts last season and scored six goals) headed the ball towards the six-yard box and it hit Chicksen on his arm. Notts responded positively and ten minutes later Rodrigues equalised when his excellent 18-yard shot entered the bottom corner of the net. 60 seconds later Rodrigues found Brunt who hit a post with his shot. Then, in the 22nd minute, the referee awarded Solihull another penalty when Jaros dived to push the ball away and was harshly adjudged to have felled a forward in the process. However, an assistant referee intervened and after a discussion the referee reversed his decision. The non-stop action continued until half time.

The second half was only a few minutes old when Kelly-Evans cleared a goal bound shot. Soon after Notts went ahead when Lacey scored, for the second consecutive match, with a powerful header from a Rodrigues corner kick. With 20 minutes remaining Solihull equalised when a fierce eight-yard shot found the corner of the net. Notts restored the lead almost immediately when Wootton found Rodrigues with an exquisite through ball and he confidently side-footed home from 18 yards. In a dramatic finale Solihull equalised for a second time with a wonderful half volley which flew past Jaros from 25 yards.

A draw was the correct result after a pulsating end-to-end encounter. The 650 Notts supporters had plenty to talk/think about on their journey home. Wow!

FA Trophy Sixth Round (Quarter Final) Fri 11 March 2022 19:45	**Notts County 1-2 Wrexham** Rawlinson 30' goals 43', 89'	Attendance 3,170 + streamers (FA permitted stream outside 14:45-17:15 blocked hours)

                          Slocombe (Capt.)
              Lacey   Rawlinson   Chicksen
       Kelly-Evans   Taylor
              Vincent   Francis   M Palmer
         Mitchell (Rodrigues 64')   Nemane (Roberts 71')

Subs: Jaros (gk), Richardson, Doyle, Rodrigues, Roberts

With three players out on loan (youngsters Ty Palmer, Knight, and Brooks), illness (Wootton and Sam) and injuries, only five substitutes, of the seven permitted in FA Trophy matches, were named, and one of those was Assistant Head Coach Michael Doyle. Slocombe, Taylor, Matty Palmer, Nemane and Mitchell returned to the starting eleven. Brunt was ineligible.

In the league Notts drew 1-1 at Wrexham at the end of August and beat them 3-1 at home in their first match of 2022. Since that visit to Meadow Lane Wrexham (third in The National League, Notts seventh) had won seven of nine league matches (the last five on the trot).

Notts dominated most of the first half. In the opening minutes Palmer shot over the crossbar and then fed Kelly-Evans in the penalty area but a crucial tackle prevented the Notts wing-back a goal scoring opportunity. The goalkeeper then pushed a Mitchell shot behind for a corner. On 17 minutes Palmer was knocked over in the penalty area, as he was about to shoot, but the referee waved play on. In any other area of the pitch it would have been a foul challenge! However, Notts weren't to be denied and on 30 minutes they deservedly took the lead when defender Chicksen floated the ball into the path of onrushing central defender Rawlinson who scored with a glancing header. But, with half-time two minutes away Wrexham equalised when a cross from the right ricocheted of the unfortunate Chicksen and the loose ball was smashed emphatically into the net from 12 yards.

At the beginning of the second half, after Mitchell had a shot pushed beyond a post for a corner, Wrexham had a period of sustained pressure. But, from the hour mark Notts again took control and Chicksen presented Vincent with an opportunity but his 25-yard shot flew inches wide with the goalkeeper beaten. Notts continued in the ascendency and a ferocious 22 yard shot from Francis smashed against the crossbar just before Wrexham worked their way into the Notts penalty area and won the match with a shot from near the penalty spot.

Although Wrexham contributed to an entertaining, high quality, encounter Notts were unlucky and certainly deserved the (not-to-be) penalty shoot-out.

Match 32	**Stockport County (1ˢᵗ) 3-0 Notts County (7ᵗʰ)**	Attendance
Tue 15 March 2022 19:45	goals 28', 47', 72'	7,951

Jaros

Lacey　　Rawlinson　　Chicksen

Richardson (Kelly-Evans 82')　　　　　　Taylor (Nemane 46')

Roberts (Mitchell 69')　　Francis　　M Palmer

Wootton (Capt.)　　Rodrigues

Subs: Kelly-Evans, Vincent, Brunt, Nemane, Mitchell
(no substitute goalkeeper)

There were five changes to the team unluckily beaten by Wrexham in the FA Trophy. Jaros (gk), Richardson, Roberts, Rodrigues, and Wootton returned in place of Slocombe (gk), Kelly-Evans, Vincent, Nemane, and Mitchell.

Stockport were positioned at the top of The National League for a good reason: since their last league defeat three months ago (11 December at Torquay) they had won 12 of 13 league matches – the exception was a 2-2 draw at home to second placed Chesterfield one month ago. In their last match, the quarter-final of the FA Trophy, they visited Suffolk and defeated Needham Market 0-3.

Stockport had the better of the opening exchanges, but goalkeeper Jaros was equal to his task and made three good saves. However, around the midpoint of the half it was Notts who had the two best chances to take the lead through Richardson. First, following a defenders attempted back pass, he intercepted the ball but, with only the goalkeeper to beat, he shot over the crossbar. Second, after a Roberts through ball to the edge of the penalty area, he dribbled around the goalkeeper, but, from a tight angle, his shot was diverted for a corner. Notts paid the price when they fell behind a few minutes later. A cross from the left landed between Rawlinson and Lacey and a header was placed beyond Jaros into the corner of the net. From then on Stockport dominated the remainder of the half.

Notts changed to a 4-4-2 formation for the second half. Stockport soon scored a second goal when a long kick by their goalkeeper found an unmarked player in the Notts half who was given time to thread a pass forward into the penalty area from where the ball was shot confidently past Jaros. Their dominance continued and they added a third when a low cross was calmly slotted home.

So, a superior Stockport avenged their 2-1 defeat at Meadow Lane in late October with a thoroughly deserved victory against a lethargic Notts, who but for Jaros would have suffered a heavier defeat. Their disappointment was enhanced by the fact they had conceded three goals in each of their last three away matches, and had dropped one below a play-off position - to eighth.

After the match Ian Burchnall revealed that the majority of the squad were either ill or recovering from illness. It was a night to forget for Notts.

Match 33 Sat 19 March 2022 15:00	**Dagenham & (9th) 1-2 Notts County (8th)** **Redbridge** goal 6'	Lacey 29' own goal 64'	Attendance 1,846 (420 Notts Supporters)

Jaros

Brindley (Kelly-Evans 46')   Rawlinson   Lacey (Sam 46')

Richardson   Chicksen

M Palmer   Arter (Francis 61')   Vincent

Wootton (Capt.)   Mitchell

Subs: Kelly-Evans, Francis, Brunt, Nemane, Sam
(no substitute goalkeeper)

After the defeat at Stockport Ian Burchnall said Notts had liaised with The National League to obtain permission to postpone that match and the Dagenham & Redbridge fixture. Illness (and injury) had decimated player availability, but the request had been turned down. Fortunately, the fitness situation had improved a little in the run-up to this match. Sam (February's National League 'Player of the Month') returned to the squad after his three-match absence through illness. The Notts debutant was Harry Arter, in central defensive midfield, signed on loan from Championship neighbours Nottingham Forest – more information on next page.

Notts defeated D&R 2-1 at Meadow Lane in late November. Although D&R were defeated (in the penalty shoot-out) by National League North York City in the quarter-final of the FA Trophy on 12

March, they had won their last three league matches by an identical score, three goals to nil. Only top of the league Stockport had scored more than their 59 (Notts 57) but defensively they had conceded 41 (Notts 40).

D&R started strongly and took an early lead. They beat Notts' offside trap and, despite Brindley's attempt to stop the forwards advance, a clinical ten-yard finish ensued. Notts almost got the equaliser in the 13th minute when Wootton found Vincent in the penalty area, and he dinked the ball over the goalkeeper, but Mitchell just failed to reach it at the back post. Ten minutes later a D&R shot hit the top of the crossbar. However, soon after, Notts equalised when Lacey met an excellent Harry Arter corner kick and glanced a powerful header into the corner of the net from six yards. It was his third league goal in the last 14 days, and his fifth of the season – not bad for a central defender.

During half-time Lacey had to retire with illness fatigue, and Brindley because of an arm injury. Notts adopted a 4-4-2 formation with Chicksen in central defence and Kelly-Evans on the left. Notts took the lead in the 19th minute of the second half with a D&R own goal. As Wootton closed in on a Richardson cross a defender turned the ball into his own net. From then on Notts were under almost constant D&R pressure, but a combination of poor finishing, good defending, and Jaros saves enabled them to get a much-needed victory. The three points meant they returned into a play-off position – seventh.

Harry Arter (age 32) signed for Notts, on loan until the end of the season, three days before the Dagenham & Redbridge match. He was with Bournemouth for ten years (from 2010) and the majority of his 300+ league appearances had been with Bournemouth as they rose from League One to the Championship, and then the Premier League. Although born in London he had made 19 international appearances for the Republic of Ireland. Arter joined Nottingham Forest in September 2020 on a three-year contract, but his first team opportunities had since become very limited. Between September and November 2021, he made six appearances on loan at League One Charlton Athletic.

On the day of the D&R match Notts announced that Matty Palmer had been added to the England 'C' squad for their fixture against Wales 'C' on 30 March. He therefore joined Cal Roberts and Richard Brindley. Unfortunately, Brindley broke his left arm towards the end of the first half against D&R and had to withdraw from the squad. He was likely to be unavailable for the majority, if not all, of Notts' remaining league matches.

With the completion of the D&R match Notts reached the three-quarter point of their 2021-22 National League season – they had just eleven fixtures to play – six at home and five away from Meadow Lane.

Although Brindley's participation in any of those matches was doubtful, there was some good news. The absence through illness situation had eased. Injured captain Kyle Cameron was expected to be available before the end of March and forgotten man Jim O'Brien had been spotted (alongside Arter) participating in a videoed training session, with a smile on his face!

Notts had been oscillating in and out of a play-off position (seventh and eighth) for the last two months since late January (12 matches). On paper their final seven matches were winnable. The eight weeks between now and the end of the season was obviously a crucial period, but also an opportunity to dispel the uncertainty and move into a commanding final position.

Match 34	**Notts County (7th) 1-0 Boreham Wood (6th)** Attendance 5,010
Tue 22 March 2022 19:45	M Palmer 14'

```
                        Slocombe
            Lacey       Rawlinson       Chicksen
  Richardson                                    Kelly-Evans
            Vincent   Arter (Francis 65')   M Palmer
            Wootton (Capt.)    Rodrigues
```

Subs: Taylor, Francis, Brunt, Nemane, Sam
(no substitute goalkeeper)

Goalkeeper Vitezslav Jaros (Czech Under-21 squad) and forward Kairo Mitchell (Grenada) were on international duty and unavailable, so Slocombe and Rodrigues returned to the starting eleven.

The first match, towards the end of November, ended in a 1-1 draw. Although Boreham Wood had enjoyed an excellent season they had struggled in recent weeks. They had won only one of their last seven league matches and had also lost 2-0 at Premier League Everton in the fifth round of the FA Cup. Five of their last six away matches had ended in defeat and they had failed to score in five of those. However, they possessed the joint best defensive record (23 conceded) but had only scored 40 – the lowest total in the top half of the league.

With five minutes played Slocombe dived at a forward's feet and the ball looped towards the Notts goal, but Rawlinson was there to head over the crossbar for a corner kick. A wonderful Rodrigues pass gave Richardson an opportunity but instead of a shot he tried to take the ball around the goalkeeper, lost control and the chance was gone. However, Notts only had to wait another few minutes before they took the lead. Kelly-Evans was tackled as he was about to attempt a shot following a Richardson cross and the ball fell to Matty Palmer near the penalty spot, and he shot confidently into the top corner of the net. Soon after Rodrigues and Kelly-Evans forced the goalkeeper into two excellent saves. Just before half-time Slocombe had to be alert to push two Boreham Wood shots away for corner kicks. Notts were excellent in the first half, in which they earned six corners, and fully deserved their half-time lead.

Notts dominated most of the second half, but despite another eight corners (a total of 14 in the match) and several near misses they were unable to extend their lead. Their free-flowing incisive movement exuded confidence, and they kept a clean sheet in the process. Promotion rivals Boreham Wood offered only the occasional threat.

Head Coach Ian Burchnall joined Notts on 25 March 2021, so this match was his first anniversary. In a memorable year his record, in league and cup, was: P61 W29 D15 L17 F107 A77 = a win percentage of 48%.

Match 35	Notts County (6th) 1-1 Chesterfield (2nd)	Attendance 10,334
Sat 26 March 2022 15:00	Wootton 45'+2 pen goal 13'	Live on BT Sport

```
                        Slocombe
          Lacey         Rawlinson        Chicksen
      Richardson                         Kelly-Evans
    Vincent (Francis 84')  Arter (O'Brien 65')   M Palmer
          Wootton (Capt.)       Rodrigues
```

Subs: Graham, Francis, O'Brien, Nemane, Sam
(no substitute goalkeeper)

Notts were unchanged following the good win over Boreham Wood, which meant Roberts was absent for the third consecutive match. Goalkeeper Jaros and forward Mitchell were still on international duty and unavailable. On the substitutes bench were two 'new' names – O'Brien and Graham.

Because of illness and injury Jim O'Brien last started a match over four months ago (7 November FA Cup first round at Rochdale, 1-1). He last appeared, briefly, as a substitute on 11 December.

On 23 March, because of Brindley's broken arm and Cameron's injury, central defender Sam Graham (age 21) was signed on loan for the rest of the season from League Two Rochdale – he played against Notts in the drawn FA Cup tie at the beginning of November. However, he was no stranger to Notts. At the start of the 2019-20 season, he made ten appearances, on loan from parent club Sheffield United, before a long-term injury ended his stay. He returned for the 2020-21 season but with only four appearances by the end of the year he was recalled by Sheffield United. In the summer of 2021, he transferred to Rochdale and had made 14 appearances before he suffered an injury in the match after the Notts cup-tie. Although now fully fit, he had been unable to regain his place in the Rochdale team. Third time lucky?

Chesterfield had played four league matches since they defeated Notts 3-1 on 1 March. The first two were drawn, followed by a victory then a 1-0 defeat at Altrincham four days ago.

On a pleasant warm and sunny afternoon, Notts made a bright start and Kelly-Evans cut into the penalty area from the left and unleashed a powerful shot, which took a slight deflection and forced goalkeeper Loach (ex-Notts) into a diving save and he tipped the ball over the crossbar. The corner kick, taken by Arter, was cleared off the line! However, Notts went behind a few minutes later, against the run of play. An excellent Chesterfield move down the left ended when a forward, inside the Notts penalty area, powerfully side-footed the ball into the net from 15 yards. From then on the match was more evenly contested until Notts equalised from the penalty spot after Rodrigues had been felled by the Chesterfield goal scorer. Wootton, despite some 'sledging' from a Chesterfield player, confidently sent the goalkeeper the wrong way with his spot kick. The last action of the half was his first goal since 19 February – eight matches ago.

At the beginning of the second half Chesterfield's Miller (a Notts player towards the end of last season when on loan from Harrogate) twice caused problems for Slocombe. First the Notts goalkeeper had to tip a cross, which deflected off Palmer, over the crossbar and five minutes later Miller's low shot hit the outside of a post. On 78 minutes Lacey headed a cross back across the six-yard box but Wootton's free header from three yards hit the top of the crossbar on its way out for a goal kick, when it looked easier to score!

Notts weren't at their best and a draw, after a good closely contested match, was probably a fair result.

With illness, injuries and international call-ups, March had been an intense month for Notts as six of their eight matches (seven league, one FA Trophy) had been against teams above them in the league table. The month started with defeat at Chesterfield and ended, 25 days later, with this drawn return fixture.

Notts' remaining nine fixtures were against teams below them in The National League. Their trip on 9 April to Devon = Torquay was the highest placed team to be faced.

Two of the nine fixtures were against rock bottom of the league Dover, home and away. While Notts and Chesterfield played out an entertaining draw, Dover were away at fourth in the table Wrexham. It wasn't a surprise that Wrexham had established a two goal lead after 20 minutes, but by half-time it was 2-2. Early in the second half a Dover player (Gyasi) scored a 12-minute hat-trick to give them a 2-5 lead. Wrexham then scored two quick goals and by the 69th minute the score was 4-5. In stoppage time (90'+1) Wrexham equalised and six minutes later the same player scored again to give a final score of 6-5. Incredible!

Match 36	**Southend Utd (13th) 0-3 Notts County (6th)**	Attendance 6,338
Sat 2 Apr 2022 15:00	Rodrigues 20', 61', 79'	

Jaros

Lacey   Rawlinson   Chicksen

Richardson   Kelly-Evans

Vincent (O'Brien 63')   Arter (Brunt 74')   M Palmer

Wootton (Capt.)   Rodrigues (Sam 85')

Subs: Graham, O'Brien, Brunt, Nemane, Sam
(no substitute goalkeeper)

Notts made one change to the side which drew with Chesterfield, Jaros was preferred to Slocombe in goal. Although Roberts played for the England 'C' team defeated (4-0) by Wales 'C' three days ago, he was absent for the fourth consecutive match. Palmer appeared as an England substitute in the second half.

After Southend were defeated 4-1 at Meadow Lane in mid-December they began a sequence of 13 unbeaten league games – eight victories and five draws. However, since that excellent run their form had deteriorated, with three defeats in the last four (LWLL).

On a sunny, but chilly, afternoon Notts made an indifferent start to the match. However, against the run of play, they went ahead in the 20th minute when Arter chipped a free kick to Rodrigues in the penalty area. His first time shot rebounded off the goalkeepers outstretched foot and hit the underside of the crossbar before it fell over the line. The remainder of the half was then more even, but throughout Jaros was impressive with his positioning and handling.

The second half burst into life on the hour mark. Notts survived a frantic goalmouth scramble during which Rawlinson made an excellent block to deny a possible Southend equaliser. In the counterattack Notts increased their lead when Wootton chased a long clearance into the penalty area and passed to Rodrigues who found the corner of the net from 15 yards with another first time shot. Five minutes later Southend were awarded a penalty. Rawlinson got into a tangle as he attempted a back pass to Jaros, the ball ran loose, and Lacey barged an attacker over. Jaros saved the (rather feeble) spot kick to make another important save, at a crucial time. With just over ten minutes remaining Notts got their third goal. Richardson ran into the penalty area and passed to Rodrigues. His first attempt on goal was blocked, but as the ball fell he lobbed it into the corner of the net from near the penalty spot.

With his (right-footed) hat trick Rodrigues reached 15 league goals - level with Wootton. Roberts was in third position with 11 goals. There were 536 Notts supporters at Southend. Torquay away was Notts' next match, for their longest journey of the season at a distance of 230 miles. COYP!

Match 37 Sat 9 Apr 2022 15:00	**Torquay Utd (11th) 5-1 Notts County (6th)** goals 10', 14', 77', 85', 90'+5 Wootton 74'	Attendance 3,130

                             Jaros
            Lacey   Rawlinson   Chicksen
       Richardson   Kelly-Evans (Sam 46')
Vincent (Nemane 46')   Arter (O'Brien 68')   M Palmer
            Wootton (Capt.)   Rodrigues

Subs: Graham, O'Brien, Brunt, Nemane, Sam
(no substitute goalkeeper)

Notts were unchanged from the side victorious at Southend.

The last time Notts played at Torquay was in mid-June 2021 when they were beaten 4-2 (after extra time) in the playoff semi-final. Only five players in that 16-man squad were in today's squad: Rawlinson, Chicksen, Kelly-Evans, Wootton, and Rodrigues. In Notts' first home match this season the teams drew 1-1. Torquay's form had been good since the beginning of December with only three league defeats in 18 matches. They were unbeaten in their last six at home and had kept a 'clean sheet' in five of those matches.

In glorious sunshine, Torquay were two goals ahead within 15 minutes. They took the lead when a shot from the edge of the penalty area was expertly curled into the top corner of the net. A second goal soon followed when a low centre, which Chicksen failed to clear near the back post, was tapped home from close range. At the mid-point of the first half Rodrigues was felled in the penalty area but the referee ignored the vociferous Notts appeals. In the 40th minute Jaros produced an excellent save to prevent a third Torquay goal and, despite a Wootton shot which flew narrowly wide a few minutes later, a hugely disappointing Notts were glad the hear the half time whistle.

A double substitution during the break meant Notts changed to a 4-2-4 formation. Sam immediately missed a great chance to reduce the deficit when, well placed and unmarked inside the six-yard box, he failed to convert a Nemane cross from the right. Notts were much improved and deservedly reduced the arrears when Richardson passed to Rodrigues who slipped the ball to Wootton, and he scored with a delightful left-footed shot into the top corner from 18 yards. However, Notts' optimism and joy was short-lived as Torquay took advantage of some poor defensive work in the latter stages of the match to score three further goals and secure, what in the end, was an emphatic victory.

So, approximate 600 supporters from Meadow Lane witnessed Notts' heaviest defeat in non-league football. They remained in sixth position, and their next five matches were against the four teams adrift near the bottom of the league, including home and away fixtures at rock bottom Dover!

Match 38	**Notts County (6th) 4-1 King's Lynn Town (21st)**	Attendance 6,722
Fri 15 Apr 2022 15:00	Wootton 24'	goal 11'
	Roberts 39'	
	Nemane 60'	
	Sam 81'	

Jaros

Richardson   Rawlinson   Graham   Chicksen

Roberts   M Palmer   Arter (Francis 88')   Nemane (Sam 76')

Wootton (Capt.) (Brunt 84')   Rodrigues

Subs: Kelly-Evans, Francis, O'Brien, Brunt, Sam
(no substitute goalkeeper)

Ian Burchnall made three changes to the team deservedly beaten at Torquay: Graham replaced the injured Lacey, Nemane was preferred to Vincent and Roberts returned after a five-match absence at the expense of Kelly-Evans.

Notts won 2-4 at King's Lynn in mid-January. Although strugglers in the relegation zone for most of the season, KL had only been beaten twice in their last nine league matches – both at home, to Torquay and league leaders Stockport. They were unbeaten in their last four: two wins and two draws.

Despite a good start by Notts, it was King's Lynn who scored first. A few quick passes down the right, and some indifferent Notts defending, resulted in the ball being prodded home from close range. Nemane nearly equalised five minutes later but his goal bound shot was cleared with the goalkeeper beaten. However, Notts did equalise when Rodrigues squared the ball to Wootton who, with good control, turned the pass into the net from six yards. Notts continued to press and as half time approached Roberts cut inside from the right and his powerful left footed shot from 17 yards flew past the goalkeeper.

Notts dominated from the start of the second half and with one hour played Aaron Nemane scored his first goal for Notts. Wootton slipped the ball to Rodrigues near the half-way line and he released Nemane down the left who ran 40 yards into the penalty area and side-stepped two defenders before he curled a delightful right-footed shot into the far corner of the net. Nemane had a chance to score a second goal a few minutes later but the goalkeeper saved the shot with his feet and the ball went behind for a corner kick. With ten minutes of the match left Notts added a fourth goal when a Roberts shot was blocked, and Sam directed the loose ball into the net from 15 yards. Only two excellent saves by the King's Lynn goalkeeper, near the end of the match, prevented Richardson and Sam scoring two further goals.

It was a comfortable victory for Notts on a warm and mostly sunny afternoon. Only two teams had been involved in matches with a larger 'For' and 'Against' goals tally than sixth placed Notts with a total of 117 (F69 A48): Dagenham & Redbridge 119 (F71 A48) and Barnet 124 (F48 A76). Rock-bottom Dover, Notts' opponents in two of their next four matches, totalled 116 (F31 A85).

Match 39	**Notts County (7ᵗʰ) 3-1 Weymouth (22ⁿᵈ)**	Attendance 6,032
Sat 23 Apr 2022 15:00	Wootton 8' goal 53'	
	Nemane 13'	
	Rodrigues 48'	

Jaros

Richardson   Rawlinson   Graham   Chicksen

Roberts   M Palmer   Arter (Francis 61')   Nemane (O'Brien 74')

Wootton (Capt.) (Sam 81')   Rodrigues

Subs: Kelly-Evans, Francis, O'Brien, Brunt, Sam
(no substitute goalkeeper)

There were no changes from squad victorious over King's Lynn.

Weymouth and Notts drew 1-1 in mid-September. Since a victory (at home to King's Lynn) on 30 October Weymouth had achieved just one league victory in 24 matches. They had failed to score in eight of their last nine matches and had been in a relegation position since the beginning of the year. Needless to say, Notts were odds-on favourites to win this fixture!

Notts "were absolutely magnificent in the first 30 minutes and it could easily have been four or five, but in the last ten minutes of the half we were poor and became complacent" – Ian Burchnall's after match interview. The first goal followed a low corner kick by Palmer which Wootton nonchalantly flicked home at the near post. The second, five minutes later, was the culmination of a fine Notts move which started with an excellent 50-yard pass by Graham to Roberts and ended when Richardson found Nemane inside the penalty area with a low cross and he confidently found the bottom corner of the net with a first-time shot. Weymouth could (should) have equalised in the final 15 minutes of the half. A shot hit a post, a header hit the crossbar, and there were other near misses and some poor finishing.

Weymouth fell further behind at the beginning of the second half when Rodrigues stroked a powerful free-kick home from 19 yards which flew past ex-Notts goalkeeper Ross Fitzsimons. However, within minutes, Weymouth reduced their deficit when a low cross from the right was side footed calmly into the corner of the net from 12 yards. Just before the end Fitzsimons made an excellent diving save from a ferocious 25-yard drive by Francis but overall the second half was fairly even. Notts seemed content to let the match stagnate and there was no repeat of the Weymouth onslaught which occurred at the end of the first 45 minutes.

Despite the victory Notts remained in seventh position, seven points behind Halifax in third place but with a match in-hand over them and the three other teams directly above Notts, who had a day off on (Easter) Monday - caused by the league consisting of 23 teams this season instead of the normal 24!

Match 40	**Dover Athletic (23rd) 0-3 Notts County (7th)**	Attendance
Tue 26 Apr 2022 19:45	Francis 60'	N/A (Av. 866)
	Roberts 83'	
	Rodrigues 90'+1	

Slocombe

Richardson   Lacey (Rawlinson 63')   Graham   Chicksen

M. Palmer (Capt.)   Francis

Roberts   Nemane (Brunt 70')   Sam (O'Brien 83')

Rodrigues

Subs: Rawlinson, Kelly-Evans, O'Brien, Brunt, Mitchell
(no substitute goalkeeper)

For the first of two matches against bottom of the league Dover in the space of six days, Ian Burchnall rotated the squad after two unchanged matches. Slocombe returned in goal, Lacey replaced Rawlinson, Francis came in for Arter (rested) and Sam deputised for the injured Wootton, who missed his first league match of the season. Matty Palmer was named as captain.

Since Notts were relegated from the English Football League they had played Dover three times – two draws in 2019-20 and an expunged 1-0 defeat at Dover on the opening day of last season, 2020-21. This was Notts' third journey to Dover this season, after the first two trips were postponed at short notice due to a waterlogged pitch.

Dover, who had experienced only two victories in 41 league and cup matches this season, had been bottom of the league throughout and had accumulated just 12 points (two wins and six draws). Last season their results were expunged for disciplinary reasons (failing to meet fixture obligations). As well as a fine, part of that punishment was a deduction of 12 points for the start of this season, so their current points total was zero! However, in their last match away at Chesterfield (5th) only two late goals in the final ten minutes by the home team turned a Dover victory into a 3-2 defeat.

Notts totally dominated throughout the first half. Whereas the Dover goalkeeper made some excellent saves, Slocombe was a spectator!

With the second half just three minutes old Dover were reduced to ten men when a player hauled down Nemane and received a second yellow card. Two minutes later Richardson had a goal disallowed for offside. Notts at last made the breakthrough on the hour through Ed Francis who scored his first Notts goal with a 25-yard cross cum shot which sailed into the far top corner of the net. With seven minutes of normal time left a long clearance by Rawlinson found Rodrigues who passed to Roberts, and he eased beyond three defenders before he placed the ball into the corner of the net. Brunt then curled a 16-yard shot against a post. In added time a Rodrigues free kick was deflected off the defensive wall into the net. Dover were fortunate to only lose by three goals!

Match 41	**Aldershot (20th) 3-1 Notts County (5th)** Attendance: 1,969
Sat 30 Apr 2022 15:00	goals 8', 34', 88' Roberts 24' (pen)

Jaros
Kelly-Evans   Rawlinson (Wootton 56')   Graham   Chicksen
M. Palmer (Capt)   Francis   Brunt (Arter 56')
Nemane (Sam 67')   Roberts   Rodrigues

Subs: Richardson, Arter, O'Brien, Wootton, Sam
(no substitute goalkeeper)

Ian Burchnall, keen to have a fit squad for the play-offs, made four changes to the side victorious at Dover: Jaros returned as goalkeeper, Rawlinson replaced Lacey, Kelly-Evans came in for Richardson and Brunt was preferred to Sam.

One of Aldershot's 11 defeats in their first 14 matches was at Meadow Lane in early September, 3-2. However, after that dreadful start to the season they improved and suffered only one defeat in the next 12 league matches. Their form then deteriorated again and, except for a 0-0 draw at home to Dover, they lost eight of their next nine matches. In their last five matches they had W2 D1 L2 – two wins, followed by two losses, and a draw in their last match. Throughout the season they had resided in the bottom half of the table.

Notts had an early chance, but Rodrigues shot wide after Nemane's cross was parried by the goalkeeper. A few minutes later Aldershot took the lead when a low cross from the right was turned home from close range. Notts equalised midway through the first half when Roberts scored from the penalty spot after Rodrigues had been fouled. Although Notts dominated from then on it was Aldershot who regained the lead following a counterattack. A forward was given time to turn and fire the ball into the corner of the net from 17 yards.

The second half was only a few minutes old when a Rawlinson back pass was intercepted but Jaros made a good save. Although Notts went close a few times it was Aldershot who sealed their victory just before the end when Graham was outmanoeuvred and an unstoppable shot from the edge of the penalty area flew into the far top corner of the net. To complete a very disappointing afternoon for Notts and their 452 travelling supporters, deep into stoppage time Kelly-Evans was sent off after he received a second yellow card. Four other Notts players were booked (given yellow cards) during the match.

So, against opponents with an extremely poor home record (only Dover had worse) Notts once again failed to get a point in Hampshire – their three National League visits to Aldershot had ended in defeat.

Match 42   **Notts County (5th) 1-0 Dover Athletic (23rd)**   Attendance: 6,523
Mon 2 May 2022 15:00   Rodrigues 18'

Slocombe

Richardson   Rawlinson   Lacey   Taylor

M. Palmer   Arter (Roberts 64')   O'Brien (Francis 77')

Rodrigues   Wootton (Capt.)   Sam

Subs: Brindley, Francis, Vincent, Roberts, Mitchell
(no substitute goalkeeper)

Following the defeat at Aldershot, Ian Burchnall made eight rotation changes - only Rawlinson, Palmer and Rodrigues also started 48 hours ago. Jim O'Brien last started a match nearly six months ago - on 7 November at Rochdale (FA Cup 1-1). Taylor had missed the last nine matches.

Notts continued were they left off six days ago against bottom of the league Dover but Sam's low cross just evaded Rodrigues and Wootton. However, Notts took the lead soon after when a superb through ball by O'Brien allowed Richardson to provide Rodrigues with an unmissable opportunity. The goal ended a sequence of 17 passes. Notts controlled the remainder of the first half but were unable to get the second goal their play deserved.

Notts also dominated the second half. Wootton had a goal disallowed (incorrectly) for offside following a goalmouth scramble and the Dover goalkeeper tipped a Rodrigues shot on to the crossbar but Notts were again unable to capitalise on their superiority.

During the match Notts had 19 attempts on goal (8 on target) and Slocombe had to make only one real save (in the 79th minute). In a defensive performance by Dover their goalkeeper was outstanding.

This match ended the loan spell of midfielder Harry Arter from Championship neighbours Nottingham Forest. Although he did not complete a full 90 minutes during his nine appearances, he helped Notts to six victories and a draw. He experienced only one defeat in the eight matches he started. In the defeat at Aldershot two days ago he was introduced as a second half substitute with Notts 2-1 down. For both Arter and Notts it was a successful loan spell despite his lack of full match fitness on his arrival in mid-March.

Match 43 Sat 7 May 2022 15:00	**Notts County (5th) 3-0 Altrincham (14th)** Attendance: 6,581 Roberts 46' (pen) Wootton 75' Rodrigues 83'

Slocombe

Brindley   Lacey   Chicksen

Richardson   Kelly-Evans (Cameron 64')

M. Palmer   O'Brien (Francis 76')

Roberts (Sam 80')   Wootton (Capt)   Rodrigues

Subs: Cameron, Rawlinson, Francis, Brunt, Sam
(no substitute goalkeeper)

There were five changes to the team which completed the double over Dover. Arter had returned to Nottingham Forest. Kelly-Evans back after a one match suspension. Brindley and Chicksen replaced Rawlinson and Taylor and Roberts came in for Sam.

Altrincham won six of their first ten matches, which included a 1-0 victory over Notts for whom it was a first defeat of the season. (Notts won 2-1 at Meadow Lane in the third round of the FA Trophy). After their good start Altrincham then had a prolonged period of poor form, but since the beginning of February they had suffered only three defeats in 15 league matches.

Notts were by far the better team in a goalless first half. Following a corner in the 20th minute the ball fell to Richardson who hit the crossbar with a powerful 16-yard shot. Just before half-time a Wootton header from a Roberts cross also hit the crossbar.

The second half was only a minute old when Notts were awarded a penalty after Roberts' arm was pulled back. He sent the goalkeeper the wrong way as he stroked the ball into the corner of the net from the spot. Notts' domination continued but in the 63rd minute Slocombe was forced into a good save when he dived to palm away a 25-yard free kick. As the match entered its final 15 minutes Notts increased their lead when four Altrincham defenders were unable to cope with a tricky dribble by Roberts – Wootton swivelled and volleyed his cross into the net from eight yards. The third goal followed eight minutes later after Sam's excellent pass released Richardson. His cross deflected off a defender and Rodrigues dived forward to head the ball into the net from ten yards. For both Wootton and Rodrigues, it was their 19th league goal of the season.

It was an impressive and deserved victory for Notts who emphatically confirmed their place in the promotion play-offs. They had scored in every home match this season – 57 goals in 27 league and cup matches.

Match 44   **Maidenhead Utd (16th) 0-1 Notts County (5th)**   Attendance 2,074
Sun 15 May 2022 15:00   Roberts 71' (pen)

Slocombe

Brindley   Lacey   Cameron (Capt.) (Rawlinson 66')

Richardson   Kelly-Evans

M. Palmer   O'Brien

Roberts (Brunt 76')   Wootton (Sam 66')   Rodrigues

Subs: Rawlinson, Taylor, Francis, Brunt, Sam
(no substitute goalkeeper)

The only change from last weekend's final home match against Altrincham was the return of club captain Kyle Cameron. (He appeared from the substitute's bench in the 64th minute of that 3-0 victory). This was his first start since he received a hamstring injury on 5 March – a 13 match absence. Chicksen was rested.

Aaron Nemane was unavailable due to a three-match suspension following an incident in the tunnel after full-time at Aldershot on 30 April.

Maidenhead had resided in the lower half of the league table for most of the season. However, they were undefeated in their last seven matches and in their previous match last weekend they won 1-3 at Grimsby.

On a wet Sunday afternoon (on a pitch with a noticeable slope) Notts dominated the goalless first half, with Roberts at the centre of much of the significant action.

The second half was even until Notts took the lead with a penalty – their third award in the last four matches. Roberts won the penalty when he was fouled in the area, and he took the kick and scored from the spot.

The victory secured a fifth-place finish for Notts and a home fixture quarter-final in the promotion play-offs. Their opponents at Meadow Lane on the evening of Monday 23 May were sixth placed Grimsby.

Play-off Quarter-Final   **Notts County (5th) 1-2 Grimsby Town (6th)**   Attendance: 12,023
Mon 23 May 2022   after extra time   Live on BT Sport
19:45   Rodrigues 72' (pen)   goals 90'+6, 119'

Slocombe
Brindley   Lacey   Cameron (Capt.)
Richardson (Kelly-Evans 113')   Chicksen
M. Palmer   O'Brien (Francis 60')
Roberts (Sam 22')   Wootton   Rodrigues (Brunt 82')

Subs: Rawlinson, Kelly-Evans, Francis, Brunt, Sam (no substitute goalkeeper)
For this match four substitute changes were allowed – three in normal time and one in extra-time.

Ian Burchnall fielded a full-strength team with just one change after the victory at Maidenhead - Chicksen replaced Kelly-Evans. It was unfortunate that Cal Roberts (four goals in the last five matches – three of which were penalties) received an ankle injury after ten minutes and halfway through the first half he had to be substituted, by Sam.

In the two league matches this season, Notts won the away fixture 0-1 but Grimsby got their revenge at Meadow Lane with a 1-2 victory. The form teams at the end of the season in The National League were Solihull, managed by Notts' previous manager Neal Ardley, Notts (won nine of their last twelve matches) and Grimsby (undefeated in their last seven away matches).

It was Grimsby who had just the better of an entertaining, 'end-to-end', but goalless first half in which they earned five corners. In the 13th minute they had a powerful header which flew narrowly wide. Shortly after coming on for Roberts, Sam produced Notts' first shot on goal, but the effort was comfortably saved by the goalkeeper. On the half hour a Rodrigues diving header from a Richardson cross just cleared the crossbar.

Notts were the first to threaten at the start of the second half when Wootton, from a Chicksen cross, missed a good chance (header) when inside the six-yard box. Grimsby retaliated with a fierce 30 yard shot which Slocombe was glad to see go just wide of a post. Two minutes later Notts got their first corner kick of the match, but it was Grimsby who gradually became the dominant team. Brindley diverted a shot for a corner, and they had a goal disallowed. However, it was Notts who opened the scoring with a penalty when a Rodrigues shot was handled in the penalty area. With Roberts off injured Rodrigues took the responsibility and, in front of the spion kop, he calmly sent the goalkeeper the wrong way as he stroked the spot kick into the corner of the net. The entertainment continued, with Slocombe again pleased to see a scuffed shot go just wide. With ten minutes to go Notts had an appeal for a second penalty turned down by the referee after Richardson's shot struck the arm of a defender. At the end of the 90 minutes there were six minutes of added time and with the last kick of the match Grimsby equalised. Richardson gave away an unnecessary free kick (a push) on the edge of the penalty area and from the subsequent goalmouth scramble the ball was squeezed into the corner of the net from six yards!

Extra time (two periods of 15 minutes) was then played. Sam had an opportunity in the first period, but his shot was blocked, before Slocombe saved a Grimsby shot. Soon after the start of the second period Brunt had a shot blocked and his follow-up was saved. With two minutes to go Slocombe pushed away a 20-yard shot. But, with a penalty shoot-out imminent Grimsby won the match with a goal similar to their equaliser – the ball was bundled home from close range following a free kick, despite Brindley's in vain attempt to clear the ball. There was still time for Notts to create a final opportunity, but Sam shot high over the crossbar.

Although Notts were not at their best, to be deprived a victory with the last kick of the match and then a penalty shoot-out in the final minute of extra-time was cruel. During the season one third of the league goals Notts conceded occurred after the 75th minute of a match – 17 of the 52.

Grimsby occupied top position in The National League for the whole of October – until defeated by Notts on 30 October. After this quarter-final victory over Notts they won at Wrexham, and then defeated Solihull in the final. In all three (away) matches they fought back after being behind, with extra-time involved. Grimsby were to be congratulated on their promotion back into League Two, at the first attempt after they were relegated at the end of last season.

At the end of their first season in The National League (2019-20) Notts were defeated in the play-off final by Harrogate. The following season (2020-21) it was the turn of Torquay to seal our fate in the semi-final. This time it was Grimsby. It meant a fourth season in non-league football for Notts, and their stressed supporters.

Final National League Table 15 May 2022

		GP	W	D	L	GF	GA	GD	Pts
1	Stockport **AP**	44	30	4	10	87	38	+49	94
2	Wrexham	44	26	10	8	91	46	+45	88
3	Solihull Moors	44	25	12	7	83	45	+38	87
4	Halifax Town	44	25	9	10	62	35	+27	84
5	**Notts County**	**44**	**24**	**10**	**10**	**81**	**52**	**+29**	**82**
6	Grimsby **P**	44	23	8	13	68	46	+22	77
7	Chesterfield	44	20	14	10	69	51	+18	74
8	Dagenham & R.	44	22	7	15	80	53	+27	73
9	Boreham Wood	44	18	13	13	49	40	+9	67
10	Bromley	44	18	13	13	61	53	+8	67
11	Torquay Utd	44	18	12	14	66	54	+12	66
12	Yeovil Town	44	15	14	15	43	46	-3	59
13	Southend Utd	44	16	10	18	45	61	-16	58
14	Altrincham	44	15	10	19	62	69	-7	55
15	Woking	44	16	5	23	59	61	-2	53
16	Wealdstone	44	14	11	19	51	65	-14	53
17	Maidenhead Utd	44	13	12	19	48	67	-19	51
18	Barnet	44	13	11	20	59	89	-30	50
19	Eastleigh	44	12	10	22	52	74	-22	46
20	Aldershot Town	44	11	10	23	46	73	-27	43
21	Kings Lynn **R**	44	8	10	26	47	79	-32	34
22	Weymouth **R**	44	6	10	28	40	88	-48	28
23	Dover Athletic **R**	44	2	7	35	37	101	-64	1

Deducted points: Dover Athletic (-12 pts)	Play-off Results	
AP = Automatic Promotion to EFL League Two **P** = Promoted to League Two after winning play-offs **R** = Relegated to National League South/North	**Notts County** 1-2 Grimsby Halifax Town 1-2 Chesterfield Wrexham 4-5 Grimsby Solihull Moors 3-1 Chesterfield	after extra time after extra time
Final at the London Stadium, Queen Elizabeth Olympic Park (now home of West Ham Utd.)	Solihull Moors 1-2 Grimsby	after extra time

Notts County National League Results 2021-22

Date	Home	Away	F-A	Scorers	Attendance	Pos
2021						
21/8		Barnet	5-0	Rodrigues (2), Roberts (pen), Wootton, O'Brien	2,067	1
28/8	Torquay Utd		1-1	Wootton	6,934	5
30/8		Wrexham	1-1	Wootton	5,454 (BT Sport)	7
4/9	Aldershot Town		3-2	Wootton, Cameron, Roberts	5,921	4
11/9		Weymouth	1-1	Roberts	1,783	5
14/9	Wealdstone		3-2	Roberts, Wootton, Cameron	5,213	5
18/9	Maidenhead Utd		1-0	Lacey	5,748	4
25/9		Altrincham	0-1		2,569	6
2/10	Woking		1-4	Rodrigues	5,807	7
5/10		Halifax Town	2-3	Rodrigues, Lacey	2,023	10
9/10		Yeovil Town	2-0	Rodrigues (2)	2,438	9
23/10	Stockport County		2-1	Wootton, Vincent	7,418	8
26/10	Bromley		1-1	Cameron	5,331	8
30/10		Grimsby Town	1-0	Rodrigues	7,213	6
13/11	Solihull Moors		2-0	Wootton, Mitchell	12,843	5
20/11		Eastleigh	0-2		2,817	6
23/11		Boreham Wood	1-1	Rodrigues	821	6
27/11	Dagenham & Redbridge		2-1	Vincent, Wootton	4,889 (BT Sport)	5
11/12	Southend Utd		4-1	Roberts, Wootton (2), Cameron	6,206	6
2022						
2/1	Wrexham		3-1	Wootton (2 inc. pen), Richardson	8,890	6
11/1		King's Lynn Town	4-2	Roberts (3), Vincent	1,505	4
25/1		Wealdstone	0-0		1,547	8
29/1		Bromley	0-1		3,606	8
5/2	Grimsby Town		1-2	Roberts	9,305	8
8/2	Barnet		6-1	Sam (2), Roberts, Rodrigues, Wootton, M Palmer	5,657	8
19/2	Eastleigh		2-0	Roberts, Wootton	5,682	8
22/2	Halifax Town		1-1	Sam	5,603	8
26/2		Woking	2-0	Rodrigues, Sam	3,141	7
1/3		Chesterfield	1-3	Sam	7,912	7
5/3	Yeovil Town		1-1	Lacey	6,943	7
8/3		Solihull Moors	3-3	Rodrigues (2), Lacey	2,120	7
15/3		Stockport County	0-3		7,951	8
19/3		Dagenham & Redbridge	2-1	Lacey, own goal	1,846	7
22/3	Boreham Wood		1-0	M Palmer	5,010	6
26/3	Chesterfield		1-1	Wootton (pen)	10,334 (BT Sport)	6
2/4		Southend United	3-0	Rodrigues (3)	6,338	6
9/4		Torquay United	1-5	Wootton	3,130	6
15/4	King's Lynn Town		4-1	Wootton, Roberts, Nemane, Sam	6,722	6
23/4	Weymouth		3-1	Wootton, Nemane, Rodrigues	6,032	7
26/4		Dover Athletic	3-0	Francis, Roberts, Rodrigues	866*	5
30/4		Aldershot Town	1-3	Roberts (pen)	1,969	5
2/5	Dover Athletic		1-0	Rodrigues	6,523	5
7/5	Altrincham		3-0	Roberts (pen), Wootton, Rodrigues	6,581	5
15/5		Maidenhead United	1-0	Roberts (pen)	2,074	5
23/5	Grimsby Town (Play-off)		1-2	Rodrigues (pen)	12,023 (BT Sport)	

* Attendance unknown – average shown

Notts County 2021-22
League +Cup 'Starts', (Sub appearances), Goals & Cards

	Name	Starts	(Sub)	Goals	Yellow/Red (Cards)
GK	Slocombe	20+4	(0+0)		0
"	Jaros	15+0	(0+0)		1
"	Patterson	9+4	(0+0)		1
"	Brooks	0+0	(0+0)		0 Unused sub x3
"	Kean	0+0	(0+0)		0 Unused sub x2
D	Cameron (Capt.)	25+4	(2+0)	4+0	7
E	Brindley	32+4	(0+0)	0+0	4
F	Chicksen	28+5	(3+0)	0+0	5
E	Lacey	26+2	(1+1)	5+0	7
N	Richardson	24+1	(0+2)	1+0	3
D	Taylor	19+6	(1+1)	0+0	2
E	Kelly-Evans	20+5	(8+1)	0+0	8/1
R	Rawlinson	19+6	(4+0)	0+1	2
S	Graham	4+0	(0+0)	0+0	0
"	Brennan	4+1	(0+0)	0+0	1
"	Parsons	1+2	(2+0)	0+0	0
M	Palmer M	43+5	(0+0)	2+0	7
I	Vincent	18+6	(5+1)	3+1	3
D	Francis	17+5	(15+2)	1+0	8
F	O'Brien	12+1	(12+1)	1+0	5
I	Brunt	4+0	(9+0)	0+0	1
E	Arter	8-0	(1+0)	0+0	4
L	Doyle	0+0	(0+0)	0+0	0 Unused sub x 2
D					(1 FAC & 1 FAT)
A	Wootton (Vice Capt.)	42+5	(1+1)	19+3	5
T	Rodrigues	41+6	(1+2)	19+2	12
T	Roberts	31+3	(5+4)	16+0	7
A	Mitchell	6+7	(21+0)	1+3	2
C	Nemane	8+4	(12+3)	2+0	3
K	Sam	8+2	(15+2)	6+2	3
E	Knight	0+0	(1+0)	0+0	0
R	Palmer Ty	0+0	(0+0)	0+0	0
S			own goals	1+1	yellow totals may not be 100% accurate
			Exc. Play-off	81+13	

Tyreace Palmer loaned to Melton Town, and then Basford United.
Lewis Knight loaned to Bradford Park Avenue (National League North) 24 Jan until the end of the season.
Tiernan Brooks loaned to Coalville Town during February – 4 March, extended until the end of the season.

Notts County League (& Cup) Goal Scorers 2021-22

Player	League	(Cup)	Total
Wootton	19*	(3)	=22* inc. 2 pens.
Rodrigues	19	(2*)	=21* inc. 1 pen.
Roberts	16*	(0)	=16* inc. 4 pens.
Sam	6	(2)	=8
Lacey	5	(0)	=5
Cameron	4	(0)	=4
Vincent	3	(1)	=4
Mitchell	1	(3)	=4
Palmer M	2	(0)	=2
Nemane	2	(0)	=2
O'Brien	1	(0)	=1
Francis	1	(0)	=1
Richardson	1	(0)	=1
Rawlinson	0	(1)	=1
Brunt	0	(0)	=0
Kelly-Evans	0	(0)	=0
Chicksen	0	(0)	=0
Brindley	0	(0)	=0
Taylor	0	(0)	=0
Arter	0	(0)	=0
Brennan	0	(0)	=0
Parsons	0	(0)	=0
Graham	0	(0)	=0
Knight	0	(0)	=0
Palmer Ty	0	(0)	=0
Doyle	0	(0)	=0
Own goals	1	(1)	=2
Total	**81**	**(13)**	**=94**

Play-off match against Grimsby (Rodrigues penalty) NOT included

Notts County FA Cup and FA Trophy Results 2021-22

Date	Home	Away	F-A	Scorers	Attendance	Round
16/10/21		Tamworth	0-0		1,813	FA Cup 4th Qualifying
19/10	Tamworth		4-0	Mitchell (2), Wootton, Vincent	2,594	Replay
7/11		Rochdale	1-1	Wootton	2,587	FA Cup 1st
16/11	Rochdale		1-2	own goal	4,416	Replay
18/12	Altrincham		2-1	Rodrigues (pen), Wootton	1,248 + 971 Streamers	FA Trophy 3rd
15/1/22	Eastleigh		2-1	Sam (2)	2,609	FA Trophy 4th
12/2		Halifax Town	2-1	Rodrigues, Mitchell	1,406	FA Trophy 5th
11/3	Wrexham		1-2	Rawlinson	3,170 + Streamers	FA Trophy 6th

Notts County Goal Times - League (& Cup) 2021-22
First 22 league (plus 4 FA Cup & 2 FA Trophy) matches

For						
0-15 min	16-30 min	31 min - HT	46-60 min	61-75 min	76-90 min	90+
1*(2)	3 (1)	8 (1)	12 (3)	9 (2)	6 (1)	1 (0)
Against						
0-15 min	16-30 min	31 min - HT	46-60 min	61-75 min	76-90 min	90+
3 (2)	1 (1)	5 (1)	2 (0)	6 (0)	5 (1)	3 (0)

*The only goal scored in the first 15 minutes came from the penalty spot!

Second 22 league (plus 2 FA Trophy) matches

For						
0-15 min	16-30 min	31 min - HT	46-60 min	61-75 min	76-90 min	90+
6 (1)	7 (1)	7 (0)	6 (0)	7 (0)	5 (1)	3 (0)
Against						
0-15 min	16-30 min	31 min - HT	46-60 min	61-75 min	76-90 min	90+
7 (0)	2 (0)	2 (1)	4 (1)	3 (0)	8 (1)	1 (0)

Notts County Home Attendances 2021-22

Att.	Opponents	Date (k.o. 15:00 unless stated)	
12,843	Solihull Moors	13 Nov	Admission prices reduced (Adults £5, Under 16 £1)
12,023	Grimsby Town	23 May (19:45)	Live on BT Sport – 2,013 from Grimsby - play-off
10,334	Chesterfield	26 Mar	Live on BT Sport – 2,719 from Chesterfield
9,305	Grimsby Town	5 Feb	
8,890	Wrexham	2 Jan	
7,418	Stockport County	23 Oct	
6,943	Yeovil Town	5 Mar	
6,934	Torquay Utd	28 Aug	First home league game of the season
6,722	King's Lynn	15 Apr	
6,581	Altrincham	7 May	
6,523	Dover Athletic	2 May	
6,206	Southend Utd	11 Dec	
6,032	Weymouth	23 Apr	
5,921	Aldershot Town	4 Sep	
5,807	Woking	2 Oct	
5,748	Maidenhead Utd	18 Sep	
5,682	Eastleigh	19 Feb	
5,657	Barnet	8 Feb (19:45)	
5,603	Halifax Town	22 Feb (19:45)	
5,331	Bromley	26 Oct (19:45)	
5,213	Wealdstone	14 Sep (19:45)	
5,010	Boreham Wood	22 Mar (19:45)	
4,889	Dagenham & Red	27 Nov (17:20)	Live on BT Sport
4,416	Rochdale	16 Nov (19:45)	FA Cup replay
3,170 +S	Wrexham	11 Mar (19:45)	FA Trophy + Streamers online
2,609	Eastleigh	15 Jan	FA Trophy
2,594	Tamworth	19 Oct (19:45)	FA Cup replay
1,248 +S	Altrincham	18 Dec (19:30)	FA Trophy + Streamers 971

	2019-20	2020-21	2021-22
National League Average:	104,207 = 5,210	Coronavirus	149,592 = 6,800
FA Cup/FA Trophy Average:	13,007 = 4,336	(COVID-19)	14,037 = 2,807
Combined Average:	117,214 = 5,096	Behind closed doors	163,629 = 6,060 Exc, play-off match

Chapter 20: The summer of 2022 - Burchnall 'out', Williams 'in'

Two days after the defeat to Grimsby in the play-off quarter final Notts issued their retained list following the conclusion of the 2021-22 season. A statement from the board of directors read:

> *We would like to place on record our gratitude to all departing players, who leave with our very best wishes for the future. As our supporters would expect, preparations for 2022-23 commenced long ago. We have identified the areas we need to improve and are in a strong position to act swiftly.*

Under contract

Sam Slocombe (Gk)
Joel Taylor
Kyle Cameron
Connell Rawlinson
Jim O'Brien
Kairo Mitchell
Cal Roberts.......... Won 2021-22 Goal of the Season v Aldershot at MeadowLane
Aaron Nemane
Ed Francis
Frank Vincent
Matt Palmer.......... Fans' and Players' Player of the Season
~~Elisha Sam~~........... Departed 1 June after he requested termination of his contract
Ruben Rodrigues... Named in The National League Team of the Season
~~Lewis Knight~~......... Departed 21 June to Gateshead (National League)

Offered new contract

Richard Brindley.... 29 May – signed new two year contract
~~Kyle Wootton~~......... Departed 9 June to Stockport County, EFL League Two
Adam Chicksen..... 20 June – signed new one year contract
Tiernan Brooks (Gk) 22 June – signed new three year contract

Under 19s offered senior contract

Luther Munakandafa Signed 6 June

Released

Dion Kelly-Evans   Joined Boreham Wood (National League)
Alex Lacey   Joined Hartlepool Utd (League Two)
Tyreace Palmer

Loan players returning to clubs

Vitezslav Jaros
Sam Graham
Jayden Richardson (Named in The National League Team of the Season)
Zak Brunt

Ian Burchnall (Head Coach) departed 27 May, followed by Michael Doyle (Assistant Head Coach) three days later. Both moved to Forest Green Rovers, EFL League One. Burchnall's record during his tenure (all competitions, excluding friendlies):

P70 W36 D15 L19 For 125 Against 85 = win percentage 51%.

The replacements for Ian Burchnall and Michael Doyle were Luke Williams and Ryan Harley - appointed on 14 June. Notts made the following announcement. There was no mention as to the length of their contracts.

Luke Williams and Ryan Harley

Luke Williams, *41, was previously head coach at Swindon Town and, most recently, assistant head coach to Russell Martin at [Championship club] Swansea City. Our board of directors feel he is the perfect man to take us forward.*

We're delighted that Luke and Ryan have joined us as our new head coach and assistant head coach. Between them they have the right management skills and experience of all EFL divisions, as well as The National League, which we believe will help us achieve our goal of promotion and getting back to where we feel we belong.

Luke's values and playing principles are aligned with our own and we feel the continuity and consistency this brings will be a huge factor in ensuring a smooth transition to his leadership. We have been very impressed not only with Luke's general character, but also his excitement about this opportunity and his fierce determination to succeed. He fully understands the pressure and expectation that comes with this role and we can see he's ready to take on the challenge.

Luke has already met with our recruitment team to discuss our current squad and ongoing transfer targets and we look forward to working closely with him to build a team which will give us the best possible chance of earning the promotion we all crave in 2022-23.

After a promising youth career was curtailed by injury at 20, Williams turned his hand to coaching.

His first major role came in the form of a three-year spell as Brighton and Hove Albion Under 21s manager, which led to his appointment as Mark Cooper's assistant at League One side Swindon Town in 2013. The pair led the Robins to the play-off final in 2014-15, losing out to Preston North End, and Williams continued in his role alongside interim chairman-manager Lee Power and then Martin Ling following Cooper's departure. Ling resigned in 2015, opening the door for Williams to take the caretaker manager's role – an opportunity he grasped with both hands as, following an excellent run of results, he was handed a five-year contract as the club's head coach with Power declaring him a 'fantastic coach' who was 'the best I've come across in 25 years.'

Unfortunately, however, Williams' control over footballing affairs was limited by the club's deployment of a director of football and Swindon found themselves in a relegation battle which resulted in the club dropping into League Two and the mutual termination of Williams' contract.

Williams made an immediate return to work by becoming head coach of Bristol City's Under 23s, with then first team manager Lee Johnson and chief executive Mark Ashton both lauding the reputation Williams held within the game as an excellent coach.

Two years later, Williams teamed up with the newly-appointed [Russell] Martin as his assistant at MK Dons before following him to the Championship when the Swans came calling. Williams left that role in February due to personal reasons.

Ryan Harley, 37, enjoyed a long playing career which saw him experience life in every division of the EFL. He also tasted non-league, winning the Conference [now The National League] play-offs with Exeter City before securing back-to-back promotions with the Grecians in League Two the following season. The midfielder also won *promotion with MK Dons in 2018-19 and coached there with Williams, who arrived at Stadium MK the following season. He also played at Brighton and Swindon during Williams' time at both clubs.*

The players returned to Meadow Lane for pre-season training, following their summer break, on Thursday 30 June. The next day the 2022-23 squad numbers were confirmed:

1 - Sam Slocombe (Gk)

2 - Richard Brindley

3 - Joel Taylor

4 - Kyle Cameron (Capt.)

5 - Connell Rawlinson

6 - Jim O'Brien

7 - Kairo Mitchell

8 - **Sam Austin NEW** Age 25. An attacking midfielder (11 league goals last season) signed from National League (North) Kidderminster Harriers, where he was captain, on a three-year contract. Named in the NL(N) Team of the (2021-22) Season. In six seasons at Kidderminster he made over 200 appearances.

9 - **Macaulay Langstaff NEW** Age 25. A striker signed from National League (North) champions Gateshead on a three-year contract. NL(N) Player of the (2021-22) Season and the league's top scorer with 28 goals. Named in the NL(N) Team of the (2021-22) Season.

~~10 - Cal Roberts~~ Transferred to Scottish Premiership club Aberdeen on 25 July – undisclosed fee

11 - Aaron Nemane

12 - Tiernan Brooks (Gk)

14 - Ed Francis

15 - **Aden Baldwin NEW** Age 25. A central defender signed on a two-year contact from League One MK Dons, where he made 16 appearances last season. Prior experience with Cheltenham Town (League Two) - five appearances - and in National League (South).

16 - **Geraldo Bajrami NEW** Age 22. A versatile defender signed from Kidderminster Harriers on a two-year contract. Before Kidderminster he had been at Birmingham City (Championship) for whom he made three appearances.

17 - Frank Vincent

18 - Matty Palmer

19 - **Cedwyn Scott NEW** Age 23. A striker signed from National League (North) champions Gateshead on a two-year contract. Named in the NL(N) Team of the (2021-22) Season. Scored 24 goals, alongside Langstaff. Before joining Gateshead he made seven appearances for Carlisle Utd (League Two). Earlier in his career he gained experience with Dundee, Berwick Rangers and Forfar Athletic in Scotland.

20 - Ruben Rodrigues

21 - **Tobi Adebayo-Rowling NEW** Age 25. A pacey right wing back signed from National League (South) Ebbsfleet on a two-year contract. Previous experience at Peterborough Utd (League One), for whom he made five appearances, and in the League of Ireland.

22 - Luther Munakandafa   23 - Adam Chicksen

On 4 July it emerged that, with the early bird and renewal period at an end, season ticket sales had surpassed last season's total. With just over a month to go before the first match of the season on Saturday 6 August at home to Maidenhead Utd, total sales had passed 3,500. Chief Executive Jason Turner was delighted so many fans had already committed to the forthcoming season.

> *"At such an early stage, hitting the 3,500 mark and selling more season tickets than we did in total last year is an incredible achievement," he said. "I think this is a great reflection of the optimism our supporters have for the new season, with a very talented head coach and several exciting signings already in place. We look forward to welcoming all our fans back to Meadow Lane and hopefully delivering the promotion we all so desperately want."*

He also commented on the news that neighbours Nottingham Forest, promoted to the Premier League via the play-offs at the end of last season, had agreed to visit Meadow Lane for a friendly on Tuesday 26 July. Meadow Lane was also the venue for Forest's pre-season friendly against Valencia four days later.

> *"Today's announcement is another reflection of the excellent relationship we have developed with our neighbours. We very much look forward to welcoming Forest to Meadow Lane for both fixtures and wish them well for the forthcoming season."*

On 8 July, following conclusion of the early bird and renewal periods, 2022-23 season tickets went on general sale.

Prices (Price per game in brackets).

Away supporters are accommodated in the Jimmy Sirrel Stand.

	Derek Pavis	Kop	Family Stand
Adult	£389 (£16.91)	£320 (£13.91)	£320 (£13.91)
65 & over	£250 (£10.87)	£230 (£10)	£230 (£10)
22-25	£190 (£8.26)	£190 (£8.26)	£190 (£8.26)
18-21	£140 (£6.09)	£140 (£6.09)	£140 (£6.09)
Under 18	£65 (£2.83)	£65 (£2.83)	£65 (£2.83)
Under 12	£20 (£0.87)	£20 (£0.87)	£20 (£0.87)

The board, staff and players all recognise the immense support of our fans which saw us ranked second in the 2021-22 National League average attendance table. Despite the club having increasing operational costs, we are also mindful of the rise in the cost of living and are committed to repaying fans' loyalty by making it as affordable as possible to follow our fortunes.

Notts' pre-season fixtures and results:

Tue 5 July: Basford United (A) – 7.45pm……………………………………………..won 1-5

Although Basford scored first, Notts were comfortable winners with goals from Rodrigues, Langstaff, Scott and Cameron, plus an own goal.

Sat 9 July: Leicester City (A – Leicester's excellent training ground) – 1 pm….won 1-2

On a hot and sunny early afternoon, a strong Leicester team took the lead on the half hour through Harvey Barnes (11 goals and 13 assists for the Premier League club last season). Notts responded positively and won with goals from Mitchell and Baldwin.

Tue 12 July: Alfreton Town (A) – 7.45pm..won 0-2

Notts were dominant throughout and should have beaten The National League (North) team by a wider margin. Roberts scored just before half-time from the penalty spot, after he had been fouled in the penalty area. Francis flicked in the second goal.

Sat 16 July: Cambridge United (A – St Neots Town FC) – 1pm.........................lost 2-0
                                                                                                                            – 3pm............................won 2-3

Two 70-minute matches (35 minutes each way) were played against Cambridge (EFL League One). Notts fielded two completely different 11's. 19 of the 22 registered players were in action. The three unavailable were Rawlinson and Rodrigues (minor injuries) and Scott (illness). One trialist and two U19's were given an opportunity. In the 1pm match Notts were beaten by two second half goals. In the 3pm match Cambridge scored two first half goals but in the second half Langstaff scored the perfect hat-trick – header, left foot, right foot – in just seven minutes!

Wed 20 July: Boston United (A) – 7.45pm...draw 1-1

The home side, of The National League (North), took an early fourth minute lead, but two minutes later Cameron scored an excellent equaliser. Notts then dominated the match and should have won. After one hour, seven changes (which included one trialist) were made to the starting eleven. Five members of the 22-man squad were unavailable through injury or illness: Rawlinson, Palmer, Austin, Langstaff and Scott. 24 hours earlier much of eastern and southern England (together with many other places in the UK) experienced their hottest day on record – a sweltering 40C, a value never before reached in the UK. Fortunately this evening was, by comparison, cool!

Tue 26 July: Nottingham Forest (H) – 7.45pm..draw 2-2

Notts' only home pre-season friendly, on the third anniversary under the ownership of Christoffer and Alexander Reedtz, gave Luke Williams and Ryan Harley, together with the six new players, an introduction to the Meadow Lane match day atmosphere. The attendance was 14,041 (5,929 Forest supporters).

                              Slocombe
                Brindley   Baldwin   Cameron (Capt.)
Nemane (Adebayo-Rowling 82')   Francis (Bajrami 64')   Chicksen (Taylor 82')
                       Austin   O'Brien (Scott 64')
          Langstaff (Mitchell 82')   Rodrigues (Vincent 82')

Unused subs: Brooks (Gk). Rawlinson, Palmer, and Munakandafa omitted

Premier League neighbours Forest didn't field a full-strength side, but it was an entertaining, skilful, and competitive match. Just before the end of an even first half Forest took the lead when Sam Sturridge scored a delightful goal when he expertly placed a right footed shot from inside the penalty area into the corner of the net. Rodrigues nearly equalised a minute later but his deflected shot hit a post and was cleared. There were three goals in the first 15 minutes of the second half. First, Langstaff produced a clinical finish after he received a slide rule pass from Rodrigues. Ribeiro Dias (aka Cafu) then restored Forest's lead with a thunderous 30-yard free kick which gave Sam Slocombe no chance. Notts' second equaliser was scored by the industrious Austin when he shot powerfully home from near the penalty spot, after the Forest goalkeeper failed to clear a searching cross from Cameron. Although there were no further goals it was Notts who dictated the final half hour, during which they created opportunities to win the match.

Head groundsman Matt Hallam, with assistance from his colleagues Jay and Shaun, had produced a superb new playing surface following the "turnover" of the pitch during the last nine weeks.

Also, 'Club News' announced the day before the match that:

> **State-of-the-art floodlights have been installed at Meadow Lane and supporters will see them in action during the pre-season friendly against Nottingham Forest.** *The new LED fittings replace the previous lamps which, having been installed in 2014, were reaching the end of their lifespan. This investment introduces technology used at top-class football venues such as Bayern Munich's Allianz Arena and Rotherham's New York Stadium, a host ground for this summer's Women's European Championships, and carries several benefits for the club including: reduced electricity charges, minimal maintenance costs, brighter white light with reduced glare and a reduced carbon footprint.*

Sat 30 July: York City (A) – 3pm……………………………………..won 0-1

For their final pre-season friendly, against fellow National League club York City, Notts fielded the following team:

                             Slocombe
Brindley (Nemane 65')   Baldwin (Francis 46')   Cameron (Capt.)
       Adebayo-Rowling   Bajrami   Taylor (Chicksen 65')
       Austin (Mitchell 75')   O' Brien (Palmer 65')
          Langstaff (Scott 57')   Rodrigues (Vincent 65')

Unused subs: Brooks (Gk). Not involved: Rawlinson (injured) and Munakandafa

Notts controlled most of the first half. After ten minutes a Cameron header hit the crossbar but ten minutes later O'Brien capitalised on a defensive error to put Notts ahead. However, they didn't show the drive and intensity they had against Forest, and other chances to increase their lead before half time were not taken. Although Scott hit a post on 70 minutes and Mitchell had a goal disallowed for offside, York had their best spell during the latter stages of the match. Notts weren't at their best but did enough to deserve their victory.

Attendance: 1,504 (175 Notts).

This match celebrated York's first ever fixture in 1922, which was a 4-2 defeat against Notts (Reserves) at Meadow Lane. Today's match formed part of their centenary celebrations. A total of 1000 limited edition programmes were printed for the occasion.

So, Notts' 21-man squad turned their attention to Saturday 6 August, when Maidenhead Utd were the opponents at Meadow Lane on the opening day of the 2022-23 National League season.

According to the bookmakers Notts were expected to finish second (to Wrexham), and therefore take part in the playoff's for the fourth time in their fourth National League campaign.

National League Winner odds

Team	BetVictor
Wrexham	– 7/4
Notts County	**– 6/1**
Chesterfield	– 8/1
Solihull Moors	– 10/1
Oldham Athletic	– 14/1
Southend United	– 14/1
FC Halifax Town	– 16/1
Boreham Wood	– 20/1
Scunthorpe United	– 20/1
Dagenham	– 20/1
Yeovil Town	– 25/1
Torquay United	– 25/1
Bromley	– 40/1
York City	– 50/1
Woking	– 66/1
Gateshead	– 66/1
Barnet	– 66/1
Maidstone	– 66/1
Dorking	– 66/1
Eastleigh	– 100/1
Aldershot Town	– 100/1
Wealdstone	– 150/1
Altrincham	– 150/1
Maidenhead United	– 150/1

Chapter 21: The 2022-23 season (first half, matches 1-23)

Back row, left to right: Joao Alves (First Team Assistant/Analyst), Matt **Palmer,** Adam **Chicksen,** Kairo **Mitchell,** Aden **Baldwin,** Joel **Taylor,** Ruben **Rodrigues,** Ian Hutton (Strength & Conditioning Coach)

Middle row, left to right: Jane Jackson (Sports Therapist), Craig Heiden (Head of Medical Services), Geraldo **Bajrami,** Connell **Rawlinson,** Tiernan **Brooks,** Sam **Slocombe,** Ed **Francis,** Richard **Brindley,** Lewis Saleem (Kit & Equipment Manager), Tom Weal (Goalkeeper Coach)

Front row, left to right: Macaulay **Langstaff,** Cedwyn **Scott,** Jim **O'Brien,** Tobi **Adebayo-Rowling,** Ryan Harley (Assistant Head Coach), Luke Williams (Head Coach), Kyle **Cameron** (Capt), Sam **Austin,** Frank **Vincent,** Aaron **Nemane**

Match 1　　　　　　　　　　**Notts County 3-0 Maidenhead Utd**　　　　Attendance 6,331
Sat 6 Aug 2022 15:00　　　Langstaff 22', 44'
Taylor 60'

```
                              Slocombe
                 Brindley        Baldwin        Cameron (Capt.)
        Taylor                                                  Chicksen
               Austin      Francis (Bajrami 83')     O'Brien (Palmer 65')
             Langstaff (Scott 76')                  Rodrigues
```

Subs: Bajrami, Palmer, Vincent, Scott, Mitchell
(no substitute goalkeeper)

Not in the squad: Brooks (Gk), Rawlinson (injured), Nemane (suspension carried over from last season), Adebayo-Rowling, Munakandafa.

The starting eleven selected by Luke Williams had five changes from the team defeated by Grimsby in the play-off match on 23 May. Three were debutants: Baldwin, Austin and Langstaff.

Notts visited Maidenhead on the final day of last season when they completed the double over them – both matches ended 1-0 to Notts. Maidenhead finished in 17th position. Only five players who started that final match started this match: Slocombe, Brindley, Cameron, O'Brien, and Rodrigues.

Macaulay Langstaff made an explosive start, in his first competitive Notts match, with two first half goals. The first was created by O'Brien and Rodrigues, and when he received the ball his 12 yard right footed shot was too powerful for the Maidenhead goalkeeper. Taylor and Austin were the providers for his second goal. This time he swiftly adjusted his feet to create space before a clinical finish from ten yards with his left foot.

The second half was 15 minutes old when Joel Taylor scored his first Notts goal, and what a goal it was. O'Brien slid the ball to him and from 25 yards he unleashed a ferocious shot which flew into the top corner of the net in front of the kop. The BBC Radio Nottingham commentator, Charlie Slater, said the ball hit the place "where the spiders live and the owls sleep".

This was a comfortable victory for Notts who controlled the match, against a disappointing Maidenhead.

Match 2	Boreham Wood (8th) 2-2 Notts County (2nd)	Attendance 1,303
Sat 13 Aug 2022 15:00	goals 38', 83' (pen.) Rodrigues 7' (pen), Mitchell 68	(inc. 537 Notts)

```
                        Slocombe
          Brindley    Baldwin (Bajrami 77')    Cameron (Capt.)
    Taylor                                              Chicksen
       Austin (Palmer 60')    Francis    O'Brien (Mitchell 60')
                   Langstaff              Rodrigues
```

Subs: Bajrami, Palmer, Vincent, Scott, Mitchell
(no substitute goalkeeper)

Following last week's victory over Maidenhead, the starting eleven and the substitutes were unchanged.

Boreham Wood finished 9th last season. Notts drew 1-1 here and won 1-0 at Meadow Lane. Dion Kelly-Evans, released by Notts last May, joined Boreham Wood in the summer. He was sent off in their 0-1 win at Southend seven days ago and was therefore suspended. Tough tackling KE was the only Notts player sent off last season, during which he made 34 appearances. Zak Brunt (in today's starting eleven for Boreham Wood) made 13 appearances for Notts during the second half of last season on loan from Sheffield Utd.

On a swelteringly hot and sunny afternoon, Notts were awarded an early penalty after the Boreham Wood goalkeeper parried a good Rodrigues shot. A defender and Langstaff tussled for the loose ball. All three ended up on the ground but it was unclear why the referee gave a penalty in the subsequent melee. Rodrigues calmly sent the goalkeeper the wrong way as he confidently placed his shot into the corner of the net. Notts dominated the next half hour but then, after Langstaff just failed to turn home a wonderful low cross by Chicksen, Boreham Wood had two chances to score. Brunt shot wide when well placed, but a minute later they equalized from inside the six yards box after the ball had pin-balled around following a corner, given after Slocombe had tipped a lob over the crossbar.

The second half was ten minutes old when Brunt 'scored' but the goal was disallowed for offside. Notts improved and regained the lead with a wonderful 20 yard shot by Mitchell, after he had received the ball from Langstaff. Boreham Wood then had a second goal disallowed for offside! However, Notts' defensive frailties were being exposed and Mitchell was adjudged to have pushed an opponent over in the penalty area following a corner. Boreham Wood equalized from the spot.

Langstaff, Mitchell and Rodrigues all went close in the final minutes, but a disappointed Luke Williams said Notts "lost the game twice and threw away two points". Five Notts players also received a yellow card.

Match 3	**Gateshead (16th) 1-1 Notts County (=1st)**	Attendance 1,825 (inc.
Tue 16 Aug 2022 19:45	goal 46' own goal 88'	598 Notts)

                        Slocombe
         Brindley   Cameron (Capt.)   Bajrami
Nemane   Chicksen
          Palmer   Francis (Mitchell 63')   O'Brien (Vincent 81')
            Langstaff (Scott 75')   Rodrigues

Subs: Taylor, Vincent, Austin, Scott, Mitchell
(no substitute goalkeeper)

Not in the squad: Brooks (Gk), Baldwin and Rawlinson (both injured), Adebayo-Rowling, Munakandafa.

Williams made three changes to the side which drew at Boreham Wood. Bajrami made his first league start for Notts, in for the injured Baldwin. Nemane was preferred to Taylor on the right and Palmer replaced Austin in midfield.

Gateshead were promoted from National League (North) at the end of last season after they had finished as champions. Their opening two matches this season had ended as 2-2 draws. In the first they lost a two-goal lead and in the second they recovered from a two-goal deficit. Two of their four goals had been scored by ex-Notts player Adam Campbell. Remember, Notts signed Langstaff and Scott from Gateshead a couple of months ago, after the pair had scored over 50 goals between them as Gateshead finished top of the league. (Just after Scott was transferred to Notts he became ill with COVID and he was still not 100% fit).

The first chance fell to Gateshead. Francis was caught in possession by Campbell who ran forward but Slocombe had advanced, and his shot hit the goalkeeper on the chest as he dived and Notts survived. A Langstaff header forced the home goalkeeper into a good save, but he was unable to hold the ball, and a defender was happy to give away a corner (one of nine Notts earned in the first half), and at the interval neither side had made a breakthrough.

The second half was only seconds old when Gateshead took the lead. A weak Cameron back pass was intercepted. Slocombe again advanced, but the forward steered the ball past him from the edge of the penalty area. Notts did not panic, and they slowly began to exert pressure on the home defence. With two minutes of normal time left they finally got the equalizer they deserved when a defender turned (the lively) Nemane's low cross into his own net.

So, Notts remained unbeaten but dropped to (equal) sixth position.

Match 4	Notts County (=6th) 2-2 Chesterfield (2nd)	Attendance 8,287
Sat 20 Aug 2022 17:20	Langstaff 60', 63' goals 16', 55'	Televised live on BT Sport

```
                        Slocombe
        Brindley    Baldwin (Bajrami 72')    Cameron (Capt.)
    Nemane                                              Chicksen
        O'Brien (Austin 58')    Palmer          Rodrigues
              Langstaff           Mitchell (Scott 58')

          Subs: Bajrami, Taylor, Francis, Austin, Scott
                    (no substitute goalkeeper)
```

Not in the squad: Brooks (Gk), Rawlinson (injured), Adebayo-Rowling, Munakandafa. Midfielder Frank Vincent released, on a month's loan, to Aldershot until the week commencing Monday 26 September.

Williams made two changes to the side which drew at Gateshead. Baldwin returned at the expense of Bajrami and striker Mitchell came in for Francis.

Chesterfield, like Notts, were defeated in the promotion play-offs at the end of last season. In the league it was a 1-1 draw at Meadow Lane, but Notts lost 3-1 in the away fixture. The Spireites were undefeated in their three matches this season with a draw and two victories.

Both sides made a good start to the match, but it was Chesterfield who went ahead with a shot from 12 yards which beat the diving Slocombe and entered the far corner of the net. The remainder of the first half was keenly contested and both sides had goal scoring opportunities, but there were no further goals.

Although the first ten minutes of the second half were fairly even, Chesterfield then increased their lead. A forward created space for himself just inside the penalty area and shot powerfully into the net. A few minutes later Notts were nearly three down when a shot by the same player hit a post. Almost immediately Notts reduced their deficit through Langstaff, who latched on to a rebound off a Chesterfield defender and lashed the ball home from 18 yards with a first time shot. The crowd were still cheering when he equalized with a diving header, following a superb cross by Austin. Both sides had chances in an exciting final half hour, and near the end Rodrigues robbed a defender and passed to Langstaff on the edge of the six-yard box but he was denied his hat-trick when a defender blocked his shot.

This end-to-end match was an excellent advertisement for non-league football, and a draw was a fair result. The Spireites had a following of 1,886 supporters. After their third successive draw Notts dropped to tenth position in the table.

Match 5 Sat 27 Aug 2022 15:00	**FC Halifax Town (24th) 1-4 Notts County (10th)** goal 83'	Langstaff 42', 60' Scott 45'+2, Mitchell 87'	Attendance 2,371 (773 Notts)

Slocombe
Brindley   Baldwin   Cameron (Capt.)
Nemane (Adebayo-Rowling 68')   Chicksen
Austin   Palmer   O'Brien
Langstaff (Mitchell 72')   Scott (Bajrami 61')

Subs: Bajrami, Francis, Mitchell, Adebayo-Rowling, Munakandafa
(no substitute goalkeeper)

Not in the squad: Brooks (Gk), Rawlinson and Taylor (both injured), Rodrigues (virus), Vincent, on loan at Aldershot. Brad Young, a 20-year-old highly rated goalkeeper, signed yesterday from Premier League Leicester City on a season-long loan. Prior to Leicester he was with Hartlepool Utd. His experience was limited to Leicester's U21 side and the England U20 squad.

Williams made two changes to the side which drew against Chesterfield. Austin replaced (the ill) Rodrigues and striker Scott, making his first league start for Notts, was preferred to Mitchell.

Halifax, like Notts, were defeated in the promotion play-offs at the end of last season. In the league Notts suffered a 3-2 defeat here with a 1-1 draw at Meadow Lane, but Notts won 1-2 here in the FA Trophy. Despite their 4th place finish last season (Notts 5th) the Shaymen had started this season with three defeats and a draw, without a goal to their credit, and were bottom of the league.

On a difficult, spongy, pitch, an uneventful first half burst into life in the final minutes with two Notts goals from the duo who scored 52 league goals for Gateshead last season. The first was scored by Langstaff who turned the ball into the net from close range following a cross by Austin. Scott scored his first Notts league goal with a header at the near post after a cross by O'Brien. In between these goals a scissor kick by a Halifax forward was brilliantly saved by Slocombe.

After a bright start to the second half by Halifax, Notts increased their lead in a counterattack. Scott, from inside the Notts half, passed to Langstaff who ran on, took the ball around the goalkeeper, and side-footed it into an empty net. Despite the setback Halifax continued to put Notts under some pressure and they scored their first goal of the season with a good finish from 15 yards. However, there was still time for Mitchell to take advantage of a poor back pass and shoot confidently into the corner of the net from the edge of the penalty area.

Match 6	**Notts County (8th) 1-0 Solihull Moors (2nd)**	Attendance 7,004
Mon 29 Aug 2022 15:00	Chicksen 65'	

Slocombe

Brindley   Baldwin   Cameron (Capt.)

Nemane   Chicksen

Palmer   Bajrami (O'Brien 90')   Rodrigues

Langstaff (Mitchell 82')   Scott (Austin 62')

Subs: Adebayo-Rowling, Francis, O'Brien, Austin, Mitchell

(no substitute goalkeeper)

Not in the squad: Brooks and Young (Gk's), Rawlinson and Taylor (both injured), Munakandafa. Vincent, on loan at Aldershot.

There were two changes to the side victorious at Halifax just 48 hours ago. In midfield, Rodrigues and Bajrami were selected ahead of O'Brien and Austin.

Solihull, managed by ex-Notts manager Neal Ardley, were defeated by Grimsby Town in the promotion play-off final at the end of last season. In the two league matches Notts won 2-0 at

Meadow Lane and drew 3-3 away in a rip-roaring encounter. The Moors had started the season well and were undefeated in their five matches. They were the league's leading scorers with 13 goals (twice scoring four goals) – Notts were second highest scorers with 12 goals.

Notts dominated a one-sided first half and had opportunities to take the lead. Slocombe was mostly a spectator – his only save was made in the sixth minute, when he dived to hold a 22-yard shot. Just before half-time a goal bound effort by Rodrigues was superbly cleared off the line by a defender, with the goalkeeper beaten.

Notts continued in the ascendency during the second half, and they deservedly took the lead when Chicksen scored in front of the kop, following a superb cross by Palmer. A sequence of 14 consecutive passes, which started in Notts' six-yard box, were made before Chicksen shot into the net from inside the Solihull six-yard box. As the match entered its final stage, Rodrigues made an audacious attempt to score from just inside the Notts half, after he spotted the goalkeeper off his goal-line, but the effort just cleared the crossbar.

This was probably Notts' best performance of the season so far. Unbeaten, high scoring, Solihull never really threatened and Notts were worthy winners. So, unbeaten Notts ended the month in fifth position. The only other unbeaten team in the league was top of the table Chesterfield.

Match 7	**Dagenham & (12ᵗʰ) 0-5 Notts County (5ᵗʰ)**	Attendance 1,722
Sat 3 Sep 2022 15:00	**Redbridge**	(421 Notts)
	Langstaff 18', 45'+1, 76'	
	Scott 40'	
	Chicken 74'	

Slocombe

Brindley Baldwin Cameron (Capt.)

Nemane (Bajrami 65') Chicksen

O'Brien (Austin 60') Palmer Rodrigues

Langstaff Scott (Francis 73')

Subs: Adebayo-Rowling, Bajrami, Francis, Austin, Mitchell
(no substitute goalkeeper)

Not in the squad: Young (Gk), Rawlinson and Taylor (both injured), Munakandafa. Vincent, on loan at Aldershot. Brooks (Gk) on loan until January 2023 to Hednesford Town of the Southern Premier Central League.

There was just one change to the side which convincingly defeated Solihull. In midfield, O'Brien was preferred to Bajrami.

Dagenham & Redbridge finished one point and one place (8ᵗʰ) outside the promotion play-offs at the end of last season, when Notts won both fixtures 2-1. This season D & R had made a mixed start: P6 W2 D2 L2 F8 A7.

Notts made an impressive start and deservedly took the lead through Langstaff's seventh goal of the season. He turned quickly and slotted the ball home from the edge of the six-yard box, after a cross by Nemane wasn't cleared. Notts continued to dominate, and a terrific 25 yard shot by Nemane hit the crossbar. Soon after, Scott turned Nemane's deflected shot home at the back post. Notts' third goal was scored by the unstoppable Langstaff during time added at the end of the half. From close range he shot home after Scott's shot had been partially saved by the goalkeeper.

Although D & R showed some improvement in the second half, Notts continued to outclass the home side and they scored two quick goals with about fifteen minutes to play. Chicken scored for the second consecutive match after he received a Rodrigues pass, created space, and the goalkeeper could only help his shot into the corner of the net. A couple of minutes later Langstaff got his hat-trick when he deflected Cameron's low shot beyond the home goalkeeper.

So, a superb Notts performance brought a third win in a week, a third clean sheet of the season and a rise to third in the league. Only Chesterfield and Wrexham were above Notts.

Match 8 Tue 13 Sep 2022 19:45	**Notts County (3rd) 2-0 Aldershot Town (21st)** Attendance 5,607 Scott 52' Langstaff 64'

```
                            Slocombe
        Brindley (Rawlinson 55')    Bajrami           Cameron (Capt.)
   Nemane                                                      Chicksen
            O'Brien        Palmer      Rodrigues
      Langstaff (Mitchell 68')              Scott (Castro 68')
```

Subs: Rawlinson, Adebayo-Rowling, Francis, Castro, Mitchell
(no substitute goalkeeper)

Not in the squad: Young (Gk), Baldwin, Austin and Taylor (injured), Vincent, on loan at Aldershot – the terms of which meant he was not in the Aldershot squad. Brooks (Gk) on loan at Hednesford Town. Munakandafa – now on loan at Basford Utd of the Northern Premier League until 11 December. The day before this fixture Quevin Castro, age 21, was signed on loan until 8 January, from Championship club West Bromwich Albion. The Portuguese attacking midfielder made his WBA debut last season against Arsenal in the EFL Cup and then made two Championship appearances as a substitute. Earlier this season he was on loan at League One Burton Albion where he made one start and substitute appearances.

There was one change to the side which thrashed Dagenham & Redbridge – Bajrami came in for the injured Baldwin.

Notts had mixed fortunes against Aldershot last season, winning 3-2 at Meadow Lane but they were defeated 3-1 away from home, as Aldershot finished just one place above the relegated clubs. This season they were in the relegation zone with five defeats and two victories.

On a pleasant autumn evening there was a one-minute silence in honour of HM Queen Elizabeth II who died on 8 September. Aldershot made the better start and gave Notts some anxious moments. Slocombe, Brindley and a post, prevented a goal for the visitors. Notts gradually asserted themselves as the half progressed but the closest they came to a goal was on the stroke of half time when Langstaff deflected a Cameron shot over the crossbar.

Notts dominated the second half, and they scored twice in the first 20 minutes. They took the lead when Bajrami moved forward and lifted the ball towards the six-yard box, where it brushed Langstaff's head on its way to Scott who bundled the ball home. The second arrived after Langstaff turned home a Nemane cross, following a sequence of ten passes.

It was a stylish victory by a team full of confidence and invention, illustrated by four successive wins and three successive clean sheets.

Match 9 Sat 17 Sep 2022 15:00	Dorking (13th) 3-1 Notts County (3rd) Wanderers goals 19', Scott 50' 90'+3, 90'+7	Attendance 2,402 (Notts 600+)

```
                        Slocombe
            Rawlinson   Bajrami       Cameron (Capt.)
   Nemane                                     Chicksen
        O'Brien (Mitchell 70')   Palmer    Rodrigues
            Scott (Castro 66')        Langstaff
```

Subs: Young (Gk), Adebayo-Rowling, Francis, Mitchell, Castro

Not in the squad: Brindley, Baldwin, Austin, and Taylor (injured), Vincent, on loan at Aldershot. Brooks (Gk) on loan at Hednesford Town. Munakandafa on loan at Basford Utd.

There was just one change to the side which defeated Aldershot. Rawlinson (not 100% fit according to Luke Williams) came in for his first start of the season, to replace the injured Brindley.

Dorking Wanderers were promoted from National League South at the end of last season, winning the play-off final after finishing in second position. They had had a mixed start to this season and were in mid-table, but their defensive record was the worst in the division with 20 goals conceded.

On an artificial grass pitch, against a part-time team, Notts had several chances to score in the first half but poor finishing and some good saves by the home goalkeeper meant they experienced a barren 45 minutes. Dorking were presented with the lead when Slocombe attempted to find Palmer with a pass, but the ball was intercepted by a Dorking player who lifted the ball into the unguarded net from 35 yards.

Notts dominated the second half and had further opportunities to equalize but were restricted to a single goal when Scott created an opportunity for himself and shot home from the edge of the penalty area. However, Notts failed to press home their superiority and Dorking completed a smash-and-grab with three minutes of the nine minutes of added time played. A shot hit a post and fell to their leading scorer who gleefully scored his second goal of the afternoon. Worse was to follow for Notts when he completed his hat-trick after Slocombe dived and got his hand to a shot, but couldn't hold the ball, and the rebound was prodded into the net.

So, Notts lost for the first time this season against a side who had suffered defeats in their last two home matches (0-5 and 1-4). If they had won, Notts would have gone to the top of the league. Football is a funny old game!

Match 10	**York City (8th) 1-3 Notts County (4th)**	Attendance 6,759
Sat 24 Sep 2022 15:00	goal 35' Castro 5',	(Notts 1734)
	Langstaff 42', 79'	

Slocombe

Brindley   Rawlinson   Cameron (Capt.)

Nemane   Chicksen

Palmer   O'Brien

Castro (Austin 65')   Rodrigues (Mitchell 83')

Langstaff (Scott 83')

Subs: Adebayo-Rowling, Francis, Austin, Mitchell, Scott
(no substitute goalkeeper)

Not in the squad: Bajrami, Baldwin, and Taylor (injured). Young (Gk). Vincent, on loan at Aldershot. Brooks (Gk) on loan at Hednesford Town. Munakandafa on loan at Basford Utd.

Luke Williams made three changes to the side defeated at Dorking. Brindley returned after his one match injury absence, but Bajrami had picked up an injury and Rawlinson took his place in central defence. Castro, who had replaced Scott from the substitutes bench twice in the last two matches, came in for his full debut.

York were promoted from National League North at the end of last season, winning the play-off final after finishing in fifth position. They had made a good start to this season and were unbeaten in their last five matches.

Quevin Castro scored with a spectacular 35-yard free kick after just five minutes. He struck the ball with such power and placement into the top corner that the goalkeeper hardly moved! Notts continued to dominate and only good saves by the home goalkeeper prevented Langstaff, Rodrigues and Nemane goals. However, York equalized following a free kick into the penalty area which wasn't cleared, and the ball was turned into the net from seven yards. After a brief spell of York pressure Notts deservedly regained the lead. Rodrigues passed to Nemane who crossed, and Langstaff scored with a powerful diving header from six yards.

With five minutes of the second half played Notts could/should have increased their lead. O'Brien and Nemane got the ball to Castro, and he crossed. Chicksen did well to reach the cross but then lifted the ball over the crossbar from inside the six-yard box. A surging Cameron run provided Langstaff with an excellent chance, but he blazed his shot over the crossbar. A superior Notts scored their third goal when a defensive error allowed Austin to present Langstaff with a one-on-one against the goalkeeper. He moved forward confidently and made no mistake as he became the leading goal scorer in the top five tiers of English football, with 12 goals. Wow!

Match 11	**Notts County (3rd) 3-1 Altrincham (23rd)**		Attendance 6,458
Sat 1 Oct 2022 15:00	Langstaff 42', 44'	goal 47'	
	Chicksen 60'		

Slocombe
Brindley   Rawlinson   Cameron (Capt.)
Adebayo-Rowling   Chicksen (Nemane 70')
Castro (Francis 55')   Palmer   Rodrigues
Scott (Austin 55')   Langstaff

Subs: Francis, O'Brien, Austin, Nemane, Mitchell
(no substitute goalkeeper)

Not in the squad: Bajrami, Baldwin, and Taylor (injured). Young (Gk). Vincent on loan (extended until 8 January 2023) at Aldershot. Brooks (Gk) on loan at Hednesford Town. Munakandafa on loan at Basford Utd.

There were two changes to the side victorious at York. Adebayo-Rowling came in for his full debut (he made a substitute appearance in match 5), in place of Nemane. Scott returned to partner Langstaff, with midfielder O'Brien a substitute.

Altrincham finished 14th at the end of last season. In their three matches against Notts they scored a 1-0 home victory but lost 3-0 in the league and 2-1 in the FA Trophy – at Meadow Lane. Last Saturday they won for the first time this season, 1-0 at home to Aldershot, and moved off the bottom of the league.

After five minutes Castro almost replicated his goal at York last Saturday, but this time his 30-yard shot crashed against the underside of the crossbar and bounced down in front of the goal line. Fifteen minutes later it was Altrincham who nearly took the lead. A forward only had Slocombe to beat, but his shot rattled the crossbar and was then cleared. Notts netted twice just before the interval when Langstaff scored with close range efforts. Scott was involved with both goals. For the first his shot was parried by the goalkeeper and Langstaff was on hand to turn the ball home. Two minutes later Scott passed to Adebayo-Rowling, who's cross was diverted on to a post but he prodded the rebound to Langstaff, and he tapped the ball into the net.

The second half was only two minute old when Altrincham capitalized on a mis-placed pass, made progress down the left and the cross was turned into the corner of the net from six yards. But Notts restored their two-goal cushion when Langstaff almost got his hat-trick, but his glancing header from Adebayo-Rowling's excellent cross was helped over the goal line by Chicksen.

Notts were not at their best and Altrincham belied their lowly league position and created several chances, but in the end Notts 'got the job done'.

Match 12	**Notts County (2nd) 1-0 Wrexham (1st)**	Attendance 10,741
Tue 4 Oct 2022 19:45	Langstaff 13'	

Slocombe

Brindley Rawlinson Cameron (Capt.)

Nemane Chicksen

O'Brien (Bajrami 34') Palmer Rodrigues

Scott (Austin 79') Langstaff (Mitchell 87')

Subs: Adebayo-Rowling, Bajrami, Austin, Mitchell, Castro
(no substitute goalkeeper)

Not in the squad: Baldwin, and Taylor (injured), Francis, Young (Gk). Vincent on loan at Aldershot. Brooks (Gk) on loan at Hednesford Town. Munakandafa on loan at Basford Utd.

For this top of the table clash, Luke Williams made two changes to the side which beat Altrincham. Nemane was preferred to Adebayo-Rowling and O'Brien returned in place of Castro.

Wrexham, like Notts, were beaten in the promotion play-offs at the end of last season, after they had finished in second position behind champions Stockport County. Since Notts were relegated into The National League at the end of the 2018-19 season Wrexham had not defeated Notts in five league meetings, although they did win at Meadow Lane in the FA Trophy in March 2022.

For the first 25 minutes of the match Notts overwhelmed Wrexham with incisive, attacking, free-flowing football. In the third minute only a goal line clearance prevented Nemane giving Notts the lead, after a Langstaff header from a Cameron cross had been saved. They deservedly took the lead ten minutes later when Langstaff scored his 15th goal of the season, following an excellent free kick routine. Chicksen passed to Rodrigues, and he nutmegged a defender to release Palmer who cut the ball back to Langstaff and he side-footed the ball into the net from near the penalty spot. Magical!

To the delight of their near 2,000 following, Wrexham were the better team for much of the second half, and Slocombe came to Notts' rescue on a number of occasions. In the 65th minute they had a goal disallowed for offside. It was a narrow escape. The match then became an end-to-end affair and both teams had opportunities to score. Throughout the match the goalkeepers were excellent.

So, after a thoroughly entertaining and exciting 100 minutes (five minutes were added at the end of each half) Notts moved to the top of the league due to an all-round good team performance, against a strong Wrexham team.

This match meant the season was one quarter through. The league table follows.

National League Table 4 October 2022

		GP	W	D	L	GF	GA	GD	Pts
1	**Notts County**	**12**	**8**	**3**	**1**	**28**	**11**	**+17**	**27**
2	Wrexham	12	8	2	2	31	10	+21	26
3	Chesterfield	12	7	3	2	24	16	+8	24
4	Bromley	12	7	2	3	19	12	+7	23
5	Solihull Moors	12	6	4	2	27	15	+12	22
6	Boreham Wood	12	6	4	2	18	11	+7	22
7	Woking	12	6	2	4	20	11	+9	20
8	Wealdstone	12	5	4	3	13	11	+2	19
9	York City	12	5	3	4	16	11	+5	18
10	Dorking Wanderers	12	5	2	5	23	26	-3	17
11	Barnet	12	5	2	5	22	25	-3	17
12	Dagenham & Red.	12	5	2	5	22	28	-6	17
13	Southend Utd	12	4	4	4	11	10	+1	16
14	Eastleigh	12	4	4	4	13	14	-1	16
15	Maidenhead Utd	12	5	1	6	12	15	-3	16
16	Oldham Athletic	12	3	3	6	13	21	-8	12
17	Gateshead FC	12	2	5	5	15	19	-4	11
18	Altrincham	12	2	5	5	14	23	-9	11
19	Halifax Town	12	3	2	7	8	19	-11	11
20	Maidstone Utd	12	3	2	7	16	29	-13	11
21	Yeovil Town	12	1	7	4	11	14	-3	10
22	Aldershot Town	12	3	1	8	14	19	-5	10
23	Scunthorpe Utd	12	2	4	6	16	23	-7	10
24	Torquay Utd	12	2	3	7	9	22	-13	9

Position 1 Automatic promotion to EFL League Two
Positions 2-7 Promotion playoffs (one team promoted)
Positions 21-24 Relegated

Match 13	Woking (7th) 2-3 Notts County(1st)	Attendance 3,267
Sat 8 Oct 2022 15:00	goals 30', Rodrigues 9' (pen.), 86' (pen.) Scott 15', 42'	(Notts 530)

```
                        Slocombe
            Brindley    Rawlinson    Cameron (Capt.)
  Nemane                                              Chicksen
            Palmer (Castro 83')  Bajrami    Rodrigues
            Scott (Austin 78')   Langstaff (Mitchell 74')
```

Subs: Adebayo-Rowling, Francis, Austin, Mitchell, Castro
(no substitute goalkeeper)

Not in the squad: Baldwin, Taylor, and O'Brien (injured), Young (Gk). Vincent, Brooks (Gk) and Munakandafa out on loan.

Bajrami replaced the injured O'Brien during the first half against Wrexham, and he remained in that midfield position. Luke Williams expected the thigh/groin injury to keep O'Brien out of action for at least four weeks.

Although Woking were defeated 2-3 at home to Wrexham a few weeks ago they had won their other four home matches this season in which they had scored nine without conceding a goal. In three home fixtures against Notts, since the Magpies were relegated from League Two, they had conceded ten goals in three defeats!

Against the run of play Notts took an early lead in their first attack after Chicksen was felled in the penalty area. Rodrigues sent the home goalkeeper the wrong way with his spot kick. Despite the setback Woking continued in the ascendency, but it was Notts who increased their lead when Scott turned home Chicksen's cross. However, Woking reduced their deficit when Slocombe was caught in possession on the edge of the six-yard box as his attempted clearance was blocked by a forward and the ball rebounded into the net. Just before the end of a bizarre first half Scott scored again after the ball had pinballed around and Langstaff gave him the opportunity to side-foot the ball into the net for Notts' third goal.

Notts controlled most of the second half and seemed content to manage the game, but they were given a fright near the end when Woking were awarded a penalty after Mitchell was adjudged to have handled the ball. Slocombe was sent the wrong way as the spot kick was stroked into the net.

It was an anticlimactic Notts performance following their display against Wrexham. A case of 'after the Lord Mayor's show', but they remained the top team in non-league football with a fourth straight victory. Although Langstaff did not score he made National League history when, for the second month in succession, he was named 'Player of the Month' for September following his August award.

FA Cup Fourth Qualifying Round	Notts County 2-3 Coalville Town	Attendance 5,060
Sat 15 Oct 2022 15:00	Austin 9', 66' goals 3', 23', 86'	

Young
Brindley   Rawlinson (Capt.)   Mahovo (Palmer 53')
Adebayo-Rowling   Taylor
Austin   Francis   Bajrami
Castro (Rodrigues 53')
Mitchell (Langstaff 67')

Subs: Slocombe (Gk), Chicksen, Palmer, Rodrigues, Nemane, Langstaff, Scott

Not in the squad: Baldwin and O'Brien (both injured). Vincent, Brooks (Gk) and Munakandafa out on loan.

Luke Williams rotated the squad and made eight changes to the team successful at Woking. Only Brindley, Rawlinson and Bajrami played in that match, and today. He gave debuts to goalkeeper Brad Young and 17-year-old Lucien Mahovo.

Coalville, members of the Southern League Premier Central - two tiers below Notts – were well placed in third position, with a 100% away record of played four, won four.

Notts got off to the worst possible start. Brindley headed a long clearance from Coalville's goalkeeper to an opponent and, after a few neat passes, Young was beaten by a good finish from 10 yards. Notts levelled six minutes later when Austin scored his first competitive Notts goal – his only previous goal was against Nottingham Forest in the pre-season friendly. On this occasion he controlled a cross by Adebayo-Rowling on the edge of the six-yard box and calmly slotted the ball home. Notts were certainly not at their best and they fell behind again when Mahovo was out maneuvered and from the subsequent cross Brindley was unable to prevent an onrushing forward stabbing the ball into the net.

With two early second half substitutions Notts' performance improved. Just after Brindley had effectively dealt with a counterattack, they equalized for a second time. An excellent cross by Taylor was too good for the goalkeeper and Austin was on hand to head the ball into the unguarded net. Notts then had opportunities to take the lead but with four minutes of normal time left they were dealt a sucker punch when poor defending allowed a forward to progress to the near post and the ball was eventually scrambled home.

A very disappointed Luke Williams gave credit to Coalville and admitted they deserved to win.

Match 14 Fri 21 Oct 2022 19:45	**Notts County (1st) 3-0 Maidstone Utd (21st)** Langstaff 44' Rodrigues 52' Scott 63'	Attendance 6,765

Slocombe
Brindley   Rawlinson   Cameron (Capt.)
Nemane (Adebayo-Rowling 66')   Chicksen
Palmer   Bajrami   Rodrigues
Scott (Austin 66')   Langstaff (Mitchell 76')

Subs: Baldwin, Adebayo-Rowling, Francis, Austin, Mitchell
(no substitute goalkeeper)

Not in the squad: O'Brien (injured), Taylor, Castro, Young (Gk). Vincent, Brooks (Gk) and Munakandafa out on loan.

After the debacle against Coalville, Luke Williams reverted to the team which defeated Woking in the last league game.

Maidstone were promoted as champions from National League South at the end of last season, but they had found life more difficult at this higher level and were in the relegation zone. Only one team had conceded more goals and they had not won since 29 August. Like Notts, they too were knocked out of the FA Cup six days ago by a team from two tiers below.

Notts took control from the start and soon had an opportunity to take the lead, but Chicksen shot into the side-netting from Nemane's low cross towards the back post. In the 20th minute Langstaff had a goal disallowed for offside. However, they eventually got a deserved lead just before half-time when Langstaff scored his 16th goal of the season. A short corner followed by a cross was headed on by Bajrami and Langstaff headed against the crossbar, but he was first to the rebound and he put the ball into the net from close range.

The second half was only minutes old when Notts doubled their lead. Rodrigues scored his first goal of the season from open play after he received the ball from Langstaff and curled a powerful shot into the corner of the net from 20 yards. His two previous goals had been penalties. Two minutes later Rodrigues was given the opportunity to score his third penalty of the season when Scott was felled in the area, but his poor spot kick was saved by the goalkeeper. However, ten minutes later Notts did increase their lead when Scott's hard low drive, from just inside the penalty area, flashed past the goalkeeper at the near post.

Slocombe had just one save to make in the whole match as Notts dominated throughout. It was their fifth consecutive league victory, and they extended their lead over Wrexham (in second place) to three points.

Match 15	**Wealdstone (12th) 1-6 Notts County (1st)**	Attendance 1,710
Tue 25 Oct 2022 19:45	goal 60' Langstaff 3',	(Notts 513)
	Chicksen 24', 43',	
	Palmer 31',	
	Nemane 46'	
	Bajrami 55'	

Slocombe
Brindley   Rawlinson   Cameron (Capt.)
Nemane (Adebayo-Rowling 65')   Chicksen
Palmer   Bajrami   Rodrigues (Baldwin 75')
Scott (Austin 65')   Langstaff

Subs: Baldwin, Adebayo-Rowling, Francis, Austin, Mitchell
(no substitute goalkeeper)

Not in the squad: O'Brien (injured), Taylor, Castro, Young (Gk). Vincent, Brooks (Gk) and Munakandafa out on loan.

Luke Williams made no changes to the team/squad which defeated Maidstone.

Notts and Wealdstone had met four times in The National League, with the Magpies victorious on three occasions and the other match drawn. This August Wealdstone won four of their first five matches, but since then had won only one of their last nine in the league. They had lost their last four matches, including a 5-3 defeat to Boreham Wood in the FA Cup.

In the third minute Rodrigues threaded a pass to Langstaff. He moved the ball forward with his left foot and shot home with his right foot from the edge of the penalty area. Wealdstone retaliated and had a goal disallowed for offside after ten minutes. They then had a couple of opportunities to equalize, but it was Notts who scored their second and again the assist came from Rodrigues. He rolled a free kick to Chicksen who hit the ball hard and low into the far corner of the net. A few minutes later Palmer scored his first goal of the season with a crisp shot from 15 yards after he had received a pass from Nemane, and Notts were three goals ahead! Following a good save by Slocombe, it was Notts who continued to give Wealdstone a lesson on how to score spectacular goals when they got a fourth with another Rodrigues assist. Chicksen controlled his cross inside the penalty area and smashed the ball into the roof of the net.

In the first minute of the second half Nemane scored his first goal of the season when his shot from the edge of the penalty area struck a defender and was deflected past the goalkeeper. Unbelievably, the Magpies got a sixth when Bajrami scored his first Notts goal after the goalkeeper pushed a Nemane cross/shot to him. On the hour Slocombe was given no chance when a Wealdstone forward smashed the ball past him from eight yards. The drama continued as Brindley committed another foul, received a second yellow card, and was sent off. Before the end Langstaff and Cameron went close, but Notts were unable to get a seventh goal.

It was Notts' biggest league win, away from Meadow Lane, since 1923 – 99 years!

Match 16	**Notts County (1ˢᵗ) 4-0 Torquay Utd (24ᵗʰ)** Attendance 7,563
Sat 29 Oct 2022 15:00	Rawlinson 27'
	Rodrigues 34' (pen)
	Castro 87', Bajrami 89'

```
                          Slocombe
             Rawlinson     Baldwin     Cameron (Capt.)
     Nemane (Adebayo-Rowling 76')                Chicksen
                 Palmer    Bajrami    Rodrigues (Castro 76')
           Scott (Austin 65')            Langstaff
```

Subs: Adebayo-Rowling, Francis, Austin, Mitchell, Castro
(no substitute goalkeeper)

Not in the squad: O'Brien (injured), Brindley (suspended), Taylor, Young (Gk). Vincent, Brooks (Gk) and Munakandafa out on loan.

Just one change to the team that thrashed Wealdstone four days ago. Baldwin, injured at the beginning of September but now fully fit, replaced the suspended (for one match) Brindley.

Torquay had given Notts some disappointments in the three previous seasons. Although Notts were undefeated at Meadow Lane against Torquay (one win, two draws) they had suffered a draw and two heavy defeats at Plainmoor – 4-2 in a semi-final promotion playoff match in June 2021 and 5-1 in the league six months ago! Currently in bottom place Torquay had not won any of their last eight league matches (three draws) and had only scored 13 league goals so far this season.

Notts soon created an opportunity, but the unmarked Chicksen headed Palmer's cross wide. Just after Nemane had been thwarted by the goalkeeper, Notts' superiority paid off when Palmer passed to Rawlinson who scored his first goal of the season with a powerful twenty yard shot into the corner of the net. Six minutes later Nemane was fouled in the penalty area and Rodrigues sent the goalkeeper the wrong way with a confident spot kick. With half-time minutes away Scott passed to Chicksen who hit the underside of the crossbar with a shot from near the penalty spot. Langstaff got to the rebound, but the goalkeeper blocked his attempt.

Notts continued to control the match in the second half. Just after Austin had arrived from the substitutes bench he shot against the crossbar from the edge of the penalty area. Notts finished the match in style with two goals in the final five minutes. Castro received the ball from Cameron, moved forward and, from 22 yards, blasted a shot into the bottom corner of the net. There was still time for Austin to pass to Bajrami and his 20-yard shot was deflected into the net.

Another dominant performance by Notts who thoroughly deserved the victory.

Luke Williams: Manager of the Month, October 2022
(Awarded in Mid-November)

Back row: Alves, Saleem, Heiden, Hutton
Front row: Jackson, Lawtey, **Luke Williams**, Weal, Harley

Luke Williams has been named October's Vanarama National League Manager of the Month – but has insisted the award will be shared by the whole backroom team at Meadow Lane.

The head coach has led us on an impressive start to the season since his summer arrival, overseeing 13 wins from 19 matches and tasting defeat only once so far. Six of those victories came during a remarkable October in which we won all our (6) league games, scoring 20 in the process – one in a huge victory against title rivals Wrexham and six in a rampant away display at Wealdstone.

And, while Williams has received huge plaudits for the team's achievements so far, he is adamant they would not have been possible without the support of his staff.

"I would firstly like to thank the people who considered us for this award, which we're truly honoured to have," said the head coach.

"I'm merely receiving it on behalf of the entire backroom staff who, since the day I've walked through the door, have been an immense support to me and have each played a huge individual role in extracting consistent performances from the team. Like in any job, people on the outside can't see the full picture – the hours of hard work, early starts, late finishes, travelling, concentration, dedication and talent that are essential to compete in this highly competitive environment. This is brilliant recognition for all of them and, as a staff, we can use this award to further strengthen our bond and continue to develop our working practices for the benefit of the team and club.

"I would also like to give a special mention to our chief executive, Jason Turner, who has been pivotal in helping me adjust to life at a new club in a new division. Jason has an encyclopaedic knowledge of the game and is an all-round great guy. He, along with our owners Chris and Alex Reedtz, provides an incredible environment for us to do our work and deserves as much credit as anyone.

"Finally, a huge thank you to our supporters who have got behind me, the staff and players since day one. Given the struggles and disappointments they have endured in recent years, I've been amazed by their spirit and passion. I, and everyone at the club, share our fans' desperation to see Notts County back in the EFL as soon as possible and our work has only just begun in trying to achieve that."

The team behind the team…

Ryan Harley (Assistant Head Coach) *Harley arrived alongside Williams this summer having crossed paths with him at Brighton, Swindon and MK Dons. A talented midfielder, he enjoyed a long playing career which saw him experience life in every division of the EFL - and his skills are still put to good use day in, day out as he regularly participates in training.*

Tom Weal (Goalkeeper Coach) *Weal joined us from Norwich City in 2021, where he was head of academy goalkeeping, but his role here has not been limited to between the sticks. He also plays a major part in a collective effort to devise our dead-ball routines, many of which have come to fruition this season.*

Craig Heiden (Head of Medical Services) and **Jane Jackson** (Sports Therapist) *Heiden, who has considerable experience from time spent in Nottingham Forest's academy and in other roles, works alongside Jackson, who joined us permanently after a successful internship, to manage our injury prevention and rehabilitation programme. They're responsible for carrying out medical assessments on new signings and also have the unenviable task of advising when a player may need to be rested due to injury!*

Ian Hutton (Strength and Conditioning Coach) *Hutton, boasting considerable experience following highly successful spells with Cheltenham Town and Solihull, is responsible for building, monitoring and managing the players' physical condition. Supporters will have seen him leading warm-ups ahead of matches, and behind the scenes he runs gym sessions for the players and uses a data-led approach to keep the squad in the best shape possible.*

George Lawtey and Joao Alves (First Team Assistants) *Lawtey, who previously worked with Williams at Bristol City, teamed up with Portugal-born Alves to take on a shared role earlier this season. The pair are responsible for editing and presenting video which showcases aspects of both our own and opposition's performances, while also coaching the players both on the training ground and in meetings.*

Lewis Saleem (Kit & Equipment Manager) *Saleem carries out a hugely important role in ensuring the staff and players' needs are met not only on matchday, but also at every training session. He is responsible for the necessary kit and equipment being ready each day, which includes many hours of driving, carrying, printing, washing and drying – and he's even taken control of our new drone which is used to analyse training from above!*

Remember, Macaulay Langstaff was awarded 'Player of the Month' in August and September

Match 17	Notts County (1ˢᵗ) 1-1 Bromley (8ᵗʰ)	Attendance 6,389
Tue 1 Nov 2022 19:45	Chicksen 17' goal 60'	

```
                        Slocombe
       Rawlinson (Brindley 76')   Baldwin        Cameron (Capt.)
   Nemane                                                      Chicksen
                 Palmer    Bajrami    Rodrigues
              Scott (Castro 76')        Langstaff
```

Subs: Brindley, Adebayo-Rowling, Austin, Mitchell, Castro
(no substitute goalkeeper)

Not in the squad: O'Brien (injured), Francis, Taylor, Young (Gk). Vincent, Brooks (Gk) and Munakandafa out on loan.

Notts fielded the same team that convincingly defeated Torquay.

This match was originally scheduled for Saturday 10 September but all fixtures on that day were postponed due to the death of HM Queen Elizabeth II two days earlier. Bromley had been in a promotion playoff position until recently, but they had suffered four successive defeats, including an exit from the FA Cup by Hereford from National League North.

Notts made a good start, but they nearly fell behind after 13 minutes. Bromley's leading scorer in recent seasons, Michael Cheek, rounded Slocombe but Baldwin made an excellent clearance to prevent a goal. Four minutes later Notts took the lead when a superb low cross by Rodrigues gave Chicksen a chance, and the goal scoring wing-back made no mistake from close range. Langstaff then had a chance but shot over the crossbar. Bromley countered but Chicksen made an important intervention. A few minutes later the Bromley goalkeeper pushed a powerful shot by Scott on to a post and out for a corner. The visitors then had a good spell and Slocombe was required to make three excellent saves in quick succession. Notts retaliated and Rodrigues intercepted the ball, exchanged passes with Langstaff, and his powerful 20-yard shot smashed against a post. At the end of an entertaining 45 minutes Notts were a little fortunate to be in the lead.

The second half started in the same end-to-end fashion. Langstaff had two chances. The goalkeeper made a fine save from the first and the second hit the crossbar, but in-between Slocombe made another excellent save. Bromley finally got the goal they had threatened on the hour mark when, from a corner, Cheek glanced a header past Slocombe. Thereafter Notts looked the more likely to score – Palmer, and Castro on two occasions, went close - but they were unable to breach the Bromley defence, despite six minutes of added time.

A draw was probably a fair result. So, Notts did not achieve an eighth consecutive victory, but they remained top of the league – one point ahead of Wrexham.

Match 18	Southend Utd (6ᵗʰ) 2-2 Notts County (1ˢᵗ)	Attendance 6,603
Tue 8 Nov 2022 19:45	goals 54', 65' Langstaff 34',	(Notts 286)
	Scott 60'	Televised on BT Sport

```
                         Slocombe
           Brindley      Baldwin      Cameron (Capt.)
   Nemane (Adebayo-Rowling 72')                    Chicksen
           Palmer    Bajrami (Austin 61')    Rodrigues (Castro 80')
                   Scott            Langstaff
```

Subs: Rawlinson, Adebayo-Rowling, Austin, Mitchell, Castro
(no substitute goalkeeper)

Not in the squad: O'Brien (injured), Francis, Taylor, Young (Gk). Vincent, Brooks (Gk) and Munakandafa out on loan.

Luke Williams made just one change to the team involved in the highly entertaining draw against Bromley – Brindley returned in place of Rawlinson.

Southend were relegated from EFL League One in July 2020 and from EFL League Two in May 2021. Last season, in The National League, they finished a mid-table 13ᵗʰ, and Notts won both matches (4-1 at Meadow Lane and 0-3 at Roots Hall, where Rodrigues scored a hat-trick.) Following a disappointing start to this season Southend were undefeated in their last nine league matches, including victories in their last four with 11 goals scored and none conceded! Southend and Notts were the current in-form National League teams, with defensive records of 11 and 15 respectively but Southend had scored only 23 to Notts' 45.

The first 30 minutes were even with both teams going close to scoring. However, it was Notts who made the breakthrough when Palmer's shot was deflected to Langstaff who, from a tight angle, fired a hard low shot home from the edge of the six-yard box.

The second half was less than ten minutes old when Southend equalized. An opponent pushed Scott in the back as he climbed to head the ball past Slocombe. Scott got his revenge a few minutes later when he received a pass from Palmer, twisted and turned just outside the penalty area and then struck a low shot expertly into the corner of the net. But soon after Cameron had made a crucial block, Notts were pegged back for a second time after Nemane misjudged the flight of a long, high, pass. A dangerous cross from the left was then turned beyond Slocombe by the unfortunate Baldwin.

Notts gave Southend some anxious moments as they searched for a third goal, but in the end they had to settle for a draw, in a competitive match against a good team.

With Wrexham victorious at Scunthorpe, Notts dropped to second place.

Match 19 Sat 12 Nov 2022 15:00	Eastleigh (8ᵗʰ) 0-2 Notts County (2ⁿᵈ) Chicksen 56', Rodrigues 74'	Attendance 3,055 (Notts 502)

Slocombe

Brindley   Rawlinson   Cameron (Capt.)

Adebayo-Rowling   Chicksen

Austin   Francis (Scott 64')   Palmer   Rodrigues (Bajrami 76')

Langstaff (Mitchell 76')

Subs: Baldwin, Bajrami, Nemane, Scott, Mitchell
(no substitute goalkeeper)

Not in the squad: O'Brien and Castro (both injured), Young (Gk). Vincent, Brooks (Gk) and Munakandafa out on loan. Today, wing back Joel Taylor was loaned to Dagenham & Redbridge for two months, until 8 January.

Luke Williams made four changes to the team involved in the entertaining draw against Southend. Rawlinson, Adebayo Rowling, Austin, and Francis (his first league start since 16 August at Gateshead) were preferred to Baldwin, Nemane, Bajrami and Scott who were all on the substitutes bench.

Notts commenced their National League journey on 3 August 2019, when they were defeated 1-0 at Eastleigh. Both subsequent trips to the south coast had ended in 2-0 defeats. In their nine home matches this season Eastleigh were unbeaten (W7 D2), including a 5-2 victory over Maidstone four days ago, and only Notts and Wrexham had superior home records. History, and Eastleigh's current home form, indicated a difficult match for Notts.

Despite their excellent home record Eastleigh were unadventurous, and it was Notts who dominated the first half. However, the Magpies only threatened the Eastleigh goal twice through Austin and Langstaff.

The second half was, initially, a more even affair but Notts took the lead through their prolific goalscoring wing back Chicksen when he scored his seventh goal of the season. The assist came from the other wing back Adebayo-Rowling who crossed to the far post where Chicksen headed home. The Magpies control and perseverance earned them a deserved second goal 18 minutes later when Scott and Rodrigues exchanged passes before Austin tapped the ball to Rodrigues and he side-footed the ball into the net from just inside the penalty area. Soon after the home goalkeeper Joe McDonnell (ex-Notts) made a brilliant save to deny Bajrami and just before the end Adebayo-Rowling's powerful shot hit a post and the ball rebounded for a throw-in.

Eastleigh offered little in the way of attack and Notts, who were worthy winners, returned to the top of the league as Wrexham were surprisingly held to a goalless draw at Wealdstone – where Notts won 1-6 on 25 October.

Match 20	**Notts County (1st) 0-0 Yeovil Town (19th)**	Attendance 16,511
Sat 19 Nov 2022 15:00		(League record)

Slocombe
Brindley   Baldwin   Cameron (Capt.)
Adebayo-Rowling   Chicksen
Austin (Castro 65')   Palmer   Rodrigues
Scott (Mitchell 75')   Langstaff

Subs: Rawlinson, Bajrami, Francis, Castro, Mitchell
(no substitute goalkeeper)

Not in the squad: O'Brien (injured), Nemane (chronic fatigue), Young (Gk). Vincent, Brooks (Gk), Munakandafa and Taylor out on loan.

There were two changes to the team which achieved a fine win at Eastleigh. Baldwin and Scott replaced Rawlinson and Francis.

This match was Notts' annual discounted fixture, with admission £5 for adults and £1 for under 16's. Last season the venture was a tremendous success – with a record National League attendance of 12,843. This previous record for a non-league match was easily broken with an attendance of 16,511 (452 from Yeovil).

The opening game of the 2022 FIFA World Cup in Qatar took place 24 hours later. With England and Wales participants (in the same group, before the last 16 knockout stage), Premier League and Championship fixtures were postponed until Boxing Day, 26 December, and 3 December respectively.

Yeovil ended a run of seven league and FA Cup matches without a victory when they defeated bottom club Gateshead in their last match. They had scored the fewest goals in the league but had a good defensive record, P19 W3 D9 L7 F16 A21.

It soon became evident that Yeovil had arrived with the intention of spoiling the party, by playing defensively with just a lone striker. The first half bombardment was almost entirely played in front of the kop. Yeovil's goalkeeper made good saves from Langstaff and Scott, and even better saves from Chicksen and Rodrigues.

Yeovil gave the Notts defence a scare at the start of the second half, but Notts were soon back on the offensive. Palmer forced the goalkeeper into another good save, and Castro's goal bound shot was deflected just wide of a post. Baldwin tried his luck from thirty yards, but his shot flew inches wide. Notts almost got the victory they deserved but Cameron's shot, from a Rodrigues corner, was clear off the goal line. In added time Chicksen missed the best chance of the match but his diving header, from Adebayo-Rowling's cross, three yards out, cleared the crossbar!

Notts last failed to score at Meadow Lane on 17 April 2021 - 41 league and cup matches ago, but their unbeaten league run (11) continued. With this draw they dropped to second – Wrexham won and returned to the top of the league.

Match 21	Scunthorpe Utd (23rd) 1-4 Notts County (2nd)	Attendance 4,196
Sat 3 Dec 2022 12:30	goal 20' Castro 23',	(Notts 1,411)
	O'Brien 32',	
	Langstaff 40',	
	Scott 85'	

                        Slocombe

        Brindley   Baldwin   Cameron (Capt.)

Adebayo-Rowling   Chicksen

Castro (Austin 53')   Palmer   O'Brien (Francis 67')   Rodrigues

                     Langstaff (Scott 75')

Subs: Bajrami, Francis, Austin, Scott, Mitchell
(no substitute goalkeeper)

Not in the squad: Rawlinson (injured), Nemane, Young (Gk). Vincent, Brooks (Gk), Munakandafa and Taylor out on loan.

Following two weeks without a match (it was the second round of the FA Cup last week) Luke Williams made two changes to the team which drew with Yeovil. O'Brien returned after injury to replace Austin and Castro was preferred to Scott.

Scunthorpe, relegated after finishing bottom of EFL League Two at the end of last season, had continued their poor form into this season. Only a slightly better goal difference was enough to keep them off the bottom of the league. They had lost their last five matches and had conceded 43 goals in their 21 matches. In 11 league matches against teams currently in 13th position and above they had taken just one point. Also, their leading scorer with nine goals was sent off (given a straight red card) on 26 November and he was therefore suspended. Two days later they changed their interim first team manager, and on 1 December a successful takeover of the club was announced!

Scunthorpe were a club in turmoil. But, against the run of play they took the lead after 20 minutes following a counterattack. Two forwards were given too much space and time and a shot from inside the penalty area beat Slocombe at his near post. However, Notts' response was almost immediate. Rodrigues slid the ball to Castro who side-footed into the corner of the net from just inside the penalty area. Ten minutes later Castro then turned provider when he teed up the ball for O'Brien who, from 25 yards, shot low and hard into the (same) corner of the net. Just before half-time another

O'Brien shot was deflected, the ball rebounded off the goalkeeper, and Langstaff scored Notts' third from ten yards.

Although Notts controlled the second half neither team were able to assert themselves until Notts scored their fourth goal when substitute Scott scored from close range after the ball had pinballed around and rebounded of a post.

Notts returned to the top of the league, one point ahead of Wrexham who could only draw 1-1 at York, and Scunthorpe dropped to the bottom.

On 7 December Notts made a surprising addition to the squad – 30-year-old John Bostock, a left-footed 6'2" (defensive) midfielder, on an 18 month contract until the summer of 2024. Since leaving League One Doncaster Rovers at the end of last season he had trained with Nottingham Forest's Under 21's to maintain his fitness and motivation, and more recently he had spent two weeks at Meadow Lane.

Head coach Luke Williams said:

"The opportunity for John to come and train with us was a pleasant surprise to say the least and, very quickly, you could see he has the physique and quality of a top player. He's powerful, very strong when he needs to protect the ball and can move freely. He doesn't need back lift – he pushes the ball around very cleanly.

"What you don't notice until a little later, however, is that he has the mentality of a top player as well. He's very bright and his attitude is superb.

"I feel really strongly that John will add value – not only as a player, but as a man. He's gone full circle in football, experiencing really high moments but also probably some low and disillusioned periods, with lots of success woven in. He's bounced back from every difficult period he's faced and is going to be able to give some really valuable help and advice to the players around him. He's someone you can't fail to respect.

"I think John could see from being around the lads that it's an ambitious group that works very hard and plays the game in an enjoyable way. He looked like he was in an

environment which suited him and for a player of his quality to fit in so well with the group is testament to the individuals we have here."

Notts provided a resume of his (15 club, inc. loans) football career to date:

Born in south London, he signed for Crystal Palace aged five and went on to earn 'wonder kid' status thanks to his performances at club and [England U16, U17 and U19] international level.

By the age of 14 he was being monitored by the biggest clubs in Europe, with Barcelona offering him a 10-year contract, only for him to continue at Palace. He was rewarded with the opportunity to become the Eagles' youngest ever player when he was selected for their FA Cup match against Watford aged 15, before following up with four Championship appearances that season.

A high-profile move to Tottenham Hotspur was to follow but, despite also becoming Spurs' youngest ever player when he made his debut in the UEFA Cup aged 16, the move didn't work out and, following loans in the EFL and MLS, he departed White Hart Lane.

Belgium was his next destination and, after becoming a fans' favourite at Royal Antwerp, he won the second tier's Player of the Season award when he helped fire OH Leuven to promotion with 13 goals and 19 assists. His success earned him moves to Lens, where he won the French second tier's Player of the Season award, and then to Bursaspor and Toulouse in Turkey and France's top tiers.

From there he returned to England with a loan spell at Nottingham Forest, before signing for Doncaster during the 2020-21 campaign. He impressed despite Rovers' relegation from League One last season and decided to turn down their offer of a new deal, paving the way for him to join us on a free transfer.

Match 22 Sat 10 Dec 2022 15:00	**Maidenhead Utd (14th) 3-4 Notts County (1st)** goals 31', 48', 67' Rodrigues 9', Castro 39', Langstaff 41', 83'	Attendance 1,467 (Notts 400)

Slocombe

Brindley   Baldwin   Cameron (Capt.)

Adebayo-Rowling   Chicksen

Castro (Austin 60')   Palmer (Bostock 80')   O'Brien (Scott 73')   Rodrigues

Langstaff

Subs: Bajrami, Bostock, Nemane, Austin, Scott
(no substitute goalkeeper)

Not in the squad: Rawlinson (injured), Francis, Mitchell, Young (Gk). Vincent, Brooks (Gk), Munakandafa and Taylor out on loan.

On 6 December, young defender Lucien Mahovo (age 17) signed a professional contract until June 2025. He made his senior debut in mid-October in the FA Cup defeat to Coalville Town. The next day Notts signed unattached midfielder John Bostock (age 30) on an 18-month contract until June 2024. These two signings increased the number of players in the professional squad to 25.

It was the same team that defeated Scunthorpe, but with two changes amongst the substitutes – Nemane for Mitchell and newcomer Bostock instead of Francis.

Maidenhead were defeated 3-0 at Meadow Lane on the opening day of the season. Since then, their form had been topsy-turvy – not helped by a disappointing number of goals scored (22 in their 22 matches) – although they had been beaten only once in their last five league matches.

With frost on a shaded strip of the sloping pitch, Notts took an early lead when an excellent team move was finished by Rodrigues who side-footed the ball home following a Cameron cross from the left. Although Notts were in control of the match, on the half hour Slocombe had to push a strong shot away for a corner from which Maidenhead equalized when the ball was bundled home from close range. It didn't take Notts long to restore, and then increase, their lead. Castro made it 1-2 when his cross from the left went all the way into the corner of the net. Langstaff made it 1-3 when he ended an incredible sequence of **28** passes (the last from Rodrigues) with a shot from just inside the penalty area.

Maidenhead reduced their deficit with the second half only three minutes old when a long throw-in was poked into the net from close range. They equalized with a goal that looked suspiciously offside, but a forward duly scored from ten yards. Notts won the seven-goal thriller with a brilliant Langstaff goal. Cameron surged forward, crossed the ball, and, with a first-time volley, Langstaff smashed the ball home from the edge of the six-yard box to score his 21st goal of the season.

Match 23	Notts County (1st) 2-0 Gateshead (23rd)	Attendance 5,539
Tue 13 Dec 2022 19:45	Francis 41' Rodrigues 61'	

<pre>
                        Slocombe
          Brindley   Baldwin   Cameron (Capt.)
   Nemane   Chicksen (Bajrami 46')
          Austin   Palmer   Francis (Bostock 62')   Rodrigues
                    Langstaff (Scott 70')
</pre>

Subs: Bajrami, Bostock, O'Brien, Castro, Scott
(no substitute goalkeeper)

Not in the squad: Rawlinson (injured), Mitchell, Young (Gk), Adebayo-Rowling, Mahovo. Vincent, Brooks (Gk), Munakandafa and Taylor out on loan.

There were three changes to the team victorious at Maidenhead. Nemane for Adebayo-Rowling, Austin for Castro, and Francis for O'Brien.

Notts earned a 1-1 draw at Gateshead in August – an own goal two minutes from time gave them a reprieve. Since then, Gateshead had struggled to find any kind of form and they were just one place off the bottom of the league.

As in many of their matches this season, Notts once again controlled most of the first half. Langstaff had a good header from 12 yards tipped over the crossbar by the goalkeeper in the tenth minute. However, Gateshead were prepared to take the initiative on occasions, unlike some other teams who had visited Meadow Lane, and Notts did not have it all their own way. With half-time in sight Notts took the lead when a Nemane shot was blocked and the rebound fell to Francis who shot into the net from the edge of the penalty area for his first goal of the season.

Notts increased their lead on the hour mark when a cross by Palmer was headed goalwards by Cameron. The ball looked destined for the corner of the net but as it fell Rodrigues was there to make sure it crossed the line. As the second half progressed the match became more one-sided but Notts, despite good opportunities created by Nemane, were unable to increase their lead as Gateshead finally looked a beaten team.

Because of injury Chicksen did not return for the second half, and Langstaff, a few minutes after he experienced a strong challenge, hobbled slowly off the pitch.

This match brought Notts to the mid-point of their season. The victory meant they remained top of the league, with a four-point advantage over Wrexham in second position and an eleven-point advantage over Chesterfield in third position. With only one defeat, 54 points and 59 goals, it was hoped Notts' excellent form would continue in the second half of the season to achieve a return to EFL League Two.

National League Table 14 December 2022

		GP	W	D	L	GF	GA	GD	Pts
1	**Notts County**	**23**	**16**	**6**	**1**	**59**	**21**	**+38**	**54**
2	Wrexham	22	15	5	2	55	19	+36	50
3	Chesterfield	21	13	4	4	43	25	+18	43
4	Woking	22	12	4	6	37	22	+15	40
5	Barnet	21	11	3	7	40	38	+2	36
6	Southend Utd	22	9	7	6	30	20	+10	34
7	Solihull Moors	21	9	6	6	35	24	+11	33
8	Boreham Wood	21	8	7	6	25	21	+4	31
9	Eastleigh	23	9	4	10	26	29	-3	31
10	Halifax Town	22	9	4	9	21	27	-6	31
11	Bromley	21	8	6	7	31	29	+2	30
12	Wealdstone	22	8	6	8	26	33	-7	30
13	Dagenham & R.	20	8	5	7	34	36	-2	29
14	Altrincham	23	7	8	8	33	42	-9	29
15	Dorking Wanderers	24	8	5	11	42	54	-12	29
16	York City	23	7	7	9	26	24	+2	28
17	Maidenhead Utd	23	8	4	11	25	31	-6	28
18	Aldershot Town	21	8	2	11	30	33	-3	26
19	Yeovil Town	22	4	11	7	17	21	-4	23
20	Maidstone Utd	24	5	6	13	30	53	-23	21
21	Oldham Athletic	21	5	5	11	22	33	-11	20
22	Torquay Utd	23	4	6	13	27	46	-19	18
23	Gateshead FC	22	3	8	11	25	38	-13	17
24	Scunthorpe Utd	23	3	7	13	27	47	-20	16

Position 1 Automatic promotion to EFL League Two
Positions 2-7 Promotion playoffs (one team promoted)
Positions 21-24 Relegated

Chapter 22: The second half of the season (matches 24-46)

FA Trophy 3rd Round Tue 20 Dec 2022 19:45	**Notts County 2-1 Chorley** Austin 33' goal 18' own goal 45'	Attendance 2,040

```
                        Young
          Brindley    Bajrami    Cameron (Capt.)
    Nemane                              Adebayo-Rowling
            Palmer    Bostock    O'Brien (Francis 68')
              Austin      Scott (Mitchell 70')
```

Subs: Slocombe (Gk), Mahovo, Francis, Cisse, Castro, Rodrigues, Mitchell

Not in the squad: Rawlinson, Chicksen, Langstaff (all injured). Baldwin rested. Vincent, Brooks (Gk), Munakandafa and Taylor - out on loan.

Luke Williams took the opportunity to 'rest and rotate'. He introduced U19's midfielder, Madou Cisse, to senior football with a place amongst the substitutes.

The match was postponed from the previous Saturday due to a frozen pitch. Chorley, a team one level below Notts, were in a solid 11th position in National League North with a record this season of P21 W8 D7 L6 F29 A21 PTS31

Although Bajrami, Palmer, and Bostock (making his first Notts start) all had opportunities in the opening exchanges, it was Chorley who took the lead. The Notts defence were slow to react to a cross from the left and a forward was able to glide the ball beyond Young. Five minutes later the same player almost scored a second, but he was unable to make contact with a cross from the right. With half time near Nemane featured in two Notts goals. For the equalizer, his cross from the left found Scott and his header was pushed away by the goalkeeper, but only to Austin who quickly tapped home the rebound from three yards. Notts took the lead when Austin passed incisively to Nemane and his low cross from the right struck a Chorley defender and rolled slowly into the corner of the net. In between the two goals the goalkeeper made an excellent save from an Austin header.

The only real scare of the second half for the Notts defence came after five minutes when Young ran out of his area to clear the ball but fouled a forward in the process. He received a yellow card and an ankle injury, although he completed the match. Notts were unable to capitalize on their superiority, mainly due to a good display by the visitor's goalkeeper. His saves denied Austin (who was excellent throughout), Bostock, and Francis.

It transpired that Young's injury was more serious than first thought, and goalkeeper Tiernan Brooks was recalled from his loan at Hednesford to provide cover for Sam Slocombe.

Match 24 Mon 26 Dec 2022 15:00	**Notts County (1ˢᵗ) 4- 1 Oldham Athletic(21ˢᵗ)** Scott 4', 43' goal 5' Cameron 9', Rodrigues 41'	Attendance 9,789

```
                        Slocombe
         Brindley       Baldwin        Cameron (Capt.)
   Nemane                                            Chicksen
         Palmer (Castro 69')        Francis (Bostock 69')
              Austin                 Rodrigues (Mitchell 69')
                         Scott
```

Subs: Bajrami, Bostock, Adebayo-Rowling, Castro, Mitchell
(no substitute goalkeeper)

Not in the squad: Rawlinson, O'Brien (trapped nerve), Langstaff, and Young (Gk) all injured. Mahovo and Brooks (Gk). Vincent, Munakandafa and Taylor out on loan.

Luke Williams reverted to the team which defeated Gateshead in the last league match, with the exception that Scott replaced the injured Langstaff.

On Christmas Day it was announced that Matt(y) Palmer had signed a new contract until the end of the 2024-25 season.

Oldham, relegated after finishing next to the bottom of EFL League Two at the end of last season, had continued their poor form into this season. They had the worst away record in The National League (no wins, four draws, seven defeats, only five goals scored) and were in the relegation zone. In nine matches against teams currently in 15ᵗʰ position and below in the league table they were undefeated, but they had managed just three points (a home victory) in twelve matches against team's 14ᵗʰ and above. Only two teams had scored fewer than their 22 goals.

Both teams scored in the first five minutes. Notts took the lead when an excellent cross by Austin was headed home by Scott from the edge of the six-yard box. Oldham equalized straightaway when, after some good passes, a shot from ten yards was swept beyond Slocombe. But, after Chicksen had hit a post on seven minutes, Notts were ahead again two minutes later. Francis took a free kick from 23 yards which the goalkeeper could only palm out to Cameron who shot powerfully into the net from the corner of the six-yard box, for his first goal of the season. In the five minutes before half time Notts scored two more goals. Under pressure from Scott the goalkeeper was unable to collect Cameron's cross and the ball rebounded off him to Rodrigues who, unchallenged, side footed the ball home from eight yards. The fourth goal came after another Cameron cross found Rodrigues who headed the ball down to Scott and he converted from close range.

Notts controlled the second half, and had a number of opportunities to score, but a resolute Oldham defence had luck on their side and they managed to prevent further goals.

31 December 2022

Our owners Chris and Alex Reedtz issued a new year's message to supporters

As we say goodbye to an eventful 2022 and welcome what's sure to be an exciting 2023, we would like to wish our fans a very happy new year and thank them for their tremendous, continued support. While 2022 didn't bring us the promotion we all wanted, we believe it has nevertheless been a year of positive progress with plenty of enjoyable and memorable moments.

Clearly, the biggest decision and challenge we faced this year was appointing the right head coach to lead us into this season following the departure of Ian Burchnall. We are, of course, very glad that we gave that responsibility to Luke Williams, who has taken us to the top of the table and established an incredibly effective and appealing style of play. Our thanks go to him, his staff and players for their excellent performance so far, which we're sure will continue into the New Year and beyond. Automatic promotion has always been our number-one aim and we're delighted to find ourselves in a strong position to go on and achieve it this season. There's still a lot of football to be played, of course, and we face very competitive opposition, but we have full belief in Luke and the team.

January brings inevitable speculation around players coming in and out – but our stance is the same as ever. We would only consider selling a player if we believed the offer would benefit our push for promotion, and we will only consider new signings who will significantly help the squad. Luke has done a brilliant job of moulding a tight-knit group of players who are consistently delivering excellent results and, while we are constantly striving for improvement, we must appreciate the work of those who have got us into this position and give them our backing.

Away from the field, we have been pleased to make several investments in the club's long-term infrastructure this year, including the installation of new state-of-the-art floodlights and the completion of Nottingham Padel Centre. In terms of future projects, we're in the final stages of approving a total replacement of the PA system at Meadow Lane, with work to begin in the New Year. We believe this significant investment will greatly enhance the match day experience for our supporters and help create a more vibrant atmosphere. We have also approved proposals for an ambitious, exciting and highly-impactful marketing project which will boost the club's efforts to attract fans of the future.

It's been very encouraging to see our supporter base continue to increase this season, with an average gate of 8,000 and more than 4,000 season ticket holders. This was also the year that we broke our own National League attendance record with an incredible crowd of 16,511 against Yeovil Town. Who knows - maybe the final match of the season against York City will give us the chance to break it again!

Match 25	**Oldham Athletic (22ⁿᵈ) 2-2 Notts County (1ˢᵗ)**	Attendance 7,312
Sun 1 Jan 2023 15:00	goals 53', 78' (pen.) Langstaff 51', Scott 57'	(Notts 1,249)

                         Slocombe
         Brindley   Baldwin   Bajrami
   Nemane   Cameron (Capt.)
              Palmer   Bostock (Castro 82')
        Austin (Scott 54')   Rodrigues
                  Langstaff (O'Brien 75')

Subs: Chicken, Francis, O'Brien, Castro, Scott
(no substitute goalkeeper)

Not in the squad: Rawlinson (not match fit), Adebayo-Rowling, Mitchell, Mahovo, and Brooks (Gk). Vincent, Munakandafa and Taylor out on loan. Brad Young (Gk) recalled by Leicester City to continue his rehabilitation from a knee injury.

For the double header return fixture, six days on, Luke Williams made three changes. Bajrami, Bostock (first league start), and (fit again) Langstaff, replaced Chicksen, Francis, and Scott respectively.

Although Notts had the most possession, the first half was a rather uneventful affair with neither goalkeeper troubled. However, the match burst into life at the beginning of the second half.

Notts took the lead when Baldwin passed to Nemane who scampered down the right, moved inside and crossed low towards the six-yard box from where Langstaff beat a defender to the ball and slotted home to score his 22ⁿᵈ goal of the season. But two minutes later Oldham equalized when, in a counterattack, Slocombe ran outside his penalty area to intercept a pass and, instead of a clearance, lost control of the ball which found Cameron. He was taken by surprise and a forward robbed him and ran on to shoot into the empty net from 25 yards. Within three minutes of his arrival from the substitutes bench, Scott restored Notts' lead. Palmer released Nemane, his cross hit a defender and fell to the unmarked Scott who scored from eight yards. There were just over ten minutes left when the referee adjudged Cameron had committed a foul following a high free kick into the penalty area. Slocombe was sent the wrong way by the spot kick. In the closing stages both teams missed an opportunity to score the winner – Notts, after Castro's astute pass released Cameron and his low cross whizzed through a crowded six-yard box. After a quick break down the left by Oldham the ball was crossed to a forward but from a few yards out he lifted the chance high over Slocombe's crossbar.

Although Notts nearly suffered a last-minute defeat, their first match of 2023 ended in frustration and disappointment as they conceded the lead twice with two preventable goals. Their lead at the top of the league was now two points over Wrexham (who had one match in hand) and nine points over Chesterfield (who had two matches in hand).

Match 26	**Aldershot Town (19th) 0-3 Notts County (1st)**	Attendance 2,039
Sat 7 Jan 2023 15:00	O'Brien 26',	(Notts 454)
	Rodrigues 56'	
	Nemane 89'	

Slocombe

Brindley   Baldwin   Cameron (Capt.) (Bajrami 66')

Nemane   Chicksen

O'Brien   Palmer   Rodrigues (Bostock 66')

Langstaff   Scott (Castro 80')

Subs: Bajrami, Francis, Bostock, Castro, Mitchell
(no substitute goalkeeper)

Not in the squad: Rawlinson (not match fit), Adebayo-Rowling (slight injury), Austin (ill), Mahovo, and Brooks (Gk).

Following the draw at Oldham on New Year's Day, Chicksen, O'Brien, and Scott were preferred to Bajrami, Bostock, and Austin.

Munakandafa, recalled from his loan at Basford Utd (22 appearances) to enable him to join National League North Boston Utd on loan until the end of the season. Taylor out on loan, at Dagenham & Redbridge, until 8 January. Notts midfielder Frank Vincent had been on loan at Aldershot for most of the season and scored one goal in his 20 appearances. The loan expired with this match, and he was omitted from the Aldershot team as a condition of the loan.

Aldershot were five points clear of the relegation zone. Notts had a comfortable 2-0 victory at Meadow Lane in mid-September. They had lost five of their last seven, including both over Christmas and the New Year.

On a windy, showery, afternoon, the teams were evenly matched in the first 25 minutes. The only opportunity of note fell to Langstaff, but his header was saved by the goalkeeper. Notts took the lead through O'Brien who scored from close range after a Langstaff shot, following a low cross by Nemane, had been blocked, and O'Brien fired the rebound home from inside the six-yard box. Notts controlled the remainder of the first half but were unable to add to their single goal.

Although Aldershot made the occasional foray into the Notts half, it was Notts who remained in control during the second 45 minutes. Rodrigues scored the second goal with a curled placement into the corner of the net from twenty yards, after he had received a Langstaff pass. In the final minute, the goalkeeper cleared a back pass straight to Nemane, who composed himself and then lifted the ball 30 yards into the empty net from near the right touchline.

Since Notts' relegation to The National League, they had been defeated in all three previous visits to Aldershot. Wrexham and Chesterfield were engaged in FA Cup third round fixtures, so these three points increased Notts' lead at the top of the league.

Match 27	**Notts County (1st) 1-1 Boreham Wood (13th)**	Attendance 6,033
Tue 10 Jan 2023 19:45	Scott 56' goal 44'	

                    Slocombe
        Brindley   Baldwin   Cameron (Capt.)
Nemane   Chicksen
        Palmer   Bostock   Rodrigues (Austin 73')
              Langstaff   Scott (Mitchell 87')

Subs: Bajrami, Francis, O'Brien, Austin, Mitchell
(no substitute goalkeeper)

Not in the squad: Rawlinson (not match fit), Adebayo-Rowling (slight injury), Vincent, Mahovo, and Brooks (Gk). Munakandafa and Taylor out on loan – Taylor's, at Dagenham & Redbridge, extended until 12 February. Quevin Castro's loan at Notts ended yesterday. Although Luke Williams wanted him to stay Castro decided to return to West Bromwich Albion "to pursue opportunities to play more regularly elsewhere".

Following the comfortable win over Aldershot, the only change was in midfield where Bostock came in for O'Brien.

Club captain Kyle Cameron was named The National League's December 'Player of the Month'. Although primarily a defender, his attacking style meant he had five goal assists (and one goal) so far this season.

Boreham Wood, although in mid table, were only five points off a playoff place, with matches in hand over some in a higher position. They held Notts to a 2-2 draw in mid-August but had won only one of their last ten in the league. In their last match they drew with League One Accrington Stanley in the third round of the FA Cup.

On a wet and windy evening Notts started impressively, and three minutes passed before a BW player touched the ball! In the fourth minute, Scott released Langstaff for a one-on-one with the goalkeeper who rushed forward and denied Notts' leading goal scorer. But, after 25 minutes, as the rain became torrential, BW nearly took the lead after Palmer was dispossessed, and a 17-yard shot hit a post. Notts retaliated and the BW goalkeeper saved shots from Nemane and Langstaff. However, the visitors took the lead just before half time after Slocombe did well to block a shot with his feet, but the loose ball was tapped home from close range by an unmarked forward.

The weather improved for the second half and, after Chicksen and Cameron had tested the goalkeeper, Bostock lifted a pass to Scott who equalized with a superb header. On 60 minutes Slocombe palmed a 25-yard free kick away for a corner, before Scott headed a Nemane cross just wide. From a BW corner kick an attacking header from near the penalty spot hit the top of the crossbar.

A Wrexham (two matches in hand) victory reduced Notts' lead at the top to three points. Chesterfield's match postponed, so their fixtures were piling up!

On Friday 13 January 2023 Club News revealed:

New contract: Luke Williams

Head coach commits to longer-term deal

We're delighted to announce that our head coach Luke Williams has signed a new contract which commits him to the club until the end of the 2026-27 season.

Williams has made an incredible impact since arriving in June, leading us to the top of the Vanarama National League table in sensational style. The free-flowing, attacking style of play he has implemented has resulted in us topping the league's scoring charts with 69 goals in 27

matches – and we've been particularly rampant away from home, averaging an incredible three goals per game on the road.

And our owners Chris and Alex Reedtz are delighted that Williams, along with his assistant Ryan Harley, have agreed to new terms.

"We have been hugely impressed with Luke both as a head coach and a colleague," they said.

"On the pitch, he has been delivering amazing results and consistently enjoyable performances, which is the combination every football club strives for. Away from the field, the board enjoy a very healthy and constructive relationship with Luke and his staff which we believe is helping to take the club to another level. We would like to place on record our thanks to Luke and Ryan for their fantastic work so far. We're very excited to see what the future holds with them at the helm."

Luke Williams, who currently has us on an 18-match unbeaten run, was equally effusive in his praise for the board.

"As a manager or head coach, it can be incredibly difficult to find a club that closely matches your own philosophy and values," he said.

"I feel very fortunate to have found that here, particularly so early in my career, and I'm so pleased that Chris and Alex have put their faith in Ryan and me. We should all be proud of the work we've done so far, but I feel it's important to stress that we're only six months into our journey together and I know that we're only going to get stronger.

"The foundations Chris and Alex have laid for this club are phenomenal and I'm honoured to be the person they want to lead the team at this very important juncture in the club's history.

"It would mean the world to me to be part of the collective effort to take Notts back into the EFL – and the prospect of what we could go on to achieve from there is incredibly exciting.

"For now, though, as clichéd as it sounds, our focus has to be on the next match and helping the players maintain the superb levels they have consistently produced so far this season."

FA Trophy 4th Round	Notts County 2-2 Maidstone Utd	Attendance 2,405
Sun 15 Jan 2023 15:00	(won 6-5* after pens.)	
	Chicksen 63', goals 40' (pen.), 57'	
	Austin 84'	

Mair

Bajrami   Rawlinson*   Baldwin*   Cameron (Capt.)

Palmer   Francis*   Austin*

Nemane (Cisse 59')   Chicksen (Gill 65')

Mitchell*

Subs: Slocombe, O'Brien, Langstaff, Fearon (U19 wing back), Cisse (U19 midfielder), Gill (U19 attacking midfielder). N.B. Six named – seven allowed.

Not in the squad, because of injury/illness: Brindley, Adebayo-Rowling, Bostock, Rodrigues, Scott, Mahovo. Vincent (cup-tied when on loan at Aldershot) and Brooks (Gk). Munakandafa and Taylor - out on loan.

Earlier in the week, goalkeeper Archie Mair was signed on loan, from Championship club Norwich City, until the end of the season. The 21-year-old, a Scotland U-21 international, had gained most of his senior experience on loan at King's Lynn Town (25 matches) when they were members of The National League, in season 2020-21. Just before Christmas he played five matches for Dartford (National League South) while on emergency loan.

Jim O'Brien, who signed for Notts (from Bradford City) in January 2019 had now been a 'Magpie' for the last four years. He played in the team relegated from League Two at Swindon on 4 May 2019 and was the only player still at the club after that defeat, except goalkeeper Tiernan Brooks who was an 'Apprentice Under Contract' at the time. O'Brien was released a few weeks later but re-signed on 1 August 2019, just two days before he played in Notts' first ever match in non-league football – a 1-0 defeat at Eastleigh.

Maidstone, comprehensively beaten 3-0 at Meadow Lane in late October, had descended towards the basement of The National League in recent weeks following six consecutive defeats. Only one team had conceded more goals than their 59. They recently sacked their manager!

New goalkeeper Mair was at fault with both Maidstone goals. For the first he passed to Baldwin just outside the penalty area who was unable to control the ball. Mair's two footed lunge then felled a forward, and he was beaten by the subsequent spot kick. For Maidstone's second he ran out of his penalty area and intercepted the ball but, under pressure, then passed to a forward who lifted the ball into the empty net from 35 yards.

Notts scored their first when Palmer's shot rebounded off a defender to Chicksen who confidently stroked the ball into the far corner of the net from seven yards. The equaliser came when Palmer crossed to Austin on the edge of the six-yard box. The goalkeeper palmed his header back to him, and he reacted quickly to shoot home. Palmer took the first of Notts' sudden death penalties, but his shot was saved and Notts disappointingly bowed out of the FA Trophy.

Match 28	**Notts County (2ⁿᵈ) 1-0 Halifax Town (16ᵗʰ)**	Attendance 7,548
Sat 28 Jan 2023 15:00	Langstaff 38'	

Slocombe
Rawlinson Baldwin Cameron (Capt.)
Nemane   Chicksen
Rodrigues Palmer O'Brien (Scott 71') Austin (Jones 75')
Langstaff

Subs: Bajrami, Bostock, Vincent, Scott, Jones
(no substitute goalkeeper)

Not in the squad: Brindley (injured), Adebayo-Rowling, Francis, Mitchell, Mahovo, Mair (Gk). Brooks (Gk) on a new (month long) loan at Boston United of National league North. Munakandafa and Taylor also out on loan.

Luke Williams made three changes to the eleven who started the last league match on 10 January, a draw at home to Boreham Wood: Rawlinson, O'Brien and Austin replaced Brindley, Bostock, and Scott.

Earlier in the week Notts signed 25-year-old winger/attacking midfielder Jodi Jones, from EFL League One Oxford United, on loan until the end of the season. Most of his career had been with Coventry City, where he appeared in the Championship, League One and League Two. On the opening day of the 2017/18 season, he scored a hat-trick against Notts playing for Coventry. Three months later his highly promising career was halted when he suffered a serious cruciate ligament injury. Since then, injury had limited his appearances but he had now fully recovered and was ready to recommence his football journey. Between September and November 2022, although born in London, he made four international appearances for Malta.

Halifax made a bad start to the season, and when Notts won at 'The Shay' on 27 August they were bottom of the league. Since then, they had slowly improved although in their last four league matches only one point had been earned – a draw and three defeats. Only Yeovil had scored fewer than Halifax's 24.

Notts made a good start and had a goal (narrowly) disallowed for offside on eight minutes after an excellent Rodrigues cross had been headed home by Langstaff. Their superiority continued and they took a deserved lead when a poor back pass was intercepted by Langstaff who rounded the goalkeeper and calmly placed the ball into the net beyond a covering defender.

The second half was all Notts, but a good defensive display by Halifax meant they did not get the goals their attacking play and domination deserved.

Notts' last two league fixtures had been postponed (frozen pitches at Chesterfield and Solihull). Wrexham had played, and won, their two matches in hand and overtaken Notts at the top of The National League with a three-point advantage. After this Notts victory both had the same points but Wrexham (FA Cup fixture this weekend) had a superior, by plus two, goal difference.

Match 29	**Solihull Moors (12th) 1-2 Notts County (2nd)**	Attendance 2,260
Tue 31 Jan 2023 19:45	goal 22' Rodrigues 36', 80' (penalties)	(Notts 894)

Slocombe
Rawlinson Baldwin Cameron (Capt.)
Nemane   Chicksen
Palmer Bajrami (Bostock 63') Rodrigues (Austin 82')
Langstaff Scott (Jones 63')

Subs: Bostock, O'Brien, Austin, Vincent, Jones
(no substitute goalkeeper)

Not in the squad: Brindley (injured), Adebayo-Rowling, Francis, Mitchell, Mahovo, Mair (Gk). Brooks (Gk), Munakandafa and Taylor out on loan.

Just two changes to the eleven which started against Halifax: Bajrami and Scott came in for O'Brien and Austin.

Solihull, managed by Neal Ardley (Notts manager November 2018-March 2021) were defeated 1-0 at Meadow Lane at the end of August. Between the start of the season on 6 August 2022 and 1 November 2022 Solihull lost only three league matches. Since then, their form had been poor with seven defeats and two victories. The second victory came in their last match, three days ago, when they won 0-3 at Dorking (the only team to inflict a league defeat on Notts).

After an uninspiring first 20 minutes it was Solihull who gained the initiative. Cameron was dispossessed just inside the Solihull half. Two forwards ran at the Notts defence, exchanged passes, and the finish was clinical from just outside the six-yard box. Notts equalized when Bajrami slid a pass to Scott in the penalty area. He was brought down, and Rodrigues sent the goalkeeper the wrong way with a confident spot kick. In the final minute of the first half Solihull breached the Notts defence and a forward ran through on goal with only Slocombe to beat but the poor shot went tamely wide.

In the first minute of the second half Solihull beat the offside trap but, after a forward had taken the ball past Slocombe he was unable to prevent the ball running out of play. Langstaff then had a great chance to put Notts ahead but, after he had received a Rodrigues pass, he dragged his shot just wide of the far post. In the 54th minute Notts got their first corner kick of the match, and a succession of corners followed as they became the dominant team. However, with ten minutes of normal time remaining, it was a second penalty which provided the opportunity to take the lead. Rodrigues took a short corner to Palmer who was barged to the ground. The Portuguese took the spot kick and shot emphatically into the roof of the net. In a final flurry Langstaff and Jones squandered good chances, but in the end Notts just about deserved the victory.

Notts gave a patchy performance, but 894 of their supporters witnessed the creation of a new club record - 20 consecutive league matches unbeaten, including 15 victories. They returned to the top of the league with a three-point lead over Wrexham (no fixture today, so, again, two matches in hand).

Match 30	Torquay Utd (21ˢᵗ) 1-2 Notts County (1ˢᵗ)	Attendance 2,621
Sat 4 Feb 2023 15:00	goal 42' Langstaff 35', Rodrigues 48' (pen)	(Notts 489)

Slocombe

Rawlinson (Bajrami 87')   Baldwin   Cameron (Capt.)

Nemane   Chicksen

Palmer   Bostock   Rodrigues   Austin (Jones 55')

Langstaff (Scott 80')

Subs: Bajrami, O'Brien, Vincent, Scott, Jones
(no substitute goalkeeper)

Not in the squad: Brindley, Adebayo-Rowling, Francis, Mahovo, Mair (Gk). Brooks (Gk), Munakandafa and Taylor out on loan. Earlier in the week striker Kairo Mitchell was loaned to fellow National League club Eastleigh for the remainder of the season.

After the record-breaking match at Solihull four days ago, Bostock and Austin were preferred to Bajrami and Scott.

Torquay had been in, or around, the relegation zone all season. They were defeated 4-0 at Meadow Lane at the end of October (at Wrexham they lost 6-0). However, they had won two of their last three league matches including a 1-1 draw at third in the league Woking four days ago.

After a combative and physical start by Torquay, Notts were awarded a series of free kicks. On 25 minutes Slocombe was required to make an excellent save to prevent a Rawlinson own goal when he clawed away his back header for a corner kick. Ten minutes later Notts took the lead after a move of eight passes ended when Rawlinson crossed to Langstaff on the edge on the penalty area. He swiveled to create space for himself before a hard, low, shot was flashed into the corner of the net. The equalizer came just over five minutes later. A counterattack, after Bostock had misplaced a pass, gave a forward a chance and he produced a good finish from near the penalty spot. Immediately after their goal Torquay substituted a player who should have been sent off by the referee. Notts, apart from the goal, had given the home goalkeeper an easy 45 minutes.

In the third minute of the second half Notts regained the lead after Rodrigues passed to Nemane, who was floored in the penalty area. Rodrigues sent the goalkeeper the wrong way with his third spot kick in four days. On 65 minutes he received a second yellow card (for hand ball as it was about to go out of play for a goal kick) and was sent off! Bearing in mind the ferocity of Torquay's play, particularly in the first half, it was a 'no common sense' decision, but technically the referee was correct. The Radio Nottingham commentary duo, Charlie Slater and ex-Notts player Mark Stallard, described the referee's control throughout as "fraught with inconsistency", and that's putting it mildly.

In the circumstances it was a tremendous performance by Notts, which Luke Williams enthused about in his after-match interview. As Wrexham also won, 1-2 at Altrincham, the positions at the top remained unchanged – Notts still first.

Match 31	**Chesterfield (5th) 1-2 Notts County (1st)**	Attendance 9,706
Sat 11 Feb 2023 17:20	goal 45'+3 Langstaff 25',	(Notts 1,961)
	Chicksen 71'	Live on BT Sport

Slocombe
Rawlinson   Baldwin   Cameron (Capt.)
Nemane   Chicksen
Jones   O'Brien (Bostock 60')   Palmer
Langstaff   Scott (Austin 78')

Subs: Brindley, Bajrami, Bostock, Vincent, Austin
(no substitute goalkeeper)

Not in the squad: Adebayo-Rowling, Francis, Mahovo, Mair (Gk). Brooks (Gk), Munakandafa, Taylor and Mitchell out on loan.

For Notts' third consecutive away fixture, there were three changes to the starting eleven which achieved the well-earned victory in Devon. With Rodrigues suspended (for this match only) **Jodi Jones** came in for his Notts debut following three substitute appearances – he tweeted **"first league start/90 minutes in 1908 days"**. O'Brien and Scott were preferred to Bostock and Austin.

Chesterfield and Notts drew 2-2 at Meadow Lane in August. Between 22 October and 24 January, Chesterfield won nine of eleven league matches, with one draw and one defeat. However, they had been defeated in their last three league matches - at Barnet and Boreham Wood, and at home to Woking four days ago. As a result, Chesterfield had been displaced from third position by Woking (now 3rd) and Barnet (now 4th).

Langstaff almost scored in the second minute after a mistake by a defender allowed him to run into the penalty area. He diverted the ball beyond the goalkeeper (ex-Notts player Fitzsimons) but his attempt lacked power and the ball was cleared. Thereafter the match was even, until the 25th minute when Notts scored an incredible goal. Slocombe's long clearance (pass) over everyone dropped to the sprinting Langstaff who, under pressure from a defender, controlled the ball and placed it beyond Fitzsimons into the corner of the unguarded net from just inside the penalty area. What a goal! However, following a corner kick, Chesterfield equalized during a goalmouth scramble with the last kick of the first half.

The second half was only four minutes old when Jones put Langstaff through on goal with only Fitzsimons to beat but the goalkeeper spreadeagled himself and made a great save. Chesterfield's efforts to stay in the match were dealt a blow in the 64th minute when a player was sent off for a bad foul on Scott, for which he received a second yellow card. Soon after Notts regained the lead. After eleven passes, Nemane ran into the penalty area and fired a hard low cross into the six-yard box where Chicksen was on hand to turn the ball home. Despite a spirited response by The Spireites, Notts secured their 12th away victory.

Wrexham, (two matches in hand) also won, remain three points behind Notts.

Match 32	**Notts County (1st) 4-1 Barnet (4th)**	Attendance 6,891
Tue 14 Feb 2023 19:45	Scott 57', goal 7' Chicksen 76' Langstaff 81', 87'	

                              Slocombe
             Rawlinson   Baldwin   Cameron (Capt.)
Adebayo-Rowling (Jones 46')   Chicksen (Vincent 84')
               Palmer   Bostock   Rodrigues
               Langstaff   Scott (Austin 75')

Subs: Bajrami, O'Brien, Vincent, Austin, Jones
(no substitute goalkeeper)

Not in the squad: Nemane (rested), Brindley, Francis, Taylor, Mahovo and Mair (Gk). Brooks (Gk), Munakandafa, and Mitchell out on loan.

There were three changes to the team victorious at Chesterfield. Adebayo-Rowling replaced Nemane, and Bostock came in for O'Brien. Rodrigues returned with Jones rested after his first full league match in over five years!

This fixture had been postponed twice – by Notts, due to a FA Trophy postponement, and by Barnet, due to a FA Cup second round fixture. It was therefore a first meeting of the season between the two clubs.

In the last two seasons Notts had won all four matches: 4-2 (H), 1-4 (A), 0-5 (A), 6-1 (H). In early October Barnet lost 7-5 at Wrexham! However, since that heavy defeat they had climbed into a play-off position with just one defeat in 15 league matches, and only five goals conceded in their last eleven. Four days ago, they won 1-2 at Torquay in the fifth round of the FA Trophy!

Early nightmare: Cameron took a short free kick to Palmer, and he passed back to Baldwin, who lost control of the ball, and a Barnet forward placed it into the unguarded net from 30 yards. Slocombe was out of his goal in a position to receive a (possible) pass. Although Rodrigues had two excellent shots well saved, Notts looked rattled and disjointed against an adventurous Barnet who went close to increasing their lead on several occasions.

Notts improved in the second half, and five minutes after a Rodrigues shot had hit the outside of a post they scored a controversial equalizer. As a Barnet player lay injured for over a minute, Notts had shots blocked before Rawlinson headed to Scott who scored from six yards. In the next ten minutes a Barnet free kick from near the touchline hit the top of the crossbar, and a Bostock 20-yard thunderbolt was tipped over by the goalkeeper. Notts then scored three quick goals. Substitute Austin nodded a Jones cross to Chicksen who finished with a close-range header. Austin's second assist came when he passed to Langstaff, and he shot powerfully home from 13 yards. Finally, Vincent crossed to Jones and his goal bound shot was chested home by Langstaff. Unbelievable!

Wrexham drew at home to third place Woking, so Notts increased their lead at the top to five points, although Wrexham still had two games in hand.

Match 33	Yeovil Town (17ᵗʰ) 1-4 Notts County (1ˢᵗ)	Attendance 3,020
Sat 18 Feb 2023 15:00 goal 66'	Langstaff 4', 90'+3, 90'+4 Rodrigues 85' (pen)	(Notts 479)

```
                        Slocombe
            Bajrami    Rawlinson    Cameron (Capt.)
    Nemane (Vincent 86')                        Chicksen
        Palmer    O'Brien (Bostock 80')    Rodrigues    Austin (Jones 70')
                        Langstaff
```

Subs: Baldwin, Francis, Bostock, Vincent, Jones
(no substitute goalkeeper)

Not in the squad: Adebayo-Rowling (ankle), Scott (shoulder), Brindley, injured, Taylor, Mahovo and Mair (Gk). Brooks (Gk), Munakandafa, and Mitchell out on loan.

There were four changes to the team that halted Barnet's progress. Bajrami and O'Brien were preferred to Baldwin and Bostock. Nemane and Austin replaced the injured Adebayo-Rowling and Scott.

Yeovil had been in the lower half of The National League all season and had drawn 14 of their 28 matches. However, their recent form was good with only one defeat in 11 league matches (seven at home), including a visit to Meadow Lane on 19 November when they held Notts to a goalless draw in front of The National League record crowd – 16,511. Yeovil had scored fewest league goals (25) but had conceded only 28, one fewer than Notts. They were bottom of the 'Total Match Goals' table with an average of 1.89 in their matches.

Notts made the ideal start when Chicksen passed to Austin who ran to the edge of the penalty area, and his excellent cross was headed home by the unmarked Langstaff. Thereafter, it was an aggressive Yeovil who held the upper hand.

In the first ten minutes of the second half Palmer created two opportunities. First, he released Nemane and his cross-cum-shot went over the angle of post and crossbar, and shortly afterwards his header put Langstaff through. He lifted the ball over the goalkeeper but, from a narrow angle, his shot hit the outside of a post. With the match finely balanced Notts, not for the first time this season, contrived to present the opposition with a goal. When Bajrami and Slocombe failed to clear the ball near the edge of the penalty area an attacker took advantage and shot into the open net. Notts were reprieved when they were awarded a penalty after Palmer was brought down. Rodrigues sent the goalkeeper the wrong way with his spot kick. There was still time for Yeovil to hit the top of the Notts crossbar, and then miss a great chance to equalize, before Langstaff scored twice to complete a hat-trick. Rodrigues passed to him, and he shot home from 18 yards, and a minute later, after a lofted Chicksen pass, his first shot was saved but he kept his composure and scored from 15 yards.

Notts were not at their best, and the scoreline was an injustice for Yeovil. Wrexham also won, but Notts improved their goal difference, now 54 to 51!

Match 34	**Notts County (1st) 4-0 Southend United (6th)** Attendance 7,237
Tue 21 Feb 2023 19:45	Langstaff 18', 55'
	Austin 23', 83'

Slocombe
Rawlinson   Baldwin   Cameron (Capt.)
Jones (O'Brien 73')   Chicksen (Bajrami 84')
Palmer   Bostock   Rodrigues   Austin
Langstaff (Francis 65')

Subs: Mair (Gk), Bajrami, Taylor, Francis, O'Brien

Not in the squad: Adebayo-Rowling, Brindley, Vincent, Nemane, Scott (all injured) Mahovo. Brooks (Gk), Munakandafa, and Mitchell out on loan.

Luke Williams made three changes to the team fortunate to win at Yeovil. Baldwin returned in place of Bajrami, Jones and Bostock came in for Nemane and O'Brien respectively.

Southend held Notts to a 2-2 draw in early November, but their form then dipped. At the end of January, a judge adjourned a hearing with **HM R**evenue **& C**ustoms (HMRC), for money owed by Southend, to 1 March. They had won all four of their February league matches and returned to a promotion playoff position. Southend had the best defensive record in The National League – only 26 conceded in their 30 matches (Notts 30 conceded in 33). Their goals tally was 41 – Notts, the league's leading scorers, had more than double (84).

Notts started the match with plenty of possession and slick, accurate, passes. They were rewarded when Rodrigues slipped the ball to Langstaff who, from just inside the penalty area, gave the goalkeeper no chance when he curled his shot into the corner of the net. Five minutes later the lead was doubled when Austin scored his first Notts league goal (he had netted four cup goals). Bostock lifted a delightful pass to Austin on the edge of the six yard box, and he dived forward to plant his header into the net. An impressive Notts controlled the remainder of the first half.

The second half was ten minutes old when Rodrigues ran with the ball from well inside the Notts half, skillfully evaded attempts to halt his progress and waited for Langstaff to get in position just outside the corner of the penalty area. He then passed as Langstaff ran on, and with power and precision he scored his 32nd goal of the season from 12 yards. Southend should have scored on 70 minutes, but an unmarked forward shot against a post from six yards. However, Notts continued their domination and at the end of a superb sequence of passes Bostock again lifted the ball to Austin on the corner of the six yard box, and he smashed the ball into the roof of the net.

A top class performance by Notts who scored four (plus) goals for the tenth time. Wrexham also won (2-0) so they remained five points behind in second place, with two matches in hand, but the goal difference was now five in Notts' favour.

Match 35	**Notts County (1st) 1-2 Dagenham &**	Attendance 7,441
Sat 25 Feb 2023 17:20	**Redbridge (10th)**	Live on BT Sport
	Rodrigues 21' goals 31', 86'	

Slocombe
Rawlinson   Baldwin   Cameron (Capt.)
Nemane (Lemonheigh-Evans 71')   Chicksen
Palmer   Bostock (Jones 56')   O'Brien (Austin 56')   Rodrigues
Langstaff

Subs: Bajrami, Francis, Austin, Jones, Lemonheigh-Evans
(no substitute goalkeeper)

Not in the squad: Adebayo-Rowling, Brindley, Vincent, Scott (all injured). Mair (Gk), Taylor, Mahovo. Brooks (Gk), Munakandafa, and Mitchell on loan.

There were two changes to the team which destroyed Southend - Nemane and O'Brien preferred to Jones and Austin. Two days ago Notts signed 26 year old Connor Lemonheigh-Evans, from League Two Stockport County, on loan for the remainder of the season. At the end of the 2020-21 season, he was named in The National League 'Team of the Season' and also named the Torquay 'Player of the Season'. Last season, on 9 April 2022, he scored a hat-trick against Notts (lost 5-1). Luke

Williams explained "He could play anywhere in front of the back line for us – and do it well. He has the football brain you need to do that".

D & R were defeated 0-5 in early September, when Langstaff scored a hat-trick. They had been a mid-table team for most of the season. In their last seven league matches they had lost five and won two – last match a 2-1 home win. 24 hours before this match their manager departed "by mutual consent".

During an entertaining first half, Notts took the lead when Rodrigues created space for himself and directed a cross-shot into the corner of the net from just outside the penalty area. Unfortunately, ten minutes later he was caught in possession in the D & R half and from the counterattack the visitors equalized.

Notts dominated the second half, but a good D & R defensive display, aided by good goalkeeping and some luck, prevented a breakthrough by the Magpies. Jones and Langstaff hit a post. Shots were blocked. The ball was cleared off the goal line, and two strong penalty appeals were turned down by the referee. Then, with 90 minutes almost up, D & R won the match with another counterattack. The goal was scored by Inih Effiong, who made 12 appearances for Notts between January-March 2021 (one goal, a penalty) when on loan from League Two Stevenage. He received a pass, ran on, and, chased by Rawlinson and Baldwin, shot powerfully into the roof of the net from 18 yards. It was a goal reminiscent of Geoff Hurst's hat-trick goal as England won the 1966 World Cup Final. After this match Baldwin was shown a red card, in the players tunnel!

So, Notts' record 25 match unbeaten league run came to a dramatic and unfortunate end, after they lost for only the second time this season. Wrexham won 3-1 and, on 28 February, won 2-1 (both matches at home) to move one point above Notts at the top, and they still had one match in hand.

Match 36	Bromley (9th) 1-1 Notts County (2nd)	Attendance 3,417
Sat 4 Mar 2023 15:00	goal 20' (pen) Langstaff 90'+3	(Notts 632)

Brooks

Rawlinson   Bajrami (Lemonheigh-Evans 46')   Cameron (Capt.)

Nemane   Chicksen

Jones   Palmer   Rodrigues   Austin (Bostock 70')

Langstaff

Subs: Mair (Gk), Taylor, Bostock, O'Brien, Lemonheigh-Evans

Not in the squad: Slocombe, Adebayo-Rowling, Brindley, Vincent, Scott (all injured), Baldwin, Mahovo. Munakandafa and Mitchell out on loan. Earlier in the week Luke Williams reluctantly allowed midfielder Ed Francis to move to fellow National League club Gateshead, on loan, for the rest of this season - "in pursuit of more regular gametime".

There were four changes to the team which unluckily suffered an unexpected defeat against Dagenham & Redbridge. One was enforced: Baldwin, who received a red card in the player's tunnel at the end of that match, missed the first of a two-match suspension, and Bajrami took his place in defence. The injured Slocombe was absent for the first time this season, so 20-year-old goalkeeper Tiernan Brooks made his Notts debut. The other two changes were in midfield, where Austin and Jones were preferred to Bostock and O'Brien.

Since Bromley drew (1-1) at Meadow Lane on 1 November, they had lost only three of 17 league matches – twice to third placed Woking and once at top of the league Wrexham. Bromley's playing surface was artificial (4G) turf.

Notts' debutant goalkeeper Tiernan Brooks had a dramatic first 40 minutes. His first involvement was to face a penalty kick after Bajrami had pulled an attacker back in the penalty area. He saved the spot kick with an outstretched leg as he dived. Ten minutes later Bromley were awarded a second penalty when an attacker ran through with only Brooks to beat, who made a superb diving save and the forward fell over him. Brooks was booked for a foul. The same player took the kick, and this time scored. Unbelievably, Bromley should have been awarded a third penalty after 37 minutes. This time Brooks was adjudged to have committed a foul after losing possession in the penalty area. Video evidence showed the foul was just inside, rather than outside, the box.

Bajrami was substituted by Lemonheigh-Evans at the start of the second half with Cameron in central defence and Chicksen to his left. Jones moved to left wing back. Notts were much improved, and L-E missed an open goal. They got a deserved equalizer in time added after the full 90. Rodrigues' defence splitting pass put Langstaff through and he sent the ball past the diving goalkeeper.

Wrexham also dropped two points after a 2-2 draw at Maidenhead, who equalized in time added at the end of the second half! Wrexham remained one point ahead with one match in hand – away at D & R in three days' time.

National League Table 8 March 2023
(after Wrexham's victory at D & R)

		GP	W	D	L	GF	GA	GD	Pts
1	Wrexham	36	27	7	2	94	34	+60	88
2	**Notts County**	**36**	**25**	**9**	**2**	**90**	**33**	**+57**	**84**
3	Woking	36	19	8	9	60	38	+22	65
4	Chesterfield	35	18	7	10	59	43	+16	61
5	Barnet	35	18	5	12	66	59	+7	59
6	Boreham Wood	35	15	13	7	43	30	+13	58
7	Eastleigh	36	17	6	13	43	38	+5	57
8	Southend Utd	34	15	8	11	44	34	+10	53
9	Bromley	36	13	13	10	50	45	+5	52
10	Wealdstone	35	14	10	11	46	50	-4	52
11	Dagenham & Red.	36	15	6	15	53	60	-7	51
12	Solihull Moors	36	13	9	14	53	52	+1	48
13	Altrincham	36	12	10	14	54	65	-11	46
14	Oldham Athletic	35	12	8	15	47	51	-4	44
15	Maidenhead Utd	36	12	7	17	40	49	-9	43
16	Halifax Town	36	11	9	16	34	42	-8	42
17	York City	36	10	9	17	43	47	-4	39
18	Aldershot Town	36	11	6	19	49	61	-12	39
19	Dorking Wanderers	35	10	7	18	50	78	-28	37
20	Yeovil Town	34	7	15	12	29	38	-9	36
	================								
21	Gateshead FC	34	7	13	14	41	52	-11	34
22	Torquay Utd	35	7	9	19	41	64	-23	30
23	Scunthorpe Utd	36	7	9	20	41	67	-26	30
24	Maidstone Utd	37	5	9	23	39	79	-40	24

Position 1 Automatic promotion to EFL League Two
Positions 2-7 Promotion playoffs (one team promoted)
With ten matches to play, Notts almost guaranteed at least a second place finish. Positions 2 & 3 have a home semi-final playoff fixture (one leg only)
Positions 4-7 have quarter-final playoff fixtures (one leg only; 4 at home to 7, 5 at home to 6)

Match 37	**Notts County (2ⁿᵈ) 3-1 Dorking Wanderers (19ᵗʰ)**	Attend. 7,060
Sat 11 Mar 2023 17:20	Langstaff 19', 52' goal 12'	Live on BT
	Palmer 85'	Sport

                              Brooks
              Rawlinson   Bajrami   Chicksen
     Nemane   Jones (Vincent 77')
                  Palmer   O'Brien (Bostock 77')
                  Rodrigues   Austin (Lemonheigh-Evans 70')
                          Langstaff (Capt.)

Subs: Mair (Gk), Bostock, Vincent, Lemonheigh-Evans (five are allowed).

Not in the squad: Slocombe, Adebayo-Rowling, Brindley, Scott (all injured), Baldwin (suspended), Cameron (ill), Taylor (contract mutually terminated), Mahovo. Munakandafa, Mitchell and Francis out on loan.

There was just one change to the team which drew at Bromley - Captain Cameron missed his first match of the season through illness and Langstaff was made captain. Notts' leading scorer was named in the England 'C' squad earlier in the week for a match against Wales 'C' on 21 March.

Dorking gave Notts their first defeat of the season on 17 September, 3-1. They had lost seven of their last ten league matches, although they had drawn and then won their last two. They were top of the 'Total Match Goals' table with an average of 3.66 per match (Notts 4ᵗʰ with 3.42 per match). Only one team had a worse away record, and a worse defensive record – bottom of the league Maidstone. Dorking had not won away from home since 13 September.

Notts had most of the possession in the first ten minutes, but Dorking then missed two chances to take the lead before they scored. A strong run by an attacker was too much for O'Brien and his cross was flicked home at the near post. However, Notts soon equalized. Nemane's low cross was palmed away by the goalkeeper and the ball hit a defender and rebounded to Langstaff who easily scored from close range. The remainder of the half belonged to Notts, but, despite some near misses, the Dorking goalkeeper was never seriously troubled.

The second 45 minutes were controlled by Notts with Brooks often called upon, not to make saves but to spray the ball forward from inside the Notts half. They took the lead when Austin gained possession after some poor defensive play and Langstaff rifled home his cross from the edge of the six-yard box. Just before his substitution Austin had a shot headed off the line. The victory was sealed with a third goal when Chicksen ran forward with the ball and passed to Rodrigues who, not for the first time this season, stroked the ball forward into the penalty area, from where Palmer confidently finished the move with a seven-yard shot.

It was a deserved victory for Notts. League leaders Wrexham also won (1-0 at home to Southend) so the gap remained four points, but Notts reduced the goal difference between them from three to two.

Match 38 Tue 14 Mar 2023 19:45	**Notts County (2nd) 3-1 Eastleigh (5th)** Rodrigues 60', 76' goal 33' (pen) Langstaff 87'	Attendance 6,058

```
                        Brooks
        Rawlinson   Baldwin (Bajrami 55')    Chicksen
            Nemane                      Jones (Vincent 77')
              Palmer            Bostock (Austin 61')
              Rodrigues         Lemonheigh-Evans
                      Langstaff (Capt.)

         Subs: Cameron, Bajrami, O'Brien, Vincent, Austin
                   (no substitute goalkeeper)
```

Not in the squad: Slocombe, Adebayo-Rowling, Brindley, Scott (all injured), Mair (Gk), Mahovo. Munakandafa, Mitchell and Francis out on loan.

Following the victory over Dorking, Baldwin returned after suspension, in place of Bajrami, and Bostock and Lemonheigh-Evans (L-E) were preferred to O'Brien and Austin. It was L-E first Notts start after three substitute appearances.

In the reverse fixture Notts won 0-2 in mid-November. Eastleigh's recent form, since a 0-4 home defeat to Maidstone in the FA Trophy on 11 February, had been very good: P8 W6 D1 L1 scored 8 against 2.

In an entertaining first half an energetic Eastleigh pressed Notts, who were forced to bring Brooks into the game on numerous occasions to start forward movement. Notts began to settle as the 30-minute mark approached but they received a setback when, following an Eastleigh corner kick, L-E was penalized for holding back an opponent and the referee gave a penalty. Brooks faced his third spot kick in three matches and was sent the wrong way by the striker. For the third consecutive match Notts conceded the first goal, but they responded well and continued to build momentum as the half came to an end.

Notts, and Rodrigues, together with Austin after he came on as a substitute, were magnificent in the second half, which they dominated throughout. The equalizer came after Nemane crossed to Langstaff, who fed Rodrigues. He mesmerized four defenders with superb close control as he advanced towards the penalty spot, from where he expertly placed the ball beyond (ex-Notts) goalkeeper McDonnell. It was Notts' 100th goal of the season – 94 in the league, 6 in the FA Trophy and FA Cup. Ten minutes later Notts were awarded a penalty after a defender handled the ball. Rodrigues took the spot kick but McDonnell made a brilliant double save! Soon after L-E headed Brooks' long clearance to Austin. His shot was deflected to Rodrigues who calmly scored from 15 yards to give Notts a deserved lead. Just before the end Langstaff took his goal tally to 36 when he headed home from a corner kick – taken by Rodrigues.

Wrexham were without a fixture, which meant they again had a match in hand over Notts, and their lead at the top was reduced to one point, but both now had a goal difference of plus 61.

Match 39	Barnet (5th) 1-1 Notts County (2nd)	Attendance 2,969
Sat 18 Mar 2023 15:00	goal 45'+3 Langstaff 42'	(Notts 1,064)

Brooks
Rawlinson   Bajrami   Cameron (Capt.)
Nemane   Chicksen
Palmer   Bostock (Jones 60')
Rodrigues   Austin (Lemonheigh-Evans 60')
Langstaff

Subs: Mair (Gk), O'Brien, Vincent, Jones, Lemonheigh-Evans

Not in the squad: Slocombe, Adebayo-Rowling, Brindley, Baldwin, Scott, Morias, (all injured), Mahovo. Munakandafa, Mitchell, Francis out on loan.

Luke Williams made three changes to the team victorious over Eastleigh. Bajrami returned for the injured Baldwin. Fit again Cameron, and Austin replaced Jones and Lemonheigh-Evans.

On 15 March Notts signed centre forward Junior Morias (age 27) from Dagenham & Redbridge on a three-year deal, for an undisclosed fee. Earlier in his career he played in League One (Peterborough Utd), League Two (Wycombe Wanderers and Northampton Town), and the Scottish Premiership (St. Mirren). More recently he had played for Boreham Wood and King's Lynn in The National League, before he joined D & R in November 2021. The experienced, Jamaican born, striker played in 57 league matches for D & R, including both against Notts this season, and scored 21 goals.

In addition to the England 'C' international recognition given to Langstaff (see 11 March), Brooks and Jones (Maltese father) were this week named in the Republic of Ireland U21 and Malta squads respectively.

Since their 4-1 defeat at Meadow Lane on 14 February, Barnet had progressed to an FA Trophy semi-final, but in seven league matches they had won three and lost four. However, they were still in a playoff position, seven points clear of eighth place.

Notts dominated the first half, and Nemane had a cross shot pushed on to the angle of post and crossbar by the home goalkeeper for one of our nine corner kicks. They took the lead just before half time when another Rodrigues defence splitting pass into the penalty area fed Nemane who slid the ball to Langstaff, and he made no mistake from eight yards. However, with the last action of the half Barnet undeservedly equalized when a header, following a long throw-in, rattled the underside of the crossbar and bounced down over the line.

The second 45 minutes were more even and both teams could have won the match. Luke Williams was very disappointed with Notts' second half display.

Wrexham won 1-2 at Bromley and extended their lead to three points, with one match in hand. Notts were becalmed in second place. The playoff's beckoned.

Community Day: Adults £10, Concessions and Under 22 £5, Under 16 £1		
The annual discounted fixture on 19 November 2022: Adults £5, U16 £1 = Att. 16,511		
Match 40	**Notts County (2nd) 4-0 Scunthorpe Utd (22nd)**	Attendance 16,086
Sat 25 Mar 2023 15:00	Chicksen 7',	(1,750 Scunthorpe)
	Own goal 12'	
	Langstaff 73', 76'	

Slocombe (Mair 16')

Rawlinson   Bajrami   Cameron (Capt.)

Nemane (Austin 63')   Chicksen (Vincent 63')

Palmer   O'Brien   Bostock   Rodrigues

Langstaff

Subs: Mair (Gk), Brindley, Austin, Vincent, Mahovo

Not in the squad: Adebayo-Rowling, Baldwin, Scott, Morias, (all injured). Munakandafa, Mitchell, Francis out on loan. Brooks and Jones absent on international duty. On Monday 20th (the day before the international match) Notts announced that Langstaff had withdrawn from the England 'C' squad "as a precaution". On Thursday 23rd (shortly after this season's deadline for player registrations) Stockport County recalled Lemonheigh-Evans, just four weeks into a loan originally expected to be until the end of the season.

There were two changes to the team which drew at Barnet. Fit again Slocombe returned in goal, and O'Brien replaced Austin. Unfortunately, Slocombe suffered an early injury after a fierce challenge by a forward in an offside confrontation, and Mair came on for his Notts league debut.

With only one away victory all season, and a poor defensive record (71 conceded), Scunthorpe had been in, or near, the relegation zone throughout. They were defeated by Notts (1-4) in early December. However, they had recently signed four new players and had won two of their last three matches, including a 4-1 victory at home to Wealdstone a week ago.

Luke Williams described this superb Notts team performance as "classy". They outplayed the visitors throughout and were soon two goals ahead. Rodrigues confused the Scunthorpe defence when he allowed a long Bajrami pass to reach Nemane, who passed the ball to Rodrigues in the penalty area. His slide rule pass through the six-yard box found Chicksen and he had a simple finish. Nemane and Rodrigues combined again five minutes later to free Langstaff, and his fierce shot cannoned off a defender into the net for an own goal. In the second half Langstaff had a shot tipped on to the crossbar by the goalkeeper, before he scored two goals in three minutes. The first (Notts' 100th league goal) a close-range header following a superb Austin cross. For the second he swept Palmer's cross into the net to score his 39th goal of the season to equal Tom Keetley's all-time Notts record for a single season set in 1930-31.

Wrexham also won (3-0 at home to York) so Notts remained in second position.

Match 41 Tue 28 Mar 2023 19:45	**Altrincham (13th) 0-2 Notts County (2nd)** Langstaff 25' Rodrigues 47' (pen)	Attendance 2,011 (Notts 638)

Mair
Rawlinson (Brindley 68')   Bajrami   Cameron (Capt.)
Nemane (Vincent 73')   Chicksen
Palmer   Rodrigues (O'Brien 55')   Bostock   Austin
Langstaff

Subs: Brooks (Gk), Brindley, O'Brien, Vincent, Jones

Not in the squad: Slocombe, Adebayo-Rowling, Baldwin, Scott, Morias, (all injured). Mahovo. Munakandafa, Mitchell, Francis out on loan.

Following the comprehensive victory over Scunthorpe, Luke Williams made two changes. With Slocombe injured, on loan goalkeeper Mair made his first Notts league start, and Austin was preferred to O'Brien.

Notts defeated Altrincham 3-1 at Meadow Lane on 1 October. Throughout the season the Greater Manchester club had hovered around mid-table. Other than for a period between mid-November and mid-January, when they were undefeated for eight matches, their form had been inconsistent. On the plus side they had reached the semi-final of the FA Trophy, and beaten Wrexham in the fourth round of that cup competition.

It was an entertaining first half, with Notts in the ascendency. However, Altrincham were lively in attack and they gave The Magpies defence a few anxious moments. After 15 minutes Mair had to race out of his penalty area to avert the danger with a headed clearance. Notts controversially took the lead after 25 minutes following a quick free kick 20 yards from goal. Bostock slid the ball to the unmarked Langstaff near the penalty spot, and the statuesque Altrincham defence watched as our talisman scored his 40th goal of the season (in his 40th match) to equal the all-time National League single season goal scoring record, set in 2017-18. Altrincham had the chance to equalize from the penalty spot five minutes later when an ungainly tackle by Cameron felled a fast moving forward, but Mair made a brilliant save by diving to his right to palm the ball away for a corner kick.

The second half was only two minutes old when Notts were awarded a penalty when a defender handled a Nemane cross. Rodrigues sent the goalkeeper the wrong way with the spot kick. Thereafter Notts controlled the remainder of the match. Austin, Palmer, and Bostock came close to increasing the lead before, with ten minutes remaining, an Altrincham shot brushed the top of Mair's crossbar. In the 90th minute Langstaff rattled the home crossbar with an 18-yard shot.

The victory lifted Notts back to the top of the league on goal difference – Notts plus 67, Wrexham plus 65, but the Welsh club now had two matches in hand.

Jason Turner

On Friday 31 March 2023 Notts announced:

We are devastated to report the loss of our much-loved chief executive, Jason Turner.

Jason, who passed away suddenly last night aged 50, was appointed in 2016 and devoted himself to the club thereafter. He was an outstanding CEO who was respected across football having also worked for Bath City, Cardiff City, Plymouth Argyle and Newport County.

A statement from his mother, Jen, and father, David, reads: "Words cannot describe our sadness following the loss of our beloved son, Jason. We know this feeling will be shared by all of his colleagues and his many, many friends. While we come to terms with this news, we ask for our family's privacy to be respected."

Charlie Slater, BBC Radio Nottingham's Notts County reporter:

Jason shunned the spotlight personally, but drove Notts County into the light.

He was completely dedicated to his role as CEO and worked harder than anyone could imagine to ensure the football club moved in the right direction.

His impact can't be underestimated and Jason is as responsible as anyone for the club's current prosperity.

He went to battle for the Magpies when they almost went out of business and helped to drag the club through testing times during Covid, establishing himself as a leading figure in The National League.

Jason was passionate, diligent and kind. His charm lit up a room and he will leave a huge hole in the club he had grown to love so dearly.

It's tragic that he won't be around to see more prosperous days in Notts County's history that are undoubtedly approaching, and that he played a big part in.

Notts boss Luke Williams said the club had "lost a special person that we all loved".

"It's fair to say we are all suffering. Jason was a unique person because everything you could imagine had a link to him and he did everything in a spectacular way. There are many reminders of how great he was, so it has been challenging."

Williams said he and everyone at Notts had the privilege to learn from Jason and that he will remain an important influence as The National League high-flyers try to return to the English Football League.

"To drop our levels would be an insult, because everything you see the lads do on the pitch was a reflection of how Jason ran the club behind the scenes. We have to override the feeling of sadness with our responsibility to show respect to him and the incredible job that he did."

"Jason will be commemorated at Friday's home game against Wealdstone. A flag in tribute to him will be displayed in the Kop stand at Meadow Lane while both sides will wear black armbands, and a minute's applause will take place before kick-off. Turner's family will also be at the match, saying they could not miss the chance to join the club and its supporters "in remembering him at what was his second home".

"We have to use that in a positive way because we know what Jason would want - he would want us to kick on and we have to use that as motivation. We know how much he thought of us and want to repay that by doing it on the pitch."

Wrexham, Notts' rivals for automatic promotion from The National League:

"We enjoyed a great working relationship with Jason, and our thoughts are with his family, friends and all at Notts County at this time."

Hollywood star Ryan Reynolds, who co-owns the Welsh club with fellow actor Rob McElhenney, also paid tribute to Turner on social media.

"Gone way too soon," Reynolds wrote. "Love and condolences to his family and the top-notch organization of Notts County."

A tribute from owners Christoffer and Alexander Reedtz, who remember a much-loved CEO

We, like so many others, were shocked and devastated by the sudden loss of our chief executive, Jason Turner, last week.

Our thoughts continue to be with his loved ones, especially his family with whom we spent several hours on Friday as we all struggled to come to terms with the news.

It's impossible for us to truly describe how huge a loss Jason will be, both as a friend and colleague who was ever-present in our lives since we acquired the club nearly four years ago.

His warm personality, combined with his encyclopedic knowledge of football, breadth of experience, contacts, passion, work ethic, high standards and belief in the club's potential made it an easy decision for us to reinstate him as CEO – and we never regretted it.

In truth, though, Jason was more than a CEO. Each day he would go over and above what we would expect of him, driven always by a fierce determination to ensure the club was operating on a level which belied its position in the footballing pyramid.

While he would never be seen on camera or heard in interviews, Jason shared our willingness and desire to communicate openly with supporters, many of whom will have either received personal correspondence from him or read the regular updates he would publish on our website since he first arrived at Meadow Lane in 2016.

He was also a staunch advocate for good and fair governance – regularly speaking up not only on behalf of our club and supporters, but others too.

We should recognise the immense contribution he made in times of crisis, especially in the months ahead of our takeover when, while he was employed as Director of Football Operations, players and staff went unpaid and the club faced an ongoing winding-up petition, while also losing its EFL status for the first time in its history.

It would have been easy for someone of Jason's experience and reputation to move on – but his love and respect for the club kept him in post, ensuring we were greeted on our arrival by the perfect man to guide us on a path to recovery.

As we continue to grieve, we must plan to honour Jason in the way he and his family deserves.

We have been overwhelmed by the flood of tributes which followed Friday's announcement and, from 9am on Tuesday, we invite supporters to visit our club shop and leave a message in a book of condolence. In time, the book will be given to Jason's parents who we know have taken great comfort from the outpouring of love and respect over the last few days.

We will also be contacting the relevant authorities to arrange for a minute's applause to take place ahead of kick-off in Friday's home match against Wealdstone – a fixture which will be dedicated to Jason and his family, who will be in attendance. More details will follow in due course.

As difficult as it has been given the circumstances, we have been in regular dialogue with our senior management team over the weekend to ensure the club is in the best possible place to continue the strides we are making both on and off the field, of which we know Jason was so proud.

We have decided that, to enable the club to adequately prepare for Friday's match, we will reopen at 10am on Monday.

We recognise the bravery and commitment of our fantastic staff, who are facing an incredibly difficult period without the guidance, friendship and leadership they had become accustomed to under Jason. We know our supporters will be sympathetic and understanding towards them as we face up to the unthinkable prospect of life without him.

From this point, the club will naturally undergo a process of re-evaluation. Paramount to this will be ensuring Jason's many responsibilities are covered in the short term so the club is able to continue operating at the excellent levels he established.

We must also all rally behind Luke Williams, his staff and players who all loved Jason so much and will, despite their anguish, be doing everything they can to honour his memory by making it a strong end to the season.

Finally, we would like to express our immense gratitude to club chaplain, Rev. Liam O'Boyle, whose incredible kindness and support is appreciated so much by so many.

Rest in peace, Jason, and thank you.

Match 42	**Notts County (2ⁿᵈ) 3-0 Wealdstone (10ᵗʰ)**	Attendance 9,786
Good Friday	Austin 8'	
7 Apr 2023 15:00	Langstaff 60'	
	Vincent 76'	

Mair

Brindley   Baldwin   Cameron (Capt.)

Nemane (Vincent 66')   Chicksen

Palmer   Bostock (O'Brien 66')   Jones (Scott 73')   Austin

Langstaff

Subs: Brooks (Gk), Rawlinson, O'Brien, Vincent, Scott

Not in the squad: Slocombe, Adebayo-Rowling, Morias, (all injured). Bajrami and Rodrigues (rested as a precaution), Mahovo. Munakandafa, Mitchell, Francis out on loan.

Luke Williams made three changes to the side victorious at Altrincham ten days ago. Brindley, Baldwin, and Jones returned in place of Rawlinson, Bajrami, and Rodrigues. This was the first match since the death of Jason Turner. It would have been his seventh anniversary at the club. Notts had been inundated with tributes from friends and colleagues in football and beyond.

The match was dedicated to Jason. His family were in attendance – they could not miss the opportunity "to join the club and its supporters in remembering him at what was his second home."

In late October Notts won 1-6 at Wealdstone! However, the team from the northern side of Greater London were not a poor side. They had spent most of the season in the top half of the league, although their recent form had been disappointing with three consecutive defeats before a draw in their last match.

Notts took an early lead when Langstaff passed to Austin who evaded a defender and swept the ball into the net, off a post, from the edge of the penalty area. Langstaff, who hit a post with a header in the first half, became The National League's highest ever scorer on the hour mark. Palmer tapped the ball back to goalkeeper Mair and his clearance found 'Macca' in the centre circle, who ran on, unchallenged, to score his 41st goal of the season from 16 yards. Substitute Vincent scored his first Notts goal of the season after Chicksen crossed from the right to Scott, but the goalkeeper saved his shot and the rebound fell to 'Vinny' who smashed the ball home from ten yards.

It was a comfortable win for Notts who achieved 100 points in a season for the first time. Wrexham, our season-long rival from North Wales, lost (3-1) at Halifax, so Notts returned to the summit of The National League. The next fixture, on Easter Monday, televised live on BT Sport: Wrexham v Notts County!

	P	W	D	L	F	A	Goal Diff	Pts
Notts County	42	30	10	2	106	36	+70	100
Wrexham	41	31	7	3	106	39	+67	100
Woking	41	22	9	10	67	42	+25	75
Chesterfield	41	21	9	11	68	47	+21	72

Match 43	**Wrexham (2nd) 3-2 Notts County (1st)**	Attendance 9,924
Easter Monday	goals 50', 69', 79' Bostock 45'+4	(Notts 1,042)
10 Apr 2023 15:00	Cameron 75'	Live on BT Sport

Slocombe

Rawlinson   Bajrami   Cameron (Capt.)

Nemane (Jones 77')   Chicksen

Palmer   Bostock   O'Brien (Austin 69')   Rodrigues (Scott 77')

Langstaff

Subs: Brooks (Gk), Vincent, Austin, Scott, Jones

Not in the squad: Brindley, Adebayo-Rowling, Baldwin, Morias, (all injured), Mair (Gk), Mahovo. Munakandafa, Mitchell, Francis out on loan.

Luke Williams made five changes to the team which defeated Wealdstone. Fit again Slocombe returned in goal, Rawlinson and Bajrami replaced Brindley and Baldwin, and O'Brien and Rodrigues came in for Austin and Jones.

Wrexham's defeat at Halifax three days ago was their first in the league since they lost 1-0 at Meadow Lane on 4 October, a sequence of 28 unbeaten matches. Their home record was P21 W20 D1 L0 F68 A18!

This match was described as the biggest and best ever non-league football match. At the end of a closely contested first half Notts took the lead with a top class 25-yard free kick by Bostock, which flew over the wall of defenders into the top corner of the net – his first Notts goal. Wrexham equalized early in the second half when Mullin got the better of Bajrami and swept a low cross from the right into the corner of the net from 15 yards. It was his 35th league goal of the season – 44th inc. cup matches. Soon after Slocombe's crossbar had been rattled by a tremendous first-time shot, Wrexham scored their second when Mullin's low cross from the right was powered home from the corner of the six-yard box. However, Notts fought back and from a Palmer cross, Cameron equalized with a diving header. Four minutes later Wrexham reclaimed the lead when a poor clearance by Bajrami was seized upon by Mullin and his pass was turned emphatically beyond Slocombe, who later made an excellent save to prevent a fourth Wrexham goal. However, in the sixth minute of added time, Notts were awarded a penalty when a defender handled the ball. With usual penalty taker Rodrigues substituted, Scott's spot kick was brilliantly saved by 40-year-old ex-England goalkeeper Ben Foster. He dived to his right and the ball flew up off his right hand, but he then clawed the ball away for a corner with his high flying left hand. An incredible end to an incredible match!

Wrexham were now three points ahead of Notts with a game in hand. Although they still had to travel to Barnet (5th) and entertain Boreham Wood (6th) some bookmakers' odds were 1/20 for Wrexham to finish as National League champions and achieve automatic promotion into League Two of the EFL.

Match 44	Notts County (2ⁿᵈ) 3-0 Woking (3ʳᵈ)	Attendance 8,520
Sat 15 Apr 2023 17:30	Austin 55', 75' Nemane 72'	Live on BT Sport

Slocombe

Rawlinson   Baldwin   Cameron (Capt.)

Jones (Nemane 68')   Chicksen

Palmer   Bostock   Rodrigues (Scott 73')   Austin

Langstaff (Morias 73')

Subs: Nemane, O'Brien, Vincent, Scott, Morias
(no substitute goalkeeper)

Not in the squad: Brindley, Adebayo-Rowling, (both injured), Bajrami, Brooks (Gk), Mair (Gk), Mahovo. Munakandafa, Mitchell, Francis out on loan.

After the hugely disappointing result at Wrexham, Luke Williams made three changes: Baldwin replaced Bajrami, Jones and Austin were preferred to Nemane and O'Brien.

Earlier in the week Luke Williams and Macaulay Langstaff received The National League monthly awards for March – Luke also won 'Manager of the Month' in October and Macaulay 'Player of the Month' in August and September.

Although Notts won 2-3 at Woking in early October, the team from Surrey had had a successful season (76 points from 42 matches) and were in contention with Chesterfield (75 points from 42 matches) for the coveted third place finish. (A second and third place finish = a home fixture in the playoff semi-final's – Notts were guaranteed at least a second-place finish). Woking were the only team who had managed to avoid defeat at Wrexham this season (2-2 draw).

Luke Williams was disappointed with Notts' first half performance, when both teams had chances to score. Notts soon took control at the beginning of the second half. Austin gave them the lead after Chicksen fed Palmer and his accurate low cross was swept beyond the goalkeeper with a first time shot from 10 yards. Within five minutes of his arrival as a substitute Nemane scored, and it was Austin who provided the assist with a teasing cross from the left into the six-yard box. Nemane managed to direct the ball goalwards and his attempt at an overhead kick confused the goalkeeper and he forced the loose ball over the line. Austin scored his second goal when he received a pass from Scott and, despite the attendance of a defender, shot home from inside the penalty area.

Substitute Morias was lively in the latter stages of the match and the debutant forced the goalkeeper into a good save with a powerful 25-yard shot.

The Barnet v Wrexham match ended goalless, so second in the table Notts were now only one point behind top of the league Wrexham. Although the north Wales team still had a match in hand, Notts improved their goal difference - Notts +72, Wrexham +68. For Notts, this 31st win of the season was a club record!

Match 45	**Maidstone Utd (24th) 2-5 Notts County (2nd)**	Attendance 2,391
Sat 22 Apr 2023 15:00	goals 70', 71' Scott 5',	(Notts 781)
	O'Brien 15', 60', 89' (pen.)	
	Rodrigues 83'	

Mair

Brindley Baldwin Cameron (Capt.)

Jones (Nemane 65') Vincent

Palmer (Morias 65') O'Brien Rodrigues Austin

Scott (Langstaff 65')

Subs: Chicksen, Nemane, Bostock, Langstaff, Morias
(no substitute goalkeeper)

Not in the squad: Adebayo-Rowling (injured), Rawlinson, Bajrami, Slocombe (Gk), Brooks (Gk), Mahovo. Munakandafa, Mitchell, Francis out on loan.

For their final away match of the season, on a 4G artificial grass pitch, there were five changes to the team victorious over high-flying Woking. Goalkeeper Mair played instead of Slocombe (adverse reaction to a previous artificial surface), Brindley replaced Rawlinson, Vincent (his first Notts start of the season) and O'Brien came in for Chicksen and Bostock, and Scott returned in place of Langstaff who had been ill earlier in the week.

Defeated 3-0 at Meadow Lane last October, bottom of the league Maidstone (already relegated to National League South) had played 23 matches since they last won a league match on 26 November. They had the worst home record in the league, and the worst defensive record (95 conceded). Only Yeovil had scored fewer goals than their 43. However, in January, they won at Meadow Lane in the fourth round of the FA Trophy, on penalties after a 2-2 draw.

Notts cruised through the first 45 minutes and scored two early goals. The first came when a defender trod on the ball, lost possession, and Scott scored from just inside the penalty area. For the second, Rodrigues passed to Jones and his cross rebounded off a defender to O'Brien, who scored from ten yards. Notts had further chances before half-time but failed to increase their lead.

O'Brien scored his second on the hour, after a Vincent shot came back off the crossbar, and a defender only cleared the ball to the Scotsman who made no mistake from 15 yards. Soon after, Luke Williams made three changes. Within minutes Maidstone scored two goals, after some poor defending, and then hit the crossbar! A shaken Notts eased the pressure when Rodrigues was fouled just outside the penalty area and his free kick was too powerful for the goalkeeper. In the last minute of normal time Rodrigues was tripped in the penalty area, and O'Brien was given the opportunity to complete his hat-trick, which he did when he sent the goalkeeper the wrong way with his spot kick. With the last kick of the match Mair made an excellent save to prevent a third Maidstone goal.

Wrexham, who won their match in hand in midweek, beat Boreham Wood 3-1 and became champions, which meant Notts were consigned to the playoffs!

Match 46	**Notts County (2nd) 1-1 York City (19th)**	Attendance 11,336
Sat 29 Apr 2023 17:30	Langstaff 45'+1 goal 89'	

Slocombe

Rawlinson (Brindley 56')   Baldwin   Cameron (Capt.)

Nemane   Chicksen

Palmer   Bostock (O'Brien 76')   Rodrigues   Austin (Scott 66')

Langstaff

Subs: Brindley, O'Brien, Vincent, Scott, Jones
(no substitute goalkeeper)

Not in the squad: Adebayo-Rowling (injured), Bajrami, Morias, Brooks (Gk), Mair (Gk), Mahovo. Munakandafa, Mitchell, Francis out on loan.

For the last league match of the season, Luke Williams made six changes to the team which defeated bottom club Maidstone in a bizarre encounter seven days ago. Slocombe returned in goal, and Rawlinson, Nemane, Chicksen, Bostock and Langstaff came in for Brindley, Jones, Vincent, O'Brien, and Scott.

York were defeated by Notts (1-3) way back in September. Although only three points above the relegation zone, York's goal difference was such that they were assured of a place in The National League next season.

Very little was seen of York as an attacking force in the first half with Notts dominant throughout. However, despite all their pressure, it was in added time at the end of the half when Notts took the lead. Rodrigues finally unlocked the York defence with a delightful pass to Langstaff, and The National League's top scorer expertly slotted the ball home for his 42nd goal of the season.

Notts continued in the ascendency during the second half, but in the 57th minute Slocombe made his first save of the match when he dived to turn a shot behind for a corner. Notts threatened to increase their lead, but the York goalkeeper was in excellent form, and he denied Austin and Scott in quick succession. In the 77th minute he was beaten by a Langstaff shot which hit a post. Notts could not get the second goal they deserved and in the last minute of normal time York equalized when a forward, who had arrived from the substitutes bench only five minutes earlier, scored with a well-placed shot. During the six minutes of added time Notts put the York defence under intense pressure with five corners but the goalkeeper continued to excel, and he made excellent saves to deny Rodrigues, Chicksen and Langstaff in a grand finale.

After the final whistle the York players celebrated, in front of their one thousand plus supporters, as if they had won promotion! The Notts players, together with Luke Williams and his staff, returned to the pitch, some with their young children, to celebrate (almost) the end of a fantastic season.

Notts' next match was the playoff semi-final, at Meadow Lane, against Boreham Wood. A victory would give them a Wembley (promotion) final!

Funeral: Jason Turner

CEO remembered in beautiful service.

Our late chief executive Jason Turner was remembered in a beautiful funeral service at St Mary's Church on 3 May.

His procession passed through the car park outside the Derek Pavis Stand, pausing for a short while in front of staff and supporters who had gathered to be with him on his final visit to Meadow Lane.

The cortege carried on to the church in the Lace Market, where club chaplain Rev. Liam O'Boyle delivered a heartfelt and touching service which included readings from some of Jason's close friends and colleagues.

After Jason was laid to rest, a celebration of his life was held in the 1862 Suite with hundreds in attendance.

Following his passing, tributes from Jason's friends and colleagues poured in and his parents, Jen and David, took great comfort from the many beautiful words.

They said:

"As a family, we have been overwhelmed by the kindness shown to us at this devastating time, particularly by Chris and Alex Reedtz, Luke Williams, the club's amazing staff and supporters.

"Losing Jason is the hardest thing we've ever experienced – but the messages, tributes and flowers have been so reassuring.

"At the recent match against Wealdstone, it was an honour to lead out the team in Jason's memory and we can't thank both clubs enough for the wonderful way they welcomed us and paid tribute to our beloved son.

"Again, from the bottom of our hearts, thank you to everyone for their thoughtfulness and respect."

The funeral of legendary Notts County reporter, Colin Slater MBE, who died on 10 January 2022 at the age of 87, also took place (on 31 January 2022) at St Mary's Church, High Pavement, Nottingham.

Chapter 23: Promotion playoffs May 2023

Promotion Playoff (Semi-Final) Sun 7 May 2023 12:30	Notts County (2ⁿᵈ) 3-2 Boreham Wood (6ᵗʰ) after extra time Baldwin 47', 90'+7 goals 37' & 45'+2 Jones 120'	Attendance 15,617 Live on BT Sport

Slocombe

Rawlinson   Baldwin (Brindley 106')   Cameron (Capt.)

Nemane   Chicksen (Jones 77')

Palmer   Bostock   Rodrigues (O'Brien 103')   Austin (Scott 65')

Langstaff

Subs: Mair (Gk), Brindley, O'Brien, Scott, Jones

Not in the squad: Adebayo-Rowling (injured), Bajrami, Vincent, Morias, Brooks (Gk), Mahovo, Munakandafa, Mitchell, Francis.

Luke Williams made no changes to the team unable to secure a deserved victory against a resilient York City eight days ago.

Both league matches this season were drawn, 2-2 and 1-1. Boreham Wood won 1-2 away at Barnet in their playoff eliminator five days ago. At the end of the season, they finished with the best defensive record (40 conceded) - two fewer than Notts who had the next best defence. However, there was a big difference in the number of goals scored – Boreham Wood 52, Notts 117!

A few days before this match Boreham Wood signed ex-Notts goalkeeper Joe McDonnell on emergency loan, from fellow National League club Eastleigh, due to an injury to their first choice 'keeper. McDonnell played eight times for The Magpies in the 2019-20 season before he signed for Eastleigh in August 2020.

Notts started well and two big chances fell to Rodrigues in the first six minutes. First, his shot was just off target after Chicksen had crossed into the six-yard box. Four minutes later Nemane dribbled past a defender and cut the ball back to the unmarked Rodrigues but, from 12 yards, he lifted his fierce shot over the crossbar. Boreham Wood retaliated, and in the 24ᵗʰ minute Slocombe made his first save of the afternoon. Soon after, Langstaff had a shot saved. Rodrigues then had another good opportunity, courtesy of Austin, but his shot was also saved by McDonnell. In the latter stages of the first half a long throw-in caused confusion in the Notts defence and a shot from the edge of the penalty area was tipped over the crossbar by Slocombe. But two minutes later the visitors beat the Notts offside trap and, despite being under pressure from Nemane, a forward bundled a low cross home from close range. Baldwin almost equalized with two shots in quick succession, both from outside the penalty area. The first flew just wide and the second McDonnell dived and pushed the ball behind for a corner. In time added Austin gave Rodrigues another chance but his shot was saved. With the last action of the half a loose Bostock pass put Baldwin under pressure. He lost the ball to a forward who ran on to the edge of the penalty area and shot confidently beyond the advancing Slocombe to give the visitors a two-goal interval lead.

The second half was only two minutes old when Notts pulled a goal back. For Baldwin it was a case of third time lucky, but it was not a lucky goal. Nemane passed to him and a thunderbolt from 35 yards flew into the bottom corner of the net, for his first ever Notts goal. One minute later Baldwin momentarily lost concentration, which almost presented Boreham Wood with a third goal. He failed to notice the presence of a forward, who took the ball beyond Slocombe, but he sprinted back to (just) deflect the goal bound shot behind for a corner. On the hour a 12-yard first time shot by Langstaff went just wide of a post, following an excellent pass by…. Baldwin! A minute later Rodrigues was fouled in the penalty area, but McDonnell dived to his right to save his spot kick and deny Notts the equalizer. It was the second time this season he had saved a Rodrigues penalty at Meadow Lane - the first was during Eastleigh's 3-1 defeat in March. From then on Boreham Wood offered little going forward. Although Bostock had a 25-yard shot saved and Langstaff twice went close, Notts could not penetrate the stubborn Boreham Wood defence. It seemed their record-breaking season would end in bitter disappointment. But, in the 97th minute the breakthrough came when, after the eighth Notts pass, substitute Jones crossed and Baldwin, on the edge of the six-yard box, knelt to plant a header beyond the helpless McDonnell.

Meadow Lane erupted!

In the first period of extra time Boreham Wood were initially the better team, but Notts soon regained control of the match. Just after the start of the second period of extra time, following a long throw-in, Slocombe had to tip a powerful header over the crossbar. Five minutes later Nemane made a brilliant sliding clearance to prevent a forward scoring Boreham Wood's third goal. In the last minute of extra time, with everyone prepared for a penalty shoot-out, Jones scored the winner with his first Notts goal. Notts usually took short corner kicks, but Palmer lifted this one into the goal mouth. A headed clearance fell to Jones near the corner of the penalty area who beat a defender and fired a rocket which was too powerful for the diving McDonnell.

Meadow Lane went berserk!

Just 24 hours after the coronation of King Charles III and Queen Camilla at Westminster Abbey, Notts County and Boreham Wood created drama of their own as Notts scored the equalizer with (almost) the last action of the second half and the winner with (almost) the last kick of extra time. At the end of this incredible match the Meadow Lane pitch was invaded by jubilant Notts supporters.

Aden Baldwin

Jodi Jones

A few hours later, in the other semi-final playoff, Chesterfield defeated Bromley (also 3-2 after extra time). So, Notts' opponents in the promotion final were our near neighbours from Derbyshire. Wembley Stadium here we come!

This pulsating, extraordinary, match was the best I have ever seen, courtesy of live coverage by BT Sport. Only Notts' two winning Wembley playoff finals in May 1990 and May 1991 possibly compare, when they achieved a place in the top tier of English football – now known as the Premier League.

@Official_NCFC May 7

> Boreham Wood FC @BOREHAM WOODFC
>
> Congratulations, @Official_NCFC! We're heartbroken, but you've had an incredible season. We wish you all the very best at Wembley. Do it for Jason (Turner)

@JohnJBostock May 8

> What a way to mark my 300th professional appearance. I've played in many teams, but none as special as this one. 300 down and many more to go by His grace. The marathon continues.
> To Jesus be all the glory.

The Wrexham FC co-owner Ryan Reynolds has stayed true to his promise after Notts County's massive victory over Boreham Wood.

It's clear the Hollywood A-lister is a man of his word after following through with his vow to root for Notts County.

The Welsh football club returned to the football league after a 3-1 victory (also over Boreham Wood) on 22 April.

The promotion battle was incredible, with both teams amassing over 100 goals, 100 points and only three defeats during the season.

Ultimately, Wrexham was the team to prevail and secure promotion by just a narrow four-point margin, leaving Notts County to battle it out in the play-offs.

Since then, Reynolds has consistently supported Notts County and revealed that he and co-owner Rob McElhenney would be championing them in the play-offs.

Despite the rivalry between the two clubs, Reynolds revealed: "It's something Rob and I feel quite strongly about. We are rooting for Notts County.

We want to see them go up to League Two and face them next year. They're incredible."

After Wrexham's impressive 3-2 victory over Notts County last month, the star told BT Sport it was a shame that there wasn't two automatic promotion spots.

He said: "I have such enormous respect for everything they've built and everything that they've done and it's just insane for me that only one goes up automatically.

"If it were different – and I think it should be – both of these clubs would be celebrating together right now.

"Because what they've done is not only created drama greater than anything you'd see in a damn movie but just something I think people will be talking about for ages."

Luke Williams (and the Meadow Lane kop)

Wembley Stadium, London

Luke Williams paid special tribute to the late Jason Turner after Notts County booked their place in The National League promotion final.

Sunday's win against Boreham Wood came four days after the funeral for the club's chief executive.

Williams, who was among those to carry the coffin, said he looked up at the memorial flag for Turner in the stands at Meadow Lane throughout the match.

"I'm sure the smile got broader," he said of Turner's image.

"Look at him, he's there. Honestly, he looks happy."

"At one point I looked across and he was frowning at me."

Williams spoke of Turner with a broad smile of his own after seeing Jodi Jones score a last-minute extra-time goal to seal an enthralling 3-2 victory.

After missing out on promotion to Wrexham despite amassing 107 points, Sunday's victory set up a final against Chesterfield at Wembley on Saturday 13 May, when Notts plan to have the memorial flag of Turner unfurled in the stands.

Williams had previously spoken about how Turner's sudden death in March had impacted the club, and would emotionally charge their bid for promotion.

After moving to within one win of securing a return to the English Football League after a four-year absence, Williams said "the whole time has been tough since Jason passed away. It's hard to explain, I'm a grown man but Jason looked after me and protected me." Williams told BBC Radio Nottingham.

"Nothing ever seemed to be a problem and I'm learning more and more that many things were a problem, he just didn't bring them to me.

"To carry all these different problems and then still come into my office with joy and be cheery all the time, and always make sure I was OK, is something I'll never forget. I owe him so much."

Promotion Playoff Final Sat 13 May 2023 15:30 Wembley Stadium	**Notts County (2ⁿᵈ) 2-2 Chesterfield (3ʳᵈ)** after extra time Bostock 87' Rodrigues 108'	goals 5' (pen), 93'	Attendance 38,138 Live on BT Sport

Notts won 4-3 after penalties
1=Langstaff, 2=Rodrigues, 3= Jones, 4=Scott
Mair saved two of the Chesterfield penalties

                    Slocombe (Mair 119')
     Rawlinson   Baldwin (Brindley 117')   Cameron (Capt.)
  Nemane   Chicksen (Jones 55')
          Palmer   Bostock   Rodrigues   Austin (Scott 65')
                            Langstaff

Subs: Mair (Gk), Brindley, O'Brien, Scott, Jones

Not in the squad: Adebayo-Rowling (injured), Bajrami, Vincent, Morias, Brooks (Gk), Mahovo, Munakandafa, Mitchell, Francis.

Luke Williams made no changes to the 16-man squad which defeated Boreham Wood in the pulsating semi-final at Meadow Lane.

In the league Notts were held to a 2-2 draw at Meadow Lane, but won 1-2 in the away fixture. Although they finished in second and third positions there was a 23-point gap in the number of points earned: Notts 107, Chesterfield 84.

Goalkeeper Sam Slocombe made two massive errors of judgement in the first five minutes. First, he failed to take a short goal kick correctly and ended up kicking the ball twice. From the resultant 11 yard indirect free kick, with all eleven Notts players standing along the goal line, he was the one who managed to save the shot, and the ball was eventually scrambled clear. Worse then followed when he ran from his six-yard area and attempted to clear the ball away from a Chesterfield forward running along the side of the penalty area. His clumsy challenge was clearly a foul and the referee had no hesitation in awarding Chesterfield a spot kick, from which they took the lead.

It took Notts some time to recover from this disastrous start, but as the first half progressed they gradually eased themselves into the match, with Nemane in particular a threat from the right, and Bostock and Palmer impressive in midfield. Although there was little to choose between the two teams, Slocombe was the busier goalkeeper.

Notts were the better team at the start of the second 45 minutes, and Austin shot over the crossbar from 17 yards after another good cross by Nemane. In the 66th minute a free-kick found Rawlinson on the edge of the six yard box, but he directed his stooping header just wide of a post. A minute later a Chesterfield shot flew through the six yard box and just wide of Slocombe's far post. Despite Notts' superiority for most of the second half, their former goalkeeper Ross Fitzsimons, in the Chesterfield goal, was rarely troubled. However, with just three minutes of normal time left Notts were presented with a goal courtesy of a mistake by Fitzsimons. Bostock took a free-kick in line with the corner of the penalty area which cleared the defence and dipped. The goalkeeper failed to hold the ball and allowed it to squirm past him at his near post into the corner of the net for the equaliser. In a pulsating finish Rawlinson had to make an excellent challenge to prevent a possible goal, and Cameron eventually cleared the subsequent goalmouth scramble.

The first period of extra time was only three minutes old when Chesterfield regained the lead. An attacker was allowed time and space to curl a lofted shot from the edge of the penalty area into the far corner of the net. Five minutes later Langstaff latched on to a Palmer pass but dragged his shot wide of the far post. Notts continued to press a tired looking Chesterfield defence and Rawlinson shot just wide after he received a pass from Scott.

The second period of extra time was only a few minutes old when Rodrigues equalized after Fitzsimons punched a Cameron cross to him on the edge of the penalty area. His downward shot hit the pitch and bounced over everyone into the net. In the last minute of extra time, with a penalty shoot-out likely, Luke Williams made a tactical switch when he changed goalkeepers - Slocombe was replaced by 22 year old Archie Mair, on loan from Norwich City.

All four goals had been scored in the goal nearest the Notts' supporters, and this goal was chosen for the penalty shoot-out.

Chesterfield took the first penalty and scored. **Langstaff equalized.** Chesterfield's second penalty was brilliantly saved by Mair who dived to his right to push the ball away. **Rodrigues then scored to made it 1-2 to Notts.** The Spireites made it 2-2 with their third penalty, before **Jones restored Notts' lead**. Mair then produced a wonder save when he again dived to his right, and the left foot of his high flying body cleared the ball! **Bostock then had the chance to win the shoot-out but he hit the crossbar with his 'Panenka' kick** (a light touch underneath the ball to direct it towards the centre of the goal, which usually deceives the goalkeeper who invariably dives to the right or the left). Mair was beaten by Chesterfield's fifth penalty, but **Scott stepped up to send Fitzsimons the wrong way with Notts' fifth penalty, and return the Magpies to League Two of the English Football League.**

This final was well referred by Matthew Corlett, who was confident, authoritative, and levelheaded throughout. It was an incredible finish to an incredible season for Notts. During the final two hours, when three goalkeepers provided the main highlights, there was, not for the first time during the last four National League seasons, despair and excitement for the 22,500 Notts supporters before Cedwyn Scott's dramatic penalty at the end.

Two of the most dramatic and emotional matches in Notts County's history, but they were once again **the oldest professional football league club in the world!**

Christoffer and Alexander Reedtz issued the following on 'Club News' a few days after the Wembley victory:

Words cannot describe how proud we are of what the club achieved at Wembley on Saturday.

Before we reflect on the day, however, we would like to offer our commiserations to Chesterfield and thank them for their gracious messages of congratulations. They played brilliantly and we have no doubt they'll be a force to be reckoned with next season.

While the team certainly didn't choose the 'easy way' in this play-off campaign, we were so impressed with the mental and physical fortitude they displayed both in the semi and final. Their will to win was evident and we're so pleased that, in the end, they, along with Luke Williams and his staff, got what they deserved for such an amazing, record-breaking season.

To witness the players lift the trophy and to join them in their celebrations in front of our 22,500 supporters, who we wholeheartedly thank for battling the travel disruption, was a dream come true and has only made us more determined to bring future successes to the club.

It was incredibly emotional to see Jason Turner's flag on display, along with his photo being held by the players on the pitch. We know this meant a lot to his parents, Jen and David, who were there with us and delighted with the outcome of the match.

As we begin preparations for our first season without Jason, we would like to announce that our boardroom will be renamed in his honour from the start of the 2023-24 campaign. Anyone who experienced Jason's warm hospitality over the course of his tenure will understand what a welcoming and engaging presence he was and we hope this gesture serves as further evidence to his family that he will never, ever be forgotten.

Throughout the season we have been hugely encouraged by the club's progress off the field, with attendances at their highest in recent history. Saturday's victory has only served to create an even bigger buzz around the club and our staff have been hard at work since full-time to ensure we capitalise on the opportunities presented by our success. We'd like to thank the incredibly hard-working behind-the-scenes team for their brilliant ongoing efforts.

Season ticket sales have already been very strong and, after selling around 4,000 last season, we expect our 2023-24 offering to receive the highest uptake of our tenure so far.

It was brilliant to see so many children and young adults at Wembley and, as ever, our season ticket pricing reflects our desire to attract people in those age groups to Meadow Lane.

We're keen to engage younger fans in other ways, too, and look forward to announcing details of a significant campaign to engage 1,000 new families in the near future.

Renovations on the Meadow Lane playing surface are already underway and we're pleased to confirm that work has begun on installing a new state-of-the-art PA system. The club has also acquired new equipment to maximise functionality of our scoreboards, so fans can expect a greatly-improved matchday experience next season.

Supporters will, of course, be keen to know details of which players will still be with us when the new campaign comes around. The club is going through the necessary processes as we speak and fans can expect an update before the end of the week.

When it comes to the recruitment of new players, fans are assured that we had been planning for life in League Two, as well as The National League, long before promotion was secured. We're excited by the new opportunities our EFL status will bring and work has begun on building a squad which we hope will compete at the top end of the division.

Several key figures from this season's squad are out of contract but, again, our fans should know that we are doing everything we can to maintain a strong nucleus of a side that has achieved so much.

Promotion doesn't only strengthen our position in the transfer market – it consolidates other areas of the club, including our excellent academy which will benefit from a significant increase in funding. We're excited to see how this positively impacts the development of the many talented young players within our ranks.

We hope our brilliant supporters continue to enjoy Saturday's success and have a wonderful, relaxing summer!

Chris and Alex

To conclude, an amazing statistic emerged after the two unforgettable playoff matches: excluding the penalty shoot-out at Wembley, out of the 240 minutes played (2x90 + 2x30 extra time) Notts were in the lead for only one minute!

A couple of days before the Wembley final The National League announced their 2022/23 'Team of the Season'. Five Notts players were selected.

Goalkeeper:

    Nathan Ashmore — Boreham Wood

Defenders:
- Jeff King — Chesterfield
- Ben Tozer — Wrexham
- KYLE CAMERON — NOTTS COUNTY
- ADAM CHICKSEN — NOTTS COUNTY

Midfielders
- Elliot Lee — Wrexham
- MATTY PALMER — NOTTS COUNTY
- RUBEN RODRIGUES — NOTTS COUNTY

Forwards
- Paul Mullin — Wrexham
- MACAULAY LANGSTAFF — NOTTS COUNTY
- Ryan Colclough — Chesterfield

Notts County's club record breaking 2022-23 season

It was difficult to keep track of the many records broken in an incredible season. Honorary club historian Michael Chappell provided:

Highest-ever points tally	107
Most wins	32
Goals scored	117 (also a 5th tier/National League record)
Fewest defeats	3
Equal-most away wins	15
Longest-ever unbeaten run	25
Best-ever goal difference	+75

Highest-ever National League attendance of 16,511 v Yeovil Town (19/11/22)

Apologies if more records were broken, but overlooked.

Macaulay Langstaff scored 42 goals, all in the league and from open play – no penalties or free-kicks.

Macaulay Langstaff's 2022-23 honours list

- National League Player of the Season
- National League Top Scorer
- Notts County Fans' Player of the Season
- Notts County Players' Player of the Season
- National League Player of the Month (3 times)
- Record set for most goals in a Notts County Season
- Record set for most goals in a National League Season
- Record set for most goals in a fifth-tier season since rebranding in 2015
- Record set for most Player of the Month awards in a National League Season

Notts County National League Results 2022-23

Date	Home	Away	F-A	Scorers	Attendance	Pos
2022						
6/8	Maidenhead Utd		3-0	Langstaff (2), Taylor	6,331	2
13/8		Boreham Wood	2-2	Rodrigues (pen), Mitchell	1,303	1=
16/8		Gateshead	1-1	og = own goal	1,825	6=
20/8	Chesterfield		2-2	Langstaff (2)	8,287 (BT Sport)	10
27/8		Halifax Town	4-1	Langstaff (2), Scott, Mitchell	2,371	8
29/8	Solihull Moors		1-0	Chicksen	7,004	5
3/9		Dagenham & Redbridge	5-0	Langstaff (3), Scott, Chicksen	1,722	3
10/9	*The home fixture against Bromley was postponed to respect the death of Queen Elizabeth II on 8 September*					
13/9	Aldershot Town		2-0	Scott, Langstaff	5,607	3
17/9		Dorking Wanderers	1-3	Scott	2,402	4
24/9		York City	3-1	Castro, Langstaff (2)	6,759	3
1/10	Altrincham		3-1	Langstaff (2), Chicksen	6,458	2
4/10	Wrexham		1-0	Langstaff	10,741	1
8/10		Woking	3-2	Rodrigues (pen), Scott (2)	3,267	1
21/10	Maidstone Utd		3-0	Langstaff, Rodrigues, Scott	6,765	1
25/10		Wealdstone	6-1	Langstaff, Chicksen (2), Palmer Nemane, Bajrami	1,710	1
29/10	Torquay Utd		4-0	Rawlinson, Rodrigues (pen) Castro, Bajrami	7,563	1
1/11	Bromley		1-1	Chicksen	6,389	1
8/11		Southend Utd	2-2	Langstaff, Scott	6,603 (BT Sport)	2
12/11		Eastleigh	2-0	Chicksen, Rodrigues	3,055	1
19/11	Yeovil Town		0-0		16,511	2
3/12		Scunthorpe Utd	4-1	Castro, O'Brien, Langstaff, Scott	4,196	1
10/12		Maidenhead Utd	4-3	Rodrigues, Castro, Langstaff (2)	1,467 (S)	1
13/12	Gateshead		2-0	Francis, Rodrigues	5,539 (S)	1
26/12	Oldham Athletic		4-1	Scott (2), Cameron, Rodrigues	9,789 (S)	1
2023						
1/1		Oldham Athletic	2-2	Langstaff, Scott	7,312 (S)	1
7/1		Aldershot Town	3-0	O'Brien, Rodrigues, Nemane	2,039 (S)	1
10/1	Boreham Wood		1-1	Scott	6,033 (S)	1
28/1	Halifax Town		1-0	Langstaff	7,548	2
31/1		Solihull Moors	2-1	Rodrigues (2 pens)	2,260 (S)	1
4/2		Torquay Utd	2-1	Langstaff, Rodrigues (pen)	2,621	1
11/2		Chesterfield	2-1	Langstaff, Chicksen	9,706 (BT Sport)	1
14/2	Barnet		4-1	Scott, Chicksen, Langstaff (2)	6,891 (S)	1
18/2		Yeovil Town	4-1	Langstaff (3), Rodrigues (pen)	3,020	1
21/2	Southend Utd		4-0	Langstaff (2), Austin (2)	7,237 (S)	1
25/2	Dagenham & Redbridge		1-2	Rodrigues	7,441 (BT Sport)	1
4/3		Bromley	1-1	Langstaff	3,417	2
11/3	Dorking Wanderers		3-1	Langstaff (2), Palmer	7,060 (BT Sport)	2
14/3	Eastleigh		3-1	Rodrigues (2), Langstaff	6,058 (S)	2
18/3		Barnet	1-1	Langstaff	2,969	2
25/3	Scunthorpe Utd		4-0	Chicksen, og, Langstaff (2)	16,086	2
28/3		Altrincham	2-0	Langstaff, Rodrigues (pen)	2,011(S)	1
7/4	Wealdstone		3-0	Austin, Langstaff, Vincent	9,786 (S)	1
10/4		Wrexham	2-3	Bostock, Cameron	9,924 (BT Sport)	2
15/4	Woking		3-0	Austin (2), Nemane	8,520 (BT Sport)	2
22/4		Maidstone Utd	5-2	Scott, O'Brien (3, 1 pen.), Rodrigues	2,391	2
29/4	York City		1-1	Langstaff	11,336 (S)	2

(S) = Streamed live (National League TV)

Notts County National League Results - Playoffs 2022-23

Date	Home	F-A	Scorers	Attendance
7/5	Boreham Wood (Playoff semi-final)	3-2 aet	Baldwin (2), Jones	15,617 (BT Sport)
13/5	Playoff final at Wembley v Chesterfield	2-2 aet	Bostock, Rodrigues	38,138 (BT Sport)

aet = after extra time Notts won the Wembley penalty shoot-out 4-3

Notts County FA Cup and FA Trophy Results 2022-23

Date	Home	Away	F-A	Scorers	Attendance	Round
15/10/22	Coalville Town		2-3	Austin (2)	5,060 (Inc. Coalville supporters 1,397)	FA Cup 4th Qualifying
20/12	Chorley		2-1	Austin, own goal	2,040	FA Trophy 3rd
15/1/23	Maidstone Utd		2-2	Chicksen, Austin *Notts lost 5-6 penalties*	2,405	FA Trophy 4th

Notts County Goal Times-League (& Cup) 2022-23, exc playoffs
First 23 league (plus 1 FA Cup) matches

For = 59						
0-15 min	16-30 min	31 min - HT	46-60 min	61-75 min	76-90 min	90+
7 (1)	6 (0)	19 (0)	11 (0)	8 (1)	8 (0)	0 (0)
Against = 21						
0-15 min	16-30 min	31 min - HT	46-60 min	61-75 min	76-90 min	90+
0 (1)	4 (1)	3 (0)	7 (0)	2 (0)	3 (1)	2 (0)

Second 23 league (plus 2 FA Trophy) matches

For = 58						
0-15 min	16-30 min	31 min - HT	46-60 min	61-75 min	76-90 min	90+
8 (0)	7 (0)	8 (2)	13 (0)	5 (1)	14 (1)	3 (0)
Against = 21						
0-15 min	16-30 min	31 min - HT	46-60 min	61-75 min	76-90 min	90+
3 (0)	2 (1)	6 (1)	2 (1)	4 (0)	4 (0)	0 (0)

Notts County 2022-23
League +Cup 'Starts', (Sub appearances), Goals & Cards, all exc. playoffs

Name	Starts	(Sub)	Goals	Yellow/Red (Cards)
Slocombe (Gk)	39+0	(0+0)		5
Brooks (Gk)	4+0	(0+0)		1
Mair (Gk) loan	3+1	(1+0)		1
Young (Gk) loan	0+2	(0+0)		1
Cameron (Capt.)	44+2	(0+0)	2+0	8
Baldwin	29+1	(1+0)	0+0	4/1
Rawlinson	27+2	(1+0)	1+0	6
Brindley	26+2	(3+0)	0+0	6/1
Bajrami	19+3	(12+0)	2+0	5
Chicksen	44+1	(0+0)	10+1	2
Nemane	35+2	(3+0)	3+0	4
Adebayo-Rowling	6+2	(5+0)	0+0	0
Taylor	2+1	(0+0)	1+0	1
Palmer	44+2	(2+1)	2+0	4
Rodrigues	43+0	(0+1)	18+0	8/1
O'Brien	21+1	(6+0)	5+0	5
Austin	20+3	(21+0)	5+4	1
Bostock	14+1	(9+0)	1+0	0
Francis	6+2	(4+1)	1+0	4
Vincent	1+0	(8+0)	1+0	0
Jones (loan)	8+0	(8+0)	0+0	3
Castro (loan)	4+1	(10+0)	4+0	1
Lemonheigh-Evans (loan)	1+0	(4+0)	0+0	0
Langstaff	44+0	(1+1)	42+0	2
Scott	21+1	(15+0)	15+0	1
Mitchell	1+2	(14+1)	2+0	1
Morias	0+0	(2+0)	0+0	0
Mahovo	0+1	(0+0)	0+0	0
Munakandafa	0+0	(0+0)	0+0	0
Cisse (U19)	0+0	(0+1)	0+0	0
Gill (U19)	0+0	(0+1)	0+0	0
Fearon (U19)	0+0	(0+0)	0+0	0
		own goals	2+1	yellow totals may not be
			117+6	100% accurate

Notts County League (& Cup) Goal Scorers & Assists 2022-23, exc. Playoffs

Name	Goals	Cup Goals	Total	Assists	
Langstaff	42	(0)	= 42	8	
Rodrigues	18*	(0)	= 18	17	* inc 8 pens
Scott	15	(0)	= 15	2	
Chicksen	10	(1)	= 11	2	
Austin	5	(4)	= 9	13	
O'Brien	5*	(0)	= 5	3	* inc 1 pen
Castro	4	(0)	= 4	1	
Nemane	3	(0)	= 3	10	
Palmer	2	(0)	= 2	7	
Cameron	2	(0)	= 2	5	
Bajrami	2	(0)	= 2	0	
Mitchell	2	(0)	= 2	0	
Bostock	1	(0)	= 1	4	
Rawlinson	1	(0)	= 1	2	
Vincent	1	(0)	= 1	0	
Francis	1	(0)	= 1	0	
Taylor	1	(0)	= 1	1	
Adebayo-Rowling	0	(0)	= 0	3	
Jones	0	(0)	= 0	1	
Slocombe (Gk)	0	(0)	= 0	1	
Mair (Gk)	0	(0)	= 0	1	
Brooks (Gk)	0	(0)	= 0	0	
Baldwin	0	(0)	= 0	0	
Brindley	0	(0)	= 0	0	
Morias	0	(0)	= 0	0	
Lemonheigh-Evans	0	(0)	= 0	0	
Mahovo	0	(0)	= 0	0	
Munakandafa	0	(0)	= 0	0	
Cisse (U19)	0	(0)	= 0	0	
Gill (U19)	0	(0)	= 0	0	
Fearon (U19)	0	(0)	= 0	0	
Own goals	**2**	**(1)**	**=3**		
Total	**117**	**(6)**	**=123**	assist totals may not be 100% accurate	

Macaulay Langstaff's goals were all from open play – no penalties or free-kicks

Note the fantastic goal contribution by full back/wing back Adam Chicksen

Notts County Home Attendances 2022-23 (k.o. 15:00 unless stated)

Att.	Opponents	Date	
16,511*	Yeovil Town	19 Nov	10th home match (£5 adults, £1 under 16)
16,086	Scunthorpe Utd	25 Mar	20th home match (£10 adults, £5 concessions and under 22, £1 under 16)
11,336 (S)	York City	29 Apr (17:30)	last (23rd) home match of the season
10,741	Wrexham	4 Oct (19:45)	6th home match
9,789 (S)	Oldham Athletic	26 Dec	12th home match
9,786 (S)	Wealdstone	7 Apr	21st home match
8,520	Woking	15 Apr	22nd home match. Live on BT Sport
8,287	Chesterfield	20 Aug (17:20)	2nd home match. Live on BT Sport
7,563	Torquay Utd	29 Oct	8th home match
7,548	Halifax Town	28 Jan	14th home match
7,441	Dagenham & Redbridge	25 Feb (17:20)	17th home match. Live on BT Sport
7,237 (S)	Southend Utd	21 Feb (19:45)	16th home match
7,060	Dorking Wanderers	11 Mar (17:20)	18th home match. Live on BT Sport
7,004	Solihull Moors	29 Aug	3rd home match
6,891 (S)	Barnet	14 Feb	15th home match
6,765	Maidstone Utd	21 Oct (19:45)	7th home match
6,458	Altrincham	1 Oct	5th home match
6,389	Bromley	1 Nov (19:45)	9th home match
6,331	Maidenhead Utd	6 Aug	1st home league match of season
6,058 (S)	Eastleigh	14 Mar (19:45)	19th home match
6,033 (S)	Boreham Wood	10 Jan (19:45)	13th home match
5,607	Aldershot Town	13 Sep (19:45)	4th home match
5,539 (S)	Gateshead	12 Dec (19:45)	11th home match
5,060	Coalville Town	15 Oct	**FA Cup 4th Qualifying**
2,405	Maidstone Utd	15 Jan	**FA Trophy 4th Round**
2,040	Chorley	20 Dec (19:45)	**FA Trophy 3rd Round**

*Record for a (National League) regular-season non-league match
(S) = Streamed live (National League TV)

League Average Attendance (2019-2023)

2019-20	2020-21	2021-22	2022-23
League Average: 104,207 = 5,210	COVID-19	149,592 = 6,800	190,980 = 8,303
Cup(s) Average: 13,007 = 4,336	COVID-19	14,037 = 2,807	9,505 = 3,168
Combined Average: 117,214 = 5,096		163,629 = 6,060	200,485 = 7,711
Last 3 home matches cancelled (COVID-19). FA Trophy and playoff semi-finals both played behind closed doors at Meadow Lane. FA Trophy semi-final: Notts lost to Harrogate and were beaten by them at Wembley in the behind closed doors playoff final.	All behind closed doors, except the last league match on 22/5 = 4,197 and a playoff match on 5/6 = 4,569 – both had attendance restrictions.	Exc. playoff match 12,023	Exc. playoff semi-final 15,617

In the Wembley playoff final 22,500 (out of 38,138) saw Notts beat Chesterfield |

Final National League Table Season 2022-23

		GP	W	D	L	GF	GA	GD	Pts
1	Wrexham **Prom**	46	34	9	3	116	43	+73	**111**
2	**Notts Co Prom**	**46**	**32**	**11**	**3**	**117**	**42**	**+75**	**107**
3	Chesterfield	46	25	9	12	81	52	+29	**84**
4	Woking	46	24	10	12	71	48	+23	**82**
5	Barnet	46	21	11	14	75	67	+8	**74**
6	Boreham Wood	46	19	15	12	52	40	+12	**72**
7	Bromley	46	18	17	11	68	53	+15	**71**
8	Southend Utd	46	20	9	17	57	45	+12	**69**
9	Eastleigh	46	19	10	17	56	57	-1	**67**
10	Dagenham & Red.	46	18	9	19	61	72	-11	**63**
11	Halifax Town	46	16	13	17	49	48	+1	**61**
12	Oldham Athletic	46	16	13	17	63	64	-1	**61**
13	Wealdstone	46	16	12	18	57	72	-15	**60**
14	Gateshead FC *	46	15	15	16	67	62	+5	**59**
15	Solihull Moors	46	15	13	18	62	66	-4	**58**
16	Dorking Wanderers	46	16	9	21	67	91	-24	**57**
17	Altrincham	46	14	14	18	68	82	-14	**56**
18	Aldershot Town	46	14	11	21	64	76	-12	**53**
19	York City	46	13	12	21	55	63	-8	**51**
20	Maidenhead Utd	46	13	11	22	47	66	-19	**50**
21	Torquay Utd	46	12	12	22	58	80	-22	**48**
22	Yeovil Town	46	7	19	20	35	60	-25	**40**
23	Scunthorpe Utd	46	8	10	28	49	87	-38	**34**
24	Maidstone Utd	46	5	10	31	45	104	-59	**25**

Playoff results   Barnet 1-2 Boreham Wood   >   **Notts Co 3**-2 Boreham Wood (aet)
                 Woking 1-2 Bromley   >   Chesterfield 3-2 Bromley (aet)

Playoff Final, Wembley Saturday 13 May **Notts Co 2**-2 Chesterfield (aet) **Notts won 4-3 after pens**.

* Deducted 1 point   Positions 21-24 Relegated to National League (N)/(S)

Chapter 24: EFL League Two - A turbulent 2023-24 season

The week after Notts County's promotion from The National League into the English Football League (League Two), they issued their retained list:

Under contract

- Tiernan Brooks (Gk) — Subsequently loaned to League of Ireland Premier Division club Cork City in 2023, and then National League Rochdale between January-April 2024
- Aden Baldwin
- Lucien Mahovo — The 18 year old defender made one EFL Trophy start. Loaned to Boston Utd in March 2024
- Geraldo Bajrami — Sustained a serious knee injury in August 2023 – no league matches played during the season
- Adam Chicksen
- Richard Brindley
- Tobi Adebayo-Rowling
- John Bostock
- Matt Palmer — Sustained a knee injury in October 2023 – out for the rest of the season
- Luther Munakandafa — The 19 year old forward made two EFL Trophy appearances, before then being loaned out twice
- Sam Austin
- Junior Morias — Injury and illness meant he was rarely involved during the season
- Cedwyn Scott — Sustained a knee injury in August 2023 – returned with four late substitute appearances in April
- Macaulay Langstaff
- **Jodi Jones** — Arrived on loan in January 2023, then accepted the offer of a permanent contract in May 2023

Offered new contract

- Sam Slocombe (Gk) — all
- Kyle Cameron — signed
- Connell Rawlinson — a new
- Aaron Nemane — contract,
- Jim O'Brien — except
- **Ruben Rodrigues** — transferred to Oxford Utd, League One, in summer 2023

Released and Loan deals expiring

- Ed Francis   (signed for Gateshead, National League)
- Frank Vincent   (signed for Dagenham & Redbridge, National League)
- Kairo Mitchell   (signed for Rochdale, National League)

- Archie Mair (Gk)   returned to Norwich City, after his heroics at Wembley

There were additions to the above 20 (contracted) players. The first four signed in pre-season, with a two-year contract.

David McGoldrick, age 35, a forward. Notts were "thrilled" to sign such an experienced player:

A return to Meadow Lane after enjoying a phenomenal 2022-23 campaign with League One Derby County, scoring 25 goals and being named Fans' and Players' Player of the Season. Unsurprisingly, he was offered the chance to stay at Pride Park but he instead decided to fulfil his long-held ambition of returning to his boyhood club.

The Nottingham-born forward progressed through our academy and made his senior debut aged just 16 in a 2-1 home defeat to Swindon Town in 2004. He went on to make another three appearances that season, which ended in relegation, before then-Premier League side Southampton signed him for an undisclosed fee. After returning to us on loan in 2005-06, he went on to establish himself at St Mary's and finished the 2008-09 season as the Saints' top scorer with 14 goals as they were relegated from the Championship.

That paved the way for a £1million move to Nottingham Forest and, while his City Ground career never really got going, a loan move to League One Coventry sparked his goal scoring into life as he finished the first half of the season with 16 from 22 appearances.

He returned to the Championship in the new year with a loan to Ipswich Town, a move which was made permanent the following season. He went on to score 45 goals in 159 appearances for the Tractor Boys before signing for Sheffield United ahead of the 2018-19 campaign.

His performances soon earned him an extension to his initial one-year deal and he repaid the Blades with a total of 15 goals to help fire them into the Premier League, scooping the Fans' Player of the Season award in the process. He went on to make 63 Premier League appearances for United, scoring 10 top-flight goals including a delightful finish against Arsenal which saw him win the club's 2020-21 Goal of the Season award. A beacon of light in a Blades side that suffered relegation to the Championship, his team-mates voted him their Players' Player of the Season and,

> *despite the following campaign being hampered by injury, he continued to have a positive influence at Bramall Lane as a mentor to younger team-mates. He departed at the end of that season, with manager Paul Heckingbottom describing him as 'a great bloke and a winner', qualities recognised by Derby as they brought him in on a one-year contract last summer.*
>
> *And it proved to be an outstanding piece of business for our near neighbours as he notched an incredible three hat-tricks on his way to scoring 22 goals in League One.*
>
> *David also boasts international experience having won 14 caps for Republic of Ireland.*
>
> *His contributions on the national stage were recognised when he was voted the FAI's Senior International Player of the Year in 2020, shortly before he retired to focus more on family and his club career.*

Dan Crowley, age 25, attacking midfielder, signed from Morecambe. League One and Championship experience. He had also played in the top tier of Dutch football. He went on to have an outstanding first season at Meadow Lane.

Will Randall-Hurren, age 26, wide midfielder, from Sutton Utd. A series of minor injuries and loss of form limited his Notts appearances.

Aidan Stone (Gk), age 23, on a free transfer from Port Vale. Experience in League Two with Mansfield, and League One with Vale. He made more appearances than Slocombe during the season, but didn't make the starting eleven after the 1-3 home defeat to Gillingham on 9 February.

In July 2023, Notts appointed Joe Palmer as their new chief executive.

The announcement began:

> *Boasting considerable EFL experience from his time as chief operating officer at Sheffield Wednesday and chief executive at AFC Wimbledon, Palmer is also highly regarded following his time at Shakhtar Donetsk where, as their executive director of strategy, commerce and marketing, he played a pivotal role in the Ukrainian club's dramatic growth during its exciting Champions League era.*

Our owners, Chris and Alex Reedtz, said:

> *"Joe impressed us during an extremely thorough recruitment process, demonstrating a wealth of leadership experience from his many years in football. We're confident he will be a great fit for the role and will do a fantastic job leading and supporting our administrative team, who have guided the club brilliantly in the wake of Jason Turner's tragic passing and our promotion back to the EFL. Joe is someone we believe can help the club reach it's huge commercial potential and we're excited to work with him."*

Palmer, who commenced his role in early August, added:

> *"I would like to acknowledge the tremendous foundations laid by my predecessor, Jason, at Meadow Lane. Unfortunately, I didn't know Jason personally but I have huge respect for the work he did and the reputation he developed not only at Notts, but everywhere he worked. The response of the football community to the shocking news of his passing showed how highly regarded he was and I'm very much looking forward to meeting his family at the Grimsby match, when the Meadow Lane boardroom will be officially renamed in his memory. I'm extremely grateful to Chris and Alex for selecting me as the man to fill the huge void left by Jason."*

> *"Notts County is one of English football's greatest treasures. It's a brilliant club and I'm categorically invested in the way the owners want to move it forward. Their data-driven, analytical and pragmatic approach is, I believe, a recipe for success and we have already begun to see that in action with the club's long-awaited return to the EFL."*

On 5 August Notts lost (5-1) their first match of the season at Sutton. Stone (goalkeeper) was sent off after 15 minutes with the score 1-0 to Sutton. O'Brien was substituted and Slocombe took over in goal. They were then unbeaten in their next eight league matches with six wins and two draws, and ascended to the top of the league in early September.

On 30 September they suffered a 5-4 defeat at Colchester, which was the start of some indifferent form. The beginning of October saw Notts beat Swindon at home, followed by a draw at Barrow. Before the end of the month Mansfield, who won 4-1, and Wrexham (won 2-0) achieved victories at Meadow Lane, but in-between Notts beat Gillingham and Newport.

In mid-November a scintillating first half performance against Bradford City earned them a 4-0 half-time lead (final score 4-2), but the following week Notts lost (4-2) at Wimbledon.

On 1 December after a shocking defensive display at home to League One Shrewsbury they exited the FA Cup in the second round, suffering a 2-3 defeat.

Three successive league defeats followed, at home to Walsall and at Harrogate and top of the league Stockport. Impressive victories at Meadow Lane, over Doncaster (3-0) and Morecambe (5-0), between Christmas and the New Year were welcome. However, Notts started 2024 with a depressing defeat (4-2) at Tranmere on New Year's Day.

To cut a long story short, Notts had lost five and drawn one in matches against teams in the top seven, and conceded 13 goals against the three bottom teams!

There were, however, two notable events in the first half of the season:

Notts played their 5,000th EFL match at Gillingham on 21 October. In their FA Cup defeat to Shrewsbury Town, 17-year-old James Sanderson scored on his debut - two minutes after his arrival from the substitute's bench.

It was understandable that during the latter part of 2023 there was increasing concern that form had become inconsistent. During what turned out to be the last two months of Luke Williams' reign, Notts' results were disappointing: P11 W4 D0 L7, including the Shrewsbury fiasco.

There were also three player updates:

Ollie Tipton, age 19, a young defender from Premier League Wolverhampton Wanderers. When he arrived in July, it was initially for a season long loan, but he was recalled by Wolves on 2 January 2024. He did not start a league game.

Lewis Macari, age 21. The defender joined on 1 September from Championship side Stoke City, on loan until January. (Stoke loaned him to Dundalk for the 2022 League of Ireland season). In mid-December he signed a permanent contract with Notts until the end of the 2026-27 season, and then made regular League Two starts from February onwards.

Dan Gosling, age 33, central midfielder. A free agent, he signed in early November on a short-term contract until 6 January 2024 when Matty Palmer was ruled out with injury for the rest of the season. An experienced Premier League and Championship player (nearly 300 appearances). During his two month stay his Notts league appearances were from the substitute's bench.

Notts ended 2023 fifth in League Two, P26 W13 D3 L10 F55 A47 Pts 42.

At the start of the season, such a lofty playoff position at the turn of the year would have been considered very acceptable. However, recent form had been erratic.

League Two table on 1 January 2024, with Notts' results to date

		GP	Pts	Home	Away
1	Stockport	26	51		2 - 1
2	Mansfield	24	49	1 - 4	
3	Wrexham	25	49	0 - 2	
4	Barrow	25	45		1 - 1
5	**Notts County**	**26**	**42**		
6	Crewe	25	41		1 - 0
7	AFC Wimbledon	25	39		4 - 2
8	Milton Keynes	24	39		1 - 1
9	Accrington	26	38	3 - 1	
10	Gillingham	25	38		1 - 2
11	Walsall	25	36	1 - 2	
12	Crawley	25	36	3 - 1	
13	Bradford	25	34	4 - 2	
14	Harrogate	25	34		3 - 1
15	Tranmere	26	33	2 - 1	4 - 2
16	Swindon	26	33	3 - 1	
17	Morecambe	24	33	5 - 0	0 - 0
18	Newport	26	31	3 - 0	
19	Doncaster	25	28	3 - 0	1 - 3
20	Grimsby	26	27	3 - 2	
21	Salford	25	23		0 - 2
22	Colchester	26	23		5 - 4
23	Sutton	25	18		5 - 1
24	Forest Green	24	17	4 - 3	

At the end of the season a finish in positions 1, 2, and 3 earned promotion into EFL League One. Positions 4-7 - a playoff campaign, the winner being the fourth promoted team - which turned out to be Crawley. Also, Doncaster, in 22nd position with only 29 points on 3 February, eventually reached the playoffs but lost to Crewe!

The bottom two (positions 23 and 24) - relegation into The National League.

Five days into the New Year, Notts announced that Luke Williams had left to become head coach at his previous club – Swansea City:

The two clubs have agreed compensation for the 43-year-old, who joins the Sky Bet Championship outfit along with his assistant Ryan Harley and coach George Lawtey.

A statement from our board of directors:

"As disappointed as we are to lose Luke, he departs with nothing but our very best wishes.

We're sure this sentiment will be shared by our supporters, who have grown to love him not only for his phenomenal achievements but also his infectious personality. He will be forever known as the man who took the world's oldest professional club back into the EFL, breaking records and creating lifelong memories along the way.

"The high-profile nature of our achievements since Luke's arrival 18 months ago, coupled with the immense respect he holds within the game, mean it's come as no surprise that he's attracted interest from higher in the pyramid. Our focus now has to be on finding a new head coach to build on the excellent foundations he's laid.

"It's important to remember that the club operates in a way that protects itself against the loss of a key figure like Luke. While his presence will naturally be missed, our vision remains the same and we're very confident of finding a suitable replacement to fit our ethos and help the club challenge for promotion to League One.

"It's still very much our intention to strengthen the squad this month and, as evidenced in the summer of Ian Burchnall's departure, we're more than capable of doing so without a head coach in place should the correct opportunity arise.

"We thank our fans for their ongoing support and will provide a further update when appropriate."

In the interim, first-team affairs will be handled by Jim O'Brien, Tom Weal and Joao Alves. O'Brien, the club's longest-serving player, possesses the UEFA A Licence and has already taken his first steps into coaching with a role in Sheffield United's academy. Weal is well known to supporters as our head of goalkeeping and set-piece coach, while Alves has been part of our first-team coaching and analysis set-up for several years.

In charge 14 June 2022 to 5 January 2024 his league record for Notts was, to use one of his favourite words, "incredible" P72 W45 D14 L13 F172 A89 Pts 149 – wins 63%.

In Jim O'Brien's first, and only, match in charge on Saturday 13 January, Notts achieved something they had not managed since their formation in 1862 – a scoreline of 5-5 - away at Grimsby Town. The Notts starting eleven was:

Stone (gk), Cameron (Capt.), Baldwin, Rawlinson, Jones, Nemane (60', 79'), Bostock, Robertson, Crowley, McGoldrick (39', 90'+2), Langstaff (45'). To the disappointment of 1,188 Notts supporters in an attendance of 7,567, Grimsby's equaliser came after 90'+5!

On 18 January 2024 came the announcement of the successor to Luke Williams:

Stuart Maynard

The 43-year-old new head coach signed a three and a half year contract. He had been manager at National League club Wealdstone since March 2021. Stuart brought with him his assistant at Wealdstone, Matt Saunders, and also his first team coach, Craig Saunders.

Joao Alves (Notts Analyst) was promoted to the role of first team coach to work alongside Stuart, Matt and Craig.

A statement from the board of directors read:

> *"We've been tracking Stuart's progress for a long time and have huge respect for the outstanding job he's done at Wealdstone on limited resources.*
>
> *"We believe he will thrive in a full-time environment and is an excellent fit for us in terms of his playing philosophy, which puts him in a strong position to settle in quickly and lead our continued push for promotion to League One.*
>
> *"Alongside Matt and Craig, he has formed a formidable and dedicated coaching team who will integrate seamlessly into our existing set-up as we look to build on the foundations we've laid during our adaptation to life back in the EFL."*

January was also notable for Notts in the transfer market with four signings, one permanent and three on loan until the end of the season:

Scott Robertson, age 22, signed on 1 January – just prior to the departure of Luke Williams, on a free transfer from League One Fleetwood Town. His contract was for two-and-a-half-years. With Bajrami and Palmer side-lined with long-term injuries Notts needed a central midfielder. He made his debut in the 5-5 draw at Grimsby, and started most matches thereafter.

Luca Ashby-Hammond (goalkeeper), age 22, arrived on 10 January from Premier League Fulham on loan. During the first half of the season he had been at fellow League Two club Crawley Town. After making his debut on 13 February he played 11 matches (Slocombe 5).

Jaden Warner, age 21, the central defender joined from Championship club Norwich City on 22 January on loan. Three Norwich appearances early in the season. Made eight Notts starts in February and March.

Charlie Colkett, age 27, the midfielder signed from fellow League Two club Crewe Alexandra on 31 January, on loan. Although a highly-rated product of Chelsea's academy, with later experience in League One and the top tier of Swedish football at Ostersunds, he only made a few substitute appearances for Notts.

On Saturday 20 January, Stuart Maynard's scheduled first Notts County match against top of the league Stockport County at Meadow Lane was postponed due to a frozen pitch. This gave everyone an additional seven days to get to know each another, before the match against fifth placed Barrow. So, he inherited a team seventh in League Two, who in 27 matches had scored 60 goals but conceded 52. In his first match, in front of 11,243 at Meadow Lane, Notts drew 1-1 against Barrow on 27 January.

Question: Name the Notts player who scored four goals, in three matches for three different 'managers', in the space of 27 days: one goal in the last match Luke Williams was head coach, two goals for one match caretaker Jim O'Brien, and the first goal for Stuart Maynard?

Clue: In 40 league and cup appearances last season he scored just three goals. **Answer:** in jumbled letters… anagram = MANNEARONEA.

Notts were defeated in five of their six matches in February. Admittedly, two were at Mansfield (Maynard's first away from home) and Wrexham. They lost both 1-0. The 1-3 home defeat to Gillingham on 9 February was the first of five consecutively at Meadow Lane. The sequence was halted on 1 April when Nemane scored in the 91st minute to earn a 3-3 draw against Milton Keynes.

Of six matches played in March, Notts lost the first two and the last two. Sandwiched in-between were two encouraging away results: a 2-2 draw at Accrington, followed by an impressive 0-3 victory at Bradford City when two of the goals were scored by recent signing Alassana Jatta. He scored his first Notts goal at Accrington in his first Notts start after a few substitute appearances.

Jatta (Age 25, born in Gambia, and 6'4") was signed on 1 February from Danish top-flight side Viborg, for an undisclosed fee, and given a two and a half year contract: For Viborg, the forward scored 21 goals in 103 appearances.

Richard Montague, who sits on Notts' board and leads on recruitment said:

> "We're really excited about the qualities Alassana will bring to our forward line in terms of his stature, pace and power. We also feel he has the energy and willingness to press relentlessly from the front, something we demand from all our forwards.
>
> "With our owners, Chris and Alex Reedtz, being involved at Viborg we also have an excellent insight into his character and therefore know he has conducted himself in a thoroughly professional, positive and hard-working manner throughout his time there.
>
> "We rate the Danish league highly and have been impressed with how he's performed at the top level over the last three seasons, so we think he can be very effective for us in League Two and at a higher level in the future. Viborg play in a relatively similar way to us, so we feel he can make a quick adaptation to life at Meadow Lane and add fresh impetus to what is already a highly potent attack.
>
> "We also know that he turned down another very attractive move to join us, which highlights his enthusiasm for the club and the ambitions we've outlined to him."

By the end of the season Jatta had scored five goals in ten appearances (6 starts).

During April 2024, the last month of the season, two important updates were posted on Notts' Club News. The first update was seen as a vote of confidence in Notts' head coach, Stuart Maynard. It was posted on 5th April, four days after Aaron Nemane scored the equaliser in time added at the end of the second half in the 3-3 draw at Meadow Lane against MK Dons. Without that goal Notts would have been defeated for a record sixth consecutive home match.

> **Our board of directors have provided an update to supporters as the 2023-24 campaign nears its conclusion.**
>
> *We'd like to begin by thanking all our fans for backing the team in tremendous numbers home and away this season. It's disappointing that it's now highly unlikely that we'll be able to reward that support with the top-seven finish we aimed for, with performance levels and league position both falling below our expectations.*
>
> *However, while we're all dissatisfied with recent results and the outcome of the season, our analysis shows that performance levels over the course of the campaign have merited a much better league position – and therefore the improvement required for us to compete for promotion next season, as will be our aim, isn't as large as the table would suggest.*

When carefully analysing our performance levels over the long term, we use metrics primarily based on goalscoring chances created/conceded and the quality of such chances. These metrics have been proven to give a more accurate guide to the quality of a team's performances than league position and, overall, they haven't been as strong as we'd hoped for this season.

However, they do clearly show that our performances have been good enough to earn a league position significantly better than the 16th place we currently find ourselves in, and we must therefore take this information into consideration when planning for the immediate future.

The metrics also show that our performance levels haven't changed significantly over the season. This may seem counter-intuitive, given the bad results we've experienced since the turn of the year, but we haven't been significantly outplayed by any team in that time and have generally created at least as many, and in some cases more, high-quality goalscoring opportunities than our opponents.

Due to the huge amount of luck and variance in results, we always try to look at the bigger picture. Many games have been lost due to fine margins and could easily have gone the other way. Conversely, we had luck on our side on a few occasions at the beginning of the season, picking up better results despite not playing better or worse than we have done in 2024.

Clearly, our weakness this season has been the high number of goals we've conceded – but it would be unfair to blame this only on our defensive players. Minimising the number of goals against us isn't just about defending our penalty area or reducing errors near our goal, it also requires the entire team to defend as a unit in order to prevent opponents reaching dangerous attacking positions in the first place. Individual mistakes that lead to a goal are always most noticeable, but it's crucial that we improve all the aforementioned aspects of our defensive play.

As you would expect, Stuart Maynard and his team are working hard on this and we believe we're on track to build a team with the right balance between attack and defence, which will concede far fewer goals and bring an improved level of performance next season.

We also look forward to the return of important players from injury, the coaching team having more time to implement their ideas and the arrival of new signings, with our preparation for summer recruitment already well underway alongside Stuart.

While we have ambitious plans to improve the club's standing in the pyramid, these are long-term and based on financial sustainability and value-based decision making. Put simply, our intention will never be to seek success 'at all costs'.

Instead, we will continue our efforts to strike the correct balance between on-field competitiveness and financial responsibility in order to safeguard the club's future, as well as to ensure we're adequately prepared for the possibility of tighter financial restrictions being imposed by governing bodies in the future.

On the issue of sustainability, we support these words from the EFL which we believe will also resonate with our fans given the difficult financial positions the club has found itself in over the course of its history: "It has been clear that the English game needs a fundamental financial reset in order to be sustainable so that all clubs can continue to serve their supporters and communities long into the future." We feel our club has the potential to be a leader in achieving sustainable success.

As proved in last season's incredible title battle with Wrexham, we know we can compete with anyone at our level regardless of budgets and we also have complete faith in our bespoke, continually-evolving data model – the efficacy of which will only be enhanced by our learnings from our first season in League Two.

Crucial to the club's on-field progress is the development of our commercial revenues, which we're pleased to say is on the right track thanks to the work of our chief executive, Joe Palmer, and his team. Joe will soon be providing a detailed overview of the tremendous progress he's overseen in his first season in post, including news of our commitment to significant further investment in infrastructure ahead of the new season.

We look forward to discussing our strategy in further detail with supporters at a post-season fans' forum. In the meantime, we ask you to continue your brilliant support of Stuart and the team between now and the end of the campaign.

Chris Reedtz, Alex Reedtz and Richard Montague – Board of Directors

The second update, three days after the one issued by the board of directors, came from CEO Joe Palmer.

Following the recent message from our board of directors, which highlighted the importance of the club maximising its commercial revenues in order to support a sustainable pursuit of their substantial, long-term footballing ambitions, I'm pleased to bring you an overview of the work that's been carried out, and the significant financial commitments Chris and Alex Reedtz have made, towards that in 2023-24.

On my arrival at the club last summer I discussed the importance of exploring innovative ideas which could open new revenue streams for years to come, rather than solely relying on 'traditional' forms of income. We set to work on this straightaway and, in February, announced plans to develop a best-in-class fanzone and events space on the perimeter of Meadow Lane.

I'm delighted to say that we have now been granted planning permission to proceed with this huge, and extremely exciting, project – and intend to open in time for the commencement of England's participation in this summer's European Championships, with the aim of providing the best destination in Nottingham for football fans to watch the eagerly-anticipated tournament unfold.

The venue, titled the Nest and boasting a capacity of more than 1,000, will be our own take on the likes of Boxpark, with work to begin soon on a comprehensive refurbishment and the installation of state-of-the-art lighting, sound and screens.

On a site previously occupied by East Midlands Fabrications on Iremonger Road, and sharing a boundary with the Derek Pavis car park.

For Notts fans, the matchday experience will be revolutionised. As I discussed following the installation of a new container bar behind the Kop, our growing fanbase deserve far more in terms of food, beverage and pre/post-match entertainment – and they can now look forward to having one of the very best provisions in English football from the start of the 2024-25 season.

Supporters will be able to watch the early and late Premier League kick-offs, sample delicious street food from a top-class rotation of vendors and quickly buy refreshments from a large bar – all within an incredibly short walk of the turnstiles. On non-matchdays, the possibilities are endless with the space lending itself perfectly to a variety of events including beer and food festivals, comedy, film screenings, e-sports and much more.

We can't wait to begin working with new partners to build a year-round schedule of events that will bring thousands of new people to Meadow Lane, while also providing a host of employment opportunities to the city.

The work is only just beginning so, if you'd like to receive regular updates on the Nest including details of how to book your place for the Euros, please register with us. We'd also be delighted to hear from businesses who'd be interested in bringing their events to us.

Continuing on the theme of matchday experience, I'm pleased to say that next season's hospitality provision will be greatly enhanced by the reconfiguration and expansion of the corporate seating area in the Derek Pavis Stand. In line with the club's growth in recent years, we're experiencing unprecedented demand for hospitality but are hampered by a limited number of premium seats, which quickly sell out for every match.

For context, our suites can accommodate up to 450 guests per match – but with only 200 premium seats available we're not even close to maximising our potential. To resolve this, we'll be relocating the press box and making some other adjustments in that area to ensure we can create a true VIP experience for all our hospitality guests from 2024-25 onwards. We're working on an exciting new range of packages, too, so I'd encourage you to register for updates on all things hospitality ahead of the new season.

An improved hospitality offering will make us a far more attractive prospect to club partners – and to help us find them I'm delighted to welcome Adam Chantrey into the brand-new role of Head of Commercial Sales. Adam brings with him a wealth of experience and contacts from his very successful time at Lincoln City and would love to hear from businesses large and small who are interested in any of our newly-developed sponsorship or advertising packages.

As part of the restructure of the commercial team, Jordan Worthington has taken on a new role as our Head of Venue, Ticketing and Retail, which will see him put the considerable knowledge he's developed across various departments to brilliant use as part of our continued efforts to provide the best possible service to fans and customers.

In line with this, the club will be undergoing a digital transformation this summer with the introduction of a brand-new website, bespoke app and retail provider. These new platforms will vastly improve the way fans interact with us across all our touchpoints and we look forward to providing more information in due course.

While there are many more projects in development, including the impending launch of our first two BTEC courses through our Learning and Innovation Centre, the final one I'd like to discuss is our commitment to a full reconstruction of the Meadow Lane pitch – the first of its kind since the stadium's redevelopment in the 1990s.

Thanks to the tremendous efforts of our groundstaff, it may come as a surprise to fans that the pitch is in desperate need of reconstruction. Both the underlying drainage system and the sub-soil base are starting to fail and require total replacement. In truth, we can count ourselves fortunate not to have had matches postponed due to waterlogging this season - and the board have agreed that now is the correct time to resolve this issue by thoroughly modernising the entire infrastructure of the pitch and its surroundings. As well as state-of-the-art drainage, which will all but eradicate the threat of waterlogging, a new hybrid SIS pitch will be installed – bringing the composition of our playing surface up to Premier League level.

The works will also allow us to meet FIFA standards in terms of playable area, meaning we'll be in a position to host top-class football events, as well as other sports such as rugby, should any proposal to do so make financial sense to us.

We'll also be taking the opportunity to install an undersoil heating system – although it's important to note that, due to the costs involved, this won't be connected to a boiler until such time we encounter consistently lengthy cold spells, where a number of matches are put at risk.

This project will begin very soon after the final home match of the season and, due to its extensive nature, it's unlikely we'll be able to host any home friendlies this summer. While it would have been possible to carry out lesser works on the pitch, the decision to do so would simply have put off the inevitability of a full reconstruction. By taking action now, we're eradicating the issues, future-proofing the club for progress up the pyramid and guaranteeing a phenomenal surface for our players, and prospective signings, to showcase the best of their abilities.

I'd like to take this opportunity to thank everyone at the club for their excellent efforts in progressing the aforementioned projects over the course of the season.

Of course, the highest debt of gratitude is owed to Chris and Alex, whose incredible vision and backing, combined with their outstanding methodology, leaves me in a position that I'm sure would be the envy of many chief executives across football. While the vast majority of their work will never be seen, their achievements since taking on the world's oldest professional club at the lowest point in its history are nothing short of remarkable and I couldn't be more excited about where this club could, and I firmly believe will, go in the future.

But we will only undertake that journey in a rational, responsible way, while always knowing that the nature of football means you can never guarantee short-term success. What you can control is your chance of being successful over time and, by delivering on what I've spoken about today, we will take the club to another level financially and move towards achieving the state of 'football utopia' by breaking even, or better still becoming profitable, while also providing one of the most competitive budgets in the *league and the best possible experience for our fans. We're already making good progress towards that but there is still so much work to do.*

We will, of course, keep you updated on our ongoing progress – including the communication of details regarding our 2024-25 ticketing programme.

Joe Palmer – CEO

After the 3-3 draw with MK Dons on 1 April, Notts won three of their remaining five matches of the season - convincing victories, 3-0 over Harrogate and 1-0 over relegation threatened Colchester, at Meadow Lane, and 1-3 at Walsall. However, a 2-5 home loss to champions Stockport County extinguished any lingering hopes of reaching a seventh place finish and a playoff place. In the final match of the season, at bottom of the league and relegated Forest Green Rovers, Notts suffered a very disappointing 1-0 defeat.

It was understandable that some supporters were questioning the appointment of Stuart Maynard. During his 19 matches Notts dropped from seventh to fourteenth at the end of the season.

His record from his arrival in January was disappointing:

P19 W5 D3 L11 F29 A34 Pts 18 (out of a possible 57). Although he was not responsible for some of the following statistics, they are included to illustrate what in many ways became a rather disappointing season for Notts:

Against the teams who finished in the top seven Notts' record was dismal:

P14 W3 D2 L9 F19 A27. They lost all six against the three promoted (Stockport, Wrexham, Mansfield) and scored only 4, conceding 15. Against the two relegated, Sutton did the double over Notts, but Notts just managed a victory at Meadow Lane over Forest Green. So, P4 W1 D0 L3 F8 A13.

As well as conceding 17 penalties (by far the highest of all 92 teams in the top four tiers) they also committed a significant number of appalling defensive errors. The total number of league goals conceded was 86 (worst defence in League Two). If cup matches are included the total number conceded was 99! On the positive side only Stockport and Mansfield scored more league goals than Notts' 89 (96 including cup competitions). Wrexham also scored 89.

Some other statistics were: the fewest fouls committed in League Two (356), and the highest number of passes (almost 28,000). With 6,000 season ticket holders, the average Meadow Lane attendance was 10,905, including 16,638 and 16,083 (versus Mansfield and Wrexham respectively). This average was their highest for over thirty years. The away following once again exceeded expectations, often greater than 1,000 supporters.

For the second successive season Macaulay Langstaff was Notts' leading scorer, and the top scorer in League Two, with 28 goals – Crowley 15, McGoldrick 12. Jodi Jones provided 24 assists (not all for Langstaff) – an English professional record. Not bad for a player who suffered over five years of injury before he joined Notts.

For info: In the three tiers above Notts the 'golden boot' was won by:

Erling Haaland 27 for Premier League champions Manchester City

Sammie Szmodics 27 (Blackburn Rovers, Championship)

Alfie May 23 (Charlton Athletic, League One)

In terms of player league appearances:

The three goalkeepers (Slocombe, Stone, and Ashby-Hammond) have already been mentioned. Brooks had two loans away from Meadow Lane. This is a problem position. Some stability is required.

In outfield positions Langstaff, Cameron, Crowley, Jones, Nemane, Baldwin, McGoldrick, Bostock, Austin, O'Brien, Brindley, and Rawlinson, were well supported by Macari (loan, then permanent signing mid-December), Robertson (signed 1 January), Palmer (until injured in October), Chicksen, Adebayo-Rowling, Warner, and Jatta (signed 1 February).

Unfortunately, Morias, Randall-Hurren, Mahovo, and Munakandafa had little game time. Youngster James Sanderson made two substitute appearances.

Gosling, Colkett, and Tipton, together with youngsters Cisse and Gill, were on the periphery of the first team squad.

Bajrami and Scott were absent for virtually the whole season through injury – neither made a league start.

Finally, to conclude an eventful season, below are the final League Two table, the Notts County 2023-24 awards, and the 2024 Retained List:

EFL League Two Final Table Season 2023-24

			Home				Away					Overall						
		P	W	D	L	F	A	W	D	L	F	A	W	D	L	F	A	GD	PTS
1	Stockport County (Promoted)	46	15	5	3	48	17	12	6	5	48	31	27	11	8	96	48	48	**92**
2	Wrexham (Promoted)	46	17	3	3	62	25	9	7	7	27	27	26	10	10	89	52	37	**88**
3	Mansfield Town (Promoted)	46	13	7	3	43	22	11	7	5	47	25	24	14	8	90	47	43	**86**
4	MK Dons	46	14	5	4	48	27	9	4	10	35	41	23	9	14	83	68	15	**78**
5	Doncaster Rovers	46	14	2	7	38	30	7	6	10	35	38	21	8	17	73	68	5	**71**
6	Crewe Alexandra	46	11	5	7	35	35	8	9	6	34	30	19	14	13	69	65	4	**71**
7	Crawley Town (Promoted)	46	11	3	9	37	30	10	4	9	36	37	21	7	18	73	67	6	**70**
8	Barrow	46	11	8	4	28	19	7	7	9	34	37	18	15	13	62	56	6	**69**
9	Bradford City	46	9	8	6	29	28	10	4	9	32	31	19	12	15	61	59	2	**69**
10	AFC Wimbledon	46	11	6	6	41	25	6	8	9	23	26	17	14	15	64	51	13	**65**
11	Walsall	46	12	6	5	35	25	6	5	12	34	48	18	11	17	69	73	-4	**65**
12	Gillingham	46	9	9	5	25	23	9	1	13	21	34	18	10	18	46	57	-11	**64**
13	Harrogate Town	46	9	3	11	35	37	8	9	6	25	32	17	12	17	60	69	-9	**63**
14	Notts County	46	12	2	9	51	42	6	5	12	38	44	18	7	21	89	86	3	**61**
15	Morecambe (deducted 3 pts)	46	8	7	8	29	29	9	3	11	38	52	17	10	19	67	81	-14	**58**
16	Tranmere Rovers	46	12	3	8	44	32	5	3	15	23	38	17	6	23	67	70	-3	**57**
17	Accrington Stanley	46	10	5	8	34	27	6	4	13	29	44	16	9	21	63	71	-8	**57**
18	Newport County	46	9	6	8	37	37	7	1	15	25	39	16	7	23	62	76	-14	**55**
19	Swindon Town	46	11	5	7	45	34	3	7	13	32	49	14	12	20	77	83	-6	**54**
20	Salford City	46	5	8	10	37	46	8	4	11	29	36	13	12	21	66	82	-16	**51**
21	Grimsby Town	46	9	5	9	34	41	2	11	10	23	33	11	16	19	57	74	-17	**49**
22	Colchester United	46	6	7	10	34	41	5	5	13	25	39	11	12	23	59	80	-21	**45**
23	Sutton United (Relegated)	46	5	9	9	33	34	4	6	13	26	50	9	15	22	59	84	-25	**42**
24	Forest Green Rovers (Relegated)	46	5	4	14	19	38	6	5	12	25	40	11	9	26	44	78	-34	**42**

Jodi Jones

- Sky Bet League Two Player of the Season
- Sky Bet League Two Team of the Season
- Fans' Player of the Season
- Players' Player of the Season
- Outstanding Achievement (24 assists)

Macaulay Langstaff

- Sky Bet League Two Golden Boot (28 goals)
- Sky Bet League Two Team of the Season

Aaron Nemane

- Goal of the Season (Walsall away)

James Sanderson

- Under 21s Player of the Season (chosen by NCFCOSA)

Two days after the defeat at Forest Green Rovers in the last match of the 2023-24 season, Notts issued their retained list, which included 17-year-old James Sanderson. The attacking midfielder signed a two-and-a-half-year professional contract in January 2024.

Under contract

- Sam Slocombe
- Tiernan Brooks
- Kyle Cameron
- Lewis Macari
- Lucien Mahovo
- Adam Chicksen
- Jodi Jones
- Aaron Nemane
- Matt Palmer
- Scott Robertson
- Dan Crowley
- Sam Austin
- James Sanderson
- Macaulay Langstaff
- David McGoldrick
- Junior Morias
- Alassana Jatta

Option taken to extend contract

- Cedwyn Scott

Out of contract, offered new deal

- Geraldo Bajrami

Under contract, available for transfer

- Aidan Stone
- Connell Rawlinson
- Will Randall

Out of contract, released

- Aden Baldwin
- Richard Brindley
- Tobi Adebayo
- Jim O'Brien
- John Bostock
- Luther Munakandafa

Loan players returning to parent club

Luca Ashby-Hammond, Jaden Warner, Charlie Colkett

The board of directors issued the following statement:

We'd like to place on record our immense gratitude to Jim O'Brien, Richard Brindley, Connell Rawlinson, John Bostock, Aden Baldwin and Tobi Adebayo for their tremendous efforts in their time at the club.

"Jim is the only member of the squad who pre-dates our arrival, having joined the battle against relegation in January 2019. He went on to be an integral part of our efforts to restore our EFL status and, having helped us achieve that in 2022-23, has this season recorded his highest number of appearances for the club (43). That fact is made all the more impressive when you consider his playing duties took a back seat in the wake of Luke Williams' departure, when he accepted the huge challenge of managing team affairs. Jim applied himself to that role with the same level of dedication that we have seen from him on the pitch week in, week out - and proved why he will go on to have an outstanding coaching career. Despite his strong performances this season, we feel

now is the right time to part ways – but he moves on having firmly established himself as an iconic figure in the history of the world's oldest professional club.

Connell and Richard were two of our earliest signings, joining shortly after our takeover as we were assembling the squad which went on to reach the play-off final in the club's first season in the National League. They were mainstays of our team as we continued to push for promotion in the years that followed – and fittingly were both on the pitch as our winning penalty ensured their efforts were rewarded in last season's Wembley final.

Their fellow defender, Aden Baldwin, can also take immense pride in what he's achieved in his time at Meadow Lane. As well as being an outstanding performer in our promotion season, we would never have reached Wembley without his two heroic goals in the semi-final against Boreham Wood.

John and Tobi are two other players who have established themselves as huge characters at the club. As well as being a thoroughly professional and calming presence away from the field, John made many excellent performances for us – not least at Wembley, where his incredibly composed display and all-important equaliser were crucial to us winning the promotion he and his team-mates so richly deserved.

Tobi also played his part in last season's success and his infectious personality, combined with the extreme qualities he possesses, will make him a very attractive prospect for many clubs this summer.

We know our supporters will always hold the aforementioned players in extremely high regard for playing such huge roles in the club's progress to this point.

Following conversations with both players, we will be making Aidan Stone and Will Randall, along with Connell, available for transfer, while also allowing Luther Munakandafa to move on in order to hopefully reach his full potential. We thank them all for their service and will work with them to find the right next step for their careers.

Looking ahead to 2024-25, we're excited about what Cedwyn and Geraldo, who has been offered new terms, can bring to the squad after a full pre-season following their long-term injuries.

Speculation about several of our high-performing, contracted players is inevitable. Nevertheless, our position is the same as ever – we do not need, nor intend, to sell any of them and would only consider offers that represented exceptional value for the club.

As they depart for their summer break, we'd like to reiterate our gratitude to the squad for their efforts in 2023-24.

For Stuart Maynard and his staff, the hard work doesn't stop as we continue our collective effort to build a squad capable of challenging for promotion next season. Excellent progress has already been made and we look forward to updating supporters on new signings, as well as the club's many exciting off-field projects, in the weeks and months ahead.

Jim O'Brien joined Notts in 2019 and was in the team relegated at Swindon in May of that year. At Wembley in May 2023 he was an unused substitute when Notts were promoted back into the EFL after defeating Chesterfield.

Goalkeeper Tiernan Brooks, a 16-year-old Notts apprentice when they were relegated, who later graduated through the academy, is now the only player who has been at Meadow Lane throughout the five seasons since relegation in May 2019.

Jim issued a farewell message to supporters:

Jim O'Brien

To my fellow Magpies,

It's with great sadness that my time with you is now over.

Firstly, I would like to thank you for welcoming me into your club at a time in my life when I was struggling to find somewhere to call 'home'. You gave me that home - and you gave me my love for football back. For that, I will forever be grateful.

There have been plenty of lows throughout my time with you - but the highs outweigh them all. The people I've met and the relationships formed along the way will be with me forever.

I have taken immense personal and professional pride in representing your wonderful and historic football club. So much so that I am now a supporter and consider it to be MY club.

Being able to play a part in the club's history, alongside some fantastic players, is something I will honour for the rest of my life. From fighting relegation to leading the team away at Grimsby, it's been some ride!

I hope you will remember me with fondness and as someone who gave everything every time I pulled on the shirt.

It's not "goodbye", it's "see you later".

Love always,

Jim x

I think this is also the time for me to conclude Notts County's history since the arrival of Alan Hardy in January 2017. As you have persevered to reach the end of the (almost) seven and a half year journey, you may wish to continue the story.

Remember, there is rarely a dull moment at Meadow Lane!

Come **O**n **Y**ou **P**ies

Acknowledgements

There are many who have contributed, knowingly and unknowingly, to the creation of this book.

The first to thank is my wife, **Linda**, also a devoted Notts fan (and occasional supporter) who has listened to my never-ending football stories for many years, and given me much support.

Arthur King, my late father, introduced me to Notts when he took me to Meadow Lane for the first time in 1957.

Andrew and John King (sons) and grandchildren **Grace, Freddie, Alfie, Zara, and Digby**, who have all listened patiently to my many Notts County stories.

Nick Richardson, Notts County's Head of Media, Communications & Marketing, for his agreement to my use of material from Notts' website and social media outlets.

Edwin Rydberg, author and publisher (Quantum Dot Press), his help, guidance, and advice was invaluable, and much appreciated.

Mick Chappell, Notts County honorary club historian.

Nick Brigham, friend and author.

Neal Ardley, Ian Burchnall, Luke Williams, and Stuart Maynard for information gained from their many excellent media interviews.

Charlie Slater and **Mark** ('get in') **Stallard** for their enjoyable BBC Radio Nottingham commentaries.

BT Sport and **National League TV** which allowed me to view some matches from my home in Harrogate.

Also **soccerstats.com, sportsmole.co.uk** and **footballwebpages.co.uk** for the provision of some useful information via the internet.

Friend **Colin Slater**, a Notts County stalwart, and BBC Radio Nottingham match commentator for many years, who sadly died in January 2022.

I am aware there may be others who are not mentioned above who also deserve an accolade. Please accept my apologies for the omission.

Roger King
Harrogate, North Yorkshire
1 May 2024

www.ingramcontent.com/pod-product-compliance
Lightning Source LLC
Chambersburg PA
CBHW081613100526
44590CB00021B/3418